SECOND EDITION

# Environmental Economics and Management
## Theory, Policy, and Applications

SECOND EDITION

# Environmental Economics and Management
## Theory, Policy, and Applications

**Scott J. Callan**
**Janet M. Thomas**
*Both of Bentley College*

The Dryden Press
**A Division of Harcourt College Publishers**

Fort Worth   Philadelphia   San Diego   New York   Austin   Orlando   San Antonio
Toronto   Montreal   London   Sydney   Tokyo

**Publisher**   Mike Roche
**Acquisitions Editor**   Gary Nelson
**Market Strategist**   Debbie K. Anderson
**Developmental Editor**   Amy Porubsky
**Project Editor**   Jon Davies
**Art Director**   Biatriz Chapa
**Production Manager**   James McDonald

Cover by Lora Gray

ISBN: 0-03-025631-3

Library of Congress Catalog Card Number: 99-74295

Copyright © 2000, 1996 by Harcourt, Inc.

Requests for permission to make copies of any part of the work should be mailed to: Permissions Department, Harcourt, Inc., 6277 Sea Harbor Drive, Orlando, FL 32887-6777.

*Address for Domestic Orders*
The Dryden Press, 6277 Sea Harbor Drive, Orlando, FL 32887-6777
800-782-4479

*Address for International Orders*
International Customer Service
The Dryden Press, 6277 Sea Harbor Drive, Orlando, FL 32887-6777
407-345-3800
(fax) 407-345-4060
(e-mail) hbintl@harcourtbrace.com

*Address for Editorial Correspondence*
The Dryden Press, 301 Commerce Street, Suite 3700, Fort Worth, TX 76102

*Web Site Address*
http://www.harcourtcollege.com

THE DRYDEN PRESS, DRYDEN, and the DP LOGO are registered trademarks of Harcourt, Inc.

Printed in the United States of America

9 0 1 2 3 4 5 6 7 8   039   9 8 7 6 5 4 3 2 1

The Dryden Press
Harcourt College Publishers

# The Dryden Press Series in Economics

Few contemporary issues have so influenced consumer behavior, corporate strategy, and public policy as environmental concerns. In the past two decades, we have witnessed changes in product design, capital investment practices, tax policies, product packaging, and technology—all because environmental issues have been integrated into private and public decision making. New industries have emerged in environmental products and services. National and international policies are being developed to preserve natural resources and ecosystems. Firms have redefined their business strategies in response to new regulations and the changing demands of more environmentally conscious consumers. As a society, we have come to recognize that economic activity and the natural environment are inexorably linked, and this profound relationship is at the core of environmental economics and management.

Teaching environmental economics is an exciting opportunity to show students the broad applicability of economic thinking. Students are more environmentally literate than they were a decade ago, and most are eager to understand how the market process can help explain and even solve environmental problems. It is, to say the least, an energizing challenge to present this evolving field to what is typically a diverse audience of students.

We wrote *Environmental Economics and Management* to give undergraduate and MBA students a clear perspective of the relationship between market activity and the environment. Our general approach is to illustrate how economic analytical tools such as market models and benefit–cost analysis can be used to assess environmental problems and to evaluate policy solutions. Along with more traditional discussions, we have incorporated the business perspective in our development of environmental decision making—a vantage point often overlooked in more conventional treatments. The presentation does not compromise economic theoretical concepts, but it does complement the theory with timely, real-world applications. In so doing, seemingly abstract concepts are given relevance through actual cases about consumers, industry, and public policy.

## Content: A Modular Approach

Organizing the vast amount of material that an environmental economics course attempts to cover is a challenge at best. Mindful of the usual time constraint in a one-semester course and the fact that the student audience can be highly varied, we devised a modular structure for the text. This approach not only organizes the presentation by major topic but also provides a format that facilitates customizing the material to suit a variety of course objectives. At the instructor's discretion, certain chapters within a given module can be omitted or covered less thoroughly without loss of continuity in the overall presentation.

The first three modules are the foundation for the course:

**Part I. Modeling Environmental Problems:** a three-chapter module illustrating how environmental problems are modeled from an economic perspective. Primary topics are the materials balance model, a review of market theory and price determination in an environmental context, and the market failure of pollution using both a public goods model and externality theory.

**Part II. Modeling Solutions to Environmental Problems:** a two-chapter module on environmental regulatory approaches, one on command-and-control and one on the market approach. Allocative efficiency and cost-effectiveness are used to analyze these, and models are developed to study various control instruments such as technology-based standards, pollution charges, deposit/refund systems, and tradeable pollution permits.

**Part III. Analytical Tools for Environmental Planning:** a five-chapter module introduced by a general model of environmental policy development followed by an in-depth investigation of risk assessment, risk management, and benefit–cost analysis. Included is a thorough presentation of benefit estimation procedures such as the contingent valuation method and the averting expenditure approach.

We also present three media-specific modules that are actually comprehensive case studies of major environmental problems and policy solutions. Using economic modeling and analytical tools, each module assesses the associated environmental risk, evaluates the policy response, and presents a benefit–cost analysis of major U.S. legislation. These three modules can be covered in any sequence following the foundational material covered in the first half of the text.

**Part IV. The Case of Air:** a three-chapter module assessing major air pollution problems and the policy initiatives aimed at controlling them. Integrated in the analysis of the Clean Air Act and its amendments are discussions of urban smog and acid rain. A comprehensive discussion of international issues such as ozone depletion and global warming also are presented. Throughout each chapter, economic modeling and benefit–cost analysis are used to facilitate the investigation of each issue.

**Part V. The Case of Water:** a three-chapter module covering the problems of ground and surface water contamination and specific policies aimed at point and nonpoint polluting sources. Two chapters are devoted to an economic analysis of the Clean Water Act, and a third conducts an analogous investigation of the recently reauthorized Safe Drinking Water Act.

**Part VI. The Case of Solid Wastes and Toxic Substances:** a three-chapter module analyzing the solid waste cycle and the use of pesticides and other toxic substances. Among the primary topics discussed are risk management of the hazardous waste stream, the Superfund controversy, market solutions to controlling municipal solid waste, and risk–benefit analysis in pesticide control.

The final module ties together the materials balance model, economic and environmental objectives, and the media-specific policy analyses to discuss the direction of future environmental policy.

**Part VII. Environmental Management in Transition**: a one-chapter module examining evolving trends in environmental policy and the objective of sustainable development. Key topics include environmental literacy, the shift toward pollution prevention, and cooperative partnerships among nations and among economic sectors to achieve environmental quality and economic prosperity.

In preparing the second edition, we updated the text, data tables, and applications to assure that students have access to the most current information. Included are discussions of the recent Kyoto Conference, President Clinton's Climate Change Initiative, and the Safe Drinking Water Act Amendments of 1996. Responding to adopters of the first edition, we added more graphical analyses throughout the text and incorporated more quantitative end-of-chapter problems as well. We also shortened most of the applications to make them more accessible and edited the general text throughout. Most of the data tables have a new, simpler presentation, and some use bar graphs to facilitate comprehension.

An important new feature of this edition is the integration of relevant Internet sites throughout the text. Many of these Web sites are highlighted in the general reading to encourage students to further explore a concept or investigate an environmental issue or law. Some are incorporated directly in review questions, facilitating an interactive approach to learning the material. All chapter-referenced Web sites are listed in the Related Web Sites section located at the end of each chapter. In addition, we include several other sites, which students and instructors might find useful.

# Pedagogical Features

In planning this text, we included a number of features to make the material interesting and accessible to students without compromising the integrity of the subject matter. Perhaps the most important of these is our extensive use of real-world **Applications** throughout the text.

**Applications:** Over 70 applications complement the presentation by illustrating the relevance of economic theory, environmental risk, and public policy. The content has been drawn from a variety of sources, including the business press, government reports, and the economic and environmental science literature. Topics range from corporate strategies to international policy formulation. These real-world cases motivate learning because they illustrate fundamental concepts in relevant, contemporary settings. They also may stimulate more in-depth study in a term paper or course project. A selection of some of the titles is:

Informing the Public through Truth in Advertising: Green Marketing Guidelines

Design for Disassembly: Materials Management at BMW

Searching for Alternatives to CFCs: The Corporate Response

Mexico City's Serious Smog Problem

Who Regulates the Quality of Bottled Water?

Taxing Gasoline Consumption: An International Comparison

Germany's Effluent Charge System

Industrial Ecosystems: When a Bad Becomes a Good

**Marginal Definitions, Key Concepts, and Acronyms:** In each chapter, **Marginal Definitions** of terms and relationships are placed adjacent to the relevant text presentation. A list of **Key Concepts** is also provided at the end of each chapter. At the end of the text, all terms are collectively presented in a convenient **Glossary.** These features call attention to important points in the text, help familiarize students with new terminology, and assist them in reviewing and self-testing their comprehension. We also have added chapter appendices of commonly used **Acronyms** throughout the media-specific modules. These act as a quick reference for students as they are reading chapters in which acronyms occur frequently.

**End-of-Chapter Learning Tools:** Each chapter concludes with a **Summary** to help students review and assimilate what they have read. Instructors also may find these summaries valuable in organizing the course and in preparing lectures. We provide conceptual and analytical **Review Questions** that can be used for regular assignments, in-class discussions, or sample test questions. We also offer a selection of **Additional Readings** (beyond those cited in the chapter) that are useful for supplementing course reading assignments. A list of **References** is included at the end of the text, which gives complete information on all sources cited in short form throughout the book. Both instructors and students should find this collection of resources helpful in conducting independent investigations of selected topics. New to the second edition is a list of **Related Web Sites** to give students and instructors selected links to online information pertaining to the chapter.

## Acknowledgments

No text is ever produced without the help and support of many individuals. In our case, we owe a debt of gratitude to Bentley College, particularly the administration, for its support of this project and our related work in environmental economics. We also thank our colleagues who offered valuable commentary and remembered to ask how the book was coming along. To our students as well, we are grateful for their input in using the text and working with the review problems and other features.

Many economists contributed to this text at various stages of the review process. Special thanks go to the reviewers of the first edition: Bill Ballard, College of Charleston; Laurie Bates, Bryant College; John Braden, University of Illinois (Urbana); Michelle Correia, Florida Atlantic University; Warren Fisher, Susquehanna University; Joyce Gleason, Nebraska Wesleyan College; Sue Eileen Hayes, Sonoma State University; Charles Howe, University of Colorado; Donn Johnson, University of Northern Iowa; Supriya Lahiri, University of Massachusetts; Donald Marron, University of Chicago; Arden Pope, Brigham Young University; H. David Robison, La Salle University; Richard Rosenberg, Penn. State University; Jeffrey Sundberg, Lake Forest College; David Terkla, University of Massachusetts; John Whitehead, East Carolina University; and Keith Willett, Oklahoma State University. We also wish to thank our review panel for the second edition, which included Mark Aldrich, Smith College; Douglas F. Greer, San Jose State University; Darwin C. Hall, California State University; Stanley R. Keil, Ball State University; and Warren Matthews, Houston Baptist University. To all of these teachers and scholars, we offer our thanks for their constructive criticism and many insightful comments. By incorporating many of their suggestions, we believe the finished text is much improved.

There are also many people to thank at our new publisher, The Dryden Press. Chief among these is Gary Nelson for his continued confidence in our work and the text. We are grateful for his dedication to this project in both its first and second editions. Special thanks also go to Amy Porubsky and Jon Davies for their assistance throughout the review and production of the text.

Finally and most importantly, we thank our spouses, Karen and David, for their patience and their continued support of our professional work.

Scott J. Callan

Janet M. Thomas

# CONTENTS IN BRIEF

# CONTENTS

# Chapter 3

**PART THREE**

**Analytical Tools for
Environmental
Planning
155**

# Chapter 6

## Environmental Decision Making:
## Public Policy Development

# Chapter 9

# Chapter 12

## Chapter 13

### Global Air Quality: Policies for Ozone Depletion and Global Warming    370

**PART FIVE**

**The Case of Water
409**

# Chapter 14

# Chapter 15

# Chapter 16

**PART SIX**

**The Case of Solid Wastes and Toxic Substances**
**519**

# Chapter 17

## Managing Hazardous Solid Waste and Waste Sites      521

# Chapter 18

SECOND EDITION

# Environmental Economics and Management

## Theory, Policy, and Applications

# I

# Modeling Environmental Problems

Environmental problems, while not new, have taken on a more significant role in business decisions and corporate planning in the past two decades. The world has become more aware of the natural environment and more sensitive to the implications of ecological damage. Individuals are altering their consumption patterns to incorporate environmental responsibility into their market decisions. Many are reordering their preferences in favor of biodegradable detergents, nonozone-depleting personal products, and recyclable packaging. Similarly, governments are responding on both a local and national level by passing environmental laws and establishing pollution monitoring networks to protect the ecology. Firms are adding environmental concerns to their list of business priorities. This corporate response is necessary, not only to comply with the growing number of regulations on production and product design, but also to remain competitive in a marketplace where many consumers are seeking environmentally responsible producers.

To comprehend this changing marketplace, it is necessary to understand the fundamentals of how markets work and the relationship between market activity and nature. Economic analysis uses models to explain the strategic decision making and the economic conditions that define the marketplace. By eliminating unnecessary detail, models allow economists to test hypotheses about economic relationships and to make predictions about behavioral and institutional reactions to changes in market conditions. As such, modeling is a fundamental tool in the study of environmental economics.

In this first module of the text, three chapters are devoted to basic models that are of direct use in understanding environmental issues. Chapter 1 develops what is called the materials balance model, which illustrates the linkages between the circular flow of economic activity and nature. In so doing, the model shows how environmental damage and resource depletion occur as a result of market decision making. This provides a forum through which the basic concepts of environmental economics are discussed. Chapter 2 focuses on the fundamentals of the market process, reviewing key concepts like supply and demand, economic efficiency, and measures of social welfare. All of this lays the foundation for Chapter 3, which explains how environmental problems occur when the market fails. Here, too, models are used to illustrate the sources of market failure and the conditions under which such an outcome arises.

1

# 1

# *The Role of Economics in Environmental Management*

As society moves through the twenty-first century, it faces an important challenge—to protect and preserve the earth's resources as it continues to develop economically. That such an objective is ambitious is evidenced by even a casual retrospective of economic history. The rapid growth and advancing technology that began in earnest with the Industrial Revolution took a tremendous toll on the natural environment. Mass transport, manufacturing processes, telecommunications, and synthetic chemicals are responsible both for the highly advanced lifestyle that society enjoys *and* for much of the environmental damage it now faces. With 20/20 hindsight, we now recognize that there was a significant trade-off between economic growth and environmental quality.

An important objective is to understand the critical relationship between economic activity and nature and use that knowledge to make better and wiser decisions. Of course, there will always be some amount of trade-off—precisely what is conveyed by economic theory. We cannot expect to have perfectly clean air or completely pure water, nor can we continue to grow economically with no regard for the future. But there *is* a solution, though it is a compromise of sorts. We first have to decide what level of environmental quality is acceptable, and then make appropriate adjustments in our market behavior to sustain that quality as we continue to develop as a society.

The adjustment process is not an easy one, and it takes time. As a society, we are still learning—about nature, about market behavior, and about the important relationships that link the two together. What economics contributes to this learning process are analytical tools that help to explain the interaction of markets and the environment, the implications of that relationship, and the opportunities for effective solutions.

In this chapter, we support these assertions with a simple but powerful model that illustrates the link between economic activity and nature. The accompanying analysis illustrates how fundamental market decisions affect the earth's natural resource stock. As we will discover, the underlying relationships motivate economic analysis of environmental issues, which is formally defined through two disciplines—natural resource economics and environmental economics, the latter being our focus in this text. With this model as a foundation, we then lay the groundwork for our course of study, starting with an introduction of basic concepts. From there, major objectives in environmental economics are identified and discussed, followed by an overview of public policy development and the role of economics in that process.

# Economics and the Environment

One of the most pervasive applications of economic theory is that it logically explains what we observe in reality. For example, through microeconomic analysis we can understand the behavior of consumers and firms and the decision making that defines what we refer to abstractly as the marketplace. This same application of economic theory can be used to analyze environmental problems—why they occur and what can be done about them. Stop to consider how pollution or resource depletion comes about—not from a sophisticated scientific level, just a fundamental perspective. The answer? Both arise from decisions made by households and firms. Consumption and production draw upon the earth's supply of natural resources. Furthermore, both activities generate by-products that can contaminate the environment. Thus the fundamental decisions that comprise economic activity are connected directly to environmental problems. To illustrate this relationship, we begin by presenting a basic model of economic activity. Then we expand it to show exactly how this connection arises.

### The Fundamental Model of Economic Activity: The Circular Flow Model

**circular flow model**
Illustrates the real and monetary flows of economic activity through the factor market and the output market.

The basis for modeling the relationship between economic activity and the environment is the same one that underlies all of economic theory—the **circular flow model.** This is typically the first model students learn about in introductory economics, and it is without question one of the more powerful explanatory tools in the field. Figure 1.1 illustrates a simple circular flow model.

First, consider how the flows operate, holding all else constant. Notice how the so-called **real flow** (i.e., the nonmonetary flow), runs counter-

| FIGURE 1.1 | THE CIRCULAR FLOW MODEL OF ECONOMIC ACTIVITY |
|---|---|

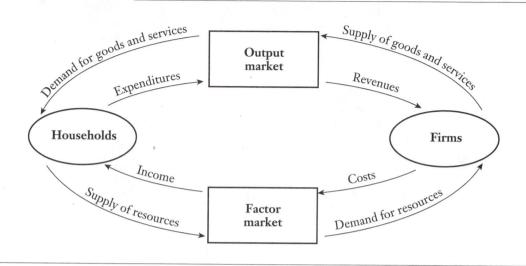

clockwise between the two market sectors, households (or consumers), and firms (or producers). Households supply resources or factors of production to the **factor market,** where they are demanded by firms to produce goods and services. These commodities are then supplied to the **output market** where they are demanded by households. Running clockwise is the **money flow.** The exchange of inputs in the factor market generates a flow of income to households, and that flow represents costs incurred by firms. Analogously, the money flow through the output market shows how households' expenditures on goods and services are revenues to firms.

Now, think about how the volume of economic activity and hence the *size* of the flow are influenced by such factors as population growth, technological change, labor productivity, capital accumulation, and natural phenomena such as drought or floods. For example, holding all else constant, technological advance would expand the productive capacity of the economy, which in turn would increase the size of the flow. Similarly, a population increase would give rise to a greater demand for goods and services, which would call forth more production and lead to a larger circular flow.

**materials balance model** Positions the circular flow within a larger schematic to show the connections between economic decision making and the natural environment.

Notice that by analyzing how the flows operate and how the size of an economy can change, we can understand the basic functioning of an economic system and the market relationships between households and firms. However, the model does not *explicitly* show the linkage between economic activity and the environment. To illustrate this interdependence, the circular flow model must be expanded to depict market activity as part of a broader paradigm called the **materials balance model.**

FIGURE 1.2

THE MATERIALS BALANCE MODEL:
THE INTERDEPENDENCE OF
ECONOMIC ACTIVITY AND NATURE

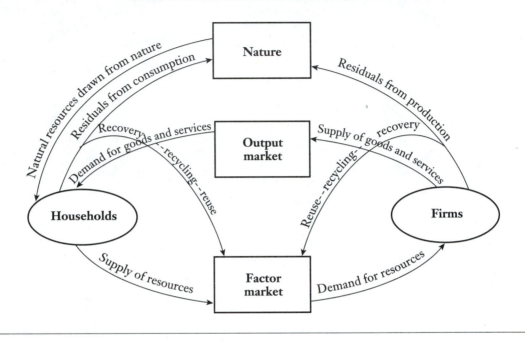

SOURCE: Adapted from Allen V. Kneese, Robert U. Ayres, and Ralph C. D'Arge. *Economics and the Environment: A Materials Balance Approach*. Washington, DC: Resources for the Future, 1970.

### The Materials Balance Model

The explicit relationship between economic activity and the natural environment is illustrated by the **materials balance model** shown in Figure 1.2.[1] Notice how the real flow of the circular flow model is positioned within a larger schematic to show the various connections between economic decision making and the natural environment.

**The Flow of Resources: Natural Resource Economics.**   Focus on the linkages between the upper block representing nature and the two market sectors—households and firms—paying particular attention to the direction of the arrows. Notice that one way an economic system is linked to

---

[1] Kneese, Ayres, and D'Arge (1970). See Chart 1, p. 9, in this source for a more detailed depiction of this model.

nature is through a flow of *materials* or natural resources that runs *from* the environment *to* the economy, specifically through the household sector. (Recall that, by assumption, households are the owners of *all* factors of production, including natural resources.) This flow describes how economic activity draws upon the earth's stock of natural resources, such as soil, minerals, and water. It is the primary focus of **natural resource economics,** which is a field of study concerned with the flows of resources from nature to economic activity.

**natural resource economics** A field of study concerned with the flow of resources from nature to economic activity.

**The Flow of Residuals: Environmental Economics.** A second set of linkages runs in the opposite direction, *from* the economy *to* the environment. This flow illustrates how raw materials entering the system eventually are released back to nature as by-products or **residuals.** Most residuals are in the form of gases released into the atmosphere, and in the short run, most are not harmful. In fact, some are absorbed naturally through what is called the **assimilative capacity** of the environment. For example, carbon dioxide emissions from the combustion of fossil fuels (i.e., oil, coal, and natural gas) can be partially absorbed by the Earth's oceans and forests. Other released gases are not easily assimilated and may cause harm even in the short term. There are also liquid residuals, such as industrial wastewaters, and solid residuals like municipal trash and certain hazardous wastes—all of which are potential threats to health and ecological systems.[2] Notice in Figure 1.2 that there are two residual outflows, one leading from each of the two market sectors, meaning that residuals arise from both consumption and production activity. This set of flows is the chief concern of **environmental economics.**

**residual** The amount of a pollutant remaining in the environment after a natural or technological process has occurred.

It is possible that the flow of residuals back to nature can be delayed—though not prevented—through **recovery, recycling,** and **reuse.** Notice in the model that there are inner flows running from the two residual outflows back to the factor market. These inner flows show that some residuals can be recovered from the stream and either recycled into another usable form or reused in their existing form. For example, Application 1.1 discusses how Germany's Bavarian Motor Works (BMW) has made advances toward designing automobiles to facilitate recycling once the vehicle has reached the end of its economic life.

**environmental economics** A field of study concerned with the flow of residuals from economic activity back to nature.

Although recycling efforts are important, keep in mind that they are only short-term measures, since even recycled and reused products eventually become residuals that are returned to nature. Indeed, what the materials balance model shows is that *all* resources drawn from the environment ultimately are returned there in the form of residuals. The two flows are balanced—a profound fact that is supported by science.

---

[2] Kneese, Ayres, and D'Arge (1970), pp. 11–12.

**APPLICATION 1.1**

# Design for Disassembly: Materials Management at BMW

Known for its well-engineered automobiles, BMW is seeking another type of distinction. The German carmaker has set its sights on building an automobile from 100 percent reusable or recyclable parts. To achieve its goal, the company has been researching an approach called "Design for Disassembly (DFD)"—a manufacturing method aimed at building a product specifically to facilitate recycling at the end of its useful life. Along with other major corporations like Volkswagen, 3M, and General Electric, BMW is investigating ways to manufacture a DFD product that is economically competitive and that stands up to the company's high standards for quality engineering.

Orchestrating a Design for Disassembly program in automobile production depends upon a coordinated effort among the manufacturer, the automobile dismantler, and the materials supplier. Manufacturers must design cars to facilitate dismantling, educate dismantlers about parts removal, and encourage suppliers to accept recovered materials from dismantlers. They also need to stipulate to suppliers that they will purchase only parts made from recovered materials.

BMW's research in DFD is part of a long-term commitment to environmentally conscious production decisions. The company has been recycling its catalytic converters since 1987. A year later, it introduced its limited-production Z1 roadster. The two-seater is totally recyclable and considered to be the first DFD product ever made. Since then, BMW has constructed a pilot plant in Bavaria dedicated solely to researching the DFD approach to manufacturing. Teams of workers at the facility systematically dismantle cars, beginning with all the fluids and oils and ending with the removal and sorting of interior materials.

A major objective is to build an automobile that can be dismantled at a relatively low cost. Long hours for the disassembly process elevates costs, which ultimately forces up car prices and reduces competitiveness—an outcome no carmaker can afford. Another key goal is to assure that parts can be readily sorted. This is particularly critical for plastics, which are more complex to recycle. Hence, producers need to find ways to reduce both the amount and the variety of materials used in production and to facilitate the sorting of recovered parts. BMW currently uses about twenty types of plastics in its automobiles, and it is looking to reduce this by a wide margin. The company also is establishing a network of recycling centers in Germany and the United States to make it more convenient for BMW owners to dispose of their cars.

BMW's efforts to advance the "Design for Disassembly" approach are well ahead of the rest of the industry, though other manufacturers have begun to follow suit. Japan's Nissan Motor Company has launched a variety of new research programs—some aimed directly at the DFD approach, others at using more recycled materials and fewer plastics in production. In the United States, manufacturers have announced plans to label plastic parts to facilitate sorting for recycling, and they have established a consortium with suppliers and recyclers. Hence, there appears to be a consensus that increasing the recyclability of automobiles is a worthwhile pursuit.

SOURCES: Ferdinand Protzman. "Germany's Push to Expand the Scope of Recycling." *New York Times*. July 4, 1992; Bruce Nussbaum and John Templeman. "Built to Last—Until It's Time to Take It Apart." *Business Week*, September 17, 1990 p. 102; U.S. Congress, Office of Technology Assessment (OTA). *Green Products by Design: Choices for a Cleaner Environment*. Washington, DC: U.S. Government Printing Office, October 1992, p. 11; Mike Knepper. "Recycling: Investment in the Future." *BMW Magazine*, January 1993, pp. 66–69.

**first law of thermodynamics** Matter and energy can neither be created nor destroyed.

**Using Science to Understand the Materials Balance.** According to the **first law of thermodynamics,** matter and energy can neither be created nor destroyed. Applying this fundamental law to the materials balance model means that in the long run, the flow of materials and energy drawn from nature into consumption and production must be equivalent to the flow of residuals that run from these activities back into the environment. Thus, when raw materials are used in economic activity, they are converted into other forms of matter and energy, but nothing is lost in the process. And, over time, all of these materials become residuals that are returned to nature. Some arise in the short run, such as waste materials during production. Other resources are first transformed into commodities and do not enter the residual flow until the goods are used up. At this point, the residuals can take a variety of forms, like carbon monoxide emissions associated with gasoline combustion or trash disposed in a municipal landfill. Even if recovery takes place, the conversion of residuals into recycled or reused goods is only temporary. In the long run, these too end up as wastes.

There is one further point. Accepting that matter and energy cannot be destroyed, it may seem as if the materials flow can go on forever. But the **second law of thermodynamics** states that nature's capacity to convert matter and energy is not without bound. During energy conversion, some of the energy becomes unusable. It still exists, but it is no longer available to use in another process. Hence, the fundamental process upon which economic activity depends is finite.

**second law of thermodynamics** Nature's capacity to convert matter and energy is not without bound.

These scientific laws that support the materials balance model communicate important, practical information to society. First, we must recognize that every resource drawn into economic activity ends up as a residual, which has the potential to damage the environment. The process can be delayed through recovery but not stopped. Second, nature's ability to convert resources to other forms of matter and energy is limited. Taken together, these assertions provide a comprehensive perspective of environmental problems and the important connections between economic activity and nature. It is the existence of these connections that motivates the discipline of environmental economics.

# Fundamental Concepts in Environmental Economics[3]

**pollution** The presence of matter or energy whose nature, location, or quantity has undesired effects on the environment.

Environmental economics is concerned with identifying and solving the problem of environmental damage, or **pollution,** associated with the flow of residuals. Although pollution is defined differently in different contexts,

---

[3] Although it is not necessary to master the rigors of environmental science, it is important to become familiar with the basic concepts used to identify environmental damage. A useful reference is the EPA's Web site, which gives a glossary of environmental terms at **www.epa.gov/OCEPA terms**.

such as within various legislative acts, it can be defined generally as the presence of matter or energy, whose nature, location, or quantity has undesired effects on the environment. Virtually any substance can be said to pollute solely on the basis of a single characteristic, such as its fundamental constituents, its geographical location, or its quantity. What this implies is that finding appropriate solutions to environmental damage depends critically upon an identification of the causes, sources, and scope of the damage.

### Identifying the Causes of Environmental Damage: Types of Pollutants

**natural pollutants**
Those contaminants that come about through nonartificial processes in nature.

One way to identify which substances are causing environmental damage is to distinguish them by their general origin—whether they are **natural pollutants** that arise from nature or whether they are **anthropogenic pollutants,** resulting from human activity.

**anthropogenic pollutants** Contaminants associated with human activity, including polluting residuals from consumption and production.

- **Natural pollutants** arise from nonartificial processes in nature, such as gases associated with the decay of animals and plants, particles from volcanic eruptions, salt spray from the oceans, and pollen.

- **Anthropogenic pollutants** are human induced and include all residuals associated with consumption and production. Examples include gases and particles from combustion and chemical wastes from certain manufacturing processes.

Of the two, anthropogenic pollutants are of primary concern to environmental economists, particularly those for which nature has little or no assimilative capacity.

### Identifying the Sources of Pollution: Classifying Polluting Sources

Once pollutants have been identified, the next step is to determine the sources responsible for their release. Polluting sources are many and varied, ranging from automobiles to waste disposal sites. Even a seemingly pristine setting like farmland can be a polluting source, if rainwater transports chemical pesticides and fertilizers to nearby lakes and streams. Because polluting sources are so diverse, they are generally classified into broadly defined categories that are meaningful to policy development. Depending on the environmental media (i.e., air, water, or land), sources of pollution are generally grouped by: (1) their mobility or (2) how readily they can be identified.

**stationary source**
A fixed-site producer of pollution, such as a building or manufacturing plant.

**mobile source** Any nonstationary polluting source, including all transport vehicles.

**Sources Grouped by Mobility.** Whether or not a polluting source remains in a single location affects how the resulting pollution can be controlled. The categories are designated simply as **stationary sources** and **mobile sources.**

- A **stationary source** is a fixed-site producer of pollution, such as a coal-burning power plant or a sewage-treatment facility.

- A **mobile source** refers to any nonstationary polluting source, such as an automobile or an airplane.

This distinction is commonly used to characterize air pollution sources, since each requires a different form of control.

**Sources Grouped by Identifiability.** In some contexts, the identifiability of a polluting source is an important factor, in which case a distinction is made between **point sources** and **nonpoint sources.**

**point source** Any single identifiable source from which pollutants are released, such as a factory smokestack, a pipe, or a ship.

- A **point source** refers to any single identifiable source from which pollutants are released, such as a factory smokestack, a pipe, or a ship.

**nonpoint source** A source that cannot be identified accurately and degrades the environment in a diffuse, indirect way over a relatively broad area.

- A **nonpoint source** is one that cannot be identified accurately and degrades the environment in a diffuse, indirect way over a relatively broad area.

This set of classifications is most commonly used in water pollution control policy because nonpoint sources are so significant to this particular problem. As these definitions suggest, pollutants released from nonpoint sources are much more difficult to control than those released from point sources.

*Identifying the Scope of Environmental Damage:*
*Local, Regional, and Global Pollution*

Although environmental damage is a universal concern, some types of pollution have detrimental effects that are limited to a single community, whereas others pose a risk over a large geographical region. The point is, the extent of the damage associated with pollution can vary considerably — an observation vitally important to policy formulation. Consequently, environmental pollution is often classified according to the relative size of its geographical impact as local, regional, or global.

**local pollution** Environmental damage that does not extend far from the polluting source, such as urban smog.

**Local Pollution.** **Local pollution** refers to environmental damage that does not extend very far from the polluting source and is typically confined to a single community. Although the negative effects are limited in scope, they nonetheless pose a risk to society and can be difficult to control. A common local pollution problem is **urban smog.** Visible as a thick yellowish haze, smog is caused by a number of pollutants that react chemically in sunlight. It is particularly severe in major cities like Los Angeles and Mexico City, as the graphic in Figure 1.3 suggests.

FIGURE 1.3    COMPARISON OF POLLUTANTS CONTRIBUTING
TO URBAN AIR POLLUTION IN MAJOR CITIES

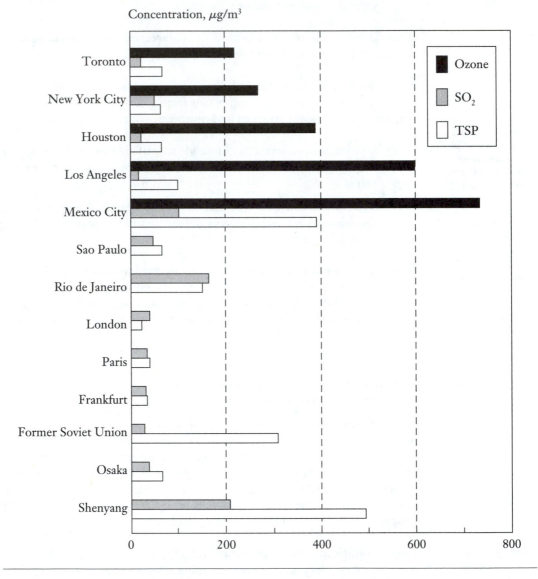

Concentration, $\mu g/m^3$

NOTES:
(i)   Ozone refers to ground-level ozone; $SO_2$ is sulfur dioxide, the condensation of which contributes significantly to particulate matter in the air; and TSP refers to total suspended particles such as dust, soot, smoke, and other contaminants.
(ii)  Concentrations are given in $\mu g/m^3$ = micrograms per cubic meter.
SOURCE: U.S. Environmental Protection Agency, Office of Air Quality Planning and Standards. *National Air Quality and Emissions Trends Report, 1991.* Research Triangle Park, NC: October 1992, Figure 6-5, p. 6-7, which is drawn from numerous sources.

| TABLE 1.1 | MUNICIPAL SOLID WASTE (TOP 50) PER CAPITA GENERATION IN SELECTED COUNTRIES | | | | |

| Country | Waste (lbs. per capita per day) | Rank | Country | Waste (lbs. per capita per day) | Rank |
|---|---|---|---|---|---|
| Australia | 4.2 | 1 | Spain | 1.9 | 26 |
| New Zealand | 4.0 | 2 | Germany | 1.8 | 27 |
| France | 4.0 | 3 | Iceland | 1.8 | 28 |
| Canada | 3.7 | 4 | Hungary | 1.6 | 29 |
| United States | 3.3 | 5 | Greece | 1.5 | 30 |
| Norway | 2.9 | 6 | Italy | 1.5 | 31 |
| Netherlands | 2.6 | 7 | Portugal | 1.5 | 32 |
| Denmark | 2.6 | 8 | Soviet Union (former) | 1.3 | 33 |
| Finland | 2.4 | 9 | Czechoslovakia | 1.3 | 34 |
| Bahrain | 2.4 | 10 | Albania | 1.3 | 35 |
| United Arab Emirates | 2.4 | 11 | Bulgaria | 1.3 | 36 |
| Saudi Arabia | 2.4 | 12 | Austria | 1.3 | 37 |
| Kuwait | 2.4 | 13 | Poland | 1.3 | 38 |
| Oman | 2.4 | 14 | Romania | 1.3 | 39 |
| Israel | 2.4 | 15 | Indonesia | 1.3 | 40 |
| Qatar | 2.4 | 16 | Colombia | 1.2 | 41 |
| Iraq | 2.4 | 17 | Guatemala | 1.1 | 42 |
| Luxembourg | 2.2 | 18 | Liberia | 1.1 | 43 |
| Switzerland | 2.2 | 19 | Cote d'Ivoire | 1.1 | 44 |
| United Kingdom | 2.2 | 20 | Malta | 1.1 | 45 |
| Belgium | 2.0 | 21 | Gabon | 1.1 | 46 |
| Sweden | 2.0 | 22 | Kenya | 1.1 | 47 |
| Japan | 2.0 | 23 | Trinidad and Tobago | 1.1 | 48 |
| Ireland | 2.0 | 24 | Cape Verde | 1.1 | 49 |
| Singapore | 1.9 | 25 | Mozambique | 1.1 | 50 |

SOURCE: "Municipal Solid Waste (top 50)," from *1993 Information Please Environmental Almanac.* Copyright © 1992 by World Resources Institute. Reprinted by permission of Houghton Mifflin Company. All rights reserved.

Another local pollution problem that is receiving increasing attention is **solid waste pollution.** Poor waste management practices can allow leaching of contaminants such as lead and mercury into soil and nearby water supplies. Beyond measures aimed at improving waste management are efforts to measurably reduce the amount of waste being generated in the first place. Examine the estimates on municipal waste generation for selected countries given in Table 1.1, which suggests a positive relationship between waste generation and industrialization.

**regional pollution**
Degradation that extends well beyond the polluting source, such as acidic deposition.

**Regional Pollution.**    Environmental pollution that poses a risk well beyond the polluting source is called **regional pollution.** An important example is **acidic deposition,** which arises from acidic compounds that mix with other particles and fall to the earth either as dry deposits or in fog, snow, or rain—thus the common reference, "acid rain." Acid rain is characterized as regional pollution because the harmful emissions can travel hundreds of miles from their source.

**global pollution**
Environmental effects that are widespread with global implications, such as global warming and ozone depletion.

**Global Pollution.**    Some environmental problems have effects so extensive that they are referred to as **global pollution.** Global pollution is difficult to control, both because the associated risks are widespread and because international cooperation is needed to achieve effective solutions. Consider, for example, the problem of **global warming.** Also known as the "greenhouse effect," global warming occurs as sunlight passes through the atmosphere to the earth's surface and is radiated back into the air where it is absorbed by so-called greenhouse gases such as carbon dioxide. Although this warming process is quite natural, certain activities such as fossil fuel combustion add to the normal level of greenhouse gases, which in turn can increase the earth's natural temperature. According to scientific models, such disruptions to normal climate patterns could affect agricultural productivity, weather conditions, and the level of the earth's oceans—all effects that are worldwide in scope.

Similarly widespread are the risks associated with **ozone depletion,** a thinning of the earth's ozone layer. The ozone layer protects the earth from harmful ultraviolet radiation, which can weaken human immune systems, increase the risk of skin cancer, and adversely affect ecosystems. In 1985, scientists discovered that a previously observed thinning of the ozone layer over the Antarctic region had become an "ozone hole" the size of North America. Ozone depletion is caused mainly by a group of chemicals known as chlorofluorocarbons, or CFCs, which had been commonly used in refrigeration, air-conditioning, packaging, insulation, and aerosol propellants. Although national governments have imposed controls on CFC usage, the main policy thrust has arisen through international agreements because of the global nature of the problem.

## Identifying Environmental Objectives

Just as fundamental environmental problems are universal, so too are the overall objectives. But articulating the specifics of these objectives *and* accepting the trade-offs that such goals imply is a process that is not without debate. Indeed, such is the substance of environmental summits, where national leaders, industry officials, and environmentalists gather to exchange ideas about appropriate objectives and to garner cooperation from one another. A case in point was the 1997 conference on global warming held in

Kyoto, Japan.[4] A more comprehensive environmental agenda was addressed at the United Nations Conference on Environment and Development (UNCED) held in Rio de Janeiro, Brazil, in 1992. Known as the Earth Summit, the event marked the twentieth anniversary of the first worldwide environmental conference in Stockholm and was attended by 6,000 delegates representing over 170 countries.[5]

Although the objective-setting process has been arduous at times and often immersed in political debate, it *is* nonetheless moving forward. Today, virtually every environmental decision is guided by what have become worldwide objectives—**environmental quality, sustainable development;** and **biodiversity.**

### Environmental Quality

**environmental quality** A reduction in anthropogenic contamination to a level that is "acceptable" to society.

Given the pervasive problems of local, regional, and global pollution, few would debate including **environmental quality** among the world's objectives. However, there *is* a lack of consensus about how to define this concept in practice. In common parlance, most of us consider environmental quality to mean clean air, water, and land. But when it is being defined to guide policy, the dilemma becomes one of deciding just how clean is clean.

The debate usually begins with asking why environmental quality should not mean the absence of all pollution. The answer is that such an objective is impossible, at least in a pure sense. Recall that some pollution is natural and therefore not controllable. Furthermore, the absence of all anthropogenic pollutants could be achieved only if there were a prohibition on virtually all the goods and services that characterize modern living. Hence a more rational perception of environmental quality is that it represents a reduction in anthropogenic contamination to a level that is "acceptable" to society. This "acceptable" level of pollution will, of course, be different for different contaminants. But in each case, certain factors are considered in making the determination. Among them are the gains to human health and ecosystems, expenditures needed to achieve the reduction, availability of technology, and the relative risk of a given environmental hazard.

Although the world has begun to make progress toward achieving environmental quality, there is still much work to be done. In some parts of the world, such as Eastern Europe and the developing nations, environmental pollution is extreme, and progress toward mitigating the effects is slow. Application 1.2 discusses some of the environmental problems China is dealing with as it strives to advance economically.

Recognizing environmental quality as a worldwide objective has triggered an awareness of its importance over a longer time horizon. Society

---

[4] For more information on the Kyoto conference and the White House Initiative on Global Climate Change, visit the Web site **www.whitehouse.gov/Initiatives/Climate/index.cgi**.

[5] Council on Environmental Quality (January 1993), p. 140.

---

**APPLICATION 1.2**

## Conflict between Economic Development and the Environment: China's View

As China attempts to develop its economy into an industrialized power, the quality of its air, water, and land resources is deteriorating. Although officials are beginning to draft pollution control plans, much of the ecological damage is going virtually unchecked. As is sometimes the case in developing economies, environmentalism is perceived as an obstacle to economic advance. Pollution controls are viewed as financial burdens that will frustrate China's progress toward industrial development. Many observers believe that unless officials change their perspective toward environmental issues, the official response to China's pollution problems will be insufficient, yielding little or no measurable improvement in environmental quality.

China's air pollution problems can be traced primarily to the country's heavy reliance on coal as an energy source. In fact, during the 1980s, its coal consumption increased from 620 million tons to more than 1 billion tons. By 1996, China was ranked as the largest producer and consumer of coal, and according to most experts, its dependence on coal is expected to at least double by 2020. Industrial centers, like Chongqing, already face severe acid rain problems because of the use of high-sulfur coal. Documented damages range from erosion of buildings to the destruction of crops and other plant life. Reportedly, trees along city streets have had to be replaced three times in the past 30 years. China's water resources are also at risk. Sewage treatment is often inadequate, even nonexistent in some locations, and industrial wastes are contaminating many of the country's rivers and streams. These are nontrivial problems, but they are particularly serious for a nation with hundreds of cities facing water shortages.

According to China's environmental protection committee, economic losses from environmental pollution are about 3 percent of China's GNP or approximately $11.5 billion per year. The country now spends about 0.7 percent of its GNP on environmental protection, which apparently is not nearly enough to address the extent and seriousness of China's pollution problems. Nonetheless, Chinese officials are reticent to allocate resources away from economic development and toward environmental cleanup and protection, accepting pollution as a necessary sacrifice to achieve industrial growth. Instead, China is relying on financial support from other countries and international organizations. Denmark is helping Chongqing build a modern sewage-treatment plant, and the World Bank is providing loans to fund major environmental efforts, including a multi-million-dollar project to clean up Beijing. Notwithstanding the significance of these international endeavors, the most important effort has come from China itself. And that can follow only if this vast nation learns to balance growth with resource preservation and the needs of future generations with those of the present.

SOURCES: Dan Biers. "China Creates Environmental Nightmare in Industrial Rush." *The Brockton Enterprise*, June 16, 1994; Charles A. Radin. "With China's 'Miracle,' Pollution Surges." *Boston Globe*, January 2, 1995, pp. 47, 50; Associated Press. "Coal Dependence Has China Looking for Pollution Solution." *The Brockton Enterprise*, November 3, 1996, p. 6.

has begun to realize that the pursuit of economic growth could so adversely affect the natural resource stock that the productive capacity and overall welfare of future generations would be threatened. The potential of such an *intertemporal* trade-off has prompted a sense of obligation to the future that has materialized into two related objectives, **sustainable development** and **biodiversity.**

## Sustainable Development

Economic growth is defined as an increase in real gross domestic product (GDP). While growth is a favorable outcome, there are nonetheless long-term environmental implications, as the materials balance model suggests. Achieving an appropriate balance between economic growth and the preservation of natural resources are the essence of the objective known as **sustainable development,** which calls for managing the earth's resources to assure their long-term quality and abundance.[6] This reminds us that the circular flow of economic activity cannot be properly understood without recognizing how it fits into the larger scheme of the natural environment. Yet only in the past decade or so have economists and society at large begun to accept this broader and more realistic view. For example, new methods are being proposed to capture the ecological effects of growth in macro-economic performance measures—an issue discussed in Application 1.3.

On a much broader scale, the *Rio Declaration*, which was drafted at the Rio Summit, outlines 27 principles to act as guidelines for global environmental protection and economic development. Similar commitments are given in the summit's 40-chapter document, *Agenda 21*, an international agenda of comprehensive environmental goals. Its text is dedicated in large part to sustainable development, with emphasis on regions where achieving this objective is particularly critical such as developing nations.[7]

**sustainable development** The management of the Earth's resources such that their long-term quality and abundance are ensured.

## Biodiversity

Another environmental objective that addresses the legacy left to future generations is the preservation of **biodiversity.** This refers to the variety of distinct species, their genetic variability, and the variety of ecosystems they inhabit.[8] There is still much that scientists do not know about the diversity of life on earth. Although approximately 2.5 million species have been identified, most estimates suggest that the actual number may be at least 5 to 10 million, and some biologists believe there may be as many as 100 million.[9] Although there are many unknowns, there is consensus within the scientific community that the variety of species on earth is important to the ecology. Beyond the preservation of a species for its own sake, it is also the case that all life on earth is connected inexorably. Hence, the loss of one species may have serious implications for others, including human life.

The longevity of any biological species can be directly threatened by exposure to pollutants or by other human actions like commercial or sport

**biodiversity** The variety of distinct species, their genetic variability, and the variety of ecosystems they inhabit.

---

[6] Council on Environmental Quality (January 1993), p. 135.

[7] Parson, Haas, and Levy (October 1992).

[8] Council on Environmental Quality (January 1993), p. 135.

[9] Raven, Berg, and Johnson (1993), p. 144.

# National Income Accounting and the Bias against Environmental Assets

Assessing a nation's macroeconomic performance is an important and complex undertaking. The objective is to monetize total production and use the result as a means to assess and monitor a nation's growth. Measures of economic activity are also useful in making international comparisons, provided the accounting methods used are standardized. Currently, the accepted methodology follows the System of National Accounts (SNA) endorsed by the United Nations, a universal accounting framework for calculating such performance measures as gross domestic product (GDP) and national income.

As defined in most introductory economics texts, GDP is a monetized value of all final goods and services produced in a country each year. Although designed to be a fully comprehensive measure of productive activity, GDP is admittedly flawed. Difficulties in attempting to capture the value of non-marketed goods, such as the value of "do-it-yourself" projects and the so-called underground economy, necessarily bias the measure. Beyond these well-known flaws, there are other inherent biases that have caused some economists and government officials to question the validity of GDP as a measure of economic welfare. Among these is the absence of consideration for the ecological damage and natural resource depletion associated with economic activity.

Recognizing this shortcoming, some economists have argued in favor of an environmentally adjusted national income measure that explicitly values natural resources as economic assets. The justifications for this proposal are based on the following considerations. Just as the SNA allows for the depreciation of physical capital, so too should it recognize the devaluation of natural resources associated with economic activity. If pesticides leach into underground springs, the damage to drinking water supplies should be monetized and explicitly recognized by the GDP measure. Likewise, if a forest is destroyed to make way for urban development, that loss should be recorded. In both cases, important assets would be depreciating, and that depreciation should be captured in the SNA income and product accounts to avoid a serious bias.

Proponents of environmentally adjusted performance measures also make a broader-based argument. They claim that ignoring the economic value of natural resources perpetuates society's failure to acknowledge the effect of economic growth on future generations. In fact, in some cases, current accounting practices falsely record environmental deterioration as a contribution to economic welfare. A case in point are increased medical expenditures associated with the effects of a toxic chemical leak or government spending for cleaning up toxic waste sites, both of which ironically *elevate* a nation's GDP measure. Hence, it is argued that an explicit accounting of resource depletion and environmental damage would correct this outcome and restore accuracy to national product and income accounts.

Officials in many nations are aware of the environmental bias in national income accounts, and some are compiling internal accounts that explicitly value natural resources and the negative effects of environmental pollution. But to date, authorities at the UN have not acknowledged the need to correct the bias against environmental assets in the SNA. The official response has been limited to developing guidelines on how individual nations should prepare their own natural resource accounts. Those in favor of environmentally adjusting the SNA view this response as grossly inadequate as long as the SNA is the universally accepted approach to measuring economic well-being.

SOURCES: Robert Repetto. "Earth in the Balance Sheet: Incorporating Natural Resources in National Income Accounts." *Environment* 34(7), September 1992, pp. 12–20, 43–45; Robert Repetto. "Accounting for Environmental Assets." *Scientific American*, June 1992, pp. 94–100.

| TABLE 1.2 | THREATENED AND ENDANGERED SPECIES IN THE UNITED STATES AS OF JUNE 1997 |
|---|---|

|  | Endangered | Threatened | Total |
|---|---|---|---|
| Mammals | 56 | 7 | 63 |
| Birds | 75 | 15 | 90 |
| Herptiles (reptiles, amphibians) | 23 | 25 | 48 |
| Fish | 65 | 40 | 105 |
| Invertebrates (snails, clams, crustaceans, insects, arachnids) | 115 | 25 | 140 |
| Plants | 528 | 113 | 641 |
| TOTAL | 862 | 225 | 1087 |

SOURCE: U.S. Department of the Interior (DOI), Fish and Wildlife Service (FWS). *Threatened and Endangered Species.* Washington, DC, June 30, 1997, as cited in *1997 Information Please Almanac,* **www.infoplease.com**.

hunting. But the major threat to biodiversity is natural habitat destruction, which affects entire ecosystems. Population growth, poverty, and economic development are primarily responsible for this destruction, which includes the harvesting of tropical forests and the engineered conversion of natural land masses into alternative uses.[10] For example, by the mid 1970s, literally half of the 200 million acres of wetlands within the contiguous United States had been lost to such uses as agriculture and urban development.[11] Biodiversity can also be jeopardized by habitat *alteration*, which is often attributed to environmental pollution. Acid rain, for example, has been linked to changes in the chemical composition of rivers and lakes as well as to forest declines in Europe and North America. Such disturbances in the natural conditions to which biological life have become adapted can pose a threat to the longevity of these species.

The extent of biodiversity loss is not known. There are, however, indications that concern about diversity loss is warranted. As of 1997, over 1,080 plant and animal groups have been classified as endangered or threatened in the United States, as shown in Table 1.2.[12] That this issue is one of global concern is evidenced by the *Convention on Biodiversity* executed

[10] Raven, Berg, and Johnson (1993), pp. 262–63, 353–58.

[11] U.S. Environmental Protection Agency (August 1988), p. 57.

[12] U.S. Department of the Interior (DOI), Fish and Wildlife Service (FWS) (June 30, 1997).

by 153 nations at the Rio Summit. Among its mandates are to find measures that identify which species are in decline and to discover reasons for the observed declines.

Collectively, the goals of environmental quality, sustainable development, and biodiversity set an ambitious agenda. As such, all of society must work toward the development of environmental policy initiatives. Central to this effort is a planning process in which public officials, industry, and private citizens participate. In the context of environmental problems, this process involves a series of decisions about assessing environmental risk and responding to it, as the following overview explains.

## Environmental Policy Planning: An Overview

Devising policy for environmental pollution relies on careful research and planning. Many disciplines play a role in the process—among them biology, chemistry, economics, law, and medicine. Input from these and other fields is used to evaluate data and make decisions that ultimately lead to specific policy prescriptions. The underlying tool that guides policy planning is **risk analysis,** which comprises two decision-making procedures: **risk assessment** and **risk management.**

### Risk Assessment

**risk assessment**
The qualitative and quantitative evaluation of the risk posed to health or the ecology by an environmental hazard.

At any point in time, there are a number of environmental objectives to be met with a limited amount of economic resources. Hence, as problems are identified, they have to be prioritized. Generally, this is done through scientific assessment of the relative risk to human health and the ecology of a given environmental hazard—a procedure known as **risk assessment.** The assessment must determine if there is a causal relationship between the identified hazard and any observed health or ecological effects. If causality is determined, scientists then attempt to quantify *how* the effects change with increased exposure to the hazard. These findings are critical, since they determine whether or not a policy response is necessary, and if so, how immediate and how stringent that policy should be.

### Risk Management

**risk management**
The decision-making process of evaluating and choosing from alternative responses to environmental risk.

Assuming the risk assessment findings warrant it, the planning process enters its next phase called **risk management.** This refers to the decision-making process of evaluating and choosing from available responses to environmental risk. In a public policy context, risk responses refer to alternative types of control instruments, such as a legal limit on pollution releases or an excise tax on pollution-generating products. The objective of risk management is clear—to choose a policy instrument that reduces the risk of harm to society. What is less obvious is how public officials determine the level of risk society can tolerate and on what basis they evaluate various policy options.

A number of risk-management strategies have been devised to guide these important decisions. These strategies use criteria to evaluate policy options. Generally, these criteria are based on measures of risk, costs, or benefits—either singularly or in comparison to one another. Two that are economic in motivation are **allocative efficiency** and **cost-effectiveness.**

- **Allocative efficiency** requires that resources be appropriated such that the additional benefits to society are equal to the additional costs incurred.

- **Cost-effectiveness** requires that the least amount of resources be used to achieve an objective.

In practice, the choice of criteria is mandated, or at least implied, by law. For example, some provisions in U.S. legislation specifically disallow cost considerations in policy formulation, implicitly blocking either an efficient or cost-effective outcome—a result that is frequently debated in the literature and one that we will analyze in later chapters.

**Government's Overall Policy Approach.** An important element of risk management is the regulatory approach selected by government. Policies calling for direct regulation of polluting are indicative of a **command-and-control approach.** This form of regulation uses rules or standards to control the release of pollution. In practice, standards either set a maximum on the amount of residuals polluters may release or they designate a pollution abatement technology that all sources must use. In either case, polluters have little or no flexibility in deciding how they comply with the law. Every polluter must meet the same standard regardless of its location, access to resources, existing emission levels, or technology. Command-and-control has been the predominant approach used in the United States over the past several decades. But in recent years, more economic incentives have been integrated into strategic policy plans, which is indicative of a shift toward a **market approach** to policy.

The **market approach** is incentive-based, meaning it attempts to *encourage* conservation practices or pollution-reduction strategies rather than force polluters to follow a specific rule. There are many policy instruments that can achieve this result, such as a charge on pollutant releases or a tax levied on pollution-generating commodities. What all such instruments

**command-and-control approach**
A policy that directly regulates polluters through the use of rules or standards.

**market approach**
An incentive-based policy that encourages conservation practices or pollution reduction strategies.

have in common is that they tap into natural market forces so that polluters' optimizing decisions will benefit the environment. Think about how private firms are influenced by profit. What a market approach does is to use this information strategically to design environmental policy. For example, if a profit-maximizing firm were discharging a chemical into a river, a market approach might be to charge that polluter a fee for every unit of chemical released. In so doing, the firm would be made to pay for the damage it caused, and that payment would erode its profits. This tactic is sometimes called the **"polluter-pays principle."** The expected outcome is that a rational, profit-maximizing firm will reduce the amount of chemicals it releases, using the least-cost method available. The favorable outcomes are that society enjoys the benefit of a cleaner environment *and* the associated costs to achieve that gain are minimized.

That such market-based strategies can be effective is validated by experience all over the world. In the United States and other industrialized nations, more market incentives are being integrated within the conventional command-and-control policy approach. In fact, in a 1987 study of 14 nations, the Organization of Economic Cooperation and Development (OECD), which supports the polluter-pays principle, found that approximately 150 economic instruments were in use across these countries.[13]

**Setting the Time Horizon.** Another element of risk management decision making is determining the most effective time plan for policy initiatives. One approach is to target policy at more immediate or *short-run* problems. These types of initiatives are referred to as **management strategies,** since their purpose is to manage an existing problem. Here, the intent is *ameliorative.* In terms of the materials balance model, such strategies attempt to reduce the damage from the flow of residuals back to the environment.

An alternative approach deals with the potential of future deterioration and is therefore preventive in purpose. This *long-term* strategy is referred to as **pollution prevention** and is implemented by reducing the flow of residuals back to nature and/or by minimizing the harmful components of residuals like toxic chemicals. Preventive strategies are becoming more prevalent in U.S. policy initiatives. In fact, the United States made a formal commitment to pollution prevention when Congress enacted the Pollution Prevention Act of 1990. There have also been some important private initiatives that support preventive strategies. One such effort is exemplified in a corporate pledge, originally known as the "Valdez Principles," which is discussed in Application 1.4.

**management strategies** Methods that address existing environmental problems and attempt to reduce the damage from the residual flow.

**pollution prevention** A long-term strategy aimed at reducing the amount or toxicity of residuals released to nature.

---

[13] OECD (1989a).

# The Coalition for Environmentally Responsible Economies: Valdez Principles

In the fall of 1989, the Coalition for Environmentally Responsible Economies (CERES) was formed. Its purpose is simple and direct—to encourage the corporate sector to assume full responsibility for the environmental consequences of its actions. The coalition comprises 14 environmental organizations, including the Sierra Club and the National Wildlife Association, plus the 325-member Social Investment Forum (SIF)—a national trade association of investment professionals concerned with social issues. To accomplish its goal, CERES embarked on a plan to draft a formal pledge document through which private firms would commit to environmental objectives.

The membership collaborated to define specific standards to which signatories of the compact would be held accountable. Biodiversity, sustainable development, and pollution prevention were among the issues considered for the final document. Ultimately, the group settled on a set of 10 guidelines originally called the "Valdez Principles," named after the infamous March 1989 Alaskan oil spill.

The next step was critical. The CERES membership invited thousands of corporations to sign the environmental pledge. With endorsements from groups that collectively control $150 billion in investment funds, CERES believed its financial clout would be effective in garnering and rewarding corporate participation. But despite a strong effort, response has been less than enthusiastic. As of 1997, only about 50 companies had agreed to commit formally to what are now known as the "CERES Principles." However, the recent 1998 endorsement of Coca-Cola Company may encourage other firms to follow suit. The 10 guidelines that make up the CERES Principles are itemized below. For more detail on these principles and a current list of endorsers, the interested reader should visit CERES' website at **www.ceres.org.**

## The CERES Principles

1. Protection of the Biosphere
2. Sustainable Use of Natural Resources
3. Reduction and Disposal of Waste
4. Wise Use of Energy
5. Risk Reduction
6. Marketing of Safe Products and Services
7. Damage Compensation
8. Disclosure
9. Environmental Directors and Managers
10. Assessment and Annual Audit

SOURCES: Keiko Ohnuma. "Missed Manners." *Sierra*, March/April 1990, pp. 24–26; Coalition for Environmentally Responsible Economies (CERES). "The Valdez Principles," USA, 1989, as reported in The Canadian Institute of Chartered Accountants. *Environmental Auditing and the Role of the Accounting Profession*, Toronto, Ontario: The Canadian Institute of Chartered Accountants, 1992, Table 2.1, pp. 7–8; Michael Parrish. "GM Signs on to Environmental Code of Conduct." *Los Angeles Times*, February 10, 1994.

# Conclusions

Concern about the risks of pollution and the threat of natural resource depletion has been expressed by private citizens, the business community, and governments all over the world. In large part, this perspective has come from a growing awareness of the delicate balance between nature and economic activity. The materials balance model illustrates the strength of this relationship and the consequences of naive decision making that ignores it.

Recognizing the implications, many nations have made measurable progress in identifying the problems and setting an agenda to address them. As that work continues, comparable efforts are under way to develop and implement solutions. To that end, policy reform, collaborative arrangements between government and industry, and international summits are being aimed at resolving environmental problems. Research scientists are working to learn more about the ecology, the diversity of species, and environmental risks. Laws are being amended to incorporate more preventive measures as well as incentive-based instruments that encourage pollution reduction and resource conservation. As this process evolves, society is changing the way it thinks about the earth's resources, the long-term consequences of its decisions, and its obligation to the future.

Economics has much to contribute to this evolution—in large part because of the interdependence between market decisions and nature. The fundamental concepts of price and optimizing behavior can be used to analyze the effectiveness of environmental policy and to develop alternative solutions. As we explore the discipline of environmental economics, we will use these same applications of theory to study the effects of environmental pollution as well as the public policy and private responses to the associated risks.

As this chapter suggests, there is a lot of ground to cover. But, the importance and relevance of the issues justify the effort. This field of study, much like the problem it examines, presents both a challenge and an opportunity—a characterization drawn from the opening address to the Rio Summit:

> The Earth Summit is not an end in itself, but a new beginning. . . . The road beyond Rio will be a long and difficult one; but it will also be a journey of renewed hope, of excitement, challenge and opportunity, leading as we move into the 21st century to the dawning of a new world in which the hopes and aspirations of all the world's children for a more secure and hospitable future can be fulfilled.[14]

---

[14] Maurice F. Strong, UNCED secretary-general. Opening address to UNCED Conference on Environment and Development, Rio de Janeiro, Brazil, June 3, 1992, as cited in Haas, Levy, and Parson (October 1992), p. 7.

# Summary

- The circular flow model is the basis for modeling the link between economic activity and nature.

- The relationship between economic activity and the natural environment is illustrated by the materials balance model.

- The first law of thermodynamics asserts that matter and energy can be neither created nor destroyed. The second law of thermodynamics states that the conversion capacity of nature is limited.

- Pollution refers to the presence of matter or energy, whose nature, location, or quantity produces undesired environmental effects. Some pollutants are natural, and others are anthropogenic.

- Sources of pollution are sometimes grouped into mobile and stationary sources. Another common classification is to distinguish point sources from nonpoint sources.

- Local pollution problems are those whose effects do not extend far from the polluting source.

- Regional pollution has effects that extend well beyond the source of the pollution.

- Global pollution problems are those whose effects are so extensive that the entire earth is affected.

- Among the most critical environmental objectives are environmental quality, sustainable development, and biodiversity.

- The underlying tool that guides policy planning is risk analysis, which comprises two decision-making procedures: risk assessment and risk management.

- Risk assessment is a scientific evaluation of the relative risk to human health and the ecology of a given environmental hazard. Risk management refers to the process of evaluating and selecting an appropriate response to environmental risk.

- Two economic criteria used in risk management are allocative efficiency and cost-effectiveness.

- A command-and-control policy approach uses limits or standards to regulate environmental pollution.

- A market approach uses economic incentives to encourage pollution reduction or resource conservation.

- Management strategies have a short-run orientation and are ameliorative in intent.

• Pollution prevention strategies have a long-term perspective and are aimed at precluding the potential for further environmental damage.

## Key Concepts

circular flow model
materials balance model
natural resource economics
residual
environmental economics
first law of thermodynamics
second law of thermodynamics
pollution
natural pollutants
anthropogenic pollutants
stationary source
mobile source
point source

nonpoint source
local pollution
regional pollution
global pollution
environmental quality
sustainable development
biodiversity
risk assessment
risk management
command-and-control approach
market approach
management strategies
pollution prevention

## Review Questions

1. a. State how each of the following factors affect the materials balance model: (i) population growth; (ii) income growth; (iii) increased consumer recycling; (iv) increased industrial recycling; (v) increased use of pollution prevention technologies.
   b. Assume that stringent pollution controls are placed on the flow of residuals released into the atmosphere. According to the materials balance model, what does this imply about the residual flows to the other environmental media, and/or the flow of inputs into the economy?

2. Faced with the oil crisis of the mid 1970s, the U.S. Congress instituted Corporate Average-Fuel Economy (CAFE) standards. (For an overview of the CAFE standards, visit the Web site **www.ita.doc.gov/industry/ basic/cafe.html.** at the U.S. Department of Commerce, International Trade Administration.) These standards were intended to increase the miles per gallon (MPG) of automobiles.
   a. Briefly describe the expected environmental effect of increasing the MPG of automobiles, holding all else constant.
   b. There has been serious criticism lodged against these standards because U.S. automakers responded by using more plastics in automobiles to make cars lighter in weight as a way to meet the more

restrictive CAFE standards. Explain how the use of this technology affects your answer to part (a). Are there any other relevant issues associated with this manufacturing decision?

3. Use your knowledge of economic principles to discuss how the market premise operates under the "polluter-pays principle."

4. Reconsider the problem of U.S. wetlands loss and the implications for biological diversity. Briefly contrast how a command-and-control policy approach to this problem would differ in intent and implementation from a market approach.

5. In your view, should employment in the forest industry be sacrificed to save the northern spotted owl? If so, by how much, and how should the extent of employment loss be determined? If not, why not?

# Additional Readings

Blum, Elissa. "Making Biodiversity Conservation Profitable: A Case Study of the Merck/INBio Agreement." *Environment* 35(4), May 1993, pp. 16–20, 38–45.

Briscoe, John. "When the Cup Is Half Full: Improving Water and Sanitation Services in the Developing World." *Environment* 35(4), May 1993, pp. 7–15, 28–37.

Commoner, Barry. "Economic Growth and Environmental Quality: How to Have Both." *Social Policy*, Summer 1985, pp. 18–26.

Cruz, Wilfrido, Mohan Munasinghe, and Jeremy Warford. "Greening Development: Environmental Implications of Economic Policies." *Environment* 38(5), June 1996, pp. 6–11, 31–38.

DiLorenzo, Thomas J. "The Mirage of Sustainable Development." *The Futurist*, September/October 1993, pp. 14–19.

Fialka, John J. "A Curious Assortment of Adversaries Assemble in Kyoto for Talks on Global Warming Treaty." *The Wall Street Journal*, December 5, 1997, p. A20.

———. "Global Warming Treaty Is Approved." *The Wall Street Journal*, December 11, 1997.

Haas, Peter M., Marc A. Levy, and Edward A. Parson. "Appraising the Earth Summit: How Should We Judge UNCED's Success?" *Environment* 34(8), October 1992, pp. 6–11, 26–33.

National Wildlife Federation. "25th Environmental Quality Index: A Year of Crucial Decision." *National Wildlife*, February/March 1993, pp. 35–41.

Raustiala, Kal, and David G. Victor. "The Future of the Convention on Biological Diversity." *Environment* 38(4), May 1996, pp. 16–20, 37–45.

Sessions, Kathy. "Building the Capacity for Change." *EPA Journal* 19(2), April–June 1993, pp. 15–19.

Smith, Emily T. "Growth vs. Environment: In Rio Next Month, a Push for Sustainable Development." *Business Week*, May 11, 1992, pp. 66–75.

Solow, Robert M. "Sustainability: An Economist's Perspective." In Robert Dorfman and Nancy S. Dorfman, eds., *Economics of the Environment; Selected Readings*. New York: W. W. Norton, 1993, pp. 179–87.

## Related Web Sites

The Coalition for Environmentally
Responsible Economies (CERES)          **www.ceres.org**

The Council on Environmental
Quality                                **www.whitehouse.gov/CEQ**

United Nations Environment
Programme (UNEP)                       **www.unep.org**

U.S. Department of Commerce,
International Trade Administration      **www.ita.doc.gov/industry/basic/cafe.html**

U.S. Environmental Protection
Agency Terms of Environment            **www.epa.gov/OCEPAterms**

White House Initiative on Global
Climate Change                         **www.whitehouse.gov/Initiatives/Climate/index.cgi**

The World Bank Group (Information on economic development
and the environment.)                  **www.worldbank.org**

# 2

# Modeling the Market Process: A Review of the Basics

According to the materials balance model, environmental problems are directly linked to market activity. The basic decisions made by consumers and firms affect both the abundance and quality of the earth's natural resource stock. Since environmental economics is concerned with resource *damage*, we need to develop a thorough understanding of how market activity gives rise to polluting residuals and why the usual market forces cannot solve the problem. From an economic perspective, environmental pollution is characterized as a market failure. Hence, environmental economics uses market failure models to analyze the problem and to identify solutions. But these models rely on a solid understanding of the market process itself.

To that end, this chapter reviews the essential components of a market and the basic concepts used in microeconomic analysis. Essentially, we will be focusing on the operation of the circular flow model, which is central to the materials balance paradigm. The fundamentals of supply and demand are reviewed to reestablish a good grasp of market behavior, the motivations for consumer and firm decision making, and price determination.

The context for our review is a hypothetical market for bottled mineral water in which competitive conditions are assumed. Through an analysis of market equilibrium, we discuss the economic criterion of efficiency—a notion used throughout the study of environmental economics to evaluate public and private responses to pollution problems. From there, we develop welfare measures, which are useful in evaluating the effect of environmental policy on society. All the analytical and modeling tools presented here will serve as the foundation for our study of market failure in the next chapter.

# Market Models: The Fundamentals

## *Defining the Relevant Market*

**market** The interaction between consumers and producers to exchange a well-defined commodity.

In economic analysis, the concept of a market is given a broader definition than in everyday usage. Specifically, a **market** refers to the interaction between consumers (or buyers) and producers (or sellers) for the purpose of exchanging a well-defined commodity. This more theoretical definition is purposefully general and abstract, since an economic market is meant to refer to the process of exchange and the conditions underlying that exchange for a broad range of economic activities. For example, this definition is as relevant to the purchase and sale of labor in the factor market as it is to the exchange of groceries at a supermarket. As we will discover in upcoming chapters, it can even be applied to an analysis of pollution control in the "market for environmental quality." Hence, one of the more critical steps in economic analysis is defining the market context for the good or service under investigation.

## *Specifying the Market Model*

Once the relevant market is defined, a model of that market and its characteristics must be specified. The form of the model varies with the objective of the prospective study and its level of complexity. Simple qualitative relationships among economic variables can be modeled using a two-dimensional graph. To quantify these relationships, models are refined through the use of equations or functions.[1] Formal testing is accomplished through empirical analysis of these theorized relationships using real-world data.[2]

# The Model of Supply and Demand: An Overview

By definition, a market exchange for any commodity comprises two sets of independent decision makers—buyers and sellers. Each is motivated by different objectives, and each is influenced and even constrained by different economic factors. Thus, modeling the exchange of a product involves the specification of these two distinct market perspectives. The decisions of sellers or producers are modeled through a **supply** function, while consumers' decisions are modeled through a **demand** function. When considered simultaneously, the resulting market model of supply and demand determines equilibrium output and price.

---

[1] For the most part, when we use equations in the text, we will specify linear relationships for simplicity.

[2] In later chapters, we examine the results of some important empirical studies in environmental economics.

## The Purpose of the Model

The primary objective of the supply and demand model is to facilitate an analysis of market conditions and any observed changes in price. An investigation of price movements can discern the presence of shortages and surpluses, the existence of resource misallocations, and the economic implications of government policy initiatives. For example, environmental economists can use supply and demand models to investigate the effectiveness of a gasoline tax in reducing gas consumption as a way to help improve urban air quality. By studying the associated changes in market conditions and movements in gasoline prices, economists can determine how consumption patterns are affected, how the tax burden is shared between the consumer and producer, and how income distribution is affected.

More complex analysis is necessary when the market system fails to operate properly. In these instances, the conventional model of supply and demand must be modified to account for those conditions that weaken the operation of market forces. Economic theory suggests that the persistence of environmental problems such as urban smog and water pollution are the result of failures or breakdowns in the market system. Of course, to understand why this is so and to begin to formulate solutions, it is necessary to have a good command of the market process, the underlying supply and demand conditions, and the mechanisms of the price system.

## Building a Basic Model: Competitive Markets for Private Goods

To develop a basic model of supply and demand, we make a number of assumptions. First, a competitive *goods* market is assumed, which is characterized by (i) a large number of independent buyers and sellers with no control over price; (ii) a homogeneous or standardized product; (iii) the absence of entry barriers; (iv) perfect information; and (v) perfect mobility of resources. Second, the market for *resources* also is assumed to be competitive. This implies that the individual firm has no control over input prices—a result that will simplify the model. Finally, the output being exchanged in the market is assumed to be a private good. A **private good** is a commodity that has two characteristics—rivalry in consumption and excludability. This means that consumption of the good by one person precludes that of another, and the benefits of consumption are exclusive to that single consumer. This assumption of a private (as opposed to a public)[3] good is critical to a conventional analysis of quantity and price determination.

**private good** A commodity that has two characteristics: rivalry in consumption and excludability.

---

[3] Public goods are excluded from our analysis because they represent a type of market failure. These are commodities like national defense and clean air, whose consumption is both nonrival and nonexclusive. That is, once a public good is provided to one consumer, it is difficult or very costly to prevent others from sharing in its consumption. A more formal development of the theory of public goods as it pertains to environmental issues will be presented in the next chapter.

# Market Demand

Demand refers to the market response of consumers who adjust their purchasing decisions to maximize their satisfaction, or what economists term "utility." There are many factors that influence consumers' decisions. However, since a key objective of market analysis is price determination, the demand function is specified as the relationship between the quantity demanded by consumers and price, holding constant all other variables that influence this decision. Economists use the Latin phrase, *ceteris paribus*, abbreviated *c.p.*, to mean "holding all else constant." Hence, **demand** is formally defined as the quantities of a good the consumer is willing and able to purchase at some set of prices during a discrete time period, *c.p.* The consumer's "ability to pay" refers to the income constraint that limits consumer choice. The "willingness to pay" is the value or benefit the consumer expects to receive from consumption of the commodity. In fact, this willingness to pay or **demand price** is considered to be a measure of the **marginal benefit (*MB*)** associated with consuming another unit of the good.

> **demand** The quantities of a good the consumer is willing and able to purchase at a set of prices during some discrete time period, *c.p.*

The key economic variables held constant when specifying demand are the wealth and income of the consumer, prices of related goods (i.e., substitute products and complementary goods), preferences, and price expectations. A change in any of these variables alters the *entire* price–quantity relationship, which represents a *change in demand*. This is distinct from the effect on consumption of a change in price, which causes only a *change in quantity demanded*. For example, consumers typically buy more of a good when it goes on sale. This is simply a change in the quantity demanded of the product in response to a price change. On the other hand, if, for example, consumers' tastes change such that they desire more of a product at *all* possible prices, the result would be a change in *demand*. A case in point is the observed shift in consumer preferences toward "environmentally friendly" products at all possible prices. Application 2.1 discusses survey data that speak to this phenomenon and its impact on market demand.

## The Law of Demand

Under conventional circumstances, the qualitative relationship between quantity demanded and price is an inverse one. Hence, a *rise* in price is associated with a *fall* in quantity demanded, and the converse is true. This relationship is referred to as the **Law of Demand,** which asserts that there is an inverse relationship between the price of a good and the quantity demanded of that good. This is a highly intuitive theory, since it is reasonable to expect consumers to view price as an obstacle that limits consumption, given their income constraints.[4]

> **Law of Demand** There is an inverse relationship between price and quantity demanded of a good, *c.p.*

---

[4] There are more advanced explanations for the Law of Demand, specifically the income effect and the substitution effect. The interested reader can refer to any microeconomics text for a discussion of these concepts.

# Consumer Demand and Environmental Issues: What Really Matters?

According to a 1991 survey of 410 New York adults, environmental safety has become an important influence on consumer decision making. Approximately 93 percent of the respondents in this survey believe that protecting the environment is a "very important factor" in their purchasing decisions. However, while this new influence on consumer demand is a viable one, only 1 in 10 of the survey respondents place environmental safety as a top priority. Product price and quality continue to be the most significant determinants of consumers' buying decisions. These findings have been supported by other sources. A 1994 national poll, for example, indicated that over 80 percent of Americans were in favor of more stringent environmental laws, yet only 54 percent were willing to incur the economic costs of achieving improved environmental quality.

Notwithstanding the strong hold that price and quality have on American buyers, the survey of New York adults *does* indicate that consumers will switch brands in favor of environmentally safer products. This change in preferences implies a shift in market demand toward these products and away from less safe substitutes. Some of the nondurable consumer product groups affected by this phenomenon are detergents, diapers, aerosol sprays, and cleaners. Overall, 44.6 percent of all survey participants say they have switched brands for environmental reasons, with a higher proportion reported for the 31- to 45-year-old age group. Gender differences also exist with respect to this switching phenomenon. Some 49.4 percent of females in the survey express a willingness to substitute toward more environmentally safe brands, while the comparable proportion for males is reported at 37.9 percent.

Recognizing the market opportunity, manufacturers are responding to this trend by promoting their brand names as "environmentally safe." The survey provides some information about the relative success of this effort across competitive commodities. Brand names such as Clorox, Arm & Hammer, Tide, L'Oreal, and Revlon are among those perceived by consumers as associated with environmentally superior products. This brand recognition suggests that the advertised commitment to environmental concerns of certain manufacturers is perceived as more credible than that of other firms.

Just as demand theory dictates, consumer decision making depends on a variety of market conditions and product characteristics. According to this survey, price continues to be a major determinant of demand, particularly in an economic slowdown. Nonetheless, environmental concerns have some effect on consumers' buying habits—at least for some nondurable products. On the supply side, manufacturers are adjusting their production and marketing strategies to respond to this change in consumer preferences and not miss out on a lucrative opportunity. Of course, the demand for some products is more sensitive to this influence than others. And as time progresses, firms will have to monitor the degree of market responsiveness to environmental concerns to determine if this is a short-term or long-term phenomenon.

SOURCES: Lorne Manly. "It Doesn't Pay to Go Green When Consumers are Seeing Red." *Adweek*, March 23, 1992, pp. 32–33; John L. Fialka. "Gore Faces Cool Response to Issue of Global Warming." *The Wall Street Journal*, August 27, 1997, p. A18.

## Modeling Individual Demand

To illustrate the Law of Demand, Table 2.1 presents hypothetical data for an individual's demand for one-liter bottles of mineral water. The values show the utility-maximizing quantity decisions in a one-month period for a set of prices ranging from $0.50 to $5.00 per bottle. Notice how the

| TABLE 2.1 | SINGLE CONSUMER'S DEMAND DATA FOR BOTTLED MINERAL WATER |
| --- | --- |

| Price in Dollars $P$ | Quantity Demanded (bottles/month) $q_d = -4P + 20$ |
| --- | --- |
| 0.50 | 18 |
| 1.00 | 16 |
| 1.50 | 14 |
| 2.00 | 12 |
| 2.50 | 10 |
| 3.00 | 8 |
| 3.50 | 6 |
| 4.00 | 4 |
| 4.50 | 2 |
| 5.00 | 0 |

inverse relationship between quantity demanded and price holds throughout. While these data give only a limited sampling of price–quantity pairs, an equation of the same relationship models *all* possible price–quantity responses for the consumer. In this case, the demand function is the simple linear relationship: $q_d = -4P + 20$, where the lowercase "$q_d$" signifies the quantity demanded of a single individual, and $P$ represents the dollar price per one-liter bottle. Notice that if any of the $P$ values from Table 2.1 are substituted into the right-hand side of the equation, the corresponding $q_d$ values can be obtained algebraically. For example, if $P = \$3$, $q_d = -4(3) + 20 = 8$.

By convention, the graphical depiction of demand uses the *inverse* form of the function; that is, $P = f(q_d)$. Solving the equation for $P$ in terms of $q_d$ generates the following: $P = -0.25q_d + 5$. The graph of this single consumer's demand curve (*d*) is shown in Figure 2.1.

### *Deriving Market Demand from Individual Demand Data*

**market demand for a private good** The decisions of all consumers willing and able to purchase a good; derived by summing the individual demands *horizontally*.

For most applications in economics, the collective decision making of *all* consumers in a given market is more relevant than that of a single consumer. Thus, the more appropriate concept is **market demand,** representing all consumers who are willing and able to purchase the commodity. This is derived by summing over the individual demand data. For private goods, this summing is done over the *quantity* levels at each demand price and is therefore referred to as "horizontal summing," since quantity is conventionally

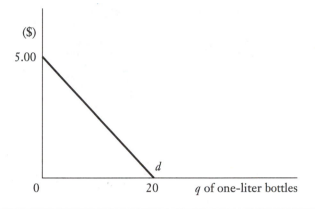

| FIGURE 2.1 | GRAPHICAL MODEL OF ONE CONSUMER'S DEMAND (*d*) FOR BOTTLED MINERAL WATER |

This graphical model of one consumer's demand (*d*) uses the *inverse* form of the function, $P = -0.25q_d + 5$, where $-0.25$ is the slope and $+5$ is the vertical intercept. The negative slope illustrates the Law of Demand.

plotted on the *horizontal* axis.[5] Even though price is the same for all consumers, quantity decisions are variable because of differences in other factors like consumer income, wealth, tastes, and expectations.

For simplicity, we first illustrate this summing procedure by adding the demand of only one other consumer to the model specified previously. Individual demand data for two hypothetical consumers, Consumers 1 and 2, are given in Table 2.2. Notice that each makes unique decisions about quantity because each has a unique income level, stock of wealth, preference ordering, and so forth. The aggregate demand for these two individuals is found by summing the two quantity columns at each price level, the result of which is shown in the far right-hand column of the table. The same method can be applied to an algebraic model by adding each pair of corresponding terms in the two demand equations. This is shown below:[6]

| | |
|---|---|
| Demand for Consumer 1: | $q_{d1} = -4P + 20$ |
| + Demand for Consumer 2: | $q_{d2} = -2P + 10$ |
| Demand for Consumers 1 and 2: | $q_{d(1+2)} = (q_{d1} + q_{d2}) = -6P + 30$ |

[5] Horizontal summing is characteristic of **private goods.** Because consumption of such goods is excludable, each individual is able to choose his or her own quantity. As we will discuss in the next chapter, this will *not* be true for public goods, an outcome with important environmental economic implications.

[6] As an exercise, verify that the price–quantity pairs given in Table 2.2 satisfy each corresponding algebraic expression.

| TABLE 2.2 | COMBINED DEMAND DATA FOR BOTTLED MINERAL WATER FOR TWO CONSUMERS, CONSUMER 1 AND CONSUMER 2 | | |
|---|---|---|---|

| Price in Dollars $P$ | Quantity Demanded by Consumer 1 (bottles/month) $q_{d1} = -4P + 20$ | Quantity Demanded by Consumer 2 (bottles/month) $q_{d2} = -2P + 10$ | Combined Quantity Demanded by Both Consumers (bottles/month) $q_{d(1+2)} = (q_{d1} + q_{d2})$ $= -6P + 30$ |
|---|---|---|---|
| 0.50 | 18 | 9 | 27 |
| 1.00 | 16 | 8 | 24 |
| 1.50 | 14 | 7 | 21 |
| 2.00 | 12 | 6 | 18 |
| 2.50 | 10 | 5 | 15 |
| 3.00 | 8 | 4 | 12 |
| 3.50 | 6 | 3 | 9 |
| 4.00 | 4 | 2 | 6 |
| 4.50 | 2 | 1 | 3 |
| 5.00 | 0 | 0 | 0 |

To derive the market demand, we use the same approach to aggregate across *all* consumers. Maintaining the characteristics of a competitive market, we assume there are 100 consumers in the market for bottled mineral water. The hypothetical data are shown in Table 2.3. For each price, we show the combined quantity values for Consumers 1 and 2 in the second column, the aggregated data for the remaining 98 consumers in the third, and the market quantity demanded, $Q_d = \Sigma q_d$, in the fourth. The corresponding equations are as follows:

| Demand for Consumers 1 and 2: | $q_{d(1+2)} =$ | $-6P + 30$ |
|---|---|---|
| + Demand for Consumers 3 through 100: | $q_{d(3...100)} =$ | $-94P + 1,120$ |
| Market demand: | | $Q_d = -100P + 1,150$ |

The graphical depiction of the *inverse* market demand curve (*D*) is shown in Figure 2.2.[7] At each price level, the horizontal distance between the vertical axis and *D* is exactly equal to the sum of the analogous horizontal intervals for each of the 100 individual demand (*d*) curves.

---

[7] The algebraic expression for the inverse market demand function is $P = -0.01Q_d + 11.5$.

| TABLE 2.3 | | | |
|---|---|---|---|
| **MARKET DEMAND DATA FOR BOTTLED MINERAL WATER** | | | |
| **Price in Dollars** $P$ | **Quantity Demanded by Consumers 1 and 2 (bottles/month)** $q_{d(1+2)} = -6P + 30$ | **Quantity Demanded by Consumers 3 through 100 (bottles/month)** $q_{d(3...100)} = -94P + 1{,}120$ | **Market Demand (bottles/month)** $Q_d = -100P + 1{,}150$ |
| 0.50 | 27 | 1073 | 1100 |
| 1.00 | 24 | 1026 | 1050 |
| 1.50 | 21 | 979 | 1000 |
| 2.00 | 18 | 932 | 950 |
| 2.50 | 15 | 885 | 900 |
| 3.00 | 12 | 838 | 850 |
| 3.50 | 9 | 791 | 800 |
| 4.00 | 6 | 744 | 750 |
| 4.50 | 3 | 697 | 700 |
| 5.00 | 0 | 650 | 650 |

| FIGURE 2.2 | |
|---|---|
| **GRAPHICAL MODEL OF THE MARKET DEMAND (*D*) FOR BOTTLED MINERAL WATER** | |

This graphical model of the market demand (*D*) for bottled mineral water uses the *inverse* market demand function, $P = -0.01Q_d + 11.5$, which represents the aggregate decisions of all consumers in the market. The market demand curve is derived using a horizontal summing procedure across all individual demand curves. Thus, at each price level, the horizontal distance between the vertical axis and *D* is exactly equal to the sum of the analogous horizontal intervals for each of the 100 individual demand (*d*) curves.

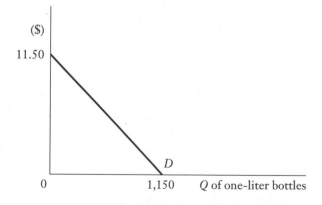

# Market Supply

On the opposite side of the market, we derive a supply relationship based on the decisions of producers who are motivated by profit. Each firm's supply decision is modeled as a function of price, even though this decision is influenced by many other variables. Hence, we say that **supply** refers to the quantities of a good the producer is willing and able to bring to market at a given set of prices during some discrete time period, *c.p.* Among the variables that potentially affect the price–quantity response of a firm are production technology, input prices, taxes and subsidies, and price expectations. Analogous to the demand side of the market, changes in these determinants affect the entire price–quantity relationship, causing a *change in supply*, while a movement in price is associated with a *change in quantity supplied*.

> **supply** The quantities of a good the producer is willing and able to bring to market at a given set of prices during some discrete time period, *c.p.*

## The Law of Supply

The qualitative relationship between quantity supplied and price is generally a positive one. That is, a *rise* in price is associated with a *rise* in quantity supplied, and the converse holds as well. This relationship is referred to as the **Law of Supply,** which asserts that there is a direct relationship between the price of a good and the quantity supplied by producers. The conventional assumption that firms are profit-maximizers suggests that a higher price should be an incentive for firms to bring more of the product to market. A contemporary example of how powerful the profit motive can be is in the context of "green markets" discussed in Application 2.2.

> **Law of Supply** There is a direct relationship between price and quantity supplied of a good, *c.p.*

A more formal justification for the Law of Supply is based on the nature of firms' costs as production is carried out. As the firm produces more output ($Q$), its **total costs ($TC$)** rise proportionally faster, meaning the ratio of the change in $TC$ (i.e., $\Delta TC$) to the change in $Q$ (i.e., $\Delta Q$) is increasing. This ratio, $\Delta TC/\Delta Q$, defines the firm's **marginal cost ($MC$)** of production, the additional cost of producing another unit of output. Since $MC$ rises as $Q$ rises, firms need to charge a higher price for each extra unit of output they produce. Hence, the existence of rising $MC$ supports the positive price–quantity relationship given by the Law of Supply.

## Modeling Individual Supply

The Law of Supply is illustrated using hypothetical data for a single producer of bottled mineral water given in Table 2.4. The quantity column shows a single firm's profit-maximizing output decisions associated with prices ranging from $0.50 to $5.00. Notice how the positive relationship between the **supply price** and quantity supplied holds throughout. The linear equation associated with these data is: $q_s = 16P - 4$, where lowercase $q_s$ is used to signify the quantity supplied by a *single* firm. Each of the price–quantity pairs given in Table 2.4 satisfies this equation.

# Profit Opportunities in Green Markets: Japan Takes the Lead

The lure of profit is one of the most powerful influences on firms' market decisions. A case in point is the entrepreneurial response to emerging industries in pollution abatement equipment and energy-saving technologies. Nowhere is the reaction more striking than in Japan. Promoting a technology-oriented solution to environmental problems, Japan's industrial sector has already taken the lead in these new high-growth "green markets."

Japan is pursuing opportunities proffered by environmental markets with a momentum virtually unmatched by any other nation. Patterned after their time-tested success in achieving dominance in other world markets, the Japanese are using a technology-based approach toward developing these new industries. For example, Toyota, Nissan, Honda, and Mazda are intensely focused on developing cleaner-running engines, superior catalytic converters, and lightweight car bodies. Fuji Electric's innovative efforts have won it world dominance in fuel-cell technology. And an ongoing research project directed by the Ministry of International Trade and Industry plans to use biotechnology to manufacture hydrogen, believed to be the energy source of the future.

Japan's approach to environmental concerns is rooted in a belief that economic growth need *not* be sacrificed to protect the ecology as long as production methods are properly adjusted through technological innovation. Some see this ideology as myopic, ignoring issues such as the destruction of rain forests and the decline of endangered species, which cannot be corrected solely through high-tech invention. Others perceive Japan's national posture as an accurate long-term assessment of how to control environmental damage and one that will allow the Japanese to achieve dominance in still another group of important industries.

Why aren't other countries' industrial sectors pursuing these opportunities with the same energy? Often the question is pointed squarely at American industry. After all, the United States generates disproportionately higher amounts of certain pollutants like sulfur oxides than Japan. Reportedly, part of the reason is that incentives at the firm level are weaker in the United States, where federal legislation is relatively lenient by Japanese standards. Another more deeply rooted issue may be that American industry tends to view environmental controls as an obstacle to growth and a negative influence on productivity.

In any case, Japanese corporations are confronting environmental problems and turning them into opportunities for growth and worldwide commercial success. There is little doubt that their head start in many environmental industries could win them market power that will be hard to surpass in the future. The message to industry in other nations is clear—"green markets" are offering lucrative profits, opportunities for commercial success, and a chance to participate directly in solving the world's environmental problems.

SOURCES: Neil Gross, "The Green Giant? It May Be Japan." *Business Week*. February 24, 1992, p. 74; Jacob M. Schlesinger. "In Japan, Environment Means an Opportunity for New Technologies." *The Wall Street Journal*, November 5, 1990; Dianne Dumanoski. "Some See Profits; We See Obstacles." *Boston Globe*, November 5, 1990.

The graphical model of the single firm's supply curve (*s*) is illustrated in Figure 2.3. Again, the convention is to plot price on the vertical axis and quantity on the horizontal, using the inverse form of the equation. In this case, the inverse supply function is $P = 0.0625q_s + 0.25$. Given the absence of extremes in the model, the supply curve has the expected positive slope in accordance with the Law of Supply and the underlying theory of rising

| TABLE 2.4 | SINGLE PRODUCER'S SUPPLY DATA FOR BOTTLED MINERAL WATER |
|---|---|

| Price in Dollars $P$ | Quantity Supplied (bottles/month) $q_s = 16P - 4$ |
|---|---|
| 0.50 | 4 |
| 1.00 | 12 |
| 1.50 | 20 |
| 2.00 | 28 |
| 2.50 | 36 |
| 3.00 | 44 |
| 3.50 | 52 |
| 4.00 | 60 |
| 4.50 | 68 |
| 5.00 | 76 |

| FIGURE 2.3 | GRAPHICAL MODEL OF ONE PRODUCER'S SUPPLY (S) OF BOTTLED MINERAL WATER |
|---|---|

The model shown is the supply (*s*) of one representative producer in the bottled mineral water market. It is based on the inverse supply function, $P = 0.0625q_s + 0.25$. Notice that this function has a slope of $+0.0625$ and a vertical intercept of $+0.25$. The positive slope supports the relationship given in the Law of Supply and the theory of rising *MC*. Since the market for bottled mineral water is assumed to be competitive, this supply curve is the firm's *MC* curve.

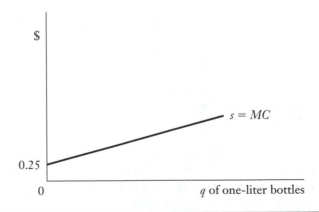

| TABLE 2.5 | COMBINED SUPPLY DATA FOR BOTTLED MINERAL WATER FOR TWO PRODUCERS, PRODUCER 1 AND PRODUCER 2 |
|---|---|

| Price in Dollars $P$ | Quantity Supplied by Producer 1 (bottles/month) $q_{s1} = +16P - 4$ | Quantity Supplied by Producer 2 (bottles/month) $q_{s2} = +16P - 4$ | Combined Quantity Supplied by Both Producers (bottles/month) $q_{s(1+2)} = q_{s1} + q_{s2}$ $= +32P - 8$ |
|---|---|---|---|
| 0.50 | 4 | 4 | 8 |
| 1.00 | 12 | 12 | 24 |
| 1.50 | 20 | 20 | 40 |
| 2.00 | 28 | 28 | 56 |
| 2.50 | 36 | 36 | 72 |
| 3.00 | 44 | 44 | 88 |
| 3.50 | 52 | 52 | 104 |
| 4.00 | 60 | 60 | 120 |
| 4.50 | 68 | 68 | 136 |
| 5.00 | 76 | 76 | 152 |

*MC.* In fact, under the assumption of competitive output markets, the firm's short-run supply curve *is* its *MC* curve.

### Deriving Market Supply from Individual Supply Data

**market supply of a private good** The combined decisions of all producers in a given industry; derived by summing the individual supplies *horizontally.*

To analyze production at an aggregated level, **market supply** of a private good is derived using a *horizontal* summing procedure over all the individual quantity decisions of firms, analogous to what is done on the demand side. However, because the output market is assumed to be competitive, the adding-up process on the supply side is simpler, since all firms are identical under such market conditions.

Just as on the demand side, we begin by illustrating the aggregation procedure using only two firms. Hypothetical data for two representative producers of bottled mineral water and their combined supply decisions are given in Table 2.5. The algebraic counterpart is as follows:

Supply by Producer 1: $\qquad q_{s1} = +16P - 4$

\+ Supply by Producer 2: $\qquad q_{s2} = +16P - 4$

Combined Supply by Producers 1 and 2: $\qquad q_{s(1+2)} = (q_{s1} + q_{s2}) = +32P - 8$

| TABLE 2.6 | MARKET SUPPLY DATA FOR BOTTLED MINERAL WATER | | |

| Price in Dollars $P$ | Quantity Supplied by Producers 1 and 2 (bottles/month) $q_{s(1+2)} = 32P - 8$ | Quantity Supplied by Producers 3 through 25 (bottles/month) $q_{s(3...25)} = 368P - 92$ | Market Supply (bottles/month) $Q_s = 400P - 100$ |
|---|---|---|---|
| 0.50 | 8 | 92 | 100 |
| 1.00 | 24 | 276 | 300 |
| 1.50 | 40 | 460 | 500 |
| 2.00 | 56 | 644 | 700 |
| 2.50 | 72 | 828 | 900 |
| 3.00 | 88 | 1,012 | 1,100 |
| 3.50 | 104 | 1,196 | 1,300 |
| 4.00 | 120 | 1,380 | 1,500 |
| 4.50 | 136 | 1,564 | 1,700 |
| 5.00 | 152 | 1,748 | 1,900 |

To bring the supply relationship up to the market level, we follow the same summing procedure for *all* firms in the industry assumed to total 25 in number. The hypothetical **market supply** data are shown in Table 2.6. For each market price, the combined supply decisions for Producers 1 and 2 are given in the second column, the aggregated data for the remaining 23 producers in the third, and the market quantity supplied, $Q_s = \Sigma q_s$, in the last. The corresponding supply equations are as follows:

| Supply by Producers 1 and 2 | $q_{s(1+2)} =$ | $32P -$ | $8$ |
|---|---|---|---|
| + Supply by Producers 3 through 25 | $q_{s(3...25)} =$ | $368P -$ | $92$ |
| Market Supply | | $Q_s =$ | $400P - 100$ |

Figure 2.4 shows the graphical model of the market supply curve ($S$) in inverse form.[8] At each price level, the horizontal distance between the vertical axis and $S$ is exactly equal to the sum of the analogous horizontal intervals for each of the 25 individual supply ($s$) curves. Furthermore, since the competitive firm's supply ($s$) curve is its $MC$ curve, the market supply ($S$) curve is in turn the horizontal sum of each of the individual firm's $MC$ curves.

---

[8] The corresponding equation for market supply in inverse form is: $P = 0.0025Q_s + 0.25$.

| FIGURE 2.4 | **GRAPHICAL MODEL OF THE MARKET SUPPLY (S) OF BOTTLED MINERAL WATER** |

This depicts the graphical model of the market supply curve (*S*) for bottled mineral water based on the inverse form of the market supply function: $P = 0.0025Q_s + 0.25$. The market supply curve is derived by summing all the individual supply curves (*s*) horizontally. Hence, at each price level, the horizontal distance between the vertical axis and *S* is exactly equal to the sum of the analogous horizontal intervals for each of the 25 individual supply (*s*) curves. And, since each individual supply (*s*) curve is the single firm's *MC* curve, the market supply (*S*) represents the horizontal sum of all of these *MC* curves.

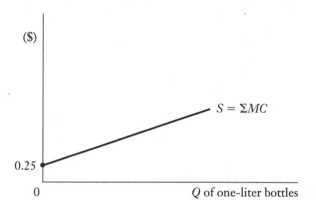

## Market Equilibrium

Thus far, we have considered each side of the market separately to develop distinct models of economic decision making. To generate a model of price determination, we must consider supply and demand *simultaneously* to allow for the interaction of consumers and producers in the marketplace. The formal theory that price is simultaneously determined by supply and demand is one of the most significant in all of economic analysis.[9]

### Equilibrium Price and Quantity

**equilibrium price and quantity** The "market-clearing" price ($P_e$) associated with the equilibrium quantity ($Q_e$), where $Q_d = Q_s$.

Together, the forces of supply and demand determine a unique **equilibrium price ($P_e$)** at which point the market system "comes to rest" or has no tendency for change. **Equilibrium or "market-clearing" price ($Pe$)** is

---

[9]This theory is attributable to Alfred Marshall, who first published this hypothesis in his *Principles of Economics* in 1890.

| TABLE 2.7 | | | |
|---|---|---|---|
| **MARKET SUPPLY AND DEMAND DATA FOR BOTTLED MINERAL WATER** | | | |
| **Price in Dollars** $P$ | **Market Quantity Supplied** $Q_s = 400P - 100$ | **Market Quantity Demanded** $Q_d = -100P + 1{,}150$ | **Market Surplus/Shortage** |
| 0.50 | 100 | 1,100 | Shortage = 1,000 |
| 1.00 | 300 | 1,050 | Shortage = 750 |
| 1.50 | 500 | 1,000 | Shortage = 500 |
| 2.00 | 700 | 950 | Shortage = 250 |
| **2.50** | **900** | **900** | **Equilibrium** |
| 3.00 | 1,100 | 850 | Surplus = 250 |
| 3.50 | 1,300 | 800 | Surplus = 500 |
| 4.00 | 1,500 | 750 | Surplus = 750 |
| 4.50 | 1,700 | 700 | Surplus = 1,000 |
| 5.00 | 1,900 | 650 | Surplus = 1,250 |

the price at which quantity demanded by consumers, $Q_d$, is exactly equal to the quantity supplied by producers, $Q_s$ (i.e., where $Q_d = Q_s$). Only at $P_e$ will the associated **equilibrium quantity ($Q_e$)** be both the profit-maximizing production level for firms and the utility-maximizing consumption level for consumers.

Market equilibrium for our hypothetical mineral water market is illustrated in Table 2.7 where market supply and demand data are presented together. Notice that equilibrium price in this market is $2.50, the only price at which quantity supplied ($Q_s$) is exactly equal to the quantity demanded ($Q_d$) of 900 units. This result can also be determined algebraically by solving the market demand and market supply equations simultaneously.[10]

Graphically, market equilibrium is modeled by diagramming the market demand ($D$) and market supply ($S$) curves together on a single coordinate system. This is illustrated in Figure 2.5. Note that equilibrium is shown as the point where $D$ and $S$ intersect or where $Q_d = Q_s$.

### Market Adjustment to Disequilibrium

If the prevailing market price is at some level other than at equilibrium, it must be the case that $Q_d \neq Q_s$, and the market is said to be in **disequilibrium.** As a consequence, consumers and producers have an incentive to make some adjustment that will restore equilibrium to the market. The

---

[10] Verify this assertion by substituting the market supply equation, $Q_s = 400P - 100$, and the market demand equation, $Q_d = -100P + 1{,}150$, into the equilibrium condition, $Q_s = Q_d$.

FIGURE 2.5 **EQUILIBRIUM IN THE MARKET FOR BOTTLED MINERAL WATER: MARKET SUPPLY AND MARKET DEMAND**

The model of market demand ($D$) and market supply ($S$) on a single coordinate system determine equilibrium price ($P_e$) and quantity ($Q_e$) at their point of intersection.

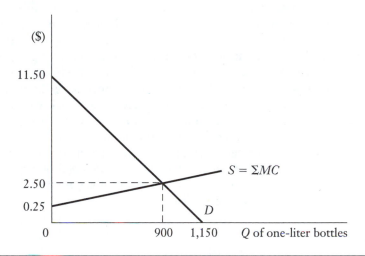

motivation for this adjustment and the process by which it is implemented depend on whether there is excess demand or excess supply.

**shortage** Excess demand of a commodity equal to $(Q_d - Q_s)$ that arises if price is *below* its equilibrium level.

**Shortage.** If the actual price, $P$, is *below* the equilibrium price, $P_e$, there is **excess demand,** meaning $Q_d$ exceeds $Q_s$ at that price level. The result is a market **shortage** of the commodity equal to $(Q_d - Q_s)$. Refer back to Table 2.7 to see the shortages arising in the mineral water market at every price below $2.50. This means that consumers want more of the good at the existing price level than firms are willing and able to provide to the market. Responding to this, firms would be willing to increase quantity supplied, moving up the market supply curve and elevating price as they do so. This process would continue until the incentive to change quantity no longer exists, which occurs when price is increased to its equilibrium level.

**surplus** Excess supply of a commodity equal to $(Q_s - Q_d)$ that arises if price is *above* its equilibrium level.

**Surplus.** When the actual price, $P$, is *above* the equilibrium price, $P_e$, firms are unable to sell all their output at the prevailing price level, and they begin to observe their inventories accumulating with unsold stock. In this case, there is **excess supply,** meaning that $Q_s$ exceeds $Q_d$ at the prevailing price level. The result is a market **surplus** equal to $(Q_s - Q_d)$. Look back at Table 2.7 to see the surpluses in the mineral water market at all prices above $2.50. Observing unsold supplies, firms would have an incentive to lower price to eliminate the surplus. This price reduction would continue until all of the unsold supplies are purchased, which occurs at the equilibrium price.

Notice how price movements serve as a signal that a shortage or surplus exists, while the stability of price suggests equilibrium. The adjustments that occur when the market is in disequilibrium happen because of the market's internal forces. As long as the assumptions of the model hold (and this is an important point), there is no need for government intervention or any other third-party mediation to achieve equilibrium. An example of how the market adjustment process operates is discussed in Application 2.3 in the context of the recycled newspaper market.

Thus far, we have examined the fundamental elements of a competitive market and illustrated how the simultaneous effect of demand and supply decisions determines equilibrium price and quantity. But we need to go beyond this point to understand the *implications* of a competitive equilibrium—first in terms of the allocation of economic resources and then in terms of the well-being of society.

## The Economic Criteria of Efficiency

Economic analysis is guided by specific criteria. One of these deals with the proper allocation of resources among alternative productive uses, referred to as **allocative efficiency.** Another is concerned with economizing on resources used in production, called **technical efficiency.** Each of these criteria is relevant to all applied economic disciplines, including environmental economics. We begin with a discussion of allocative efficiency.

### Allocative Efficiency

As illustrated by the materials balance model, the way a market system uses resources is critical, not only for production and consumption, but also for the natural environment. But how is the resource allocation to be evaluated? The answer is through a procedure that involves the following two elements:

- an assessment of benefits and costs; and
- the use of marginal analysis.

We have already introduced these elements in our prior discussion of demand and supply. Now we use them to draw important conclusions about decision making and equilibrium under competitive conditions—first at the *market* level and then at the *firm* level.

# Recycling Efforts and the Volatile Market for Newsprint

The amount of trash generated in the United States has risen from 88 million tons in 1960 to 208 million tons in 1995. Of this tonnage, nearly 40 percent is paper and paper products. In a logical move, many communities established paper recycling programs in the 1980s. The first step was to encourage individuals and firms to bring paper wastes to collection centers. According to EPA statistics shown below, this recovery stage has met with some success.

Although these data suggest that society responded responsibly to the waste disposal dilemma, they belie a very real problem. In their haste to reduce paper waste in landfills, many communities failed to recognize the need to create a market for recovered materials. The recovery stage of the recycling process generates a supply of used materials. But if there is insufficient demand for these materials, communities face a glut of recovered wastes.

| Types of Paper Waste | Percent Recovered | | |
|---|---|---|---|
| | 1980 | 1990 | 1995 |
| Corrugated boxes | 37.4 | 48.0 | 64.2 |
| Newspaper | 27.3 | 38.0 | 53.0 |
| Books and magazines | 8.3 | 20.9 | 47.1 |
| Office papers | 21.8 | 26.5 | 44.3 |

SOURCE: U.S. Environmental Protection Agency, Office of Solid Waste and Emergency Response. *Characterization of Municipal Solid Waste in the United States, 1996 Update.* Washington, DC: U.S. EPA, May 1997, Table 16, p. 65, and Table 21, p. 73.

This potential problem became a reality for recovered newspapers, which grew by 34 percent over a five-year period in the late 1980s. The excess supply sent the price of used newsprint plummeting—a financial dilemma for many American cities and towns. According to a *Business Week* report, towns in New Jersey that used to *sell* the material for $20 per ton later had to *pay* as much as $10 a ton to get rid of it. Hence, the price actually fell to a negative value. Similar scenarios were reported by communities throughout the northeastern United States.

To correct the excess supply of recovered newspapers without facing dramatic price declines, it was necessary to stimulate market demand. Virtually all levels of government took an active role. A number of state governments passed laws requiring newspapers to be partly printed on recycled paper. In 1993, President Clinton signed Executive Order 12873, calling for all printing and writing paper to contain at least 20 percent recovered paper (which was to increase to 30 percent on December 31, 1998). The EPA established clearinghouses and hotlines to bring together suppliers and demanders of recyclables. Added influences were the thriving domestic economy and the rising demand of developing nations, whose growth required new sources of paper inputs.

Taken together, market demand swamped existing supplies, and in 1995, there was a shortage of recycled newsprint. Just as predicted by economic theory, the shortage placed upward pressure on price, which rose to between $100 and $200 per ton. But the boom in the market was temporary. By the following year, still more market fluctuations tipped the scales again—this time in the opposite direction. By 1996, excess supplies and falling demand drove prices back to the $20 per ton level of the early 1990s.

The lessons are clear. First, recycling is a complex process, and collection is just one step in that process. For recycling to be successful, there have to be complete markets—both supply *and* demand. Second, the market for recovered paper can be volatile. Although a supply of recovered paper is assured by routine recycling practices, the same is not true for demand. With the unpredictability of market demand, price in this market is anything but stable.

SOURCES: Michael Alexander. "The Challenge of Markets: The Supply of Recyclables Is Larger Than the Demand." *EPA Journal*, July/August 1992, pp. 29–33; Dori Jones Yang et al. "Recycling Is Rewriting the Rules of Papermaking." *Business Week*, April 22, 1991, pp. 100H–101H; Vicky Cahan. "Waste Not, Want Not? Not Necessarily." *Business Week*, July 17, 1989, pp. 116–17; *Los Angeles Times*, "Newspaper Recycling Booming," *Brockton Enterprise*, July 11, 1995, p. 18. Chris Reidy. "Economics of Recycling Paper Take a Tumble." *Boston Globe*, July 24, 1996, pp. A1, A16.

**Evaluating Resource Allocation at the Market Level.** Competitive markets are considered to be an ideal, a standard by which other market conditions are evaluated. If we look carefully at what is conveyed by a competitive equilibrium, we can better appreciate this characterization. At equilibrium, we know that market demand intersects market supply. But what does this mean in terms of resource allocation? Recall that we argued that prices along a demand curve are measures of marginal benefit ($MB$). Each demand price communicates the *value* consumers place on the *next* or *marginal* unit of the good based on the added benefit they expect to receive from consumption. On the supply side, there is also a marginal interpretation, but here the prices are measures of economic *cost*. Since the market supply in a competitive market is the horizontal sum of each firm's marginal cost ($MC$) curve, each supply price represents the additional cost of resources needed to produce another unit of the good. Economic costs include both the *explicit* or "out-of-pocket" costs associated with production and all *implicit* costs based on the highest-valued alternative use of any economic resource.

Taking these two interpretations together, we arrive at an important result. At the competitive equilibrium, the value society places on the good is equivalent to the value of the resources given up to produce it, or $MB = MC$. By definition, this result assures that there is an efficient allocation of scarce economic resources, or that **allocative efficiency** is achieved. **Allocative efficiency** requires that the additional value society places on another unit of the good is equal to what society must give up in scarce resources to produce it. Recognizing this outcome as part of the competitive model is important, but it is just as critical to understand *why* it arises. For that, we need to focus on the decision making of individual producers under these market conditions.

**allocative efficiency** The economic criterion that society's valuation of an additional unit of the good be equivalent to the value of the resources used to produce it.

**Evaluating Resource Allocation at the Firm Level.** Starting from a general perspective, the assumed motivation governing firm decision making is profit maximization. We further assume that the choice variable for producers is output. Hence, all firms, regardless of competitive conditions, choose the level of output that will maximize profit. **Total profit ($\pi$)** is defined as **Total revenue ($TR$)** − **Total costs ($TC$).** $TR$ is simply the dollar value of the firm's sales, found as the product of market price ($P$) and the quantity of output sold ($q$) (i.e., $TR = P \cdot q$). Total costs ($TC$) include all economic costs associated with producing the output.

**total profit** Total profit ($\pi$) = Total revenue ($TR$) − Total costs ($TC$).

To find the $q$ that achieves the highest possible $\pi$, the firm makes its decisions *at the margin*, considering the relative benefits and costs of producing each *additional* unit of output. From the firm's perspective, the benefit is measured by $TR$ and the cost by $TC$. Thus it considers the profit implications of each successive unit of output by looking at the associated *changes* in $TR$ and $TC$. If producing the *next* unit of output adds more to its $TR$ than it does to its $TC$, the firm increases production. If production adds more to $TC$ than to $TR$, production is decreased. The process goes on until there is no incentive to continue, or when the *change in TR* ($\Delta TR$) from increasing output is equal to the *change in TC* ($\Delta TC$). At this point, the *change in $\pi$* ($\Delta\pi$) from producing the last unit of output is zero, and any further increase in output would cause $\pi$ to decline. Thus, at this precise point, $\pi$ is at its maximum.[11]

Notice that the entire decision-making process relies on *changes*, which is the definition of marginal analysis. In this context, the relevant marginal variables are as follows:

- **Marginal revenue (*MR*)** is the change in total revenue (*TR*) associated with a change in production level; that is, $MR = \Delta TR/\Delta q$.

- **Marginal cost (*MC*)** is the change in total costs (*TC*) associated with a change in production level; that is, $MC = \Delta TC/\Delta q$.

- **Marginal profit (*M$\pi$*)** is the change in total profit ($\pi$) associated with a change in production level; that is, $M\pi = \Delta\pi/\Delta q$.

Thus, the firm implicitly makes its $\pi$-maximizing decisions according to the following rules:

The firm increases production as long as $MR > MC$ or as long as $M\pi > 0$.

The firm contracts production as long as $MR < MC$ or as long as $M\pi < 0$.

**profit maximization**
Achieved at the output level where $MR = MC$ or where $M\pi = 0$.

The firm achieves **profit maximization** at the output level where $MR = MC$, or where $M\pi = 0$.

Notice that the individual firm's optimal output level occurs at precisely the point where the marginal benefit *to the firm* of doing so, *MR*, is exactly offset by the marginal cost of the resources it uses, *MC*. Although this outcome validates the use of benefits and costs at the margin, it does not necessarily result in an allocatively efficient outcome. Why? Because *MR* is the marginal benefit *to the firm*, which is *not* necessarily equal to the marginal benefit *to society*, which is measured by price, *P*. In fact, the only way the firm's optimizing behavior achieves allocative efficiency is if *MR* is equal to *P*, and this equivalency occurs only under competitive conditions. To understand this, we need to reconsider how the firm's profit-maximizing decision is affected by a competitive market.

As a price taker, each firm in a competitive market must accept the market-determined price as a given. It is unable to charge a higher price, since by assumption its product is identical to that of all other firms in the

---

[11] This, of course, assumes that in the short run the firm's revenues cover its variable costs. If not, it will shut down. In the long run, the firm produces as long as its total revenues cover all of its total costs. If not, it will exit from the market.

market. Thus, if it were to *raise* price, consumers would demand none of its output and buy from other suppliers. Moreover, the firm has no incentive to *lower* price, since it can sell all it wants at the market-determined price. (Recall that the single firm is small compared to the entire market, so "selling all it wants" means that its output adjustments are, in a relative sense, insignificant.)

Since the competitive firm has no control over prevailing market conditions, it faces a price that is constant. Consequently, each additional unit the firm sells raises its total revenue by an amount exactly equal to the price of the good. This outcome translates to an important equality that is unique to competitive markets, namely that $P = MR$. Thus, although competitive firms follow the profit-maximizing decision rules derived above, the equilibrium outcome is markedly different in that allocative efficiency is assured automatically. This is summarized in the following derivation:

$\pi$-maximization requires: $\qquad\qquad\qquad\qquad\qquad MR = MC$

Competitive markets imply: $\qquad\qquad\qquad\qquad\qquad P = MR$

Thus, $\pi$-maximization for competitive firms requires: $\quad P = MC$

Now it should be clear why the competitive *market* equilibrium achieves allocative efficiency—because every firm in that market independently produces where $P = MC$.

To illustrate this outcome, Table 2.8 presents selected revenue and cost data for a representative firm in our mineral water market. First, let's confirm that $P = MR$ at all output levels. In accordance with the competitive model, notice that the prices faced by the firm are constant at the market-determined equilibrium price ($P_e$) of $2.50. The $MR$ values are found by calculating the change in $TR$ divided by the change in $q$. So, for example, when output rises from 28 units to 36 units, generating an increase in $TR$ from $70 to $90, $MR = \Delta TR/\Delta q = (\$90 - \$70)/(36 - 28) = \$20/8 = \$2.50$. As this calculation is repeated for all changes in $q$ shown in the table, $MR = \$2.50$ in every case—exactly equal to $P_e$.

Now let's examine how the firm chooses a production level that maximizes profit. As predicted by the competitive model, the $MC$ values shown in the last column of the table are the same as the set of prices associated with the firm's supply schedule. To guide its production decisions, the firm considers the $MC$ of production relative to the $MR$ at each output level. In this case, the profit-maximizing equilibrium output occurs at $q_e = 36$, where $MR = MC = \$2.50$. And, since $P = MR$ at all $q$ levels, this decision also assures that $P = MC$, indicating that resources are being allocated to production in an efficient manner. Figure 2.6 illustrates this equilibrium.

Two final observations are worth noting. First, be sure to recognize why alternative output decisions would not maximize profit. Notice in Figure 2.6 that at any output level *below* $q_e$, the firm's $MR$ exceeds $MC$, meaning

| TABLE 2.8 | | | | |
|---|---|---|---|---|
| **REVENUE AND COST DATA FOR A REPRESENTATIVE FIRM IN THE BOTTLED MINERAL WATER MARKET** | | | | |

| Price in Dollars $P_e$ | Quantity $q$ | Total Revenue $TR$ | Marginal Revenue $MR$ | Marginal Cost $MC$ |
|---|---|---|---|---|
| 2.50 | 4 | $ 10.00 | $2.50 | $0.50 |
| 2.50 | 12 | 30.00 | 2.50 | 1.00 |
| 2.50 | 20 | 50.00 | 2.50 | 1.50 |
| 2.50 | 28 | 70.00 | 2.50 | 2.00 |
| 2.50 | 36 | 90.00 | 2.50 | 2.50 |
| 2.50 | 44 | 110.00 | 2.50 | 3.00 |
| 2.50 | 52 | 130.00 | 2.50 | 3.50 |
| 2.50 | 60 | 150.00 | 2.50 | 4.00 |
| 2.50 | 68 | 170.00 | 2.50 | 4.50 |
| 2.50 | 76 | 190.00 | 2.50 | 5.00 |

| FIGURE 2.6 | |
|---|---|
| **THE COMPETITIVE FIRM'S PROFIT-MAXIMIZING EQUILIBRIUM** | |

The profit-maximizing equilibrium for the competitive firm occurs at $q_e = 36$, where $MR = MC = \$2.50$. Since $P = MR$ at all $q$ levels, it must be the case that $P = MC$ at equilibrium, indicating that resources are allocated efficiently. At any $q$ *below* $q_e$, $MR > MC$, meaning $M\pi > 0$. Hence, the firm can *increase* $\pi$ by expanding production. Conversely, at all output levels *above* $q_e$, $MR < MC$, meaning $M\pi < 0$, or $\pi$ is declining. So, the firm is better off contracting production. Only at $q_e = 36$ is $M\pi = 0$, meaning that further additions to $\pi$ are not possible and $\pi$ is at its maximum.

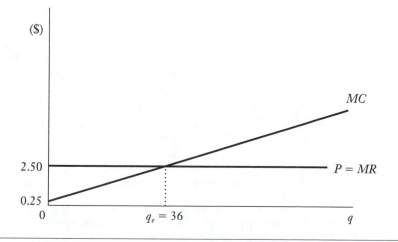

that its $M\pi$ is greater than zero. Hence, the firm can *increase* $\pi$ by expanding production. Conversely, at all output levels *above* $q_e$, its $MR$ is less than $MC$, meaning its $M\pi$ is less than zero or its $\pi$ is declining. So, the firm is better off contracting production. Only at $q = 36$ is $MR = MC$ or $M\pi = 0$, meaning that further additions to $\pi$ are not possible or that $\pi$ is at its maximum.

The second observation is that each of the other 24 firms in the bottled mineral water market would follow this same decision-making process, and each would arrive at the same $q_e$ of 36 since competitive firms are identical. Therefore, the market equilibrium quantity ($Q_e$) is equal to 900 units—the product of the number of firms in the market, 25, and the firm-level $q_e$ of 36. Notice that this result confirms the equilibrium quantity determined from the market supply and demand model.

### Technical Efficiency

**technical efficiency**
Production decisions that generate maximum output given some stock of resources.

Another important economic criterion used in market analysis is **technical efficiency.** This refers to production decisions that generate maximum output, given some stock of resources, or (saying the same thing from a slightly different perspective), decisions to produce a given output level using a minimum amount of resources. In the context of the materials balance model, achieving technical efficiency preserves the stock of natural resources and minimizes the subsequent generation of residuals arising from resource use. Furthermore, given the relationship between production and costs, technical efficiency implies that economic costs are minimized when producing a given level of output. When viewed from this perspective, it becomes apparent that technical efficiency is an application of the more general cost-effectiveness criterion introduced in Chapter 1.

A key point is to understand that market forces can achieve technical efficiency as long as competitive conditions prevail. To remain viable, the competitive firm must minimize costs, since it cannot raise price to cover the added expense of inefficient production. Were it to attempt such a strategy, demand for its product would fall to zero, since there are many other firms bringing the same product to market at a lower price. Recognizing how technical efficiency is achieved under such ideal market conditions helps economists determine *why* it is not being met in some other market context. More importantly, the magnitude of a technically inefficient decision can be assessed by comparing the resulting costs to what they *would* be if the market were allowed to operate freely.

## Welfare Measures: Consumer Surplus and Producer Surplus

In economics, an important objective is to assess the gains and losses to society associated with any event that alters market price. The supply and demand model provides the information necessary to perform these types of analyses, using concepts known as **consumer surplus** and **producer surplus.** By comparing these measures before and after a market disturbance, it is possible to quantify how society has been affected.

### Consumer Surplus

**consumer surplus**
The net benefit to buyers estimated by the excess of the marginal benefit (*MB*) of consumption over market price (*P*), aggregated over all units purchased.

To get a sense of the logic of consumer surplus, we start with a general working definition. **Consumer surplus** is a measure of net benefit accruing to buyers of a good estimated by the excess of what they are willing to pay over what they must actually pay, aggregated over all units of the good purchased in the market. Notice that consumer surplus depends on two distinct notions of price—one that measures a *willingness to pay*, and one that measures what is *actually paid.* The series of prices consumers are willing to pay for various quantities of a good are those that define the demand curve. And as discussed, each demand price is a measure of the Marginal Benefit (*MB*) associated with consumption. Conversely, the price that consumers must actually pay is the prevailing market price (*P*) determined by *both* demand and supply.

There are two major differences between these prices. First, they have different determinants. The demand price (*MB*) is determined *solely* by demand, a sort of psychic price based on how consumers value a good. On the other hand, market price (*P*) arises from the forces of supply and demand and is driven by *both* producer and consumer incentives. Second, while there is a whole series of demand prices, there is only one market price charged for *all* units sold. The result? Once the market price is determined, *all* units are sold for that single price—even those for which the demand price is much higher. Hence, consumers receive a surplus benefit for every unit purchased whose demand price exceeds the market price.

To illustrate consumer surplus graphically, Figure 2.7 reproduces the market demand for mineral water derived previously. Added to the diagram is a reference price line drawn horizontally at the equilibrium price level of $2.50. Notice that for every output level up *to* the equilibrium quantity of 900, the demand price is higher than the market price. So each unit purchased yields consumers a surplus benefit over and above what they had to pay for it. For example, for the first bottle of mineral water, consumers are willing to pay a price of $11.49 based on the market inverse demand function.[12] But they actually have to pay only $2.50. Thus, they receive a net benefit from consuming the first unit of the good equal to the excess of $11.49 over $2.50, or $8.99. Geometrically, this amount is measured as the vertical distance from the demand curve to the price line at $Q = 1$, shown in Figure 2.7 as distance *ab*.

---

[12]The price of $11.49 is found by substituting $Q_d = 1$ into the inverse demand function, $P = -0.01Q_d + 11.5$.

| FIGURE 2.7 | CONSUMER SURPLUS IN THE COMPETITIVE MARKET FOR BOTTLED MINERAL WATER |
|---|---|

For the first bottle of mineral water, consumers' demand price is $11.49, but the market-determined price is only $2.50, so they receive a net benefit from this first bottle of water equal to $11.49 − $2.50 = $8.99, shown as the vertical distance *ab*. Aggregating this net benefit over all units of water consumed yields the measure of consumer surplus shown as the triangular area *WXY*. The dollar value of this area is (½ · 900 · $9.00) = $4,050.

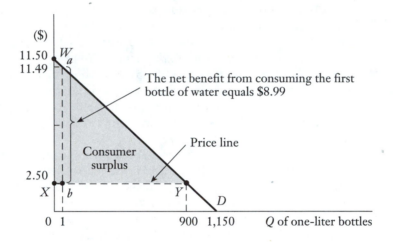

Since consumers receive a net benefit for every unit purchased up to the equilibrium point, this value must be aggregated over all units consumed to derive the measure of **consumer surplus.** Graphically, this is the triangular area above the price line and below the demand curve. In Figure 2.7, the consumer surplus for mineral water is the area labeled *WXY.* This makes sense, since the entire area under the demand curve is a measure of total benefit from consumption (i.e., the aggregation of the marginal benefit from each unit of the good), and the rectangular area under the price line is the total expenditure on the good. Thus the difference between the two is the net benefit to the consumer.

The dollar value of consumer surplus can be found by calculating the area of the triangle that represents it in the graphical model.[13] In Figure 2.7, the base of the *WXY* triangle is the horizontal distance from the vertical axis to the equilibrium quantity or 900. The height is $9.00, which is the difference between the vertical intercept of the demand curve, $11.50, and the price line, $2.50. Thus the dollar value of consumer surplus in this market is ½ · 900 · $9.00 = $4,050.

---

[13] Recall that the formula for finding the area of a triangle is ½ · Base · Height.

The applicability of consumer surplus stems from the fact that its magnitude is related to equilibrium price and quantity. So any disturbance to market equilibrium will change the size of consumer surplus. Since this surplus is a measure of consumer benefit, any change in its value can be used to assess the associated gain or loss to consumer welfare.

### Producer Surplus

**producer surplus**
The net gain to sellers of a good estimated by the excess of market price (*P*) over marginal cost (*MC*), aggregated over all units sold.

On the supply side of the market, the comparable measure of welfare is **producer surplus.** It is a measure of net gain accruing to sellers estimated by the excess of the market price (*P*) of a product over the marginal cost (*MC*) to produce it, aggregated over all units sold.

Based on our discussion of supply decisions, we know that firms must charge a price for their product that covers *MC*. Further, we know that the competitive market supply curve is the horizontal sum of all firms' *MC* curves. Therefore, since market price is determined by the intersection of market supply and demand, it must be the case that *P* = *MC* at a competitive equilibrium. However, at every output level below equilibrium, *MC* is *lower* than *P*. So, firms are actually willing to supply these smaller quantities at prices below what is dictated by the market. The price that firms are "willing to accept" for each output level is their supply price, and it is this price that is reflected in the *MC* curve. Thus, at each quantity below equilibrium, firms accrue a net gain measured by the excess of *P* over *MC*.

This net gain is illustrated in Figure 2.8. The diagram shows the competitive market supply for mineral water, which is also the *MC* curve, and a reference line drawn horizontally at the equilibrium price of $2.50. For every unit of output supplied *to* the equilibrium point at 900 units, producers receive a surplus equal to the excess of *P* over *MC*. For example, for the first unit of mineral water produced, the *MC* is $0.2525 based on the market supply function.[14] But firms can sell this first bottle at the market-determined price of $2.50. Thus, the net gain associated with this unit of output is the excess of $2.50 over $0.2525, or $2.2475. Geometrically, this is the vertical distance from the supply curve to the price line at $Q = 1$, labeled as distance *cd* in Figure 2.8.

Just as on the demand side of the market, this net gain must be aggregated over all units sold up to the equilibrium quantity to find the measure of producer surplus. Graphically, this is the sum of all the vertical distances between the *MC* curve and the price line, or the triangular area bounded by the *MC* curve and the price line, up to the equilibrium point. In Figure 2.8, this is shown as the area labeled *XYZ*.

Using the same method as described for consumer surplus, the dollar value of producer surplus can be found by calculating its representative

---

[14] The supply price, or *MC*, of producing the first unit of output is found by evaluating the market supply function at $Q_s = 1$, or $MC = 0.0025(1) + 0.25 = \$0.2525$.

| FIGURE 2.8 | PRODUCER SURPLUS IN THE COMPETITIVE MARKET FOR BOTTLED MINERAL WATER |
|---|---|

For the first bottle of mineral water produced, the *MC* is $0.2525, based on an evaluation of the market supply function at $Q_s = 1$. But since firms can sell this bottle at a price of $2.50, they receive a net gain of $2.50 − $0.2525, or $2.2475, shown as the vertical distance *cd*. Aggregating this gain over all units sold yields the measure of producer surplus represented by the triangular area *XYZ*. The dollar value of this area is ($1/2 · 900 · $2.25) = $1,012.50.

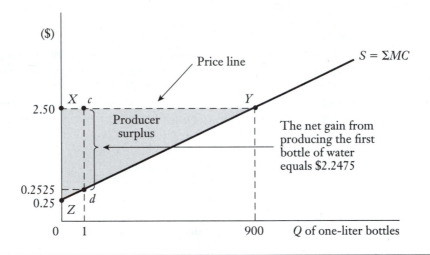

triangular area depicted in the graphical model. Referring to Figure 2.8, the base of the triangle *XYZ* has a magnitude of 900, and its height is $2.25, found as the difference between the price line at $2.50 and the vertical intercept of the supply curve, $0.25. Thus, producer surplus at equilibrium in the mineral water market is $1/2 · 900 · $2.25 = $1,012.50. Notice that the magnitude of producer surplus, just like consumer surplus, is based on equilibrium price and quantity. Hence, any market disturbance will change its value and thus provide a way to assess any associated welfare gain or loss to firms.

### The Welfare of Society: Sum of Consumer and Producer Surplus

**society's welfare**
The sum of consumer surplus and producer surplus.

Economists use the *sum* of consumer and producer surplus to capture the gains accruing to both sides of the market, or **society's welfare.** Applying this concept to the market for bottled mineral water, we see that society enjoys a surplus valued at $4,050 + $1,012.50, or $5,062.50. Because this surplus is based on a competitive equilibrium, its value is maximized. This is so because of the efficient allocation of resources that characterizes a competitive market. Put another way, it is not possible to reallocate resources to improve society's welfare. By default, this implies that any market outcome that does not meet the criterion of allocative efficiency has a negative effect on society's well-being. In such an instance, the loss can be monetized by comparing the resulting sum of consumer and producer surplus to what it *would* be if allocative efficiency were achieved.

### Measuring Welfare Changes

By way of illustration, let's consider a hypothetical policy initiative in the mineral water market that forces up price above *MC* to $6.50 per unit. To measure the effect on society's welfare, we need to compare the post-policy level of consumer and producer surplus to the benchmark competitive level of $5,062.50. We begin by reproducing the model of the mineral water market in Figure 2.9, adding to the diagram the policy price and quantity of $6.50 and 500 respectively.[15] Capital letters A through F have been added to facilitate our discussion. The benchmark level of consumer surplus is represented in this diagram by the area (A + B + C) and producer surplus by the area (D + E + F).

Now we determine the comparable surplus values under the policy-determined price and quantity. At the $6.50 price level, consumer surplus is reduced to the triangular area A valued at $1,250. This new value is $2,800 *lower* than it was before the policy, so we know that the policy generates a net *loss* to consumers. The producer surplus at the $6.50 price level is area (B + D + F) valued at $2,812.50, found by summing the area of the rectangle (B + D) and the area of the triangle (F). Since this magnitude is $1,800 *higher* than the original surplus, we see that producers enjoy a net *gain* as a result of the policy.

Finally, consider the overall effect. The total surplus under the new policy is $1,250 + $2,812.50 or $4,062.50, which is $1,000 less than the original value. Although producers enjoy a net gain of $1,800, it is outweighed by the loss to consumers of $2,800. Hence the new pricing policy causes a decline in society's welfare of $1,000. This change can be confirmed geometrically by looking at the areas representing surplus before and after the policy:

Change in consumer surplus: $\quad\quad$ $(A) - (A + B + C) = -(B + C)$

+ Change in producer surplus: $\quad$ $(B + D + F) - (D + E + F) = +(B - E)$

Net loss to society: $\quad\quad\quad\quad\quad\quad\quad\quad\quad$ $= -(C + E)$

---

[15] At a price of $6.50, $Q_s > Q_d$, so the quantity exchanged in the market is $Q_d$. Thus, quantity is found by substituting $6.50 into the demand equation as follows: $Q_d = -100(6.50) + 1,150 = 500$.

| FIGURE 2.9 | **DEADWEIGHT LOSS TO SOCIETY UNDER A PRICING REGULATION IN THE BOTTLED MINERAL WATER MARKET** |

At the allocatively efficient equilibrium, area (A + B + C) is the consumer surplus valued at $4,050, and area (D + E + F) is the producer surplus valued at $1,012.50, for a total welfare measure of $5,062.50. Under a pricing policy that sets price at $6.50, consumer surplus falls to $1,250, shown as area (A), producer surplus increases to $2,812.50 shown as area (B + D + F) for a new total welfare measure of $4,062.50. Consumers incur a net loss of −(B + C) valued at $2,800, while producers gain +(B − E) valued at $1,800. Thus, as a result of this policy, there is a **deadweight loss to society** of −(C + E) valued at $1,000.

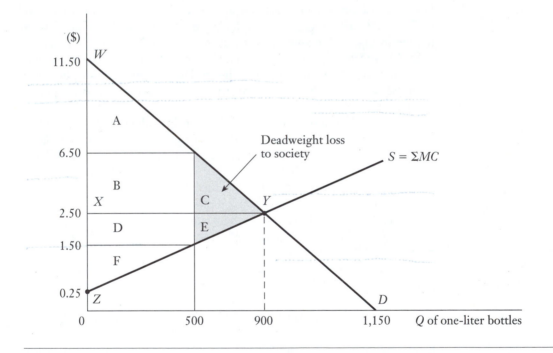

deadweight loss to
society   The net
loss of consumer and
producer surplus due
to an allocatively
inefficient market
event.

Area (C + E), valued at $1,000 is referred to as the **deadweight loss to society** because it was once a part of the surplus accruing to producers and consumers under allocatively efficient conditions, but as a result of the policy is lost or unaccounted for. Notice that area B, while a loss to consumers, is a gain to firms. Thus it is redistributed from one market sector to another. While some may view this outcome as unfair, the relevant point is that such transfers are not inefficient, since the amount is captured somewhere within the market system. What *is* problematic is that the policy generates a loss to society as a whole because it forces $P$ above $MC$, violating the allocative efficiency criterion.

## Conclusions

Understanding the fundamentals of how markets operate is an important basis for the study of environmental economics. To that end, we have limited our discussion in this chapter to the circular flow model—reviewing the mechanics of supply and demand, the signaling mechanism of price, and the importance of marginal analysis—all within the context of a classical competitive market system. Competitive markets establish a benchmark that helps economists evaluate the effects of market failures and market disturbances, both of which are important to environmental economics. From a practical perspective, we can assess the effects of environmental pollution or any policy initiative using allocative efficiency as a criterion. Furthermore, these effects can be measured by quantifying the associated changes in consumer and producer surplus.

It is also the case that the competitive model illustrates how an economic system operates in the absence of any condition that impedes natural market forces. Recognizing how a fully functioning market performs is necessary to understanding the economic perception of environmental pollution as a market failure—the subject of our next chapter. To make this transition, we will expand our analysis to the full materials balance model, allowing for the interdependence of the circular flow with the natural environment. Using the modeling tools shown in this chapter and expanding on the concepts of marginal benefits and costs, we will develop more elaborate market models that explicitly account for this interdependence. These models will show *how* and *why* the market fails to correct environmental damage, which in turn will suggest approaches to finding effective policy solutions.

## Summary

- A market refers to the interaction between consumers and producers for the purpose of exchanging a well-defined commodity.

- A competitive market model is characterized by a large number of independent buyers and sellers who cannot control market price, a homogeneous product, the absence of entry barriers, perfect information, and perfect mobility of resources.

- Demand is a relationship between quantity demanded ($Q_d$) and price ($P$), holding constant all other factors that may influence this decision such as wealth, income, prices of related goods, preferences, and price expectations.

- The Law of Demand posits an inverse relationship between quantity demanded and price, *c.p.*

- Market demand for a private good is found by summing the individual demand horizontally.

- Supply is a relationship between quantity supplied ($Q_s$) and price ($P$), holding constant all other supply determinants such as technology, input prices, taxes and subsidies, and price expectations.

- The Law of Supply states there is a direct relationship between quantity supplied and price, *c.p.*

- Market supply for a private good is found by summing the individual supplies horizontally.

- The equilibrium or market-clearing price ($P_e$) is the price at which $Q_d = Q_s$. If price is above (below) its equilibrium level, there is a surplus (shortage) of the commodity, which will put pressure on the prevailing price to fall (rise) toward its equilibrium level.

- Allocative efficiency requires that the additional value society places on another unit of a good is precisely equivalent to what society must give up in scarce resources to produce it.

- All profit($\pi$)-maximizing firms expand (contract) output as long as the associated additional revenue ($MR$) is greater (lower) than the increase in costs ($MC$). The $\pi$-maximizing level of output occurs where $MR = MC$, or where marginal profit ($M\pi$) = 0.

- Competitive firms are price-takers. Since $P = MR$ for competitive firms, the $\pi$-maximizing output level at $MR = MC$ is also the point where $P = MC$, the condition signifying allocative efficiency.

- Technical efficiency arises when the maximum amount of output is produced from some fixed stock of resources.

- Consumer surplus measures the net benefit accruing to buyers measured as the excess of what they are willing to pay, $MB$, over what they must actually pay, $P$, aggregated over all units purchased.

- Producer surplus measures the net gain accruing to sellers estimated as the excess $P$ over $MC$, aggregated over all units sold.

- Society's welfare is measured as the sum of consumer and producer surplus, which is maximized when allocative efficiency is achieved.

- The deadweight loss to society measures the net change in consumer and producer surplus caused by an allocatively inefficient market event.

# Key Concepts

market

private good

demand

Law of Demand

market demand for a private good

supply

Law of Supply

market supply of a private good

equilibrium price and quantity

shortage

surplus

allocative efficiency

total profit

profit maximization

technical efficiency

consumer surplus

producer surplus

society's welfare

deadweight loss to society

# Review Questions

1. Suppose $Q_d = 200 - 4P$ and $Q_s = 100$. Describe market demand and market supply in a given market.
   a. Algebraically find equilibrium price and quantity, and support your answer graphically.
   b. What is unusual about this market? Give an example of a good or service that might be characterized in this way.

2. In 1995, the Food and Drug Administration (FDA) published new labeling standards for bottled water. (The full text of the final rule can be found at **vm.cfsan.fda.gov/~lrd/n095-323.txt**.) Prior to that time, bottlers could sell regular tap water under a bottled water label. In fact, the FDA estimated that approximately 25 percent of the supply of bottled water was nothing more than ordinary tap water. Consider how these tougher standards eliminated 25 percent of the supply of bottled water. If market demand is unaffected, what qualitative impact would this labeling change have on equilibrium price and quantity for bottled water? Support your answer with a graphical model.

3. Reconsider the implications of the revised labeling standards discussed in Question 2 in the context of the hypothetical market for bottled water modeled in the text. Recall that the market demand and market s upply equations are:

$$Q_d = -100P + 1,150; \ Q_s = 400P - 100,$$

   where    $P_e = \$2.50$ and $Q_e = 900$.

   Now, suppose the change in standards results in a new market supply of $Q_s' = 400P - 350$, with no change in market demand.
   a. Determine the new $P_e'$ and $Q_e'$ for bottled water. Do your results agree with your intuitive answer to Question 2?

b. Graphically illustrate the market for bottled water before and after the change in labeling standards. Be sure to label all relevant points.

c. Compare the values of consumer and producer surplus before and after the change in labeling standards. Is this result expected? Why or why not?

4. a. Describe a real-world government policy that creates a market surplus. Be sure to carefully define the relevant market.

b. Explain the efficiency implications of such a policy. Be specific.

c. In the instance you have described, what is the government's motivation for intervening in the market in this way?

## Additional Readings

Friedman, Milton. *Capitalism and Freedom*. Chicago: University of Chicago Press, 1962.

Heilbroner, Robert L. *The Worldly Philosophers*. New York: Simon and Schuster, 1980.

Jenkinson, Tim (Ed.). *Readings in Microeconomics*. New York: Oxford University Press, 1996.

Mankiw, N. Gregory. *Principles of Microeconomics*. Fort Worth, TX: Dryden Press, 1998.

Nicholson, Walter. *Intermediate Microeconomics and Its Application*. Fort Worth, TX: Dryden Press, 1997.

Pindyck, Robert S., and Daniel Rubinfeld. *Microeconomics*. Upper Saddle River, NJ: Prentice-Hall, 1998.

## Related Web Sites

U.S. Food and Drug Administration Final
Rule on bottled water ..... **vm.cfsan.fda.gov/~lrd/n095-323.txt**

*Greening the Government: A Guide to
Implementing Executive Order 12873*
"Federal Acquisition, Recycling, and Waste
Prevention" (referenced in Application 2.3) ..... **www.ofee.gov/html/guide.htm**

# 3

---

## *Modeling Market Failure*

---

According to the circular flow model, free markets provide desired goods and services to the market, resolve shortages and surpluses, and eliminate inefficiency through the pricing mechanism—all without government intervention. This is a remarkable result, given that consumers and producers are not motivated by altruistic goals but rather are driven by their own self-interest. As first described through Adam Smith's metaphor, the "invisible hand," this market outcome comes about as if consumers and firms are guided to make decisions that enhance the well-being of society.[1] Recognizing the efficiency and welfare implications of a competitive equilibrium underscores what is at stake when something impedes the market process that underlies it. A case in point is the persistence of pollution.

When we consider the circular flow in the fuller context of the materials balance model, we become aware of how economic activity generates residuals that can damage natural resources. But we need to look further to understand the economics of why pollution *persists* in the absence of third-party intervention. Why is the market unable to respond to environmental pollution, or can it? The most immediate answer is that pollution is a **market failure** that distorts the classical market outcome.

From an economic perspective, environmental problems persist because they implicitly violate the assumptions of a fully functioning market. The incentive mechanisms that normally achieve an efficient solution are unable to operate, and government has to intervene. However, if the market failure is understood, incentives can be restored through environmental policy. Conceptually, the idea is to ferret out the conditions that cause the pricing system to break down, make the necessary adjustments to the underlying conditions, and then let the power of the market work toward a solution.

---

[1] Smith (1937), p. 423 (originally published in 1776).

This chapter provides the analytical tools necessary for understanding market failure in the context of environmental problems. The discussion centers around the development of two economic models. The first is based on the public goods characteristics of environmental quality. The second uses what is known as externality theory to show how market incentives fail to capture the effects of pollution associated with production or consumption. Finally, the two models are linked through a discussion of property rights and their role in environmental market failures.

## Environmental Problems: A Market Failure

Classical microeconomic theory predicts an efficient outcome given certain assumptions about pricing, product definition, cost conditions, and entry barriers. If any of these assumptions fails to hold, market mechanisms cannot operate freely. Depending on which assumption is violated, the result will be any of a number of inefficient market conditions, collectively termed **market failures.** These include imperfect competition, imperfect information, public goods, and externalities. For example, if we relax the assumption of freedom of entry in the competitive model, some degree of market power will develop. As this occurs, society's welfare declines, and resources are allocated inefficiently.

**market failure** The result of an inefficient market condition.

Economists model environmental problems as market failures using either the theory of public goods or the theory of externalities. Each is distinguished by how the market is defined.

- If the market is defined as "environmental quality," then the source of the market failure is that environmental quality is a **public good.**

- If the market is defined as the good whose production or consumption generates environmental damage, then the market failure is due to an **externality.**

While each of these models suggests a different set of solutions, the theories are not totally unrelated. And in the context of environmental problems, both are exacerbated by a third type of market failure, **imperfect information.** We begin by analyzing the market failure aspect of public goods.

## Environmental Quality: A Public Good

**public good** A commodity that is nonrival in consumption and yields benefits that are nonexcludable.

Economists distinguish public goods from private goods by examining their inherent characteristics—*not* by whether they are provided publicly or privately.[2] A **public good,** or more technically a *pure* public good, is one

---

[2] For a good discussion of this distinction, see Rosen (1995), Chapter 5.

that possesses the following characteristics: (1) it is **nonrival** in consumption, and (2) its benefits are **nonexcludable**.[3] At the other extreme is a pure private good, which is characterized by rivalness and excludability. Recall that in the last chapter, one of the assumptions underlying the market model was that the commodity being exchanged was a private good.

### Characteristics of Public Goods

**nonrivalness** The characteristic of indivisible benefits of consumption such that one person's consumption does not preclude that of another.

**Nonrivalness** refers to the notion that the benefits associated with consumption are *indivisible*, meaning when the good is consumed by one individual, another person is not preempted from consuming it at the same time. Consider, for example, the network television broadcast of the NBA championship finals. The benefits to the existing television audience are completely unaffected when another individual tunes in to view the broadcast. Contrast this result to what happens when a private good is consumed, such as a personal computer. Once someone is using the computer, that consumption activity prohibits another person from using it at the same time.

**nonexcludability** The characteristic that makes it impossible to prevent others from sharing in the benefits of consumption.

**Nonexcludability** means that preventing others from sharing in the benefits of a good's consumption is not possible (or prohibitively costly in a less strict sense). An example of a good with this characteristic is a jogging path. It would be virtually impossible to ration the use of the path to a select group of runners. In contrast, consider the inherent excludability of a conventional private good such as hotel lodging. Exclusive rationing of hotel services to the consumer paying for them is easily accomplished, and the associated benefits accrue solely to that single consumer.

Although nonrivalness and nonexcludability may seem similar, they are not identical. A good way to distinguish them is as follows. Nonrivalness means that rationing of the good is not *desirable*, while excludability means rationing of the good is not *feasible*.[4] In fact, it is possible for a good to possess one of these attributes but not the other. Reconsider the examples for each characteristic given above. While a televised NBA game is a nonrival good, it can be made excludable by broadcasting it via a cable network only to subscribers who have paid for it and by scrambling the signal to everyone else. Likewise, provision of the jogging path, while nonexcludable absent prohibitively high costs, does not possess the nonrivalry attribute. Use of the path by more and more runners would lead to congestion, which would affect every consumer of the jogging path.

Two classic examples of public goods cited consistently in the literature are a lighthouse and national defense. Contemplate the services provided by these goods to see that the benefits of each are both nonrival and

---

[3] Much of the important work in the theory of public goods is credited to Samuelson (1954), (1955), and (1958).

[4] Stiglitz (1988), pp. 119–23.

nonexcludable. A more contemporary and, from our perspective, more relevant example of a public good is environmental quality.[5] Just like the lighthouse, cleaner air, for example, is both nonexcludable and indivisible. Consider the futility of trying to restrict the benefits of air quality to a single person. It's unreasonable to think that others could be excluded from the consumption of a cleaner air supply just because another person has paid for it. Moreover, once the air is made cleaner for one person, others could simultaneously enjoy the benefits of breathing more healthy air.

So, what then is the problem? Having accepted the assertion that environmental quality is a public good, we still need to explain why this, or any public good for that matter, is a market failure. To do this, we must develop a model of a public good.

# Modeling a Public Goods Market for Environmental Quality

Public goods generate a market failure because the nonrivalness and nonexcludability characteristics prevent natural market incentives from yielding an allocatively efficient outcome. To illustrate this assertion, we reintroduce the supply and demand model but redefine the market as the public good, air quality.[6] It turns out that by changing the market definition from a private to a public good, the conventional derivation of market demand is no longer viable. And this modeling dilemma is at the root of the public goods problem.

### Allocative Efficiency in the Market for a Public Good

Just as in the private goods case, achieving an allocatively efficient equilibrium in a public goods market depends upon the existence of well-defined supply and demand functions. To develop these functions for air quality, we adjust the market definition so that output can be quantified. Air quality can be defined as "an acceptable level of pollution abatement," which we assume for discussion purposes is some percentage reduction in sulfur dioxide ($SO_2$) emissions.

**Market Supply for Air Quality.**   Although the market supply of a public good often represents government's decisions about production as opposed to those of private firms, the general derivation of the supply function is analogous to what we developed in the previous chapter for a private

---

[5] Alternatively, we could define environmental pollution as a public "bad."

[6] To direct attention solely to the public goods aspect of the model, we continue to assume competitive markets. This prevents confounding the market failure of public goods with that of imperfect competition. Further, the assumption of competitive markets allows the market supply curve to be modeled as the horizontal sum of all producers' marginal cost curves, just as was done for the private goods case in the previous chapter.

| TABLE 3.1 | HYPOTHETICAL SUPPLY DATA IN THE MARKET FOR AIR QUALITY MEASURED AS A PERCENTAGE OF SULFUR DIOXIDE ($SO_2$) ABATEMENT PER YEAR |
|-----------|------------------------------------------------------------------|

| Quantity Supplied $Q_s$ (% of $SO_2$ abatement) | Market Supply Price $P = 4 + 0.75Q_s$ ($ millions) |
|:---:|:---:|
| 0 | 4.00 |
| 5 | 7.75 |
| 10 | 11.50 |
| 15 | 15.25 |
| 20 | 19.00 |
| 25 | 22.75 |
| 30 | 26.50 |

good. We begin by assuming that there is some number of hypothetical producers, each of which is willing and able to supply various reductions in $SO_2$ at different price levels, *c.p.* The aggregation of these production decisions gives rise to market supply, which we assume is represented by the data given in Table 3.1. Price ($P$) is measured in millions of dollars, and quantity supplied ($Q_s$) is measured as a percentage of $SO_2$ abatement. The algebraic counterpart for these data is:

Market supply:     $P = 4 + 0.75Q_s$

**Market Demand for Air Quality.**   On the demand side, the model for a public good is quite different from that for a private commodity. Recall from the previous chapter that the market demand for a private good is found by summing the demands of individual consumers *horizontally*. It is as if each consumer were asked: "What *quantity* of this good would you consume at each of the following prices?" But this question is not relevant to the demand for a public good because once such a commodity is provided, it is available at the *same quantity* to all consumers—a direct consequence of the nonrivalness characteristic. How then *is* market demand determined for a public good if quantity is not a decision variable?

**market demand for a public good**  The aggregate demand of all consumers in the market derived by summing their individual demands *vertically*.

The key is to recognize that the *demand price* for a public good is variable, even though the quantity is not. So the relevant question in deriving this demand must be: "What *price* would you be willing to pay for each of the following quantities?" In theory, each consumer should express a unique **"willingness to pay (WTP)"** for the public good based on the benefits each expects to derive from consumption. The **market demand for a public good** is the aggregate demand for all viable consumers in the

| TABLE 3.2 | HYPOTHETICAL DEMAND DATA IN THE PUBLIC GOODS MARKET FOR AIR QUALITY MEASURED AS A PERCENTAGE OF SULFUR DIOXIDE ($SO_2$) ABATEMENT PER YEAR |
|---|---|

| Quantity Demanded ($Q_d$) (% of $SO_2$ abatement) | Consumer 1's WTP $p_1 = 10 - 0.1Q_d$ ($) | Consumer 2's WTP $p_2 = 15 - 0.2Q_d$ ($) | Combined Demand Price for Consumer 1 and 2 $p_1 + p_2 = 25 - 0.3Q_d$ ($) |
|---|---|---|---|
| 0 | 10.00 | 15.00 | 25.00 |
| 5 | 9.50 | 14.00 | 23.50 |
| 10 | 9.00 | 13.00 | 22.00 |
| 15 | 8.50 | 12.00 | 20.50 |
| 20 | 8.00 | 11.00 | 19.00 |
| 25 | 7.50 | 10.00 | 17.50 |
| 30 | 7.00 | 9.00 | 16.00 |

NOTE: WTP = Willingness to pay.

market. It is derived by summing each individual demand *vertically* to determine the market price ($P = \Sigma p$) at each and every possible market quantity ($Q$), *c.p.*

To illustrate this procedure in the market for $SO_2$ abatement, we initially focus on only two consumers. The scenario is that we conduct a survey, asking the two consumers how much each would be willing to pay each year for various amounts of $SO_2$ abatement, *c.p.* The results of this hypothetical inquiry are given in Table 3.2. The quantity demanded ($Q_d$) column shows a selection of possible abatement levels to be provided to all consumers. The demand prices or WTP responses are labeled $p_1$ and $p_2$ for Consumer 1 and Consumer 2, respectively. These responses are based upon the following demand equations, which are expressed in inverse form to signify that price is the decision variable:

Demand for Consumer 1: $\quad p_1 = 10 - 0.1Q_d$

Demand for Consumer 2: $\quad p_2 = 15 - 0.2Q_d$

Notice that each consumer's WTP response for a given $Q_d$ is unique. For example, for a 5-percent reduction in $SO_2$, Consumer 1 is willing to pay $9.50 per year, while Consumer 2 is willing to pay $14.00 per year. These responses differ because each consumer is distinguished by a unique level of income, wealth, preferences, and so forth. In this context, we might expect the two consumers to have distinct preferences for air quality and even disparate views about the associated benefits. For example, perhaps Con-

**FIGURE 3.1**

## COMBINED DEMAND OF TWO CONSUMERS FOR AIR QUALITY (SO₂ ABATEMENT)

The demand curve labeled $(d_1 + d_2)$ represents the combined consumption decisions of two hypothetical consumers for air quality. For any given quantity on this curve, the corresponding price is equal to the vertical sum of the individual price responses for that same quantity as given on $d_1$ and $d_2$.

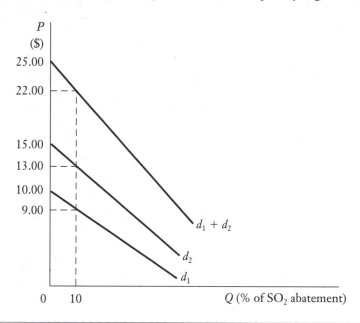

sumer 2's WTP is higher because he or she is a member of an environmental group and is more aware of the benefits of cleaner air.

To find the combined demand for air quality, the individual price responses at each quantity level are added together. The far-right column of Table 3.2 shows the result of this aggregation. The algebraic counterpart is found by summing each pair of corresponding terms on the right-hand side of each equation:

| Demand for Consumer 1: | $p_1 = 10 - 0.1Q_d$ |
|---|---|
| + Demand for Consumer 2: | $p_2 = 15 - 0.2Q_d$ |
| Demand for Consumers 1 and 2: | $p_1 + p_2 = 25 - 0.3Q_d$ |

The graphical model is shown in Figure 3.1. For any given quantity on the combined demand curve $(d_1 + d_2)$, the corresponding measure of price is equal to the vertical sum of the individual price responses for that same quantity based on the demand curves, $d_1$ and $d_2$.

| TABLE 3.3 | HYPOTHETICAL MARKET DEMAND AND MARKET SUPPLY DATA FOR AIR QUALITY MEASURED AS A PERCENTAGE OF SULFUR DIOXIDE ($SO_2$) ABATEMENT PER YEAR |
|---|---|

| Quantity Supplied $(Q_s)$ (% of $SO_2$ abatement) | Market Demand Price $P = 25 - 0.3Q_d$ ($ millions) | Market Supply Price $P = 4 + 0.75Q_s$ ($ millions) |
|---|---|---|
| 0 | 25.00 | 4.00 |
| 5 | 23.50 | 7.75 |
| 10 | 22.00 | 11.50 |
| 15 | 20.50 | 15.25 |
| **20** | **19.00** | **19.00** |
| 25 | 17.50 | 22.75 |
| 30 | 16.00 | 26.50 |

Having developed the general procedure, we now bring the demand relationship up to the market level by assuming that the combined demand of the two consumers represents the decisions of 1 million consumers. Notice that this conversion means that price ($P$) is now denominated in millions of dollars, which corresponds to the scale of the market supply function. More formally, the market demand function is specified as:

$$\text{Market demand:} \qquad P = 25 - 0.3Q_d$$

**Equilibrium in the Air Quality Market.** To find equilibrium in the market for $SO_2$ abatement, we begin by combining the market demand and supply data in Table 3.3. We observe that $Q_e$ is equal to 20 percent, the point where both the supply price and demand price are equal to $19 million, $P_e$. This result can also be found algebraically by solving the equations for market supply and demand simultaneously.[7] The corresponding graphical model is shown in Figure 3.2, where the intersection of the market supply ($S$) and market demand ($D$) curves identifies $P_e$ and $Q_e$.

*Assessing the Implications*

Determining $P_e$ and $Q_e$ for the abatement of any kind of pollution is a significant result. As will become apparent in upcoming chapters, it is this

[7] Verify this assertion by setting the market demand equation, $P = 25 - 0.3Q_d$, equal to the market supply equation, $P = 4 + 0.75Q_s$, recognizing that $Q_s = Q_d$ at equilibrium.

| FIGURE 3.2 | **MARKET SUPPLY AND MARKET DEMAND**<br>**FOR AIR QUALITY ($SO_2$ ABATEMENT)** |

Assuming the market for $SO_2$ abatement is competitive, equilibrium price $P_e$ of $19 million and equilibrium quantity $Q_e$ equal to 20 percent abatement represent an allocatively efficient solution. $Q_e$ represents the optimal level of *abatement* measured from *left to right* and implicitly the optimal level of *air pollution* measured from *right to left*. Notice that the optimal level of pollution is not zero.

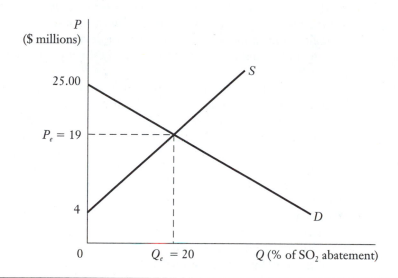

result to which economists refer when addressing market-based solutions to environmental pollution. Notice in Figure 3.2 that $Q_e$ represents the efficient or optimal level of *abatement* measured from *left to right* and implicitly the optimal level of *pollution* measured from *right to left*. And, as the model suggests, this optimal level is not necessarily zero.[8]

From a general perspective, abating at the 100-percent level to reduce pollution to zero involves prohibitive opportunity costs. These include the forgone production and consumption of any good generating even the smallest amount of pollution. Given our present technology, a zero-pollution world would be one without electricity, advanced transportation systems, and virtually all manufactured products. Thus it makes little sense to argue for the elimination of all pollution in our environment.[9]

---

[8] Of course, a zero optimal level of pollution is *possible* under certain conditions, though this is the exception rather than the rule.

[9] One of the classic research papers that discusses this economic view of pollution is Ruff (1970).

## Understanding the Market Failure of Public Goods Markets

As we stated at the outset, the achievement of an allocatively efficient outcome in a public goods market depends on the identification of well-defined demand and supply functions. Although we developed both functions for our hypothetical market for air quality, market demand was identified only because we implicitly made one critical assumption—that consumers would reveal their willingness to pay (WTP) for $SO_2$ abatement. But without third-party intervention, the nonexcludability of this or any public good makes it difficult if not impossible to ascertain such information. And if consumers' WTP responses are unknown, market demand cannot be identified, and an efficient outcome cannot be obtained. It is precisely the inability of free markets to capture the WTP for a public good that causes the market failure.

Consider the meaning of demand in the context of private versus public goods. In general, market demand captures the aggregate value of the expected benefits associated with consumption. If the good is private—that is, excludable—its benefits can be obtained only through purchase. Thus the consumer's WTP for a private good is a suitable proxy for the anticipated marginal benefits of consumption. However, in the case of a public good that is nonexcludable, the consumer can share in its consumption even when it is purchased by someone else. Hence there is no incentive for a rational consumer to volunteer a WTP for something he or she can consume without having to pay for it. Formally, this problem is known as **nonrevelation of preferences,** which in turn is due to the more basic dilemma of **free-ridership.** The rational consumer astutely recognizes that the benefits of a public good are accessible simply by allowing someone else to purchase it. So the consumer becomes a "free-rider." Individual preferences about the public good remain undisclosed, and thus market demand is undefined. When the public good is environmental quality, the consequence can be serious ecological damage. A case in point is the pollution that threatens Boston Harbor discussed in Application 3.1.

If we relax the conventional assumption of perfect information, adding more realism to the model, the identification of market demand becomes even more obscure. In many public goods markets, consumers are not fully aware of the benefits associated with consumption. This is certainly the case for environmental quality. Most people are not knowledgeable about all the health, recreational, and aesthetic benefits associated with pollution abatement. So, even if consumers could be induced to express their WTP for a cleaner environment, it is highly likely that the resulting demand price would underestimate the true benefits. This added complication is due to **imperfect information**—another source of market failure.

What can be concluded from all of this? As we initially claimed, market forces alone cannot provide an allocatively efficient level of a public good. This realization helps to explain what we observe in public goods markets—intervention by some third party, typically government. But to

**nonrevelation of preferences** Arises when a rational consumer does not volunteer a WTP due to the lack of a market incentive to do so.

**free-ridership** Recognition by a rational consumer that the benefits of consumption are accessible without paying for them.

# Boston Harbor: The Changing Condition of an Environmental Public Good

During the 1988 presidential campaign, the environmental degradation of Boston Harbor became a highly charged political issue. Wanting to promote an image as the prospective "environmental President," then Vice President Bush focused the nation's attention on what he called the "dirtiest harbor in America." Political motivations aside, Bush was, at least in spirit, accurate in his assessment of the famous harbor that for a century has suffered the ill effects of public and industrial waste dumping. Boston Harbor and its nine beaches have been fouled by pollutants ranging from raw sewage to heavy metals like lead and mercury.

Why did the condition of this vital natural resource decline to such a deplorable state? While the specifics are complex and entangled with bureaucracy and local politics, the bottom line is that the harbor became seriously polluted because clean waterways are a public good. A cleaner Boston Harbor possesses the requisite characteristics of a public good, namely, nonexclusivity and nonrivalness in consumption. The result is the typical free-ridership problem that characterizes the market failure aspect of all public goods. No one is willing to reveal their preferences for a cleaner harbor and accept a share in the financial responsibility as long as the associated benefits can be enjoyed without having to pay for them. In addition, most harbor users are not fully aware of the benefits of cleaning it up. So no one accepts responsibility for the preservation and protection of a waterway that is in a very real sense commonly owned. The unfortunate outcome is that industries have used the harbor as a dumping ground for chemical discharges, and residents have left their trash on the harbor's beaches.

As predicted by theory, third-party intervention—implemented in this case through a federal court order—was necessary to initiate corrective action to save the harbor. The federally mandated plan, to be spearheaded by the Massachusetts Water Resources Authority (MWRA) at **www.mwra.state.ma.us**, calls for a $6.1-billion reconstruction of the area's sewage treatment facilities. To meet this expenditure, the Massachusetts government contributed the relatively small sum of $29 million, and the federal government committed only another $350 million. Consequently, the remaining $5.7 billion will be funded through increased rates charged by the MWRA to their 2.5 million customers.

While a plan of such proportions will take years to implement fully, interim results are encouraging. Thus far, discharges of toxic metal and PCBs by the MWRA have been reduced by some 50 percent. Also, the MWRA has halted the destructive dumping of sludge into the harbor from its two major plants. The data below offer some evidence of the success of this third-party action.

| Year | Toxic Metal Discharges (pounds per day) | Harbor Beach Closings (due to high bacteria) | Fish Liver Cancer (% of winter flounder) |
|------|------|------|------|
| 1988 | 1,322 | 42 | 11.6 |
| 1989 | 982 | 55 | 3.2 |
| 1990 | 761 | 43 | 5.0 |
| 1991 | 741 | 49 | 2.8 |
| 1992 | 648 | 22 | < 3.0 |

SOURCE: Woods Hole Oceanographic Institute, reported by Allen (September 6, 1992).

SOURCES: Scott Allen, "Boston Harbor's Waters Have Started to Heal: Cleanup Helping to Shed 'Dirtiest Label.'" *Boston Globe*, September 6, 1992; Eric Jay Dolin, "Boston Harbor's Murky Political Waters." *Environment* 34(6), July/August 1992, pp. 7–11, 26–33; D. Doneski, "Cleaning Up Boston Harbor: Fact or Fiction?" *Boston College Environmental Affairs Law Review* 12, Spring 1985, p. 567.

what degree should government become involved in the market process, and what tasks should government perform to achieve an efficient solution? These are difficult questions, but the underlying theories that identify the public goods problem suggest approaches to solving it.

### *The Solution: Government Intervention*

In practice, a common means by which government responds to the dilemma of free-ridership and nonrevelation of preferences is through **direct provision of public goods.** Simple observation reveals that many public goods, such as fire protection, parks, and roadways, are provided by government. Similarly, government is involved in the preservation of natural resources and the provision of environmental quality. Among the government agencies whose responsibilities include the environment are the Corps of Engineers, the Federal Energy Regulatory Commission, and, of course, the Environmental Protection Agency (EPA).

An alternative government response is the use of **political procedures and voting rules** aimed at identifying society's preferences about public goods.[10] For example, members of Congress are responsible for discerning their constituents' views on environmental issues and representing their interests in developing legislation. Other environmental laws such as "bottle bills" are enacted at the state level through majority voting rules on state referenda.

Responding to the problem of imperfect information, governments regularly provide **education and public information** to citizens about public goods. The EPA, for example, allocates some of its resources to educating the public about the benefits of a cleaner environment. And the Federal Trade Commission (FTC) issued *Green Marketing Guidelines* to improve the accuracy of advertised environmental claims about products and product packaging—an effort discussed in Application 3.2.

## Environmental Problems: Externalities

**externality** A spillover effect associated with production or consumption that extends to a third party outside the market.

Another way to model environmental problems is through the use of **externality** theory, an approach that uses a different perspective to analyze the source of the market failure. Instead of defining the market as environmental quality or pollution abatement, this approach specifies the relevant market as the good whose production or consumption generates environmental damage *outside of* the market transaction.[11] Any such effect that is *external to* the market is aptly termed an **externality.**

---

[10] Such approaches are suggested by public choice theory, a subdiscipline of applied microeconomics. For an overview of public choice theory, see Rosen (1995), Chapter 7; or Stiglitz (1988), Chapter 6.

[11] Recall from the materials balance model that residuals are generated by *both* producers and households.

# Informing the Public through Truth in Advertising: Green Marketing Guidelines

Strategic labeling of products to promote their environmental attributes had become a growing business trend in the 1970s and early 1980s. This so-called green marketing was used by businesses to make their products more appealing to an emerging group of environmentally minded consumers. Using claims such as "environmentally safe," "biodegradable," or "made with 100% recycled material" on product packaging, firms could gain market share without having to reduce product price. However, as consumers' awareness of environmental issues grew, so too did their demand for *accurate* "green" labeling and their skepticism about advertised ecological promises.

An often cited case of misleading advertising was Mobil Corporation's use of a biodegradable label to market its new line of Hefty trash bags in the late 1980s. Unfortunately for Mobil, its decision came in the midst of a controversy about the relevance of degradable products. Scientists had pointed out that the absence of oxygen and sunlight for wastes buried in a landfill would deter the degradation process. In response to this finding, Mobil attempted to preempt any legal attacks by adding a disclaimer to its packaging. But its reaction came too late. In 1990, Mobil was faced with several lawsuits, charging it with deceptive advertising and consumer fraud (Lawrence 1991). Ultimately, Mobil paid $150,000 in damages to six states to settle the lawsuits.

Reacting to the Mobil case as well as countless other incidents of misleading ecological claims, consumers demanded that environmental claims be accurate and independently substantiated. Would the marketplace resolve the problem on its own? Not likely. No single producer wanted to be the only one that qualified its environmental claims in the name of accuracy, only to run the risk of losing market share. At the same time, the individual consumer lacked the information and the financial resources to take on corporate giants participating in this not-so-truthful eco-advertising. It was obvious that government had to step in to solve the dilemma.

In response to a call for action from consumer, industry, and environmental groups, the Federal Trade Commission (FTC), on July 28, 1992, announced environmental marketing guidelines for industry developed in consultation with the Environmental Protection Agency (EPA) and the Office of Consumer Affairs. These guidelines are summarized below. For more detail, visit the FTC's Web site at **www.ftc.gov/bcp/grnrule/guides92.htm**.

### General Guidelines for "Green Marketing"

- Product labels that state environmental claims should be clear and sufficiently prominent to avoid deception.

- It should be clear whether the environmental claim refers to the product, its packaging, or both.

- Claims of environmental benefits should not be overstated.

- Manufacturers that make environmental claims through comparison with other products should clearly state the basis for comparison and be prepared to substantiate the claim.

Although the guidelines are voluntary, businesses will likely cooperate to preserve their image as environmentally conscious enterprises. In so doing, accuracy of information about the product and the effects of its consumption on the environment should improve.

SOURCES: Adam Snyder, "The Color of Money." *SuperBrands*, 1992, pp. 30–31; Jennifer Lawrence. "Mobil." *Advertising Age*, January 29, 1991, p. 12; U.S. Environmental Protection Agency, Office of Solid Waste and Emergency Response, "FTC Announces Environmental Marketing Guidelines for Industry." *Reusable News*, Fall 1992, pp. 1, 8; "State Your Claim." *EPA Journal* 18(3), July/August 1992, p. 10.

## The Basics of Externality Theory

Microeconomic theory argues that price is the most important signaling mechanism in the market process. Equilibrium price communicates the marginal value consumers assign to a good and the marginal costs incurred by firms in producing it. Under ordinary conditions, this theory predicts the realities of the market remarkably well. But there are instances when price fails to capture *all* the benefits and costs associated with a market transaction. Market failures such as these occur when a third party is affected by the production or consumption of a commodity. Such a third-party effect is called an **externality.** If the external effect generates *costs* to a third party, it is a **negative externality.** If the external effect generates *benefits* to a third party, it is a **positive externality.**

**negative externality**
An external effect that generates costs to a third party.

**positive externality**
An external effect that generates benefits to a third party.

Although the notion of an externality may seem obscure, it is nonetheless familiar conceptually. If an individual purchases an unsightly satellite dish and installs it in his or her front yard, that action imposes costs to neighbors in the form of declining property values—a negative externality not reflected in the price of the satellite dish. Conversely, if one firm conducts research that advances a production process, there is a benefit to the entire industry—a positive externality not accounted for in the research investment decision.

Common to both examples is a spillover effect occurring outside the market transaction, which is not captured by the price of the commodity being exchanged. If price does not reflect *all* the benefits and costs associated with production and consumption, it is unreliable as a signaling mechanism, and the market fails. An important consequence is that scarce resources are misallocated. If consumption generates external benefits, the market price undervalues the good, and *too little* of it is produced. If there is a negative externality, the market price does not reflect the external costs, and *too much* of the commodity is produced. An example of this latter phenomenon is the congestion and pollution in Tokyo associated with merchants' overuse of the "just-in-time" delivery system. Application 3.3 gives an inside look at this unusual dilemma.

## Environmental Externalities

Of interest to environmental economists are externalities that damage the atmosphere, water supply, natural resources, and the overall quality of life. The classic case is the negative externality associated with *production* activities. For example, the provision of air transportation causes noise pollution, damages air quality, and reduces the value of nearby residential properties. These are very real costs that are not absorbed by airlines or by air travelers. Since they are incurred by parties *outside* the market transaction, they are not captured in the price of airline tickets. There are also environmental externalities associated with *consumption*. A good example is the cost of waste disposal associated with consuming products with excess or

APPLICATION 3.3

## Tokyo's Just-in-Time Deliveries Create a Negative Externality

In an ironic turn of events, Tokyo's traffic congestion and air pollution have been worsened by local merchants' use of an efficiency-driven system known as "just-in-time" (JIT) deliveries. The just-in-time production system was developed and refined by the Toyota Motor Company during the late 1950s and early 1960s. This efficiency concept is based on the premise that firms should operate with a minimum amount of inventory to avoid waste and minimize costs. Hence, raw materials and product components should arrive only just before they are needed in manufacturing. For the system to work, deliveries of inputs must be made frequently and in a timely manner to achieve maximum efficiency.

Over the years, the use of JIT production allowed Japanese manufacturers to bring their output to market at a substantially reduced cost. The system's success in Japan's industrial sector is partly responsible for the nation's dominant position in many international markets. Following the lead of their industrial counterparts, several Japanese service industries began to institute JIT delivery systems. Thousands of convenience stores, grocery markets, and department stores concentrated in Japan's capital city now maintain only a minimum stock, relying on frequent deliveries from suppliers—sometimes as often as every few hours. The result? Just-in-time delivery in this densely populated city has backfired. Adapted incorrectly, the system designed to save time is perversely wasting time. The parade of delivery trucks through the city streets slows traffic to a crawl, contributes to air pollution, and wastes fuel.

Few would question that *appropriate* use of the JIT concept generates efficiency gains and resource productivity and thus substantially reduces private costs. However, Japan's local merchants have unwittingly compromised the integrity of the concept, as evidenced by delivery trucks filled to only half their capacity. When the system is misused, as is the case in Tokyo, there are external costs to society. These include the waste of fuel, increased urban air pollution, and longer commutes for workers—none of which is reflected in the price of convenience goods and grocery products. Hence, there is a true negative externality associated with the use of the JIT delivery system by Tokyo's merchants.

In response to the dilemma, Japan's Ministry of International Trade and Industry set up an advisory group to examine the problem and suggest possible solutions. Current information on the Ministry's assessment of the use of JIT by Japan's service sector can be found at **www.jef.or.jp/news/com_pro. html**.

SOURCES: Michael Schrage, "In Tokyo, 'Just-in-Time' Deliveries in Need of Administrative Guidance." *Boston Globe*, March 22, 1992; Walter E. Goddard. *Just-in-Time: Surviving by Breaking Tradition.* Essex Junction, VT: Oliver Wight Limited Publications, Inc.,

nonbiodegradable packaging. Application 3.4 discusses how this type of externality affected the market for CDs.

There are also positive externalities that help to explain the persistence of environmental problems. Consider the market for pollution abatement equipment, such as scrubbers. Scrubbers are elaborate systems used to clean emissions from producers' smokestacks. When a producer of electricity, for example, purchases and installs a scrubber system, the benefits of cleaner air accrue to all people living in the nearby area. Since these individuals are not a part of the market transaction, the external benefits are not captured in the scrubber system's price. Resources are misallocated, and too few scrubbers are exchanged in the marketplace.

APPLICATION 3.4

## An Industry Response to a Negative Consumption Externality: CD Product Packaging

Introduced into the U.S. market in 1982, compact disks (CDs) originally were packaged in two boxes. The outer box was a 6-by-12-inch cardboard package, known in the industry as the "long box." Inside the long box was a 5-by-5½-inch "jewel box" constructed of clear plastic, which housed the CD. The jewel box, which continues in use today, generally is saved by the consumer as a protective container for the CD when not in use. However, the long box had no practical value beyond identifying the contents at the point of sale. In fact, most consumers discarded the long box immediately after purchase, so this part of the packaging ended up in landfills or burned in municipal incinerators.

Of the 250 million CDs sold in 1990, an estimated 23 million pounds of CD packaging were discarded. Think about the costs associated with the generation and disposal of this much waste—costs that are external to the purchase and sale of CDs. The producer of the CD does not consider these external costs as part of its production expenditures, so they are not reflected in the CD's price. Who then bears the costs? Society as a whole has to pick up the tab, the classic symptom of a negative externality—in this case, one associated with consumption.

The obvious question is to ask why the long box was used at all in packaging CDs. Music company executives defended this packaging with two arguments. First, its large size helped to deter shoplifting. The second and more important justification was to facilitate CD sales. The 6-by-12-inch long box allowed retailers to use existing display racks originally designed for 12-by-12-inch record albums. According to one industry official, the long box saved retailers an estimated $100 million in redesign costs for their display units.

Despite the industry's arguments, followers of the "green movement" pressured the industry to find an alternative to the wasteful packaging. In 1991, a "Ban the Box" campaign materialized to eliminate the long box from CD packaging. Environmentally minded recording artists joined the crusade, demanding that a more environmentally friendly package design be developed.

Industry officials searched for a new design that would facilitate retailers' display needs *and* ameliorate environmentalists. After weighing all the options, the recording industry agreed in 1992 to a voluntary ban on the long box, and since April 1993, CDs are shipped without the objectionable packaging. The standard practice by most American companies has become the use of the shrink-wrapped jewel box.

The CD packaging controversy is an important example of how externalities persist in the marketplace. Wasteful CD packaging was used for a full decade before any action was taken. In this case, the third-party intervention came not from government but from environmentalists who made market participants aware of how their decisions adversely affected the environment. In so doing, the industry recognized the implications in terms of long-term revenues and responded appropriately.

SOURCES: Meg Cox. "Music Firms Try Out 'Green' CD Boxes." *The Wall Street Journal,* July 25, 1991; Peter Newcomb. "'Ban the Box'." *Forbes,* May 13, 1991, p. 70; Debbie Galante Block. "CD Jewel Box Only, or Alternatives Too?" *Tape-Disc Business,* June 1993, p. 12.

Notice that there is a qualitative relationship between the external benefits associated with pollution abatement and the external costs of pollution-generating commodities. They are just the inverse of one another. If the market is defined as the abatement equipment industry, there is a *positive* externality, and the external benefits are *improved* health, natural resources, aesthetics, etc. If the market is defined as electricity production, for example, there is a *negative* externality, and the external costs are the *damages* to health, natural resources, and aesthetics. Which of the two models is relevant depends solely upon which market is specified.

### The Relationship between Public Goods and Externalities

Environmental externalities are those affecting all environmental media — air, water, and land — all of which have public goods characteristics. What this implies is that while public goods and externalities are not the same concept, they are closely related. In fact, if the externality affects a broad segment of society and if its effects are nonrival and nonexcludable, the externality *is* itself a public good.[12] If, however, the external effects are felt by a more narrowly defined group of individuals or firms, then those effects are more properly modeled as an externality.[13]

## Modeling Environmental Damage as a Negative Externality

Having established the basics of what externalities are conceptually, we now develop a formal model of a negative environmental externality. We elect to model an externality associated with *production*, since this approach addresses the source of most environmental pollution.

### Defining the Relevant Market

As always, one of the first steps in model building is the determination of the relevant market. In this case, we define the market as refined petroleum products. This is a fitting choice, since refined petroleum plants have been cited by the EPA as one of the industrial point sources polluting water supplies through direct discharge of toxic chemicals into rivers and streams. According to EPA statistics, an estimated 4.1 million pounds of toxic chemicals were released to surface waters by the refined petroleum industry in 1995.[14] Among the associated external costs are serious health risks for individuals using the rivers and streams.

### Modeling the Private Market for Refined Petroleum

To avoid confounding the analysis with the market failure of imperfect competition, we assume that the private market for refined petroleum is

---

[12] Technically, if the externality provides *benefits* to a large component of society, it is a public *good*; if the opposite is true, the externality is a public *"bad."*

[13] For further discussion of the relationship between externalities and public goods, the interested reader is referred to Holtermann (1972).

[14] See U.S. EPA, Office of Policy, Planning, and Evaluation (March 1991), p. 4-2; U.S. EPA, Office of Pollution Prevention and Toxics (April 1997), Table 4-10, p. 28.

competitive. The hypothetical supply and demand relationships for refined petroleum products are modeled as follows:

Supply:   $P = 10.0 + 0.075Q$

Demand:   $P = 42.0 - 0.125Q$,

where $Q$ is measured in thousands of barrels per day, and $P$ is the price per barrel.

Recall from the previous chapter that supply represents the marginal costs of production and demand the marginal benefits of consumption, both based on *private* or *internal* decision making. In markets such as this one where there are also external costs associated with production, it is necessary to explicitly distinguish internal or private costs from external costs. Thus we will formally refer to the supply function as the **marginal *private* cost (MPC)** of production. For consistency, we will also refer to the demand relationship as the **marginal *private* benefit (MPB)** function even though it is assumed that there are no external benefits associated with production or consumption of refined petroleum. Hence the two functions are restated as:

$$MPC = 10.0 + 0.075Q$$

$$MPB = 42.0 - 0.125Q$$

### Inefficiency of the Competitive Equilibrium

Given the usual assumptions about the underlying motivations of supply and demand, the competitive market clears where $MPB = MPC$, or equivalently where marginal profit ($M\pi$) or ($MPB - MPC$) = 0. Solving the $MPB$ and $MPC$ equations simultaneously yields a competitive market price, $P_c$, of \$22 per barrel and a market quantity, $Q_c$, of 160,000 barrels. The corresponding graphical model is shown in Figure 3.3, where equilibrium occurs at the intersection of the $MPB$ and $MPC$ curves.

The problem with this equilibrium is that it ignores the external costs to society of the contaminated water supplies caused by refined petroleum production. Remember, natural market forces motivate firms to satisfy their own interests, not those of society. The costs of the water pollution are *external* to the market exchange and consequently not factored into private market decisions. The implications are serious since allocative efficiency requires that marginal benefits be equal to *all* marginal costs of production. Since the external costs are not included in private decision making, the $MPC$ undervalues the opportunity costs of production, and the resulting output level is too high.

From a practical perspective, economists want to identify and monetize these external costs. But assigning a dollar value to negative externalities is difficult. Think about trying to monetize the damage to aquatic life

FIGURE 3.3

## COMPETITIVE EQUILIBRIUM IN THE MARKET FOR REFINED PETROLEUM

The intersection of the *MPB* and *MPC* curves identifies the competitive equilibrium in the refined petroleum market, where $P_c = \$22$ per barrel and $Q_c = 160,000$ barrels. This equilibrium ignores the external costs of contaminated water supplies caused by production of refined petroleum products. Therefore, the *MPC* undervalues the true opportunity costs of production, and the competitive output level is too high.

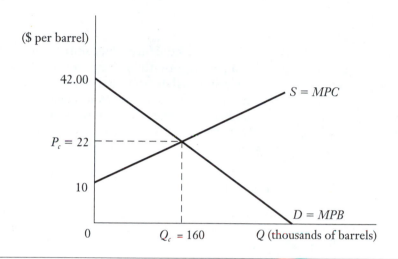

from water pollution or the increased health risks from swimming in a polluted lake. Although there are economic methods to approximate these costs, they are not straightforward. So we will defer discussion of these to later chapters. For now, we will simply argue that these costs do exist and assume for the present that they can be quantified.

### Modeling the External Costs

To complete our exposition of the refined petroleum market, we model the hypothetical **marginal external cost (*MEC*)** function as:

$$MEC = 0.05Q$$

Think about the economic interpretation of this equation. Based on the constant slope of 0.05, the *MEC* due to water pollution is increasing at a constant rate of 0.05 with respect to oil production. Since $Q$ is measured in thousands of barrels, this value implies that for every additional 1,000 barrels of refined oil produced, the marginal external costs of pollution rise by $0.05 per barrel.

## Modeling the Marginal Social Costs and Marginal Social Benefits

To achieve allocative efficiency, the external costs must be considered in determining equilibrium price and quantity. To accomplish this, the *MEC* must be added to the firm's *MPC* to derive the **marginal social cost (MSC)** equation as shown below:

**marginal social cost (MSC)** The sum of the marginal private cost (*MPC*) and the marginal external cost (*MEC*).

$$MSC \quad = MPC + MEC$$
$$= 10.0 \ + 0.075Q + 0.05Q$$
$$MSC \quad = 10.0 \ + 0.125Q$$

The *MSC* is relevant to production decisions, since it captures all the costs of producing refined petroleum—the private costs of production *and* the external costs of environmental damage to society.

On the demand side, there is an analogous benefit relationship called the **marginal social benefit (MSB),** which is the sum of the *MPB* and any marginal external benefit (*MEB*). Since we have assumed there are no positive externalities, the *MEB* is zero, so the *MPB* equals the *MSB* in this case.

**marginal social benefit (MSB)** The sum of marginal private benefit (*MPB*) and marginal external benefit (*MEB*).

## The Efficient Equilibrium

Once determined, the *MSC* must be set equal to the *MSB* function to solve for the efficient equilibrium price, $P_e$, and quantity, $Q_e$. In this case, the efficient level of refined petroleum products is 128,000 barrels per day sold at a market price of $26 per barrel. Compare this to the competitive equilibrium of $Q_c = 160,000$ and $P_c = $22$. As we asserted, the competitive equilibrium in the presence of a negative externality is characterized by an overallocation of resources to production. Furthermore, the competitive price is too low, since the *MEC* is not captured by the market transaction.

The comparative results are shown graphically in Figure 3.4. Geometrically, the *MSC* curve is found by vertically summing the *MEC* curve and the *MPC* curve, since costs are measured on the vertical axis. The intersection of *MSC* and *MSB* identifies the efficient equilibrium at $P_e = $26$ and $Q_e = 128,000$. The graph also shows the competitive equilibrium at $P_c = $22$ and $Q_c = 160,000$, which corresponds to the intersection of *MPC* and *MPB*. Notice that at $Q_c$, *MSB* is *below MSC*. This signifies that society is giving up more in scarce resources to produce petroleum than it gains in benefits from consuming it. To restore the equality of *MSB = MSC*, signifying allocative efficiency, output must be decreased—precisely what is predicted by theory.

An alternative way to analyze the two equilibria is to examine the corresponding levels of $M\pi$. At the competitive equilibrium, we know that $M\pi = 0$, since that point is defined where *MPB = MPC*. At the efficient equilibrium, we know that *MSB = MSC*, which can be reexpressed as *MSB − MSC* = 0 or equivalently where *MPB − MPC = MEC*. Hence, we

| FIGURE 3.4 | COMPARING COMPETITIVE AND EFFICIENT EQUILIBRIA USING MARGINAL BENEFIT AND MARGINAL COST: THE REFINED PETROLEUM MARKET IN THE PRESENCE OF A NEGATIVE EXTERNALITY |
|---|---|

The MSC curve is found as the vertical sum of the *MEC* and the *MPC* curves. The intersection of *MSC* and *MSB* identifies the efficient equilibrium point at $P_e$ = \$26 and $Q_e$ = 128,000. Notice how this compares to the competitive equilibrium where $P_c$ = \$22 and $Q_c$ = 160,000, corresponding to the intersection of *MPC* and *MPB*. At $Q_c$, *MSB* is *below MSC*, which means that society is giving up more in scarce resources to produce petroleum than it gains in benefits from consuming it.

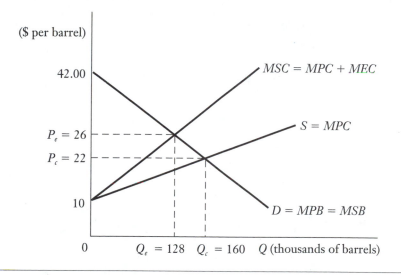

**competitive equilibrium**  The point where marginal private benefit (*MPB*) equals marginal private cost (*MPC*) or where marginal profit ($M\pi$) = 0.

**efficient equilibrium**  The point where marginal social benefit (*MSB*) equals marginal social cost (*MSC*), or where marginal profit ($M\pi$) = marginal external cost (*MEC*).

conclude that at the efficient equilibrium point, $M\pi = MEC$. These derivations are summarized below:

**Competitive equilibrium:**

$$MPB = MPC$$
$$MPB - MPC = 0$$
$$M\pi = 0.$$

**Efficient equilibrium:**

$$MSB = MSC$$
$$MPB + MEB = MPC + MEC$$
$$MPB - MPC = MEC \text{ (since } MEB = 0)$$
$$M\pi = MEC.$$

| FIGURE 3.5 | COMPARING COMPETITIVE AND EFFICIENT EQUILIBRIA USING MARGINAL PROFIT AND MARGINAL EXTERNAL COST: THE REFINED PETROLEUM MARKET IN THE PRESENCE OF A NEGATIVE EXTERNALITY |

The efficient equilibrium is shown where $M\pi$ intersects *MEC* at $Q_e$ = 128,000 barrels. At this point, both $M\pi$ and *MEC* equal $6.40. The competitive equilibrium where $Q_c$ = 160,000 occurs where the $M\pi$ function crosses the horizontal axis or where $M\pi$ = 0. The *MEC* evaluated at this point is equal to $8. Since at the competitive equilibrium $M\pi \neq MEC$, the result is not efficient.

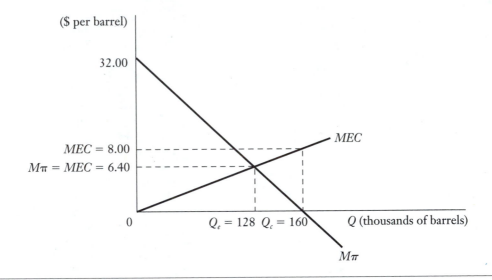

These $M\pi$ relationships are illustrated in Figure 3.5. There is a direct correspondence between the curves in this graph and those in Figure 3.4. The $M\pi$ function in Figure 3.5 is equivalent to the vertical distance between the *MPB* curve and the *MPC* curve shown in Figure 3.4. The *MEC* function in Figure 3.5 is equivalent to the vertical distance between the *MSC* and the *MPC* curves in Figure 3.4. The efficient equilibrium, where $Q_e$ = 128,000, occurs where $M\pi$ intersects the *MEC* function. At this point, notice that the *MEC* and $M\pi$ are equal to $6.40 per barrel:

$$MEC = 0.05Q = 0.05(128) = \$6.40;$$

$$M\pi = MPB - MPC = 42.0 - 0.125(128) - (10.0 + 0.075(128)) = \$6.40.$$

The competitive equilibrium, where $Q_c$ = 160,000, occurs where the $M\pi$ function crosses the horizontal axis or where $M\pi$ = 0. However, *MEC* evaluated at this point equals \$8 (i.e., $MEC = 0.05(160) = \$8$). Thus, at the competitive equilibrium, $M\pi \neq MEC$, indicating the result is inefficient.

The interpretation of this outcome is as follows. In the presence of a negative externality, efficiency requires that firms set their production levels such that the price covers not only private but also external costs at the margin. In this case, the external costs are the damages to the environment, and these should be accounted for by producers in their profit decisions.

### Measuring the Welfare Gain to Society

One important conclusion of the preceding analysis is that efficiency in the market for refined petroleum would improve if output were restricted by 32,000 barrels per day (i.e., $160,000 - 128,000$). Such an output adjustment would increase society's welfare. To illustrate this, the $MPC$, $MSC$, and $MPB$ curves are reproduced in Figure 3.6 with some added notation. Use this model to consider the separate effects on the refineries and on society associated with this output restriction. From the firms' perspective, there is a loss in profits. Notice that as $Q$ falls from 160,000 to 128,000, refineries lose profit, measured as the excess of $MPB$ over $MPC$ for each unit of output. Aggregating all the $M\pi$ values between $Q_e = 128,000$ and $Q_c = 160,000$ defines the triangular area $WYZ$, representing the total loss in profits. However, from the vantage point of society, there is a measurable gain equal to the accumulated *reduction* in $MEC$ associated with the output decline. This reduction in external costs represents the decrease in health and ecological damage. Geometrically, this gain is area $WXYZ$. Hence, on net, society gains an amount equal to the triangular area $WXY$ due to the restoration of efficiency.

In sum, if production of a commodity generates a negative externality, the market will yield an inefficient solution with too many resources allocated to production. If that externality were somehow accounted for within the market, society as a whole would gain. Of course, the operative issue is *how* to account for externalities such that efficiency can be restored.

### Market Failure Analysis

It is important to understand the lack of incentive in the natural market process to explicitly account for external costs. Petroleum refineries are motivated by *private* gain, not *social* gain. Although these firms may be aware of the environmental damage associated with their production, there is no incentive—in fact, there is a disincentive—for them to absorb these costs. Doing so would affect profits negatively. It would be as if firms offered to pay for the external costs on society's behalf. But there is no market incentive for a rational firm to incur higher costs than it has to, even if it is for the good of society. To expect firms to behave otherwise is to refute the underpinnings of the market process and the free enterprise system.

These assertions should not deter society's efforts to solve the problems of environmental damage. Quite the contrary. Market failure models

FIGURE 3.6

## ASSESSING THE NET GAIN TO SOCIETY OF RESTORING EFFICIENCY IN THE REFINED PETROLEUM MARKET

To restore efficiency, $Q$ would have to be reduced from 160,000 to 128,000 barrels. As this output restriction occurs, refineries lose profit, represented as the triangular area WYZ. But at the same time, society gains the associated decline in damages to health and the ecology shown as area *WXYZ*. Thus, on net, society gains by the triangular area *WXY* due to the restoration of efficiency.

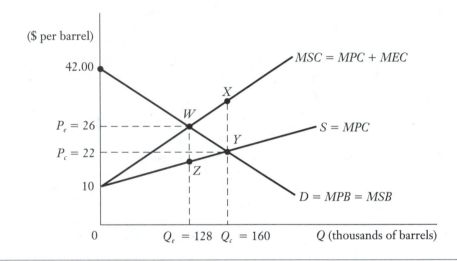

give us a better understanding of *why* we observe increasing damage to the physical environment as industrial production has intensified throughout the world. The theory also explains the persistence of environmental problems from a market perspective and the need for government regulation where such problems arise. Finding appropriate policy solutions is not easy, but the process is facilitated by an understanding of how and why markets fail. On that point, if we consider both the public goods problem and the externality model we have examined, an important common element leads us to the source of virtually all environmental problems—the **absence of property rights.**

## The Absence of Property Rights

In every model presented thus far in this chapter, the market has failed to provide an efficient solution. Using basic elements of economic theory, we have demonstrated *how* the market fails and even quantified the failure in terms of the overproduction of output. While in each case, the failure has been examined conceptually, we have not yet focused on the underlying root of the problem.

Reconsider the negative externality model, and recall the assertion that an externality *is* a public good if it affects a broad segment of society. In our model, the external cost is damage to water supplies, which indeed fits that characterization. Furthermore, clean water possesses the two distinguishing characteristics of a public good. Now recall our public goods model in which the relevant market was defined as "air quality." What do these two public goods have in common? The answer is that in each case, the **property rights** of the good are undefined, and as a result, markets for these goods are virtually nonexistent. **Property rights** are the set of valid claims to a good or resource that permits use of that good or resource and the transfer of its ownership through sale. These rights are generally limited by law and/or social custom.

In the context of environmental public goods, it is unclear who "owns" the rights to water supplies, or who "owns" the rights to the air. For example, do swimmers own the right to clean water or do refineries hold the rights to pollute it? Do individuals own the right to breathe clean air or do polluting firms own the right to contaminate it? Since there are no clear-cut answers to these questions, there is no built-in market mechanism to resolve environmental problems. It turns out that property rights are critically important to the sound functioning of the market system. In fact, as pointed out by Nobel laureate Ronald Coase, the assignment of property rights alone can provide for an efficient solution even in the presence of an externality.[15]

### The Coase Theorem

Coase's exposition about property rights and their relevance to externality problems is so significant that it has come to be known as the **Coase Theorem.** This theorem posits that proper assignment of property rights to any good, even if externalities are present, will allow bargaining between the affected parties such that an efficient solution can be obtained, regardless of which party is assigned those rights. Two important caveats of this theory are noteworthy:

- The predicted outcome is conditioned upon the assumption of costless transactions.

- The result implicitly assumes that the damages associated with the externality are accessible and measurable.

**property rights**
The set of valid claims to a good or resource that permits use of that good or resource and the transfer of its ownership through sale.

**Coase Theorem**
Assignment of property rights, even in the presence of externalities, will allow bargaining such that an efficient solution can be obtained.

---

[15] In 1991, Ronald Coase received the Nobel Prize in economics for his pioneering work in the theory of transactions costs and other concepts that link economic theory and the law (Coase 1960). Much of his research is highly relevant to the economics of environmental problems.

To illustrate the Coase Theorem, we revisit our market model of refined petroleum to see how the assignment of property rights and bargaining can restore efficiency. To operationalize the theory, we impose the assumptions given above, and test the theory's prediction by examining the outcome under two different assignments of rights to some hypothetical river. One is that private individuals hold the rights to the river for recreational use, and the other is that refineries hold the rights to release toxic chemicals into the river.[16]

### Bargaining When Property Rights Belong to the Refineries

We begin by assigning the property rights to the petroleum refineries. This means that the refineries have the "right to pollute" the river as part of their production processes. While this assignment of rights may appear to be perverse, recall that according to the Coase Theorem this should have no effect at all on the outcome. Moreover, such an approach emphasizes the power of the theory.

Remember that the refineries are interested in producing petroleum products up to a level that maximizes profit—by itself, not an objectionable motive in a free enterprise system. The pollution they cause is an unintended by-product of production. Nonetheless, the recreational users of the river *are* harmed by the associated pollution, or more formally, their utility is negatively affected. Knowing that the refineries have the right to pollute and given their own motivation to maximize utility, recreational users have an incentive to negotiate. For each unit change in output, they would be willing to pay the refineries *not* to pollute up to an amount equal to the associated negative effect on their utility. The refineries, on the other hand, would be willing to accept payment *not* to pollute as long as that payment were greater than the loss in profits from cutting back production.

The terms of the negotiation can best be understood by examining Figure 3.7, which is a replication of the negative externality model. As before, $Q_c$ represents the profit-maximizing competitive equilibrium, and $Q_e$ the efficient equilibrium. We assume the market is at $Q_c$ when the bargaining begins, since this is the point that the owners of the rights, the refineries, would choose. Each party's bargaining position is given below in the context of the cost and benefit curves in the diagram:

Recreational users: Willing to offer a payment, $\rho$, such that $\rho < (MSC - MPC)$

Refineries: Willing to accept a payment, $\rho$, such that $\rho > (MPB - MPC)$

---

[16]Although it would be more realistic to assume that only a single refinery were involved in a bargaining scenario about the use of a river, it is simpler to approach the problem from an industry perspective so that we can use the same data and graphical models developed in the negative externality discussion.

FIGURE 3.7

### BARGAINING IN THE REFINED PETROLEUM MARKET WITH THE ASSIGNMENT OF PROPERTY RIGHTS

If the refineries own the rights to the river, bargaining begins at $Q_c$ and continues to $Q_e$. This is so because, at all output levels between these points, the payment $\rho$ satisfies the condition: $MEC > \rho > M\pi$, which is acceptable to both parties. If the recreational users own the rights, bargaining begins at $Q = 0$ and continues up to $Q_e$. This occurs because, at all output levels between these points, the payment $\rho$ satisfies the condition: $M\pi > \rho > MEC$, which is acceptable to both parties.

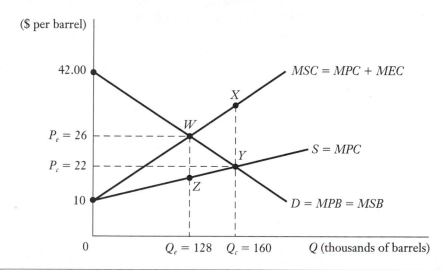

Note that the value of $(MSC - MPC)$ measured vertically is simply the $MEC$, the value of the marginal damage incurred by the recreational users for each added unit of production. The vertical distance measured by $(MPB - MPC)$ is the $M\pi$ earned by the refineries for each extra unit of output produced. In theory, the bargaining between the two groups should continue as long as the payment is greater than the refineries' loss in profit, but less than the recreational users' damage. In the context of the model, payment $\rho$ will be acceptable to both parties as long as the following condition holds:

$$(MSC - MPC) > \rho > (MPB - MPC) \text{ or equivalently,}$$

$$MEC > \rho > M\pi$$

Find these vertical distances on Figure 3.7. Note that at the competitive equilibrium, $Q_c$, the refineries' $M\pi$ equals zero, or $(MPB - MPC) = 0$. On the other hand, the $MEC$ at $Q_c$ is some positive value, or $(MSC - MPC) > 0$, represented as distance $XY$. Thus, bargaining between the parties is feasible at the competitive equilibrium, since $MEC > M\pi$ at $Q_c$. Moreover, since this condition holds for all output levels between $Q_c$ and $Q_e$, the parties will continue to bargain all the way to $Q_e$, where negotiation ceases. The reason? Because at $Q_e$, $(MSC - MPC)$ is exactly equal to $(MPB - MPC)$, or $MEC = M\pi$, each measured as distance $WZ$. Output reductions beyond that point would generate a loss in profits to the refineries that is greater than what the recreational users would be willing to pay, or $M\pi > MEC$, so bargaining would break down.

This is a profound result. Under the assumptions of Coase's model, assigning the property rights to the refineries will lead to bargaining between the parties, which ultimately generates an efficient outcome without any third-party intervention.

### Bargaining When Property Rights Belong to the Recreational Users

Now reconsider the model with the property rights assigned to the recreational users. Recall that according to the Coase Theorem, an efficient outcome can be obtained regardless of which of the affected parties controls the property rights. So we should expect to obtain the same result as before. The starting point at which bargaining begins, however, differs. If the recreational users hold the rights to the river, technically the refineries cannot produce at all unless they pay for the rights to pollute. Thus we assume that the point at which bargaining begins is at $Q = 0$.

The recreational users pursue their rights to a clean river, not to obstruct production of the refineries, but to maximize their utility. Nonetheless, the refineries' profit objective is affected detrimentally. Hence it is they who have a market-based motivation to bargain with the recreational users in an attempt to get them to accept payment for their rights to the river. The terms of the bargaining are analogous to the previous scenario except that now the refineries are in the "offering" position and the recreational users are in the "accepting" position.

Refer back to Figure 3.7 and consider the two sides' relative positions at $Q = 0$. For each unit change in output, the refineries are willing to pay for the right to pollute (and thus the right to produce output), up to an amount equal to the $M\pi$ received from production, measured as the vertical distance between $MPB$ and $MPC$. The recreational users are willing to "trade off" their rights to clean water only if they receive payment greater than the damage they incur as the river becomes polluted. This damage is, of course, the $MEC$, measured as the distance between $MSC$ and $MPC$. Thus each party's bargaining stance is as follows:

| | |
|---|---|
| Refineries: | Willing to offer a payment $\rho$ such that $\rho < (MPB - MPC)$ |
| Recreational users: | Willing to accept a payment $\rho$ such that $\rho > (MSC - MPC)$ |

Hence there is opportunity for bargaining to proceed as long as the following condition holds:

$$(MPB - MPC) > \rho > (MSC - MPC) \text{ or equivalently,}$$

$$M\pi > \rho > MEC$$

The model presented in Figure 3.7 confirms that this condition holds at $Q = 0$ and continues to hold for all output levels up to $Q_e$. At $Q_e$, bargaining ceases, since at that point $(MPB - MPC)$ is exactly equal to $(MSC - MPC)$, or $M\pi = MEC$, each represented by distance $WZ$. Note that beyond $Q_e$, the marginal damage associated with increased production exceeds the addition to profit that the refineries would receive, or $MEC > M\pi$, so bargaining would break down. Thus, the assignment of property rights, this time to the recreational users, leads to an efficient outcome without any government intervention.

### Limitations of the Coase Theorem

Coase's model yields an extremely powerful result and one that underscores the significance of property rights to the market process, regardless of which party is assigned those rights. However, as was stated at the outset, the model's prediction of an efficient outcome depends on two very limiting assumptions: that transactions are costless; and that damages are accessible and measurable. Thus, for the theory to hold in practice, at minimum it must be the case that very few individuals are involved on either side of the market.

The reality of the refinery market, and in fact of most markets, is that there are many affected parties on both sides of the market. There would be nontrivial costs associated with attempting to reach a consensus within each group about the bargaining terms even before the negotiation could begin. Undoubtedly, legal counsel would be necessary, adding still more to the transactions costs. Then there is the difficult problem of identifying the sources of the damage and attempting to assign a value to that damage. As more parties are involved, this task would become increasingly difficult.

### Common Property Resources

**common property resources** Those resources for which property rights are shared.

It turns out that the delineation of property rights need not be completely missing for a market problem to exist. If property rights exist in some form but are ill defined, the outcome will also be an inefficient one. Such is the case for what are termed **common property resources**, which represent another source of externalities and therefore market failures. **Common property resources** are those for which property rights are shared by some group of individuals.

Notice that according to this definition, common property resources fall somewhere on a continuum between the extremes of pure public goods and pure private goods. Unlike pure public goods, common property resources are not accessible to everyone, meaning there is some measure of excludability.[17] However, since the property rights extend to more than one individual, they are not as clearly defined as they are for pure private goods. Some classic examples of common property resources are fisheries and animal populations.

In the case of common property resources, the problem is that public access without any control leads to resource exploitation, which in turn generates a negative externality. The problem arises because each co-owner makes decisions about using the resource based only on private costs and benefits, ignoring how that decision would affect other owners. For example, consider a lake stocked with fish for use exclusively by members of a local community. Unless the catch is limited in some way, each person would fish from the lake based on private motivations, ignoring how the associated decline in the fish population would negatively affect others' ability to share in the benefits. Furthermore, each individual would have no incentive to consider the ultimate cost of restocking the lake, since his or her personal share of that cost would be small. The result is overuse or depletion of the scarce resource.

### The Solution: Government Intervention

From an economic perspective, the general solution to externalities, including those affecting the environment, is to *internalize the externality*—force the market participants to absorb the external costs or benefits. One way this can be accomplished is through the assignment of property rights. In our model, when the refineries owned the rights to pollute, the recreational users internalized the externality through their payment offer. Conversely, when the recreational users owned the rights to clean water, the refineries internalized the external cost by paying for the right to pollute. But how do these rights get assigned in the first place? In practice, the government would have to make this determination as well as enforce limitations on these rights for the good of society.

Other approaches to internalizing environmental externalities are policies that change the effective price of a product by the amount of the associated external cost or benefit. In the petroleum refinery market, for example, the price per barrel of oil could be forced up by the amount of the *MEC*, perhaps by a unit tax. More recent policy prescriptions involve the most direct form of internalizing environmental externalities, which is to establish a market and a price for pollution. These approaches will be investigated in later chapters, all of which are rooted in market failure theory.

---

[17] Put another way, one can think of public goods as an extreme case of common property resources, when the group that shares the property rights consists of all individuals.

# Conclusions

From an economic perspective, environmental problems persist because they are market failures. Whether we model pollution as a negative externality or as damage to environmental public goods, we observe conditions that impede natural market forces. At the root of the dilemma is the absence of property rights. Because no one owns the atmosphere or the earth's water bodies, there are no market incentives to pay for the right to protect these resources or for the right to pollute them. The result is a misallocation of economic resources and a decline in society's welfare. Some third-party mediation, typically government, is necessary to correct the market failure and reach an efficient equilibrium.

But how strong a presence should government be in affected markets? And how should government go about the difficult task of developing effective policy solutions? Although market failure models communicate what the overall approach should be, there are many practical issues that have to be addressed. In theory, we know that the value of an environmental externality must be internalized so that the efficient solution can be identified. But *how* in practice is this accomplished, and is this a practical solution? Are there methods that determine some proxy measure of the costs and benefits of pollution abatement? Or are there better alternative solutions or more reasonable objectives that should be pursued?

In the next two chapters, we will begin to address these questions by investigating various policy solutions, ranging from legislated regulations to market-based initiatives. Using the analytical modeling tools developed thus far, we will critically evaluate different policy approaches to reducing environmental pollution.

# Summary

- There are two basic explanations for the economic assessment of environmental problems as market failures: environmental quality is a public good; and pollution-generating products are associated with externalities.

- A pure public good is one that is both nonrival and nonexcludable in consumption.

- Market demand for a public good is found by summing individual demand curves vertically.

- The market failure of public goods exists because demand is not readily identified. The market failure arises because of nonrevelation of preferences, which in turn is due to free-ridership.

- Even if consumers revealed their willingness to pay, the resulting price would likely underestimate the good's true value due to imperfect information.

- Governments respond to the public goods problem through direct provision of public goods, political procedures and voting rules, and offering education and information.

- An externality is a third-party effect associated with production or consumption. If this effect generates costs, it is a negative externality; if it yields benefits, it is a positive externality.

- In the presence of a negative (positive) externality, the competitive equilibrium is characterized by an overallocation (underallocation) of resources such that too much (too little) of the good is produced.

- In a negative externality model, the competitive price is too low since the marginal external cost (*MEC*) is not captured by the market transaction.

- To identify the efficient equilibrium, the *MEC* must be added to the *MPC* to derive the marginal social cost (*MSC*), which must be set equal to the marginal social benefit (*MSB*).

- The source of the public goods problem and externalities in private markets is that property rights are not defined.

- The Coase Theorem argues that under certain conditions the assignment of property rights will lead to bargaining between the parties such that an efficient solution can be obtained.

- If property rights exist but are ill defined, such as in the case of common property resources, the market solution is inefficient because of the presence of externalities.

- Solutions to market failures typically involve government intervention, which may include regulation, tax policy, or market-based solutions.

## Key Concepts

| | |
|---|---|
| market failure | positive externality |
| public good | marginal social cost (*MSC*) |
| nonrivalness | marginal social benefit (*MSB*) |
| nonexcludability | competitive equilibrium |
| market demand for a public good | efficient equilibrium |
| nonrevelation of preferences | property rights |
| free-ridership | Coase Theorem |
| externality | common property resources |
| negative externality | |

# Review Questions

1. Use economic analysis to evaluate the following statement: "The only amount of acceptable pollution is no pollution at all."

2. Using the theory of public goods, explain the logic of *why* in some resort communities, the ownership of waterfront homes also includes some defined area along the beach.

3. Recall the model of the refined petroleum market given in the text. Use the following graph to answer the questions below.

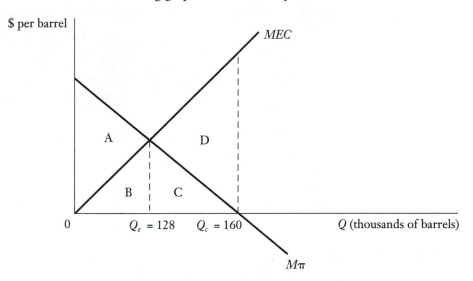

a. Give the economic interpretation of areas A, B, C, and D.
b. Which area represents the loss to the petroleum refineries due to the restoration of efficiency? To which area in Figure 3.6 in the text is this area equivalent?
c. Which area represents the net gain to society? Should the reduction in output from $Q_c$ to $Q_e$ take place? Why or why not?

4. Using the graph shown in Question 3, describe the bargaining process between the refineries and the recreational water users, assuming the refineries have the rights to pollute.

5. Suppose you serve on an environmental policy planning board for the federal government. Your task is to propose a policy initiative aimed at reducing urban air pollution, using the assignment of property rights according to the Coase Theorem. Assume that the major polluters to be targeted are commuter bus companies and that the major parties affected are the collection of city dwellers—residents and workers. Describe your proposal in detail, and include the following:

      a. Whether the rights are to be assigned to city dwellers or to bus companies.

      b. How these rights are to be defined.

      c. How the rights are to be distributed to the parties.

      d. Whether the rights are to be auctioned or sold, and if so, at what price.

## Additional Readings

Bator, F. M. "The Anatomy of Market Failure," *Quarterly Journal of Economics* 72, 1958, pp. 351–79.

Braden, John B., and Charles D. Kolstad, eds. *Measuring the Demand for Environmental Quality*, Amsterdam: North Holland, 1991.

Cornes, Richard, and Todd Sandler. *The Theory of Externalities, Public Goods, and Club Goods*, Cambridge: Cambridge University Press, 1987.

Dasgupta, Partha. "The Environment as a Commodity." In Dieter Helm, ed., *Economic Policy towards the Environment.* Cambridge: Blackwell Publishers, 1991.

Hardin, Garrett. "The Tragedy of the Commons," *Science* 162, December 13, 1968, pp. 1243–48.

Head, John G. "Public Goods and Public Policy." Reprinted in John G. Head, ed., *Public Goods and Public Policy.* Durham, NC: Duke University Press, 1974.

Hyman, David N. *Public Finance: A Contemporary Application of Theory to Policy.* Fort Worth, TX: The Dryden Press, 1996.

## Related Web Sites

American Petroleum Institute (industry strategies to protect the environment) — **www.api.org/pasp/step/standards.htm**

Massachusetts Water Resources Authority — **www.mwra.state.ma.us**

News on logistics policies from Japan's Ministry of International Trade and Industry (referenced in Application 3.3) — **www.jef.or.jp/news/com_pro.html**

U.S. Federal Trade Commission Green Guidelines — **www.ftc.gov/bcp/grnrule/guides92.htm**

# II

# *Modeling Solutions to Environmental Problems*

Recognizing the risks of environmental pollution helps us to appreciate what's at stake if the problem goes unchecked. Knowing how the market functions helps us to accept its inability to correct the problem on its own. Solutions to reduce the effects of polluting residuals must come from outside the market, generally in the form of government policies and programs. But how does government go about designing policy to address the problem of environmental pollution? What objectives does it establish to protect society's health and welfare, and what kinds of policy instruments does it use to implement those objectives? These are tough questions, and in this two-chapter module, we will begin to answer them.

At the outset, we know that government solutions will not eliminate pollution entirely. The laws of science and the materials balance model tell us that much. However, determining exactly where environmental targets should be set is one of the more difficult and even controversial elements of policy development. So too is the specific approach undertaken by government to intervene in pollution-generating markets. Governments all over the world use a variety of policy instruments aimed at reducing environmental risks, some more successful than others. These range from regulations that directly control the activities of polluters to incentive-based plans that use market forces and the price mechanism to achieve a cleaner environment.

In this module, we introduce this broad range of policy alternatives by exploring both conventional and economic solutions to environmental degradation. Conventional policy is the subject of Chapter 4, where we investigate the traditional use of standards to define environmental objectives along with the command-and-control approach to implementing these standards. In Chapter 5, we examine the market approach, which has recently been adopted by the United States and other nations as a secondary form of environmental control policy. By means of economic modeling and the criteria of allocative efficiency and cost-effectiveness, we evaluate the implications of using these different regulatory strategies to solve the complex problem of environmental pollution.

# 4

# Conventional Solutions to Environmental Problems: The Command-and-Control Approach

In the previous chapter, the public goods model and the theory of externalities were used to show how pollution is the result of market failures—failures that arise because of the absence of property rights. Since no one owns the atmosphere or the earth's rivers and streams, there is no market incentive to prevent or correct contamination of these resources. According to the Coase Theorem, assigning property rights would solve the dilemma, but only under certain limiting conditions. The bottom line is that government must act as a third-party mediator in those markets where pollution problems arise.

Recognizing the need for government to correct environmental market failures is an important observation gained through economic modeling, but it is only a first step. We also can use these models to determine *how* government should respond to achieve effective policy solutions. For example, economic theory maintains that government should set objectives to achieve allocative efficiency, balancing social benefits and costs at the margin. Although it is unlikely that these benefits and costs can be determined exactly, the efficiency criterion is useful in assessing policy objectives relative to their optimal level. It is also the case that the criterion of cost-effectiveness can be used to evaluate how these objectives are being implemented—even one set at something other than its efficient level.

Our objective in this chapter is to analyze government's use of *conventional* policy solutions to respond to environmental market failure. We begin by providing an overview of environmental standards and their role in policy development. Allocative efficiency is used to assess the level at which standards are set to define environmental objectives. Next, we provide an overview of the two broadly defined approaches to implementing these standards-based objectives—the **command-and-control approach** and the **market approach.** Finally, we investigate the cost-effectiveness of the command-and-control approach, the more conventional of the two, deferring an analysis of the market approach to the next chapter.

# The Use of Standards in Environmental Policy

Standards are the fundamental basis of most environmental policies. In the United States, setting standards follows a lengthy set of procedures involving scientific research and a series of reviews. The EPA is charged with the oversight of these tasks and for making a formal recommendation about how these standards are to be defined. Ultimately, the standards are legislated by Congress and subsequently monitored for compliance and enforced by the EPA.[1]

## Types of Environmental Standards

When environmental standards are defined in the law, they can be specified as **ambient standards, technology-based standards** or **performance-based standards. Ambient standards** designate the desired quality level of some element of the environment, such as the outdoor air or a body of water. These standards typically are expressed as a maximum allowable concentration of some pollutant in the ambient environment. The United States uses ambient standards to define both air quality and water quality. In each case, the ambient standard is not directly enforceable, but serves as a target level to be achieved through a pollution limit, which is in turn implemented through one of the other types of standards.

**ambient standard** Designates the quality of the environment to be achieved.

As its name implies, a **technology-based standard** stipulates the type of abatement control that must be used by all regulated polluting sources. In practice, the EPA is responsible for researching available technologies and evaluating their relative effectiveness in accordance with certain criteria outlined in the law. It then selects the "best" technology, which subsequently must be adopted by all regulated polluters.[2] The motivation is straightforward—to assure a specific limit on pollution releases by controlling *how* that limit is to be achieved. For example, to reduce sulfur dioxide emissions, the EPA might require all coal-burning power plants to use a scrubber system, forcing each one to achieve the same level of abatement in precisely the same way.

**technology-based standard** Designates the equipment or method to be used to achieve some abatement level.

---

[1] In subsequent chapters, we will elaborate on these processes that define environmental policy development. For access to information on environmental regulations and rulings on the Internet, students can visit the Web site, **www.epa.gov/epahome/rules.html**.

[2] The meaning of "best" in this context is one that is often the subject of debate, an issue we will investigate in upcoming chapters.

**performance-based standard** Specifies a pollution limit to be achieved but does not stipulate the technology.

The alternative type of environmental standard is performance-based. A **performance-based standard** specifies an emissions limit to be achieved by every regulated polluter, but does not stipulate the technology to be used to achieve that limit. By definition, performance-based standards are more flexible than their technology-based counterparts. They implicitly allow polluting sources to choose *how* they will reduce pollution releases as long as they meet the statutory emissions limit.

### The Economic Implications of Using Standards

Although the use of standards sounds straightforward enough, there are two important economic implications to be considered. The first deals with the *level* at which standards are set—an important issue since standards define environmental quality objectives. For example, a standard that limits carbon monoxide emissions defines an "acceptable level" of that pollutant for society. From an economic perspective, the relevant issue is whether that level achieves **allocative efficiency.** If not, there is a welfare loss to society.

A second implication of using standards relates to *how* they are implemented across polluting sources. Policy implementation is concerned with the selection of **control instruments** such as pollution limits or taxes. The decision determines not only whether the objectives are realized but also whether they are achieved in a **cost-effective** manner. If not, resources are wasted, which imposes costs to society.

We can investigate these implications through a two-part economic evaluation that centers around the following questions:

- Are the standards being used to define environmental objectives set at a level that is **allocatively efficient?** That is, does the marginal social cost of pollution abatement equal the marginal social benefit?

- Given some predetermined environmental objective, is the implementation of that objective conducted in a **cost-effective** manner?

## Are Environmental Standards Set at an Allocatively Efficient Level?

**allocatively efficient standards** Standards set such that the associated marginal social cost ($MSC$) of abatement equals the marginal social benefit ($MSB$) of abatement.

Since standards define environmental objectives, it is important to determine whether these objectives are set to achieve **allocative efficiency.** This condition holds if resources are allocated such that the associated benefits and costs to society are equal at the margin. Therefore, we need to develop these benefit and cost concepts specifically for the pollution abatement market, expanding upon what was presented in the previous chapter. Our objective is to learn precisely what is required to identify an allocatively efficient abatement level so that we can assess the likelihood of the government achieving such an outcome by setting a standards-based environmental objective.

### The Marginal Social Benefit of Abatement

As pollution is abated, the social gains are all the benefits associated with a cleaner environment, such as improvements in health, ecosystems, aesthetics, and property. If we measure how these benefits increase relative to increases in abatement, we arrive at the **marginal social benefit (*MSB*) of abatement.** It is equally correct to think of this *MSB* as a measure of the *reduction in damages or costs* caused by pollution.[3] In theory, if we were to add up all the marginal reductions in environmental external costs across every market where pollution is reduced, we would arrive at the *MSB*. We have actually modeled damage reduction, though in a limited context, in our discussion of bargaining in the previous chapter. By paying refineries to pollute less, recreational users of the river gained the *reduction* in the marginal external cost (*MEC*) associated with refined petroleum production. A real-world case where damages were shown to be directly attributable to industrial pollution is in the town of Catano, Puerto Rico, the subject of Application 4.1.

> **marginal social benefit (*MSB*) of abatement** A measure of the additional gains accruing to society as pollution is reduced.

From a market perspective, the *MSB* of abatement is society's *demand* for pollution abatement or, equivalently, its demand for environmental quality.[4] Just as the recreational users were *willing to pay* the refineries for a cleaner river, society is *willing to pay* for a cleaner environment. We expect this willingness to pay to decline with increasing levels of abatement, just as the Law of Demand predicts. Hence, the *MSB* is modeled as a negatively sloped relationship.

### The Marginal Social Cost of Abatement

On the supply side, we need to model the costs incurred by society as polluting sources reduce their releases of contaminating residuals. This relationship is referred to as **the marginal social cost (*MSC*) of abatement.** To gain a more tangible sense of what the *MSC* represents, it is easier to think of it as comprising two parts:

> **marginal social cost (*MSC*) of abatement** The sum of all polluters' marginal abatement costs plus government's marginal cost of monitoring and enforcing these activities.

1. an aggregation of the marginal costs of every polluter's abatement activities; and

---

[3] Technically, the *MSB* also includes the reduction in social costs from attempting to avoid the effects of pollution, such as the costs of air purification systems, bottled water, or water filtration systems.

[4] Although we generally model demand as the *MPB*, which differs from the *MSB* by the amount of any marginal external benefit (*MEB*), in this context there is no *MEB* since the demanders are *all* of society. Thus there are no third parties to which any external benefits could accrue.

## Industrial Pollution and Damages to Human Health: Catano, Puerto Rico

For years, the people of Catano, Puerto Rico blamed their persistent health problems on the town's severe air pollution. The residents live with a barrage of emissions released by a nearby oil refinery, a sewage sludge incinerator, ships in San Juan Bay, and a parade of 18-wheelers transporting goods from nearby docks. According to the island dwellers, however, most of the problem is caused by two giant power plants operated by the Puerto Rico Electric Power Authority. Together, the two facilities house 10 generating units with a combined capacity of 1,086 megawatts, and they release an average of 100 million pounds of sulfur dioxide emissions into Catano's atmosphere each year. One of the town's residents leading the charge against the utility says that Catano's air can be likened to a "toxic soup."

Acting on the residents' complaints, several agencies conducted health studies. Findings by a Puerto Rico Medical Association study showed that cancer rates in Catano were nearly twice the national average. The report found approximately 362 incidents of cancer for every 100,000 residents in Catano in the 1987–88 study year—a dismal statistic compared to Puerto Rico's average rate of 199 in 100,000. Still more disturbing evidence came from a U.S. public health service investigation, which found an alarming rate of respiratory disease among the people of Catano. Since it is well-known that long-term exposure to sulfur dioxide causes respiratory ailments, this latter report validated the suspicion that the utility's emissions were the primary cause of health damages in the town.

Responding to these disturbing medical reports, the EPA began its own study of the area, focusing on the power plants. What they found confirmed the accusations of Catano's residents. Pollutant releases from the plants were in violation of air quality regulations. The EPA conducted what are called opacity tests, which measure the amount of light that can pass through emissions. The results showed that the opacity levels of the power plants' emissions were two to four times the allowable limit. These results were forwarded to the U.S. Justice Department to bring Puerto Rico's utility back into compliance.

SOURCE: Karl Ross. "Some Foul Air in Puerto Rico." *Boston Globe*. January 7, 1993.

2. the marginal costs government incurs to monitor and enforce those activities.

Let's begin with the first part by considering a representative polluter and how it goes about the task of abating its emissions.

**Firm-Level Marginal Abatement Cost.** Referring once again to our discussion of bargaining under the Coase Theorem, recall that refineries reduced their toxic releases by decreasing output. In that case, the marginal cost to refineries of abating pollution was forgone profit, modeled as a movement from right to left along the marginal profit ($M\pi$) curve. Hence, if the decision variable is output, each polluting firm faces a marginal abatement cost equal to its *forgone $M\pi$*. However, such a model implicitly assumes that polluters can meet an environmental standard *only* by reducing

**APPLICATION 4.2**

## Abatement Costs: The Promise of Remediation Technology

Soil contamination is an environmental problem of major proportions. This seemingly esoteric subject has captured world attention in large part because of the damage caused by major oil spills. The 1989 *Valdez* incident, for example, despoiled Alaskan shorelines with 11 million gallons of oil. Such disasters are international news both because the environmental implications are severe *and* because the abatement costs are so staggering. Adding to these concerns is the well-publicized problem of deliberate hazardous waste dumping. Many landfill sites have become contaminated with cancer-causing substances, ranging from polychlorinated biphenyls (PCBs) to heavy metals. Based on EPA estimates, there are more than 30,000 contaminated sites throughout the United States.

Projected abatement costs to clean up the 1,300-plus worst U.S. hazardous waste sites bears an impressive price tag that might be as high as $750 billion, according to some estimates. In 1992, actual accumulated expenses for abating 84 sites were reported to be $11 billion. Oil-spill abatement expenses are no less disturbing. Exxon spent $3 billion to clean up the beaches damaged by the *Valdez* oil spill. These and other clean-up expenditures prompted new research to find lower cost-abatement technologies.

Recently, scientists have made important strides in contaminated-soil abatement using a technology called **bioremediation.** Bioremediation is a relatively low-cost technique that relies on bacteria that consume waste materials. Fertilizer sprays are used to stimulate the feeding of these microorganisms, which accelerates the usually lengthy process of returning soil to its original state. Used for some 50 years to clean waste water treatment plants, the process is now being employed to abate toxic contaminants. In its most successful application to date, bioremediation helped to clean up the oily mess left by the *Valdez* on Alaskan beaches. Within three weeks, the soil was restored down to a foot below the surface.

Reportedly, contractors are charging in the range of $50 to $100 per ton for this innovative process. The table below shows how this cost compares to that of more conventional methods like on-site or off-site incineration.

| Abatement Method | Per Ton Abatement Cost ($) |
|---|:---:|
| On-site soil incineration | 300 |
| Off-site soil incineration | 1,000 |
| Bioremediation | 50–100 |

Many believe that bioremediation holds great promise for the environment. Such technological advances provide decision makers with a wider range of alternatives to abate pollution and greater opportunities to find cost-effective solutions.

SOURCES: U.S. Environmental Protection Agency, Office of Communications, Education, and Public Affairs. *Securing Our Legacy, An EPA Progress Report 1989–1991.* Washington, DC: April 1992, p. 27; Peter Hong and Michele Galen. "The Toxic Mess Called Superfund." *Business Week*, May 11, 1992, pp. 32–34; Robert D. Hof, "The Tiniest Toxic Avengers." *Business Week*, June 4, 1990, pp. 96, 98; Associated Press. "Updating Previous Big Spills." *Boston Globe*, January 6, 1993, p. 6.

FIGURE 4.1

## THE SINGLE POLLUTER'S MARGINAL
## ABATEMENT COST (*MAC*)

A typical *MAC* curve is positively sloped and increasing at an increasing rate. Notice that as the firm continues to abate from $A_1$ to $A_2$, the *MAC* increases by a proportionately greater amount from $MAC_1$ to $MAC_2$. This reflects the fact that as the abatement process continues and the environment becomes cleaner, it becomes increasingly difficult and therefore more costly to remove each additional unit of pollution.

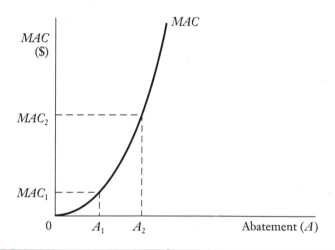

output—a very limiting assumption. Since other methods are available, we need to expand upon this output-based specification.

As a profit-maximizer, the polluting firm is implicitly a cost-minimizer. Thus, to meet an emissions standard, it will consider *all* available abatement options and select the *least-cost* method. In addition to reducing the level of production, these options may include installing some type of abatement technology or altering a production process. To allow for the fact that polluters choose from a menu of available abatement methods, we model what is conventionally called a **marginal abatement cost (*MAC*)** function. This relationship measures the change in economic costs associated with reducing pollution using the least-cost method. Application 4.2 on page 104 discusses the importance of choosing a least-cost abatement technology to clean up oil spills and hazardous wastes.

**marginal abatement cost (*MAC*)** Measures the change in costs associated with reducing pollution using the least-cost method.

Each polluting source likely faces a unique *MAC* curve. The firm's location, the type of contaminants it releases, the nature of its production, and the availability of technology are among the factors that affect the shape and position of the *MAC* curve. However, a typical *MAC* curve is positively sloped and increasing at an increasing rate, as shown in Figure 4.1.

**FIGURE 4.2**

## THE EFFECT OF COST-SAVING TECHNOLOGY ON THE POLLUTER'S *MAC* CURVE

Changes in a firm's abatement options change the position of the *MAC* curve. For example, this model shows how the introduction of a new cost-saving abatement technology would pivot the *MAC* downward to *MAC'*.

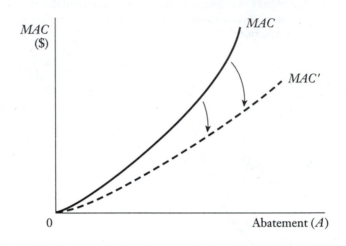

Think about the intuition of this model. When pollution levels are high, the addition of virtually any type of abatement technology will likely be quite effective. So, although costs are rising, they are doing so at a fairly slow rate relative to the abatement being accomplished. But, as this process continues and the environment becomes cleaner, it becomes very difficult to remove still more pollution. Thus the added costs relative to the abatement achieved increase at a much faster rate.

Should a firm's abatement options change, the position of its *MAC* would be affected. For example, the introduction of a cost-saving abatement technology would pivot the *MAC* downward, as shown in Figure 4.2.[5] Notice that at each abatement level, *MAC'* is below *MAC*. Likewise, a polluter's *MAC* for one pollutant might be lower than for that of another. Consequently, an *MAC* function generally is defined for a particular contaminant at a *given* level of technology.

**market-level marginal abatement cost function ($MAC_{mkt}$)** The horizontal sum of all polluters' *MAC* functions.

**Market-Level Marginal Abatement Cost.** The aggregation of all polluters' *MAC*s represents the **market-level *MAC* function ($MAC_{mkt}$)** defined as the horizontal sum of each polluter's *MAC*, or $MAC_{mkt} = \Sigma MAC_i$

---

[5] A firm's *total* abatement costs are represented as the area under the *MAC* up to the abatement level required by the standard, assuming no fixed costs. Thus, the effect of the cost-saving technology on total abatement costs is implicitly shown as the reduction in the area under the firm's *MAC*.

| FIGURE 4.3 | **DERIVING THE MARGINAL SOCIAL COST OF ABATEMENT** |
|---|---|

To derive the *MSC* function, the *MCE* is vertically added to the $MAC_{mkt}$. At any abatement level (*A*), the *MCE* is shown as the vertical distance between $MAC_{mkt}$ and *MSC*. Notice that this distance increases with higher abatement levels. As pollution standards become more stringent, polluters have a greater tendency to evade the law, which in turn calls for more sophisticated and thus more costly monitoring and enforcement programs.

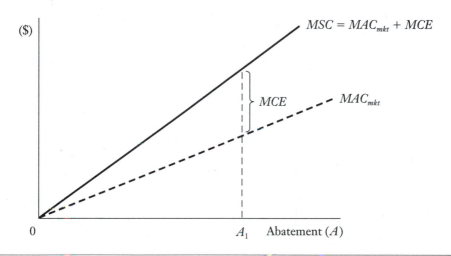

for all *i* firms. This is exactly the same procedure used to derive market supply in Chapter 2. In this context, the horizontal summing assures that the $MAC_{mkt}$ represents least-cost decisions, since it effectively sets each *MAC* equal at every abatement level.

**marginal cost of enforcement (*MCE*)** Added costs incurred by government associated with monitoring and enforcing abatement activities.

**Marginal Cost of Enforcement.** Now consider the second element of the marginal social cost of abatement (*MSC*). To the $MAC_{mkt}$ function, we need to add the marginal costs incurred by government for enforcement and monitoring of abatement activities. This component is commonly referred to as the **marginal cost of enforcement (*MCE*).** Figure 4.3 illustrates how the *MCE* is added vertically to the $MAC_{mkt}$ to derive the *MSC* function. (For simplicity, all functions are assumed to be linear.) At any abatement level (*A*), the *MCE* is represented as the vertical distance between $MAC_{mkt}$ and *MSC*. Notice that this distance is increasing with higher abatement levels. As pollution standards become more stringent, polluters have a greater tendency to evade the law, which in turn calls for more sophisticated and thus more costly monitoring and enforcement programs. Figure 4.4 presents a graphic of U.S. expenditures for the 1975 to 1994 period on abatement, monitoring, and research to improve the efficiency of abatement and monitoring.

| FIGURE 4.4 | U.S. POLLUTION AND CONTROL EXPENDITURES |

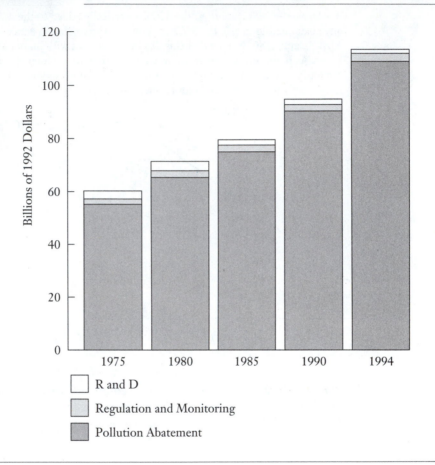

Data from C. R. Vogan. "Pollution Abatement and Control Expenditures, 1972–94." *Survey of Current Business.* Washington, DC: GPO, September 1996, cited in *Council on Environmental Quality*, 1997, Table 10, p. 402.

### *Are Abatement Standards Set Efficiently?*

From our discussion in Chapter 3, we know that the *MSB* and the *MSC* simultaneously determine the efficient level of abatement. This result is illustrated in Figure 4.5 where, for simplicity, it is assumed that both functions are linear. The efficient level of abatement, $A_e$, occurs at the intersection of the two functions. Whether or not the government sets environmental standards to achieve this level depends on a variety of considerations. There are four factors in particular that suggest this outcome is highly unlikely: (1) the existence of legislative constraints; (2) imperfect information; (3) regional differences; and (4) nonuniformity of pollutants.

| FIGURE 4.5 | THE ALLOCATIVELY EFFICIENT AMOUNT OF POLLUTION ABATEMENT |

In the market for pollution abatement, the efficient level, $A_e$, occurs at the intersection of the *MSB* and *MSC* curves.

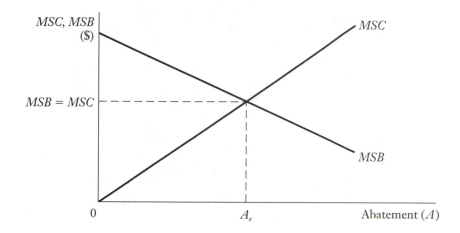

**benefit-based standard** A standard set to improve society's well-being with no consideration for the associated costs.

**Legislative Constraints.** First of all, the reality of a standards-based approach is that it does not necessarily set pollution limits to account for the associated benefits and costs. In fact, under U.S. law, many standards are said to be **benefit-based,** meaning they are set at a level to improve society's well-being with no allowance for balancing with the associated costs. For example, under the U.S. Clean Air Act, air quality ambient standards are motivated solely by the anticipated benefits of improved health and welfare. As long as costs are not accounted for in the standard-setting process, resources likely will be overallocated to abatement.

**Imperfect Information.** Even when a cost-benefit balancing *is* called for by law, the absence of full information would likely prevent the government from identifying the *MSB* and *MSC* of abatement. Let's consider the *MSB* relationship first. Recall from our discussion of market failure in Chapter 3 that pollution abatement is a public good. As such, its demand, which *is* the *MSB* curve, is not readily identified due to the problem of non-revelation of preferences. There are methods used in practice to *estimate* the value society places on the damage reductions associated with abatement. However, given the inherent difficulty of trying to monetize such intangibles as health improvements and longevity of life, the probability of modeling *MSB* accurately is quite low.

There are similar problems in identifying the *MSC*. In addition to estimating the *MCE*, the government also would have to know the *MAC* for

FIGURE 4.6

## SETTING AN ENVIRONMENTAL QUALITY STANDARD: IS IT ALLOCATIVELY EFFICIENT?

If the government were to set an abatement standard at $A_0$, the *MSB* would be higher than the *MSC*, meaning that society places a higher value on the gain from reducing pollution than the resources needed to achieve it. Hence the $A_0$ standard would be too lenient. On the other hand, if the standard were set at $A_1$, it would be considered too restrictive. Only at $A_e$ would society accept the legal limit as allocatively efficient.

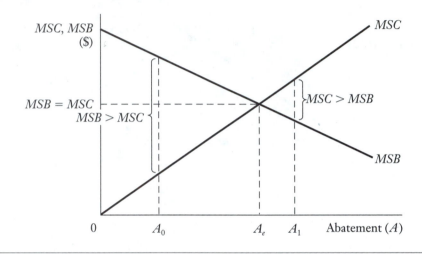

every polluter. Obtaining this firm-level information would be virtually impossible given the diversity of production and abatement techniques across polluting sources. Furthermore, the *MAC* must also account for the *implicit* costs of abatement, which are difficult to determine. In this context, implicit costs would have to capture any unemployment associated with production declines, the potential loss of consumer choice if products were eliminated or altered, and any price and income effects arising from abatement requirements.[6]

In the absence of perfect information, it is highly probable that the government will unknowingly establish the abatement standard at some level other than the allocatively efficient one, even if that was the legislated intent. Figure 4.6 reproduces the market for abatement at equilibrium, comparing the allocatively efficient outcome, $A_e$, with two other possible abatement levels, $A_0$ and $A_1$. If the standard is set at $A_0$, the *MSB* would be greater than the *MSC*, meaning that society places a higher value on reducing pollution than it must give up in resources to achieve it. Hence society would consider the $A_0$ standard to be too lenient. Conversely, a standard set

---

[6] In a later chapter, we will investigate the methods used in practice to estimate the benefits and costs of improving environmental quality.

---

| FIGURE 4.7 | THE EFFECT OF REGIONAL DIFFERENCES ON ACHIEVING ALLOCATIVE EFFICIENCY |
|---|---|

This model shows how regional-specific conditions can give rise to different optimal levels of abatement. Although the *MSC*s are identical, that is, $MSC_X = MSC_Y$, the *MSB* in region X is *lower* than for that of region Y, that is, $MSB_X < MSB_Y$. Thus, the allocatively efficient abatement level for region X, $A_X$, is lower than for region Y, $A_Y$. Consequently, a single national standard of abatement cannot be optimal for both regions.

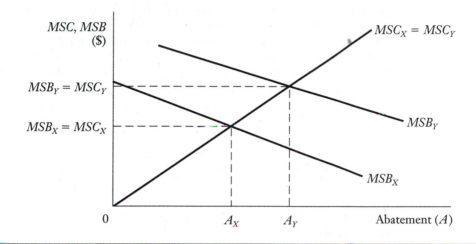

---

at $A_1$ would be considered too restrictive. Only at $A_e$ would society consider the legal limit to be allocatively efficient. However, the information needed to find this optimal level of pollution abatement is immense.

**Regional Differences.** Even if the law permits a balancing of costs and benefits *and* if full information were available, there is a qualifier on the use of $A_e$ as a national standard across all polluting sources. Why? Because this optimal level is determined from *MSB* and *MSC*, both of which assume the absence of regional-specific abatement benefits and costs. The only way $A_e$ would be allocatively efficient in all regions is if the respective *MSB* and *MSC* functions defined for those locations were identical.

By way of example, consider two hypothetical regions X and Y that have identical *MSC* functions (i.e., $MSC_X = MSC_Y$), but different *MSB* functions such that $MSB_X$ is *lower* than $MSB_Y$ at all abatement levels. Such a disparity might be due to differences in income, education, or population across the two locations. In any case, at most, only one of the two locations would consider a nationally determined $A_e$ as efficient. Look at Figure 4.7, which superimposes the *MSB* and *MSC* for each region on the same diagram. The allocatively efficient level of abatement in region X, $A_X$, is much lower than that for region Y, $A_Y$. So there is no way that a single national standard of abatement—even one that *is* efficient on a national level— would be optimal for both regions.

**Nonuniformity of pollutants.** An inefficient outcome can also arise within the same region, if changes in releases from polluting sources do not have a uniform impact on the environment. This can occur if the relationship between the change in pollutant releases and the change in exposure is nonlinear, or not directly proportional. The nonuniformity can also arise when polluting sources are located at varying distances from an exposed population or ecosystem, even if their pollution releases are identical.[7] Generally, the further away from a source is an affected population, the lower is the associated damage, since there is greater opportunity for dilution of contaminants.[8] This in turn would mean that the *MSB* of abatement varies inversely with the distance between a source and the affected population or resource. Thus, even with equal *MSC* of abatement, the efficient level of abatement would not be the same for all polluting sources. Consequently, just as in the case of regional differences discussed above, a nationally determined abatement standard would not be optimal for all sources.

What we can surmise from this assessment is that in most real-world applications, at least one of the factors—legislative constraints, imperfect information, regional differences, or nonuniformity of pollutants—will be present. Hence there is a very low probability that pollution abatement standards will be set at an allocatively efficient level. Accepting this, we must rely on a different criterion to evaluate, not where the standards are set, but how they are implemented.

## General Approaches to Implementing Environmental Policy

**cost-effective policy**
A policy that meets an objective using the least amount of economic resources.

**command-and-control approach**
Uses limits or technology-based restrictions to control pollution directly.

Our preceding analysis makes a strong case that a government-established environmental standard will be set at something other than its allocatively efficient level. While this outcome is unfortunate, it *is* possible that even a nonoptimal environmental standard can be implemented using the least amount of resources. If so, the policy is said to be **cost-effective.** Whether or not this "second-best" criterion is met depends on the method used to bring about the desired reduction in pollution.

Most governments, including that of the United States, use a number of different policy tools to achieve environmental quality, as Application 4.3 explains. However, it is helpful at the outset to collapse these down into two broad categories. One is the **command-and-control approach,** which uses

---

[7] National Acid Precipitation Assessment Program (November 1991), Chapter 3, Section 3.1.

[8] More technically, this relationship can be captured by what is called a transfer coefficient. For detail, see Tietenberg (1996), pp. 339-41.

# Methods Used by Government to Reduce Environmental Pollution

According to the Relative Risk Reduction Strategies Committee of the EPA's Science Advisory Board Web site at **www.epa.gov/science1/index.html**, there are six categories of risk-reducing policy tools that governments should consider when addressing any environmental problem. Two of these are the more conventional broad-based categories of **Conventional Regulations,** such as standards, use restrictions, and product design; and **Market Incentives,** such as pollution charges and permit systems. The other four major groups are as follows:

### Scientific and Technical Measures

Research and development to suggest promising solutions and to improve understanding of problems like the potential for global warming.

Innovations in pollution prevention and pollution control technology, such as the development of ecologically safe, cost-effective methods to manage contaminated sediments.

### Provision of Information

Improving communication to producers, consumers, and/or state and local governments about risks of environmental problems and threats to communities. (For example, new home buyers could be provided with the results of radon tests, and state and local governments could be given technical information to support their efforts in addressing indoor air pollution.)

### Enforcement

Implement more vigorous enforcement of existing laws and regulations. (Suggested options include: (1) the use of statistical techniques in enforcement to ensure that all classes of potential violators are properly inspected; and (2) the imposition of penalties that create incentives for compliance with existing environmental laws.)

### Cooperation with Other Government Agencies and Nations

Promotion of interagency cooperation to reduce environmental risk. (Environmental authorities typically have limited jurisdiction, but other government bodies make decisions that affect the environment. This necessitates a cooperative approach to environmental issues.)

Promotion of cooperation with other nations through such means as international conventions aimed at problems like global warming or acid rain.

SOURCE: U.S. Environmental Protection Agency, Science Advisory Board. *Reducing Risk: Setting Priorities and Strategies for Environmental Protection.* Washington, DC, September 1990, p. 15.

**market approach**
Uses incentive-based instruments and market forces to motivate abatement.

pollution limits or technology-based restrictions to directly regulate polluting sources. The second is the **market approach,** which uses incentive-based policy tools to motivate abatement through market forces.

Of the two, command-and-control is the more conventional approach, dominating environmental policy in most nations. This nearly universal reliance on direct regulation seems to have evolved from an attempt to gain immediate control of what was initially an unfamiliar and urgent social dilemma. Though well intentioned, the use of inflexible regulations and pollution limits—often imposed uniformly across all polluters—has not met with consistent success. Hence, over time, policy makers began to look for alternatives. The United States and other industrialized countries have gradually integrated more market-based solutions into their environmental policy programs. Combining incentive-oriented control instruments with more conventional methods seems to be indicative of a trend in environmental policy. However, the *relative* gains of market-based solutions cannot be fully appreciated without assessing the cost-effectiveness of the command-and-control approach.

## Is the Command-and-Control Approach Cost-Effective?

The practical basis for assessing the command-and-control approach according to the cost-effectiveness criterion is to determine whether society is incurring higher costs than necessary to achieve a given level of environmental quality. For discussion purposes, let's consider the abatement standard as the socially desirable (as opposed to efficient) outcome, perhaps motivated to protect human health. To achieve cost-effectiveness, policy makers must determine the relative costs of all control instruments that can achieve this objective and select the one that minimizes costs. Given this general premise, we can identify two command-and-control decisions that may violate the cost-effectiveness criterion. The first is the use of a technology-based standard, and the second is the use of uniform standards. We discuss each of these in turn.

### The Cost-Ineffectiveness of the Technology-Based Standard

Recall from the beginning of the chapter that there are three types of standards—the ambient standard, the performance-based standard, and the technology-based standard. Take a minute to reread the definitions of each of these control instruments, and think about the cost implications of each. What should be apparent is that the technology-based standard potentially prevents the polluter from minimizing the costs of achieving a given abatement level. Remember that the *MAC* curve is defined under the assumption that the polluter selects the *least-cost* available method. If the government *forces* polluters to use a specific technology to meet an emissions limit, it is impeding the firm's incentive to abate in a cost-effective manner. Unless the mandated technology happens to be the least-cost abatement approach for *all* polluters, at least some will be forced to operate *above* their respective *MAC* curves. This in turn means that society is incurring costs higher than the *MSC* of abatement. The outcome is a waste of economic resources with no additional benefits accruing to society.

If instead a performance-based standard were used, each polluter could select the means by which it achieves a given objective. Without further guidance, it would follow its self-interest and choose the least costly abatement method. Society would still gain the benefits of a cleaner environment, but fewer resources would be used to achieve that gain. A word of caution is in order, however. Although there are potential cost advantages to using performance-based standards over technology-based standards, this selection does not by itself assure a cost-effective solution. In fact, regardless of which type of standard is used, resources will be wasted if they are imposed *uniformly* across polluters.

### The Cost-Ineffectiveness of Uniform Standards

Under a strict command-and-control framework, standards often are imposed *uniformly* across groups of polluting sources.[9] The operative question is whether such a policy approach is cost-effective. The answer? The use of uniform standards across polluting sources will waste economic resources as long as abatement cost conditions differ among those sources. Of course, the reality is that there are many factors that might give rise to such differences. One is the age of the polluter's physical plant. Newer facilities typically are designed and built with the most advanced pollution control equipment, making them capable of meeting an abatement standard at a much lower marginal cost than their less modern counterparts. Another relevant factor is regional differences in input prices. There is no reason to expect firms in different locations to face the same costs of labor, land, and capital. And as long as input prices vary, so too will polluters' costs to achieve a given abatement standard.

Accepting the likelihood of abatement cost differences among polluters, we need to explore why this would make the use of uniform standards cost-ineffective. The problem is that uniform standards under a command-and-control framework force high-cost abaters to reduce pollution as much as low-cost abaters, so more resources than necessary are used to achieve a cleaner environment. Cost savings could be realized by having more of the abatement accomplished by polluters who can do so at a relatively lower cost. We use a simple analytical model to illustrate this important assertion.

To begin, assume there are only two polluting sources in a given region, each of which generates 10 units of pollution for a total of 20 units released into the environment. The government determines that emissions must be reduced by 10 units across the region to achieve the "socially desirable level

[9]In some contexts, pollution limits vary across major industrial groups but are applied uniformly *within* each of these.

of pollution." Each firm faces different abatement cost conditions modeled as follows:[10]

Polluter 1's Marginal Abatement Cost ($MAC_1$):   $MAC_1 = 2.5(A_1)$;

Polluter 1's Total Abatement Costs ($TAC_1$):   $TAC_1 = 1.25(A_1)^2$,

where $A_1$ is the amount of pollution abated by Polluter 1.

Polluter 2's Marginal Abatement Cost ($MAC_2$):   $MAC_2 = 0.625(A_2)$;

Polluter 2's Total Abatement Costs ($TAC_2$):   $TAC_2 = 0.3125(A_2)^2$,

where $A_2$ is the amount of pollution abated by Polluter 2.

Now, assume that the government implements the 10-unit standard *uniformly*, requiring each polluter to abate by 5 units (i.e., $A_1 = A_2 = 5$). At this level, the $MAC$ for Polluter 1 is \$12.50 [$MAC_1 = 2.5(5) = \$12.50$], and its $TAC$ is \$31.25 [$TAC_1 = 1.25(5)^2 = \$31.25$]. For Polluter 2, $MAC_2$ is \$3.13, and $TAC_2$ is \$7.81. Thus, the total abatement costs for the region, (absent the costs of monitoring and enforcement), equal \$39.06, which represents the value of resources used by polluters to meet the standard. The question is, could the same standard be achieved at a lower cost?

Notice that Polluter 2 has an abatement cost advantage over Polluter 1. For example, the fifth unit of abatement costs Polluter 2 \$9.37 less than Polluter 1. Therefore, it would be cheaper if Polluter 2 were to do more of the abating. Of course, it would have to have an incentive to do this, and the two firms would have to negotiate to arrive at some mutually beneficial agreement.[11] But no such opportunity is allowed when the government forces every polluter to abate by the same amount. Thus, we conclude that the use of uniform standards under a conventional command-and-control approach does not achieve the cost-effectiveness criterion, as long as $MAC$ conditions differ across polluters.

Could the government reallocate abatement levels across the two polluters to achieve a cost-effective solution? The answer is yes, and it turns out that economic theory conveys exactly how this result could be achieved. If each polluter were to abate to the point where the corresponding level of $MAC$ is equal across firms, the **cost-effective abatement criterion** would be achieved. This means that the environmental standard would be met at minimum cost. This result is one application of what microeconomic theory calls the **equi-marginal principle of optimality.**

To illustrate the cost savings of such an approach, let's return to our two-polluter model. We need to find the abatement levels for each polluter

**cost-effective abatement criterion** Allocating abatement across polluting sources such that the $MAC$s for each source are equal.

---

[10] Assuming no fixed costs, the total abatement costs ($TAC$) for a given abatement level, $A$, is simply the aggregation of the $MAC$ at each abatement level up to $A$. Graphically, this means that the $TAC$ for abatement level $A$ is the area under the $MAC$ curve up to point $A$.

[11] In a real-world setting, there would also be transactions costs associated with the negotiations between the two firms.

FIGURE 4.8

### THE COST-EFFECTIVE SOLUTION
### IN A TWO-POLLUTER MODEL

The model shows the *MAC* curves for two firms, Polluter 1 and Polluter 2, diagrammed on the same graph. Polluter 1's abatement level, $A_1$, is measured left to right on the horizontal axis, and Polluter 2's abatement, $A_2$, right to left. The horizontal axis measures from 0 units of abatement up to the 10-unit limit imposed by the regulatory authority, so that every point represents a *combined* abatement level that satisfies the standard. In accordance with the equi-marginal principle of optimality, the intersection of the two *MAC* curves yields the cost-effective solution, where $A_1 = 2$ and $A_2 = 8$. At this point, notice that $MAC_1 = MAC_2 = \$5.00$.

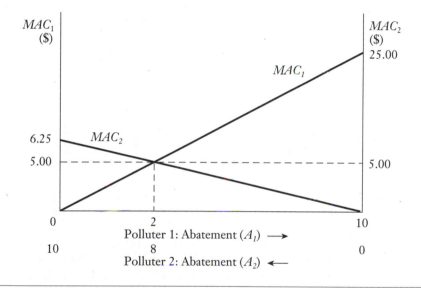

where their respective *MAC*s are equal, holding the combined abatement level at 10 units to meet the standard. Algebraically, the steps in the solution are:

**Step 1:**
Set $MAC_1 = MAC_2$:                    $2.5A_1 = 0.625A_2$

**Step 2:**
Set $A_1 + A_2 =$ Abatement Standard:   $A_1 + A_2 = 10$

**Step 3:**
Solve the equations simultaneously:   $A_1 = 2;$   $A_2 = 8$

This same result is shown graphically in Figure 4.8. Both firms' *MAC* curves are plotted on the same diagram. For Polluter 1, $A_1$ is measured horizontally *left to right;* whereas for Polluter 2, $A_2$ is measured *right to left.* The horizontal axis measured in either direction ranges from 0 units of abatement up to the 10-unit requirement imposed by the regulatory authority. Thus every point on this axis represents a *combined* abatement level that satisfies the standard. Notice that the intersection of the two *MAC* curves yields the cost-effective solution, $A_1 = 2$ and $A_2 = 8$. At this point, $MAC_1 = MAC_2 = \$5.00$.

If each polluter were given these firm-specific abatement targets, the total costs of achieving the environmental objective would be minimized. These costs can be calculated from each firm's *TAC* equation, substituting in the cost-effective abatement levels:

$$TAC_1 = \quad 1.25(2)^2 = \$ \ 5.00$$

$$TAC_2 = 0.3125(8)^2 = \$20.00$$

By following the equi-marginal principle of optimality, the total cost to society of achieving the 10-unit abatement standard is \$25.00—a \$14.06 savings over the uniform standards approach. Equivalently, this \$14.06 represents the unnecessary costs incurred by society when a uniform standard is imposed across nonidentical polluters.

As a final point, it is reasonable to ask how in practice the government could arrive at these firm-specific abatement standards within a command-and-control framework. The answer is that it would have to know the abatement cost conditions for every firm it was regulating. Of course, this kind of information would be virtually impossible to determine, particularly when thousands of individual sources are being controlled. But there is a way around the problem—though not within the command-and-control approach. As we will discover in the next chapter, there are instruments under the market approach that can arrive at this same cost-effective solution without specific knowledge of polluters' costs. How? By using market incentives and the price mechanism in place of inflexible rules.

## Conclusions

In this chapter, we have begun to evaluate solutions to environmental problems by focusing on the more conventional policy tools used in practice—the use of standards to define environmental objectives and the command-and-control approach to implementing those objectives. Even at this introductory level, we were able to reach some important conclusions. It is apparent, for example, that government-mandated environmental standards are not likely to be set at an efficient level. Beyond those instances when the law does not allow for the requisite balancing of benefits and costs, there is still an information problem. Policy makers would need extensive data to measure the marginal costs and benefits of abatement accurately. Hence, in all likelihood, the level at which environmental objectives are set will not be allocatively efficient.

Accepting this realization, cost-effectiveness becomes the relevant criterion by which to assess the command-and-control approach and compare it to the market approach. Thus far, our investigation shows that the use of uniform standards under a command-and-control framework likely wastes economic resources. Cost savings can be realized if polluters reduce emissions up to the point where their marginal costs of doing so are equal. But how can such a result be achieved in practice? The answer requires an investigation of alternative control instruments, in particular those characterized as part of the market approach to environmental policy.

In sum, although our findings in this chapter are important, they are nonetheless incomplete. We still must learn how market-based initiatives are designed and how they compare to their command-and-control counterparts—precisely the agenda of our next chapter. This part of our analysis is particularly relevant given the recent move by the United States and other nations to integrate market-based instruments into what had been an exclusively command-and-control approach to environmental policy. To appreciate this trend and what it means for society, we must understand how market instruments operate and evaluate their effectiveness in achieving environmental goals.

# Summary

- There are three basic types of standards used in environmental control policy: ambient standards that designate the level of environmental quality; technology-based standards that indicate the abatement method to be used by polluters; and performance-based standards that specify an emissions limit to be achieved by polluters.

- An environmental standard achieves allocative efficiency if resources are allocated such that the marginal social benefit (*MSB*) of abatement is equal to the marginal social cost (*MSC*) of abatement.

- The *MSB* measures the additional gains to society associated with the reduction in damages caused by pollution.

- The MSC is the horizontal sum of the market-level $MAC$ ($MAC_{mkt}$) plus the government's marginal cost of enforcement ($MCE$).

- Four factors suggest that a government-mandated abatement standard is not likely to meet the allocative efficiency criterion: (1) the existence of legislative constraints; (2) imperfect information; (3) regional differences; and (4) nonuniformity of pollutants.

- Governments generally use one of two approaches to implement environmental policy: the command-and-control approach, or the market approach.

- Two aspects of the command-and-control approach may violate the cost-effectiveness criterion: the use of technology-based standards, and the use of uniform standards.

- Since technology-based standards dictate a specific abatement method to polluting sources, they prevent the polluter from minimizing costs.

- Uniform standards force high-cost abaters to reduce pollution as much as low-cost abaters, so more resources than necessary are used to achieve the benefits of a cleaner environment.

- To achieve a cost-effective outcome, the allocation of abatement responsibilities across polluting sources must be such that the *MAC* is equal across polluters.

## Key Concepts

ambient standards
technology-based standards
performance-based standards
allocatively efficient standards
marginal social benefit of abatement (*MSB*)
marginal social cost of abatement (*MSC*)
marginal abatement cost (*MAC*)

market-level marginal abatement cost function ($MAC_{mkt}$)
marginal cost of enforcement (*MCE*)
benefit-based standards
cost-effective policy
command-and-control approach
market approach
cost-effective abatement criterion

## Review Questions

1. One of the major problems in applying the Coase Theorem in practice is the existence of high transactions costs. Propose an approach that a third party could institute that would reduce these costs sufficiently so that bargaining could proceed. How likely is the solution to be efficient and why?

2. Using a graph of the pollution abatement market, model a situation where the allocatively efficient level of abatement occurs at 100 percent, or equivalently where pollution is zero. Referring to the relative position of the *MSC* and *MSB* curves, explain such an outcome intuitively.

3. a. Under a strict command-and-control framework, suppose abatement standards are set equally across polluters. Assume the total

abatement target is 30 units. Show the cost implications using three graphs, each of a different polluter with a unique *MAC* curve drawn to depict a "low-cost abater," a "moderate-cost abater," and a "high-cost abater." On each graph, identify the abatement level corresponding to a uniform standards approach, and show the level of *MAC* at that point and the area corresponding to *TAC*.

b. Now refer directly to your model and summarize what would happen *qualitatively* to the abatement levels of each firm if the equi-marginal principle of optimality were used. Explain intuitively why this would be cost-effective.

4. It is well documented that the carbon monoxide (CO) emissions from combustible engines increase in colder climates. This in turn implies that the associated damages are expected to be less severe in summer months than in winter. Nonetheless, air quality control authorities use a standard for CO that is uniform throughout the year with no allowance for seasonal effects. Use this information and the following model to answer the questions below.

$$MSB \text{ of CO abatement in winter } = 350 - 0.5A$$

$$MSB \text{ of CO abatement in summer} = 140 - 0.2A$$

$$MSC \text{ of CO abatement } = 0.2A,$$

where $A$ is the level of CO abatement.

a. Graph the *MSB* and *MSC* functions on the same diagram.

b. Assume the government sets a uniform standard for winter and summer at $A = 500$. Support or refute this policy based on the criterion of allocative efficiency, using your model to explain your response.

c. If you were in charge of setting policy for CO emissions, what action would you recommend to assure an allocatively efficient outcome across the two seasons?

# Additional Readings

Buck, Susan. *Understanding Environmental Administration and Law.* Covelo, CA: Island Press, 1996.

Crandall, Robert W. "Is There Progress in Environmental Policy?" *Contemporary Economic Policy*, January 1995, pp. 80–83.

Kneese, Allen V., and Charles Schultz. *Pollution, Prices, and Public Policy.* Washington, DC: The Brookings Institution, 1975.

Portney, Paul R. "EPA and the Evolution of Federal Regulation." In Paul R. Portney, ed., *Public Policies for Environmental Protection.* Washington, DC: Resources for the Future, 1990, pp. 7–25.

Spence, A. M., and M. L. Weitzman. "Regulatory Strategies for Pollution Control." In A. E. Friedlander, ed., *Approaches to Controlling Air Pollution*. Boston: MIT Press, 1979, pp. 199–219.

U.S. Environmental Protection Agency, Science Advisory Board. *Reducing Risk: Setting Priorities and Strategies for Environmental Protection*. Washington, DC, September 1990.

## Related Web Sites

U.S. EPA, Laws and Regulations, Access to
Environmental Regulations and Proposed Rules    **www.epa.gov/epahome/rules.html.**

U.S. EPA, Science Advisory Board
(as referenced in Application 4.3)    **www.epa.gov/science1/index.html**

# 5

# Economic Solutions to Environmental Problems: The Market Approach

Though the market fails to correct environmental problems on its own, the incentives that define the market process can be put to work by policy makers. Recommended for some time by economists, the **market approach** to environmental policy has begun to be adopted by governments as part of their overall response to the risks of pollution. Distinct from the more traditional use of command-and-control instruments, the market approach uses price or other economic variables to provide incentives for polluters to reduce harmful emissions.

Economists are strong proponents of the market approach because it can achieve a cost-effective solution to environmental problems. How? By designing policy initiatives that allow polluters to respond according to their own self-interest. Market instruments are aimed at bringing the external costs of environmental damage back into the decision making of firms and consumers. Taking its cue directly from market failure theory, the market approach attempts to restore economic incentives by assigning a value to environmental quality or, equivalently, by pricing pollution. Once done, firms and consumers adjust their optimizing behavior to the resulting change in market conditions.

Awareness of the gains associated with market-based instruments is growing in both the private and public sectors. Thus it is important to understand this alternative policy approach and its advantages over more traditional forms of regulation. To that end, this chapter examines the theory and the practical implications of control instruments based on market incentives. Economic modeling will be the primary tool of analysis, and the criteria of allocative efficiency and cost-effectiveness will serve as the means by which assessments are made.

To provide a framework for our investigation, we begin with a brief overview of the major categories of market-based instruments: pollution charges, subsidies, deposit/refund systems, and pollution permit trading systems. We then use these categories to structure the economic analysis. Taking each one in turn, we develop models of specific instruments, assess the results, and provide examples of how each is used in practice.

## A Descriptive Overview

**market approach**
Uses incentive-based instruments and market forces to motivate abatement.

What distinguishes the **market approach** from the command-and-control approach is the way in which environmental objectives are *implemented* as opposed to the level at which those objectives are set. From a practical perspective, standards-based objectives are set at a socially desirable rather than an efficient level. Where the market approach parts company with the command-and-control approach is in *how* it attempts to achieve those objectives, that is, in its design of policy instruments.

### Identifying Types of Market Instruments

Since there are many types of control instruments that use market incentives, it is helpful to classify these into major categories. As described in Table 5.1, these categories are: **pollution charges, subsidies, deposit/ refund systems,** and **pollution permit trading systems.** Nations all over the world have begun to use these market-based instruments to help control pollution. In fact, an international survey of 14 nations found that 11 market instruments on average were being used in each country as of 1987.[1] Every type of economic instrument was identified by the survey as part of national policy across all environmental media. Although the market approach continues to be a secondary form of control, its use in national policy prescriptions speaks to its importance as part of the full range of available solutions to environmental problems. A brief description of each of the major categories of market instruments follows.

**Pollution Charges.** **Pollution charges** are fees imposed on polluting sources that vary directly with the amount of contaminants released to the environment. These pricing instruments have broad applicability, since they can be implemented in a variety of ways. Among these are **effluent** or **emission fees** assessed directly on pollution releases, **product charges** levied on pollution-generating commodities, **user charges** imposed on

---

[1] Organisation for Economic Co-operation and Development (OECD) (1989a).

| TABLE 5.1 | A TAXONOMY OF MARKET-BASED INSTRUMENTS |
|---|---|

| Market Instrument | Description |
|---|---|
| Pollution charge | A fee charged to the polluter that varies with the quantity of pollutants released. It can be implemented through any one of the following: |
| | **Effluent or emission charge**<br>A fee based on the actual discharge of pollution. |
| | **Product charge**<br>An upward adjustment to the price of a pollution-generating product based on its quantity or some characteristic responsible for the pollution. Product charges may be implemented through *tax differentiation*, that is, levying different taxes on goods based on their potential effect on the environment. |
| | **User charge**<br>A fee levied on the user of an environmental resource based on the costs for treatment of emissions or effluents that adversely affect that resource. |
| | **Administrative charge**<br>A service fee for implementing or monitoring a regulation or for registering a pollutant with an authority. |
| Subsidy | A payment or tax concession that provides financial assistance for pollution reductions or plans to abate in the future. |
| Deposit/refund | A system that imposes an up-front charge to pay for potential pollution damages that is returned for positive action, such as returning a product for proper disposal or recycling. |
| Pollution permit trading system | The establishment of a market for "rights to pollute," using either credits or allowances. |
| | **Credits**<br>With a **credit system,** polluters earn marketable credits for emitting below an established standard. |
| | **Allowances**<br>Under an **allowance system,** permits give polluters the right to release some amount of pollution, which can be increased or decreased through trading. |

SOURCES: U.S. EPA, Office of Policy, Planning, and Evaluation. *The United States Experience with Economic Incentives to Control Pollution*, Washington, DC, July 1992; Organisation for Economic Cooperation and Development. *Economic Instruments for Environmental Protection*. Paris: OECD, 1989a.

users of natural resources, and **administrative charges** for environmental services such as the registration of hazardous chemicals. The type of pollution charge employed in practice depends on the environmental medium affected and the nature of the problem. For example, effluent charges are often used to control noise and water pollution, whereas user charges are commonly employed for wastewater treatment and solid waste disposal.

**Subsidies.** **Subsidies** are payments made for reducing pollution levels or for developing plans to do so in the future. Sometimes referred to as the "carrot" versus the "stick" approach, subsidies give polluting sources an incentive to increase abatement activity—just the opposite of taxes, which penalize polluting activities. They might be effected through direct payments, grant programs, loans at below-market interest rates, or tax concessions.[2]

**Deposit/Refund Systems.** As its name suggests, the **deposit/refund system** has two components. It imposes an up-front charge, the **deposit**, to pay for *potential* environmental damage. This fee is later returned as a **refund** for some positive action like returning a product for proper disposal or recycling.

**Pollution Permit Trading Systems.** A fairly recent addition to the market approach is the **pollution permit trading system.** Under such a system, the government issues a fixed number of permits or "rights to pollute" and then allows a market to develop by letting polluters trade these rights among themselves. In practice, pollution permits are defined either as **credits** or **allowances.** Credit-based systems, the most common of the two, allocate permits to polluting sources based on their *current* emission levels relative to the allowable limit. For every unit of pollution emitted below the standard, the polluter receives a credit. Allowance-based systems, which are starting to gain acceptance, are based on *future* pollution levels. The number of allowances issued communicates the maximum emission level the polluter must achieve to meet an environmental objective. If the polluter emits less than what is mandated, it can either hold the unused allowances for future use or sell them to another polluter. If it cannot achieve the limit, it must buy allowances from another polluting source.

# Pollution Charges

**pollution charge**
A fee that varies
with the amount of
pollutants released.

The theoretical premise of a **pollution charge** is to internalize the cost of environmental damages by pricing the pollution-generating activity. The motivation follows what is known as the **"Polluter-Pays Principle (PPP)"**—a position rooted in the belief that the polluter should bear the costs of control measures to maintain an acceptable level of environmental quality.[3] We begin by modeling a **product charge** implemented as a tax—the classical solution to negative externalities.

---

[2] OECD (1989a), p. 15.
[3] OECD (1989a), p. 27.

| FIGURE 5.1 | THE IMPLEMENTATION OF A PIGOUVIAN TAX TO ACHIEVE EFFICIENCY |
|---|---|

The model illustrates the use of a Pigouvian tax to achieve efficiency in the market for some pollution-generating product, $Q$. By setting the per unit tax exactly equal to the $MEC$ at $Q_e$, shown as distance $ab$, the $MPC$ shifts up to $MPC_t$. Equilibrium output is then determined by the intersection of $MPC_t$ and $MSB$, which establishes an allocatively efficient production level at $Q_e$.

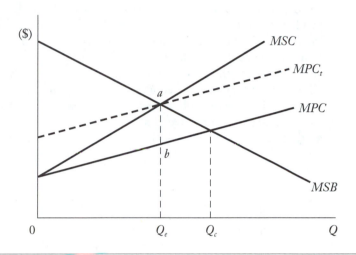

### Modeling a Product Charge as a Per Unit Tax

Consider a good in a competitive market whose production generates a negative environmental externality. Because producers base their decisions solely on the marginal private cost ($MPC$) of production, ignoring the marginal external cost ($MEC$) of the environmental damage, too many resources are allocated to production. As shown in Figure 5.1, firms produce at output level $Q_c$, where the marginal social benefit ($MSB$) of consuming the good is equal to the marginal private cost ($MPC$) of producing it.[4] Notice that the equilibrium output, $Q_c$ is higher than the efficient level, $Q_e$, which corresponds to the point where the $MSB$ equals the marginal social cost ($MSC$).

**product charge**
A fee added to the price of a pollution-generating product.

The policy motivation of a **product charge** is to induce firms to internalize the externality by taking account of the $MEC$ in their production

[4]As we have done in previous discussions, we are implicitly assuming there is no marginal external benefit (MEB) in the market for this good, so that MPB = MSB.

**Pigouvian tax** A unit charge on a good whose production generates a negative externality, such that the charge equals the *MEC* at $Q_e$.

decisions. One way this can be done is by imposing a unit tax on the pollution-generating product exactly equal to the *MEC* at the efficient output level, $Q_e$. This type of tax is called a **Pigouvian tax,** named after the English economist A. C. Pigou, who initially formulated the theory. As illustrated in Figure 5.1, this policy instrument effectively shifts the *MPC* curve up by distance *ab* to $MPC_t$, which generates an equilibrium at the efficient output level.

**Assessing the Model.** In theory, the Pigouvian tax forces firms to lower production to the efficient output level. While theoretically pleasing, this instrument is difficult to impose in practice and is not commonly used. Why? One problem is the difficulty of identifying the dollar value of *MEC* at $Q_e$ and hence the level of the tax. A second is that the model implicitly allows only for an output reduction to abate pollution—an unrealistic restriction. To address both of these reservations in this context, we consider a more practical alternative. The pollution charge can be implemented as an **emission charge,** a tax levied on the pollution, instead of as a product charge. By moving out of the product market, the model does not restrict the polluter's response to an output reduction.

### Modeling an Emission Charge: The Single Polluter Case

**emission or effluent charge** A fee imposed directly on the actual discharge of pollution.

An **emission or effluent charge** assigns a price to pollution, typically through a tax. Once this price mechanism is in place, the polluter can no longer ignore the effect of its environmental damages on society. The pollution charge forces it to confront those damages, pay for them, and in so doing, consider the damages as a part of its production costs. Faced with this added cost, the polluting firm can either continue polluting at the same level and pay the charge, or it can invest in abatement technology to reduce its pollutant releases and lower its tax burden. Based on normal market incentives, it will choose whichever action minimizes its costs.

It is fairly simple to model an emission charge that allows polluters to make cost-minimizing decisions. To begin, we assume that the government sets an abatement standard at some "acceptable level," $A_s$. Now we consider a policy that presents the polluter with the following options to be undertaken singularly or in combination:

- The polluter must pay a constant per unit tax, $t$, on the difference between its existing abatement level, $A_i$, and the standard, $A_s$, such that Total Tax $= t(A_s - A_i)$; and/or

- The polluter incurs the cost of abating.

In Figure 5.2, we graph these options from a single firm's perspective using marginal curves. Since the per unit tax is constant at $t$, the marginal tax (*MT*) curve is a horizontal line at that tax level. The cost of abating at the

## MODELING AN EMISSION CHARGE
## FOR THE SINGLE FIRM

The model illustrates the decisions of a single polluter, faced with the options of either paying a tax $= t(A_s - A_i)$ and/or incurring the cost of abating. The tax burden is represented by the marginal tax ($MT$) curve, and the firm's marginal cost of abating is shown as the $MAC$ curve. In this case, the cost-minimizing firm will abate up to level $A_o$, since up to that point $MAC < MT$. Its total abatement costs ($TAC$) are represented by area $0aA_o$. Beyond $A_o$ and up to the standard, $A_s$, the firm will opt to pay the taxes, since $MT < MAC$ in that range. Its tax burden is represented by area $A_oabA_s$. Hence the total costs to the polluter of complying with this policy are shown as area $0abA_s$.

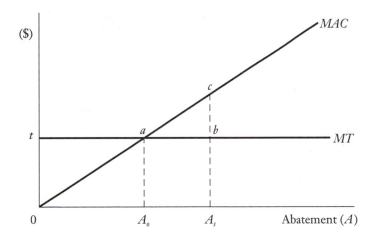

margin is shown as the marginal abatement cost ($MAC$) curve. At each unit of $A$, the cost-minimizing firm will compare $MAC$ to $MT$ and choose the lower of the two. In our model, the firm will abate up to $A_o$, since up to that point $MAC$ is below $MT$. Assuming no fixed costs, total abatement costs ($TAC$) are represented by the area under $MAC$ up to $A_o$, or area $0aA_o$. Notice that these costs are lower than what the taxes would be up to $A_o$, shown as area $0taA_o$. Beyond $A_o$ and up to $A_s$, the firm will opt to pay the tax, since $MT$ is lower than $MAC$ in that range. The firm's total tax payment for not abating between $A_o$ and $A_s$ is represented by area $A_oabA_s$, which is smaller than the cost of abating that amount, which is area $A_oacA_s$. In sum, the total costs to the polluter of complying with this policy are area $0abA_s$, which comprises the following two elements:

1. Area $0aA_o$, the total cost of abating $A_o$ units of pollution; and

2. Area $A_oabA_s$, the tax on pollution not abated up to $A_s$.

FIGURE 5.3

## THE EFFECT OF TECHNOLOGY IMPROVEMENT ON THE FIRM'S LEAST-COST DECISION MAKING

A technological advance causes the *MAC* to pivot downward to *MAC'*. As a result, if the firm is faced with the option of abating or paying the unit tax at each abatement level up to $A_s$, it would be better off abating all the way up to $A_s$. Hence, the technological change helped the firm avoid paying any emission charges.

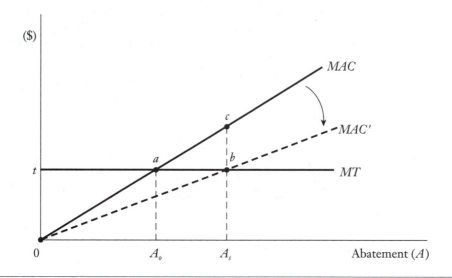

**Assessing the Model.**   Be sure to recognize that the emission charge stimulates the natural incentives of the polluter. At any point in time, there are *static* incentives that motivate the firm to choose among the available options given its existing technology. Seeking to satisfy its own self-interest to maximize profit, the polluter makes a least-cost decision between paying the tax or abating. The result is that the externality is internalized, using the least amount of resources.

There are also *dynamic* incentives that encourage the firm to advance its abatement technology. More efficient abatement techniques would allow the firm to reduce pollution more cheaply and enjoy the associated cost savings. Furthermore, the lower abatement costs might even allow the firm to avoid paying any emission charges. Consider the effect of a hypothetical technological advance, shown in Figure 5.3 as a downward pivot in the *MAC* to *MAC'*. In this case, if the firm were faced with the same set of policy options based on $A_s$, it would be better off abating all the way up to that standard.

*Modeling an Emission Charge: The Multiple Polluter Case*

To evaluate the cost-effectiveness of an emission charge across multiple polluters, we return to the two-polluter model used in the last chapter. As before, we assume that the government imposes a 10-unit abatement standard for the region. The cost functions are repeated below to facilitate discussion:

Polluter 1's Marginal Abatement Cost ($MAC_1$):  $MAC_1 = 2.5(A_1)$

Polluter 1's Total Abatement Costs ($TAC_1$):      $TAC_1 = 1.25(A_1)^2$,

where $A_1$ is the amount of pollution abated by Polluter 1.

Polluter 2's Marginal Abatement Cost ($MAC_2$): $MAC_2 = 0.625(A_2)$

Polluter 2's Total Abatement Costs ($TAC_2$):      $TAC_2 = 0.3125(A_2)^2$,

where $A_2$ is the amount of pollution abated by Polluter 2.

Let's assume that the government imposes the same emission charge as in the single firm case above; that is, Total Tax $= t(A_s - A_i)$. In this case, since $A_s = 10$, the emission charge becomes $t(10 - A_i)$. We also assume that the tax rate, $t$, is set at \$5, so Total Tax $= \$5(10 - A_i)$ for each polluter.

Now consider each firm's response to the tax. As we proceed, refer to Figure 5.4, which reproduces the model used in Chapter 4, adding a horizontal line ($MT$) at \$5 to represent the emission charge. When faced with the \$5–per unit charge, Polluter 1 would compare the relative cost of $MT$ and $MAC_1$ for each incremental unit of abatement, just as in the single-firm case. It would abate as long as $MAC_1 < MT$, and pay the tax when the opposite is true. Thus, Polluter 1 would abate up to the point where $MAC_1 = MT$, which occurs at $A_1 = 2$, and pay the tax on the remaining 8 units. Polluter 2 would proceed in the same way, abating to the point where $MAC_2 = MT$ at $A_2 = 8$ and paying the tax on the remaining 2 units. The corresponding calculations are:

**Polluter 1:**
Abates up to the point where $MAC_1 = MT$:   $2.5(A_1) = \$5$, or $A_1 = 2$
Incurs Total Abatement Costs of:                  $TAC_1 = 1.25(2)^2 = \$5$.
Incurs Total Tax payment of:                       Total Tax $= 5(10 - 2)$
                                                                  $= \$40$.

**Polluter 2:**
Abates up to the point where $MAC_2 = MT$:   $0.625(A_2) = \$5$,
                                                                  or $A_2 = 8$
Incurs Total Abatement Costs of:                  $TAC_2 = 0.3125(8)^2$
                                                                  $= \$20$.
Incurs Total Tax payment of:                       Total Tax $= 5(10 - 8)$
                                                                  $= \$10$.

| FIGURE 5.4 | EFFECT OF AN EMISSION CHARGE IN A TWO-POLLUTER MODEL |
|---|---|

The model shows the *MAC*s for Polluter 1 and Polluter 2 and the emission charge imposed as a unit tax of $5 represented by the *MT* curve. The horizontal axis measures the 10-unit abatement standard imposed by government. Each firm abates as long as its $MAC < MT$, and pays the emission charge on all units of pollution not abated. In this case, Polluter 1, the high-cost abater, abates 2 units and pays $40 in taxes on the remaining 8. Polluter 2, the low-cost abater, abates 8 units and pays taxes of $10 on the remaining 2. At this point, $MAC_1 = MAC_2 = \$5$, which indicates the least-cost allocation of abatement responsibilities across the two firms.

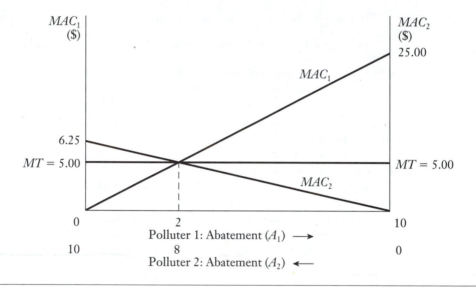

**Combined Values for the Region:**
Total level of abatement $= 10 = A_s$
Total Abatement Costs $= \$25$
Total Tax Payments $= \$50$

There are two important observations to make about these results. First, the $5 unit tax achieves the 10-unit abatement level. Second, this objective has been achieved using the cost-effective allocation of abatement resources across polluters.[5] Since each polluter abates to the point where its *MAC*

---

[5] Recall from the previous chapter that using a uniform standard under a command-and-control approach generates total abatement costs of $39.06.

equals *MT*, all *MAC*s are equal—precisely in accordance with the cost-effective abatement criterion. Notice that most of the abating is done by the low-cost abater, Polluter 2. The high-cost polluter, Polluter 1, abates less but pays much higher emission charges in the form of taxes.

**Assessing the Model.**    The emission charge exploits each polluter's natural incentive to pursue a least-cost strategy. As a result, the low-cost abaters do most of the cleaning up, and the high-cost abaters pay more in taxes to cover the greater damages they cause. The benefits to society are not affected by *who* does the abating, but the costs are. In this case, costs are minimized because Polluter 2 does most of the abating. It does so, not because it is motivated by society's objectives, but because it is in its own best interest to do so. An added advantage of this approach is that the tax generates revenues to the government, which could be used to help finance the costs of enforcement and monitoring.

Having underscored the advantages of the emission charge, there are nonetheless several caveats that deserve mention. The first concerns the setting of the emission charge itself. Realistically, the government will not know the tax rate at which polluters' abatement levels collectively meet the standard and therefore will have to adjust the tax until the environmental objective is achieved.[6] Such an adjustment process can be time-intensive. Another consideration is the potential increase in monitoring costs. Monitoring is likely to be more complex when each polluting source responds to a policy based on its own internal operations. There are also distributional implications to be considered. As polluting firms pay higher taxes, part of the tax burden is shared with consumers in the form of higher prices. There may also be job losses linked to polluters' adjusting to the tax burden or changing their technologies to increase abatement. Finally, firms may try to evade a tax by disposing of pollutants illegally. To minimize the potential of such activity, government may have to strengthen its monitoring program, which adds to administrative costs.

### Pollution Charges in Practice

Internationally, the pollution charge is the most commonly used market-based instrument. OECD's survey of 14 nations found that 81 pollution charges were in use during 1987 out of a total of 153 identified market instruments. Several countries, including Japan and Switzerland, use **effluent charges** to control the noise pollution generated by aircraft. Germany and

---

[6]For example, if the government had set the tax at too low a level, say \$4, each polluter would have abated to the point where its *MAC* equals \$4. The result would have been $A_1 = 1.6$ and $A_2 = 6.4$ for a combined abatement level of 8 units—too low to satisfy the objective. So, the government would have had to raise the tax until the combined total reached the 10-unit abatement standard.

## Taxing Gasoline Consumption: An International Comparison

According to Kazuo Aichi, former chief of Japan's environmental agency, "Gasoline is too cheap in the United States and should be taxed more to cut energy use." Aichi's argument is motivated in part by ongoing disagreements between the United States and some of its industrialized counterparts about the appropriate response to problems like resource depletion and global air pollution. Fueled by the alleged lack of U.S. cooperation at the 1992 Rio Earth Summit, Aichi's criticism of U.S. policy on fuel taxes underscores the importance of the price mechanism in encouraging conservation.

To better understand the objection to American policy, consider how the U.S. tax on gasoline compares to what is imposed by other industrialized countries.

**Gasoline Prices and Taxes by Country (February 1998)**

| Country | Total Gasoline Price per Gallon (in U.S. dollars) | Tax Rate % of Price |
|---|---|---|
| United States | 1.13 | 34 |
| United Kingdom | 4.26 | 81 |
| France | 4.00 | 82 |
| Germany | 3.19 | 77 |
| Italy | 4.00 | 76 |
| Japan | 3.02 | 59 |
| Spain | 2.95 | 69 |
| Canada | 1.38 | 55 |

SOURCE: International Energy Agency, Paris, France, **www.iea.org/stat.htm**.

These data validate Aichi's claim that the price of gasoline in the United States *is* cheap in a relative sense, and much of the difference is due to a lower tax rate. Notice that the gasoline tax is between 69 and 82 percent of the unit price in European nations, 55 percent in Canada, and 59 percent in Japan. The comparatively low tax rate of 34 percent in the United States reflects its fuel tax policy.

Beyond this cursory assessment of Aichi's commentary, there is the more important issue of the economic intent of a gasoline tax. In addition to boosting government revenues, taxing a commodity like gasoline is designed to internalize the negative externalities of consumption. External to the market for gasoline are air pollution problems caused by operating gasoline-powered motor vehicles. Other negative externalities are highway congestion and the increased risk of traffic accidents. These adverse effects have one thing in common—they extend to parties beyond those engaged in the market transaction. Consequently, the costs of these damages are not reflected in the price, and too much gasoline is brought to market. As other nations have apparently learned, raising the tax on gasoline can reduce consumption and bring the associated social costs and benefits closer together.

SOURCES: Associated Press. "Japanese Environmentalist Says Gas Too Cheap in U.S." *Brockton Enterprise*, February 2, 1992; Anne Reifenberg and Allanna Sullivan. "Rising Gasoline Prices: Everyone Else's Fault." *The Wall Street Journal*, May 1, 1996, pp. B1, B8; James Tanner. "Carbon Tax to Limit Use of Fossil Fuels Becomes Embroiled in Global Politics." *The Wall Street Journal*, June 9, 1992, p. A2.

Italy are among the nations employing effluent charges to protect water resources.[7]

A common use of a **product charge** is as a tax on lubricant oils, such as that employed in Finland, France, Germany, Italy, and the Netherlands. Finland also uses a product charge to support its deposit/refund system by heavily taxing beverage containers that are *not* returnable. Other targeted products include pesticides, fertilizers, mercury- and cadmium-containing batteries, and fuels.[8] Application 5.1 on page 134 gives an overview of the international experience with gasoline taxes aimed at internalizing the external costs of consumption.

# Environmental Subsidies

An alternative market approach to reducing environmental damage is to pay polluters *not* to pollute through an **environmental subsidy.** There are two major types of subsidies—**abatement equipment subsidies** and **pollution reduction subsidies.** We discuss each of these in turn.

*Modeling an Abatement Equipment Subsidy*

**abatement equipment subsidy** A payment aimed at lowering the cost of abatement technology.

**Abatement equipment subsidies** are aimed at reducing the costs of abatement technology. Since subsidies are "negative taxes," they have a similar incentive mechanism to pollution charges except that they reward for *not* polluting as opposed to penalizing for engaging in polluting activities. In practice, abatement equipment subsidies are implemented through grants, low-interest loans, or investment tax credits, all of which give polluters an incentive to invest in abatement technology.

From a theoretical perspective, we argue that these subsidies attempt to internalize the *positive* externality associated with the consumption of abatement activities. If a subsidy were offered for the installation of specific abatement equipment, such as scrubbers, the effect would be to encourage a higher quantity demanded of this equipment by lowering the effective price. To achieve an efficient equilibrium, the subsidy would have to equal the marginal external benefit (*MEB*) of scrubber consumption measured at the efficient output level. Notice that this is analogous to a Pigouvian tax, and in fact, this type of subsidy is known as a **Pigouvian subsidy.**

**Pigouvian subsidy** A per unit payment on a good the consumption of which generates a positive externality such that the payment equals the *MEB* at $Q_e$.

A model of a hypothetical competitive market for scrubbers would be:

$$MSC = 70.0 + 0.5Q, \qquad MPB = 350.0 - 0.9Q$$
$$+ \, MEB = \phantom{0}56.0 - 0.2Q$$
$$MSB = 406.0 - 1.1Q,$$

---

[7] OECD (1989a), pp. 31–50.
[8] OECD (1989a), pp. 55–60.

| FIGURE 5.5 | A PIGOUVIAN SUBSIDY IN THE MARKET FOR SCRUBBERS |
|---|---|

In the market for scrubbers, there is a positive externality associated with their consumption. Hence, the true measure of benefits to society is given by the *MSB*, which is the vertical sum of the *MPB* and the *MEB*. If a Pigouvian subsidy were provided to purchasers of scrubber systems equal to the *MEB* at the efficient output level, 210 scrubbers would be traded in the market instead of the competitive output level of 200. In this case, the Pigouvian subsidy is $14 million labeled as distance *KL*. Notice that the effective price to polluters would be the efficient market price *less* the amount of the subsidy paid by the government, which in this case is ($175 − $14) or $161 million.

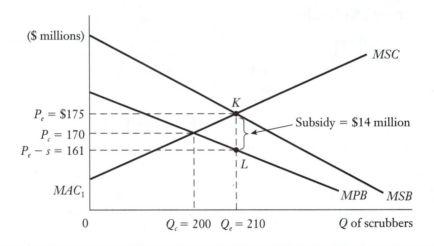

where $Q$ is the number of scrubber systems produced in a year and *MSC*, *MPB*, and *MEB* are denominated in millions of dollars.[9] The corresponding graph is given in Figure 5.5. The competitive equilibrium is found where $MPB = MSC$, or at $Q_c = 200$ and $P_c = $170$ million. However, the efficient equilibrium occurs where $MSB = MSC$, or at $Q_e = 210$, and $P_e = $175$ million. In an unregulated competitive market, too few scrubbers are exchanged at too low a price because the external benefits of a cleaner environment are not recognized by the market participants. If a subsidy ($s$) were provided to demanders (i.e., polluters), equal to the *MEB* at the efficient output level, more scrubbers would be traded. In this case, the Pigouvian subsidy would equal $MEB = 56.0 − 0.2(210) = $14$ million, shown as distance *KL* in Figure 5.5. The effective price to polluters would

---

[9] For simplicity, we assume there are no marginal external costs (*MEC*), so that $MPC = MSC$.

be the efficient market price *less* the subsidy, or $(P_e - s)$, which in this case is ($175 − $14) or $161 million.

**Assessing the Model.**   Just as in the case of a Pigouvian tax, one problem with implementing a Pigouvian subsidy is measuring the *MEB*. Monetizing the marginal external benefits of such intangibles as better health and more stable ecosystems is difficult at best. Hence it is not likely that a subsidy of abatement equipment will achieve allocative efficiency. However, its associated effect of encouraging greater consumption because of an effectively lower price should still occur.

Even setting aside the difficulty in achieving an efficient outcome, equipment subsidies may have other drawbacks. One commonly cited criticism is that this type of control instrument biases polluters' decisions about how best to abate. Subsidies affect relative prices, making other alternatives less attractive to polluters from a financial perspective. However, some of these abatement alternatives might be more effective in reducing pollution. For the same reason, innovation of a potentially superior abatement system could be discouraged as long as the government is subsidizing existing equipment. Finally, subsidies must be financed through taxes or government borrowing. Thus, they effectively redistribute income from society to polluters, an outcome some view as unacceptable despite the associated gains of a cleaner environment.

## Modeling a Per Unit Subsidy on Pollution Reduction

**per unit subsidy on pollution reduction**
A payment for every unit of pollution removed below some predetermined level.

An alternative type of subsidy is one based on emission or effluent reductions, called a **per unit subsidy on pollution reduction.** In this case, the government agrees to pay the polluter a subsidy ($s$) for every unit of pollution removed below some predetermined level, $Z_o$. This is modeled as:

$$\text{Per unit subsidy} = s(Z_o - Z_i),$$

where $Z_i$ is the actual level of pollution. Suppose, for example, the standard $Z_o$ is set at 200 tons of emissions per month, and the subsidy ($s$) is set at $100 per month. Then, if a polluter reduces its emissions to 180 tons per month, it would receive a subsidy of $100(200 − 180), or $2,000.

**Assessing the Model.**   On the plus side, a per unit pollution reduction subsidy *might* be less disruptive than an equipment subsidy, since it is established independent of the abatement method used and thus avoids any technological bias. On the other hand, these subsidies can have the perverse effect of elevating pollution levels in the aggregate. How does such a paradox arise? Because a per unit subsidy effectively lowers a polluter's unit

# State Subsidies for Recycling Programs

Some state governments have implemented subsidies as a way to encourage recycling. Many subsidies are imposed as one-time tax incentives. Among the more common subsidy instruments are investment tax credits for recycling facilities and sales tax exemptions on the purchase of recycling equipment. The premise for these applications is that once the incentives establish the infrastructure to support recycling, the activity should become self-directed.

The listing below itemizes some of the approaches being used by state governments throughout the United States. For more information, visit the website of the Environmental Industry Associations at **www.envasns.org**.

| State | Description of the Tax Incentive |
| --- | --- |
| California | Tax credits for the cost of equipment used to manufacture recycled products. Development bonds for manufacturing products with recycled materials. |
| Colorado | Income tax credits for investment in plastics recycling technology. |
| Florida | Sales tax exemptions on recycling machinery purchased after July 1, 1988. Tax incentives to encourage affordable transport of recycled materials from collection centers to processing sites. |
| Illinois | Sales tax exemptions for recycling equipment. |
| Indiana | Property tax exemptions for buildings, equipment, and land used in recycling wastes into new products. |
| Iowa | Sales tax exemptions. |
| Kentucky | Property tax exemptions to recycling industries. |
| Maine | Tax credits to businesses of 30 percent of the cost of recycling equipment. Subsidies to municipalities for transport costs of scrap metal. |
| Maryland | Income tax deduction of 100 percent of expenses for furnace conversion to burn used oil and for the purchase and installation of equipment for recycling used Freon. |
| New Jersey | Fifty percent investment tax credit to businesses for recycling vehicles and equipment. Six percent sales tax exemption on recycling equipment purchases. |
| N. Carolina | Corporate income tax credits and exemptions for recycling equipment and facilities. |
| Oregon | Income tax credits for recycling equipment and facilities. Special tax credits for property or machinery used to collect, transport, or process reclaimed plastics. |
| Texas | Franchise tax exemptions for sludge recycling corporations. |
| Utah | Payment of $21 per ton to tire recyclers for tires recycled or incinerated for energy recovery. |
| Virginia | Tax credit of 10 percent of the cost of machinery or equipment used for processing recyclable materials. |
| Washington | Exemption from motor vehicle rate regulation for vehicles used to transport recovered materials. |
| Wisconsin | Sales tax exemptions for waste reduction and recycling equipment and facilities. Property tax exemptions for certain equipment. |

SOURCES: Drawn from National Solid Waste Management Association (NSWMA). *Recycling in the States: Mid-Year Update 1990.* Washington, DC: NSWMA, October 1990, with permission of National Solid Waste Management Association.

costs, which in turn raises its profits. If the industry has limited entry bar-riers, these profits would signal entrepreneurs to enter the industry. In the long run, although each *individual* polluter reduces its emissions, the sub-sidy may cause the market to expand such that *aggregate* emissions end up higher than they were originally.[10] The dilemma could be solved if entry were prohibited, or at least limited in some way. Whether or not this is fea-sible, or even desirable depends on the industry structure, the extent of en-vironmental damage, and the associated costs.

### Environmental Subsidies in Practice

There are many instances where environmental subsidies are used in prac-tice. Italy's *Decree of August 31, 1987*, for example, allows for direct subsi-dies to industries that change manufacturing technologies to reduce waste disposal.[11] In the United States, the most common use of subsidies is fed-eral funding for projects like publicly owned wastewater treatment works (POTWs).[12] Subsidies also are employed to encourage the use of energy-saving products, such as energy-efficient lighting. Many state governments use subsidies in the form of tax incentives to encourage recycling activi-ties. An overview of some of these programs is given in Application 5.2 on page 138.

# Deposit/Refund Systems

**deposit/refund system** Imposes an up-front charge to pay for potential damages and returns it for returning a product for proper disposal or recycling.

The potentially perverse consequences of abatement subsidies suggest that pollution charges might be a better alternative. In some contexts, however, pollution charges can be costly to administer because of the associated ex-pense of monitoring and enforcement. Recall that one of the drawbacks of pollution charges is that they may encourage illegal disposal of con-taminants. This potential problem is an important motivation for using a **deposit/refund system.** Operationally, deposit/refund systems attach a front-end charge—the deposit—for the *potential* occurrence of a damag-ing activity, and guarantee a return of that charge—the refund—upon as-surance that the activity has not been undertaken. This market instrument combines the incentive characteristic of a pollution charge with a built-in mechanism for controlling monitoring costs. It is used mainly to capture the difference between the private and social costs of improper waste dis-posal, with its most common targets being beverage containers and lead-acid batteries.

---

[10] For further detail, see Baumol and Oates (1975), Chapter 12.

[11] OECD (1989a), pp. 79–80.

[12] U.S. EPA, Office of Policy, Planning, and Evaluation (July 1992), p. 6-1.

## The Economics of Deposit/Refund Systems

Improper or illegal waste disposal gives rise to a negative externality. The external costs include health damages, such as lead contamination from discarded lead-acid batteries, and aesthetic impairment from litter and trash accumulation. Deposit/refund systems are intended to force the potential polluter to account for both the marginal private cost ($MPC$) and the marginal external cost ($MEC$) of improper waste disposal, should that activity be undertaken.

Like the pollution charge, the deposit component of the system is intended to capture the $MEC$ of improper waste disposal. It forces the polluter to internalize the cost of any damage it may cause by making it absorb this cost *in advance*. Unique to the deposit/refund system is the refund component, which introduces an incentive to dispose of wastes properly and prevent environmental damage from taking place at all. Taken together, the deposit/refund system targets the *potential* polluter instead of penalizing the *actual* polluter, using the refund to reward appropriate behavior.

## Modeling a Deposit/Refund System

A model of a deposit/refund system is shown in Figure 5.6. From left to right, the horizontal axis measures *improper* waste disposal ($IW$) as a percentage of all waste disposal activity. Implicitly then, the percentage of *proper* waste disposal ($PW$) is measured right to left. Thus, if 25 percent of all wastes are improperly disposed of, by default 75 percent are disposed of appropriately and safely.

The $MPC_{IW}$ includes expenses for collecting and illegally dumping wastes plus the costs of improperly disposing recyclable wastes, such as the expense of trash receptacles, collection fees paid to a refuse company, and the opportunity costs of forgone revenue associated with recycling. The $MSC_{IW}$ includes the $MPC_{IW}$ plus the $MEC_{IW}$, represented implicitly as the vertical distance between $MSC_{IW}$ and $MPC_{IW}$. The $MPB_{IW}$ is the demand for improper waste disposal. It is motivated by the avoidance of time and resources to collect wastes, bring nonrecyclables to a landfill, and haul recyclables to a collection center.[13] Since we assume no external benefits in this case, $MPB_{IW} = MSB_{IW}$. In the absence of environmental controls, equilibrium is determined by the intersection of $MSB_{IW}$ and $MPC_{IW}$, or $Q_{IW}$. The efficient equilibrium occurs where $MSC_{IW}$ equals $MSB_{IW}$, or at $Q_e$, which is smaller than $Q_{IW}$. Once again, we observe that in the presence of a negative externality, too much improper waste disposal is produced because market participants do not consider the full impact of their actions.[14]

---

[13] The $MPB_{IW}$ measured left to right is equivalent to the $MPC_{PW}$ measured right to left.

[14] This analysis could equivalently be modeled by specifying the market as "proper waste disposal." In such a specification, there would be a *positive* external benefit from *proper* disposal of wastes, which would be equivalent to the reduction in external costs from reducing *improper* waste disposal.

---

FIGURE 5.6

## MODELING A DEPOSIT/REFUND SYSTEM
## IN THE MARKET FOR WASTE DISPOSAL

Improper waste disposal $(IW)$ is measured left to right on the horizontal axis as a proportion of all waste disposal activity. Hence the percentage of proper waste disposal $(PW)$ is measured right to left. To correct the negative externality associated with improper waste disposal, a deposit/refund system is instituted with the deposit set equal to the $MEC_{IW}$ measured at $Q_e$. The deposit, labeled as distance $ab$, elevates the $MPC_{IW}$ up to $MSC_{IW}$, forcing the market participants to establish a new equilibrium at the socially optimal level. The result is an increase in the proportion of wastes properly disposed of from $Q_{IW}$ to $Q_e$.

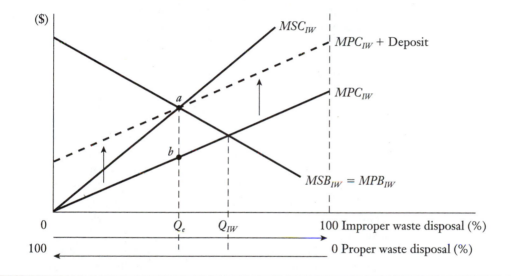

To correct the negative externality, assume that a deposit/refund system is instituted whereby the deposit equals the $MEC_{IW}$ at $Q_e$. This is labeled as distance $ab$ in Figure 5.6. Once imposed, the deposit effectively elevates $MPC_{IW}$ up by distance $ab$, forcing the market participants to a new equilibrium at $Q_e$. In so doing, a percentage of waste disposal is converted from improper methods to appropriate ones measured by the distance $(Q_{IW} - Q_e)$. Notice that the deposit serves the same function as a pollution charge. The critical difference is that the refund helps to deter improper waste disposal. The potential polluter has an explicit incentive to dispose of wastes properly, since doing so allows it to reclaim the deposit. Should disposers choose instead to discard their wastes illegally, at least they will have paid for the external costs in advance. Authorities also have the flexibility to adjust the deposit or refund amounts to enhance the built-in incentives.

**Assessing the Model.** The value added of the deposit/refund system is that the refund encourages environmentally responsible behavior without adding significantly to government's monitoring and compliance costs. What makes this instrument unique is that once established, the incentives operate with limited supervision.

Another advantage of the deposit/refund instrument is that it can be used to encourage more efficient use of raw materials. An inordinate amount of used products and materials ends up in landfills or burned in incinerators, when they could be recycled. The availability of recycled products and wastes can help slow the depletion of such virgin raw materials as aluminum and timber and may result in associated price declines as well.[15] Charging firms a deposit on raw materials acts as a tax, encouraging more efficient use of resources *during* the production process. The refund encourages proper disposal or recycling of raw material waste at the *end* of the production phase. Firms that elect to ignore this incentive face not only conventional disposal costs but also the opportunity cost of the forgone refund.

### Deposit/Refund Systems in Practice

Perhaps the best-known applications of deposit/refund systems are those used to encourage proper disposal of beverage containers. In the United States, such programs typically are initiated through state "bottle bills." As of 1997, 10 states had passed legislation requiring deposits on beer and soft drink containers. Application 5.3 discusses the mechanics of these state-level initiatives. Oregon, the first state to enact a "bottle bill," reports that roadside litter was reduced by 75 to 85 percent just two years after its bill became law.[16] The state of Michigan reported a 95 percent return rate in the first year after it instituted its program.[17] Similar results have been observed in other countries as well. Finland, Norway, the Netherlands, and Sweden report return rates on beverage containers ranging from 70 to 90 percent after instituting a deposit/refund system.[18]

Other state initiatives are aimed at encouraging responsible disposal of used tires and lead-acid batteries. Proper discard of lead-acid batteries is of particular concern due to the health risks of lead exposure. According to the EPA, lead-acid batteries represent approximately 65 percent of the lead found in municipal solid wastes.[19] Sweden and Norway have had some

---

[15] As an exercise, model the demand and supply of aluminum. Now assume that a deposit/refund system has been imposed on aluminum containers. Show how an increase in recycled aluminum is expected to affect this market.

[16] U.S. EPA, Office of Policy, Planning, and Evaluation (July 1992), p. 4-1.

[17] Porter (1983), pp. 177–94.

[18] U.S. EPA, Office of Policy, Planning, and Evaluation (July 1992), pp. 9-4–9-5.

[19] U.S. EPA, Office of Policy, Planning, and Evaluation (March 1991), p. 2-18.

# The Mechanics of a Deposit/Refund System: "Bottle Bills"

Currently, 10 states have passed bottle bills—California, Connecticut, Delaware, Iowa, Maine, Massachusetts, Michigan, New York, Oregon, and Vermont. While each state's law is unique, there are similarities that characterize how a deposit/refund system is designed for beverage containers. The following is a brief description of the phases outlining the structure of such a system.

**Phase 1:** A deposit is paid by the retailer to the bottler or wholesaler for each beverage container received. If the product is a soft drink, retailers pay the deposit to the bottler; for beer, the retailer pays the wholesaler.

**Phase 2:** Consumers pay the same deposit to the retailer as part of the product's purchase price.

**Phase 3:** After the beverage is consumed, the consumer returns the used container to the retailer who refunds the consumer for the amount of the initial deposit.

**Phase 4:** Retailers reclaim the deposit from either the bottler or wholesaler when they return the empty container. In addition, bottlers and wholesalers typically pay a per unit handling fee to retailers to cover their costs to collect and return the containers.

Notice from this four-step process that bottle bills are self-implementing. Once the deposit system is in place, market forces take over. There is a natural incentive for consumers and retailers to return used containers so they can recover their deposits.

So why haven't more states passed bottle bills? Voter opposition to these bills exists for a variety of reasons. One is the perverse outcome caused by the availability of substitute containers not covered by a bottle bill. For example, if a bottle bill requires a deposit only on aluminum containers, some consumers may purchase the product in plastic just to avoid the deposit. Such a response occurred in New York, where consumption of soft drinks in plastic containers rose from 39 to 52 percent following the passage of the state's bottle bill. The response is problematic because plastic is not as recyclable as aluminum, and disposal of plastic containers adds more to the *volume* of the solid waste stream than other types of beverage containers.

Another reason for voter opposition is the opportunity cost of participating in a deposit/refund program—the value of time to collect, clean, store, and transport containers to retailers. Some consumers view these costs as outweighing the value of refunds. As cost-minimizers, these individuals would make the rational decision *not* to participate in a deposit/refund program. Finally, there is some controversy about what proportion of collected containers are recycled versus the proportion that ends up in landfills. Other skeptics believe that bottle bills have a relatively small effect on the size of the solid waste stream.

How valid are these concerns? To answer this, deposit/refund systems must be evaluated using benefit–cost analysis. The appraisal should make use of information from those states that *do* have bottle bills about the associated energy savings, reduction in littering, recovery rates, and changes in consumption patterns. As these data are examined, consumers and industry will be better able to make informed decisions about proposals in their own states and to tailor a deposit/refund system to better meet the needs of their regions.

SOURCES: U.S. Environmental Protection Agency, Office of Policy, Planning, and Evaluation. *Economic Incentives: Options for Environmental Protection.* Washington, DC, March 1991, Chapter 2; U.S. Environmental Protection Agency, Office of Policy, Planning, and Evaluation. *The United States Experience with Economic Incentives to Control Environmental Protection.* Washington, DC, July 1992, Chapter 4.

success using deposit/refunds to reduce the improper disposal of junk cars. Interestingly, both charge a deposit that is actually less than the refund, presumably to further enhance the incentive to return unwanted vehicles for proper disposal or recycling.[20]

# Pollution Permit Trading Systems

**pollution permit trading system** Establishes a market for "rights to pollute" by issuing tradeable pollution credits or allowances.

**pollution credits** Tradeable permits issued for emitting below an established standard.

**pollution allowances** Tradeable permits that indicate the maximum level of pollution that may be released.

Thus far, we have illustrated that market instruments can be used to set prices for polluting and abatement activities. It is also possible for government to use the price-quantity relationship in the opposite direction—by establishing the quantity of pollution or abatement to be achieved and letting the market determine the price. With perfect information, either approach is viable, and both will lead to the same outcome. However, pricing instruments can be problematic in that the government does not know in advance what price will achieve a quantity-based environmental objective. Consequently, it has to monitor the quantity response to some initially established price and continually make adjustments until the proper pollution level is achieved—essentially a "trial and error" process. It may be more efficient to use a policy instrument that operates from the *known* variable, that is, the socially desirable quantity of pollution or abatement, and let the market establish the price. Such is the underlying premise of a **pollution permit trading system,** which can be implemented through the use of credits or allowances. Under a **pollution credit** system, a polluter earns marketable credits only if it emits below an established standard. If instead the trading system uses **pollution allowances,** each permit gives the bearer the right to release some amount of pollution. These too are marketable, so that polluters can buy and sell allowances as needed based on their access to abatement technologies and their cost conditions.

## The Structure of a Pollution Permit Trading System

A system of marketable pollution permits has two components: (1) the issuance of some fixed number of permits in a region; and (2) a provision for trading these permits among polluting sources within that region. The total number of permits issued is bound by whatever level of pollution is mandated by law as "acceptable." For example, if the level were set at 200 units of emissions, a maximum of 200 one-unit permits could be issued. Any polluter releasing emissions not authorized by permits would be in violation of the law. Once the permits are distributed, polluters are allowed to trade them with one another. A bargaining process should develop, which gives

---

[20] U.S. EPA, Office of Policy, Planning, and Evaluation (July 1992), p. 9-5.

rise to a *market* for "pollution rights." Following their own self-interest, polluters either purchase these "rights to pollute" or abate—whichever is the cheaper alternative. High-cost abaters will have an incentive to bid for available permits, while low-cost abaters will have an incentive to abate and sell their permits on the open market. The result is a cost-effective allocation of abatement responsibilities.[21]

The tradeable permit system accommodates environmental objectives defined at an aggregate level. For example, in the United States, air pollution policies are designed to achieve national ambient air quality standards within well-defined regions. But within any region, some polluters might perform above the standard and others below it, which is acceptable as long as in the aggregate the region is in compliance. This is exactly how the permit system operates—controlling the total amount of emissions in a region, but not the releases for each source within that region.[22] The trading component of the permit system capitalizes on differences in polluters' abatement technologies and opportunities. Sources that can abate efficiently are given the incentive to do so because they can sell their unused permits to their less-efficient counterparts. As long as the environmental goal is achieved in the aggregate, the benefit to society is the same whether every firm does an equal amount of abating or if the task is undertaken by a select few. However, the costs will be markedly lower if abatement is done by more efficient polluters.

### Modeling a Pollution Permit System for Multiple Polluters

To illustrate the operation of a permit system, we return to our two-polluter model, where each firm faces distinct abatement costs:

Polluter 1:  $TAC_1 = 1.25(A_1)^2$
$MAC_1 = 2.5(A_1)$

Polluter 2:  $TAC_2 = 0.3125(A_2)^2$
$MAC_2 = .625(A_2)$

Prior to any government intervention, we assume that each firm releases 10 units of pollution for an aggregate amount of 20 units in their region. The government has determined that the "acceptable" level of pollution for this region is 10 units, and it decides to reach this objective by using a

---

[21] Trading is critical to the cost-effective outcome. For example, if the permits were allocated equally across all polluters and no trading were allowed, the result would be no different than a command-and-control system of uniform standards.

[22] Contrast this scenario with a command-and-control instrument that forces every polluting source to meet identical standards of emission or effluent levels. Such instruments equalize the *level of control* across polluters rather than equalizing the *marginal costs of control*.

tradeable permit system. It therefore issues 10 permits, each of which allows the bearer to emit 1 unit of pollution. For simplicity, assume that the government allocates five permits to each polluter.[23] Under the rules of the permit system, each firm is required to hold a permit for each unit of pollution released and undertake abatement on all remaining units.

Based on the *initial* allocation of permits, each polluter must abate 5 units of pollution. This initial condition, termed Round 1 of the permit system, is summarized as follows:

### ROUND 1: Government Issues Five Permits to Each Polluter

Polluter 1:  Current pollution level:  10 units
Number of permits held:  5
Abatement required:  5 units

$$MAC_1 = 2.5 \ (A_1) \ = 2.5 \ (5) \ = \$12.50$$
$$TAC_1 \ = 1.25(A_1)^2 = 1.25(5)^2 = \$31.25$$

Polluter 2:  Current pollution level:  10 units
Number of permits held:  5
Abatement required:  5 units

$$MAC_2 = 0.625 \ A_2 \ = 0.625 \ (5) \ = \$3.125$$
$$TAC_2 \ = 0.3125(A_2)^2 = 0.3125(5)^2 = \$7.81$$

If the permit system did not allow for trading, each firm would have no choice but to abate 5 units each. While the environmental objective would be met, it would not be achieved in a cost-effective manner. The combined abatement cost for both sources without trading is \$39.06.[24]

Now consider how the result changes when permit trading is allowed. Since the two firms face different *MAC* levels at the end of Round 1, there will be an incentive for trade. Polluter 1 has an incentive to buy permits from Polluter 2 as long as the purchase price of each permit is less than its $MAC_1$. Likewise, Polluter 2 has an incentive to sell permits to Polluter 1 as long as it can obtain a price greater than its $MAC_2$. Suppose that at Round 2 of the trading process, the two firms agree on the purchase and sale of one permit at a price of \$8.00.[25] Polluter 1 purchases one permit from

---

[23] The government could have introduced the permits through a direct sale, assigning a price to each permit, or through an auction. Either method has the advantage of generating revenue to the government, which could be used to absorb some of the administrative costs of the permit system.

[24] Recall from the last chapter that this is precisely the same expenditure incurred by the two polluters if a uniform standard is used under a command-and-control approach.

[25] Any negotiated price between $MAC_1$ and $MAC_2$ would be acceptable. The ultimate selling price within that range would be determined by the two firms' relative bargaining strengths.

Polluter 2, giving Polluter 1 the "right" to pollute 6 units and the obligation to abate 4 units. Polluter 2 now possesses the "right" to release 4 units of pollution, which means it must abate 6 units. Round 2 is summarized as follows:

### ROUND 2: Polluter 1 Purchases One Permit from Polluter 2

Polluter 1:
Current pollution level: 10 units
Number of permits held: 6
Abatement required: 4 units

$$MAC_1 = 2.5 \ (A_1) \ = 2.5 \ (4) \ = \$10.00$$
$$TAC_1 = 1.25(A_1)^2 = 1.25(4)^2 = \$20.00$$
Cost of one permit purchased $= \$\ 8.00$

Polluter 2:
Current pollution level: 10 units
Number of permits held: 4
Abatement required: 6 units

$$MAC_2 = 0.625 \ \ A_2 \ \ = 0.625 \ (6) \ = \$\ 3.75$$
$$TAC_2 = 0.3125(A_2)^2 = 0.3125(6)^2 = \$11.25$$
Revenue from one permit sold $= \$\ 8.00$

This outcome can be analyzed from two perspectives—that of society and that of the firm. From the vantage point of society, the total costs of abating 10 units of pollution are now $31.25, which is $7.81 *less* than the costs without permit trading. Qualitatively, this is exactly what should result, since trading has brought the two firms' *MAC* values closer together. Polluter 1 now faces a lower $MAC_1$ of $10, (compared to $12.50 in Round 1), and Polluter 2, a higher $MAC_2$ of $3.75, (compared to $3.125 in Round 1).

Next, consider the gains that accrue to each firm as a result of the trade. Polluter 1 is better off, since its total expenditures have decreased. Its outlay for abating plus the cost of the added permit is $28.00 (i.e., $TAC_1$ of $20.00 plus the cost of the additional permit at $8.00), which is $3.25 less than its $TAC_1$ in Round 1. Likewise, Polluter 2 is better off since its net expenditures associated with abating and trading are $3.25, (i.e., $TAC_2$ of $11.25 minus the revenue received from selling one permit at $8.00), which is $4.56 less than its $TAC_2$ at the end of Round 1.

Since there is an incentive for trade as long as the two firms face different *MAC* levels, it should be apparent that Round 2 does not represent a cost-effective solution. After the exchange of one permit, Polluter 1 still faces a higher *MAC* level than Polluter 2 (i.e., $10.00 for Polluter 1 versus $3.25 for Polluter 2). Thus, it is in each polluter's best interest to continue to trade. The "rule of thumb" is that in the presence of differing *MAC*s among polluting sources, high-cost abaters have an incentive to purchase permits from low-cost abaters, and low-cost abaters have an incentive to sell them. The result? Low-cost abaters will do what they do best—clean up the environment, and high-cost abaters will pay for the "right" to pollute by buying more permits. Trading will continue until the incentive to do so no longer exists—when the *MAC*s across both firms are equal. At precisely this point, the cost-effective solution is obtained.

Applying this equi-marginal principle to our model, the final round, or equilibrium, is as follows:

> **FINAL ROUND: *Polluter 1 Purchases a Total of Three Permits from Polluter 2:***
> ***Equalization of* MAC *across Polluters Is Achieved***

| Polluter 1: | Current pollution level: | 10 units |
| | Number of permits held: | 8 |
| | Abatement required: | 2 units |

$$MAC_1 = 2.5 \ (A_1) \ = 2.5 \ (2) \quad = \$ 5.00$$
$$TAC_1 \ = 1.25(A_1)^2 = 1.25(2)^2 \quad = \$ 5.00$$
Cost of three permits purchased[26] $= \$20.00$

| Polluter 2: | Current pollution level: | 10 units |
| | Number of permits held: | 2 |
| | Abatement required: | 8 units |

$$MAC_2 = 0.625 \quad A_2 \ = 0.625 \ (8) \ = \$ \ 5.00$$
$$TAC_2 \ = 0.3125(A_2)^2 = 0.3125(8)^2 = \$20.00$$
Revenue from three permits sold $= \$20.00$

At this point, each polluter faces an *MAC* of $5, and society's total cost to achieve the environmental objective is $25. (Notice that the $20 payment for permits should not be included in society's abatement costs, since this amount is just a *transfer* from one firm to another.) As predicted, the low-cost abater, Polluter 2, is doing most of the abating at 8 units, while the high-cost abater, Polluter 1, abates only 2 units.

**Assessing the Model.**   It's no coincidence that the final abatement allocation for these two firms is identical to what results if a $5 pollution charge is imposed. Logically, the outcome is the same because both instruments use incentives that operate through the polluter's *MAC*. There are, however, three important differences. First, with a pollution charge, the

---

[26]We assume that the second permit was sold for $7 and the third for $5. These values plus the $8 price for the first permit results in a total payment of $20 for permits.

government has to search for the price that will bring about the requisite amount of abatement. In the permit system, trading establishes the price of a "right to pollute" without outside intervention. Secondly, the pollution charge generates tax revenues on all units of pollution not abated, while there are none from the permit system. This distinction may be critical in jurisdictions facing tight fiscal budgets. However, a trading system *can* be designed to generate revenues, if the government sells or auctions off the initial allocation of permits. Thirdly, the trading system is more flexible in that the number of permits can be adjusted to change the environmental objective. If the objective is too stringent, more permits can be introduced. If it is too lenient, the government, environmental groups, or concerned citizens can buy up permits, effectively reducing the amount of pollution allowed in the affected region.

There is some measure of controversy surrounding the use of trading systems. Economists typically tout the advantages of a system that so explicitly uses the market process. Noted economist Alan Blinder has argued in favor of market-based environmental policy instruments for some time. He points to the inherent cost savings, the elimination of bureaucratic interference, and the potential for much-needed government revenues.[27] On the other side of the coin, opponents argue that trading systems can create "pollution hot spots"—localized areas facing high concentrations of pollutants where most of the permit buying takes place. Another objection is the potential for elevated administrative costs to keep records of trades and the emissions of buyers and sellers.[28] Hypotheticals aside, the true test will be in observing how these permit systems perform in practice.

### Pollution Permit Trading Systems in Practice

Of all the available control instruments, tradeable permit systems are by far the most market-oriented form of environmental policy. Proposed for years by economists,[29] these systems are still in the early stage of development, with much of the evolution taking place in the United States. Attempting to combat the adverse effects of acid rain, the Clean Air Act Amendments of 1990 establish an allowance-based trading program to control sulfur dioxide emissions.[30] Application 5.4 describes the major events that characterized the first day of official trading on March 31, 1993.

---

[27] See, for example, Blinder (July 10, 1989 and August 24, 1987).

[28] Mandel (May 22, 1989).

[29] See, for example, Ruff (1970).

[30] These important amendments and the legislation dealing with emissions trading will be discussed at length in upcoming chapters

**APPLICATION 5.4**

## Fighting Acid Rain with Pollution Rights: The First Annual Auction

In March of 1993, the first annual auction of rights to release sulfur dioxide ($SO_2$) emissions was held. The event was administered by the largest commodity exchange in the world—the Chicago Board of Trade (CBOT). While most of the available permits are allocated by the EPA directly to the nation's largest polluting sources, a relatively small number—150,000 one-ton permits per year—are set aside in what is called an "Auction Subaccount" for direct sale. Selected by the EPA to conduct the one-day auction each year, the CBOT receives no remuneration from the agency and may not charge for its services.

Most of the bids in the 1993 auction came from the nation's major utilities—the largest $SO_2$ polluters. A case in point is Illinois Power, a utility responsible for releasing about 240,000 tons of sulfur dioxide emissions each year. This facility was unable to operate on the 171,000 permits issued by the EPA, so it bought some of the 75,000 to 125,000 more it needed from other utilities at about $225 each. It subsequently submitted bids for another 5,000 permits at the 1993 auction. For Illinois Power and others like it, the costs to abate were apparently greater than the expected outlay to purchase permits.

Despite the predominance of utilities in the bidding, there was at least one important exception—a nonprofit, environmental group called National Healthy Air License Exchange. According to the group's president, any permits bought in the auction would be retired and kept off the market. That private citizens can exercise such a tangible influence over environmental policy is one of the advantages of an emissions trading program. National Healthy Air License Exchange submitted bids for 1,100 permits but came away with only one for which it paid $350. Nonetheless, the organization was able to participate in the auction and eliminate some emissions from the atmosphere—all without the help of political lobbyists or public officials.

In an apparently altruistic move, Northeast Utilities of Connecticut donated 10,000 of its permits to the American Lung Association just before the auction. The association retired the permits to keep them out of the bidding process. The utility, which did not need the permits to operate, could have sold them for an estimated value of some $3 million on the open market. However, the gesture was not totally without financial incentive. Northeast was expected to enjoy tax deductions for the contribution that would offset any sacrifice of pollution rights' revenues. Hoping to encourage other such donations, Northeast Utilities and the American Lung Association established a repository for permits donated by other utilities.

How did the bidders fare in the first pollution rights auction? Rights to emit the 150,000 tons of $SO_2$ were purchased by utilities, brokers, and environmentalists for a total of $21 million. Permit prices ranged from $122 to $450. The largest single purchaser was Carolina Power and Light Co., a utility that bid for and won over 85,000 permits. In accordance with the law, all auction proceeds went to the EPA, which then allocates the funds to those utilities from which the permits were originally obtained.

SOURCES: Jeffrey Taylor. "Auction of Rights to Pollute Fetches about $21 Million." *The Wall Street Journal*, March 31, 1992; Jeffrey Taylor and Dave Kansas. "Environmentalists Vie for Right to Pollute." *The Wall Street Journal*, March 26, 1992; Scott Allen, "Rights to Pollute Given Up." *Boston Globe*, March 20, 1993; Jeffrey Taylor and Rose Gutfeld, "CBOT Selected to Run Auction for Polluters." *The Wall Street Journal*, September 25, 1992.

# Conclusions

No environmental policy instrument is without flaws. In truth, this less-than-perfect outcome should be expected. The market process works as well as it does because it operates autonomously, without external guidance. So it should not be surprising that any attempt to correct a market problem by imposing third-party controls is likely to have its share of pitfalls.

This line of defense is precisely the motivation of market-based policy approaches. The aim is not to add more restraint but to restore the market forces that broke down in the first place. In one form or another, market-based instruments effectively assign a price to environmental goods like clean air and water. Once this signaling mechanism is in place, polluters are forced to internalize the costs of pollution damage and adjust their decisions accordingly.

Of course, not all market-based instruments are well suited to all environmental problems. Both the nature of the problem and the market context must be understood before any policy can be implemented with success. Environmental problems are complex, both in origin and in implication. Likewise, today's markets are sophisticated and dynamic. However, evidence is beginning to accumulate that the link between the two is a fundamental step toward finding solutions.

# Summary

- The market approach to pollution control uses economic incentives and the price mechanism to achieve a government-mandated environmental standard.

- The major categories of these market-based instruments are: pollution charges, subsidies, deposit/refund systems, and pollution permit trading systems.

- A pollution charge is a fee that varies with the quantity of pollutants released. It can be implemented as an effluent or emission fee, a product charge, a user charge, or an administrative charge.

- A Pigouvian tax is a unit charge on the pollution-generating product equal to the *MEC* at the efficient level of output.

- An emission charge is a fee levied directly on the actual release of pollutants. Given a choice of abating, paying the fee, or employing a mix of abatement technology and tax payments, the profit-maximizing polluter will choose the most cost-effective strategy.

- In the case of multiple polluters facing a given abatement standard, the emission charge yields a cost-effective allocation of abatement responsibilities where the *MAC*s for all sources are equal.

- Abatement equipment subsidies are aimed at reducing the costs of abatement.

- If the subsidy equals the *MEB* at the efficient level of production, it is called a Pigouvian subsidy.

- Per unit pollution reduction subsidies pay the polluter for abating beyond some predetermined level.

- A deposit/refund system imposes an up-front charge to pay for potential pollution damage and later refunds it for returning a product for proper disposal or recycling. The deposit is intended to capture the MEC of improper disposal, and the refund provides an incentive to properly dispose of or recycle wastes.

- A pollution permit trading system involves the issuance of tradeable "rights to pollute" based on a given environmental objective. Following natural incentives, polluters will either purchase these rights or abate—whichever is the cheaper alternative.

# Key Concepts

market approach
pollution charge
product charge
Pigouvian tax
emission or effluent fee
abatement equipment subsidy
Pigouvian subsidy

per unit subsidy on pollution
   reductions
deposit/refund system
pollution permit trading system
pollution credits
pollution allowances

# Review Questions

1. In an article titled, "Environmentalist Predicts Marked Change in U.S. Policy," which appeared in the December 7, 1992, issue of the *Boston Globe*, Jessica Mathews, then vice president of the World Resources Institute, is quoted as saying that U.S. environmental policy will be undergoing major changes. She argues that subsidies encouraging the use of scarce resources will be abandoned and that the prices of goods using these resources will rise to reflect their true environmental cost.
   a. Illustrate Mathews's prediction by using appropriate market diagrams, both before and after a subsidy is in use.
   b. Mathews also asserts that future policy will include tax differentials, whereby taxes will be reduced or removed on productive activity such as savings and imposed on nonproductive negative externalities like pollution.

      (i)  Give the economic intuition of this tax proposal.

     (ii)  Give an example of a *current* polluting activity that might be taxed in the future. Graphically illustrate your example and explain its significance to environmental quality control.

  c.  Visit the OECD's environmental economics Web site **www.oecd.org/env/eco/issues.htm#eistr** and read the section called "Green Tax Reform." Explain the notion of an "employment double dividend" as it relates to the tax differentials to which Mathews refers.

2.  Despite economists' support of a market approach to environmental policy, command-and-control continues to dominate the policy of most nations. Explain why this is the case. In your response, cite and then comment on some of the common criticisms of market-based initiatives.

3.  Assume that there are two firms each emitting 20 units of pollutants into the environment for a total of 40 units in their region. The government sets an aggregate abatement standard of 20 units. The polluters' cost functions are as follows:

Polluter 1:    $TAC_1 = 10 + 0.75(A_1)^2$
$MAC_1 = 1.5(A_1)$

Polluter 2:    $TAC_2 = 5 + 0.5(A_2)^2$
$MAC_2 = A_2$

  a.  What information does the government need to support an assertion that the 20-unit abatement standard is allocatively efficient?

  b.  Suppose the government allocates the abatement responsibility equally such that each polluter must abate 10 units of pollution. Graphically illustrate this allocation and analytically assess the cost implications.

  c.  Now assume that the government institutes an emission fee of $16 per unit of pollution. How many units of pollution would each polluter abate? Is the $16-fee a cost-effective strategy for meeting the standard? Explain.

  d.  If instead the government used a pollution permit system, what permit price would achieve a cost-effective allocation of abatement? Compare this allocation to the equal allocation standard described in part (b).

## Additional Readings

Hanneman, W. Michael. "Improving Environmental Policy: Are Markets the Solution?" *Contemporary Economic Policy*, January 1995, pp. 74–79.

Kelman, Steven. *What Price Incentives? Economists and the Environment*. Boston: Auburn House, 1981.

McCann, Richard J. "Environmental Commodities Markets: 'Messy' versus 'Ideal' Worlds." *Contemporary Policy Issues* 14, July 1996, pp. 85–97.

Nichols, Albert L. *Targeting Economic Incentives for Environmental Protection.* Cambridge, MA: MIT Press, 1984.

Oates, Wallace. "Green Taxes: Can We Protect the Environment and Improve the Tax System at the Same Time?" *Southern Economic Journal*, April 1995, pp. 915–22.

Repetto, Robert, Roger C. Dower, Robin Jenkins, and Jacqueline Geoghegan. *Green Fees: How a Tax Shift Can Work for the Environment and the Economy.* Washington, DC: World Resources Inc., November 1992.

Stavins, Robert N. "Harnessing Market Forces to Protect the Environment." *Environment*, 31(1), January–February 1989, pp. 5–7, 28–35.

Stavins, Robert N., and Bradley W. Whitehead. "Dealing with Pollution: Market-Based Incentives for Environmental Protection." *Environment*, 34(7), September 1992, pp. 6–11, 29–42.

Tietenberg, T. H. *Emissions Trading: An Exercise in Reforming Pollution Policy.* Washington, DC: Resources for the Future, 1985.

Wirth, Timothy E., and John Heinz. *Project 88: Harnessing Market Forces to Protect Our Environment: Initiatives for the New President.* Washington, DC: December 1988.

## Related Web Sites

Energy Information Administration (provides information on energy-related issues) **www.eia.doe.gov/index.html**

Environmental Industry Associations (referenced in Application 5.2) **www.envasns.org**

Organisation for Economic Co-operation and Development **www.oecd.org**

# III

# *Analytical Tools for Environmental Planning*

Economics uses powerful models to explain environmental market failures and the policy solutions used to address them. With these models as a foundation, we can now move to the practical implications of environmental planning, the process through which government identifies environmental risks, prioritizes them, and responds with a policy plan. The planning process involves difficult decisions: determining which hazards pose the greatest threat to society, where to set policy objectives, and which control instruments to use. These decisions are guided by analytical tools designed to evaluate environmental risks and assess the costs and benefits of minimizing them.

This planning or decision-making process is actually part of a broader paradigm known as public policy development, a series of events that typically begins at the grassroots level of society and eventually leads to scientific investigation, congressional debate, and legislative enactment. Every segment of society and virtually every discipline plays a role. Understanding the entirety of public policy development gives context to environmental decision making and explains how it is affected by science, technology, politics and the law, and fiscal constraints.

In this module, we conduct an in-depth investigation of environmental planning and the analytical tools of decision making, all within the broader framework of government policy development. In Chapter 6, we present a conventional public policy model, which we tailor to environmental issues. This customized model identifies the planning phase as one called environmental decision making and risk analysis. In Chapter 7, we study the two components of risk analysis known as risk assessment—the identification of risk, and risk management—the formulation of a risk response. Among several risk management strategies available to policy makers is benefit–cost analysis, an economic tool used in guiding environmental policy decisions. Because of its potential significance, the final three chapters of the module are devoted to an investigation of this important analytical tool. Chapter 8 explains how economists measure and monetize environmental benefits. Chapter 9 presents the analogous discussion for costs, and Chapter 10 shows how both sets of results are used in a comparative evaluation to guide policy decisions.

# 6

# *Environmental Decision Making: Public Policy Development*

As we learned in the last module, there are many kinds of policy instruments government can use to control pollution, ranging from uniform standards to tradeable pollution permits. Now we are prepared to investigate *how* such policies are designed and implemented in practice. It turns out that the means by which government first becomes involved in any market failure and how it ultimately responds through policy are elements of a highly complex process. Our goal is to understand how this process works in the context of **environmental public policy development.**

Logically, it makes sense that policy makers have to start by understanding the extent of the environmental damage. Then they must establish an environmental quality objective and begin to consider various policy options capable of achieving it. Once a course of action is selected, it must be formally adopted through the legislature and then implemented by government agencies. Finally, the policy is monitored through an ongoing evaluation process. Collectively, these tasks define environmental public policy development and the decision-making process that supports it.

In this chapter, we explore this series of events using an established model of public policy development tailored to highlight environmental decision making. Of course, in practice, policy development rarely follows the same path, nor is it an entirely objective procedure. Nonetheless, a general model can guide us through what is usually a complicated and often politically charged process. Think of it as a sort of blueprint that shows how the pieces fit together and what supports the structure rather than all the detail of complex reality.

# A Model of Environmental Public Policy Development

In the United States, environmental public policy development does not typically originate at the White House or on Capitol Hill or even at a local town hall. Well before any governing body begins to take action on a public issue, the environmental problem must first be identified—something that usually occurs at the grassroots level of society. Following this, the problem has to be communicated to the public sector. The objective is to elicit government's help by convincing the appropriate public official or agency that the problem should be added to what is usually an already crowded agenda. Once done, the decision making begins—a process that involves assessing the damages to society, setting an objective, evaluating possible solutions, and implementing some type of initiative. Finally, once the policy has been set in motion, monitoring and enforcement activities take over to assure that the policy is achieving its stated objective.

In practice, the process we have just described in a few sentences is a complex one. In fact, for policies aimed at pervasive problems like air pollution or hazardous waste disposal, the complete series of steps can take years to accomplish. Because of this, public policy analysts have developed models that give structure to the process and make it easier to understand. One fairly general paradigm of public policy development is illustrated in Figure 6.1.[1] Notice from the graphic that this model breaks down the process into a series of more manageable steps: problem formation, policy agenda, policy formulation, policy adoption, policy implementation, and policy evaluation.

Adapting this model to investigate environmental policy development is accomplished by grouping the six steps into a more compact three-phase procedure. This customized approach is presented in Figure 6.2. First, problem formation and policy agenda define **Phase I: Identification of the Environmental Problem.** The next three steps—policy formulation, policy adoption, and policy implementation—are combined into **Phase II: Environmental Decision Making and Risk Analysis.** Finally, policy evaluation is classified as **Phase III: Environmental Policy Appraisal.** This approach shows that, while decision making in Phase II is the operational basis for environmental policy development, it is but one part of an interdependent progression of events.

**identification of the environmental problem** Awareness of an environmental hazard and the process of convincing government to respond.

## *Phase I: Identification of the Environmental Problem*

Identification of an environmental issue begins with **problem formation**—the recognition of a *public* dilemma, meaning one that affects some segment of society as opposed to a single individual. Sometimes the signs of a problem are obvious, like medical wastes washed up on local beaches or smog

---

[1] See Anderson, Brady, and Bullock III (1978), and Anderson (1975).

| FIGURE 6.1 | THE PUBLIC POLICY PROCESS |
|---|---|

PROBLEM FORMATION
Initial Recognition of the Problem

↓

POLICY AGENDA
Adding the Problem to Government's Agenda

↓

POLICY FORMULATION
Evaluating Options and Proposing a Solution

↓

POLICY ADOPTION
Gaining Support for and Legislating Policy

↓

POLICY IMPLEMENTATION
Executing the Solution through a Policy Instrument

↓

POLICY EVALUATION
Assessing the Effectiveness of Policy

SOURCES: Adapted from James E. Anderson, David W. Brady, and Charles Bullock, III. *Public Policy and Politics in America*. North Scituate, MA: Duxbury Press, 1978; James E. Anderson, *Public Policy-Making: Decisions and Their Implementation*. New York: Praeger,

| FIGURE 6.2 | ENVIRONMENTAL PUBLIC POLICY DEVELOPMENT |
|---|---|

PHASE I: IDENTIFICATION OF THE ENVIRONMENTAL PROBLEM

Problem formation
Policy agenda

↓

PHASE II: ENVIRONMENTAL DECISION MAKING AND RISK ANALYSIS

Risk analysis } → { Policy formulation
Policy adoption
Policy implementation

↓

PHASE III: ENVIRONMENTAL POLICY APPRAISAL

Policy evaluation

that impairs breathing and visibility. In other instances, the signals are more subtle—so much so that it takes people a long time to notice that there might be a problem. For example, residents of a community might begin to realize that there has been a higher than normal number of unexplained birth defects within its population or that the incidence of cancer is suspiciously high. If an environmental problem is the suspected cause, such as a contaminated water supply, citizens will most likely elicit government's help to identify the source of the problem and discover ways to correct it.

Recognizing a problem or a potential hazard is a significant step, but it is just the beginning. What must happen next is that citizens must convince public officials that the issue is sufficiently important to be added to government's **policy agenda.** In theory at least, there are a number of ways this can be accomplished. For example, depending on the scope of the problem, individuals might express their grievances at a town meeting, or they might contact the governor of their state. Larger and potentially more damaging problems will likely require federal intervention. In such instances, individuals might bring the problem to the attention of a senator or congressional representative. Of course, in practice, it is difficult for an individual to summon government action, particularly at the federal level. Consequently, private individuals often form coalitions to strengthen their chances of success, a practice that has been effective in bringing environmental issues to national attention. As environmental awareness has grown, so too have the ways in which concerns are communicated from the grassroots level to public officials. Application 6.1 discusses survey data on what American citizens are doing to influence the environmental agenda of public and private decision makers.

Once government officials are first made aware of a suspected environmental problem, they have to make certain that any claim of environmental damage can be substantiated. Even if that is achieved, there are no guarantees that the problem will be placed on an official agenda. For one thing, government has to make a judgment about which of the many problems it learns about are most in need of an official response. Resources are limited—even at the federal level of government. Given an already busy agenda, the public sector might have no alternative but to take no action at all or at least defer intervention to a later date. Its evaluation of the *relative* importance of a public problem and its inherent risks involves not only a systematic appraisal but also some subjective value judgments. There are also political pressures that affect how a policy agenda is set. Every public official knows that this agenda becomes a track record by which constituents evaluate accomplishments and failures. Hence the process that connects policy formation to policy agenda is not without its share of gray areas. In any event, once an environmental problem does reach an official public agenda, government must begin the task of formulating an appropriate policy response.

# How American Citizens Are Influencing Environmental Agenda

Since the first Earth Day in 1970, Americans have become increasingly active in environmental issues and more aggressive in influencing environmental agenda. According to recent public opinion polls, 78 percent of Americans consider themselves to be environmentalists. But are such self-acclamations supported by bona fide actions? Survey results suggest that they are. Individuals report that they are recycling newspapers, glass, and aluminum, and that their communities are orchestrating coordinated efforts to clean up polluted beaches and littered roadsides. Even more telling are survey statistics showing rising participation rates in "green" activities over time. Between March 1989 and March 1991, the proportion of individuals recycling newspapers nearly doubled, and those returning beverage bottles and cans grew from 41 to 48 percent. More recent polls indicate that this latter statistic has continued to rise, estimated at 58 percent in 1992.

Beyond these activities, individuals and consumer groups have also begun to use the market to communicate their views on environmentally damaging products. By purchasing only goods produced by environmentally responsible firms, consumers are sending market signals to the business community. Recognizing the potential profit implications, some firms are responding by eliminating wasteful packaging and minimizing the use of toxic substances in production processes.

Private citizens also are becoming more involved in the political process that guides environmental policy. Some are contributing money to environmental groups and other organizations whose agenda matches their own. Often, these contributions support lobbying efforts aimed at communicating specific environmental concerns to Congress and other government officials. Other individuals choose a more direct route by contacting their government representatives to voice their opinion or to volunteer their services to some environmental endeavor.

All told, it seems that Americans are making a commitment to protect and preserve the environment. Consider the following survey data collected by the Roper Organization for the 1991–1992 period.

| Activity | 1992 | Percentage Change from 1991 |
|---|---|---|
| Return bottles and cans to a store and/or recycling center | 58 | 10 |
| Recycle newspaper | 43 | 6 |
| Sort trash to separate from recyclable material/garbage | 35 | 3 |
| Use biodegradable, low phosphate detergents | 29 | 0 |
| Buy products in pumps, not aerosols | 28 | −3 |
| Use biodegradable plastic garbage bags | 28 | 2 |
| Check labels for environmental safety | 24 | NA |
| Buy products made of/packaged in recycled paper | 19 | 1 |
| Buy products in refillable packages | 18 | NA |
| Compost household/yard waste | 18 | NA |
| Avoid products from companies not environmentally responsible | 12 | −2 |
| Take bags to the market | 10 | −2 |
| Cut back on auto use | 8 | −2 |
| Avoid restaurants using Styrofoam containers | 8 | −1 |
| Contribute money to environmental groups | 8 | 0 |
| Write letters to politicians on environmental issues | 4 | −2 |

SOURCES: Frederick Allen and Gregg Sekscienski. "Greening at the Grassroots: What Polls Say about American's Environmental Commitment." *EPA Journal* 18(4), September/October 1992, pp. 52–53; U.S. Environmental Protection Agency, Office of Communications, Education, and Public Affairs. *Securing Our Legacy: An EPA Progress Report 1989–1991.* Washington, DC, April 1992, p. 9.

**environmental decision making and risk analysis**
Assessing the magnitude of the problem and developing an appropriate policy response.

**risk assessment**
The qualitative and quantitative evaluation of the risk posed by an environmental hazard.

**risk management**
Evaluating and choosing from alternative policy responses to environmental risk.

## Phase II: Environmental Decision Making and Risk Analysis

**Policy formulation** is the first step in environmental decision making. It is during this stage that two important and highly interrelated functions are performed. First, government must formally assess the magnitude of the environmental problem and the risk it poses to society—a procedure referred to as **risk assessment.** Second, it must develop an appropriate policy response—part of the process known as **risk management.** In the next chapter, we will elaborate on these important risk-based procedures. For now, we consider the issues that are at stake when these processes are undertaken as part of environmental policy development.

Perhaps the most important decision made during policy formulation is determining what is to be accomplished by government regulation. Implicitly, these objectives dictate how stringent the ultimate policy response will have to be. In extreme cases, the goal might be an outright ban of the suspected contaminant.[2] In the United States, such an uncompromising approach has been used to control some cancer-causing substances, such as polychlorinated biphenyls (PCBs) and dichloro-diphenyl-trichloroethane (DDT). Although such hard-line policies are disruptive to economic activity, the objective-setting decision is clear-cut. If the threat to society is so severe as to warrant such action, there is no room for compromise.

Aside from extremes, the conventional case calls for seeking a middle ground somewhere between status quo and an outright ban. In these instances, government officials are faced with the tough decision of identifying an "acceptable" level of pollution. But what exactly is an "acceptable" level of pollution, and how is such a determination made? Economic theory argues that "acceptable" should be guided by allocative efficiency—setting the target where the *MSC* and *MSB* of abatement are equal. In practice, however, the uncertainties associated with measuring these costs and benefits leave public officials with the dilemma of making inferences or using some alternative criterion.

Once environmental objectives are defined, officials begin to consider alternative control instruments capable of realizing these goals. Available options range from command-and-control approaches to more flexible market-based instruments. Economic theory can and sometimes does guide the policy maker in selecting from among alternative control policies, using the criteria of allocative efficiency or cost-effectiveness. However, because of the difficulty in measuring the expected benefits of improved environmental quality, officials most often are guided by cost-effectiveness.

Following the selection of an appropriate policy proposal, the **policy adoption** stage begins. Adopting public policy into law is a complex undertaking, particularly at the national level. In the United States, the

---

[2] Such an objective would be justified on economic grounds only if the *MSC* of abatement were less than or equal to the *MSB* of abatement at the 100 percent abatement level.

customary procedure is for the proposal to be submitted to Congress where it is debated and discussed before a vote is called for. The proposal must be approved by the House of Representatives and the Senate, and finally by the president of the United States.[3] Of course, not all proposals are adopted, and among those that eventually do become law, most are amended along the way.

Many factors influence this process—economic conditions, international trade implications, politics, and public opinion. In addition to national and global interests, regional economic impacts must also be considered. A case in point was President Clinton's 1993 plan to preserve the national forests and protect endangered species such as the northern spotted owl. The Clinton plan met with resistance from congressional representatives from the northwestern United States and from the logging industry, both of whom shared a common concern about the potentially adverse economic effects on the Northwest region. Finally, special interest groups are a highly visible and often influential element of the environmental policy process—among them, environmentalists, corporate officials, and labor unions. In fact, a strong lobbying force for the United Mine Workers biased certain of the provisions in the 1977 Clean Air Act Amendments to protect the jobs of high-sulfur coal miners.[4]

Once an environmental policy is ratified by Congress, it must then be executed, monitored, and enforced—all part of **policy implementation.** In the United States, implementation is done by administrative agencies, and it generally involves coordination between federal and state governments. As it applies to the environment, this coordination is referred to as **environmental federalism.** Among the U.S. agencies responsible for environmental policy implementation are the Food and Drug Administration (FDA), the Office of Safety and Health Administration (OSHA), and, of course, the Environmental Protection Agency (EPA)—the largest federal agency in the United States.[5]

To assure compliance, monitoring systems must be established. As environmental regulations have become more sophisticated, so too have monitoring and enforcement procedures. According to the EPA, criminal enforcement has become a powerful means to assure compliance. During 1996, a record number of 221 individuals and corporations were charged in EPA criminal cases. Of this sum, 33 corporate defendants and 107 individuals pleaded or were found guilty. Aggregate jail time for the year was 1,160

**environmental federalism** The coordination and delegation of tasks among levels of government to develop and implement environmental policy.

---

[3] Some policies are issued directly through executive order by the president or handed down by the Supreme Court.

[4] We will elaborate on this historical and highly controversial issue in our study of clean air policy in upcoming chapters.

[5] Within the EPA, the Office of Policy, Planning, and Evaluation (OPPE) has the overall responsibility for implementation, a major undertaking given that the EPA administers nine comprehensive environmental protection laws.

| FIGURE 6.3 | THE ECONOMIC IMPLICATIONS OF MONITORING AND ENFORCEMENT COSTS |

$A_e$ signifies the efficient level of abatement, which is determined by the intersection of *MSC* and *MSB*. The *MSC* includes all polluters' marginal abatement costs ($MAC_{mkt}$) plus the government's marginal cost of enforcement (*MCE*). The *MCE* is represented by the vertical distance between $MAC_{mkt}$ and *MSC*. If the *MCE* is not accounted for in setting an abatement objective, too many resources will be allocated to that activity. The result of such a decision is shown as $A_1$, determined by the intersection of *MSB* and $MAC_{mkt}$.

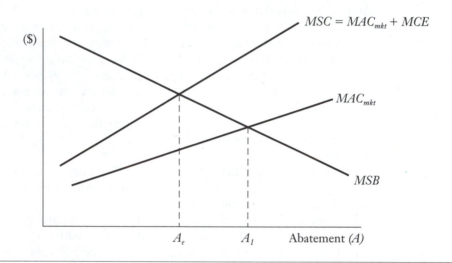

months compared to 860 months for 1995. There were also $76.7 million in criminal fines and restitution imposed, which again represented a sharp rise over the $23 million in 1995.[6]

There are important economic implications associated with monitoring and enforcement activities. Reconsider the market for pollution abatement, which is reproduced in Figure 6.3. The efficient level of abatement, $A_e$, is determined by the intersection of the *MSC* and *MSB* curves. Recall that the *MSC* includes the aggregate of all polluters' marginal abatement costs ($MAC_{mkt}$) plus government's marginal cost of enforcement (*MCE*), where the *MCE* is represented by the vertical distance between $MAC_{mkt}$ and *MSC*. If the *MCE* is not accounted for in setting an objective level of abatement, too many resources will be allocated to that activity. Referring to Figure 6.3, notice that such an omission would cause the target

[6]U.S. EPA, Office of Enforcement and Compliance Assurance. *FY 1996 Enforcement and Compliance Assurance Accomplishments Report.* Washington, DC: last updated February 18, 1998, **es.epa.gov/oeca/ 96accomp/index.html**.

abatement level to be set at $A_1$, at the intersection of $MSB$ and $MAC_{mkt}$, which is well above $A_e$.

**environmental policy appraisal** Evaluating policy using criteria such as allocative efficiency, cost-effectiveness, and equity.

*Phase III: Environmental Policy Appraisal*

The final step in the planning process, **policy evaluation,** is aimed at appraising the effectiveness of environmental initiatives and initiating reform as needed. The operative issues in this phase are to determine how well the policy is achieving its objectives and to identify any unanticipated negative effects on society. Consider, for example, provisions in the 1990 Clean Air Act Amendments that call for the use of cleaner gasolines. These are expected to reduce harmful air pollutants in nine of the nation's dirtiest cities by at least 15 percent.[7] Part of the evaluation of this set of provisions will be to determine whether the targeted reduction has been achieved and whether there have been any unexpected effects on society, such as worker displacement or other losses caused by fuel-switching.

An *economic* ex-post policy appraisal uses benefit–cost analysis guided by the same criteria used in policy formulation—allocative efficiency and cost-effectiveness. Relying on well-defined criteria such as these provides a way to quantify the evaluation and lend objectivity to what is a very difficult process.

**environmental equity** Concerned with the fairness of the environmental risk burden across segments of society or geographical regions.

While both efficiency and cost-effectiveness are rooted in resource allocation, another criterion called **environmental equity** has a different perspective. It considers the *fairness* of the risk burden across geographical regions or segments of the population. Policy officials have begun to place an increasing emphasis on environmental equity. In fact, President Clinton's Executive Order 12898 specifically directs all federal agencies to incorporate environmental justice into their policy and decision-making activities.[8] Pollution problems such as exposure to hazardous waste sites and urban smog are locationally oriented, and there is some evidence to suggest that income and cultural factors are linked to the locational decisions of certain population groups. Consequently, public officials are trying to rectify existing inequities and to incorporate the equity criterion into future decision making.[9]

# The Key Players in Environmental Decision Making

An important observation to make about environmental policy development is that it involves the interdependence of many individuals from the private and public sectors. Each group of participants, albeit from a

---

[7] Council on Environmental Quality (January 1993), p. 12.

[8] This executive order can be accessed at **www.npr.gov/library/direct/orders/264a.html**.

[9] For a collection of articles on the issue of environmental equity, see Heritage (March/April 1992).

FIGURE 6.4    PLAYERS IN THE ENVIRONMENTAL
PUBLIC POLICY PROCESS

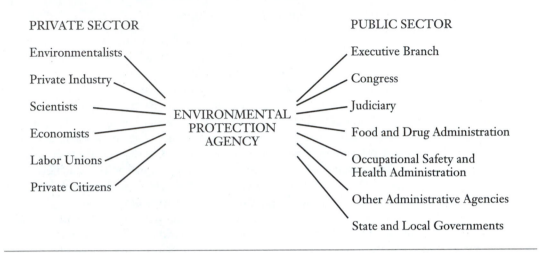

PRIVATE SECTOR

Environmentalists

Private Industry

Scientists

Economists

Labor Unions

Private Citizens

ENVIRONMENTAL
PROTECTION
AGENCY

PUBLIC SECTOR

Executive Branch

Congress

Judiciary

Food and Drug Administration

Occupational Safety and
Health Administration

Other Administrative Agencies

State and Local Governments

SOURCE: Adapted from James W. Vaupel. "Truth or Consequences: Some Roles for Scientists and Analysts in Environmental Decisionmaking." In Wesley A. Magat, ed., *Reform of Environmental Regulation.* Cambridge, MA: Ballinger Publishing Company, 1978, Figure 5-3, p. 75.

different vantage point, plays a significant role in environmental decision making and the formulation of policy. Not unlike the more general model of an economic system, each set of players in the policy development process operates from a unique set of motivations, yet each offers much-needed expertise to the outcome. On balance, the process would suffer immeasurably without any one of them.

There are any many ways to categorize the individuals who are instrumental to environmental policy development. Using the broadest classification, there are two major groups—the public sector and the private sector. The schematic in Figure 6.4 shows the different parties included in each sector with the EPA acting as a sort of liaison between them. At the other extreme is a classification based on profession or discipline—a very long list indeed. Seeking a middle ground, we consider five broadly defined groups of key players in environmental public policy development. These are: **environmentalists, private industry, scientists, economists,** and **government and its agencies.**[10] Notice that this classification is a comprehensive cross section of society with many professions implicitly represented within

---

[10] Of course, these groups are not mutually exclusive. That is, an individual who is a member of an environmental group might also be a scientist or an industry official. However, the purpose of the groupings is not to divide the population into distinct categories but rather to consider the motivation and importance of those who most influence policy.

each category. Although government leaders have the final say in determining policy, their decisions are influenced by virtually every segment of society. This assertion will become clearer as we look at the five identified groups in more detail.

### Environmentalists[11]

Private citizen interest in environmental issues has evolved considerably over the past century.[12] Beginning in the late 1800s, society became concerned with preserving natural resources and wilderness areas, a period referred to as the conservationist era. It was during this time that environmental groups such as the Sierra Club (1892) and the National Audubon Society (1905) were founded. While this interest in conservation was distracted at times by political and economic crises, the stream of consciousness was never completely broken. Society's continued interest in nature and resource preservation was largely the result of efforts by high-visibility groups like the Sierra Club.

During the 1950s, more complex issues like overpopulation and pollution began to gain national attention. This shift in focus signified that conservationism was evolving into the environmentalist movement that continues today. But it was the decade of the 1960s that witnessed a surge in public awareness of environmental pollution. Rachel Carson's notable book, *Silent Spring* (1962), warned of the dangers of the pesticide known as DDT. Across the Atlantic at about the same time, Britain's Nature Conservancy revealed that all of the seabirds' eggs it had collected along England's coastlines had been contaminated with organochloride pesticides. A similar report was released in 1969, when the dumping of PCBs was blamed for the 50,000 to 100,000 dead seabirds found on Britain's beaches.

Public reaction to these and other accounts was direct and aggressive. In the United States, several new environmental groups were formed. Among them were the Environmental Defense Fund (1967), Friends of the Earth (1969), and the Natural Resources Defense Council (1970). A parallel reaction occurred in other parts of the world. In the United Kingdom, for example, a British chapter of Friends of the Earth was founded, along with Greenpeace and the Conservation Society.[13] Meanwhile, membership in existing environmental groups skyrocketed throughout the 1960s. The environmental movement was under way, further evidenced by the celebration of the first Earth Day in 1970.

Of course, there are differences in the *relative* effectiveness ronmental groups. According to public policy analysts, me visit www.

---

[11] To access a comprehensive list of environmental groups and We envirolink.org/library/index.html.

[12] For a more detailed analysis of this evolution, see Dun

[13] Vogel (1986), pp. 40–41.

| TABLE 6.1 | SELECTED ENVIRONMENTAL ORGANIZATIONS | | |
|---|---|---|---|

| Organization | Year Founded | Membership | Budget ($ millions) |
|---|---|---|---|
| Sierra Club | 1892 | 550,000 | 50.0 |
| National Audubon Society | 1905 | 550,000 | 44.9 |
| Nature Conservancy | 1951 | 720,000 | 337.0 |
| National Wildlife Federation | 1936 | 5,000,000 | not available |
| Environmental Defense Fund | 1967 | 300,000 | 25.4 |
| Natural Resources Defense Council | 1970 | 350,000 | 27.5 |
| Greenpeace USA | 1971 | 600,000 | 32.0 |

SOURCES: Robert Cameron Mitchell, Angela G. Mertig, and Riley E. Dunlap. "Twenty Years of Environmental Mobilization: Trends among National Environmental Organizations." In Riley E. Dunlap and Angela G. Mertig (Eds.), *American Environmentalism: The U.S. Environmental Movement, 1970–1990.* Philadelphia, PA: Taylor and Francis New York, Inc., 1992, pp. 13 and 18; Jeffrey St. Clair and Bernardo Issel. "A Field Guide to the Environmental Movement." July 28, 1997, Hoosier Environmental Council, **www.envirolink.org/envlib/orgs/hecweb/archive/fieldguide.htm**.

power, and status are important determinants of a group's ability to influence government decisions and business practices.[14] Following this line of thought, Table 6.1 gives membership and budget data for some major environmental organizations. Much of the observed variability across associations is related to the kinds of activities that dominate each group's agenda. Notice that Greenpeace USA, which has a varied and aggressive agenda, has about 600,000 memberships and controls a budget of $32 million.

Two emerging trends suggest that a new phase may be evolving in the environmentalist movement. One is the formation of cooperative efforts between environmentalists and corporations. Both groups have recognized the advantages of working together even though their primary objectives differ. This new phenomenon has given rise to some productive alliances, as Application 6.2 explains. A second trend is an apparent slowdown in society's support of environmental groups. Starting in the early 1990s, membership in and financial support of major associations like Greenpeace and the Sierra Club began to drop. The reported reasons are many, including a perception that environmentalism is already well entrenched in the public agenda and a belief that other social issues such as homelessness and crime are now in greater need of support.[15]

## *Private Industry* [16]

Another important player in environmental decision making is private industry. As regulatory controls have been put in place, industry has had to

[14]Anderson et al. (1978), p. 9.

ppel (October 21, 1994).

site that offers a variety of resources about environmental industry is **www.enviroindustry.com**.

# Working Together: Strategic Environmental Partnerships

In the recent past, Corporate America and environmental groups have been perceived as archenemies, with the business sector's profit motive pitted against the social objectives of environmentalists. Although the two groups are still at odds on many issues, they are starting to work together. Through government-sponsored programs and various independent organizations, the two are coordinating their efforts to find environmental solutions that are also good for business.

Why the about-face? The move is mutually beneficial. Firms continue to be motivated by their bottom line—that much hasn't changed. What *is* different is that environmentally responsible decision making has become a determinant of a firm's profit position. Consumers are not tolerant of businesses that ignore the ecological and health implications of their actions. The bad PR that accompanies a lawsuit brought by an environmentalist group is not something firms can afford. Furthermore, environmental regulations are adding to firms' costs. Such cost increases give businesses a market incentive to function more efficiently and to *prevent* pollution rather than absorb the costs of cleaning it up. These strategic adjustments and changes in corporate culture have set up the perfect opportunity for firms and environmentalists to learn from one another and to find a common ground.

For its part, government is fostering such cooperative relationships wherever it can. A good example is the President's Council on Sustainable Development (PCSD) formed in 1993 via Executive Order 12852. The council comprises 25 members, representing the corporate world, nonprofit organizations, and government. Among the council's objectives are to formulate policy recommendations for U.S. strategy on sustainable development and to respond to the recommendations outlined in the international agenda of the Rio Summit, *Agenda 21*.

Beyond the cooperative efforts fostered through national affiliations, there are also partnerships developing independently between corporations and environmental groups. A case in point are alliances between the nonprofit environmental group, Environmental Defense Fund (EDF), and major corporations. No stranger to working for or against corporations, the EDF has been influencing environmental policy since it was founded in 1967, including its instrumental role in the U.S. 1972 decision to ban DDT. In 1990, EDF began a collaborative waste management program with the fast-food giant, McDonald's Corporation. As a result, the corporation has made waste reduction an integral part of its management decisions. More recently, EDF formed a strategic alliance with General Motors (GM)—this one aimed at improving air quality.

So far, environmental partnerships like these seem to be succeeding. Environmentalists are winning battles against pollution, and firms are finding ways to support corporate environmentalism while trimming sums from their operating and compliance costs.

### Affiliations of the President's Council on Sustainable Development

| | | |
|---|---|---|
| Interface, Inc. | U.S. Department of the Interior | U.S. Department of Education |
| World Resources Institute | U.S. Department of Housing and | Browning-Ferris Industries, Inc. |
| Natural Resources Defense | Urban Development | City of Tulsa, Oklahoma |
|    Council | U.S. Department of Commerce | U.S. Department of Agriculture |
| U.S. Small Business Administration | S.C. Johnson & Son, Inc. | U.S. Department of Transportation |
| The Dow Chemical Company | Environmental Defense Fund | Columbia River Inter-Tribal Fish |
| Center for Neighborhood | Enron Corporation |    Commission |
|    Technology | General Motors Corporation | Zero Population Growth |
| U.S. Environmental Protection | Sierra Club | Marion County, Oregon |
|    Agency | U.S. Department of Energy | The Nature Conservancy |

SOURCES: Council on Environmental Quality. *Environmental Quality, 23rd Annual Report.* Washington, DC: U.S. Government Printing Office, January 1993, pp. 183–92; Rose Gutfeld. "Environmental Group Doesn't Always Lick 'em; It Can Join 'em and Succeed." *The Wall Street Journal,* August 20, 1992; "President's Council on Sustainable Development," **www.whitehouse.gov/PCSD/index-plain.html**.

| FIGURE 6.5 | POLLUTION ABATEMENT EXPENDITURES FOR SELECTED INDUSTRIES |
|---|---|

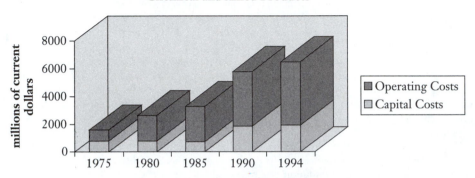

### Chemical and Allied Products

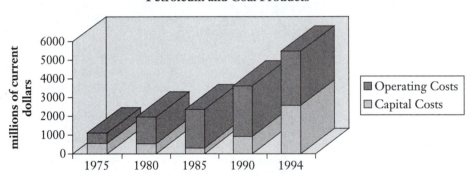

### Petroleum and Coal Products

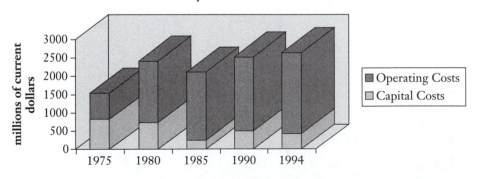

### Primary Metals Industries

SOURCE: U.S. Department of Commerce, Bureau of the Census. *Pollution Abatement Costs and Expenditure.* Current Industrial Reports. Washington, DC: GPO, annual, as cited in Council on Environmental Quality, 1997, Table 13.

absorb the costs of abatement technology. Figure 6.5 on page 170 presents abatement cost data for a selection of U.S. industries over the 1975 to 1994 period. The magnitude of these costs confirms that private industry has a vested interest in how environmental policy is formulated. Of course, some industries are more directly affected than others. Look at the expenditures for the chemicals and allied products group. These account for the largest industrial share of abatement expenditures—a direct reflection of the amount and toxicity of pollution released by this industry to all environmental media.

Increased awareness of environmental issues, better enforcement, and technological advances in pollution abatement have all contributed to greater cooperation between industry and other sectors of the economy. In the United States, a number of corporate–government partnerships have evolved with the specific aim of finding innovative ways to reduce pollution. One of these is an EPA-sponsored program called Green Lights. This plan encourages industry to install energy-efficient lighting that conserves energy *and* reduces operating costs.[17] Such cooperative arrangements will likely continue to be a part of environmental policy development. Both industry and government have a stake in the outcome, and each has a contribution to make along the way. Industry has the technological expertise to find cost-effective ways to abate and the knowledge to anticipate market implications of policy initiatives. Government has the resources and the span of control to assimilate market data on new technologies, which can help firms make sound decisions in responding to environmental policy.

## Government and Its Administrative Agencies

Throughout the world, governments are giving priority to environmental issues. This shift in emphasis began to take hold in the 1960s and 1970s, just as the environmental movement was gaining strength. Evidence of this change is the number of major environmental laws passed during that period, as Table 6.2 indicates.[18]

At the federal level of government in the United States, there is a complex infrastructure responsible for public policy design and implementation. In addition to the three branches of government and the array of committees, subcommittees, and commissions, there is also a contingent of administrative agencies dedicated to these tasks. Major environmental policy issues are, of course, the responsibility of the EPA. Established in 1970, the EPA was created by President Nixon from various components of existing federal agencies and executive departments.[19] Today, the EPA

---

[17] For a full discussion on industry's participation in a variety of cooperative and proactive programs, see U.S. EPA, Office of Pollution Prevention (October 1991).

[18] The dates given show the year in which the original legislation was passed. Many of these laws are still in force, but have undergone numerous reauthorizations and revisions over time.

[19] The EPA's mission statement can be accessed at **www.epa.gov/epahome/epa.html**.

| TABLE 6.2 | | SELECTED ENVIRONMENTAL LAWS IN THE UNITED STATES AND BRITAIN | |
|---|---|---|---|

| Selected U.S. Legislation | Year Enacted | Selected U.K. Legislation | Year Enacted |
|---|---|---|---|
| Clean Air Act | 1963 | Clean Air Act | 1956 |
| Clean Air Act Amendments | 1965 | Estuaries and Tidal Water Act | 1960 |
| Solid Waste Disposal Act | 1965 | Radioactive Substances Act | 1960 |
| The Air Quality Act of 1967 | 1967 | Rivers (Prevention of Pollution) Act | 1961 |
| National Environmental Policy Act | 1969 | Water Resources Act | 1963 |
| The Resource Recovery Act | 1970 | Medicines Act | 1968 |
| Clean Air Act Amendments | 1970 | Countryside Act | 1968 |
| The Federal Water Pollution Control Act of 1972 | 1972 | Clean Air Act | 1968 |
| | | Town and Country Planning Act | 1968 |
| The Federal Environmental Pesticide Control Act of 1972 | 1972 | Deposit of Poisonous Waste Act | 1972 |
| Safe Drinking Water Act | 1974 | Water Act | 1973 |
| Toxic Substances Control Act | 1976 | Dumping at Sea Act | 1974 |
| | | Health and Safety at Work Act | 1974 |
| The Resource Conservation and Recovery Act of 1976 | 1976 | Control of Pollution Act | 1974 |
| Clean Air Act Amendments | 1977 | The Conservation of Wild Creatures and Wild Plants Act | 1975 |
| The Federal Environmental Pesticide Control Act Amendments | 1977 | Endangered Species (Import and Export) Act | 1976 |
| Clean Water Act Amendments | 1977 | Town and Country Planning Act | 1980 |
| Comprehensive Environmental Response, Compensation, and Liability Act | 1980 | | |

operates as an independent agency headed by a president-appointed administrator who oversees its vast infrastructure. To gain a general sense of the EPA's organization and internal hierarchy, refer to the schematic in Figure 6.6. The growth rate of the EPA since its creation has been substantial. Look at the rise in its budget authority and workforce shown in Figure 6.7.[20]

---

[20] U.S. EPA, Office of Communications, Education, and Public Affairs (April 1992), p. 46. For complete data on the EPA's budget, visit **www.epa.gov/ocfo**.

FIGURE 6.6    STRUCTURE OF THE U.S. ENVIRONMENTAL PROTECTION AGENCY

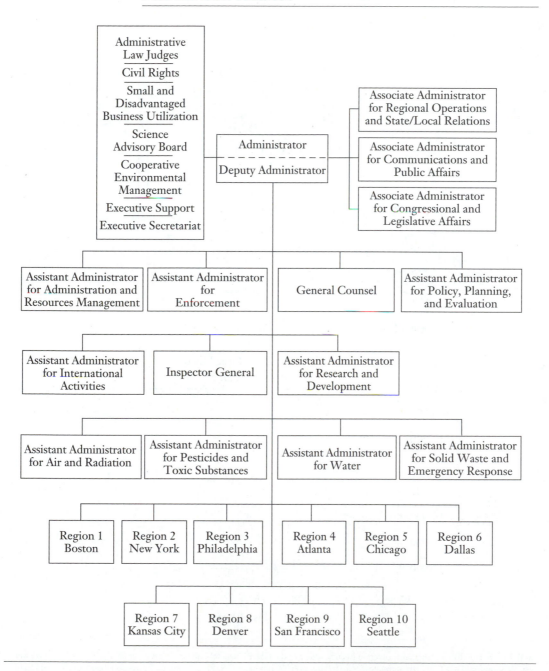

SOURCE: U.S. Environmental Protection Agency, Information Access Branch, Information Management and Services Division. *Access EPA.* Washington, DC, 1991, p. 8.

**FIGURE 6.7**   EPA BUDGET AND STAFF DATA

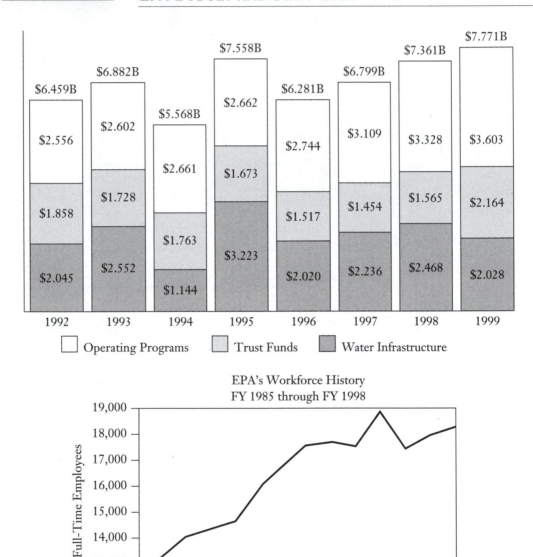

SOURCES: U.S. Environmental Protection Agency, Office of the Chief Financial Officer. *Summary of EPA's FY1999 President's Budget*. Washington, DC, 1998, **www.epa.gov/ocfo/99budget/1999bib.htm**; U.S. Environmental Protection Agency, Office of Human Resources and Organizational Services. "EPA's Workforce: EPA's Workforce History" (last update: June 26, 1997), **www.epa.gov/epahrist/growth.htm**.

Some environmental issues fall under the jurisdiction of federal agencies other than the EPA. For example, policies aimed at occupational-specific environmental hazards, such as worker exposure to asbestos, are assigned to the Occupational Safety and Health Administration (OSHA). Issues relating to the contamination of foods or the use of food additives such as saccharine are the responsibility of the Food and Drug Administration (FDA).

Integration of effort across administrative agencies, executive departments, and branches of government is directed by the National Environmental Policy Act (NEPA) of 1969. This legislation guides the formulation of all federal environmental policy and also requires that the environmental impact of *all* public policy decisions be formally addressed. According to NEPA:

> "The Congress authorizes and directs that, to the fullest extent possible . . . all agencies of the Federal Government shall—
>
> > Utilize a systematic, interdisciplinary approach which will insure the integrated use of the natural and social sciences and the environmental design arts in planning and in decision making which may have an impact on man's environment; . . .
> >
> > Include in every recommendation or report on proposals for legislation and other major Federal actions significantly affecting the quality of the human environment, a detailed statement by the responsible official on the environmental impact of the proposed action, . . ."[21]

The provisions of the NEPA are not just political rhetoric. In fact, there has been a history of complaints filed against government agencies for failing to comply with this act, particularly its requirement for submitting an "Environmental Impact Statement (EIS)" on any proposed legislation or major federal initiative. Application 6.3 discusses the EIA requirement, its litigation history, and its impact on the negotiations for the North American Free Trade Agreement (NAFTA).

### Scientists[22]

Scientific research is critical to environmental policy development. For example, policy makers rely on marine biologists and chemists to assess the impact of surface water contamination on aquatic life and marine ecosystems. Such research helps public officials understand the implications of water pollution, which in turn guides the formulation of policy. As a direct

---

[21] Title I. "Declaration of National Environmental Policy"; Sec.102(1)(A) and Sec.102.(1)(E) of the National Environmental Policy Act of 1969 as amended.

[22] A comprehensive website on environmental science information is the Environmental News Network at **www.enn.com**.

## Environmental Impact Statements under the NEPA

The National Environmental Policy Act (NEPA) is a broad-based set of rulings that outlines the nation's overall position on environmental issues. Among its provisions is a requirement for an Environmental Impact Statement (EIS), which according to law is to entail the following:

(i)   The environmental impact of the proposed action,
(ii)  Any adverse environmental effects which cannot be avoided should the proposal be implemented,
(iii) Alternatives to the proposed action,
(iv)  The relationship between local short-term uses of man's environment and the maintenance and enhancement of long-term productivity, and
(v)   Any irreversible and irretrievable commitments of resources which would be involved in the proposed action should it be implemented.

Since the NEPA was passed in 1969, literally thousands of EISs have been completed by a variety of federal agencies. During 1994 alone, 532 EISs were completed by major federal agencies and executive departments. However, not all federally proposed actions have complied with the law, and in some cases lawsuits have been filed. For example, in 1994, 106 cases were filed against government agencies or departments for failure to file an EIS or for incomplete documents. But of the hundreds of cases filed to date, none captured greater world attention than one involving the North American Free Trade Agreement (NAFTA).

In a stunning federal court decision handed down in 1993, a judge ruled that the filing of an EIS was required for negotiations of the NAFTA between the United States, Mexico, and Canada. The case originally had been brought before the District Court of Washington DC in August 1992 as *Public Citizens v. Office of the U.S. Trade Representative* for failure to file an EIS for NAFTA and for the Uruguay round of negotiations under the General Agreement on Tariffs and Trade (GATT). Among the plaintiffs in the case was the Sierra Club, a major lobbying environmental group. The district court dismissed the case, and a subsequent court of appeals ruling stated that the plaintiffs had failed to identify a final agency action. Responding to President Bush's announcement of an agreement on NAFTA on September 12, 1992, a new court action was filed—this time arguing the need for an EIS only for NAFTA.

The 1993 decision by Judge Charles B. Richey stirred up another round of debate centered on the economic and environmental implications of open trade among the three nations. Judge Richey was assertive about his position, writing in his decision:

> "An impact statement is essential for providing Congress and the public with the information needed to assess the present and future environmental consequences of . . . the NAFTA."

Critics complained that filing an EIS could take years—a delay they believed could mean the end of NAFTA. Responding to Judge Richey's ruling, then U.S. trade representative Mickey Kantor stated that the government would appeal the decision. Interestingly, in September of 1993, Judge Richey's ruling was reversed—not because of the anticipated delays, but because NAFTA is a presidential action not covered by the NEPA. And in December 1993, President Clinton signed NAFTA into law.

SOURCES: Council on Environmental Quality. *Environmental Quality, 25th Anniversary Report.* Washington, DC: U.S. Government Printing Office, 1997, pp. 51, 534–45; Dianne Dumanoski. "Activists Cite Trade Rules as a Force Shaping Nature." *Boston Globe*, July 1, 1993, p. 13; Peter G. Gosselin. "Environmental Ruling Blocks Free Trade Pact." *Boston Globe*. July 1, 1993, p. 1; Michael York. "President Wins One on NAFTA; Court Reverses Order to Study Environment." *Washington Post*, September 25, 1993, p. A1.

consequence of this kind of scientific study, the U.S. government has allocated significant resources to the restoration of threatened water bodies, including the Great Lakes, the Gulf of Mexico, Puget Sound, and Chesapeake Bay.[23]

Government also needs the scientific community to study health effects from exposure to contaminants and to identify population-specific sensitivities, such as the higher susceptibility of young children to lead poisoning. This research is guided by the science of toxicology, the study of poisons and their effects. This relatively young discipline has grown in significance as chemicals have become more prevalent in our society and as synthetic chemicals have been developed—a trend that has led to more complex and serious pollution problems. There is little question that environmental policy would be ill defined without the evidence that can be provided through scientific research and analysis.

## Economists

Over the past two decades, economics and market forces have become increasingly important to the design of environmental policy. Revisions to U.S. legislation, such as the 1990 Clean Air Act Amendments, incorporate more market-based instruments than ever before. Many state governments have begun to follow suit, using incentives to *encourage* abatement rather than imposing command-and-control limits or restrictions. As this trend has evolved, the role of economists in policy development has become more prominent.

The use of economic analysis in U.S. public policy decisions is in large part the result of President Reagan's Executive Order 12291—a mandate that explicitly called for federal decision makers to consider the benefits and costs of all major regulatory acts.[24] This requirement was subsequently extended by President Clinton's Executive Order 12866.

Why is benefit–cost analysis so important in this context? The answer is simple economics. Industrialized nations have to allocate scarce resources among the needs of many national issues. Thus efficiency and cost-effectiveness have become the relevant criteria for deciding how best to use available resources. Yet these criteria can be applied in practice only if the associated costs and benefits have been estimated. Hence, as environmental policy has advanced, so too has the need for economists to define, measure, and interpret these concepts in the context of environmental initiatives. In this relatively new application, benefit–cost analysis is still under development, and there is much new ground to break. In upcoming chapters, we will investigate this work, examine how economists arrive at these estimated values, and discuss the direction of new research.

[23] U.S. EPA, Office of Communications, Education, and Public Affairs (April 1992), p. 29.

[24] See Federal Register, February 17, 1981, pp. 13193–13194.

# Conclusions

Environmental degradation affects all of society, and there is little doubt that government is needed to assess the damages, evaluate the implications, and formulate a policy response. By itself, the public policy process is a complex one. However, the task is that much more difficult when the objective is to reduce environmental damage. Environmental problems are not easy to solve, and there is scientific uncertainty about many of the underlying issues. What *is* certain is that policy decisions have implications about the quality of life for today's society and for future generations. Recognizing the challenge and the significance of environmental decision making is in large part why *all* segments of society participate in the public policy process.

Private citizens are often the catalyst for environmental policy development. Through their efforts in identifying environmental problems, both as individuals and as members of environmental groups, many new laws have been passed to protect and preserve the environment. Scientists provide the research needed to identify health and ecological risks—a critical element of environmental decision making. Armed with scientific data, government agencies can make more informed policy decisions.

For its part, industry also contributes to public policy development through technological advance and cooperative endeavors with environmental groups and government agencies. In their search for better solutions, governments are calling upon the expertise of economists to analyze and assess the use of market-based instruments in environmental policy. Economists are also needed to estimate the social benefits and costs of major policy proposals. Such efforts are instrumental not only to policy formulation, but also to the appraisal stage during which initiatives are assessed and often amended.

Taken together, it is apparent that all segments of society contribute to environmental policy development. In the next chapter, we will learn more about this collective effort by focusing on Phase II of our model—environmental decision making and risk analysis. In our study of risk assessment, we will explore how many scientific fields contribute to policy makers' understanding of environmental hazards. Even more disciplines are involved in risk management—among them, economics and the law. Such an interdisciplinary collaboration has become the cornerstone of environmental decision making.

# Summary

- Public policy development can be modeled as a series of six steps: problem formation, policy agenda, policy formulation, policy adoption, policy implementation, and policy evaluation.

- To tailor the model to environmental policy development, the six-step paradigm is recast as a three-phase model—Phase I: Identification of the problem; Phase II: Environmental decision making and risk analysis; and Phase III: Environmental policy appraisal.

- Five groups of major players are identified in environmental policy development: environmentalists, private industry, scientists, economists, and government.

- Environmental groups have a long history of activism and continue to influence public policy today. According to analysts, membership size, power, and status are key determinants of their overall strength.

- Private industry exerts an important influence on environmental policy decisions. Business and government are beginning to work together to control pollution.

- At the U.S. federal level of government, a complex infrastructure is responsible for environmental policy formulation and implementation. Integration of effort is directed through the National Environmental Policy Act (NEPA) of 1969.

- Scientific research is critical to sound environmental decision making, particularly in assessing environmental risk.

- Over the past two decades, economics and market forces have become increasingly important to environmental policy. This is due in part to President Reagan's Executive Order 12291, which requires that government officials consider the benefits and costs of all major regulatory acts.

## Key Concepts

identification of the environmental
   problem
environmental decision making
   and risk analysis
risk assessment

risk management
environmental federalism
environmental policy appraisal
environmental equity

## Review Questions

1. Use economic theory to explain why the "acceptable" level of pollution established by policy makers is rarely set at a zero level. Graphically illustrate a case where a zero level of pollution would be allocatively efficient.

2. Find a recent example of how an environmental group has influenced the direction of public policy. Discuss why in this instance the group was successful in its efforts.

3. Look at the membership of the President's Council on Sustainable Development given in Application 6.2. Choose any two of the affiliates and contrast their motivations for being in this group.

4. Visit the website of the Environmental Defense Fund (EDF), and scan one of their recent annual reports listed at **www.edf.org/pubs/ AnnualReport/**. Summarize one of the cooperative efforts between EDF and a private firm or a government agency and identify the gains to each participant.

5. Discuss the possible trade-offs that may exist between abatement and enforcement activities. How will these trade-offs affect the allocatively efficient level of pollution abatement?

## Additional Readings

Bullard, Robert D. "Overcoming Racism in Environmental Decisionmaking." *Environment* 36(4), May 1994, pp. 11–20, 39–44.

Commoner, Barry. *Making Peace with the Planet*. New York: W. W. Norton, 1993.

Gutfeld, Rose. "Environmental Group Doesn't Always Lick 'em; It Can Join 'em and Succeed." *The Wall Street Journal*, August 20, 1992.

Landy, Marc K., Marc J. Roberts, and Stephen R. Thomas. *The Environmental Protection Agency: Asking the Wrong Questions: Nixon to Clinton*. New York: Oxford University Press, 1994.

Morgenstern, Richard D. *Economic Analyses at EPA: Assessing Regulatory Impact*. Baltimore, MD: World Resources Institute, 1997.

Portney, Paul R. "EPA and the Evolution of Federal Regulation." In Paul R. Portney, (Ed.). *Public Policies for Environmental Protection*. Washington, DC: Resources for the Future, 1990, pp. 7–25.

## Related Web Sites

| | |
|---|---|
| Envirolink (organizational resources) | **www.envirolink.org/library/index.html** |
| Environmental Defense Fund | **www.edf.org** |
| Environmental Industry Website (information about environmental industries) | **www.enviroindustry.com** |
| Environmental News Network | **www.enn.com** |
| President Clinton's Executive Order 12898 on Environmental Justice | **www.npr.gov/library/direct/orders/264a.html** |

| | |
|---|---|
| Sierra Club | **www.sierraclub.org** |
| United Nations Environment Programme (UNEP) | **www.unep.org** |
| U.S. EPA FY 1996 Enforcement and Compliance Assurance Accomplishments Report | **es.epa.gov/oeca/96accomp/index.html** |
| U.S. EPA's Mission | **www.epa.gov/epahome/epa.html** |
| U.S. EPA's Office of the Chief Financial Officer (for EPA budget data) | **www.epa.gov/ocfo** |
| White House Virtual Library | **library.whitehouse.gov.** |

# 7

# *Environmental Risk Analysis*

In our model of environmental public policy development, we identify Phase II of the model as environmental decision making and risk analysis. It is during this phase that scientists identify and evaluate the risks of an environmental hazard and communicate their findings to policy makers. Based on this communication of risk, public officials must decide an appropriate course of action to reduce that risk. These two processes, known as risk assessment and risk management, involve difficult and sometimes controversial decisions. The decision making is difficult because there is uncertainty about environmental hazards and the implications for the ecology and human health—particularly over the long term. The controversy arises because there is no clear consensus about how government should respond to what *is* known about a given hazard. Accepting that all environmental risk cannot be eliminated, policy makers have to determine how much risk society can tolerate—a decision about which there is usually much debate. They must also decide what policy to use to achieve whatever risk level is deemed acceptable. How do public officials justify choosing one policy instrument over another? What criteria guide this decision-making process, and are they appropriate?

From an economic perspective, managing environmental risks should be guided by the costs and benefits associated with abatement. Unfortunately, there are often insufficient data to fully assess these benefits and costs. So policy makers have to rely on best available estimates or use an alternative risk management strategy. What are these alternative strategies, and what criteria are used to motivate them? These and other issues in risk analysis comprise our agenda in this chapter.

# Concept of Risk

**risk** The chance of something bad happening.

**Risk** is a somewhat obscure notion, yet all of us have some intuitive sense of what it is. After all, while most of us choose not to dwell on it, risk—or the chance of something bad happening—is part of life. Accepting that risk is a pervasive phenomenon, we also know that some risks can be minimized or even avoided, provided they have been recognized. This realization suggests that dealing with risk involves two tasks. The first is *identifying* the degree of risk, and the second is *responding* to it. Individuals participate in both activities, although usually not in any systematic fashion. As a matter of course, they usually formulate a *perception* of risk, not based on scientific data, but rather on a subjective or even instinctive level. These perceptions, however unscientific, are what determine how an individual responds to risk. A person might choose to accept the risk as is, find ways to reduce it, or try to avoid it entirely.

While all of this seems to imply that dealing with risk is strictly a private exercise, it turns out that risk analysis is also an important part of public policy development. Why? Because at its very core, policy is a formal response to risks faced by society. Since the government is devising a response for society as a whole, it cannot rely on individual perceptions of risk that are highly subjective, often uninformed, and possibly off the mark. Instead, the policy maker must use a systematic assessment of risk before devising a policy response.

### Classifying Risk: Voluntary and Involuntary Risk

Attempting to impose structure on obscure concepts is always difficult. Yet it is precisely in these instances that order is needed. That there are a number of ways researchers and other analysts classify risk seems to bear out this observation. One of the more common approaches is to consider two broad risk categories: **voluntary risk** and **involuntary risk.**

**voluntary risk** A risk that is deliberately assumed at an individual level.

**Voluntary Risk.**   As the label suggests, **voluntary risks** are those that are deliberately assumed at an individual level. That is, they are the result of a conscious decision. Every day, we make private decisions to engage in activities that implicitly add or subtract some amount of risk that we as individuals elect to accept.

Most voluntary risks arise from personal activities, such as driving a car, flying in an airplane, or drinking coffee. Because these risks are self-imposed, individuals can and do make decisions to respond to them. In particular, they adjust their personal exposure level to the underlying hazards. For example, skydiving is a personal activity associated with the risks of serious injury or premature death. An individual might choose to respond to these risks by avoiding the activity entirely. In so doing, exposure to the hazard and the risks to that individual are reduced to zero.

Since voluntary risks are self-imposed and the potential outcome is confined to a single person, the public sector typically is not involved or at most plays a limited role. When government *does* intervene, it is usually confined to identifying potentially dangerous conditions or products and communicating that information to society. In so doing, the government is helping people with the tasks of identifying and assessing risk, but it is *not* imposing a response decision. Providing information helps individuals perceive risks more accurately, so that *they* can make more informed private decisions about how to minimize or avoid them. This communication might be accomplished through product labeling—a sort of one-on-one information stream directly to the consumer, or through public service announcements that inform the general population about certain hazards.[1]

**involuntary risk**
A risk beyond one's control and not the result of a willful decision.

**Involuntary Risk.**   People also are exposed to hazards that are beyond their control. Here, the risks are **involuntary,** since they do not arise from a willful decision. A classic example of involuntary risk is the likelihood of property damage and personal injury caused by a natural disaster. The risk of being harmed by a hurricane or an earthquake is not self-imposed, yet the chance of such an event, while relatively small, exists nonetheless. Environmental hazards, such as air pollution or toxic waste sites, are another source of involuntary risk. Here, the hazard is often chemical exposure that arises as an externality of production. In such cases, the risk is considerable because the effects are pervasive and the potential harm extends to human health and the ecology.

Characteristic of involuntary risk is that individual responses are limited. Although personal exposure to the hazard can be adjusted, absent extreme behavior the risk cannot be reduced to zero. For example, to reduce personal risk of harm from an earthquake, an individual can avoid living in places prone to such occurrences like the San Francisco area. Such a response would decrease that individual's risk of harm from earthquakes, but the risk still exists. Similarly, to decrease one's risk of the effects of dirty air, one could avoid living in cities like Los Angeles or Mexico City. Again, the risk of harm is reduced, but not eliminated.

Because the sources of involuntary risk are beyond the control of private individuals, the associated threat is a *public* problem. Hence, government tries to control society's exposure to some involuntary risks. For chemical contaminants, government assumes most of the responsibility using legislated controls. Occasionally, regulations are passed that forbid both production and consumption of an environmental contaminant. By banning a dangerous chemical, government reduces society's risk of exposure to zero. In the more conventional and less extreme case, government limits the use of the chemical or controls its release into the environment.

---

[1] Recently, the EPA has undertaken what it calls its Consumer Labeling Initiative (CLI) to improve information and understanding of household product labels. To learn more about this project, visit their Web site at **www.epa.gov/opptintr/labeling/**.

**Distinguishing between Voluntary and Involuntary Risks.** To illustrate the difference between voluntary and involuntary risk, consider the voluntary risk of smoking cigarettes. As researchers learned more about the associated health risks like lung cancer and heart disease, the government disseminated this information through public service announcements and by placing warnings on cigarette packages. But the individual decision to smoke, or in this context the response to the voluntary risk, remained a private decision because the risk was believed to extend *only* to the smoker. As research progressed, it became apparent that "passive" or "secondhand" smoke presents a risk to persons *other than* the smoker. This discovery meant that what was originally perceived as a voluntary risk posed a threat to others that was very much beyond their control—an involuntary risk. As such, passive smoke was considered a public problem, and government began to assume a more aggressive position on smoking. For more on the risks of passive smoke, see Application 7.1.

### Defining Environmental Risk

One of the more important concerns of environmental decision makers is determining the involuntary risk of exposure to hazards such as pollutant emissions and toxic substances, known as **environmental risk.** Notice that two elements determine the extent of environmental risk—the hazard itself and exposure to that hazard. The **hazard** is the source of the damage or the negative externality, such as poisonous emissions from factories or toxic chemicals dumped into a river. **Exposure** refers to the pathways between the source of the damage and the affected population or resource. While both hazard and exposure define environmental risk, each can independently affect the outcome. That is, some hazards are relatively minor but affect a large part of the population; others, like certain chemicals, are dangerous, but exposure to them is limited.

Because risk analysis is central to environmental decision making, policy makers have devised methods to assess, characterize, and respond to environmental risk. These interdependent methods are referred to as **risk assessment** and **risk management,** each of which will be investigated in some detail.

**environmental risk**
The probability that damage will occur due to exposure to an environmental hazard.

**hazard** The source of the environmental damage.

**exposure** The pathways between the source of the damage and the affected population or resource.

## Risk Assessment in Environmental Decision Making[2]

**risk assessment**
Qualitative and quantitative evaluation of risk from the presence or use of pollutants.

**Risk assessment** refers to the qualitative and quantitative evaluation of the risk to health or the environment by the actual or potential presence and/or use of certain pollutants. In practice, environmental risk assessment is conducted by scientists who gather, analyze, and interpret data about a given contaminant. In the United States, the EPA uses a paradigm of this

[2]Much of the following is drawn from Patton (January/February/March 1993), pp.10–15.

## EPA Declares Secondhand Smoke a Carcinogen

In January 1993, the EPA released a long-awaited report presenting its conclusion that environmental tobacco smoke, also known as "passive" or "secondhand" smoke, is a human carcinogen responsible for the lung cancer deaths of 3,000 nonsmokers each year. Other reported risk estimates include the increased incidence of asthma in children and the higher risk of bronchitis and pneumonia in infants under 18 months old. The EPA's report was based on the findings of a scientific advisory panel, which reviewed evidence from a collection of U.S. studies.

The EPA's announcement alarmed the general public, but it also stimulated debate about the agency's treatment of the matter. Harsh criticism was mounted about the two-year delay between the EPA's initial draft report on environmental smoke and its formal announcement. In 1990, the EPA had concluded its review of the risks of passive smoke and prepared a first draft report. However, the final report was delayed while the agency and the tobacco industry disputed the validity of its findings. At the same time, the EPA's indoor air research program terminated its work on tobacco smoke. According to the agency's critics, this halt in tobacco research *and* the delay in announcing its conclusions were the result of the EPA's succumbing to pressure from the tobacco industry. The EPA denied the allegation, asserting that its research on tobacco ended because the work had been completed, and it wished to move on to study other pollutants. EPA officials further argued that the 1993 announcement was connected to their risk assessment division, whose research was not affected by any changes within the agency's indoor air program.

Other questions were raised about the methods the EPA used to arrive at the risk estimates. In fact, soon after the report was issued, tobacco growers and cigarette manufacturers jointly filed suit against the EPA. The objective was to obtain a declaration that the agency's report is null and void as it was based on faulty scientific evidence, invalid procedures, and manipulated data. Notwithstanding the motivation of the plaintiffs, it has been reported that the agency *did* adjust the statistical confidence level of the scientific studies down from 95 percent to 90 percent. This adjustment allowed one of the studies to show a statistically significant increased risk of lung cancer in nonsmokers from exposure to passive smoke. Without the adjustment, no single study arrives at such a conclusion.

Responding to the allegation, EPA administrator Carol Browner said she stands firmly behind the report. In July 1993, the Justice Department filed a motion to dismiss the lawsuit. Although the legal challenge of the initial report is still pending, a new, more comprehensive government study confirmed the initial link between secondhand smoke and lung cancer incidence, and also found it caused higher rates of heart disease, sudden infant death syndrome, and asthma.

SOURCES: U.S. Environmental Protection Agency. *Environmental Progress and Challenges: EPA's Update.* Washington, DC, August 1988, p. 32; National Research Council, Committee on Passive Smoking, Board on Environmental Studies and Toxicology. *Environmental Tobacco Smoke: Measuring Exposures and Assessing Health Effects.* Washington, DC: National Academy Press, 1986; Timothy Noah. "EPA Declares 'Passive' Smoke a Human Carcinogen." *The Wall Street Journal,* January 6, 1993, p. B1; Andrea Shalal-Esa. "Tobacco Industry Sues EPA over Secondhand Smoke Report." *Boston Globe,* June 23, 1993, p. 41; Associated Press. "EPA Warns of Exposure to Smoke." *Boston Globe,* July 23, 1993, p. 9; Associated Press. "Quietly, EPA Drops Some Tobacco Research." *Boston Globe,* January 7, 1993, p. 3; Paul Raeburn and Gail DeGeorge. "You Bet I Mind." *Business Week,* September 15, 1997.

process first presented by the National Academy of Sciences (NAS) in 1983.[3] This model specifies risk assessment as a series of four steps, or "fields of analysis," as they are known. These are: **hazard identification,**

---

[3] National Academy of Sciences (1983).

---

| FIGURE 7.1 | THE RISK ASSESSMENT PROCESS |
|---|---|

RISK ASSESSMENT
Qualitative and Quantitative Evaluation of Risk

Scientific Research ⟶ Hazard Identification
and Data Collection
↓
Dose-Response Analysis
↓
Exposure Analysis
↓
Risk Characterization
↓
RISK MANAGEMENT
Formulating Policy Responses to Risk

---

SOURCE: National Academy of Sciences. *Risk Assessment in the Federal Government: Managing the Process.* Washington, DC: U.S. Government Printing Office, 1983.

**dose–response analysis, exposure analysis,** and **risk characterization.** Figure 7.1 shows the flow of information through these four steps as well as between risk assessment and risk management.

### Hazard Identification

**hazard identification** Scientific analysis to determine if a causal relationship exists between a pollutant and any adverse effects.

The first step of risk assessment is known as **hazard identification.** It is in this stage that scientists analyze data to determine if a causal relationship exists between a pollutant and adverse effects on the ecology or human health. Causality in this context refers to a linkage between an environmental agent and the observed effect that is *believed* to exist based on a consensus within the scientific community.[4]

Ecological effects are any changes in the natural environment, such as crop damage, soil contamination, or fish kills. Under most public policies, these are viewed as secondary to human health effects. However, the two are *not* independent. Over time, human health is adversely affected if ecological health deteriorates. For example, damage to soil and crops may negatively affect economic productivity, human fitness, and the quality of life. In fact, a recent report on environmental risk conducted by the EPA's Science Advisory Board (SAB) recommends that the EPA devote more attention to reducing ecological risks and to recognizing the link between

---

[4]Kuhn (1970), cited in Lave (1982b), pp. 36–37. The interested reader should refer to Lave (1982a) for more detail on the problems of establishing causality in the context of hazard identification.

---

**APPLICATION 7.2**

## A Model for Assessing Ecological Risks

The primary objective of U.S. environmental policy is to reduce risks to human health. While no arguments have been made about this priority, per se, there *is* concern that the EPA has not given enough attention to ecological risks. In its 1990 report, the EPA's Science Advisory Board (SAB) argues that the EPA's lack of response to threats to ecosystems is inappropriate, since there is little difference between human life and the ecology in the natural environment. According to the report:

"... human beings are part of an interconnected and interdependent global ecosystem, and past experience has shown that change in one part of the system often affects other parts in unexpected ways. National efforts to evaluate relative environmental risks should recognize the vital links between human life and natural ecosystems. Up to this point, they have not." (U.S. EPA, Science Advisory Board, September 1990, p. 9)

In response to this criticism, the EPA developed guidelines aimed specifically at ecological risk assessment. Published in a 1992 report titled *Framework for Ecological Risk Assessment*, the agency outlines the following three-stage process:

**Problem formulation:** This phase is aimed at identifying the goals of risk assessment as well as its overall extent and focus. Ultimately, the objective is to formulate a conceptual model, which identifies the ecological resources to be protected, the data needed to complete the assessment, and the analytical methods to be employed.

**Analysis:** This step studies the extent of ecological contamination and the relationship between the stressor (i.e., contaminant) and the affected resource. The aim is to determine the cause-and-effect relationship and the degree of damage.

**Risk characterization:** In this final step, the results of the analysis are assimilated and evaluated to identify the probability of harm associated with a given stressor.

In 1996, the EPA's *Proposed Guidelines for Ecological Risk Assessment* were published in the Federal Register. These are designed to expand upon the 1992 report. A main focus of the proposed guidelines is the interaction between risk assessors and risk managers during the first and final phases of risk assessment. The complete proposal can be accessed at **www.epa.gov/ORD/WebPubs/ecorisk/guide.pdf**.

SOURCES: U.S. Environmental Protection Agency, Risk Assessment Forum. *Framework for Ecological Risk Assessment*. Washington, DC, February 1992; "A Step Toward Ecological Risk Guidelines." *EPA Journal* 19(1), January/February/March 1993, p. 33; U.S. Environmental Protection Agency, Risk Assessment Forum. *Proposed Guidelines for Ecological Risk Assessment*. Washington, DC: U.S. EPA, August 1996.

ecological health and human health.[5] Read Application 7.2 for more on this issue.

Identifying the health consequences of exposure to an environmental contaminant is a high priority. Several scientific methods are used to gather

---

[5] U.S. EPA, Science Advisory Board (September 1990).

| TABLE 7.1 | SCIENTIFIC METHODS TO IDENTIFY AN ENVIRONMENTAL HEALTH HAZARD | |

| Scientific Method | Definition | Description |
|---|---|---|
| Case Cluster | Based on the observation of an abnormal pattern of health effects within some population group. | This is the simplest method of hazard identification, but it is effective only if the observed health symptoms are very unusual or if the frequency of occurrence is extremely high. However, in either case, formal analysis and follow-up testing are needed to validate a causal relationship. |
| Animal Bioassay | A study based on the comparative results of lab experiments on living organisms both before and after exposure to a given hazard. | Statistical models are used to extrapolate data from laboratory animal responses to approximate a human response. This is a costly method, and there are concerns about its reliability. One concern is that an observed linkage between exposure and an animal response does not necessarily mean that the same response will occur in humans. Another is that most animal bioassays use larger doses than what would be encountered by the human population. Researchers exaggerate the dosage to assure that the experiment will produce a measurable effect. If a lower dose were used, the same experiment would have to be performed on hundreds or even thousands of animals before observing an effect. |
| Epidemiology | The study of the causes and distribution of disease in human populations based on characteristics like age, gender, occupation, and economic status. | Because epidemiology research is based on direct observation of humans, no extrapolation of results from animals to humans is necessary. However, because epidemiology studies draw directly from reality, they are not fully controlled experiments. In a fully controlled experiment, exposure and dose amounts are carefully monitored so that only these factors are responsible for any observed response. |

SOURCE: Lester B. Lave. "Methods of Risk Assessment." In Lester B. Lave, ed. *Quantitative Risk Assessment in Regulation*, Washington, DC: The Brookings Institution, 1982, pp. 23–54.

the evidence needed to identify an environmental health hazard, some more reliable than others. Three common methods are **case clusters, bioassays,** and **epidemiology,** which are described in Table 7.1.[6]

### Dose–Response Analysis

**dose–response relationship** A quantitative relationship between doses of a contaminant and the corresponding reactions.

Once a chemical substance has been identified as a hazard, scientists must investigate its potency by quantifying the ecological or human response to various doses. This element of risk assessment determines the **dose–response relationship.** Using data collected in the hazard identification

---

[6]For more detail on these and other hazard identification methods, see Lave (1982b), which also provides an analysis of the strengths and weaknesses of each approach.

**threshold** The level
of exposure to a haz-
ard up to which no
response exists.

stage, dose–response analysis attempts to develop a complete profile of the effects of an environmental pollutant. An important aspect of this analysis is determining if some level of exposure to the hazard is "safe." More formally, scientists call this a **threshold** level of exposure, which is the point up to which no response exists based on scientific evidence.

To determine the dose–response relationship, researchers first conduct two types of extrapolations from the data obtained through hazard identification.

- **The high-to-low dose extrapolation:** to adjust for the high exposure levels used in laboratory or other test conditions; and

- **The laboratory-to-natural extrapolation:** to infer how the effects observed in the laboratory or test environment would differ under conditions existing in nature. (This includes the adjustment to infer a human response from the results of laboratory animal studies.)

Then the researcher assigns a general functional form to the expected relationship between exposure and response and uses a statistical model to estimate it quantitatively.

Consider for example, estimating the dose-response relationship associated with exposure to carbon monoxide (CO), a gas released from the incomplete combustion of carbon-based fuels like gasoline. At relatively small doses of CO, the individual may experience drowsiness. At higher exposure levels, visual perception may be impaired as well as learning ability. As the exposure level increases, death results. It is the purpose of the dose-response analysis to estimate quantitatively at what exposure levels each of these effects occurs and all the intermediate dose-to-response relationships as well.

Like any statistical study, estimating a dose-response relationship requires the researcher to make initial assumptions. These include which factors are being controlled when defining the relationship and what the underlying relationship looks like.[7] Figure 7.2 (a), (b), and (c) illustrates three hypothetical dose-response functional forms. Common to each depiction is a positive relationship between dose level and response. What differs among them is the *rate* at which the response increases with the dosage. For example, in panel (a) of Figure 7.2, the dose-response relationship is linear, meaning that the rate of increase between dose and response is constant. Notice also that this curve begins at the origin. This means that a response is expected no matter how small the dose or, equivalently, that no identifiable threshold level has been observed. Contrast this with the relationship shown in panel (b). In this case, there is also a constant rate of change between dose levels and response but only beyond dose

---

[7] See Lave (1982b), pp. 43–47, for further information.

| FIGURE 7.2 | HYPOTHETICAL DOSE–RESPONSE RELATIONSHIPS |

These graphs illustrate three hypothetical dose–response functional forms. Panel (a) shows a linear dose-response function, meaning that the rate of increase between dose and response is constant. Because the function starts at the origin, it implies that no threshold level has been observed. The relationship in panel (b) also shows a constant rate of change between dose levels and response but only beyond dose level $D_t$. Up to and including that point, there is no response at all, meaning that there is an identified threshold at $D_t$. Panel (c) depicts a cubic relationship drawn from the origin, showing that the response level initially increases at an increasing rate up to dose level $D_o$ and then increases at a decreasing rate thereafter.

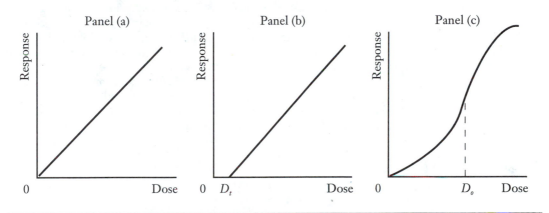

level $D_t$. Up to and including that point, there is no response at all, meaning that the hazard represented by this relationship has an identified threshold at $D_t$. Finally, panel (c) shows a cubic (or S-shaped) relationship drawn from the origin. Here, the response level increases at an increasing rate up to dose level $D_o$ and then increases at a decreasing rate beyond that point.

The scientific results derived from hazard identification and dose-response analysis provide general information about the risks of an environmental hazard based on some *known population* as defined by the laboratory or test conditions. This general information can then be used as a basis for assessing the risk to a *potentially exposed population* in a specific context. The EPA has established a database of identified environmental hazards and their estimated dose–response relationships for use by researchers and the general public. Referred to as the Integrated Risk Information System (IRIS), this database is designed to improve risk assessment by lending consistency and efficiency to what is a difficult and time-intensive process. See Application 7.3 for more on what IRIS offers and how it is used in practice to facilitate the remaining steps of the risk assessment process.

APPLICATION 7.3

## EPA's IRIS: A Health Effects Database

Risk assessment of environmental health hazards has become a well-structured process. In large part, this is a consequence of the paradigm presented by the National Academy of Sciences (NAS) in its 1983 publication, *Risk Assessment in the Federal Government: Managing the Process.* Of the four steps outlined in this model—hazard identification, dose–response analysis, exposure analysis, risk characterization—the first two provide scientific findings about the risk of a contaminant based on laboratory studies. By design, these findings can then be used to assess the risk posed by that same contaminant under actual conditions, using the latter two steps of the NAS model.

Because of the applicability of hazard identification and dose-response analysis, the EPA added structure to the risk assessment process by creating a repository of EPA consensus views on the health risks of environmental contaminants. Established in 1986, this database of consensus opinions comprises the Integrated Risk Information System, referred to by its acronym IRIS. Originally accessible only to EPA officials and staff, IRIS was made available to the general public in 1988. Today, the public can access IRIS through the Internet at **www.epa.gov/ngispgm3/iris/intro.htm**.

There are three sections in the database: carcinogen assessment data for oral and inhalation exposure, noncancer health effects from oral exposure, and noncancer health effects from inhalation exposure. The database was developed and is maintained by two work groups, each of which comprises a panel of scientists from a multitude of disciplines and several EPA program areas.

As each group arrives at a consensus on a given pollutant, a summary is prepared and added to IRIS. Each summary includes a risk assessment table, which gives a risk number or relative risk value (i.e., a probability value for carcinogenic effects, a reference dose [RfD] for oral exposure to noncarcinogenic effects, or a reference concentration [RfC] for inhalation exposure to noncarcinogenic effects). The risk value is supported by a synthesis and discussion of the relevant preliminary scientific data used to form the consensus. A full reference listing is also provided to direct the reader to the studies upon which the consensus is based. Drinking water health advisories and any EPA regulatory actions relevant to the pollutant are itemized along with supplemental data, which may include acute health hazard information, chemical and physical properties of the substance, and major uses of the pollutant. These summaries assure consistency and efficiency in conducting exposure analysis and risk characterization. Currently, there are over 530 substances for which summaries are given within IRIS.

SOURCES: Linda Tuxen. "EPA's IRIS Data Base: Accessing the Science." *EPA Journal* 19(1), January/February/March 1993, pp. 22–23; U.S. Environmental Protection Agency, Environmental Criteria and Assessment Office. *IRIS Data Base*, Research Triangle Park, NC: U.S. EPA, 1993.

### Exposure Analysis

**exposure analysis**
Characterizes the sources of an environmental hazard, concentration levels at that point, pathways, and any sensitivities.

The process through which a generalized dose-response relationship is applied to specific conditions for an affected population is called **exposure analysis.** Exposure analysis characterizes the following:

- the sources of the environmental hazard

- the concentration levels at the source point

- the pathways from the source to the affected population

- any sensitivities within the population group

To illustrate, consider conducting an exposure analysis for lead. The potentially affected target group is the general population. The sources of lead are many, including painted surfaces, factory emissions, improperly fired ceramic cookware, lead-acid batteries, lead water pipes, and lead-soldered cans. Since lead is ubiquitous, there are many pathways by which sources of this contaminant reach the population. Lead exposure can occur through inhalation of contaminated air, ingestion from drinking contaminated water or eating contaminated food, and direct ingestion of lead particles. Existing research also shows that sensitivity to lead exposure is greater for unborn babies, infants, and young children.

## Risk Characterization

**risk characterization** Description of risk based on an assessment of a hazard and exposure to that hazard.

The final phase of risk assessment is called **risk characterization**—the objective of the entire process. **Risk characterization** is a complete description of the form and dimension of the expected risk based on the assessment of its two components—the identified hazard and exposure to that hazard. More than just an assimilation of the previous steps, the description includes both a **quantitative** and **qualitative** risk evaluation.

The **quantitative** component identifies the magnitude of the risk and provides a way to compare one risk with another. Risk can be measured as a probability that an event will occur, using a numerical value that quantifies the likelihood of occurrence in some time period. Some probabilities are based on what are called **actuarial risks,** those determined from factual data. Actuarial risk measures are found by calculating the number of victims of a given hazard relative to the total number exposed. For example, the actuarial risk of deaths per year from driving an automobile has been estimated at 24 in 100,000, or 0.024 percent. The likelihood of premature death from being struck by lightning is 0.00005 percent, or 5 people for every 10 million. Other probability measures such as the carcinogenic risks associated with chemical exposure are based, not on actual data, but on inferences derived from animal bioassays or epidemiological studies. For example, the risk of getting cancer in a year from drinking chlorinated water has been estimated to be 0.0008 percent or 8 in 1 million persons exposed.[8]

Other environmental risks such as noncarcinogenic health risks are quantified as the exposure level to a hazard that can be tolerated over a lifetime without harm. This is communicated as a **reference dose (RfD)** expressed as:

RfD = milligrams of a pollutant per body weight per day.

Thus, an RfD for pollutant X of 0.005 milligrams/kilogram/day means that exposure to 0.005 milligrams of pollutant X per kilogram of body weight each day over a lifetime should cause no harm.

---

[8]The estimates of risk presented in this section are given in Scheuplein (January/February/March 1993), pp. 16–17.

## The Dynamics of Risk Assessment: The Case of Dioxin

A family of chemical compounds called dibenzo-p-dioxins are considered by some scientists to be the single most deadly of all synthetic compounds. Named as one of the contaminants responsible for the evacuation of residents in Love Canal, New York, in 1980 and Times Beach, Missouri, in 1983, dioxins were classified by the United States in 1985 as probable, highly potent, human carcinogens. Over time, new evidence has called this initial risk assessment into question, suggesting the need for further scientific inquiry. In a broad sense, what this reevaluation implies is that risk assessment is a dynamic process.

The chronicle of events surrounding the reassessment of dioxins is a good case study to observe this dynamic process in action. A summary is given below:

| Time Period | EPA Actions |
| --- | --- |
| 1980–1985 | Following the disaster at Love Canal, the EPA begins to assess the risks of exposure to dioxins. In 1985, the EPA concludes that dioxin is a probable human carcinogen. |
| 1988 | Based mainly on scientific judgment, the EPA writes a draft document to revise its initial risk assessment of dioxin. The draft suggests that dioxin may not be as potent as originally stated in the 1985 assessment. |
| 1990 | A conference of 30 scientific experts agree that the health effects of dioxin in humans can be predicted from the measured effects obtained through animal studies. They further agree that a new risk assessment model needs to be developed to accommodate current understanding of how dioxin affects the human body. |
| 1991 | In January, the National Institute for Occupational Safety and Health (NIOSH) releases new data relating to the cancer mortality of dioxin-exposed workers. |
| | In April, the EPA begins work on a reassessment of *all* risks of dioxin. As part of its tasks, the agency is to develop a dose-response model with the help of outside prominent scientists. The EPA holds meetings to inform the public of its progress and to ask for comments. |
| 1992 | In August, the EPA issues drafts of human health and exposure assessment documents. As part of the review process, the EPA schedules a series of public meetings. |
| 1994 | The EPA releases its draft report, reaffirming its earlier findings that human exposure to dioxin at high levels may cause cancer and at low levels may lead to serious health consequences. Public meetings are held to receive comments. |
| 1995 | The Science Advisory Board (SAB) reviews the documents and requests that two sections of the reassessment be reviewed again. |
| 1997 | Peer review and SAB re-review of the revised sections are scheduled. |

SOURCES: Peter W. Preuss and William H. Farland. "A Flagship Risk Assessment: EPA Reassesses Dioxin in an Open Forum." *EPA Journal* 19(1), January/February/March 1993, pp. 24–26; Associated Press. "Study: Dioxin Health Threat Much Worse Than Suspected." *Brockton Enterprise*, September 12, 1994; U.S. Environmental Protection Agency, Office of Research and Development, National Center for Environmental Assessment. *Dioxin and Related Compounds* (last revised February 10, 1998), **www.epa.gov/nceawwwl/dioxin.htm**.

The **qualitative** element of the characterization gives context to the numerical risk value. It gives a description of the hazard, an assessment of exposure that notes any susceptible population groups, an identification of the data used, the scientific and statistical methods employed, and all underlying assumptions. Any scientific uncertainties, data gaps, or measurement errors that distinguish the findings are pointed out as well. All this information characterizes the reliability of the results and facilitates further research.

It is important to realize that risk assessment is not a fixed evaluation, but rather part of a dynamic process. The assessment changes as new information and better analytical methods become available—exactly what has occurred in assessing the risk of exposure to dioxin, the subject of Application 7.4 on page 194.

# Risk Management in Environmental Decision Making: Responding to Risk

**risk management**
Evaluating and selecting from among regulatory and non-regulatory risk responses.

While the objective of risk assessment is to *identify* risk, it is the goal of **risk management** to *respond* to it. More to the point, risk management is concerned with formulating and implementing policy to reduce society's risk of a given hazard. To evaluate various policy options, the decision maker must consider not only the information given by the risk characterization, but also such factors as technological feasibility, implementation costs, and other economic implications. Notice from Figure 7.3 that while risk assessment is dominated by the work of scientists, risk management relies on many fields.

Implementation of the risk management process involves a series of decisions aimed at two major tasks: (1) to determine what level of risk is "acceptable" to society; and (2) to evaluate and select the "best" policy instrument to achieve that risk level. None of the underlying decisions are unidimensional, and realistically none can be made with complete objectivity. However, there are strategic approaches used to guide the decision making, some of which are mandated by law. We begin with a brief discussion of these two major tasks of risk management, which lays the groundwork for an analysis of risk management strategies.

## The Tasks of Risk Management

**Determining "Acceptable" Risk.** The universal objective of all risk management strategies is to reduce risk. However, for each policy proposal, the public official must decide how much of a reduction is appropriate. Although risk is a function of both hazard and exposure, only one of these—exposure—can be controlled. So, when the risk manager decides the amount of risk reduction to be achieved, the exposure level is determined

| FIGURE 7.3 | DISCIPLINES IN RISK ANALYSIS |
|---|---|

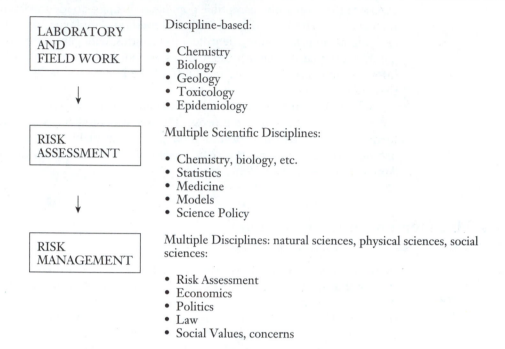

LABORATORY AND FIELD WORK

Discipline-based:

- Chemistry
- Biology
- Geology
- Toxicology
- Epidemiology

RISK ASSESSMENT

Multiple Scientific Disciplines:

- Chemistry, biology, etc.
- Statistics
- Medicine
- Models
- Science Policy

RISK MANAGEMENT

Multiple Disciplines: natural sciences, physical sciences, social sciences:

- Risk Assessment
- Economics
- Politics
- Law
- Social Values, concerns

SOURCE: Dorothy E. Patton. "The ABCs of Risk Assessment: Some Basic Principles Can Help People Understand Why Controversies Occur." *EPA Journal* 19(1), January/February/March 1993, p. 12.

**"acceptable" risk**
The amount of risk determined to be tolerable for society.

implicitly . This in turn dictates how stringent public policy must be. In setting the level of **"acceptable" risk,** the policy maker confronts a difficult but necessary question. Should the policy eliminate the risk by reducing exposure to zero, or should some compromise be struck at some positive risk level, and if so, where? [9]

If the acceptable risk level is set at zero, the policy must reduce society's exposure to zero (assuming no threshold level). While this action eliminates the associated health and ecological damage, such a stringent policy is likely to cause economic problems. For example, if the hazard is a chemical used in manufacturing, reducing exposure to zero means that its use must be prohibited. Such a ban may force plant closings and create job losses.

Conversely, if some positive level of risk is deemed "acceptable," then the decision maker is setting policy that allows exposure and therefore some amount of damage. To help guide this difficult decision, policy makers

[9] For an excellent discussion of the political and legal processes involved in environmental standard-setting as it applies to "acceptable" risk, see Marchant and Danzeisen (1989).

**de minimis risk** A negligible level of risk such that reducing it further would not justify the costs of doing so.

sometimes use the concept of *de minimis* risk. **De minimis risk** refers to a negligible level of risk such that reducing it further would not justify the costs of doing so.[10] This concept is sometimes equated to the risk of a natural hazard like a lightning strike or an earthquake.[11] Once the baseline is established, the decision maker might use **comparative risk analysis** to evaluate how the positive risk level compares to other risks currently faced and "accepted" by society. This sort of analysis has been used to communicate the relatively unfamiliar risks associated with exposure to radon, a naturally occurring gas that can be harmful when trapped indoors. See Application 7.5 for a discussion of how the risks of radon exposure are expressed in terms of the risks from more familiar activities such as X-rays and cigarette smoking.

**Evaluating and Selecting a Policy Instrument.**  Once the degree of risk and hence the stringency of policy have been determined, the second task of risk management is to decide what type of policy instrument to use. Here, the decision maker has to first evaluate alternative policies that can achieve the "acceptable" risk level and then select the "best" option from among them. Recall from chapters 4 and 5 that the options will likely include some that are command-and-control and others that are market-based. In making the decision, the risk manager considers the magnitude of risks, benefits, and/or costs associated with each available control instrument. In fact, there are risk management strategies that define exactly *how* this evaluation is to be done.

## Risk Management Strategies

Executing the two tasks of risk management—determining the "acceptable" risk level and choosing the appropriate policy instrument—requires a systematic evaluation of available options. From an economic perspective, the most important considerations are:

- the level of risk established;
- the benefits that accrue to society from adopting the policy; and
- the associated costs of implementing the policy.

Several risk management strategies have been developed over time, each of which outline *how* these factors are to be evaluated. The most prevalent of these are: **comparative risk analysis, risk–benefit analysis,** and **benefit–cost analysis.**

---

[10] For example, the United States generally does not regulate cancer risks measured at less than 1 additional case per 1 million people. This does not mean that they will never intervene if the risk is smaller — only that as a general rule they choose not to.

[11] Krimsky and Golding (1991), p. 105.

## Using Comparative Risks to Communicate the Dangers of Radon

Over the past 10 years public awareness of radon has improved, but many people still are unaware of the potential risks. The result? Government is faced with a public policy problem. Although the risk of exposure to radon is involuntary, government cannot directly intervene because radon pollutes a part of the environment that is beyond its jurisdiction—the *indoor* air.

Exposure to radon is an involuntary risk because it is a natural hazard. It is a radioactive gas caused by the decaying of uranium found in soil deposits and rocks. Outdoors, as radon is released, it dissipates quickly and poses no adverse health effects. It becomes a potential problem only if it enters homes and buildings through cracks in basements or foundations. If radon is trapped indoors, it can accumulate to dangerous levels. It is odorless and colorless, so people are unaware of its presence and are exposed to it quite involuntarily. Research studies suggest that long-term exposure to radon causes lung cancer. The EPA estimates that chronic exposure may be responsible for 7,000 to 30,000 lung cancer deaths per year, ranking it second only to smoking as a cause of lung cancer.

The EPA along with the surgeon general and various national health associations have joined forces to educate society about the little-known but potentially dangerous problem of radon. People have been encouraged to measure the radon level in their homes using readily available test kits. Brochures have been prepared by government and other associations to disseminate facts about radon to home owners. Yet all of this well-intentioned information is useful only if it is communicated in a way that is meaningful to the general public. To accomplish this, the government uses **comparative risks.**

Radon concentration levels are measured in units of picocuries per liter (pCi/l). Risk estimates for lifetime exposure to various levels are given as the number of lung cancer deaths in a given population. To communicate these estimates more effectively, comparable lifetime risks of more familiar activities are provided, as shown in the table below.

If the indoor radon level is 4 pCi/l or above, the EPA recommends that some action be taken to correct the problem. But the first step is proper risk communication. Using comparative risks to explain an otherwise unfamiliar hazard can be an effective means to help society recognize and respond to the health risk of radon exposure.

| Radon (pCi/l) | Risk of Dying from Radon (Number of persons out of 1,000) | Comparative Risk |
|---|---|---|
| 200 | 440–700 | More than 60 times nonsmoker risk |
| 100 | 270–630 | 4-pack-a-day smoker |
| 40 | 120–380 | 2,000 chest X-rays per year |
| 20 | 60–210 | 2-pack-a-day smoker or 100 times the risk of drowning |
| 10 | 30–120 | 1-pack-a-day smoker or 100 times the risk of dying in a home fire |
| 4 | 13–50 | 5 times a nonsmoker risk or 100 times the risk of dying in a plane crash |
| 2 | 7–30 | 200 chest X-rays per year or 2 times the risk of dying in a car crash |
| 1 (Average indoor level) | 3–13 | Nonsmoker risk of dying of lung cancer |
| 0.2 (Average outdoor level) | 1–3 | 20 chest X-rays per year |

SOURCES: U.S. Environmental Protection Agency. *Environmental Progress and Challenges: EPA's Update.* Washington, DC, August 1988, pp. 35–37; U.S. Environmental Protection Agency, Office of Communications, Education, and Public Affairs. *Securing Our Legacy: An EPA Progress Report 1989–1991*, Washington, DC, April 1992, p. 15; U.S. Environmental Protection Agency, U.S. Department of Health and Human Services, and U.S. Public Health Service. *A Citizen's Guide to Radon: The Guide to Protecting Yourself and Your Family from Radon.* Washington, DC, May 1992, p. 12.

| TABLE 7.2 | SCIENTIFIC RANKINGS OF ENVIRONMENTAL PROBLEMS |
|---|---|

| Environmental Problem | Relative Risk Ranking |
|---|---|
| Ambient air pollutant | High risk to human health |
| Worker exposure to chemicals in industry and agriculture | High risk to human health |
| Indoor pollution | High risk to human health |
| Contamination of drinking water | High risk to human health |
| Habitat alteration and destruction | High risk to natural ecology and human welfare |
| Species extinction and loss of biological diversity | High risk to natural ecology and human welfare |
| Stratospheric ozone depletion | High risk to natural ecology and human welfare |
| Global climate change | High risk to natural ecology and human welfare |
| Herbicides/pesticides | Medium risk to natural ecology and human welfare |
| Contamination of surface waters | Medium risk to natural ecology and human welfare |
| Acid deposition | Medium risk to natural ecology and human welfare |
| Airborne toxics | Medium risk to natural ecology and human welfare |
| Oil spills | Low risk to natural ecology and human welfare |
| Groundwater contamination | Low risk to natural ecology and human welfare |
| Radionuclides | Low risk to natural ecology and human welfare |
| Thermal pollution | Low risk to natural ecology and human welfare |
| Acid runoff to surface waters | Low risk to natural ecology and human welfare |

SOURCES: U.S. Environmental Protection Agency, Science Advisory Board. *Reducing Risk: Setting Priorities and Strategies for Environmental Protection*. Washington, DC, September 1990; U.S. Environmental Protection Agency, Office of Communications, Education, and Public Affairs. *Securing Our Legacy, An EPA Progress Report 1989–1991*. Washington, DC, April 1992, p. 9.

**comparative risk analysis** An evaluation of relative risk.

**Comparative Risk Analysis.** Just as comparative risk analysis helps the risk manager select an "acceptable" risk level, it also can be used to help officials identify which risks are most in need of an official response. The EPA's Science Advisory Board (SAB) has prepared a ranking of environmental problems by degree of risk, shown in Table 7.2.[12] The ranking was based on the best available data and scientific information and considered such factors as severity of effects and the number of people exposed. The SAB specifically advises that EPA programs should be guided by the principle of **relative risk reduction,** meaning the agency should order its policy decisions to reduce the most severe environmental risks first. The board's view on using comparative risk analysis is clear. In its report, the SAB asserts:

> "If priorities are established based on the greatest opportunities to reduce risk, total risk will be reduced in a more efficient way, lessening threats to both public health and local and global ecosystems. . . ."

---

[12] U.S. EPA, Science Advisory Board (September 1990); *EPA Journal* (January/February/March 1993), p. 19.

| TABLE 7.3 | PUBLIC PERCEPTIONS OF ENVIRONMENTAL PROBLEMS |

| Environmental Problem | Percent Responding that Problem Is Very or Extremely Serious |
|---|---|
| Hazardous waste | 89 |
| Oil spills | 84 |
| Air pollution | 80 |
| Solid waste disposal | 79 |
| Atmospheric damage | 79 |
| Nuclear waste | 78 |
| Contaminated water | 77 |
| Forest destruction | 76 |
| Ocean pollution | 75 |
| Endangered species | 67 |
| Threats to wildlife | 65 |
| Pesticide use | 60 |
| World population | 57 |
| Poor energy use | 56 |
| Global warming | 56 |
| Reliance on coal/oil | 53 |
| Wetland development | 50 |
| Radon gas | 35 |
| Indoor air pollution | 27 |
| Electromagnetic fields | 19 |

SOURCE: U.S. Environmental Protection Agency, Office of Communications, Education, and Public Affairs. *Securing Our Legacy, An EPA Progress Report 1989–1991.* Washington, DC, April 1992, p. 9.

One difficulty associated with setting risk-based priorities is that the rankings set by government often differ from how society *perceives* environmental risks. Look at Table 7.3 to see the ranking of environmental problems based on general public perception, and compare it to the SAB's ranking given in Table 7.2. This dichotomy of views presents a dilemma to officials attempting to gain support for policy proposals. Therefore, it is important that government communicate scientific findings to the public to improve its understanding of environmental risk.[13]

Comparative risk analysis can also be used to select from among alternative control instruments. Used in this context, the approach is often called **risk–risk analysis.** This risk management strategy involves a comparison of the estimated risk probabilities or risk-ranking scores from two or more policy options. For example, the decision maker might compare the relative risks of two different mandates for hazardous waste treatment,

---

[13] U.S. EPA, Science Advisory Board (September 1990), p. 12.

such as land disposal versus incineration, and propose whichever approach is more effective in reducing risk.[14] Implicitly, the objective of a risk–risk strategy is risk minimization, with no explicit consideration allowed for associated costs.

**risk–benefit analysis**
An assessment of risks along with the benefits to society of not regulating that hazard.

**Risk–Benefit Analysis.** An alternative risk management strategy, called **risk–benefit analysis,** simultaneously considers the benefits to society of *not* regulating an environmental hazard along with the level of associated risk. Here, the objective is to maximize the expected benefits *and* simultaneously to minimize the risk. Although it may seem perverse, it is true that the source of some environmental hazards offers benefits to society. Think about gasoline, which during combustion gives off emissions that present a health risk. Nonetheless, gasoline *does* benefit society by fueling motor vehicles. Hence, if the risk manager were to assess only the risks in this case, the solution might be to ban gasoline. Yet, if the risk-reduction strategy were balanced with a consideration of benefits, the risk manager would have to consider how a reduction in gasoline usage would diminish society's well-being.

The use of a risk–benefit strategy is commonly mandated in environmental law. An example is found in the Toxic Substances Control Act (TSCA). This law requires the EPA simultaneously to consider the health and environmental effects, the degree of exposure to the substance, *and* the benefits the substance provides to society in use. A similar mandate is called for in the Federal Insecticide, Fungicide, and Rodenticide Act (FIFRA).[15]

**benefit–cost analysis** A strategy that compares the *MSB* of a risk reduction policy to the associated *MSC*.

**Benefit–Cost Analysis.** President Reagan's Executive Order 12291 is largely responsible for the more intensified use of **benefit–cost analysis** in formulating environmental policy. President Clinton's Executive Order 12866 continues to support this risk management strategy.[16] Benefit–cost analysis can identify an "acceptable" risk level based on the criterion of **allocative efficiency.** For incremental risk reductions, the decision maker would compare the monetized value of social benefits with the associated costs to find the efficient risk level where the *MSB* and *MSC* of risk reduction are equal. Equivalently, this corresponds to the risk level that maximizes the difference between *TSB* and *TSC*.

Often, environmental law establishes the risk reduction to be achieved, which means that the level of associated benefits has been predetermined. In such cases, the risk manager can still use benefit–cost analysis but with a different objective in mind. Here, the goal would be to select a policy

---

[14]U.S. Congress, Office of Technology Assessment (OTA) (1983), pp. 226–27.

[15]*EPA Journal* (January/February/March 1993), p. 15. We will have much more to say about TSCA and FIFRA in later chapters.

[16]To access President Clinton's Executive Order 12866, the appropriate website is **www.npr.gov/library/ direct/orders/2646.html.**

instrument that meets the legislated risk objective at least cost. If the selection is made properly, the initiative will achieve the economic goal of **cost-effectiveness** rather than allocative efficiency.

Finally, benefit–cost analysis can be used in the policy appraisal stage much in the same way it is used to find an "acceptable" risk level. At this stage, allocative efficiency is used to evaluate the effectiveness of an ongoing initiative. In practice, estimates of the *MSB* and *MSC* at the risk level achieved by policy are compared to see if they are equivalent. If not, the risk manager knows that the policy needs to be amended to correct the resource misallocation.

# Conclusions

While most policy decisions are difficult and even controversial, those made in the context of environmental issues are particularly so. Indeed, much of what environmental policy makers struggle with is how to deal objectively and fairly with the risks posed by environmental hazards. Such is the purpose of risk analysis and its two components, risk assessment and risk management.

Scientists provide the data and analysis needed for risk assessment. As a result of their research, public officials gain valuable information about the nature of environmental hazards and the risks of exposure. Armed with a characterization of the risks involved, government can make better and more informed policy decisions. Through risk management strategies, such as comparative risk analysis and benefit–cost analysis, "acceptable" risk levels can be determined and alternative policy instruments can be evaluated objectively using well-defined criteria. Independent of how the "acceptable" risk level is determined, estimates of the social benefits and costs of a policy are useful in evaluating the effectiveness of policy initiatives after they have been adopted into law. These data can guide proposals for legislative amendments that characterize the dynamic process of environmental policy development.

The use of benefit–cost analysis as a decision rule is becoming more prevalent in public policy decision making. While monetizing environmental costs and benefits is an attempt to provide an impartial guideline to the risk manager, the task can be difficult to execute in practice. It also has been the source of some controversy. Think about the dilemma of assigning a dollar value to saving a life or restoring coastal waters. Consequently, economists are continuing to research better methods and more comprehensive data to improve their estimates of benefits and costs. In the next three chapters, we will explore the fundamental steps of benefit–cost analysis and assess the contribution of this risk management strategy to environmental decision making.

# Summary

- Voluntary risks are deliberately assumed at an individual level. Involuntary risks arise from exposure to hazards beyond the control of individuals.

- Environmental risk measures the likelihood that damage will occur due to exposure to an environmental hazard. The hazard is the source of the damage, and exposure refers to the pathways between this source and the affected population or resource.

- Risk assessment is the qualitative and quantitative evaluation of the health or ecological risk posed by an environmental hazard. This can be modeled as a series of four steps: hazard identification; dose–response analysis; exposure analysis; and risk characterization.

- Hazard identification uses scientific data to determine if a causal relationship exists between an environmental agent and adverse health or ecological effects. Several methods are used, including case clusters, bioassays, and epidemiology.

- A dose–response relationship quantitatively shows how a biological organism responds to a toxic substance as exposure changes. An important objective is to identify if there is a threshold level of exposure, the point up to which no response is observed.

- Exposure analysis characterizes the conditions faced by the potentially affected population.

- Risk characterization is a quantitative and qualitative description of expected risk.

- The quantitative component of risk characterization provides a means to gauge the relative magnitude of the risk. Risk might be measured as a probability or as a reference dose (RfD).

- The qualitative component of risk characterization gives context to the numerical measure of risk and includes a description of the hazard, an assessment of exposure, an identification of the data, the scientific and statistical methods used, and any uncertainties in the findings.

- Risk management is concerned with formulating and implementing a policy response to reduce society's risk of a given hazard. Several risk management strategies are used in practice, including comparative risk analysis, risk–benefit analysis, and benefit–cost analysis.

- Comparative risk analysis, known in some contexts as risk–risk analysis, involves an evaluation of relative risk. This can be used to help officials identify which risks are most in need of an official response. It also can be used to select among alternative control instruments.

- Risk–benefit analysis is aimed at maximizing expected benefits *and* minimizing risk simultaneously.

- Benefit–cost analysis evaluates alternative risk levels by comparing the value of the expected gains with the associated costs. If the "acceptable" risk level maximizes the difference between *TSB* and *TSC*, the outcome will be allocatively efficient. If the law establishes the risk level to be achieved, a cost-effective solution can be realized by selecting the least-cost policy instrument that achieves the risk objective.

## Key Concepts

| | |
|---|---|
| risk | threshold |
| voluntary risk | exposure analysis |
| involuntary risk | risk characterization |
| environmental risk | risk management |
| hazard | "acceptable" risk |
| exposure | *de minimis* risk |
| risk assessment | comparative risk analysis |
| hazard identification | risk–benefit analysis |
| dose–response relationship | benefit–cost analysis |

## Review Questions

1. Refer to Tables 7.2 and 7.3 and investigate how the public's perception of the risk of indoor pollution compares with the ranking given by the EPA's Science Advisory Board. How is this comparison relevant to the use of comparative risk analysis in communicating the hazards of radon as discussed in Application 7.5? (Or access the radon report directly at **www.epa.gov/iaq/radon/pubs/citguide.html#riskcharts**.)

2. Comment on the following statement: "Without exposure, there is no risk."

3. Other than those mentioned in the chapter, give several real-world examples of how government has provided public information to enhance the identification of a voluntary risk.

4. a. Interpret the shape of the dose–response function in Figure 7.2 (c).
   b. Does this dose–response relationship suggest the presence of a threshold level? If so, where is it? If not, why not?

5. a. Verbally describe what an RfD of 0.002 for some pollutant Z means.
   b. Graphically sketch a dose–response function for pollutant Z, assuming that the dose–response relationship increases at a decreasing rate throughout. Label the RfD on your diagram.

6. Suppose you are using risk–benefit analysis to evaluate a policy aimed at limiting the use of a pesticide applied to grain crops. Describe the risks and benefits that would have to be estimated to conduct this analysis properly.

## Additional Readings

Ahearne, John F. "Integrating Risk Analysis into Public Policymaking." *Environment* 35(2), March 1993, pp. 16–20, 37–39.

Carnegie Commission on Science, Technology, and Government. *Risk and the Environment: Improving Regulatory Decision Making.* New York: Carnegie Commission, June 1993.

Chess, Caron, and Billie Jo Hance. "Opening Doors: Making Risk Communication Agency Reality." *Environment* 31(5), June 1989, pp. 11–15, 38–39.

Davies, Terry. "Congress Discovers Risk Analysis." *Resources,* Winter 1995, pp. 5–8.

Hattis, Dale. "Drawing the Line: Quantitative Criteria for Risk Management." *Environment* 38(6), July/August 1996, pp. 10–15, 35–39.

Johnson, F. Reed, Ann Fisher, V. Kerry Smith, and William H. Desvouges. "Informed Choice or Regulated Risk? Lessons from a Study in Radon Risk Communication." *Environment* 30(4), May 1988, pp. 13–15, 30–35.

Manes, Christopher. *Green Rage.* Boston: Little, Brown, 1990.

Smith, Kirk R. "Air Pollution: Assessing Total Exposure in the United States." *Environment* 30(8), October 1988, pp. 10–15, 33–38.

## Related Web Sites

EPA's Consumer Labeling Initiative (CLI)

**www.epa.gov/opptintr/labeling/**

Integrated Risk Information System (IRIS)

**www.epa.gov/ngispgm3/iris/intro.htm**

On-line version of EPA's *A Citizen's Guide to Radon: The Guide to Protecting Yourself and Your Family from Radon.* May 1992

**www.epa.gov/iaq/radon/pubs/citguide.html**

On-line version of EPA's *Proposed Guidelines for Ecological Risk Assessment.* August 1996

**www.epa.gov/ORD/WebPubs/ecorisk/guide.pdf**

President Clinton's Executive Order 12866

**www.npr.gov/library/direct/orders/2646.html**

Risk Assessments for Toxic Air Pollutants

**www.epa.gov/oar/oaqps/air_risc/3_90_024.html**

# 8

# *Assessing Benefits for Environmental Decision Making*

Risk assessment and risk management are central to the decision-making process that guides environmental policy. Once the degree of environmental risk has been identified, public officials begin the critical task of formulating policy. Ultimately, the objective is to minimize risk, which represents a benefit to society. But meeting this objective is not an unconstrained decision. There are opportunity costs. Public officials must consider that resources used to reduce smog are no longer available to clean the Great Lakes or to save the California condor or to improve public education. How do policy makers come to grips with such tough decisions? There is no simple answer, and in fact, most would argue that the public sector wrestles with this problem on an ongoing basis. Yet there are decision-making strategies that can be effective in environmental policy development—among them, benefit–cost analysis.

Benefit–cost analysis underlies much of economic theory. For example, the balancing of revenues and costs at the margin to maximize profit is an application of benefit–cost analysis. In the broader context of policy decisions, benefit–cost analysis is used to evaluate the associated gains and losses to society as a whole. In every case, the basic principle is the same—an efficient solution results if benefits and costs are balanced at the margin.

Having said this, it should be apparent that the theoretical footing of benefit–cost analysis is sound. However, applying this theory in practice is not so clear-cut. In order to use benefit–cost analysis to guide environmental decisions, the associated social benefits and costs have to be *quantified.* Yet there are many intangibles involved that are difficult to measure in monetary terms, such as longevity of human life, improved aesthetics, and the preservation of ecosystems. Although the process is difficult, it is critically important. Governments everywhere are spending huge sums to develop and implement environmental policy. In the United States alone, the annual expenditure is about $120 billion. Such large appropriations cannot be made without understanding the economic implications on both sides of the ledger. Hence there is no debate that policy makers need reliable measures of social benefits and costs to help guide these important decisions.

In this chapter, we explore the motivation for valuing environmental benefits and the methods used to measure them. We start by presenting the conceptual issues of how and why society values natural resources and environmental quality. This theoretical framework supports our subsequent investigation of various benefit estimation methods. Once this side of the analysis is complete, we conduct an analogous study of costs in Chapter 9. All of this lays the groundwork for studying how the two elements come together in a benefit–cost analysis—the subject of Chapter 10.

# Identifying and Valuing Environmental Benefits: Conceptual Issues

As a starting point, we need to establish the appropriate level of analysis for assessing policy-induced environmental benefits. From previous chapters, we know that these health and ecological gains can be assessed as damage reductions. The key is to recognize that the relevant measure is the *change* in damage reductions brought about by policy. In practice, these changes are called **incremental benefits.**

**incremental benefits**
The reduction in health, ecological, and property damages associated with an environmental policy initiative.

*How damages change w/ policy.*

## *Defining Incremental Benefits*

To assess the social benefits attributable to environmental policy, decision makers must find out how health, ecological, and property damages *change* as a consequence of that policy. This focus on the *change* in damages instead of their absolute level is not new. Economic theory is concerned with effects that occur *at the margin.* These too are changes, though they are infinitesimal—measured *at a point.* When the relevant change is over a discrete range, it is referred to as **incremental** rather than **marginal.** Since policy evaluation is concerned with identifying damage reductions over some discrete time period, the appropriate measure of benefits is incremental.

To identify incremental benefits, the analyst must compare the actual or expected benefits to society *after* some policy is implemented to a baseline measure of *current* conditions. Environmental benefits are commonly separated into categories, such as improvements in human health, aesthetics, the economy, recreation, property, and the ecology. Application 8.1 discusses how incremental benefits were estimated to support an important revision in U.S. air quality standards for particulate matter.

APPLICATION 8.1

# Incremental Benefit Estimates for Revising U.S. Particulate Matter Standards

During 1983, the EPA prepared a Regulatory Impact Analysis (RIA)* for a proposal to tighten the air quality standard for particulate matter. Particulate matter (PM) refers to a broad class of contaminants that are emitted into the air as small particles. As part of the requirements of the RIA, the EPA had to estimate the incremental benefits of this proposal.

Relying on the findings of scientific studies, the EPA determined that exposure to PM is linked to such health problems as respiratory and cardiovascular disease. The agency further found that the associated welfare effects include: (1) soiling of buildings and materials; (2) increased acidic deposition through releases of sulfate particles; and (3) visibility impairment. Using this qualitative assessment as a basis, the EPA had to estimate to what extent these damages would be reduced by the proposed change in the PM standard and then monetize its findings.

To illustrate the inherent variability in quantifying environmental benefits, the table below presents the series of benefit estimates actually used in the EPA's evaluation. For each benefit class, the letters A through F indicate the various procedures used to derive the estimates.

**Incremental Benefit Estimates by Aggregation Procedure (billions of 1980 dollars)**

| Benefit Class | Procedure | | | | | |
| --- | --- | --- | --- | --- | --- | --- |
| | **A** | **B** | **C** | **D** | **E** | **F** |
| Mortality | 1.12 | 1.12 | 1.12 | 12.72 | 12.72 | 13.84 |
| Acute morbidity | 0.00 | 1.32 | 10.65 | 10.65 | 10.65 | 11.97 |
| Chronic morbidity | 0.12 | 0.12 | 0.12 | 0.12 | 11.40 | 11.40 |
| Soiling and materials (household sector) | 0.00 | 0.00 | 0.73 | 0.73 | 3.14 | 13.85 |
| Soiling and materials (manufacturing sector) | 0.00 | 0.00 | 0.00 | 0.00 | 1.30 | 1.30 |
| Total incremental benefits | 1.24 | 2.56 | 12.63 | 24.24 | 39.22 | 52.36 |

Procedure A is the most conservative, since its total of $1.24 billion includes only the benefits of reduced mortality and chronic illness. At the other end of the spectrum, Procedure F is the most comprehensive. It includes *all* expected health and welfare benefits—the reductions in mortality and morbidity plus the reduced soiling and material damages. According to this latter approach, the incremental benefits of tightening the PM standard are valued at $52.36 billion.

Beyond the differences in aggregation across the six procedures, there is also variability in how the individual benefit categories are valued. For example, according to Procedures A through C, mortality benefits are monetized at $1.12 billion, but Procedures D and E place a value on this same category of $12.72 billion, and Procedure F an even higher value of $13.84 billion.

An important inference to be made from these data is that benefit assessment is not an exact science. Rather, it relies on approximations based on a consensus of experts and supported by available scientific evidence. Often, as is the case here, a *range* of benefit estimates is considered, each based on certain underlying assumptions.

*An RIA was required under President Reagan's Executive Order 12291.

SOURCES: Mathtech Inc. *Benefit and Net Benefit Analysis of Alternative National Ambient Air Quality Standards for Particulate Matter, Volume I.* Prepared for U.S. Environmental Protection Agency, Economic Analysis Branch, Office of Air Quality Planning and Standards. Research Triangle Park, NC: U.S. EPA, March 1983, pp. 1–52; U.S. Environmental Protection Agency, Office of Policy Analysis, Office of Policy, Planning, and Evaluation. *EPA's Use of Benefit–Cost Analysis, 1981–1986.* Washington, DC, August 1987.

## Defining Primary and Secondary Environmental Benefits

Within the broad category of incremental benefits are two types of damage-reducing effects, **primary environmental benefits** and **secondary environmental benefits.** A **primary environmental benefit** is a damage-reducing effect that is the *direct* consequence of implementing policy. Compare this with the concept of a **secondary environmental benefit,** which is an *indirect* gain to society associated with the implementation of policy.

**primary environmental benefit** A damage-reducing effect that is a direct consequence of implementing environmental policy.

**Primary Environmental Benefits.** Most environmental policy actions are aimed at increasing primary benefits, particularly those associated with human health. Health benefits include both decreased mortality, such as a reduction in the risk of cancer deaths, and reduced morbidity, such as a lower incidence of respiratory ailments. Other primary benefits include more stable ecosystems and improved aesthetics. Still others are economic, such as a more prosperous fishing industry due to the enactment of clean water regulations. What these benefits have in common is that they are a *direct* outcome of environmental policy.

**secondary environmental benefit** An indirect gain to society that may arise from a stimulative effect of primary benefits or from a demand-induced effect to implement policy.

**Secondary Environmental Benefits.** Secondary environmental benefits arise *indirectly* from a policy change. One source might be the stimulative effect of a primary benefit, such as higher worker productivity that results from the primary benefit of improved health. Higher productivity increases the availability of goods and services, which may lead to a decline in prices. Since these gains are stimulated by a primary benefit and arise indirectly, they are considered secondary benefits. An alternative source is a demand-induced change, such as the increased demand for labor to implement a new policy. In this case, the economic gains of an improved labor market are secondary benefits.[1]

## Conceptually Valuing Environmental Benefits

What is the value to society of cleaner air or water? What value does society place on cleaning up a hazardous waste site? As we've discussed in previous chapters, both questions could be answered directly *if* the commodity in each case were a private good traded in the open market. Then demand prices would convey the marginal benefit of each additional unit of the good. The problem is that environmental quality is a public, nonmarketed good. The absence of prices and the dilemma of nonrevelation of preferences cloud a determination of how society values a cleaner environment. In theory, if we could *infer* society's demand for environmental

---

[1] There is some debate about whether secondary benefits ought to be considered when assessing public policy proposals, since it is argued that these indirect gains in one market or region are offset by losses in another. There is also the practical problem of trying to measure these types of benefits. Hence many researchers exclude them from their analyses. See, for example, Haveman and Weisbrod (1975).

FIGURE 8.1

### MARGINAL SOCIAL BENEFIT (*MSB*) AND TOTAL SOCIAL BENEFITS (*TSB*) OF AIR QUALITY (% SO₂ ABATEMENT)

The market demand curve for $SO_2$ abatement represents the marginal social benefit (*MSB*) of air quality. At the hypothetical level of abatement, $A_1$, the corresponding *MSB* is the vertical distance from the horizontal axis at that point up to the curve. The total social benefits (*TSB*) associated with $A_1$ are shown as the shaded area under the *MSB* up to that point.

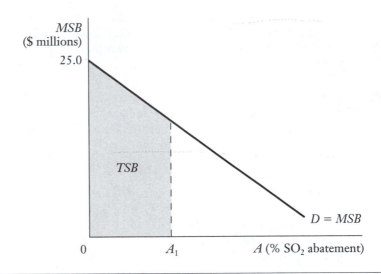

quality, we could then measure the incremental benefits associated with any environmental policy.

To illustrate this assertion, we return to our model of air quality based on $SO_2$ pollution abatement, which we introduced in Chapter 3. Recall that since demand for this public good represents society's decisions, it is both the marginal private benefit (*MPB*) and the marginal social benefit (*MSB*) of air quality. Thus, we can refer to the demand for $SO_2$ abatement as *MSB* $= 25 - 0.3A$, where *MSB* is measured in millions of dollars and $A$ is the percentage of $SO_2$ abated. The graphical model of this relationship is shown in Figure 8.1. At each level of abatement, *MSB* is measured as the vertical distance from the horizontal axis up to the demand curve. The total social benefits (*TSB*) for any abatement level are measured as the aggregation of these vertical distances, or the area under the MSB up to that point.[2] In Figure 8.1, the *TSB* for some hypothetical abatement level, $A_1$, is shown as

---

[2] Recall from Chapter 2 that the area beneath the demand curve and above the market price is consumer surplus, or the *net* benefit enjoyed by consumers. Notice that this net benefit is exactly equal to the total benefits received minus the total dollar value paid for the good. In fact, if a commodity has a zero market price, total benefits would be exactly equal to consumer surplus.

FIGURE 8.2

## MODELING INCREMENTAL SOCIAL BENEFITS FOR AIR QUALITY (% SO$_2$ ABATEMENT) USING THE *MSB* FUNCTION

The *MSB* at the baseline abatement level of 20 percent is $19 million, and *TSB* is the area under the *MSB* up to that point, or $440 million. If a policy were proposed to increase SO$_2$ abatement to 25 percent, *MSB* would be $17.5 million and *TSB* would rise to $531.25 million. Thus, the incremental benefits are measured as the difference between the two *TSB* values, or $91.25 million. In this model, incremental benefits are shown as the shaded area under the *MSB* between the two abatement levels.

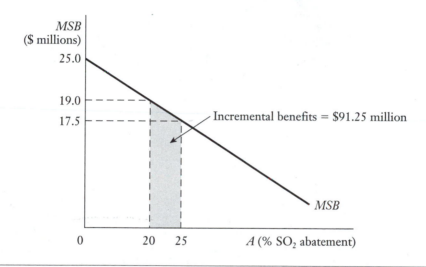

the shaded area under the demand curve up to $A_1$. Using this model, we can measure the incremental benefits from a policy-induced increase in SO$_2$ abatement in three steps:

1. Find the baseline level of *TSB* *before* the policy is undertaken.

2. Find the new level of *TSB* that would arise *after* the policy is implemented.

3. Subtract the baseline *TSB* from the post-policy *TSB* to determine incremental benefits.

Suppose that the current level of SO$_2$ abatement is 20 percent, and the objective is to find the incremental benefits of a policy that increases abatement to 25 percent. First, find the baseline *TSB*. Referring to Figure 8.2, notice that *MSB* at the 20 percent abatement level is $19 million. *TSB* at this level is the area under the *MSB* up to that point or $440 million. This dollar value represents society's **willingness to pay (WTP)** for the

---

| FIGURE 8.3 | MODELING INCREMENTAL SOCIAL BENEFITS FOR AIR QUALITY (% $SO_2$ ABATEMENT) USING THE *TSB* FUNCTION |

An alternative way to model the incremental benefits of improving air quality is to graph the relationship between *TSB* and $SO_2$ abatement. At each abatement level, *TSB* is the vertical distance from the horizontal axis up to the curve. The model shows the *TSB* for the 20 percent baseline abatement level and for the 25 percent post-policy abatement level as $440 million and $531.25 million, respectively. The incremental benefits are shown as the vertical distance between the two points on the *TSB* curve, or $91.25 million.

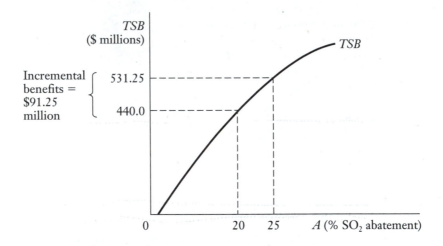

---

benefits achieved when 20 percent of $SO_2$ emissions are abated. Next, do the analogous calculations for the proposed abatement increase to 25 percent. At this post-policy abatement level, *MSB* is $17.5 million and *TSB* is $531.25 million. Finally, the incremental benefits are found as the difference between the two *TSB* values or $91.25 million. This is shown as the shaded area in Figure 8.2.

An alternative model of the same result is shown in Figure 8.3 where *TSB* is graphed directly with $SO_2$ abatement. In this model, the *TSB* associated with a given abatement level is measured simply as the vertical distance up to the curve and not as an area. Identify on the graph the pre- and post-policy levels of *TSB* corresponding to the 20 and 25 percent abatement levels. Notice that the incremental benefits of $91.25 million are measured as the vertical distance between these two *TSB* levels.

Both models assume that society's valuation of environmental quality, or equivalently its demand for pollution abatement, can be identified. However, since there is no explicit market for this commodity, the valuation cannot be obtained from observing market-determined prices. Instead, inferences must be made about *how* society derives value or utility from various levels of environmental quality.

### User versus Existence Value[3]

Discovering how society values a good is difficult in the absence of market prices. Even if the dilemma of nonrevelation of preferences could be overcome, the value of a good like clean air or water is difficult to quantify because of the many intangibles involved. While economists recognize that some of these intangibles are immeasurable, they still need some sense of how the benefits of environmental quality are *perceived* by society. Fortunately, theories have been advanced that can help.

From a purely conceptual vantage point, it is generally recognized that society derives utility from environmental quality through two sources of value: **user value** and **existence value.** User value refers to the utility or benefit received from usage of or access to an environmental good. In contrast, **existence value** is the utility or benefit received from an environmental good simply through its continuance as a good or service. Collectively, these components measure society's total valuation of an environmental good, expressed as follows:

> **user value** Benefit derived from physical use or access to an environmental good.

> **existence value** Benefit received from the continuance of an environmental good.

Total value of environmental quality = User value + Existence value.

**User value.**   Consider the benefits of using a lake. If an individual swims in a lake, that person is deriving utility by physically using the natural resource. Likewise, a commercial fishing fleet derives user benefit from catching fish from the lake. In both cases, benefits are derived from directly consuming services provided by the resource. These activities, both recreational and commercial, generate benefits that yield **direct user value.** This valuation helps to determine what the individual or the fishing fleet would be willing to pay to maintain or improve the lake's quality.

> **direct user value** Benefit derived from directly consuming services provided by an environmental good.

Continuing with the same example, another individual might receive utility from simply looking at a view of the lake. Here, the utility is derived from the lake's aesthetic qualities. This type of activity involves using the lake in a less immediate way than swimming in it or fishing from it. Hence, it is said to yield **indirect user value.** Both direct and indirect user value are elements of society's total valuation of environmental quality.[4]

> **indirect user value** Benefit derived from indirect consumption of an environmental good.

**Existence value.**   Society also receives benefits from environmental goods beyond the utility associated with direct or indirect use. Think about

---

[3] Much of the following is drawn from Mitchell and Carson (1989), Chapter 3.

[4] While these examples involve present period consumption, economists also have begun to examine how society expects to benefit from consumption in some future period. This valuation concept, which adds uncertainty to benefit assessment, is referred to as option value. For detail on this concept, see Mitchell and Carson (1989), Chapter 3; and Johansson (1991).

APPLICATION 8.2

## The Endangered Species Act

In 1973, the Endangered Species Act was passed by Congress to "*. . . provide a means whereby the eco-systems upon which endangered species and threatened species depend may be conserved.*" Officially, the act protects the biodiversity of the earth—the diversity of genes, species, ecosystems, and the interaction among them. An important outcome of this act was the creation of a formal list of biological organisms in danger of extinction, *regardless of their direct or indirect use to humans.* Originally numbering 109 in 1973, the list of endangered and threatened species in the United States includes nearly 1,100 species as of 1997.

When the Endangered Species Act was originally proposed and through its subsequent reauthorizations, arguments have been made to justify its passage on economic grounds. One was that species were to be protected because they may serve a direct benefit to mankind that scientific study had not yet discovered. Some justification for this argument is found in the recent discovery that a compound called taxol found in the bark of Pacific yew trees holds promise for the treatment of certain cancers. Approximately 60 pounds of yew bark are needed to produce enough taxol to treat one cancer patient, and the Pacific yew is a slow-growing species being harvested by timber companies at a rapid rate. Notice that this discourse focuses on the **user value** of environmental resources.

Just as strong in their position were those who asserted that environmental resources offer benefits that span a much broader range than their direct or indirect value in human consumption. Here the premise is that species should be protected based on a presumed right of survival—evidence of the role of **existence value** in benefit assessment.

There is not now, nor is there likely to be, a consensus about whether user value is relevant to the benefit assessment of biodiversity. What *is* clear is that society recognizes and appreciates existence value—an issue that continues to emerge in the ongoing deliberation about biodiversity and economic development.

SOURCES: Jerry Adler and Mary Hager. "How Much Is a Species Worth?" *National Wildlife*, April/May 1992, pp. 4–14; Council on Environmental Quality. *Environmental Quality: 23rd Annual Report.* Washington, DC: U.S. Government Printing Office, January 1993, pp. 17–28.

how people value such natural resources as the great rain forests, the Grand Canyon, or the bald eagle. Consumption does not explain how or why society values these resources. Yet we know that society as a whole is willing to pay to preserve them. In such circumstances, benefits accrue to society from simply knowing that these resources exist and are being preserved. This component of total valuation is referred to as **existence value.**

While seemingly abstract, existence value is an important motivation for privately funded conservation efforts and for many environmental policy initiatives. A case in point is the Endangered Species Act, which provides for the protection and preservation of certain animals, birds, fish, and plants threatened by extinction.[5] As discussed in Application 8.2, this act is

[5] To view the text of the Endangered Species Act and to research information on endangered species, visit the U.S. Fish and Wildlife Service's endangered species home page at **www.fws.gov/r9endspp/endspp. html**.

an example of the U.S. government's recognition of existence value. Other tangible evidence is the willingness of society to support the work of environmental groups, such as the National Wildlife Federation, the Sierra Club, and the National Audubon Society—groups whose agendas focus on preserving resources that many of their benefactors never expect to use or even see firsthand.

One of the earlier discussions of existence value is presented by Krutilla (1967), who asserts:

> "When the existence of a grand scenic wonder or a unique and fragile ecosystem is involved, its preservation and continued availability are a significant part of the real income of many individuals."[6]

Since this early work, economists have been studying various theories about the motivations for existence value. In a text about valuing public goods, Mitchell and Carson (1989) classify the motives for existence value as **vicarious consumption** and **stewardship,** among others.

**vicarious consumption** The utility associated with knowing that others derive benefits from an environmental good.

Vicarious consumption refers to the notion that individuals value a public good for the benefit it provides to others whether or not these "others" are known personally. This suggests that the utility derived is *interdependent*—that an individual can and does receive benefit from the knowledge that others are enjoying the public good. **Stewardship** arises both from a sense of obligation to preserve the environment for future generations *and* from the recognition of the intrinsic value of natural resources. In sum, we can express the total valuation of environmental quality as:

**stewardship** The sense of obligation to preserve the environment for future generations.

$$\text{Total value} = \quad \text{User value} \quad + \quad \text{Existence value}$$
$$= (\text{direct and indirect} + (\text{vicarious consumption}$$
$$\text{user value}) \qquad \text{and stewardship value})$$

Recognizing how society values an environmental resource is important for identifying the social benefits of a policy proposal. It also helps economists decide which estimation method might be most effective in quantifying those benefits. Yet the question remains—how do economists assign dollar values to nonmarketed environmental goods like clean water, human health, and the spotted owl? Remember that the objective is to *monetize* or find the **WTP** for changes in user and existence value arising from a policy-driven increase in environmental quality.

---

[6]Krutilla attributes the birth of conservation economics to A. C. Pigou, an English economist who wrote: ". . . it is the clear duty of government, which is the trustee for unborn generations as well as for its present citizens, to watch over, and if need be, by legislative enactment, to defend, the exhaustible natural resources of the country from rash and reckless spoliation" (Pigou, 1952).

## Approaches to Measuring Environmental Benefits: An Overview[7]

Economists have made great strides in developing methods to estimate the benefit of environmental quality improvements. For the most part, these methods are aimed at estimating primary benefits, implicitly assuming that secondary benefits are insignificant—likely offset by secondary costs. A review of the extensive literature on the subject shows that several methods are used in practice. Some are better than others at quantifying the more intangible benefits of improved environmental quality, including the somewhat elusive concept of existence value.

To organize our discussion of benefit measurement methods, we rely on a general classification introduced by Smith and Krutilla (1982), which places the various measurement techniques into two broad categories—the **physical linkage approach** and the **behavioral linkage approach.** A summary of selected benefit valuation methods within each approach is presented in Table 8.1.

### *Physical Linkage Approach to Environmental Benefit Valuation*

**physical linkage approach** Estimates benefits based on a technical relationship between an environmental resource and the user of that resource.

Methods within the physical linkage category use some tangible attribute of the environment to make a connection to the individual through which benefits can be observed or inferred and subsequently valued. More formally, the **physical linkage approach** measures benefits based on a technical relationship between the environmental resource and the user of that resource. A common estimation procedure that uses this approach is the **damage function method.** This method uses a functional relationship to capture the link between a contaminant and the associated damages. Based on this function, incremental benefits are measured as the reduction in damages due to a policy-induced decrease in the contaminant. This damage reduction is then monetized to obtain a dollar value of the benefits brought about by the policy.

### *Behavioral Linkage Approach to Environmental Benefit Valuation*

**behavioral linkage approach** Estimates benefits using observations of behavior in actual markets or survey responses about hypothetical markets.

In general, the **behavioral linkage approach** to quantifying benefits is based on observations of behavior in *actual* markets or survey responses about *hypothetical* markets for environmental goods. Another element of behavioral linkage methods deals with how closely the behavior or responses are linked to the environmental good. Techniques that assess responses immediately related to environmental changes are broadly termed **direct methods.** As shown in Table 8.1, two types of direct methods are the **political referendum method,** which relies on *actual* market information,

---

[7]This section is drawn mainly from Mitchell and Carson (1989), particularly pp. 74–78, and Cropper and Oates (1992).

| TABLE 8.1 | A SYNOPSIS OF BENEFIT ESTIMATION METHODS |
|---|---|

**The Physical Linkage Approach**

| | |
|---|---|
| Damage Function Method | Uses a model of the relationship between levels of a contaminant and observed (or statistically inferred) environmental damage to estimate the damage reduction arising from a policy-induced decline in the contaminant. |

**The Behavioral Linkage Approach**

**Direct Methods**

| | |
|---|---|
| Political Referendum Method | Uses the *actual* market of a public good by monitoring voting results from political referenda on proposed changes in environmental quality. |
| Contingent Valuation Method (CVM) | Employs surveys to inquire about individuals' willingness to pay (WTP) for environmental improvements based on *hypothetical* market conditions. |

**Indirect Methods**

| | |
|---|---|
| Averting Expenditure Method (AEM) | Assesses changes in an individual's spending on goods and services that are *substitutes* for personal environmental quality to assign value to changes in the overall environment. |
| Travel Cost Method (TCM) | Values a change in the quality of an environmental resource by assessing the effect of that change on the demand for a *complementary* good. |
| Hedonic Price Method (HPM) | Uses the theory that a good is valued for the attributes it possesses to estimate the implicit or hedonic price of an environmental attribute and identify its demand as a means to assign value to policy-driven improvements in quality. |

and the **contingent valuation method (CVM),** which uses *hypothetical* market data. **Indirect methods** are those that examine responses, not about the environmental good itself, but about some set of market conditions related to it. Three examples of indirect benefit estimation methods are the **averting expenditure method (AEM),** the **travel cost method (TCM),** and the **hedonic price method (HPM).**

The published literature on benefit valuation methods is extensive. Many research papers present specific empirical findings, and numerous texts focus on the methodology itself. We offer only an overview of the operational issues associated with the more common methods used by researchers.[8]

---

[8]To study any of these methods in detail, consult the references cited along the way and the list of additional readings given at the end of the chapter.

# Estimation under the Physical Linkage Approach

## *The Damage Function Method*

**damage function method** Models the relationship between a contaminant and its observed effects as a way to estimate damage reductions arising from policy.

When using the **damage function method,** the researcher specifies a model of the relationship between an environmental contaminant and some type of observed damage.[9] A generalized damage function is shown in Figure 8.4. The levels of some environmental contaminant ($C$) are measured horizontally, and the total damages ($TD$) due to exposure to that contaminant are measured vertically.[10] Once the function is specified, the analyst uses the model to estimate the damage reduction from any policy-induced decline in the contaminant. At this point, the reduction is measured in nonmonetary units—it might be the number of acidified lakes, acres of damaged forests, or number of premature deaths. Ultimately, this reduction must be assigned a monetary value, either by using market prices if available or by employing some estimation technique.

To illustrate the procedure, look at Figure 8.4 and assume that a policy initiative is expected to reduce the contaminant from $C_0$ to $C_1$. Based on the damage function model, this proposal would reduce damage (or equivalently, increase benefits), by the vertical distance between $TD_0$ and $TD_1$. If, for example, the damage reduction was diminished injury to wheat crops, this vertical distance might be measured as thousands of bushels of wheat. Having quantified the incremental benefit, a simple way to monetize it would be to multiply the number of bushels by the market-determined price.

**Assessing the Damage Function Method.** Although the damage function method is useful, it has limitations. First, by construction it estimates only one aspect of incremental benefits. In our example, the measured benefits are increased wheat crops. In most cases, a contaminant reduction would give rise to other types of gains, perhaps increases in other crops or improvements in human health. Hence, a full assessment of benefits, using the damage function approach, would require that the same estimating procedure be performed for *every* type of damage reduction. Second, the procedure is only a first-step approach in that it is not capable of simultaneously monetizing the benefits it quantifies.

**Applications of the Damage Function Method.** Recognizing the limitations of the damage function method, analysts typically use it for measuring a *specific* type of incremental benefit as opposed to performing a

---

[9] If the benefit assessment is the reduction in adverse effects to a *biological organism*, the analyst would use a **dose–response function,** which is a particular type of damage function. Recall from Chapter 7 that scientists use dose–response functions in the risk assessment process.

[10] The model shown is a cubic relationship, but this is just one possible functional form for a damage function. For more on this issue, see, for example, Halvorsen and Ruby (1981), p. 106.

| FIGURE 8.4 | **MEASURING INCREMENTAL BENEFITS USING THE DAMAGE FUNCTION METHOD: A PHYSICAL LINKAGE APPROACH** |

A damage function shows the relationship between an environmental contaminant ($C$) and the total damages ($TD$) due to exposure to that contaminant. Once the function is specified, the analyst can use it to estimate the damage reduction from any policy-induced decline in the contaminant. This damage reduction represents incremental benefits measured in nonmonetary units.

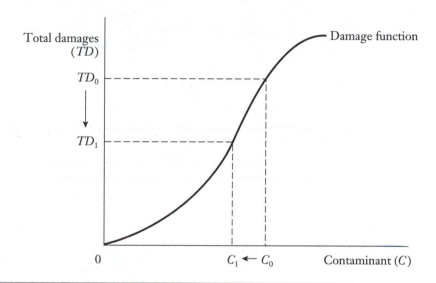

comprehensive benefit assessment. Furthermore, the context is often one where market-determined prices can be used to monetize the gain.

To illustrate, consider a benefit assessment of the Clean Air Act provisions aimed at reducing ozone in the lower atmosphere or troposphere. According to scientific evidence, one type of benefit associated with reducing tropospheric ozone is an increase in crop yields.[11] Conceptually, these agricultural benefits could be modeled by measuring the change in consumer and producer surpluses associated with an increase in crop yields. Figure 8.5 models this policy-induced effect as an increase in crop supply from $S_0$ to $S_1$, which in turn causes a price decline from $P_0$ to $P_1$.

Consider first the size of the surpluses prior to any policy change, using supply curve, $S_0$. Consumer surplus is the area below the demand curve and above the market price, or area $P_0ab$. Producer surplus is the area

---

[11] The interested reader may wish to consult Kopp and Krupnick (1987) for results of an empirical investigation that estimates the agricultural benefits of ozone reduction.

## MODELING INCREMENTAL BENEFITS
## OF AN OZONE-REDUCING POLICY

The increase in crop yields associated with a hypothetical ozone-reducing policy can be modeled as a shift in crop supply from $S_0$ to $S_1$. Prior to the policy, consumer surplus is area $P_0ab$, and producer surplus is area $P_0be$, for a total of area $eab$. After the policy is implemented and supply shifts to $S_1$, consumer surplus becomes area $P_1ac$, and producer surplus becomes area $P_1ce$, for a total of area $eac$. Thus, the incremental benefit is area $ebc$ (i.e., $eac - eab$). Consumers definitely gain, since consumer surplus rises from $P_0ab$ to $P_1ac$. Producers lose area $P_0bfP_1$, which is transferred to consumers, but they also gain area $efc$. Whether or not the gain of $efc$ exceeds the transfer of $P_0bfP_1$ depends on the shapes of the supply and demand curves and the magnitude of the supply shift.

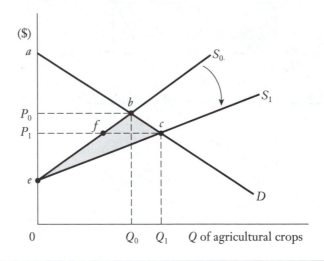

above the supply curve and below the market price, or area $P_0be$. Thus the total surplus *prior* to a policy change is area $eab$. After the ozone-reducing policy is implemented and supply shifts to $S_1$, consumer surplus becomes area $P_1ac$, and producer surplus becomes area $P_1ce$. Thus the total surplus *after* the policy change is area $eac$. The operative question is whether society is better off as a result. Since the total surplus increased from $eab$ to $eac$, the answer is yes, and the incremental benefit can be quantified as area $ebc$ (i.e., $eac - eab$).

Notice, however, that the *distribution* of benefits is not as easily determined. Consumers definitely gain, since consumer surplus rises from $P_0ab$ to $P_1ac$. But the same assertion cannot be made about producers. Some of the original producer surplus, area $P_0bfP_1$, has been transferred to consumers, but there is also a gain to producers of area $efc$. Whether or not the

## Valuing Agricultural Benefits: The Case of Tropospheric Ozone Reductions

The National Acid Precipitation Assessment Program (NAPAP) was launched as an investigative plan to gather information for formulating policy on acidic deposition. According to NAPAP's 1990 report, scientific research has been unable to find a consistent adverse effect on crop yields caused by acidic deposition. However, there *is* well-documented evidence that elevated levels of tropospheric ozone can diminish crop yields. In fact, estimates of this damage range from 2 to 56 percent, depending on such factors as crop species, location, and exposure levels. Thus a key part of NAPAP's research dealt with quantifying the incremental benefits that would result from an ozone-reducing policy initiative.

Modeling techniques to measure environmental benefits were employed in the NAPAP study of ozone's effects on agricultural yields. The final report presents the following estimates of changes in consumer and producer surplus for alternative ozone policies:

| Changes in Ozone (%) | Change in Surplus (billions of 1989 dollars) | | |
| --- | --- | --- | --- |
| | Consumer Surplus | Producer Surplus | Total Surplus |
| −10 | 0.785 | −0.046 | 0.739 |
| −25 | 1.637 | 0.095 | 1.732 |
| +10 | −1.044 | 0.215 | −0.829 |
| +25 | −2.659 | 0.453 | −2.206 |

SOURCE: NAPAP (November 1991), Table 4.9-6, p. 401.

Under the first scenario, a 10-percent reduction in ozone concentrations is estimated to increase total surplus by approximately $739 million. Of this amount, consumer surplus would increase by $785 million, while producer surplus is expected to decline by $46 million. Conversely, a more restrictive ozone policy, such as a 25-percent reduction, would increase the benefits to both producers and consumers and elevate the change in total surplus to $1,732 million. These findings have important implications about the distribution of these incremental benefits across buyers and sellers. Notice that consumers and producers do not respond symmetrically to increases in ozone levels. In fact, if ozone levels were to *increase* either by 10 or 25 percent, society as a whole would lose, but producers would actually benefit. According to the NAPAP report, this gain to producers arises because of farmers' ability to pass on the higher costs of depleted supplies to consumers in the form of higher prices.

SOURCE: National Acid Precipitation Assessment Program. *1990 Integrated Assessment Report.* Washington, DC: NAPAP Office of the Director, November 1991, pp. 55, 154–56, 398–401.

gain of *efc* exceeds the transfer of $P_0 bf P_1$ depends on the shapes of the supply and demand curves and the magnitude of the shift in supply. Consequently, to measure the incremental benefits of policy *and* to determine the distribution of these benefits, sophisticated models must be used. Application 8.3 presents the actual results of such a benefit estimation conducted as part of a U.S. air quality assessment.

# Direct Estimation Methods under the Behavioral Linkage Approach

The so-called **direct methods** under the behavioral linkage approach estimate environmental benefits according to responses or observed behaviors directly tied to environmental quality. Although there are a number of direct methods available to researchers, we consider only one representative example—the **contingent valuation method (CVM).**

## *The Contingent Valuation Method (CVM)*

**contingent valuation method (CVM)** Uses surveys to elicit responses about *WTP* for environmental quality based on hypothetical market conditions.

When market data are unavailable or unreliable, economists can use alternative estimation methods that rely on *hypothetical* market conditions. Such methods typically use surveys to inquire about individuals' willingness to pay (WTP) for some environmental initiative. This survey approach to benefit estimation is known as the **contingent valuation method (CVM)** because the results are dependent or *contingent* upon the hypothetical market devised. This market serves as the context for a series of survey questions. The critical assumption is that properly designed surveys can elicit responses comparable to those arising under actual situations. In some sense, the survey instrument helps to finesse the problem of nonrevelation of preferences that characterizes public goods.

Implementing this survey approach involves the following three tasks:[12]

 The construction of a detailed model of the hypothetical market, including the characteristics of the good and any conditions that affect the market.

2. The design of a survey instrument to obtain an unbiased estimate of individuals' WTP.

3. An assessment of the truthfulness of survey respondents' answers.

**Assessing the CVM.** The CVM is favored by researchers because of its applicability to a variety of environmental goods and its capacity to assess existence value as well as user value. However, because this approach makes inferences about actual markets from a hypothetical model, it is subject to the biases that typically plague a survey-dependent study. Table 8.2 lists common sources of bias associated with the CVM.

Responding to the potential bias, economists continue to make improvements to the CVM. For instance, some researchers are adding more detail to their hypothetical models. Others have improved the design of the

---

[12] For more detail on the specific elements of a CVM analysis, the interested student is referred to Mitchell and Carson (1989); Cummings, Brookshire, and Schultz (1986); and Smith and Desvousges (1986).

| TABLE 8.2 | CLASSIFICATION OF BIASES ENCOUNTERED IN CONTINGENT VALUATION STUDIES |
|---|---|

### General Biases

| | |
|---|---|
| Strategic: | An individual may have an incentive *not* to reveal his or her true preferences about an environmental good when responding to questions about willingness to pay (WTP). This bias may arise from the free-ridership problem typically associated with public goods. |
| Information: | If there is insufficient information about the commodity being valued, the individual's WTP response may not be equivalent to their actual WTP. |
| Hypothetical: | Because the market is hypothetical, the respondent may view the questions as unrealistic, and respond with an equally unrealistic estimate of WTP. |

### Survey Instrument-Related Biases

| | |
|---|---|
| Starting point: | Some survey instruments use predefined ranges of values to guide responses. The starting points of these ranges can influence the respondent's answers about WTP. |
| Payment vehicle: | To make the responses more factual, the survey questions about value are often tied to a specific payment vehicle, such as an increase in taxes or an adjustment on a utility bill. The selection of the payment vehicle used in the survey may influence how an individual responds to questions about WTP. |

### Procedural Biases

| | |
|---|---|
| Sampling: | Problems may arise due to the specific sampling procedure used by the researcher. |
| Interviewer: | The respondent's answers may be influenced by the individual asking the questions. |

SOURCE: Adapted from: V. Kerry Smith and William H. Desvousges. *Measuring Water Quality Benefits.* Norwell, MA: Kluwer-Nijhoff Publishing, 1986, Figure 4-1, p. 73.

survey instrument. Some surveys include maps to illustrate the location of the good or photographs of the commodity and the area affected by its provision.[13] Whatever the form, the objective is the same—to make the hypothetical market situation as factual and as close to actual conditions as possible.

**Applications of the CVM.**   Researchers have used the CVM in a variety of contexts to estimate environmental benefits. An important application is in estimating the value of a statistical human life.[14] In a recent review of

[13] Brookshire and Crocker (1981).

[14] A statistical life saved is related to the concept of environmental risk introduced in Chapter 7. For example, if an environmental policy lowers the risk of death from 2 in 100,000 persons exposed to 1 in 100,000 exposed, the incremental benefit of that policy is one human life saved.

these findings, these estimates were reported as falling within a range of $1.6 million to $4.0 million ($1986).[15]

Another common focus of CVM studies is to measure society's WTP for water quality improvements. Two examples are a study by Smith and Desvousges (1986), which examines a specific water body—the Mononga-hela River in Pennsylvania—and an analysis by Carson and Mitchell (1988), which estimates a generalized measure across all U.S. water sites. The study by Smith and Desvousges finds that the average household in five western Pennsylvania counties is willing to pay $25 ($1981) per year to improve the Monongahela River from boatable to fishable quality. Carson and Mitchell's nationwide survey shows that the average respondent is willing to pay $80 ($1983) per year for water quality improvements. How can the differ-ence be explained? Since the valuation in the national survey is higher than the more localized finding of Smith and Desvousges, the difference may be attributable to existence value. Why? Because the respondents in the more general survey are willing to pay for water quality improvements through-out the United States, even though they do not expect to use those water bodies themselves.[16]

Incremental benefits from air quality improvements also have been es-timated using CVM. In fact, some argue that the CVM is particularly use-ful for valuing visibility improvements at national parks, where existence value is likely to be significant. One study by Schulze and Brookshire (1983) seems to support this hypothesis. These researchers find that the *user value* of improving visibility at the Grand Canyon from 70 to 100 miles is under $2 ($1988) per visitor per day. In contrast, they estimate the comparable *ex-istence value* at $95 ($1988) per household per year to prevent diminished visibility at the Grand Canyon.[17]

Because the CVM is capable of capturing existence value, it has been used to value ecological benefits, such as preserving an endangered species. For example, one study estimates that individuals would be willing to pay $22 ($1983) per year to save the whooping crane.[18] Another finds that people would pay $11 per year to preserve the bald eagle.[19] There is, how-ever, an important caveat. While the value of preserving an entire ecosys-tem is typically what is of interest in policy analysis, many CVM studies focus on a single species. Yet the sum of species-specific valuations is gen-erally lower than the valuation of an entire area.[20]

---

[15] Cropper and Oates (1992), p. 713.

[16] Cropper and Oates (1992), pp. 716–17.

[17] Notice that for user value the WTP is appropriately given on a *per visitor* basis, while the existence value is quoted for *households* who may never visit the site.

[18] Bowker and Stoll (1988).

[19] Boyle and Bishop (1987).

[20] Cropper and Oates (1992), pp. 719–20.

# Indirect Estimation Methods under the Behavioral Linkage Approach

For some environmental proposals, direct estimation procedures like the CVM might not be viable. In these cases, economists use **indirect methods,** which make inferences about markets or conditions that are linked to the environmental good under investigation. Three such methods dominate the literature: the **averting expenditure method (AEM);** the **travel cost method (TCM);** and the **hedonic price method (HPM).**

## *Averting Expenditure Method (AEM): An Indirect Approach Using Substitutes*

**averting expenditure method (AEM)** Estimates benefits as the change in spending on goods that are *substitutes* for a cleaner environment.

To indirectly estimate the WTP for such nonmarketed commodities as cleaner air or water, the **averting expenditure method (AEM)** uses changes in spending on goods that are *substitutes* for environmental quality. The motivation for this approach is quite intuitive. Exposure to pollution causes damages that negatively affect an individual's utility. Consequently, people undertake "averting" actions by purchasing goods and services that improve their *personal* environmental quality, such as the indoor air or a private drinking water supply.[21]

Table 8.3 gives some common examples of what individuals do to reduce the effects of pollution on their personal environment. Notice that in each case the averting action involves an expenditure on a substitute good or service. Therefore, if the general environment is improved by some policy initiative, the individual can spend *less* on these substitute goods. It is precisely this decline in averting expenditures that gives an *indirect* estimate of the individual's WTP for the associated incremental benefits. For instance, faced with a contaminated drinking water supply, an individual might purchase bottled water or install a water-filtering system. If a government policy improves the public drinking water supply, the individual can spend less on these substitute commodities. This reduction in spending identifies the incremental benefits provided by the drinking water policy.

We model the AEM in Figure 8.6, where the relevant market is defined as *personal* environmental quality ($X$). The demand curve ($d$) is also the marginal benefit ($MB$) function, and each supply ($s$) relationship is modeled as a marginal cost ($MC$) curve.[22] The critical assumption is that each $MC$ curve represents the averting expenditures on environmental quality

---

[21] The reference to an individual's "personal" environment was first used by Bartik (1988) to describe the use of the AEM to value nonmarginal improvements in the environment.

[22] Since we are modeling *personal* environmental quality, the marginal benefits and costs accrue to a single individual. To avoid confusion, we use the simple labels of *MB* and *MC* so as not to infer a distinction between private and social decisions, which is irrelevant in this unique situation.

| TABLE 8.3 | AVERTING ACTIONS TO REDUCE RISKS OF EXPOSURE TO POLLUTION | |

| Pollution | Effect | Averting Action |
|-----------|--------|-----------------|
| Air pollution | Material soiling | Clean or repaint material surfaces; use protective covers; move to new location. |
| | Health problems | Install air purifiers or air conditioners; schedule more frequent visits for medical examinations; purchase medications to alleviate respiratory symptoms; move to new location. |
| Water pollution | Material soiling | Install water filtration system; purchase cleaning products and rust removers; move to new location. |
| | Health problems | Install water filtration system; purchase bottled water; move to new location. |
| Hazardous waste site | Aesthetic degradation | Install fencing or shrubbery; move to new location. |
| | Health problems | Test water supply for contamination; install air filtration or air conditioner; move to new location. |
| Noise pollution | Health problems | Install sound-deadening insulation; purchase medication to aid sleeping; move to new location. |

SOURCE: Adapted from Timothy J. Bartik. "Evaluating the Benefits of Non-marginal Reductions in Pollution Using Information on Defensive Expenditures." *Journal of Environmental Economics and Management* 15, 1988, pp. 111–26, Table 1.

substitutes to achieve various levels of *personal* environmental quality ($X$), given some level of *overall* environmental quality ($E$). In our diagram, $MC_0$ represents the marginal cost of averting expenditures at the existing level of overall environmental quality, $E_0$. As overall environmental quality improves to $E_1$, the individual spends less (or incurs lower costs) to achieve each level of personal environmental quality, and the $MC$ curve moves downward to the right, becoming $MC_1$.

At the initial equilibrium when overall environmental quality is $E_0$, the individual's personal environmental quality is $X_0$, where $MB$ and $MC_0$ intersect. At this point, total averting expenditures are the area under the $MC_0$ curve up to $X_0$, or area $0abX_0$. After the policy improves overall environmental quality to $E_1$, the individual's marginal cost curve shifts to $MC_1$. At the new equilibrium where $MB$ and $MC_1$ intersect, personal environmental quality increases to $X_1$, and averting expenditures change to area $0acX_1$. Now we can use this information to monetize the incremental benefits of the improvement in overall environmental quality from $E_0$ to $E_1$.

The key is to compare averting expenditure levels before and after the policy change *for the same level of personal environmental quality*. As we

| FIGURE 8.6 | **MEASURING INCREMENTAL BENEFITS USING THE AVERTING EXPENDITURE METHOD (AEM): A BEHAVIORAL LINKAGE APPROACH** |
|---|---|

$MC_0$ represents the individual's averting expenditures at the *existing* level of overall environmental quality, $E_0$, and $MC_1$ is based on a higher level $E_1$ arising from a policy change. When overall environmental quality is $E_0$, personal environmental quality is $X_0$, and averting expenditures are area $0abX_0$. After a policy increases overall environmental quality to $E_1$, personal environmental quality increases to $X_1$, and averting expenditures change to area $0acX_1$. To achieve $X_1$ in the absence of the policy change, the individual would be willing to spend an amount equal to area $0abcX_1$. Thus, the individual's WTP for the incremental benefits is the difference between $0abcX_1$ and $0acX_1$, or triangular area *abc*. An alternative valuation is based on the *original* level of personal environmental quality, $X_0$, where incremental benefits would be the difference between $0abX_0$ and $0adX_0$, or area *abd*.

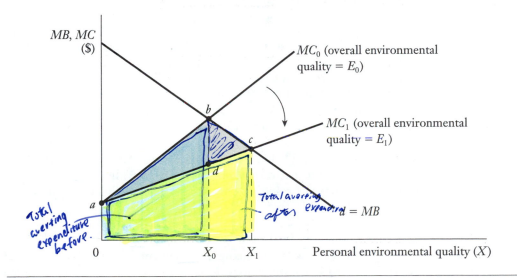

determined, post-policy averting expenditures for $X_1$ are represented by area $0acX_1$. Let's compare this to what the individual would be willing to spend to achieve $X_1$ without the influence of the policy. This is found by calculating the area under the original $MC_0$ curve up to $X_1$ and bounded by $MB$, or area $0abcX_1$. Thus, the individual's WTP for the incremental benefit is the difference between the two areas, $0abcX_1$ and $0acX_1$, or the triangular area *abc*.

An alternative valuation could be based on a constraint that holds personal environmental quality level at its original level, $X_0$. This approach might be preferred since the calculation is simpler, requiring information only on the two *MC* curves rather than both the *MC* curves and the *MB* curve. Under this scenario, the incremental benefits would be the difference between areas $0abX_0$ and $0adX_0$, or the area *abd*. This smaller area can be interpreted as a lower bound for the WTP valuation.[23]

**Assessing the AEM.**   A drawback of the AEM arises from the phenomenon known as *jointness of production.* This refers to the fact that some averting expenditures yield benefits beyond those associated with a cleaner environment. Consider, for example, the averting expenditures on an air-conditioning system. While the system does reduce certain health risks of air pollution, it also provides comfort. Hence the savings in expenditures arising from a clean air policy initiative cannot be attributed solely to the incremental benefits of that policy.

**Applications of the AEM.**   A number of studies have used the AEM to value a statistical life. Blomquist (1979) focuses on the averting action of wearing seat belts in automobiles to reduce mortality risk. This study estimates the incremental benefit of a life saved as ranging between $380,000 and $1.4 million ($1986). Dardis (1980) conducts the same sort of analysis using expenditures on smoke detectors, and monetizes the value of a statistical life at $460,000 ($1986).[24] Notice how these estimates are lower than those derived using the CVM. One explanation is that the use of seat belts and smoke detectors is not a decision of *degree* but rather one of use versus nonuse. In such instances, the decision to engage in the activity is based on whether the individual believes doing so is worthwhile. Consequently, individuals answer affirmatively as long as the marginal benefit exceeds marginal cost, causing the resulting estimate to be generally undervalued.[25]

*Travel Cost Method (TCM): An Indirect Approach Using Complements*

**travel cost method (TCM)** Values benefits by using the *complementary* relationship between the quality of a natural resource and its recreational use value.

An alternative approach to valuing environmental benefits is the **travel cost method (TCM),** which uses the *complementary* relationship between the quality of a natural resource and its recreational use value. Simple observation suggests that the demand for the recreational use of an environmental resource, such as a lake or a national forest, increases as its quality improves. Therefore, as this demand function shifts with a change in environmental quality, the resulting change in consumer surplus can be used to assess the associated incremental benefits.

---

[23] Bartik (1988).

[24] These estimates are reported in Fisher, Violette, and Chestnut (1989).

[25] Cropper and Oates (1992), pp. 713–14.

---

| FIGURE 8.7 | MEASURING INCREMENTAL BENEFITS |
| --- | --- |

**USING THE TRAVEL COST METHOD (TCM):**

**A BEHAVIORAL LINKAGE APPROACH**

$D_0$ is the recreational demand for a lake at some preexisting environmental quality level, $E_0$. $D_1$ is the new demand curve after a policy improves the lake's quality to $E_1$. The price line at $P_0$ is the admission fee. Before the policy is implemented, the number of visits to the site is $V_0$, and consumer surplus is area $abP_0$. After the policy is put into effect, the number of visits increases to $V_1$, and consumer surplus increases to area $cdP_0$. The *change* in consumer surplus, area *acdb*, represents the incremental benefits of improving the lake's quality from $E_0$ to $E_1$.

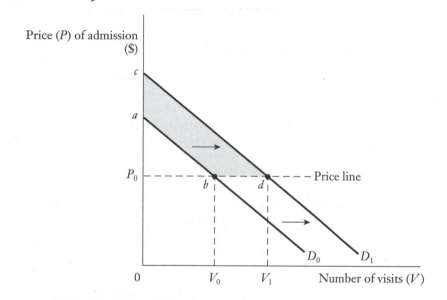

We model the travel cost method (TCM) in Figure 8.7, assuming recreational demand has been identified properly.[26] Two demand curves for the recreational use of a lake are shown in the diagram—$D_0$ and $D_1$. $D_0$ is the relevant demand at some preexisting environmental quality level, $E_0$. $D_1$ is the new demand curve after a policy has been implemented to improve the lake's quality to $E_1$. A price line is drawn at $P_0$ to represent the

---

[26]One technique used to identify a recreational demand curve is called the Clawson-Knetch (1966) method. This method uses travel costs to a recreational site, visitation rates, and other socioeconomic data to estimate recreational demand. Smith and Desvousges (1986) provide an excellent review of how this approach has been revised over time.

admission fee to use the lake. Before the policy is implemented, the number of visits to the site is $V_0$, where visitors enjoy a consumer surplus equal to area $abP_0$. After the policy is put into effect, the total number of visits increases to $V_1$, and consumer surplus increases to area $cdP_0$. The resulting *change* in consumer surplus, shown as area $acdb$ (i.e., area $cdP_0$ minus area $abP_0$), estimates the incremental benefits to visitors associated with improving the lake's quality.[27]

**Assessing the TCM.**   A disadvantage of the TCM is that it can estimate only user value and not existence value—an omission likely to create bias. Furthermore, the method focuses on recreational use, making it ineffective for estimating benefits that might accrue to commercial users of a resource. Finally, the TCM has been found to generate estimates that are biased downward if access to a site is deterred by congestion.[28]

**Applications of the TCM.**   Because of its limitations, the TCM is commonly used to value improvements to water bodies used mainly for recreation. For example, a study by Mullen and Menz (1985) uses the TCM to value acid rain damages to the Adirondack, New York, lake region. Other studies have used the procedure to value the benefits of improving water quality from boatable to fishable conditions. These findings tend to vary considerably. Consider the following results from three independent analyses, all measured as WTP per person per day in 1982 dollars:

Vaughan and Russell (1982):         Between $4.68 and $9.37;

Smith and Desvousges (1985):       Between $0.06 and $29.92; and

Smith, Desvousges, and
McGivney (1983):                            Between $1.04 and $2.15.[29]

Part of the reason for the inconsistent valuations is that TCM estimates tend to be sensitive to the site under study. While demographic variables across regions can be controlled for, there are other site differences, such as aesthetics, access to major highways, and substitute recreational opportunities that are difficult to quantify and control for. Consequently, it is unlikely that the TCM can determine a *generalized* value of improved water quality.[30]

---

[27] Notice that even if there were no entry fee to use the lake, the model would be the same except that consumer surplus would be the entire area under each demand curve. In such an instance, the resulting change in consumer surplus would extend to the horizontal axis.

[28] Smith and Desvousges (1986), p. 220.

[29] These comparisons are discussed in Smith and Desvousges (1985).

[30] For more detail on the *TCM*, the reader should consult Cropper and Oates (1992); or Mitchell and Carson (1989), Chapter 3.

*Hedonic Price Method (HPM): An Indirect Approach Using Product Attributes*

**hedonic price method (HPM)**
Uses the estimated hedonic price of an environmental attribute to value a policy-driven improvement.

The **hedonic price method (HPM)** is based on the theory that a good or service is valued for the attributes or characteristics it possesses.[31] This perception of value suggests that *implicit* or *hedonic prices* exist for product attributes, and these can be determined from the explicit price of the product. In environmental economics, researchers use this technique to value the environmental attributes of certain commodities.

Housing markets have been a classic context for hedonic environmental pricing studies. Such analyses assume that the market price of a home is determined by the implicit value of its many characteristics, such as location, number of baths, lot size, and the environmental quality of the community. Hence, changes in any of these characteristics are capitalized into the price of the property. The conventional model specifies the market price of a house, *P*, as a function of its attributes. A simplified version of such a model is:

$$P = f(X_1, X_2, \ldots X_n, E),$$

where each *X* variable represents some housing attribute, like lot size or number of baths, and the *E* variable signifies the associated environmental quality. As any one of these characteristics increases in magnitude, the price of the property, *P*, increases.[32] It is this *marginal* price that is the implicit value of that attribute. Thus, as environmental quality improves, the resulting increase in property value can be used to estimate the associated incremental benefits.

Another common context for the HPM is wage analysis. Here the method is used to explain wage differentials that might be associated with occupational risks, including those of environmental origin. Similar to hedonic studies of housing prices, hedonic wage (*w*) models generally are specified as:

$$w = g(Z_1, Z_2, \ldots Z_n, E).$$

The *Z* variables would include such attributes as the age, gender, education, and experience of the worker. The *E* variable would be some measure of occupational-specific environmental risk, such as the dangers faced by hazardous waste handlers or by engineers in a nuclear power plant. These workers are expected to receive a higher wage than those who are not so exposed to compensate them for the added risk exposure. This wage differential is used to value the incremental benefits to workers of reducing occupational risk.

---

[31] Lancaster (1966).

[32] This assumes that each attribute is specified as a favorable property characteristic.

The HPM uses a statistical procedure known as regression analysis to determine the implicit price of any environmental variable. In simple terms, the idea is to decompose an *explicit* price, such as the price of a house or the wage rate, into its *implicit* price components, one of which is the price of environmental quality ($E$). Once the implicit price of $E$ is determined, the demand for environmental quality can be estimated. This in turn can be used to measure changes in consumer surplus arising from policy-driven improvements in environmental quality.

**Assessing the HPM.** The appeal of the HPM is that it is highly intuitive. It approaches the problem of monetizing incremental benefits in a logical way, directly using market prices. Its major disadvantage is that it requires a fairly complicated empirical model. Furthermore, the method calls for extensive data on product characteristics, which are often unavailable or incomplete. If an important product attribute is missing, it will not be possible to determine the connection between a change in an explicit price and a change in environmental quality.

**Applications of the HPM.** One application of the HPM is in measuring how the siting of hazardous waste facilities affects prices of nearby properties.[33] Hedonic wage differential studies have been used to estimate the value of a statistical life saved as a result of reducing occupational risk. For example, Thaler and Rosen (1976) estimate that society's WTP for saving one additional life is between $440,000 and $840,000 ($1986). A more recent finding is presented by Moore and Viscusi (1988), who estimate the value at approximately $5.4 million.[34] The complex specification and data requirements of the HPM are partly responsible for the varying results across studies.

# Conclusions

As a risk management strategy, benefit–cost analysis can be used to set policy objectives and to select the "best available" control instrument to achieve those objectives. However, its success in guiding these important decisions hinges on the accuracy of benefit and cost measurements. In this chapter, we have focused on the conceptual issues of benefit valuation and some of the estimation methods used in practice. Of all the available benefit valuation techniques, there is no clear consensus about which is consistently

---

[33] For a recent study that looks at the impact of hazardous waste sites on property values, see Kohlhase (1991). Examples of hedonic price models that attempt to value air quality include a study by Harrison and Rubinfeld (1978) and an analysis done by Freeman (1979). Freeman's paper also provides an excellent survey of the major issues surrounding the HPM.

[34] These results are reported in Fisher, Violette, and Chestnut (1989).

superior. The diversity of approaches reflects both the complexity of the task *and* a recognition of its importance in public policy decision making.

For each estimation method, we examined the underlying theory and the measurement technique, assessed the effectiveness of the approach, and surveyed a selection of empirical results. From a general perspective, our investigation uncovered some of the difficulties inherent in any social benefit estimation—difficulties that are often magnified in an environmental context. The primary challenge is in monetizing gains that involve many intangibles not traded in the marketplace. Hence economists have had to devise methods to quantify these intangibles using something other than explicit prices.

On balance, research efforts in measuring social benefits have been fruitful. Progress has been made in fine-tuning estimation procedures, in recognizing which methods are most useful for which contexts, and in interpreting the results. The efforts are important to support the use of benefit–cost analysis as a risk management strategy and ultimately to devise better policy solutions. Of course, all of this necessitates that comparable progress be made on the cost side of the analysis, which is the focus of the next chapter.

# Summary

- To assess incremental benefits attributable to environmental policy, policy makers must determine how health, ecological, and property damages *change* as a result of that policy initiative.

- A primary environmental benefit arises as a *direct* consequence of implementing policy, whereas a secondary environmental benefit is an *indirect* gain arising either from the primary benefit or some demand-induced effect.

- Conceptually, if we could infer society's demand for environmental quality, we could measure incremental benefits, since this demand represents the marginal social benefit of abatement (*MSB*).

- It is generally recognized that society derives utility from environmental quality based on its user value and its existence value.

- User value refers to the benefit received from physical utilization or access to an environmental resource. Existence value is the benefit received from the continuance of the resource based on motives of vicarious consumption and stewardship.

- There are two major types of benefit measurement techniques: the physical linkage approach and the behavioral linkage approach.

- The damage function method is based on a technical model between levels of some contaminant and damages due to exposure to that contaminant. Incremental benefits can be estimated as the damage reduction achieved from any policy-induced decline in the contaminant.

- The contingent valuation method (CVM) is a survey approach that determines individuals' willingness to pay (WTP) for some environmental improvement based on hypothetical market conditions.

- The averting expenditure method (AEM) uses expenditures on goods that are substitutes for environmental quality to indirectly determine the WTP for a cleaner environment.

- The travel cost method (TCM) relies on identifying the recreational demand for an environmental resource, which is a complementary good to environmental quality. As environmental quality is improved, recreational demand increases, and the associated benefits can be estimated as the change in consumer surplus.

- The hedonic price method (HPM) is based on the theory that implicit or hedonic prices exist for individual product attributes, including those related to environmental quality.

## Key Concepts

| | |
|---|---|
| incremental benefits | physical linkage approach |
| primary environmental benefits | behavioral linkage approach |
| secondary environmental benefits | damage function method |
| user value | contingent valuation method (CVM) |
| existence value | |
| direct user value | averting expenditure method (AEM) |
| indirect user value | |
| vicarious consumption | travel cost method (TCM) |
| stewardship | hedonic price method (HPM) |

## Review Questions

1. Is it possible for an *individual's* valuation of an environmental commodity to include both user and existence value? Explain briefly.

2. Contrast the averting expenditure method (*AEM*) with the travel cost method (*TCM*) and discuss the relative strengths and weaknesses of each.

3. Refer back to Application 8.3 and the estimated changes in consumer and producer surplus reported by the NAPAP for various ozone policies. Graphically model the result of a 25 percent *increase* in tropospheric ozone to show *qualitatively* the distribution of benefits reported

by the NAPAP. (Note: Do not attempt to arrive at the numerical values for the changes in surplus values. Show only how the consumer, producer, and total surpluses *change* in accordance with the reported findings.)

4. One of the strengths of the contingent valuation method (CVM) is its ability to capture existence value. How can the researcher take advantage of this, yet avoid some of the biases of such a survey-based approach?

5. a. Suppose you are part of a research team evaluating a proposal to clean up a hazardous waste site. You are in charge of assessing the incremental benefits. Which method would you choose to derive the estimation? Explain briefly.

   b. Based on your selection, outline your research plan for this specific estimation problem. Be sure to identify the following in your outline: a general description of your model, the relevant market for your model, the primary variables of interest, the data requirements, and any potential bias in your results.

## Additional Readings

Abdalla, Charles W., Brian Roach, and Donald J. Epp. "Valuing Environmental Quality Changes Using Averting Expenditures: An Application to Groundwater Contamination." *Land Economics* 68(2), May 1992, pp. 163–69.

Bresnahan, Brian W., Mark Dickie, and Shelby Gerking. "Averting Behavior and Urban Air Pollution." *Land Economics* 73(3), August 1997, pp. 340–57.

Brookshire, D. S., M. A. Thayer, W. D. Schulze, and R. C. d'Arge. "Valuing Public Goods: A Comparison of Survey and Hedonic Approaches." *American Economic Review* 72, 1982, pp. 165–76.

Clawson, Marion. *Methods for Measuring the Demand for and Value of Outdoor Recreation*. Washington, DC: Resources for the Future, 1959.

Common, M., I. Reid, and R. Blamey. "Do Existence Values for Cost Benefit Analysis Exist?" *Environmental and Resource Economics*, no. 9, March 1997, pp. 225–38.

Kneese, Allen V. *Measuring the Benefits of Clean Air and Water*. Washington, DC: Resources for the Future, 1984.

Mendelsohn, Robert. "Modeling the Demand for Outdoor Recreation." *Water Resources Research* 23(5), May 1987, pp. 961–67.

Mjelde, James, Richard M. Adams, Bruce L. Dixon, and Philip Garcia. "Using Farmers' Actions to Measure Crop Loss Due to Air Pollution." *Journal of Air Pollution Control Association* 34(4), April 1984, pp. 360–64.

Portney, Paul R. "The Contingent Valuation Debate: Why Economists Should Care." *Journal of Economic Perspectives* 8(4), Fall 1994, pp. 3–18.

Resources for the Future. "The Politics of Protecting Species." *Resources*, no. 128, Summer 1997.

Smith, V. Kerry, "Can We Measure the Economic Value of Environmental Amenities?" *Southern Economic Journal* 56(4), April 1990, pp. 865–78.

Smith, V. Kerry, and William H. Desvousges. "Averting Behavior: Does It Exist?" *Economics Letters* 20(3), 1986, pp. 291–96.

## Related Web Sites

Benefit Estimation Methods
(Resources for the Future
assisted NAPAP by survey-
ing the literature on benefit
measurement.)              www.rff.org/proj_summaries/files/burtraw_emit_trade.htm

Economics and the
Endangered Species Act
(research conducted by
Resources for the Future)   www.rff.org/proj_summaries/files/ando_econ_esa.htm

U.S. Fish and Wildlife
Service's endangered
species home page           www.fws.gov/r9endspp/endspp.html

# 9

# Assessing Costs for Environmental Decision Making

In the previous chapter, we began our formal study of benefit–cost analysis with the theory and measurement of environmental benefits. Equally critical is the analysis of environmental costs—the costs of environmental improvement. In this phase of risk management, the policy maker must consider the value of *all* economic resources allocated to reducing environmental risk. Unlike the benefit side, the challenge here is not in assigning a monetary value to costs, since most are already expressed in money terms. Instead, the more critical issue is in identifying all the resources used to design, implement, and execute the policy prescription.

Few would debate that identifying environmental costs is a major undertaking. Think about the amount of government spending necessary to support the scientific research, the network of administrative agencies, and the labor force needed to implement a major environmental initiative. Add to that the billions of dollars spent by private businesses on abatement equipment and labor to comply with environmental regulations. Identifying these expenses on such a massive scale is in itself a tremendous task. But there is another element of cost analysis that adds to the difficulty— the premise that *economic* costs, and not simply *accounting* costs, are to be determined.

In this chapter, we discuss all of these issues, beginning with an overview of the fundamentals—much as we did on the benefit side. In particular, we start by defining incremental costs, the distinction between explicit and implicit costs, and the concept of valuing environmental costs. Once done, we address actual cost estimation methods used in practice today. Finally, we discuss the more prevalent ways in which environmental costs are classified and reported.

# Identifying and Valuing Environmental Costs: Conceptual Issues

Just as is the case for benefits, the appropriate level of analysis for evaluating the cost of an environmental initiative is **incremental costs.** The rationale is to allow a comparison between post-policy expenditures and their pre-policy level, which we call the baseline.

## Defining Incremental Costs

Starting with the basics, we know that environmental costs must be defined in incremental terms. The motivation for using incremental variables is to capture *changes* brought about by policy. In this case, the relevant change is the increase in costs associated with policy-induced improvements in environmental quality. **Incremental costs** are calculated by first identifying the existing level of environmental expenditures, then estimating the costs after the policy is implemented, and finally finding the difference between the two.

**incremental costs**
The change in costs arising from an environmental policy initiative.

From an economic perspective, incremental costs should reflect changes in *economic* costs. As discussed in Chapter 2, economic costs are a more accurate measure of resource utilization than are accounting costs, since they include both **explicit** (i.e., out-of-pocket) **costs** and **implicit costs.** However, since the latter are not readily identifiable, analysts often derive incremental cost values based solely on explicit expenditures.

## Explicit Environmental Costs

**explicit costs**
Administrative, monitoring, and enforcement expenses paid by the public sector plus compliance costs incurred by all sectors.

The **explicit costs** of implementing an environmental policy include the administrative, monitoring, and enforcement expenses paid by the public sector as well as the compliance costs incurred by virtually all sectors of the economy. Explicit costs and their components are easier to identify than their benefit counterparts, since most of the resources used to implement pollution control policies are traded in private markets. Those associated with the use of economic resources—land, labor, and capital—are rents, wages, and interest, respectively. Since these resources are traded on the open market, expenditures are based on market-determined input prices. However, these expenditures are not made simultaneously, and some are less controllable than others in the short run. Recognizing this, economists classify costs into two components: (i) **fixed costs,** which are not controllable in the short run and do not depend on production levels; and (ii) **variable costs,** which have the opposite characteristics. In the context of environmental policy implementation and compliance, the accounting equivalents of these categories are **capital costs** and **operating costs,** respectively.

**capital costs** Fixed expenditures for plant, equipment, construction in progress, and production process changes associated with abatement.

**Capital and Operating Costs.** According to U.S. government guidelines provided by the Department of Commerce and used by the EPA, capital and operating costs have specific meanings. **Capital costs** are expenditures for plant, equipment, construction in progress, and the costs of

**operating costs**
Variable expenditures incurred in the operation and maintenance of abatement processes.

changes in production processes that reduce or eliminate pollution generation. **Operating costs** are those incurred in the operation and maintenance of pollution abatement processes, including spending on materials, parts and supplies, direct labor, fuel, and research and development.[1]

A critical distinction between these two categories is in how costs are related to the level of abatement. A capital cost is incurred regardless of the amount of pollution abated, analogous to the economic definition of fixed cost. Examples include the installed price of a scrubber system to control air pollution, construction costs of a wastewater facility, and the purchase of acreage to use as a landfill. Notice that these capital costs are incurred prior to making any of the investments operational and are independent of whether the capital is ever used to abate pollution. Conversely, operating costs are directly related to the quantity of abatement, comparable to the economic definition of variable costs. Examples include the costs of monitoring emissions and the costs of labor to run an abatement facility.

## Implicit Environmental Costs

**implicit costs** The value of any nonmonetary effects that negatively influence society's well-being.

Although the explicit costs of abatement appear to be comprehensive, it turns out that these costs convey only part of the story. There are also **implicit costs**—those concerned with any nonmonetary effects that negatively affect society's well-being. These include the value of diminished product variety arising from a ban on certain inputs, the time costs of searching for substitutes, and the reduced convenience that environmental control policies might impose. While implicit costs are arguably an important factor, identifying and measuring these in practice is another issue entirely. In fact, most analyses fail to fully capture these values, ignoring effects that represent real costs to society. The result? Many environmental cost assessments are seriously understated—a problem that has yet to be fully resolved.

## Conceptually Valuing Environmental Costs

What economic resources are used to achieve cleaner air or water? And what are the costs of these resources? Ideally, one should determine the *social costs* of environmental policy to answer these questions.

**social costs** Expenditures needed to compensate society for resources used so that its utility level is maintained.

In theory, the **social costs** of any policy initiative are the expenditures needed to compensate society for the resources used so that its utility level is maintained. This compensation would have to account for all the price, output, and income effects that arise from a given regulation.[2] One example

---

[1] U.S. EPA, Office of Policy, Planning, and Evaluation (December 1990), pp. 1-2–1-3, in accordance with U.S. Department of Commerce, Bureau of the Census. *Government Finances*, various years and U.S. Department of Commerce, Bureau of Economic Analysis. "Pollution Abatement and Control Expenditures," published periodically in *Survey of Current Business*.

[2] In earlier chapters, we argued that one of these effects might be the forgone profits caused by firms' reducing production levels to lower pollution releases.

FIGURE 9.1 MARGINAL SOCIAL COST (*MSC*) AND TOTAL SOCIAL COSTS (*TSC*) OF AIR QUALITY (% SO$_2$ ABATEMENT)

The market supply for sulfur dioxide (SO$_2$) abatement represents the marginal social cost (*MSC*) of air quality. For each abatement (*A*) level, the associated marginal social cost (*MSC*) is shown as the vertical distance from the horizontal axis up to the supply curve. Total social costs (*TSC*) for any abatement level are measured as the area under the *MSC* up to that point. Thus, the shaded area represents the *TSC* to achieve abatement level $A_1$.

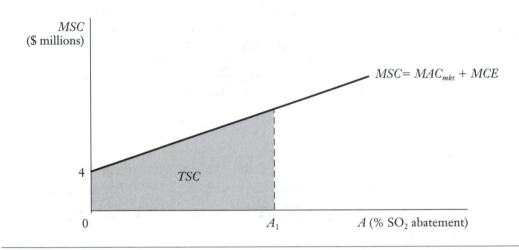

is the increased price of automobiles caused by the cost of abatement equipment like catalytic converters. Another is the higher price of household products arising from the use of recyclable packaging and the costs of more highly regulated labeling. There are also real income changes, such as those caused by higher taxes needed to support regulatory expenses. Beyond these effects are implicit or nonmonetary costs, which also have to be identified and monetized. Examples include the inconvenience of using public transportation or car pools in response to new urban air quality policies or the search costs to find nontoxic substitute products.

From a modeling perspective, we capture marginal social costs (*MSC*) by the supply of the public good, environmental quality. While the demand for a public good can only be inferred, the supply function can be identified directly in the same manner used for a private good. Let's reconsider the market supply model presented in Chapter 3 that represents the marginal social cost (*MSC*) of sulfur dioxide (SO$_2$) abatement. The function is specified as $MSC = 4 + 0.75A$, where *MSC* is measured in millions of dollars, and *A* is a percentage of SO$_2$ abatement. In Chapter 4, we argued that the *MSC* is the vertical sum of the market-level marginal abatement costs (*MAC$_{mkt}$*) plus the government's marginal cost of enforcement (*MCE*). The graphical model is shown in Figure 9.1. Analogous to the benefit side,

| FIGURE 9.2 | **MODELING INCREMENTAL COSTS FOR AIR QUALITY (% $SO_2$ ABATEMENT) USING THE *MSC* FUNCTION** |

At the baseline abatement level of 20 percent, the *MSC* equals $19 million, and the *TSC* is the area under the *MSC* up to that point or $230 million. At the post-policy abatement level of 25 percent, the *MSC* is $22.75 million, and the corresponding *TSC* is $334.375 million. Therefore, the difference between the two *TSC* values, or $104.375 million, represents the incremental costs to achieve the additional 5 percent abatement of $SO_2$ emissions. These incremental costs are shown as the shaded area.

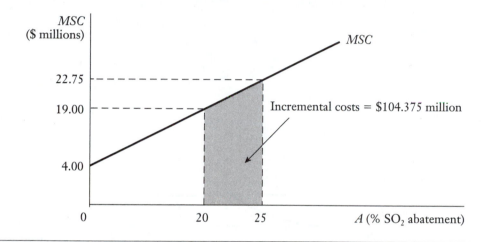

notice that for each abatement level, *MSC* is shown as the vertical distance from the horizontal axis up to the supply curve. Total social costs (*TSC*) for any abatement level are measured as the area under the *MSC* up to that point. The shaded area in Figure 9.1 represents the *TSC* to achieve an abatement level of $A_1$.

Just as on the benefit side, the incremental cost assessment follows a logical three-step process:

1. Find the baseline level of *TSC* *before* the policy is undertaken.

2. Find the new level of *TSC* that would arise *after* the policy is implemented.

3. Subtract the baseline *TSC* from the post-policy *TSC* to determine incremental costs.

To illustrate this procedure, consider the incremental costs of a policy-induced increase in $SO_2$ abatement from 20 to 25 percent. First, identify the baseline level of *TSC* when *A* equals 20 percent. Referring to Figure 9.2, notice that the *MSC* at this abatement level is $19 million, and the

FIGURE 9.3

## MODELING INCREMENTAL COSTS FOR AIR QUALITY (% SO$_2$ ABATEMENT) USING THE *TSC* FUNCTION

An alternative way to model the incremental costs of SO$_2$ abatement is to graph *TSC* directly as a function of various abatement levels. Then the *TSC* associated with any abatement level is found simply as the vertical distance from the horizontal axis up to the *TSC* curve. Notice that at the pre- and post-policy abatement levels, 20 and 25 percent respectively, the corresponding *TSC* levels are $230 million and $334.375 million, respectively. Thus the difference, or $104.375 million, is simply the vertical distance between the two cost values.

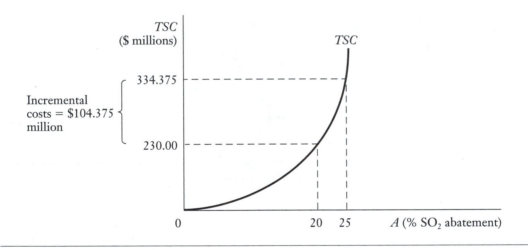

corresponding *TSC* is the area under the *MSC* curve up to that point, or $230 million. Second, we determine the post-policy *TSC* to increase abatement to 25 percent. Following the same steps, the *MSC* when *A* equals 25 is $22.75 million, and the *TSC* is $334.375 million. So, the difference between the two *TSC* values, or $104.375 million, represents the incremental costs to achieve the additional 5 percent abatement of SO$_2$ emissions.

Figure 9.3 presents an alternative model that graphs *TSC* directly with the percentage of SO$_2$ abatement. In this case, the *TSC* associated with any abatement level can be found simply as the vertical distance from the horizontal axis up to the **TSC** curve. To determine incremental costs from this model, begin by identifying the pre- and post-policy abatement levels, 20 and 25 percent respectively, and the corresponding *TSC* levels, $230 million and $334.375 million. The difference, or $104.375 million, is shown as the vertical distance between the two cost values.

In practice, to assess properly the social costs of an environmental initiative, the analyst would have to measure changes in social welfare, perhaps by estimating changes in consumer and producer surplus. This is a complex undertaking, but there is some evidence that doing so improves the accuracy of cost assessments. A study by Hazilla and Kopp (1990) estimates the social costs of U.S. air and water quality control policies. According to this research, there is a significant difference between social costs and the explicit cost estimates typically used in practice. In fact, these researchers recommend that policy makers adjust their procedures to consider more of a general equilibrium approach to cost analysis than is currently in place. However, available methods to execute this more comprehensive cost assessment are too cumbersome and unreliable to be employed as a regular practice. So, at least for the present, cost analysis continues to be based solely upon explicit expenditures, although it is generally acknowledged that such an approach understates the true social costs.

# Estimation Methods for Measuring Explicit Costs

**engineering approach** Estimates abatement expenditures based on least-cost available technology.

Two major approaches are used by economists to estimate incremental environmental costs—the **engineering approach** and the **survey approach.** The **engineering approach** estimates abatement expenditures based on the least-cost available technology needed to achieve some level of pollution abatement. The **survey approach** derives estimated abatement expenditures directly from polluting sources. While each of these is quite distinct, a common practice is to use a combination approach that draws from both. First, the survey approach is used to solicit information about available technologies and existing market conditions. Then the engineering approach is employed to estimate dollar values based on the collected data. What follows is a brief discussion of each approach with some mention of their respective shortcomings.

**survey approach** Polls a sample of firms and public facilities to obtain estimated abatement expenditures.

## The Engineering Approach

The **engineering approach** to expenditure estimation relies on the knowledge of experts in abatement technology. Based on the state of the art in abatement, engineers and scientists are called upon to identify combinations of equipment, labor, and materials needed by polluters to comply with a policy mandate. Then capital and operating costs for all feasible abatement designs are estimated. Finally, the analyst selects the least-cost model from among these technology-based designs and uses the result to estimate the *aggregate* incremental cost for all affected polluting sources.

While theoretically reasonable, the engineering approach is not without problems. For one thing, the procedure is difficult to implement for *proposed* environmental controls, since there is uncertainty about price movements, availability of raw materials, and future energy costs. Even absent these forecasting problems, there are inherent difficulties with any aggregation procedure of this magnitude. Most comprehensive policy initiatives affect a wide range of industries and public facilities. To properly account for these, the engineering approach would have to be customized

| TABLE 9.1 | SURVEY APPROACH TO POLLUTION ABATEMENT AND CONTROL EXPENDITURES FOR 1994 | |
|---|---|---|

| Title of Survey | Source | Proportion of Cost Data Determined by the Survey |
|---|---|---|
| Pollution Abatement Costs and Expenditure (MA-200) | Bureau of Census | 21 |
| Government Finances* | Bureau of Census | 22 |
| Value of New Construction Put in Place | Bureau of Census | 10 |
| Federal Funding for Pollution Control | Bureau of Economic Analysis | 5 |
| Structures and Equipment Survey | Bureau of Census | 5 |
| Steam-Electric Plant Operation and Design | Department of Energy | 2 |

NOTE:

*This line item is not the title of one particular survey. Rather, several sources make up the survey of government finance data. For example, the Bureau of Economic Analysis gathers information from Energy Information Agency reports and the EPA.

SOURCE: Drawn from Christine R. Vogan. "Pollution Abatement and Control Expenditures, 1972–94." *Survey of Current Business.* Washington, DC: Department of Commerce, Bureau of Economic Analysis, September 1996, Table 10, p. 54.

to suit each type of production setting. If ignored, the results would likely suffer from the averaging process. Even if industry-specific values were derived, the heterogeneity of firms and the unique market conditions that each faces could not be captured in such a generalized estimate. Finally, because the approach is based on the least-cost abatement design, it explicitly assumes that all firms are cost-effective or technically efficient entities—an assumption that likely understates the true costs incurred.

## The Survey Approach

In contrast to the engineering approach, the **survey approach** relies directly on polluting sources instead of external experts to provide data for the estimation. Similar to the contingent valuation method for estimating benefits, the survey approach polls a sample of firms and public facilities to inquire about existing or projected environmental expenditures. To illustrate the applicability of this approach, Table 9.1 lists the surveys used to gather U.S. cost data in 1994. Also given are the government sources responsible for administering each survey. Approximately 65 percent of the information used for 1994 cost reporting was obtained from some type of survey. Notice that these surveys target both private and public sector costs of abatement and control.[3]

On the plus side, the survey method is a more direct means to obtain abatement cost data than the engineering approach. However, there are also disadvantages. First, it implicitly assumes that polluting sources are sufficiently well-informed to provide reasonable estimates. Second, there is an inherent bias. Polluting sources have an incentive to offer inflated values to government officials, since they recognize that higher costs will increase the probability that the proposed regulation will be rejected.

Just as in benefit assessment, no cost estimation method is perfect. In fact, this realization is what has motivated researchers to use a combination of the engineering and survey methods. The objective is to attempt to have the best of both worlds and to minimize potential bias. Given the growing emphasis on benefits and costs in environmental policy decisions, efforts such as these are ongoing to improve the accuracy of environmental cost estimation.

## Cost Classifications in Practice

As part of cost assessment, analysts are interested in determining the *composition* of environmental control costs. The motivation may be that some component of costs, such as spending on water quality control or the abatement costs incurred by private industry, has particular relevance to a policy decision. More importantly, information about the composition of control costs gives policy makers a clearer sense of how resources are being allocated to achieve environmental objectives—critical information for evaluating policy on the basis of allocative efficiency. Similarly, adjustments to correct for environmental inequities require knowledge about how the cost burden is distributed across economic sectors. Because of the diversity of objectives in cost assessment, there are different cost classifications used to obtain different kinds of information. An overview of some of the more commonly used classifications follows.

### Cost Classifications by Economic Sector

Policy analysts are often concerned with how environmental costs are distributed across the public and private sectors of the economy. For instance, the costs of policy revisions that strengthen monitoring and enforcement programs shift a higher cost burden to the public sector, possibly at all levels of government. This in turn would shift up the *MCE* and hence

---

[3] For the remaining 35 percent of the cost information needed, the Bureau of Economic Analysis uses various *indirect* costing methods, most of which also use some type of survey information. See Vogan (1996), pp. 54–55.

| TABLE 9.2 | U.S. POLLUTION ABATEMENT AND CONTROL EXPENDITURES BY SECTOR, 1975–1994 (IN BILLIONS OF 1992 DOLLARS) |
|---|---|

| | Pollution Abatement | | | | | Regulation & Monitoring | | Research & Development | | | |
| | Private | | Government | | | | | | | | |
| Year | Personal | Business | Fed. | State | Other | Fed. | State | Private | Fed. | State | Total |
|---|---|---|---|---|---|---|---|---|---|---|---|
| 1975 | 7.70 | 38.89 | 1.02 | 4.15 | 11.18 | 0.90 | 0.64 | 1.45 | 1.07 | 0.12 | 67.06 |
| 1980 | 11.01 | 49.65 | 0.81 | 4.72 | 12.86 | 1.31 | 0.78 | 1.82 | 0.98 | 0.10 | 84.04 |
| 1985 | 15.51 | 53.62 | 1.61 | 6.26 | 10.68 | 0.73 | 0.87 | 1.21 | 0.52 | 0.03 | 91.02 |
| 1990 | 9.97 | 62.29 | 1.90 | 11.04 | 12.68 | 0.89 | 1.03 | 1.03 | 0.47 | 0.02 | 101.30 |
| 1994* | 9.30 | 73.05 | 2.13 | 15.17 | 12.49 | 1.21 | 0.89 | 0.66 | 1.16 | 0.08 | 116.12 |

NOTES: Some totals may not agree due to independent rounding.

All of personal spending is used to purchase and operate motor vehicle emission abatement devices.

State government spending includes expenditures by local authorities.

Other government spending refers to government enterprise fixed capital for publicly owned electric utilities and public sewer systems.

*1994 values are preliminary.

SOURCE: Christine R. Vogan. "Pollution Abatement and Control Expenditures, 1972–94." *Survey of Current Business.* Washington, DC: Department of Commerce, Bureau of Economic Analysis, September 1996, Table 11, pp. 57–63.

the *MSC* of abatement. Conversely, tighter abatement requirements will change the cost distribution more toward private industry. To illustrate, consider the U.S. trend data for 1975 to 1994 classified by economic sector in Table 9.2. The expenditures are broken down by major function—pollution abatement, regulation and monitoring, and research and development.

As the data in Table 9.2 indicate, the aggregate level of real spending on environmental issues has grown fairly steadily in the United States, up to $116.12 billion ($1992) in 1994. Furthermore, spending by each sector has shown a similar growth pattern, so much so that the relative proportions of total costs borne by each have remained fairly constant. However, the cost burden is not shared equally across the economy. Private business spending has represented about 60 to 65 percent of the total, public sector spending has accounted for about 25 to 30 percent, with the personal private sector responsible for the remainder.

These data also show that for all economic sectors, the greatest proportion of spending is allocated to abatement, although private business absorbs the highest dollar amount. To see this distribution more clearly, look at Table 9.3, which gives a breakdown of the 1994 cost data. Notice that aggregate spending on abatement was 96.6 percent of the total, with most of it borne by the business sector, primarily for operating expenses. In fact, business operating expenses for abatement were nearly twice the

| TABLE 9.3 | DECOMPOSITION OF U.S. POLLUTION ABATEMENT AND CONTROL EXPENDITURES BY SECTOR FOR 1994 |
|-----------|-----------------------------------------------------------------------------------------|

| | Constant (1992) Dollars in Billions (percentages given in parentheses) | |
|---|---|---|
| | Allocation by Sector | Sub-Total by Category |
| **Pollution Abatement** | | |
| Personal Consumption | 9.30 (8.0%) | |
|     Durable goods    9.30 | | |
|     Nondurable goods    0.00 | | |
| Business | 73.05 (62.9%) | |
|     Capital    26.44 | | |
|     Operating    46.61 | | |
| Government | 29.77 (25.6%) | |
|     Federal    2.13 | | |
|     State and Local    15.17 | | |
|     Other    12.49 | | |
| Subtotal pollution abatement | | 112.13 (96.6%) |
| **Regulation and Monitoring** | | |
| Government | 2.10 (1.8%) | |
|     Federal    1.21 | | |
|     State and Local    0.89 | | |
| Subtotal regulation and monitoring | | 2.10 (1.8%) |
| **Research and Development** | | |
| Private | 0.66 (0.6%) | |
| Government | 1.24 (1.1%) | |
|     Federal    1.16 | | |
|     State and Local    0.08 | | |
| Subtotal research and development | | 1.90 (1.6%) |
| **Grand Total** | | 116.12 (100.00%) |

NOTES: Some totals may not agree due to independent rounding.

All of personal spending is used to purchase and operate motor vehicle emission abatement devices.

State government spending includes expenditures by local authorities.

Other government spending refers to government enterprise fixed capital for publicly owned electric utilities and public sewer systems.

SOURCE: Christine R. Vogan. "Pollution Abatement and Control Expenditures, 1972–94." *Survey of Current Business.* Washington, DC: Department of Commerce, Bureau of Economic Analysis, September 1996, Table 11, pp. 57–63.

level of capital outlays. For the personal private sector, all of the spending is for the purchase and operation of abatement equipment for motor vehicles. Notice that all the spending was on durable goods at $9.3 billion. Application 9.1 takes a closer look at how this category of spending has been affected by tougher regulations on emissions from motor vehicles.

# Abatement Control Costs on Motor Vehicles

Virtually all cars on the road today are equipped with pollution abatement equipment. In response to tougher legislation, automakers have shifted from using so-called "low-tech" equipment, such as engine timing devices, to more sophisticated "high-tech" equipment, like catalytic converters and computerized emission control systems. As this technological transition has evolved, analysts have examined how this trend has affected private spending on abatement control and how it has altered the composition of that spending.

The data below are expenditures by the personal private sector on motor vehicle abatement devices over the 1975–1994 period. Durable goods expenditures refer to capital costs, and nondurable goods expenditures refer to operating and maintenance costs.

### Personal Expenditures on Air Pollution Abatement and Control 1975–1994 (billions of 1992 dollars)

| Year | Durable Goods | Nondurable Goods | Total Personal Consumption |
|------|---------------|------------------|----------------------------|
| 1975 | 3.3 | 4.4 | 7.7 |
| 1980 | 5.9 | 5.1 | 11.0 |
| 1985 | 10.6 | 4.9 | 15.5 |
| 1990 | 9.6 | 0.4 | 10.0 |
| 1994 | 9.3 | 0 | 9.3 |

SOURCE: Christine R. Vogan. "Pollution Abatement and Control Expenditures, 1972–94." *Survey of Current Business.* Washington, DC: Department of Commerce, Bureau of Economic Analysis, September 1996, Table 11, pp. 57–63.

These data show how expenditures have changed with strengthening U.S. air quality policy initiatives. Total personal consumption grew by over 100 percent between 1975 and 1985, and the 1975 value shown is nearly twice what it was in 1972 when these data were first recorded. Notice also that in 1994, spending was $9.3 billion, reflecting a 40 percent decline from the 1985 level. However, much of this decline is attributable to a fall in unit sales of automobiles over the period.

Another important observation is how the trend toward more capital-intensive regulations influenced the *composition* of abatement costs. For example, spending on catalytic converters began with the 1975 model year, which explains why the $3.3 billion spent on durable goods in 1975 is an 80-percent increase over the 1974 level of $1.8 billion. Similarly, rising spending throughout much of the 1980s reflects the costs of more sophisticated high-tech equipment introduced during that period.

The nondurable goods component of expenditures shows relatively little movement through the 1970s and 1980s. Yet there were major shifts taking place in the *composition* of these costs as well. For example, in the pre-1975 model years, most operating expenses were attributable to fuel consumption penalties (i.e., higher fuel usage due to abatement control equipment), and increased maintenance costs. In later-model cars, fuel price penalties (i.e., higher prices for unleaded gasoline) became the more important component of nondurable expenditures. Why? Because devices like catalytic converters and computer controls improve fuel economy, decreasing the fuel consumption penalty, and extend the life of exhaust systems, reducing maintenance costs. Since the 1980s, however, fuel price penalties have also shown signs of decline. Again, the primary explanation is technology. Improvements in the production of nonlead octane boosters as well as scale economies caused a reduction in the price differential between leaded and unleaded fuel. As a result, nondurable goods expenditures fell to zero in 1994.

SOURCE: Christine R. Vogan. "Pollution Abatement and Control Expenditures, 1972–94." *Survey of Current Business.* Washington, DC: Department of Commerce, Bureau of Economic Analysis, September 1996, Table 11, pp. 57–63.

| | TABLE 9.4 | U.S. POLLUTION ABATEMENT AND CONTROL EXPENDITURES DISAGGREGATED BY ENVIRONMENTAL MEDIA FOR 1975–1994 (BILLIONS OF 1992 DOLLARS) |
| --- | --- | --- |

| Year | Air | Water | Solid Waste |
| --- | --- | --- | --- |
| 1975 | 28.25 | 28.60 | 10.71 |
| 1980 | 37.00 | 34.17 | 14.11 |
| 1985 | 39.13 | 33.38 | 19.36 |
| 1990 | 30.27 | 39.67 | 32.74 |
| 1994 | 35.84 | 40.40 | 39.79 |

SOURCE: Christine R. Vogan. "Pollution Abatement and Control Expenditures, 1972–94." *Survey of Current Business*. Washington, DC: Department of Commerce, Bureau of Economic Analysis, September 1996, Table 11, pp. 57–63.

### Cost Classifications by Environmental Media

Another important policy consideration is the distribution of expenditures by environmental media (i.e., air, water, and solid waste). Table 9.4 shows U.S. abatement and control expenditures for 1975 through 1994 disaggregated by environmental media. Such information helps policy makers examine how resources are allocated across environmental problems and how this allocation changes from period to period. Notice, for example, that a rough estimate of the incremental costs of air quality regulations during the 1990 to 1994 period is $5.57 billion ($1992). Of course, a more accurate assessment would require a more complex series of calculations. For one thing, analysts are usually interested in assessing the costs of a policy once it has been fully implemented. So the appropriate analysis would extend over the relevant period of years, and the expenditure data would have to be adjusted to account for overlap with other regulations.

## Conclusions

Environmental cost assessment and estimation is a critical element of risk management. Although more tangible than benefit assessment, the valuation of environmental costs has its share of complexities. Chief among these is the divergence between the social costs of an environmental initiative and the explicit costs estimated in practice. In the absence of better techniques that can capture implicit costs, incremental cost estimates are generally assumed to be biased downward.

As economists search for a practical solution to this problem, they also look for ways to improve their estimates of explicit costs. The combined use of the survey and engineering approaches appears to be one way that greater accuracy can be achieved. Related to these efforts are attempts to classify cost data in ways that are meaningful to policy evaluation procedures and to the formulation of new programs and initiatives. The motivation is simple. Policy makers are having to make important decisions based in part on the results of environmental cost estimation. In the next chapter, we will explain precisely how environmental policy is influenced by both benefit and cost estimates when they are systematically considered in a formal benefit–cost analysis.

## Summary

- Environmental cost analysis is concerned with incremental costs, or the change in explicit and implicit costs to society, incurred as a result of government policy. Since implicit costs are not readily identifiable, analysts generally derive incremental costs based solely on explicit expenditures.

- Explicit costs of implementing an environmental policy include the administrative, monitoring, and enforcement expenses paid by the public sector as well as the compliance costs incurred by virtually all sectors of the economy.

- Capital costs are expenditures for plant and equipment used to reduce or eliminate pollution.

- Operating costs are those incurred in the operation and maintenance of abatement processes.

- Implicit costs are those concerned with any nonmonetary effects that negatively affect society's well-being.

- The social costs of any policy initiative are the expenditures needed to compensate society for the resources used so that its utility level is maintained.

- Conceptually, the supply of environmental quality can be used to model the marginal social cost of abatement ($MSC$), which is the vertical sum of the market-level marginal abatement cost function ($MAC_{mkt}$) and the marginal cost of enforcement ($MCE$).

- The engineering approach to cost estimation is based on the least-cost available technology needed to achieve a given level of abatement.

- The survey approach to cost estimation relies on estimated abatement expenditures obtained directly from polluting sources.

- Because of the diversity of objectives in environmental cost assessment, costs are commonly communicated through various classifications, such as R & D costs grouped by economic sector and abatement expenditures categorized by environmental media.

## Key Concepts

| | |
|---|---|
| incremental costs | implicit costs |
| explicit costs | social costs |
| capital costs | engineering approach |
| operating costs | survey approach |

## Review Questions

1. Consider a policy proposal to impose more stringent controls on automobile tailpipe exhausts. Distinguish between the explicit and implicit costs of this proposal and support your discussion with several specific examples of each.

2. Of the two approaches to cost estimation, which in your view likely produces the most reliable estimates? Explain.

3. Suppose the *MSC* of cleaning Puget Sound is modeled as $MSC = 10 + 1.4A$, where $A$ is the percentage of phosphorus abated, and *MSC* is measured in millions of dollars.
   a. Find the incremental costs of a policy initiative that increases the phosphorus abatement level from its baseline of 30 to 45 percent.
   b. Graphically illustrate using the *MSC* function, labeling clearly where incremental costs are shown.
   c. Repeat part (b) using the *TSC* function directly.

## Additional Readings

Cairncross, Frances. *Costing the Earth*. Boston: Harvard Business School Press, 1991.

Hartman, Raymond S., David Wheeler, and Manjula Singh. "The Cost of Air Pollution Abatement." *Applied Economics* 29, June 1997, pp. 759–74.

Lee, Dwight R. "Economics and the Social Costs of Smoking." *Contemporary Policy Issues* 9(1), January 1991, pp. 83–92.

Palmer, Karen, Hilary Sigman, and Margaret Walls. "The Cost of Reducing Municipal Solid Waste." *Journal of Environmental Economics and Management* 33, June 1997, pp. 128–50.

U.S. Environmental Protection Agency, Office of Solid Waste and Emergency Response. *Full Cost Accounting for MSW Management: A Handbook*. Washington, DC: September 1997.

Weyant, John P. "Costs of Reducing Global Carbon Emissions." *Journal of Economic Perspectives* 7(4), Fall 1993, pp. 27–46.

## Related Web Sites

The Cost of a Clean Environment (a project conducted by Resources for the Future and the EPA to estimate the opportunity cost of environmental regulations).

**www.rff.org/proj_summaries/files/harrington_clean_enviro.htm**

# 10

# Benefit–Cost Analysis in Environmental Decision Making

Should the national limit on sulfur dioxide emissions be tightened? Would society be better off if a tradeable permit system were used instead of technology-based standards to control water pollution? These are the kinds of questions dealt with by environmental decision makers. Analytical tools like benefit–cost analysis can help them find answers. Benefit–cost analysis begins with identifying and monetizing environmental benefits and costs — the subject of the previous two chapters. From this point, these preliminary estimates must be adjusted and then compared systematically to arrive at a decision. These critical steps that link benefit and cost estimates to a decision rule complete the strategic process of benefit–cost analysis.

Adjustments to estimated values are necessary because incremental costs and benefits from a given policy initiative are not realized immediately. Instead, they accrue over a period of years. Think about the implementation of a major policy initiative like the Clean Air Act or the Superfund Amendments. Such legislation takes years to put into effect. While some policy costs are incurred right away, others accrue at various points in time in the future. Similarly, the benefits are not realized in a single period. It takes time before the gains from an environmental policy are achieved. In the first place, there is a lag between risk reduction and realized improvements in human health and welfare. Furthermore, even if the effects were immediate, government-mandated reductions in contamination typically are phased in over a period of years.

How do these time differences affect the result? There are two considerations. One is that costs and benefits realized in some future period are not valued as highly as those achieved immediately. Thus future costs and benefits have to be adjusted downward to be comparable to those incurred in the present. A second adjustment is needed to account for expected changes in the price level over time. For example, the value of costs and benefits measured in today's dollars will be much higher in future dollars during periods of inflation. Without adjusting for these time-oriented differences, the benefit–cost analysis would yield biased results, and any policy decision based upon them would be misguided.

Once benefit and cost estimates are adjusted for time differences, they then must be compared to one another. But on what basis is the comparison made? Is it sufficient for the benefits to outweigh the costs, or must the numerical difference between the two be at a particular level? What if the law precludes the analysis by predetermining the benefit level to be achieved? The answers to these questions are found in understanding the decision rules that guide benefit–cost analysis. Of particular interest are the implications of those rules for meeting economic criteria—an important issue in policy evaluation.

The growing prominence of benefit–cost analysis as a risk management strategy is an important reason for understanding how it is undertaken, what it implies from an economic perspective, and how it has come to be required by the U.S. government in major policy decisions. To that end, this chapter presents and analyzes these aspects of benefit–cost analysis. We begin by giving a thorough exposition of the procedures used to adjust preliminary benefit and cost estimates for time differences. Next, we explore the policy evaluation process and the decision rules used in practice to guide that process. Once done, we consider how the role of benefit–cost analysis in U.S. policy making has evolved into a major tool for guiding legislative decisions. We conclude with an inside look at how benefit–cost analysis was used in the U.S. decision to tighten the lead standard for gasoline.

## Adjusting for the Time Dimension of Environmental Benefits and Costs

Critical to any environmental benefit–cost analysis is to reconcile the timing of benefits and costs. First, benefits and costs do not necessarily accrue at the same time. Furthermore, even if they did, they are not realized immediately. Although an environmental policy evaluation is made in the current period, the effects of that policy typically extend well into the future. Consequently, decision makers must be forward thinking in their evaluation of a policy proposal and must make projections about its future implications. To support these forecasts, benefit and cost estimates must be adjusted to account for the fact that the value of a dollar is not constant over time. Two types of time-oriented modifications are necessary. One is **present value determination,** which accounts for the opportunity cost of money. The second is **inflation correction,** to adjust for changes in the general price level. We examine each of these procedures in turn.

### Present Value Determination

Opportunity cost is one of the most pervasive concepts in economic thinking. It means that the highest valued alternative of any decision represents the full cost of that decision, whether it arises in production, consumption, or even purely financial transactions. To understand the concept in this latter context, consider the following simple scenario. Assume a friend asks to borrow $200 today, promising to pay back the loan one year from today. What amount of money would the payback have to be to maintain your well-being or utility level? (To keep things simple, assume there is no inflation.) Economically, the answer depends on the opportunity cost of money—its highest valued alternative use. If the $200 could be invested to yield a 5-percent return, then the opportunity cost of the loan is $10. Therefore, the appropriate payback should be $210, or [$200 + ($200 · 0.05)]. Technically, this calculation represents the conversion of the loan value in the *present period* into its value in the *future period*. Mathematically, the conversion for a one-year period is achieved using the following simple formula:

$$FV = PV + r \cdot PV = PV(1 + r),$$

where:

$FV$ = future value

$PV$ = present value and

$r$ = rate of return.

This equation shows that the future value ($FV$) of a dollar is equal to its present value ($PV$) plus the opportunity cost of not using the dollar in the present period ($r \cdot PV$). If the future valuation is to account for more than one time period ($t$), the above formula becomes:

$$FV = PV(1 + r)^t,$$

where:

$t = 0, 1, 2, \ldots T$ is the number of periods.

Inverting the problem, we can argue that $210 received one year from now is equivalent to having $200 today, or [$210/(1 + 0.05)]. This conversion

**present value determination** A procedure that discounts a future value (*FV*) into its present value (*PV*) by accounting for the opportunity cost of money.

procedure is called **present value determination** because it involves **discounting** a future value (*FV*) into its present value (*PV*). Mathematically, the calculation is performed using a rearrangement of the formula given above, as follows:

$$PV = FV[1/(1 + r)]$$

In this form of the equation, $r$ is called the **discount rate,** and the term $1/(1 + r)$ is called the **discount factor.** If the discounting involves more than one time period ($t$), the formula is written as:

**discount factor** The term, $1/(1 + r)^t$, where $r$ is the discount rate, and $t$ is the number of periods.

$$PV = FV[1/(1 + r)^t],$$

where:

$[1/(1 + r)^t]$ is the discount factor.

Discounting is the procedure economists use to adjust the value of environmental benefits and costs accruing in the future.

Notice that the discount rate ($r$) is the one variable element in present value determination. As this rate is elevated, the *PV* is decreased, and of course, the converse is true. Since the magnitude of the discount rate affects the conversion, its selection is critically important to benefit–cost analysis. In the context of environmental policy development, this rate can directly affect which proposals meet a given criterion and which are rejected out of hand. Because of the implications, discount rate selection is one of the more commonly debated points in the literature on present value analysis.

How *is* the discount rate selected for public policy decision making? While there are many considerations, one important position is that this rate should reflect the **social opportunity cost** of funds allocated to the provision of a public good. Why? Because monies used to support public policy initiatives are perceived as a *transfer* from the private sector. Therefore, it is argued that the discount rate used for public policy—called the **social discount rate**—should reflect the rate of return that *could* be realized through private spending on consumption and investment, assuming the same level of risk.[1]

**social discount rate** Discount rate used for public policy initiatives based on the social opportunity cost of funds.

Since 1992, the U.S. government has maintained a policy that its agencies use a social discount rate of 7-percent in their benefit–cost analyses.[2] The operative issue is whether this 7-percent rate reflects the social

[1] For an excellent discussion of the social discount rate and the opportunity cost of public funding, see Sassone and Schaffer (1978), Chapter 6.

[2] U.S. Office of Management and Budget (October 29, 1992).

opportunity cost of public expenditures. Since this rate is stated in **real** terms, that is, net of inflationary effects, the **nominal** rate is roughly equivalent to the sum of the inflation rate and the 7-percent rate. Inflation over the past several years has been about 3 percent, which means that the nominal social discount rate is about 10 percent. If this rate is meant to capture the social opportunity cost of funds, it must be the case that society could earn a 10-percent return through private investment. Beyond this issue, there are also conceptual arguments about what *should* determine this rate, a question about which there is no clear consensus.[3]

**inflation correction** Adjusts for movements in the general price level over time.

**nominal value** A magnitude stated in terms of the current period.

## Inflation Correction

Preliminary cost and benefit estimates must also be modified to account for movements in the general price level over time. To adjust a dollar amount in the present period for expected inflation in the *next* future period, the value must be converted to its **nominal value** for that period. The conversion uses a measure of price such as the consumer price index (CPI) as shown below:

$$\text{Nominal value}_{\text{period } x+1} = \text{Real value}_{\text{period } x} \cdot (\text{CPI}_{\text{period } x+1}/\text{CPI}_{\text{period } x}) \text{ or}$$

$$\text{Nominal value}_{\text{period } x+1} = \text{Real value}_{\text{period } x} \cdot (1 + p),$$

where $p$ is the rate of inflation between period $x$ and $x + 1$. The more generalized formula for any number of ($t$) periods is as follows:

$$\text{Nominal value}_{\text{period } x+t} = \text{Real value}_{\text{period } x} \cdot (1 + p)^t.$$

Inverting the formula allows for the conversion of a nominal value to its **real value,** as follows:

**real value** A magnitude adjusted for the effects of inflation.

$$\text{Real value}_{\text{period } x} = \text{Nominal value}_{\text{period } x+t}/(1 + p)^t.$$

**deflating** Converts a nominal value into its real value.

This conversion procedure, sometimes called **deflating,** is used to assess changes over a period during which there has been inflation.[4] To illustrate, look back at the cost data presented in Table 9.2 of the last chapter. Notice that all of the annual dollar values are expressed in 1992 dollars. This is done to avoid confounding changes in control costs over time with changes in the general price level. For example, the *Survey of Current Business* reports

---

[3] For further reading on this important public policy matter, see a series of articles in the March 1990 issue of the *Journal of Environmental Economics and Management* as well as Quirk and Terasawa (1991).

[4] Notice that the deflating formula is identical in form to the present value formula, except that the inflation rate, $p$, is substituted for the discount rate, $r$.

that the *nominal* value of abatement costs rose from \$104.8 billion in 1992 to \$110.1 billion in 1993.[5] Although these values imply an \$5.3-billion increase in abatement expenditures, part of the increase is due to a 2.6-percent inflation rate over the period. To correct for the price effect, the \$110.1 billion measured in 1993 dollars must be deflated to 1992 dollars. Using the formula given above, the result is \$107.3 billion (i.e., \$110.1 billion/[1 + [0.026]$^1$]). Thus, the *real* increase in abatement costs over the 1992 to 1993 period is (\$107.3 − \$104.8) billion, or \$2.5 billion measured in 1992 dollars.

### A Summary of Deriving Time-Adjusted Benefits and Costs[6]

**present value of benefits (PVB)**
The time-adjusted magnitude of incremental benefits associated with an environmental policy change.

The time-adjusted magnitudes for incremental benefits and costs are referred to as the **present value of benefits (PVB)** and the **present value of costs (PVC)**, respectively. The steps to measure the **present value of benefits (PVB)** in *real* terms are:

1. Monetize all present and future incremental benefits in nominal terms ($B_t$) where $t$ refers to the appropriate time period ($t = 0, 1, 2, \ldots T$).

2. Deflate each of the $B_t$, converting to real dollars ($b_t$):
$b_t = B_t/(1 + p)^t$.

3. Select the appropriate real social discount rate, ($r_s$).

4. Discount the $b_t$ for each period as $b_t/(1 + r_s)^t$.

5. Sum the discounted $b_t$ values over all $t$ periods to find the **present value of benefits** in real dollars as $PVB = \Sigma(b_t/(1 + r_s)^t)$.

**present value of costs (PVC)** The time-adjusted magnitude of incremental costs associated with an environmental policy change.

Analogous steps yield a measure for the **present value of costs (PVC)** in *real* terms, as follows:

1. Monetize all present and future incremental costs in nominal terms ($C_t$) where $t$ refers to the appropriate time period ($t = 0, 1, 2, \ldots T$).

2. Deflate each of the $C_t$, converting to real dollars ($c_t$):
$c_t = C_t/(1 + p)^t$.

3. Maintain the same real social discount rate ($r_s$) used in discounting future benefits.

---

[5] Vogan (1996).

[6] The following presentation derives the time-adjusted values in *real* terms. The procedure is analogous for finding *nominal* values, as long as all magnitudes including the discount rate are properly adjusted.

4. Discount the $c_t$ for each period as $c_t/(1 + r_s)^t$.

5. Sum the discounted $c_t$ values over all $t$ periods to find the **present value of costs** in real dollars as $PVC = \Sigma(c_t/(1 + r_s)^t)$.

### An Example: Time-Adjusted Incremental Benefits

To illustrate how these steps might be carried out in practice, consider a hypothetical benefit assessment. Suppose an analyst is using the averting expenditure method (AEM) to monetize the incremental benefits of improved water quality. As part of the assessment, the analyst must estimate an individual's averting expenditures on a water-filtering system.[7] Assume the system has an initial capital cost (i.e., purchase and installation) of $200 and a useful economic life of 5 years. Further, assume that annual operating costs for general maintenance and filters are quoted as $30 in nominal terms due at the end of each year.[8] Part of the objective of the AEM is to determine the overall cost to the individual of purchasing, installing, and maintaining this filtration system, accounting for both the opportunity cost of money and expected inflation.

Assume for simplicity that prices are expected to rise on average 5 percent each year. Using the conversion formula defined earlier, the real value of the operating costs at the end of the first year will be: $\$30.00/(1.05)^1 = \$28.57$. At the end of the second year, the real costs will be $\$30.00/(1.05)^2 = \$27.21$, and so forth. Table 10.1 presents these calculations for each year of the system's economic life.

A further adjustment is necessary to find the present value of these future expenditures based on the opportunity cost of money. Assuming the proper discount rate ($r$) is 10 percent in real terms,[9] the present value ($PV$) of each year's inflation-adjusted expenditures is found using the discounting formula. For example, the $PV$ of the first year's operating costs is $\$25.97 = \$28.57(1/(1.10)^1)$. For the second year, the $PV$ of the $27.21 real expenditure is $\$22.49 = \$27.21(1/(1.10)^2)$, and so forth. These calculations are given along with the price adjustments in Table 10.1.

To complete the analysis, all of the time-adjusted annual operating costs are added to the initial capital outlay of $200. Notice that the $200 is unaffected by the conversion procedures, since it is incurred in the present period. Overall, the $PV$ of the filtering system expressed in real dollars is $299.39.

---

[7] For an actual study of this type of analysis, see Abdalla (1990).

[8] The timing of the annual expenditures is a critical element of the discounting process. For illustrative purposes, assume that all annual costs are incurred at the *end* of each year. For more detail on this or any other discounting issue, see any public finance text, such as Rosen (1995).

[9] Because the annual costs have been converted to their real values, the discount rate must also be expressed in real terms to adjust for the effect of inflation on the rate of return. Alternatively, one can express all the cost values in nominal terms and use the nominal discount rate.

| TABLE 10.1 | ASSESSING THE VALUE OF FUTURE OPERATING COSTS OF A WATER FILTERING SYSTEM |
|---|---|

**Adjustments for Inflation**
**(assuming an annual inflation rate of 5%)**
$$\text{Real value}_{\text{period } x+t} = \text{Nominal value}_{\text{period } x}/(1 + p)^t$$

| Year | Expenditure in Nominal Terms | Future Expenditure in Real Dollars |
|---|---|---|
| 1 | $30.00 | $28.57 = $30/(1.05)^1 |
| 2 | $30.00 | $27.21 = $30/(1.05)^2 |
| 3 | $30.00 | $25.92 = $30/(1.05)^3 |
| 4 | $30.00 | $24.68 = $30/(1.05)^4 |
| 5 | $30.00 | $23.51 = $30/(1.05)^5 |

**Adjustments for Opportunity Cost**
**(assuming a real annual discount rate ($r$) of 10%)**
$$PV = FV[1/(1 + r)^t]$$

| Year | Future Value (FV) | Discount Factor $[1/(1 + r)^t]$ | Present Value (PV) |
|---|---|---|---|
| 0 | $200.00 | 1.0000 = 1/(1.10)^0 | $200.00 |
| 1 | $ 28.57 | 0.9090 = 1/(1.10)^1 | $ 25.97 |
| 2 | $ 27.21 | 0.8264 = 1/(1.10)^2 | $ 22.49 |
| 3 | $ 25.92 | 0.7513 = 1/(1.10)^3 | $ 19.47 |
| 4 | $ 24.68 | 0.6830 = 1/(1.10)^4 | $ 16.86 |
| 5 | $ 23.51 | 0.6209 = 1/(1.10)^5 | $ 14.60 |

Total Present Value in Nominal Terms: $299.39

## The Final Analysis: Comparing Environmental Benefits and Costs

The final phase of any benefit–cost analysis involves comparing the time-adjusted incremental benefits and costs and arriving at a decision based on their relative values. In the context of environmental policy, remember that the subject of the analysis is either the setting of a policy objective or the selection of a control instrument. During policy formulation, the analysis is carried out over a series of possible options and used to identify the "best" solution among them.[10]

The first step of this comparative evaluation is to determine if an option is *feasible* from a benefit–cost perspective. This step is essentially a zero-one decision made for every option under consideration—to accept or to reject. All of the "acceptable" options are then evaluated in a second step, where they are assessed *relative* to one another on the basis of a decision rule. At this point, a single "best" solution can be identified.

[10]Benefit–cost analysis is also used in the policy appraisal phase to evaluate an *existing* policy initiative.

*Step One: Determining Feasibility*

To distinguish feasible from infeasible options, the analyst must compare the time-adjusted values of incremental benefits and incremental costs for each option under study. A common way to do this is to form a **benefit–cost ratio** of $(PVB/PVC)$ and compare the result to unity. If the ratio for a policy option exceeds 1, it is counted among the feasible solutions; if not, it is rejected.

**benefit–cost ratio**
The ratio of *PVB* to *PVC* used to determine the feasibility of a policy option if its magnitude exceeds unity.

> If (PVB/PVC) for a given option > 1, the option is considered feasible.

An equivalent test for feasibility is to find the **present value of net benefits (PVNB),** which is $(PVB - PVC)$, and compare the result to 0. If this differential is greater than 0, the policy option is feasible; if not, it is rejected.

**present value of net benefits (PVNB)**
The differential of $(PVB - PVC)$ used to determine the feasibility of a policy option if its magnitude exceeds zero.

> If $(PVB - PVC)$ for a given option > 0, the option is considered feasible.

What both rules communicate is that feasibility is implied if the benefits associated with a policy proposal *outweigh* the costs incurred.

Although any policy option satisfying the $(PVB/PVC) > 1$ condition necessarily meets the requirement that $(PVB - PVC) > 0$, the equivalency ends there. First, the magnitudes of the two expressions have different interpretations. The numerical value of the $(PVB/PVC)$ ratio conveys the benefits of a policy option *per dollar of costs incurred*. For example, a ratio of 4.2 means that for every dollar of costs imposed on society, there are $4.20 in realized benefits. The value of $(PVB - PVC)$ measures the dollar value of *excess benefits*. So it directly communicates the net gain to society. Second, although it might be tempting to think that either measure could be used to rank feasible projects and arrive at the same "best" solution, such a hypothesis is incorrect. In fact, of the two measures, only the benefit–cost differential can be used to establish such a ranking. Why? Because the benefit–cost ratio is not reliable for comparing feasible policy proposals.

Attempts to use the benefit–cost ratio for any kind of ranking among options will lead to ambiguous results. The problem arises because of the inherent uncertainty about whether to consider an event as an increase in costs or a reduction in benefits. Suppose, for example, that a policy option is expected to create some amount of unemployment. Should the value of that unemployment be counted as a negative benefit or a positive cost? Intuitively, it should be apparent that either approach is correct and should not affect the outcome. However, although the choice would not affect the value of the *PVNB*, it would change the benefit–cost ratio. A simple example will illustrate.

Assume that this hypothetical policy option is expected to cause unemployment valued at $2 million after discounting and adjusting for inflation. Excluding this effect, suppose also that the *PVB* is $18 million and the *PVC* is $10 million. If the $2 million is counted as a negative benefit, the benefit–cost ratio would have a value of 1.6. If instead the $2 million is counted as a cost, the ratio would be 1.5. Try the same experiment with the *PVNB* to see that in either case the result is consistent at $6 million. What this example implies is that in the second step of evaluation, only the *PVNB* is useful in guiding the decision to select among feasible projects.

### Step Two: Decision Rules to Select among Feasible Options

In practice, the decision-making process used to evaluate feasible options is guided by one of the following economic criteria: **allocative efficiency,** or **cost-effectiveness.** Adding the dimension of time to these criteria, the decision rules are as follows:

> For **allocative efficiency:** Maximize the present value of net benefits (*PVNB*).

> For **cost-effectiveness:** Minimize the present value of costs (*PVC*) based on a preestablished benefit objective.

In the United States, the determination about which decision rule to use is generally dictated by the legislation or by presidential executive order—an issue we will explore later in the chapter. For now, notice that both rules involve some type of optimization to guide the selection of the "best" available option.

**maximize the present value of net benefits (*PVNB*)**
A decision rule to achieve allocative efficiency by selecting the policy option that yields greatest excess benefits after adjusting for time effects.

**DECISION RULE: Maximize the Present Value of Net Benefits (*PVNB*).** As noted above, the **present value of net benefits (*PVNB*)** is a benefit–cost differential found as the difference between the **present value of benefits (*PVB*)** and the **present value of costs (*PVC*).** Thus, this decision rule calls for choosing the option that yields to society the highest amount of excess benefits after adjusting for time effects. According to basic microeconomic theory, the point at which benefits exceed costs by the greatest amount corresponds to where $MB = MC$ or where resources are allocated efficiently. Hence we can summarize this decision rule in the following way:

> To achieve allocative efficiency, maximize $PVNB = (PVB - PVC) = \Sigma[b_t/(1 + r_s)^t] - \Sigma[c_t/(1 + r_s)^t] = \Sigma[(b_t - c_t)/(1 + r_s)^t]$ for all $t$ periods ($t = 0, 1, 2, \ldots T$) among all feasible alternatives.[11]

---

[11] An important caveat is that the efficiency criterion will be assured only if *all* feasible options are considered. In practice, only a subset of possibilities is ever evaluated. If the efficient solution does not happen to be in this subset, the decision rule will identify the most efficient option of those considered, but the efficiency criterion will not be satisfied in a strict sense.

**minimize the present value of costs (PVC)** A decision rule to achieve cost-effectiveness by selecting the least-cost policy option that achieves a pre-established objective.

**DECISION RULE: Minimize the Present Value of Costs (*PVC*).** The decision rule to minimize the present value of costs (*PVC*) guides the policy maker to select the least-cost option among those capable of achieving some preestablished objective. This is an explicit directive to set policy based on the criterion of cost-effectiveness. Of the two economically based decision rules, this one is the more common. The reason is that the law often predetermines the level of environmental benefits to be achieved through its definition of an environmental quality objective. When this is the case, the *PVB* is essentially fixed, leaving only *PVC* as a decision variable.

Before the cost comparison is done, the analyst has to first eliminate any options that do not achieve the requisite benefit level. Once done, the *PVC* is calculated for the remaining possibilities, and the option that incurs the lowest costs is selected. This decision rule can be summarized as follows:

To achieve cost-effectiveness, minimize $PVC = \Sigma[c_t/(1 + r_s)^t]$ for all $t$ periods ($t = 0, 1, 2, \ldots T$) among all feasible alternatives that achieve a predetermined benefit level.[12]

# Reservations about the Use of Benefit–Cost Analysis

While benefit–cost analysis is a viable risk management strategy, it is not without flaws. In fact, as a tool of environmental decision making, it has been the object of a fair amount of scrutiny. Critics of benefit–cost analysis generally point to two sources of concern. The first is the inherent problem of measuring and monetizing environmental costs and benefits accurately. The second refers to potential equity problems not addressed by this approach.

## Measurement Problems

Attempting to measure and assign a dollar value to environmental benefits and costs is unquestionably a major challenge of using benefit–cost analysis. As we indicated in Chapter 8, estimation is particularly problematic on the benefit side, where many intangibles are involved. Not only is it difficult to identify all the health and ecological benefits of a policy proposal, but assigning a dollar value to these gains is difficult at best. In fact, this measurement problem is often used to support the use of cost-effectiveness as an alternative criterion to allocative efficiency. On the opposite side of the analysis, capturing implicit costs is the primary source of difficulty.

---

[12] Just as with the efficiency-based decision rule, the cost-effectiveness solution will be obtained only if it is among the feasible options being considered. Since it is not practical for decision makers to consider more than a small number of possibilities, it is likely that the selected option will not be the true cost-minimizing solution, though it will be the least-cost alternative among those evaluated.

Solving this problem continues to be the objective of ongoing research. Finally, the selection of the social discount rate, which affects the present value of both benefit and cost estimates, is the subject of much debate—even among proponents of the benefit–cost approach.

### Equity Issues

In an objective assessment of benefit–cost analysis, equity concerns are not unfounded. The decision rules in benefit–cost analysis do not consider *how* the benefits and costs are distributed across various segments of society. Yet it is possible that the distribution of incremental benefits might be highly skewed, so that some group of consumers or some industrial sector receives less than its fair share. Similarly, the distribution of costs might be such that some economic sector bears an inequitable share of the burden. Of course, either problem is less troublesome if the same inequity occurs on both the benefit and the cost side, such as lower benefits matched by lower costs. However, there is no assurance that this will be the case.

Even proponents of benefit–cost analysis do not dismiss the measurement problems or potential inequities associated with benefit–cost analysis. So it is important that policy makers understand the implications and make adjustments for any noted shortcomings. In the interim, economists are continuing to research better estimation techniques. And many researchers and government officials are working to analyze and correct inequities associated with environmental policy decisions. Finding ways to improve the results is worth the effort. As a risk management strategy, benefit–cost analysis adds vital information to a very difficult undertaking. Furthermore, in the United States, benefit–cost analysis is required of all major policy proposals—a decision that has a long history behind it.

## U.S. Government Support of Benefit–Cost Analysis[13]

Most policy analysts point to the Flood Control Act of 1936 as the first U.S. federal legislation that explicitly acknowledged benefits and costs in a public policy initiative. According to this mandate, federal funds could be allocated to water projects only if the associated benefits were found to exceed the costs. Notice that this is precisely the feasibility rule based on $(PVB - PVC) > 0$ that we discussed earlier. Since this historic first, the use of economic theory as a decision-making tool has been promoted in many public policy settings—a practice that continues into present-day rule making. See Application 10.1 for recent examples of congressional efforts to legislate the use of costs, benefits, and risk analysis in environmental rule making.

---

[13] Part of this discussion is drawn from the following: Andrews (1984), pp. 43–85; and U.S. EPA, Office of Policy Analysis, Office of Policy, Planning, and Evaluation (August 1987), pp. 2-1–2-6.

# Benefits, Costs, and Risk Analysis in Environmental Rulemaking

During the 103d Congress, over a dozen bills and amendments were introduced that dealt with risk analysis. Among these was Senate Bill 110, proposed as the Environmental Risk Reduction Act of 1993 and introduced by Senator Daniel Patrick Moynihan (D–N.Y.). One of the bill's objectives was to make the major findings of the EPA's 1990 report called *Reducing Risk* part of federal law. This report summarizes an EPA Science Advisory Board study of how the United States could improve its efforts to reduce environmental risk.

According to the proposal, the Environmental Risk Reduction Act would have advanced the integration of risk assessment and benefit–cost analysis in the environmental decision-making process. As Senator Moynihan stated in a recent article,

> "I am convinced that risk ranking and cost-benefit analysis are valuable tools for making environmental decisions. They are not our only tools, but they do offer the means to set priorities and to measure success."

As part of its proposed requirements, the Senate bill called for quantitative estimates of risk exposure, an understanding of the alternatives available to reduce this exposure, and accurate estimates of the benefits and costs associated with these alternatives.

Senator Moynihan was aggressive about the bill's intent. Referring to U.S. annual spending of 2.2 percent of its GNP on environmental protection, he argued:

> "While this may not be too much money to spend on environmental protection, it is too much to spend unwisely."

Despite Moynihan's efforts, the proposed legislation was not passed by the 103d Congress.

Similar bills were proposed by other congressional officials, most notably two amendments proposed by Senator Johnston of Louisiana. The original amendment would have required the EPA to consider relative risk reduction, costs, and benefits for all proposed and final regulations. A revised version was introduced in Congress' second session. Intended to provide statutory strength to the intent of Clinton's Executive Order 12866, the Johnston amendments were added to many pending environmental bills. Interestingly, according to Terry Davies (1995), *"The lack of action on environmental legislation during the 103d Congress was due, to a great extent, to an inability to reach an acceptable compromise on the amendment's language."* Ultimately, the amendments were attached to a Department of Agriculture bill that was enacted, but the amendments were applicable only to regulations initiated by that department.

A more recent congressional effort dealing with environmental risk is a bill titled, The Regulatory Improvement Act of 1998. Introduced by Senator Levin of Michigan to the 105th Congress, this bill closely follows Clinton's Executive Order. One of its major provisions deals explicitly with benefit–cost analysis, requiring this decision rule for all regulations imposing costs over $100 million or otherwise adversely affecting the economy. At the proposed and final rule-making stages, a benefit–cost analysis would include an estimate of the anticipated benefits and costs, an analysis of regulatory alternatives, an assessment of whether the benefits justify the costs, and a determination of whether the rule-making objectives can be achieved in a more cost-effective manner or with greater net benefits than other alternatives.

SOURCES: "The Regulatory Improvement Act of 1998: Purpose and Summary," **http://thomas.loc.gov/cgi-bin/cpquery/ 1?cp105:./temp/~cp105V5Sn:e3633**. Martin R. Lee. "Environmental Protections: From the 103rd to the 104th Congress." *Congressional Research Service Report to Congress*, #95-58ENR, January 3, 1995; Senator Daniel Patrick Moynihan. "A Legislative Proposal: Why Not Enact a Law That Would Help Us Set Sensible Priorities." *EPA Journal*, January/February/March 1993, pp. 46–47; Jenifer Heath. "Moynihan Bill Sets Goals." *Water Environment and Technology*, July 1993, pp. 28–30; U.S. Environmental Protection Agency, Science Advisory Board. *Reducing Risk: Setting Priorities and Strategies for Environmental Protection.* Washington, DC: U.S. EPA, September 1990; Terry Davies. "Congress Discovers Risk Analysis." *Resources*, Winter 1995, pp. 5–8.

| TABLE 10.2 | | A RECENT HISTORY OF U.S. REGULATION USING ECONOMIC ANALYSIS | |
|---|---|---|---|
| **Act/Executive Order** | **Year** | **Title of Analysis** | **Type of Analysis** |
| OMB October 1971 Memo | 1971 | Quality of Life (QOL) Review | Costs, benefits |
| Executive Order 11821 | 1974 | Inflation Impact Statement (IIS) | Cost, benefits, inflationary impacts |
| Executive Order 11949 | 1976 | Economic Impact Statement (EIS) | Costs, benefits, economic impacts |
| Executive Order 12044 | 1978 | Regulatory Analysis | Costs, economic consequences |
| Regulatory Flexibility Act | 1980 | Regulatory Flexibility Analysis | Impacts on small businesses |
| Executive Order 12291 | 1981 | Regulatory Impact Analysis (RIA) | Costs, benefits, net benefits |
| Executive Order 12866 | 1993 | Economic Analysis | Costs, benefits, net benefits |

SOURCE: U.S. Environmental Protection Agency, Office of Policy Analysis, Office of Policy, Planning, and Evaluation. *EPA's Use of Benefit–Cost Analysis: 1981–1986*. Washington, DC, August 1987, Table 2-1, p. 2-2.

Over the past 30 years, U.S. presidents have used the power of the office to require economic analysis in federal regulatory decision making. Table 10.2 lists some of the presidential executive orders and other directives that specifically call for the consideration of benefits and/or costs in policy decisions. To understand the economic thinking in policy decisions, we consider the instruments called for in the most recent of these directives, namely the **Regulatory Impact Analysis (RIA),** and Clinton's **Economic Analysis (EA).**

### Executive Order 12291: Regulatory Impact Analysis (RIA)[14]

While the framework for considering the benefits and costs of regulatory proposals had existed under previous administrations, it was not until President Reagan's first term in office that the *efficiency criterion* was explicitly made a part of the regulatory review process. In 1981, Reagan signed Executive Order 12291, which outlined requirements that federal agencies had to follow in proposing or reviewing any major rule or regulation. Under Section 1 of this Executive Order, a "major rule" referred to any regulation expected to have an annual effect of at least $100 million or otherwise adversely affect the economy.

---

[14]For more detail concerning this Executive Order, see Federal Register 46, February 17, 1981: 13193-98.

Section 2 outlined the requirements that all agencies had to follow in developing new regulatory actions or assessing existing ones. Specifically, it called for the following:

"In promulgating new regulations, reviewing existing regulations, and developing legislative proposals concerning regulations, all agencies, to the extent permitted by law, shall adhere to the following requirements:

(a) Administrative decisions shall be based on adequate information concerning the need for and consequences of proposed government action;

(b) Regulatory action shall not be undertaken unless the potential benefits to society for the regulation outweigh the potential costs to society;

(c) Regulatory objectives shall be chosen to maximize the net benefits to society;

(d) Among alternative approaches to any regulatory objective, the alternative involving the least net cost to society shall be chosen; and

(e) Agencies shall set regulatory priorities with the aim of maximizing the aggregate net benefits to society, taking into account the condition of the particular industries affected by regulations, the conditions of the national economy, and other regulatory actions contemplated for the future."

Unlike prior references to economic considerations, this set of requirements *explicitly* called for the achievement of economic criteria in adopting regulatory actions. **Allocative efficiency** is referenced in paragraphs (c) and (e), which called for maximizing net benefits. The criterion of **cost-effectiveness** is referenced in paragraph (d), which required that the selection from among alternatives fulfilling a given objective be made on the basis of least net cost to society.

Taken out of context, paragraphs (c) and (d) suggest that these economic criteria were to have been met by every new policy proposal. However, there is a caveat in the first sentence of Section 2, given in the phrase "to the extent permitted by law." Because of this wording, many major environmental laws precluded the EPA from using either allocative efficiency or cost-effectiveness in establishing and implementing policy. Look at the list of EPA regulations in Table 10.3. Notice that some rulings, such as the primary and secondary air quality standards established by the Clean Air Act, do not consider economic costs at all. Hence, the level of environmental quality under these provisions is set to achieve some objective other than maximizing net benefits or cost-effectiveness.

Although the law was to prevail over the requirements of the executive order, all major regulations still had to be accompanied by what is called a

**TABLE 10.3**  TYPE OF ANALYSIS SPECIFIED IN SELECTED U.S. ENVIRONMENTAL LEGISLATION

| Act/Regulation | Benefits | | | Costs | | |
| --- | --- | --- | --- | --- | --- | --- |
| | Pollution Reduction | Health | Welfare/ Environment | Compliance Costs | Cost-Effectiveness | Economic Impacts |
| **Clean Air Act** | | | | | | |
| Primary standards | X | | | | | |
| Secondary standards | | | X | | | |
| Hazardous air pollutants | | X | | | | |
| New-source standards | X | * | * | ** | ** | ** |
| Motor vehicle standards*** | X | X | X | X | X | X |
| Aircraft emissions | X | X | X | X | | X |
| Fuel standards*** | X | X | X | X | | |
| **Clean Water Act** | | | | | | |
| Private treatment works | X | | **** | X | X | X |
| Public treatment works | X | | | | | |
| **Safe Drinking Water Act** | | | | | | |
| Maximum contaminant level goals | | X | | | | |
| Maximum contaminant levels | | | | X | | X |
| **Toxic Substance Control Act** | X | X | X | X | X | X |
| **Resource Conservation and Recovery Act** | | X | X | | | |
| **Comprehensive Environmental Response, Compensation and Liability Act** | | | | | | |
| Reportable quantities | | X | X | | | |
| National Contingency Plan | X | | | | X | |
| **Federal Insecticide, Fungicide and Rodenticide Act** | | | | | | |
| Data requirements | | | X | | | |
| Minor uses | X | X | X | X | X | X |
| **Atomic Energy Act** | | | | | | |
| Radioactive wastes | X | X | X | | | |
| Uranium mill tailings | X | X | X | X | X | X |

NOTES:

*Includes non-air-quality health and environmental impacts only.

**Statute refers only to "cost."

***Type of analysis depends on grounds for control.

****Includes non-water-quality environmental impacts only.

SOURCE: U.S. Environmental Protection Agency, Office of Policy Analysis, Office of Policy, Planning, and Evaluation. *EPA's Use of Benefit–Cost Analysis: 1981–1986.* Washington, DC, August 1987, Table 3-1, p. 3-2.

**Regulatory Impact Analysis (RIA)** A requirement under Executive Order 12291 that called for specific information about the potential benefits and costs associated with a "major" federal regulation.

**Regulatory Impact Analysis (RIA)** described in Section 3(d) of the executive order:

"To permit each proposed major rule to be analyzed in light of the requirements stated in Section 2 of this Order, each preliminary and final Regulatory Impact Analysis shall contain the following information:

(1) A description of the potential benefits of the rule, including any beneficial effects that cannot be quantified in monetary terms, and the identification of those likely to receive the benefits;

(2) A description of the potential costs of the rule, including any adverse effects that cannot be quantified in monetary terms, and the identification of those likely to bear the costs;

(3) A determination of the potential net benefits of the rule, including an evaluation of effects that cannot be quantified in monetary terms;

(4) A description of alternative approaches that could substantially achieve the same regulatory goal at lower cost, together with an analysis of the potential benefits and costs and a brief explanation of the legal reasons why such alternatives, if proposed, could not be adopted; and

(5) Unless covered by the description required under paragraph (4) of this subsection, an explanation of any legal reasons why the rule cannot be based on the requirements set forth in Section 2 of this Order."

The guidelines of Section 3(d) left little doubt about the importance of identifying and monetizing the potential costs and benefits of any policy proposal or regulatory review process. In that sense, the RIA was an uncompromising work assignment for economists engaged in policy formulation.

### Executive Order 12866: Economic Analysis (EA)

In September of 1993, President Clinton signed Executive Order 12866, which replaced Reagan's Executive Order 12291.[15] Nonetheless, it continued Reagan's commitment to economic fundamentals in policy formulation and evaluation. Essentially, the Clinton directive requires that all costs and benefits of available regulatory alternatives be considered in deciding whether to regulate and how to regulate. Among the executive order's

---

[15] To access the complete text of Clinton's executive order, visit **www.npr.gov/library/direct/orders/2646.html**.

"Principles of Regulations" that pertain directly to economic criteria are the following:

> "When an agency determines that a regulation is the best available method of achieving the regulatory objective, it shall design its regulations in the most cost-effective manner to achieve the regulatory objective.
>
> Each agency shall assess both the costs and the benefits of the intended regulation and . . . propose or adopt regulation only upon a reasoned determination that the benefits of the intended regulation justify its costs."

**Economic Analysis (EA)** A requirement under Executive Order 12866 that called for information on the benefits and costs of a "significant regulatory action."

Similar to Reagan's executive order, this one applies to all "significant regulatory actions," which includes those expected to have an annual impact on the economy of at least $100 million or some adverse effect. For each such action, the agency involved is required to prepare an **Economic Analysis (EA),** which acts as the successor to the Regulatory Impact Analysis (RIA).

The Office of Management and Budget formed an interagency group to determine "best practices" for preparing an Economic Analysis (EA) under the new executive order. After two years of effort, the group released its guidance on implementation of the president's executive order in 1996.[16] The report states that any EA should include information that allows decision makers to determine that:

> "There is adequate information indicating the need for and consequences of the proposed action;
>
> The potential benefits to society justify the potential costs, . . . unless a statute requires another regulatory approach;
>
> The proposed action will maximize net benefits to society, . . . unless a statute requires another regulatory approach;
>
> Where a statute requires a specific regulatory approach, the proposed action will be the most cost-effective, including reliance on performance objectives to the extent feasible;
>
> Agency decisions are based on the best reasonably obtainable scientific, technical, economic, and other information."

Notice how the EA follows the same logic and economic criteria outlined in an RIA. It too explicitly calls for a maximization of net benefits, or where otherwise required under the law, that a proposed action be the most cost-effective.

---

[16] The text of this report can be accessed at **www1.whitehouse.gov/WH/EOP/OMB/html/miscdoc/riaguide.html.**

Implementing either an EA or an RIA is a major undertaking in order to satisfy the requirements to assess environmental costs and benefits properly. To better illustrate exactly how economic criteria are used in a regulatory context, it is helpful to study a real-world example. So we next investigate the EPA's use of the net benefits decision rule in its RIA for the phasedown of lead in gasoline.

# A Regulatory Impact Analysis (RIA): Reducing Lead in Gasoline [17]

Petroleum refiners began using lead additives as an inexpensive source of octane in the 1920s. By adding lead to gasoline, refiners were able to reduce engine knock and increase engine performance. However, these gains were not without consequence. Coincident with the increased use of lead additives, researchers observed a link between lead exposure and adverse health effects such as mental and cardiovascular disorders. Acting on the growing body of scientific evidence, the EPA was charged with the responsibility of achieving a reduction in the lead content of gasoline.

In 1985, the existing U.S. lead standard was 1.1 grams per leaded gallon (gplg). As part of its plan to reduce society's exposure to lead, the EPA proposed tightening this standard to 0.1 gplg effective January 1, 1986. Since such a policy change came under the legal definition of a "major" rule, the EPA was required to conduct a Regulatory Impact Analysis (RIA). This in turn meant that the agency had to examine the costs, benefits, and net benefits of approaches that could be used to meet the more stringent lead standard.

## Estimating the Incremental Benefits of the Lead Standard Proposal

An important element of the benefit assessment for the RIA was an evaluation of the predicted health improvements associated with the lead standard proposal. Based on the findings of scientific studies, the EPA conducted tests to determine the relationship between human blood lead levels and leaded gasoline usage. Figure 10.1 shows the correlation between these two variables.

As part of the risk assessment process, the EPA also analyzed scientific findings to find out if any population groups were more susceptible to the health risks of lead exposure. Even then, there was already an abundance of scientific evidence about the effects of lead exposure on children. According to the final report of the RIA, *"these effects range from relatively subtle changes in biochemical measurements at low doses to severe retardation and even*

---

[17] The following is drawn from U.S. EPA, Office of Policy Analysis (February 1985)

| FIGURE 10.1 | CORRELATION BETWEEN LEAD IN GASOLINE AND AVERAGE BLOOD LEAD LEVELS |

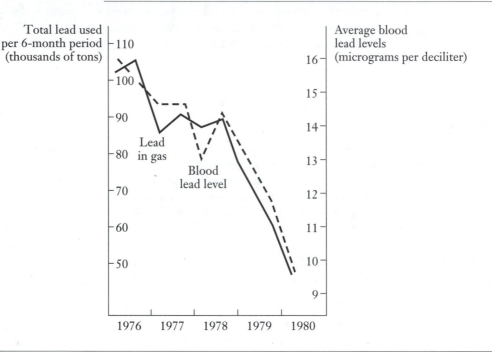

SOURCE: Lily Whiteman. "Trades to Remember: The Lead Phasedown." *EPA Journal* 18(2), May/June 1992, p. 38.

*death at very high levels.*" Based on the evidence, it was clear that an important incremental benefit of tightening the lead standard would be improvements in the health of children. To monetize children's incremental health benefits, the EPA used two measures: (1) savings in medical care expenditures, and (2) savings in compensatory educational expenditures. These attempted to capture the benefits of improving physiological health and cognitive development. Using these predefined measures, the EPA estimated that the value of incremental health benefits for children would be approximately $600 million in 1986—the first full year of the revised lead standard. (This value and all others given in the RIA report are expressed in 1983 dollars.)

Another element of the EPA's study of lead-related health effects was an examination of the evidence linking lead exposure to blood pressure levels in adult males. Much of the agency's analysis was based on the findings of two very recent scientific studies. Because of this, the EPA stated that their findings on this health issue were to be viewed as preliminary and *not* to be considered for the subject rule making. Hence, results were presented in the RIA for informational use only.

Using statistical models, the EPA estimated the relationship between blood lead levels in adult males and blood pressure levels. Based on the results, models were constructed to estimate the associated incremental benefits of reductions in cardiovascular-related death and various disorders delineated as follows: (1) hypertension; (2) myocardial infarctions; (3) strokes; and (4) deaths. To monetize the benefits of reducing *nonfatal* health effects, the EPA used the dollar value of medical care costs, expenditures on medications, and lost wages. For *fatal* cases, the EPA used existing estimates of a statistical life and selected a magnitude of $1 million per life saved. Taken together, the monetized values of the incremental benefits per case were reported in the RIA as follows: $220 per case of hypertension; $60,000 per heart attack; $44,000 per stroke; and $1 million per life saved. In the aggregate, the incremental benefits of the lead ruling associated with adult male health were reported over a six-year period and ranged from $5.897 billion in 1986 to $4.692 billion in 1992.

Three types of nonhealth benefits were analyzed in the RIA: (1) reduction in harmful emissions caused by misfueling (i.e., the use of leaded gasoline in vehicles requiring unleaded gasoline); (2) lower maintenance costs; and (3) increased fuel economy. Misfueling causes harmful emissions because leaded gasoline damages a car's catalytic converter, which is designed to abate such pollutants as hydrocarbons (HC), carbon monoxide (CO), and nitrogen oxides ($NO_x$). Thus, the lower lead content was expected to slow the rate at which catalytic converters are damaged, which in turn would reduce these emissions. Furthermore, the new standard was expected to reduce misfueling because it would increase production costs of leaded gasoline, thus reducing the price differential between leaded and unleaded fuel.

To estimate the incremental benefits of reducing misfueling damage, the EPA assumed that the new lead standard would eliminate about 80 percent of the misfueling. Accounting for all the associated damage reductions, the EPA estimated that the resulting decrease in emissions of HC, CO, and $NO_x$ would yield incremental benefits of approximately $222 million in 1986. In addition, the values for reduced maintenance expenditures and for increased fuel economy for 1986 were estimated to be $914 million and $187 million, respectively.

## Estimating the Incremental Costs of the Lead Standard Proposal

On the cost side of the analysis, the EPA had to define, quantify, and monetize the social costs of the proposed lead ruling. The RIA defines real social costs as, *"the costs of real resources that are used to comply with the rule (i.e., the extra energy, capital, labor, etc. that are needed to meet the tighter lead standard)."* To approximate these costs, the EPA used estimates of the change in manufacturing costs of gasoline and other petroleum products arising from the new lead ruling. The agency used an engineering cost model of the refinery

| TABLE 10.4 | THE REGULATORY IMPACT ANALYSIS (RIA) FOR REDUCING LEAD IN GASOLINE: THE EPA'S ESTIMATES OF INCREMENTAL BENEFITS AND COSTS |
|---|---|

| | Monetized Benefits and Costs of Reducing Lead in Gasoline (millions of 1983 dollars) | | | | | | | |
|---|---|---|---|---|---|---|---|---|
| | 1985 | 1986 | 1987 | 1988 | 1989 | 1990 | 1991 | 1992 |
| **Monetized Benefits** | | | | | | | | |
| Children health effects | 223 | 600 | 547 | 502 | 453 | 414 | 369 | 358 |
| Adult blood pressure | 1,724 | 5,897 | 5,675 | 5,447 | 5,187 | 4,966 | 4,682 | 4,692 |
| Conventional pollutants | 0 | 222 | 222 | 224 | 226 | 230 | 239 | 248 |
| Vehicle maintenance | 102 | 914 | 859 | 818 | 788 | 767 | 754 | 749 |
| Fuel economy | 35 | 187 | 170 | 113 | 134 | 139 | 172 | 164 |
| Total Monetized Benefits | 2,084 | 7,821 | 7,474 | 7,105 | 6,788 | 6,517 | 6,216 | 6,211 |
| **Monetized Costs** | | | | | | | | |
| Total Refining Costs | 96 | 608 | 558 | 532 | 504 | 471 | 444 | 441 |
| **Net Benefits** | 1,988 | 7,213 | 6,916 | 6,573 | 6,284 | 6,045 | 5,772 | 5,770 |
| **Net Benefits Excluding Adult Blood Pressure** | 264 | 1,316 | 1,241 | 1,125 | 1,096 | 1,079 | 1,090 | 1,079 |

NOTES: The above estimates are reported under the assumption of partial misfueling.

Sums may not equal totals shown due to rounding.

SOURCE: U.S. Environmental Protection Agency, Office of Policy Analysis. *Costs and Benefits of Reducing Lead in Gasoline, Final Regulatory Impact Analysis.* Report No. EPA-230-05-85-006, Washington, DC, February 1985, p. E-12.

industry, which was originally developed for the Department of Energy. First, the model was specified under the existing or baseline lead content standard. Then it was reestimated, using the new standard. The difference between the two yielded the incremental cost estimate.

In general, real manufacturing costs were found to decrease over the seven-year period under study, due mainly to the expected decline in the demand for leaded gasoline. Year-to-year cost estimates suggested a relatively small impact on refiners. For example, tightening the standard from 1.1 gplg to the proposed rule of 0.1 gplg yielded an incremental cost estimate of $608 million in 1986, the first full year of the proposed rule, and $441 million in 1992.

### Putting It All Together: Benefit–Cost Analysis

Table 10.4 summarizes the EPA's estimates of the *real* incremental benefits and costs associated with tightening the lead standard from 1.1 gplg to 0.1 gplg. Notice that the magnitudes show that the net incremental benefits of the proposed rule are positive and quite substantial. Including the benefits of reducing adverse effects on adult blood pressure, the magnitudes range from $7,213 million in 1986 to $5,770 million in 1992. Since the evidence for the adult blood pressure benefits was not well established, the EPA chose to rely on the net benefit estimates *excluding* these benefits to defend the economic feasibility of the proposed rule change. Using this more conservative estimate, net benefits still were found to be positive for each forecasted year. In fact, the estimates are above $1 billion for each of the seven full years affected by the proposed ruling.

Finally, to adjust for time differences over the period, the EPA conducted a present value analysis of their net benefit estimates. Using the conservative estimate that excludes blood pressure effects and selecting a *real* social discount rate of 10 percent, the present value of net benefits (*PVNB*) over the period was estimated to be $5.9 billion ($1983).

### The Final Decision

Following the estimation of incremental benefits and costs required in the RIA, the EPA officially announced a low-lead standard of 0.1 gplg effective January 1, 1986. The decision was supported by the economic evidence that the more stringent lead standard would be beneficial to society.

# Conclusions

In its most fundamental form, environmental policy is aimed at minimizing society's risk of exposure to environmental hazards. For a litany of reasons, this objective is at once one of the great challenges faced by society today and one of its more important responsibilities. While all of society is involved in public policy development, most of the detail of formulating, implementing, and monitoring regulatory provisions falls in the hands of public officials. By itself, this fact supports the need for analytical tools such as benefit–cost analysis to guide the decisions that define environmental policy.

While not without flaws, benefit–cost analysis is a useful strategic approach to environmental decision making. Its objectivity is its primary strength in helping officials evaluate the social gains and the opportunity costs of their decisions. Choosing between a policy that reduces mortality risk to save one more life in a million exposed or a regulation that will reduce the risk of birth defects by 10 times that amount is a tough decision by any measure. Yet, these kinds of decisions are precisely what environmental policy development is all about. Every resource allocated to save a national forest is one less resource available to clean rivers and streams. Every dollar spent to clean a hazardous waste site is one less dollar available to save an endangered species. Such is the dilemma that confronts every society as it makes decisions about how to allocate scarce resources, and such is the fundamental premise of economic thought.

Guiding decision making is the purpose of benefit–cost analysis. Explaining what this analytical tool can accomplish, how it is implemented, and what it fails to achieve have been the primary objectives of this chapter. Since benefit–cost analysis is becoming a more dominant force in public policy decisions, it is critical that we comprehend how it influences environmental regulations and how, in so doing, it affects the quality of our lives.

# Summary

- In benefit–cost analysis, two types of time-oriented adjustments are necessary—present value determination and inflation correction.

- To discount a future value $(FV)$ into its present value $(PV)$, use the conversion formula $PV = FV[1/(1 + r)^t]$, where $t$ is the number of periods, and $[1/(1 + r)^t]$ is the discount factor.

- To adjust a value in the present period for expected inflation in the future period, it must be converted to its nominal value for that period, using the formula: Nominal value$_{period\ x+t}$ = Real value$_{period\ x}$ · $(1 + p)^t$, where $p$ is the rate of inflation.

- Time-adjusted incremental benefits and costs are referred to as the present value of benefits $(PVB) = \Sigma[B_t/(1 + r_s)^t]$ and the present value of costs $(PVC) = \Sigma[C_t/(1 + r_s)^t]$, respectively.

- The first step of benefit–cost analysis identifies feasible options. A policy option is feasible if the $(PVB/PVC)$ for that option $> 1$ or if $(PVB - PVC) > 0$.

- The second step of benefit–cost analysis evaluates all "acceptable" options *relative* to one another on the basis of a decision rule.

- One decision rule is to maximize the present value of net benefits $(PVNB)$, which equals $\Sigma[B_t/(1 + r_s)^t] - \Sigma[C_t/(1 + r_s)^t]$, among all feasible alternatives to achieve allocative efficiency. Another is to minimize the present value of costs $(PVC)$, which equals $\Sigma[C_t/(1 + r_s)^t]$ among all feasible alternatives that attain a predetermined benefit level to achieve cost-effectiveness.

- Measuring and monetizing intangibles, the selection of the social discount rate, and capturing implicit costs are among the concerns of using benefit–cost analysis. Another problem is the potential for an inequitable distribution of costs and benefits.

- Over the past 30 years, U.S. presidents have required economic analysis in federal regulatory decision making. Two instruments that call for some type of benefit and/or cost considerations in policy decisions are the Regulatory Impact Analysis (RIA) required by Executive Order 12291, and the Economic Analysis (EA) called for in Executive Order 12866.

- Section 2 of President Reagan's Executive Order 12291 and more recently President Clinton's Executive Order 12866 explicitly call for the achievement of allocative efficiency and cost-effectiveness in adopting regulatory actions.

- In the RIA for evaluating a proposal to tighten the lead standard, the EPA estimated that the present value of the net benefits (*PVNB*) was $5.9 billion ($1983). The EPA officially announced a low-lead standard of 0.1 gplg effective January 1, 1986.

## Key Concepts

present value determination
discount factor
social discount rate
inflation correction
real value
nominal value
deflating
present value of benefits (*PVB*)
present value of costs (*PVC*)

benefit–cost ratio
present value of net benefits (*PVNB*)
maximize the present value of net benefits (*PVNB*)
minimize the present value of costs (*PVC*)
Regulatory Impact Analysis (RIA)
Economic Analysis (EA)

## Review Questions

1. Suppose industry abatement costs rise from $850 million in 1998 to $1,000 million in 1999 in nominal terms, and that the CPI is 100 in 1998 and 106 in 1999.
   a. Evaluate the change in costs over the period in real terms, first in 1998 dollars, and then in 1999 dollars.
   b. Are your answers the same? Explain why or why not.

2. To examine the implications of selecting various discount rates, reconsider the water filtration system example in the text, but change the discount rate from 10 percent to 5 percent.
   a. Find the present value of the system.
   b. Now compare this present value with the one calculated under the assumption of a 10-percent rate. Explain the difference intuitively.

3. Refer to the RIA for the revised lead ruling discussed in the chapter.
   a. Mathematically confirm that the estimate of the present value of net benefits (*PVNB*) is approximately $5.9 billion as stated.

b. Discuss how the *PVNB* would have changed if the EPA had used a social discount rate of 8 percent.

4. Recently, the EPA proposed an increase in the national air quality standards for particulate matter (PM). Since the change was considered a major rule, the agency was required to conduct an RIA and assess the potential costs and benefits of the proposed standard. The completed RIA can be accessed at **ttnwww.rtpnc.epa.gov/naaqsfin/ria.htm**. As part of this RIA, benefit and cost data for the *existing* standard were given and are replicated below.

| Control Region | Annual Control Cost ($1990 millions) |
|---|---|
| Midwest/Northeast | 380 |
| Southeast | 2 |
| South Central | 230 |
| Rocky Mountain | 210 |
| Northwest | 140 |
| West | 130 |
| National | 1,100 |

SOURCE: Table C1, Appendix C: "Costs and Benefits of Achieving the Current PM10 and Ozone Standard."

| Benefit Category | Monetized Benefits ($1990 billions) |
|---|---|
| Mortality | |
| Short-term exposure | 2.950 |
| Long-term exposure | 2.860 |
| Chronic bronchitis | 2.010 |
| Hospital admissions | |
| Total respiratory | 0.022 |
| Congestive heart failure | 0.003 |
| Ischemic heart disease | 0.005 |
| Upper respiratory systems | |
| Asthma attacks | 0.001 |
| Work loss days | 0.015 |
| Minor restricted activity days | 0.057 |
| Consumer cleaning cost savings | 0.039 |
| Visibility | 0.320 |
| Total benefits | |
| Using short-term mortality | 5.400 |
| Using long-term mortality | 5.300 |

SOURCE: Table C1, Appendix C: "Costs and Benefits of Achieving the Current PM10 and Ozone Standard."

a. Examine the control cost estimates, and provide a plausible explanation as to why there are incremental costs differences across regions for meeting the PM standard.
b. Economically, can you justify the PM standard? Explain.
c. List some of the limitations associated with benefit–cost analysis. Which of these are applicable to this particular economic analysis? Explain.

## Additional Readings

Baumol, William J. "On the Social Rate of Discount." *American Economic Review*, September 1968, pp. 788–802.

Crandall, Robert W. "Is There Progress in Environmental Policy?" *Contemporary Economic Policy*, January 1995, pp. 80–83.

Cropper, Maureen L., and Wallace E. Oates. "Environmental Economics: A Survey." *Journal of Economic Literature* 30, June 1992, pp. 675–740.

Cropper, Maureen L., and Paul R. Portney. "Discounting Human Lives." *Resources* 108, Summer 1992, pp. 1–4.

Dorfman, Robert. "An Introduction to Benefit–Cost Analysis." In Robert Dorfman and Nancy Dorfman, eds., *Economics of the Environment: Selected Readings*. New York: W. W. Norton, 1993.

Halvorsen, Robert, and Michael G. Ruby. *Benefit–Cost Analysis of Air-Pollution Control*. Lexington, MA: D. C. Heath, 1981.

Kopp, Raymond J., Alan J. Krupnick, and Michael Toman. "Cost–Benefit Analysis and Regulatory Reform: An Assessment of the Science and the Art." Discussion Paper 97-19, Resources for the Future, January 1997.

Krupnick, Alan J., and Paul R. Portney. "Controlling Urban Air Pollution: A Benefit–Cost Assessment." *Science* 252, April 26, 1991, pp. 522–28.

Merrifield, John. "Sensitivity Analysis in Benefit–Cost Analysis: A Key to Increased Use and Acceptance." *Contemporary Economic Policy*, July 1997, pp. 82–92.

Peskin, Henry M., and Eugene P. Seskin. *Cost Benefit Analysis and Water Pollution Policy*. Washington, DC: The Urban Institute, 1973.

"White House Issues Benefit–Cost Guidance, Ending Months of Debate." *Inside EPA's Risk Policy Report*, Washington, DC: Inside Washington Publishers, January 31, 1996.

## Related Web Sites

Circular No. A-94 Revised (guidelines and discount rates for benefit–cost analysis of federal programs)

**www1.whitehouse.gov/WH/EOP/OMB/html/circulars/a094/a094.html**

Complete text of Clinton's Executive Order 12866

**www.npr.gov/library/direct/orders/2646.html**

| | |
|---|---|
| Complete text of the Office of Management and Budget's "Economic Analysis of Federal Regulation Under Executive Order 12866" | **www1.whitehouse.gov/WH/EOP/OMB/html/miscdoc/riaguide.html** |
| Congressional Research Service Report for Congress "Cost–Benefit Analysis: Issues in Its Use in Regulation" | **www.cnie.org/nle/rsk-4.html** |
| Congressional Research Service Report for Congress "Risk Analysis and Cost–Benefit Analysis of Environmental Regulations" | **www.cnie.org/nle/rsk-5.html** |
| Cost–Benefit Analysis: Project Summaries Resources for the Future, Washington, DC | **www.rff.org/methods/cost_benefit.htm** |
| Regulatory Impact Analysis (RIA) on the new standard for particulate matter (PM) | **ttnwww.rtpnc.epa.gov/naaqsfin/ria.htm** |

# IV

## *The Case of Air*

Technically, there has been some form of air pollution as long as the earth has supported life. Yet air pollution did not begin to be a pervasive problem until the Industrial Revolution. The combination of population growth, motorized transportation, and manufacturing activity that characterized the nineteenth century also marks the period when air quality became a real concern. As industrial growth proceeded on its course, so too did air pollution, though few realized the severity of the problem in those early days of industrial development.

In the United States, as urban smog became more apparent in cities like Los Angeles and Philadelphia, pressure began to mount for public officials to take action. Local communities and some state governments began to enact air quality laws. But it was literally decades before the federal government took an active role in what was fast becoming a worldwide problem.

Over the past four decades, U.S. air quality control policy has evolved into a comprehensive body of laws, with the most recent revisions embodied in the 1990 Clean Air Act Amendments. These extensive provisions are supported by an equally sophisticated infrastructure to implement controls and monitor compliance. In addition, international conferences have begun to address worldwide air pollution problems, like global warming and ozone depletion.

Overall, there has been a good deal of progress. We have a much better sense of the implications of air pollution, thanks in part to medical and scientific research. As knowledge advanced, we have become better able to find solutions. And many nations have begun substituting economic incentives for command-and-control approaches to regulating air quality. Understanding the extent of this progress and analyzing what has been accomplished requires a fairly thorough examination of the facts and some sense of the evolution of policy.

To that end, this module provides a multi-step approach to learning about air quality problems and policy solutions, using economics as an analytical tool. We begin in Chapter 11 with a broad-based analysis of U.S. air quality control policy and the standard-setting process that defines clean air for the nation. In Chapter 12, we investigate how U.S. standards are implemented through control instruments aimed at mobile and stationary sources. A particular focus is an analysis of how well these initiatives reduce urban air pollution and acidic deposition. Finally, in Chapter 13, global air pollution is explored with an in-depth discussion of international policy and various proposals aimed at ozone depletion and global warming.

# 11

---

## *Defining Air Quality: The Standard-Setting Process*

---

One of the most important elements of clean air policy development is determining the target level of air quality that legislative initiatives are to achieve. In simpler terms, policy makers have to decide how clean is clean air. In the United States, standards or emissions limits are used to define a national level of air quality that will protect human health and the ecology. Many factors influence the standard-setting process that ultimately guides U.S. policy. Among these are such determinants as technological feasibility, energy requirements, and economic considerations. But more fundamentally, a determination has to be made about which substances in the atmosphere present a risk to society and the extent to which these substances can and should be controlled.

This important determination proceeds from the basic premise that the earth's atmosphere comprises a specific combination of various gases. Nitrogen and oxygen account for 99 percent, and other gases such as carbon dioxide and helium make up the remainder—a composition critical to supporting life on earth. Any substances that contaminate or disrupt this natural composition pose an environmental risk and are potential targets for clean air policy. Identifying these contaminants is important, but it is only part of the story. Ultimately, a decision must be made about how much of any contaminant society can tolerate—an issue of some debate. What *is* clear is that we cannot entirely avoid the risks of air pollution without incurring unreasonable opportunity costs.

To understand this assertion, consider the following. Some contaminants in the atmosphere are **natural pollutants,** such as pollen, dust particles from volcanic disturbances, gases from decaying animals and plants, even salt spray from the oceans. Because these pollutants occur naturally, they are virtually beyond human control. Other contaminants are

**natural pollutants**
Those contaminants that come about through nonartificial processes in nature.

283

**anthropogenic pollutants** Those contaminants associated with human activity.

**anthropogenic,** meaning they are caused by human activity. These include such substances as carbon monoxide from automobile tailpipe exhausts, sulfur dioxide emissions from electricity generation, and toxic chemicals released from manufacturing plants. Although these types of pollutants *are* controllable and generally present a greater environmental risk than natural contaminants, they cannot be avoided completely without incurring the unrealistic opportunity cost of the absence of industrial activity. Consequently, we must accept the reality that our air quality will *not* be synonymous with a zero pollution level. But just what level of pollution is "acceptable," and how should it be determined?

Based on economic theory, we know that an *efficient* level of air quality is identified where the marginal social benefits of cleaner air are balanced with the marginal social costs incurred to achieve it. Furthermore, we recognize that market-based instruments can be used to reduce the negative externalities from pollution-generating activities and to encourage the positive externalities associated with abatement. These theories can and sometimes do guide policy decisions. However, as is often the case, the real-world complexities of the democratic process, scientific uncertainty, and political pressures tend to delay or even prohibit the realization of this economic approach.

Our goal in this chapter is to explore the realities of clean air policy development by studying how the process has evolved in the United States. It is of particular interest to examine how the government uses standards to define air quality for the nation and to evaluate critically the implications of using a standards-based approach. To organize the presentation, we begin by discussing the following aspects of U.S. air quality policy:

- its evolution and development
- its primary objectives
- its standards-based definition of air quality
- the infrastructure it establishes for implementation

Once done, we conduct a two-part benefit–cost analysis—the first as an overall appraisal of the Clean Air Act and its amendments, and the second as an evaluation of the standard-setting process. An appendix at the end of the chapter provides a reference of the acronyms used in our discussions.

## An Overview of Air Quality Legislation in the United States

On November 15, 1990, President Bush signed into law extensive changes in air quality policy in the form of the 1990 Clean Air Act Amendments. This legislative landmark received strong congressional support. Its hallmark is the integration of market-based policy instruments. The amendments came only after years of political battles, false starts, and a chronicle of events that underscores the importance of environmental issues and the complexity of drafting policy to deal with them.

## In the Beginning

Prior to the 1950s, all air quality legislation in the United States had been enacted by state and local governments, most of which have a rather extensive history of laws aimed at cleaner air. Logically, the earliest of these were passed during the Industrial Revolution.[1] Even in contemporary times, state and local governments have typically taken the lead. The most notable example is California, whose often pathbreaking legislation has been in direct response to the smog problem in Los Angeles. In 1961, California passed the first state-level air pollution law to control motor vehicle emissions. This legislation followed many years of struggle between California officials and the American automobile industry, the subject of Application 11.1. In fact, a decade had passed since a 1951 study by Dr. A. J. Haagen-Smit of the California Institute of Technology scientifically confirmed that automobile emissions were a major contributor to smog formation.

At the federal level, the legislative history of air pollution initiatives is much shorter. In fact, there were no *national* air quality laws until the Air Pollution Control Act of 1955 was passed, and there was no truly comprehensive legislation until the Clean Air Act of 1963 was enacted—nearly a century after state and local governments had begun to take action. From that point on, there were a series of revisions and new initiatives that helped form U.S. policy as it is now defined. Look at Table 11.1 for a synopsis of the major federal laws that map out this legislative evolution.

Notice in the table that during the 1960s there were many policy revisions, many of which gradually shifted authority away from the states and toward the federal level. However, it was the decade of the 1970s that marked the turning point in the history of U.S. air quality legislation. Through the 1970 Clean Air Act Amendments, Congress established national standards for air quality and authorized the newly created Environmental Protection Agency (EPA) to administer and implement its policy.

Much of the impetus for these major changes started at the grassroots level. Chronicles of environmental degradation, some with ominous predictions, had begun to appear on bookstore shelves.[2] In 1970, the first Earth Day was celebrated, signifying society's growing interest in environmental issues. In 1972, the Stockholm Conference on the Human Environment was held, the largest international symposium on the environment to date.[3] Throughout the decade, membership in environmental groups grew at a record-setting pace.

---

[1] See Stern (1982) for a thorough historical perspective on U.S. air quality laws.

[2] The classic example of such writings is *Silent Spring* by Rachel Carson, published in 1962.

[3] One of the outcomes of this conference was the creation of the United Nations Environment Programme (UNEP). Visit their Web site at **www.unep.org**.

## California Smog and the Automobile Industry

California's severe smog problem motivated its early attempts in the 1950s to gain the support of the automobile industry in solving its dilemma. Despite the evidence connecting motor vehicle emissions to smog production revealed in Dr. A. J. Haagen-Smit's 1951 study, the automobile industry denied that auto emissions were a major contributor to the problem and argued that the source of urban smog required further investigation. The result was a volley between the industry and the state government that accomplished little throughout the 1950s.

In 1959, manufacturers acknowledged that the engine's design was an important source of the emissions problem. In 1961, automakers began to install engine ventilation devices on all new cars sold in California to control these emissions, a technology change that was eventually mandated under California law. However, this technology was not new. In fact, it had been developed in the 1930s. Apparently weary of the lack of progress, the California government attempted to force the issue. Legislation was passed calling for the installation of equipment to control vehicle exhausts as soon as it was developed either by the major automakers or by any three independent manufacturers. The automobile producers asserted that such technology simply did not exist. Yet, in June 1964, the state confirmed that independent parts manufacturers could provide the needed add-on equipment at a reasonable cost and mandated its installation on all new vehicles starting with the 1966 model year. Predictably, the automakers announced in August 1964 that they had the capability to install their own devices on 1966 models, despite the fact that in March they had claimed that 1967 was the earliest model year by which they could accommodate the change.

Not only were the major auto producers using delay tactics, but the measure of their innovative effort was unimpressive. Ford and General Motors developed only a simple air pump, while Chrysler's solution, marketed as a "clean air package," involved only minor alterations to its fuel and carburetion system. It was later discovered that Chrysler's "solution" contributed significantly to nitrogen oxide emissions.

Why were there such significant delays? Part of the answer is based on economic theory. If there had been a demand for cleaner-running cars, competitive firms would have recognized the advantage of being the first to satisfy that demand as well as the threat to their survival of being left behind in what is often a race to innovate. However, it is not at all clear that such a demand existed, and even if it had, market incentives were thwarted by the market power possessed by the "Big Three"—General Motors, Ford, and Chrysler. The giant automakers enjoyed a position of market strength that was protected by entry barriers from the threat of any innovative entering firms. In 1953, the three firms formally pooled their efforts by forming a committee to jointly investigate the pollution problem. Later, in 1955, they executed a cross-licensing agreement to share access to any patents on emission controls. In so doing, they effectively removed the incentive for any one of them to find an innovative solution. (It turns out that in 1969 the Department of Justice filed suit against the Big Three, charging them with collusive attempts at hindering the advancement of pollution control technology. The suit was settled by a consent decree that ended the cross-licensing agreement.)

SOURCES: Lawrence White. *The Regulation of Air Pollutant Emissions from Motor Vehicles.* Washington, DC: American Enterprise Institute for Public Policy Research, 1982, Ch. 3; U.S. Senate, Staff of the Subcommittee on Air and Water Pollution of the Committee on Public Works. *The Impact of Auto Emission Standards.* Washington, DC: U.S. Government Printing Office, October 1973; Eugene P. Seskin. "Automobile Air Pollution Policy." In Paul R. Portney, ed., *Current Issues in U.S. Environmental Policy.* Baltimore: The Johns Hopkins University Press, 1978, pp. 68–104.

| TABLE 11.1 | A BRIEF RETROSPECTIVE OF U.S. AIR QUALITY LEGISLATION |
|---|---|
| Air Pollution Control Act of 1955 | This was the first federal legislation on air pollution. Its focus was limited, aimed primarily at providing federal appropriations to state governments in support of research and training on air quality. |
| Clean Air Act of 1963 | This was the first comprehensive federal air quality legislation, though it continued to place the onus of air quality control on states. Emissions regulations for stationary sources were established, and the secretary of the Department of Health, Education and Welfare (HEW) was empowered to set up a liaison committee with the auto industry to study the effects of motor vehicle emissions. |
| Motor Vehicle Air Pollution Control Act of 1965 | The HEW secretary was authorized to set emission standards on new motor vehicles, but there was no statutory deadline by which this was to be accomplished. |
| 1965 Clean Air Act Amendments | The HEW was authorized to establish the first federally mandated mobile emissions standards. Maximum emissions of carbon monoxide and hydrocarbons were set for new motor vehicles, starting with the 1968 model year. |
| Air Quality Control Act of 1967 | Air quality control regions (AQCR) were to be established across the country. The HEW was to determine air quality criteria for common air pollutants and was to identify available control technologies. States were to set and implement ambient air quality standards for their designated regions based on results of federal research on the effects of air pollution. The federal government could intervene if it did not approve of the states' decisions. |
| 1970 Clean Air Act Amendments | National Ambient Air Quality Standards (NAAQS) were established for stationary sources, and emissions limits were set for mobile sources. Both were to be implemented through formalized State Implementation Plans (SIPs). New source performance standards (NSPS) were established at more stringent levels than for existing sources. |
| 1977 Clean Air Act Amendments | Previously set deadlines for meeting air quality objectives were modified. AQCRs were reclassified into attainment and nonattainment regions. The objective was to protect regions that were "cleaner" than what was required by the NAAQS. These regions were termed "PSD" areas to indicate "prevention of significant deterioration." |

SOURCES: Arthur C. Stern, "History of Air Pollution Legislation in the United States." *Journal of the Air Pollution Control Association* 32(1), January 1982, pp. 44–61; Edwin S. Mills. *The Economics of Environmental Quality*. New York: W. W. Norton, 1978, pp. 189–94; Paul R. Portney. "Air Pollution Policy." In Paul R. Portney, ed., *Public Policies for Environmental Protection*. Washington, DC: Resources for the Future, 1990a, pp. 27–96; Sidney M. Wolf, *Pollution Law Handbook: A Guide to Federal Environmental Laws*. New York: Quorum Books, 1988, Chapter 2.

**TABLE 11.2**   AN OVERVIEW OF THE CLEAN
AIR ACT AMENDMENTS OF 1990

### Title I. Provisions for Attainment and Maintenance of National Ambient Air Quality Standards

Summary:   Amends and extends provisions for achieving the National Ambient Air Quality Standards (NAAQS), and regulates changes in State Implementation Plans (SIPs) for nonattainment areas.

### Title II. Provisions Relating to Mobile Sources

Summary:   Establishes more stringent emissions controls, and extends the vehicle useful life for most emissions standards to 10 years or 100,000 miles. New provisions address the use of reformulated gasoline, oxygenated fuels, and alternative fuels in certain nonattainment areas. Prohibits leaded gasoline after December 31, 1995.

### Title III. Hazardous Air Pollutants

Summary:   Lists 189 toxic pollutants as the basis for setting emissions controls. Maximum Achievable Control Technology (MACT) standards are to be established for all listed source categories within a 10-year period.

### Title IV. Acid Deposition Control

Summary:   Establishes a market-based allowance program to achieve a permanent 10-million-ton reduction in sulfur dioxide emissions by January 1, 2000. A national cap on sulfur dioxide emissions of 8.9 million tons from utilities is established beginning January 1, 2000. Mandates a 2-million-ton reduction in nitrogen oxide emissions.

### Title V. Permits

Summary:   Requires states to establish permit programs to facilitate compliance with the new amendments. Requires all major sources of air pollution to have federal permits to operate.

### Title VI. Stratospheric Ozone Protection

Summary:   All Class I and II substances contributing to ozone depletion are to be identified and listed by the EPA. Outlines a phase-out program for both classifications. Allowances are to be issued by the EPA and a procedure established to facilitate trading that will result in a net reduction in production and consumption of ozone-depleting substances.

### Title VII. Provisions Relating to Enforcement

Summary:   Strengthens enforcement by an increased range of civil and criminal penalties for violations and by the establishment of new authorities.

### Title VIII. Miscellaneous Provisions

Summary:   Programs are established to control air pollution from sources on the Outer Continental Shelf. Negotiations with Mexico are authorized to improve air quality in border regions. Funds are allocated to support studies aimed at evaluating sources of visibility impairment and to assess progress in visibility in Class I areas.

### Title IX. Clean Air Research

Summary:   The EPA is to establish research programs associated with air pollution. The National Acid Precipitation Assessment Program (NAPAP) is reauthorized, and its responsibilities are modified and expanded. Cost–benefit analysis is specifically mandated as the decision rule to be used by the NAPAP in implementing the new amendments, the first such directive in any major environmental legislation.

| TABLE 11.2 | (CONTINUED) |
| --- | --- |

**Title X. Disadvantaged Business Concerns**

Summary: The EPA is to require that not less than 10 percent of funding for research relating to the 1990 Amendments be made available to disadvantaged firms.

**Title XI. Clean Air Employment Transition Assistance**

Summary: A training and employment services program is established for eligible workers who have been laid off or terminated due to compliance with the 1990 Amendments.

NOTE: For an online overview of the 1990 Clean Air Act Amendments, visit **www.epa.gov/oar/caa/overview.txt**.

SOURCES: Council on Environmental Quality, *Environmental Quality, 22nd Annual Report.* Washington, DC: U.S. Government Printing Office, March 1992, pp. 12–17; U.S. Environmental Protection Agency, Office of Air and Radiation. *The Clean Air Act Amendments of 1990 Summary Materials.* Washington, DC, November 15, 1990; U.S. Environmental Protection Agency, Office of Air and Radiation. *Clean Air Act Amendments of 1990: Detailed Summary of Titles.* Washington, DC, November 30, 1990.

Recognizing the need for further policy reform, Congress passed still more amendments to the Clean Air Act in 1977. Among its many provisions, the 1977 Amendments strengthened the law to protect areas in the country that already met national air quality standards. Meanwhile, the EPA developed new programs to give state governments viable alternatives through which they could satisfy federal requirements. Although some of these had a market orientation, there was no question that the use of standards as well as federally controlled procedures to implement them would continue to be the fundamental basis of air quality legislation.

### Current U.S. Policy

With this chronicle of policy reform behind it, Congress passed into law some of the most comprehensive legislation in its history—the 1990 Clean Air Act Amendments. These map out national directives for reducing the risks of air pollution. The 1990 Amendments are extensive. As shown in Table 11.2, there are eleven major sections that comprise the new and revised statutes.

Notice from the table that certain of the titled sections use market-based approaches, such as Title IV and Title VI. Yet, the underlying structure continues to be command-and-control oriented. In particular, the objectives of U.S. policy are to be met using national air quality standards, which effectively define a common air quality level for the nation. These standards in turn are implemented through an extensive infrastructure that facilitates federal oversight. The uniformity of such an approach impedes the achievement of allocative efficiency or cost-effectiveness. To verify this assertion, we begin by examining the statutory objectives of the Clean Air Act.

# Defining the Objectives of Air Quality Control

The current objectives of U.S. air quality policy were originally defined in the first comprehensive federal body of law on air quality control—the Clean Air Act of 1963. Chief among these is:

> ". . . to protect and enhance the quality of the Nation's air resources so as to promote the public health and welfare and the productive capacity of its population."

To achieve the nation's objectives, the government must understand the risks of air pollution and the abatement necessary to reduce these risks to an acceptable level. The first step is to identify the primary causes of air pollution and to isolate those contaminants deemed most harmful.

### Identifying Major Air Pollutants

**criteria documents**
Reports that present an evaluation of scientific evidence on the properties and effects of known or suspected pollutants.

Consider the extraordinary responsibility of determining which pollutants are most responsible for air pollution and setting the proper level at which to control them. Such a decision-making process is complex given the wide range of human sensitivity to pollutants, the uncertainty about health and welfare effects—particularly over the long term, and the enormous task of assessing the effects of various *combinations* of pollutants. In the United States, official reports called **criteria documents** present available scientific evidence on the properties and effects of any known or suspected pollutant.[4] This evidence is used to identify common air pollutants known to present a risk to health and the environment. Officially, these **criteria pollutants** are identified substances known to be hazardous to health and welfare. As of 1999, there are six identified criteria pollutants in the United States:

**criteria pollutants**
Substances known to be hazardous to health and welfare, characterized as harmful by criteria documents.

- Particulate matter (PM-10 and PM-2.5),[5]

- Sulfur dioxide ($SO_2$),

- Carbon monoxide (CO),

- Nitrogen dioxide ($NO_2$),

- Tropospheric ozone ($O_3$), and

- Lead (Pb).

---

[4]The documents are so named because the assessment process is to be based on descriptive factors called **criteria.** These criteria are characteristics of pollutants and their potential health and welfare effects.

[5]PM-10 refers to particles less than 10 micrograms in diameter, and PM-2.5 has the analogous meaning. The latter was added in 1997.

| TABLE 11.3 | HEALTH AND WELFARE EFFECTS OF THE SIX CRITERIA POLLUTANTS |
| --- | --- |

| Criteria Pollutant | Major Effects |
| --- | --- |
| Particulate matter (PM) | HEALTH: Breathing symptoms; aggravation of existing respiratory and cardiovascular disease; impairment of the body's natural defense systems; damage to lung tissue; carcinogenesis; and premature mortality.<br><br>WELFARE: Damage to materials; soiling; and visibility impairment. |
| Sulfur dioxide (SO₂) | HEALTH: Adverse effects on breathing; respiratory illness; alterations to the lung's defenses; and aggravation of existing respiratory and cardiovascular disease.<br><br>WELFARE: Foliar damage on trees and crops; contributes to acidic deposition, which in turn causes acidification of waterways, accelerated corrosion of buildings and monuments, and visibility impairment. |
| Carbon monoxide (CO) | HEALTH: At elevated levels causes impairment of visual perception, work capacity, manual dexterity, learning ability, and performance of complex tasks. |
| Nitrogen dioxide (NO₂) | HEALTH: Lung irritation; reduced resistance to respiratory infection; may cause higher incidence of acute respiratory disease in children if exposure is continued or frequent.<br><br>WELFARE: Contributes to ozone formation and acidic precipitation, which in turn affect terrestrial and aquatic ecosystems. |
| Ozone (O₃) | HEALTH: Reduced lung functioning; damage to lung tissue; increased sensitivity of the lung to other irritants.<br><br>WELFARE: Reduction in crop yields; foliar damage to crops and trees; damage to ecosystems. |
| Lead (Pb) | HEALTH: Damage to kidneys, liver, nervous system, and blood-forming organs: changes in fundamental enzymatic, energy transfer, and homeostatic mechanisms in the body; particularly susceptible to low doses are fetuses, infants, and children who may suffer damage to the central nervous system. |

SOURCE: U.S. Environmental Protection Agency, Office of Air Quality Planning and Standards, *National Air Quality and Emissions Trends Report, 1992*, Washington, DC, October 1993.

Table 11.3 summarizes the health and welfare effects of exposure to these pollutants, which are critical to the identification process.

A second group of contaminants identified by U.S. legislation are the so-called **hazardous air pollutants** or **air toxics.** These are noncriteria pollutants that may contribute to irreversible illness or increased mortality.[6] What distinguishes these substances from the criteria pollutants is that the associated risk is much greater, although typically a much smaller

**hazardous air pollutants**  Noncriteria pollutants that may cause or contribute to irreversible illness or increased mortality.

[6] Visit **www.epa.gov/ttn/uatw/hapindex.html** to access the EPA's Health Effects Notebook for Hazardous Air Pollutants.

segment of society is affected. The 1990 Clean Air Act Amendments include a list of 189 identified hazardous air pollutants, which is to be periodically revised as needed.[7] Prior to 1990, only eight such substances had been identified and placed under the EPA's control.[8] It was precisely because of this lack of regulatory action that a more aggressive policy was enacted in the 1990 Amendments.

# Setting Standards as a National Definition of Air Quality

Once the EPA identifies the major air pollutants, it then establishes **national standards** for them. These standards set maximum allowable levels for each pollutant to be met by all polluting sources. The two major categories of potentially controllable sources are stationary and mobile.

**stationary source**
A fixed-site producer of pollution, such as a building or manufacturing plant.

- A **stationary source** is any building or structure that emits pollution, such as a coal-burning power plant.

- A **mobile source** refers to any transport vehicle that generates pollution, such as an automobile or truck.

**mobile source** Any nonstationary polluting source, including all transport vehicles.

By establishing national standards, the federal government implicitly defines air quality for the entire country—a practice that is not exclusive to the United States. For example, Japan and some European countries also use a standard-setting approach to communicate an acceptable level of air quality for society. While the specifics vary across countries, in almost every case the list of identified air pollutants coincides with those named as criteria pollutants in the United States.[9]

## Standards for Criteria Air Pollutants

**National Ambient Air Quality Standards (NAAQS)**
Maximum allowable concentrations of criteria air pollutants.

In the United States, the standards for the six criteria pollutants are called **National Ambient Air Quality Standards (NAAQS).** Within this group are two subcategories—primary and secondary NAAQS:

**primary NAAQS**
Set to protect public health from air pollution, with some margin of safety.

- **Primary NAAQS** are set to protect public health, with some margin of safety.

- **Secondary NAAQS** are intended to protect public welfare.

**secondary NAAQS**
Set to protect public welfare from any adverse, non-health effects of air pollution.

---

[7] For current information on hazardous substances, visit the EPA's Unified Air Toxics Web site at **www.epa. gov/ttn/uatw/pollsour.html**.

[8] The eight substances are asbestos, beryllium, mercury, vinyl chloride, benzene, radionuclides, inorganic arsenic, and coke oven emissions.

[9] For an overview of certain nation's environmental policies as well as links to related sites, visit the Web site of the Organisation for Economic Co-operation and Development (OECD), Environmental Issues at **www.oecd.org/env/** or the site of the United Nations Environment Programme (UNEP) at **www.unep.org**.

Originally established under the 1970 Clean Air Act Amendments, these standards have been revised from time to time. In fact, the law requires that the criteria and the NAAQS be reviewed by the EPA every five years. The primary and secondary NAAQS in effect as of 1999 are given in Table 11.4. Notice that none of the standards are set at a zero concentration level. Thus, if we accept these standards as the nation's definition of air quality, then we must conclude that acceptable air quality does not mean the absence of all criteria pollutants.

### Standards for Hazardous Air Pollutants

U.S. law also calls for the establishment of **National Emission Standards for Hazardous Air Pollutants (NESHAP)** for every major source of the listed hazardous air pollutants. These are intended to protect public health and the environment, taking into account the costs to attain the standards, any nonair-quality health and environmental impacts, and energy requirements.

The NESHAP are to attain the maximum degree of reduction for each air toxic achievable, referred to as **maximum achievable control technology (MACT).** Where possible, this reduction should achieve a complete prohibition of the substance. Polluters can use various methods to meet these standards such as substituting less harmful inputs or enclosing production processes to eliminate hazardous emissions.

## Establishing an Infrastructure to Implement the Standards

To implement national standards, the United States has established an infrastructure that involves both federal and state governments. It is defined through two components: (1) State Implementation Plans (SIPs); and (2) Air Quality Control Regions (AQCRs).

### State Implementation Plans

Coordination between the two major levels of government is achieved through State Implementation Plans (SIPs). A **State Implementation Plan (SIP)** is an EPA-approved procedure of how a state intends to implement, monitor, and enforce the NAAQS and the NESHAP.[10]

The SIP system follows a federalist format by delegating certain tasks to different jurisdictions. The standard setting is assigned mainly to the federal level to standardize air quality across the country. State governments

**National Emission Standards for Hazardous Air Pollutants (NESHAP)**
Standards set to protect public health and the environment that are applicable to every major source of any identified hazardous air pollutant.

**maximum achievable control technology (MACT)**
The control technology that achieves the degree of reduction to be accomplished by the NESHAP.

**State Implementation Plan (SIP)**
A procedure outlining how a state intends to implement, monitor, and enforce the NAAQS and the NESHAP.

---

[10] The NAAQS represent the *minimum* requirements to be attained by every state. However, at its discretion, a state can submit a plan to achieve more stringent standards. For more information on SIPs, visit **www.epa.gov/oar/oaqps/emission.html#sip**, or to directly view the section in the Clean Air Act that refers to SIPs, visit **www.epa.gov/oar/caa/caa110.txt**.

| TABLE 11.4 | NATIONAL AMBIENT AIR QUALITY STANDARDS (NAAQS) IN EFFECT IN 1999 |
|---|---|

| Pollutant | Primary Standard | | Secondary Standard | |
|---|---|---|---|---|
| | Averaging Time | Concentration | Averaging Time | Concentration |
| Particulate matter (PM-10) | Annual arithmetic mean | 50 $\mu$g/m$^3$ | | Same as primary |
| | 24-hour | 150 $\mu$g/m$^3$ | | Same as primary |
| Particulate matter (PM-2.5) | Annual arithmetic mean | 15 $\mu$g/m$^3$ | | Same as primary |
| | 24-hour | 65 $\mu$g/m$^3$ | | Same as primary |
| Sulfur dioxide (SO$_2$) | Annual arithmetic mean | 80 $\mu$g/m$^3$ (0.03 ppm) | 3-hour | 1300 $\mu$g/m$^3$ (0.50 ppm) |
| | 24-hour | 365 $\mu$g/m$^3$ (0.14 ppm) | | |
| Carbon monoxide (CO) | 8-hour | 9.0 ppm (10 mg/m$^3$) | | No secondary standard |
| | 1-hour | 35 ppm (40 mg/m$^3$) | | No secondary standard |
| Nitrogen dioxide (NO$_2$) | Annual arithmetic mean | 0.053 ppm (100 $\mu$g/m$^3$) | | Same as primary |
| Ozone (O$_3$) | Maximum daily 1-hour average | 0.12 ppm (235 $\mu$g/m$^3$) | | Same as primary |
| | 8-hour average | 0.08 ppm (157 $\mu$g/m$^3$) | | Same as primary |
| Lead (Pb) | Maximum quarterly average | 1.5 $\mu$g/m$^3$ | | Same as primary |

NOTES: For some criteria pollutants, both a long-term and a short-term standard are given. The long-term standards give either a quarterly or annual mean level that may not be exceeded. The short-term standards are the upper-bound for 1-, 3-, 8-, or 24-hour averages that may not be exceeded more than once per year. The standard for O$_3$ limits the expected number of days per calendar year with daily maximum concentrations over 0.12 ppm to be less than or equal to one.

ppm = parts per million.

$\mu$g/m$^3$ = micrograms per cubic meter.

mg/m$^3$ = milligrams per cubic meter.

Values given in parentheses are approximately equivalent concentrations.

A direct hyperlink to these standards is **www.epa.gov/airs/criteria.html**.

The PM and Ozone standards were revised in July 1997. For an overview of these revisions, see the EPA's Fact Sheet at **ttnwww. rtpnc.epa.gov/naaqsfin/o3pm.htm**.

SOURCE: U.S. Environmental Protection Agency, Office of Air Quality Planning and Standards. *National Air Quality and Emissions Trends Report, 1994*. Research Triangle Park, NC, October 1995, Table 2-1, p. 2-2.

| TABLE 11.5 | NUMBER OF NONATTAINMENT AREAS FOR THE NAAQS POLLUTANTS AS OF 1998 |

| Pollutant | Number of Nonattainment Areas |
|---|---|
| Particulate matter (PM-10) | 78 |
| Sulfur dioxide (SO$_2$) | 35 |
| Carbon monoxide (CO) | 28 |
| Nitrogen dioxide (NO$_2$) | 1 |
| Ozone (O$_3$) | 57 |
| Lead (Pb) | 10 |

NOTE: Unclassified areas are not included in the totals.

SOURCE: U.S. Environmental Protection Agency, Office of Air Quality Planning and Standards. "USA Air Quality Nonattainment Areas," **www.epa.gov/airs/nonattn.html**, effective January 27, 1998.

are responsible for implementing the standards and monitoring polluters within their jurisdictions, since their knowledge of the immediate region gives them an advantage in doing so.

### Air Quality Control Regions

**air quality control regions (AQCRs)** Geographical areas designated by the federal government within which common air pollution problems are shared by several communities.

To coordinate states' responsibilities, **Air Quality Control Regions (AQCRs)** are defined within each state's jurisdiction. These are geographical areas designated by the federal government within which common air pollution problems are shared by several communities.

Currently, 247 AQCRs have been designated across the United States. These well-defined geographical areas are monitored to determine if the region is in compliance with the national standards. Today, a number of AQCRs still have not met the current NAAQS for one or more of the six criteria pollutants. Table 11.5 provides information on these nonattainment areas as of 1998. As these data indicate, regions have the greatest difficulty achieving the particulate matter and ozone standards, with 78 and 57 regions respectively still classified as nonattainment for these contributors to urban smog.

### Reclassification of AQCRs to Protect "Clean Air Areas"

In 1972, the Sierra Club filed suit against the EPA for failing to protect areas that were "cleaner" than what was required by law.[11] The environmental group argued that the existing NAAQS were aimed solely at *improving* air quality in areas that did not meet the standards. The concern was that

---

[11] See *Sierra Club* v. *Ruckelshaus*, D.D.C. 1972.

nondegradation areas, as they are called, would be allowed to deteriorate to the existing national standards. The Sierra Club claimed that the lack of protection for nondegradation areas was a violation of the law, since one of the statutory purposes of the Clean Air Act is to *protect* as well as *enhance* the quality of the nation's air resources. Ultimately, the group won the suit, and in 1974 a new program was established to protect these already "clean" areas.

The new "clean air areas" program redefined the structure of federal air pollution control and played a significant role in directing future policy decisions. States had to reassess their AQCRs so that they could identify the following three groups: (1) regions that met the standards; (2) regions that did not meet the standards; and (3) regions with insufficient data to confirm a classification. Regions meeting or exceeding national standards were re-designated as areas targeted for **prevention of significant deterioration** or **PSD areas.** Those that did not were designated as **nonattainment areas.**

Once determined, every PSD area was to be designated as Class I, II, or III—a progressive classification based on the maximum concentration of criteria pollutants allowed. Class I areas, the most stringently controlled, include wilderness areas and national parks. The law specifically prohibits a redesignation of these areas.[12] There is also a declaration in the law that enhancing and protecting visibility in these Class I areas was to be a new national goal. One outcome of these new classifications is the nation's on-going effort to improve visibility in Grand Canyon National Park—the first use of the visibility protection law.[13]

**prevention of significant deterioration (PSD) areas**
AQCRs meeting or exceeding the NAAQS.

**nonattainment areas**
AQCRs not in compliance with the NAAQS.

### 1990 Reclassification of Nonattainment Areas by Criteria Pollutant

In response to the nation's persistent problem of urban air pollution, the 1990 Amendments reclassify all nonattainment areas for the pollutants most responsible—ozone, carbon monoxide, and particulate matter—into new progressive categories based on existing pollutant concentrations. For example, ozone nonattainment areas are reclassified into five groups—marginal, moderate, serious, severe, and extreme. These new categories not only identify the severity of pollution but also provide some justification to set more stringent regulations in those areas with higher pollution levels.

### Monitoring Air Quality across Regions

Determining the compliance status of each region and the assessment of air quality for the nation depends on a systematic measurement of the six

---

[12] Other than these initially classified Class I areas and certain other exceptions, states can redesignate classifications for PSD areas in accordance with very specific rules.

[13] Visit the Web site **www.nmia.com/~gcvtc/final.html** to access the final recommendations of the Grand Canyon Visibility Transport Commission. This commission was created by the 1990 Clean Air Act Amendments to work on improving visibility at national parks located on the Colorado plateau.

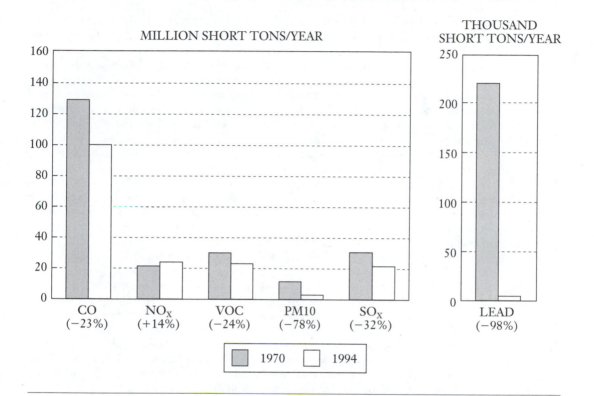

NOTE: For direct access to EPA's *National Air Quality and Emissions Trends Report, 1996,* visit **www.epa.gov/oar/aqtrnd96/**.

SOURCE: U.S. Environmental Protection Agency, Office of Air Quality Planning and Standards. *National Air Quality and Emissions Trends Report, 1994.* Research Triangle Park, NC: October 1995, Figure 1-1, pp. 1–2.

criteria pollutants. In general, this is accomplished either by estimating the emissions level of each pollutant or by measuring the ambient concentration of each in some volume of air.

**Estimating Pollutant Emissions Levels.** It is not feasible to measure actual pollutant emissions levels on a national scale, so instead they are *estimated.* In the United States, best available engineering methods are used to derive annual emissions estimates for over 450 source categories, which include almost all anthropogenic sources. These are then aggregated to determine regional and national emissions trends. The graphic in Figure 11.1 shows emissions estimates for the six criteria pollutants in 1994 compared to those for 1970. According to these estimates, there have been reductions in most emissions (the exception being $NO_X$) over the long run. Some of these reductions are the result of policy initiatives. The most substantial

## Market Incentives to Phase Out Lead Emissions

Even skeptics of market solutions to environmental problems are hard pressed to deny the success story of lead banking and trading. Touted by economists and environmentalists alike, the use of market instruments in reducing lead emissions was undeniably a victory.

Lead is a toxic heavy metal that poses a serious health hazard if ingested or inhaled. Unfortunately it is ubiquitous, showing up in paints, plastics, lead-acid batteries, plumbing compounds, and gasoline. Its use in gasoline began in the 1920s, when refineries recognized it as the cheapest available source of octane. But by the 1960s and 1970s, evidence had begun to accumulate that linked lead exposure to mental disorders and cardiovascular disease. Research also showed that lead levels in the bloodstream were directly and immediately associated with changes in the lead content of gasoline. In addition to the health threat, lead was also found to adversely affect the performance of catalytic converters being installed in new cars to meet tougher standards on tailpipe emissions.

In 1973, the EPA responded by requiring that unleaded gasoline be made available by 1974 and by establishing a limit on the average lead concentration of *all* gasoline (both leaded and unleaded), sold by a given refiner. Nonetheless, lead concentrations remained high, averaging about 2.0 grams per gallon in 1975, in part because of misfueling (i.e., using leaded fuels in vehicles designed to use only unleaded gasoline). During the 1980s, new evidence revealed that the health threat was even more serious than originally believed. On every front, the consumption of leaded gasoline generated negative externalities, and existing policy was not tough enough or effective enough to solve the problem.

The EPA's ultimate policy response was to tighten the lead standard and use market incentives to achieve it. In 1982, the EPA established a new standard based only on leaded gasoline—1.1 grams per leaded gallon (gplg) effective July 1, 1985. Subsequently, the standard was made progressively more stringent through a series of steps, calling for a concentration of 0.5 gplg after July 1, 1985, 0.1 gplg after January 1, 1986, and a complete ban by 1996. To accomplish this phasedown, the agency introduced a program of **credits** issued to refineries for reductions that surpassed those required by law. These credits could then be *banked* for use during a subsequent stage of the phasedown or *traded* with older refineries unable to meet the reductions by the statutory deadlines.

The end result was that the refineries best able to meet the required standards did so, compensating for their less efficient counterparts who were effectively given more time to retrofit their production processes. According to EPA reports, 73 percent of all refiners participated in the trading program in the second quarter of 1984. Ultimately, the plan cost the nation $220 million *less* than what it would have cost under a strict command-and-control approach of standard setting, and this savings came about with no change in the benefits of lead reduction. Since 1970, airborne lead emissions have fallen by a remarkable 98 percent. The difference is only that the method used to achieve the reductions minimized costs.

SOURCES: Lily Whiteman. "Trades to Remember: The Lead Phasedown." *EPA Journal* 18(2), May/June 1992, pp. 38–39; U.S. Environmental Protection Agency, Office of Policy, Planning, and Evaluation. *The United States Experience with Economic Incentives to Control Environmental Pollution.* Washington, DC, July 1992, pp. 5-7–5-8; U.S. Environmental Protection Agency, Office of Policy Analysis. *Costs and Benefits of Reducing Lead in Gasoline: Final Regulatory Impact Analysis.* Washington, DC, February 1985.

| TABLE 11.6 | NATIONAL AMBIENT CONCENTRATIONS OF THE SIX CRITERIA POLLUTANTS, 1985–1994 |

| Year | Particulate Matter (PM-10) ($\mu$g/m$^3$) | Sulfur Dioxide (SO$_2$) (ppm) | Carbon Monoxide (CO) (ppm) | Nitrogen Dioxide (NO$_2$) (ppm) | Ozone (O$_3$) (ppm) | Lead (Pb) ($\mu$g/m$^3$) |
|---|---|---|---|---|---|---|
| 1985 | * | 0.009 | 6.9 | 0.022 | 0.124 | 0.29 |
| 1990 | 29.9 | 0.008 | 5.9 | 0.020 | 0.114 | 0.08 |
| 1994 | 26.6 | 0.007 | 5.0 | 0.020 | 0.109 | 0.04 |

NOTES: $\mu$g/m$^3$ = micrograms per cubic meter.

ppm = parts per million.

*Prior to 1987, the standards for particulate matter were based on total suspended particulates and not on PM-10.

All data are composite averages based on all sites in the national monitoring network.

SOURCE: U.S. Environmental Protection Agency, Office of Air Quality Planning and Standards, *National Air Quality and Emissions Trends Report, 1994*. Research Triangle Park, NC, October 1995, Table A-1, pp. A-2–A-3.

decline observed is for lead, which is the result of the EPA's lead phase-out program, a market-based plan discussed in Application 11.2.

**Measuring Pollutant Concentrations.** Pollutant concentration levels are actually *measured* at air monitoring station sites located throughout the country. Most of these sites are in urban regions characterized by relatively high pollutant concentrations and population exposure. All sites report their data to the EPA via an air-monitoring network. Table 11.6 presents trend data of ambient concentrations for the six criteria pollutants from 1985 to 1994.

## Economic Analysis of U.S. Air Quality Policy

If we consider the evolution of U.S. air quality legislation that began in 1955, it is clear that the nation's control policy has become more comprehensive over time. There is now a vast infrastructure to implement and monitor national air quality objectives. This includes the establishment of AQCRs, an intergovernmental system of SIPs, and a network of monitoring sites. But is it reasonable to assess U.S. accomplishments by the number of provisions that now define air quality legislation or by the more elaborate implementation and monitoring systems that have been established? These may be *indicators* that the United States is attempting to strengthen policy, but do they suggest that policy is any more effective?

It seems simple enough to argue that the bottom line in assessing regulatory policy is whether or not any headway has been made in achieving cleaner air. However, such an argument is a gross oversimplification of what is in fact a much more complex problem. Look back at the trend data shown in Figure 11.1 and Table 11.6. Collectively, these data suggest that U.S. air quality has improved over time. Although this is likely true to a point, there are many factors that must be considered before drawing conclusions. Among these are the accuracy of the emissions estimates and the determination of what part of any observed improvement is actually attributable to effective policy. Even if these factors are accounted for, there is the challenge of converting any policy-driven air improvements to monetized values of social benefits, such as reduced health risks, increased visibility, and the preservation of the ecology. Finally, one must consider the full extent of the costs borne by society to achieve whatever progress has been made. These costs should include not only explicit expenditures for compliance, monitoring, and enforcement, but also implicit costs due to shifts in production technology, substitution of fuels and other inputs, and changes in available goods and services.

Collectively, these are the tasks that comprise an economic analysis of environmental policy. By systematically estimating and evaluating the costs and benefits associated with the Clean Air Act, one can determine whether U.S. air control policy is **allocatively efficient.** Recall from previous chapters that the decision rule assuring an efficient outcome is the **maximization of net benefits**—the point where the associated **marginal social costs** and **marginal social benefits** are equal. To illustrate this approach, we present a two-part benefit–cost investigation of U.S. air policy. The first part assesses the overall efficiency of the Clean Air Act. The second considers the efficiency of the standard-setting process itself.

# A Benefit–Cost Analysis of the Clean Air Act

## A Benefit–Cost Analysis of the Pre-1990 Clean Air Act

There is a fair amount of research that evaluates the efficiency of *specific* air quality control provisions. Far less prevalent are comprehensive analyses assessing the Clean Air Act in its entirety. Drawn from the work of other researchers, one such investigation was conducted by Paul Portney (1990a), an economist and researcher at Resources for the Future in Washington, DC. With careful reservations, Portney offers a very telling comparison of the social benefits and costs associated with U.S. policy *prior to* the enactment of the 1990 Clean Air Act Amendments. Beyond the implications of the results, the study illustrates the practical value of benefit–cost analysis and the difficulties of using this strategy to evaluate policy on a comprehensive scale.

| TABLE 11.7 | ANNUALIZED CONTROL COSTS FOR AIR (IN MILLIONS OF 1986 DOLLARS) | | | | |
|---|---|---|---|---|---|
| **Target** | **1972** | **1980** | **1987** | **1995** | **2000** |
| Stationary sources | 6,230 | 13,298 | 18,960 | 25,188 | 29,725 |
| Mobile sources | 1,345 | 4,010 | 7,469 | 11,097 | 14,140 |
| Undesignated sources | 341 | 327 | 250 | 207 | 184 |
| Air Pollution Total | 7,916 | 17,635 | 26,679 | 36,493 | 44,049 |

NOTE: Data for 1995 and 2000 are projected.

SOURCE: U.S. Environmental Protection Agency, Office of Policy, Planning, and Evaluation. *Environmental Investments: The Cost of a Clean Environment, A Summary*. Washington DC, December 1990, p. 3-2.

**Total Social Costs.**   Any cost analysis of environmental policy involves the challenge of estimating the total costs to society from having to adapt to legislated provisions. These include both explicit and implicit costs. In the United States, explicit or out-of-pocket expenditure data are collected mainly by the Department of Commerce. These are the actual compliance and operating costs associated with air quality controls. Cost data for selected years are shown in Table 11.7.[14] Although important, these explicit cost data are insufficient for an economic benefit–cost analysis. Why? Because they do not account for implicit costs to society, such as higher priced products, loss of employment from production and technology conversions, and restrictions on consumers' choice sets.

Portney's analysis derives social cost estimates of the Clean Air Act primarily from the work of two other researchers, Michael Hazilla and Raymond J. Kopp (1990). These researchers use a model of the U.S. economy to estimate how prices and income change with the implementation of policy aimed at both air and water quality. Ultimately, their measure of social costs is based on an assessment of how social welfare changed as a result of the environmental legislation. Portney then approximates what proportion of these social costs were attributable to *just* the air quality regulations. Three annual social cost estimates are derived: $4.5 billion for 1975, $13.7 billion for 1981, and $33.0 billion in 1985—all stated in 1984 dollars. Each of these magnitudes is an estimate of the explicit *and* implicit costs of the pre-1990 U.S. clean air laws at different points in time, and each can be interpreted as the value of resources given up by society to implement air quality control legislation.

---

[14]These costs are deflated to remove any inflationary effects and broken down by year (to present annualized data), by sector of the economy (i.e., EPA, non-EPA federal, state government, local government, and private sector), and by type (i.e., capital versus operating costs).

**Total Social Benefits.**   Estimating the total social benefits of the Clean Air Act involves a systematic process comprised of a series of steps:

- Analyze the data that measure the trend in air quality over time.

- Control for external influences on air quality to determine the amount of improvement due solely to public policy initiatives.

- Determine the benefits gained by society from the air quality improvement and monetize them so that they can be compared to the associated costs.

Given the availability of air quality trend data, it might seem that the only difficulty in executing the first step is in choosing which of these data to employ. While there is some truth to this supposition, it is nonetheless shortsighted. It turns out that most of the available air quality data is not totally reliable or at least is limited in some way. This is not to say that these data are not useful, rather that they have limitations that must be acknowledged in order for the analysis to have validity.

A case in point are U.S. emissions data. Recall that these data are not actual measurements, but rather estimates determined by the EPA. It is important to understand how these estimates are calculated, to know exactly what information the data are conveying, and to be aware of the limitations imposed by the estimation procedure. Ambient concentration data are also imperfect measures of U.S. air quality. Although these data are based on actual measurements, the monitoring system in the United States, while improving, is currently less than adequate.

Another important consideration is that all national statistics, by construction, disguise regional and local differences. Even when national data suggest that the ambient air is improving, there are some parts of the country, such as urban areas, that continue to face serious air pollution problems. Such localized variations are hidden by the averaging process. Finally, it is necessary to recognize that not all observed changes in air quality are attributable to policy. In truth, there are many factors other than regulatory controls that influence air pollution, many of which are simply beyond our control.

Acknowledging these issues, Portney's estimate of social benefits for the pre-1990 clean air laws relies on a comprehensive survey and synthesis report conducted by another noted economist, A. Myrick Freeman (1982). Using ambient air concentration data from 1970 to 1978, Freeman translates improvements in pollution levels for the period into several benefit categories, using links established in existing research studies. These categories are: improvements in human health; decrease in damage to vegetation; decrease in materials damage; lower cleaning costs; and enhanced aesthetics and visibility. Monetized values for each are derived, resulting in the following estimates expressed in 1984 dollars:

- Health impacts:        $27.2 billion

- Vegetation:              0.5 billion

- Materials:               1.1 billion

- Cleaning:                4.8 billion

- Property values:        3.7 billion

Aggregating these values, Portney estimates the total value of social benefits as of 1978 at $37.3 billion. While only an approximation, the estimate suggests that society ought to be willing to pay $37.3 billion for the improvements to health, property, and the environment brought about by the clean air laws in effect at that time.[15]

**Benefit–Cost Comparison.**    The final step in the analysis is to compare the estimates of social costs and social benefits and interpret the result. Notice, however, that in the context of the Portney study, the two independently estimated components are valued for different periods. The relevant social cost estimate is as of 1981, but the comparable estimate of social benefits is as of 1978. Making one final concession, Portney suggests that the social benefits are likely to be higher in 1981 than their estimated value in 1978. He justifies this by observed improvements in air quality through the period as well as increases in the general population, meaning that more people would gain from the improvements. Thus, the $37.3 billion magnitude is treated as a viable, albeit conservative, benefit estimate for 1981. Comparing this value with the 1981 social cost estimate of $13.7 billion, Portney offers a qualified conclusion that the total social benefits (*TSB*) of pre-1990 clean air legislation outweigh the total social costs (*TSC*), at least for 1981.

While Portney suggests that this assessment is likely reasonable for 1981, he is adamant that the conclusion cannot be made without reservations. For example, Freeman attributes all the observed changes in air quality to the Clean Air Act, an assumption that biases the benefit estimates upward. Further, Portney cautions that even if the estimates are reasonable, they cannot be generalized beyond 1981. For instance, he points out that estimated social costs rise sharply in 1985 to $33.0 billion, an increase that is not likely to be matched by higher social benefits. Moreover, the benefit and cost magnitudes are estimated as *total* rather than *marginal* values, which does not convey sufficient information to assess allocative efficiency. Even though the *TSB* of clean air policy exceed *TSC*, there is no reason to assume that abatement controls are at their efficient level. Such an evaluation can be made only by finding out whether the *marginal* social

---

[15] For a complete analysis of Freeman's work, see Portney (1990a), pp. 54–60, or consult the original source, Freeman (1982).

FIGURE 11.2

## A BENEFIT–COST ANALYSIS OF U.S. AIR QUALITY CONTROLS AS OF 1981

In all three depictions of U.S. policy, the *TSB* of $37.3 billion at the 1981 abatement level, $A_{1981}$, is higher than the *TSC* of $13.7 billion. What differs is the location of $A_{1981}$ relative to the efficient level of abatement, $A_e$. In Figure 11.2(a), $A_{1981}$ is equal to $A_e$, since at this point, the slope of *TSB* is equal to the slope of *TSC*, meaning that the vertical distance between *TSB* and *TSC* is maximized. In Figure 11.2(b), $A_{1981}$ is to the *left* of $A_e$, indicating that *too little* abatement has been legislated. Just the opposite case is depicted in Figure 11.2(c), where *too much* abatement is imposed by law. Without specific *marginal* benefit and cost data, there is no way to know whether or not the 1981 controls corresponded to an efficient abatement level.

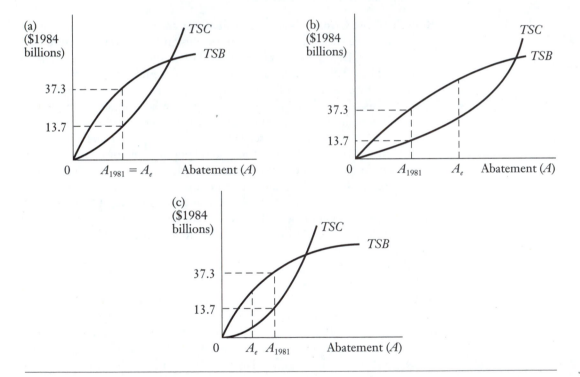

Values drawn from Paul R. Portney. "Air Pollution Policy." In Paul R. Portney, ed., *Public Policies for Environmental Protection*. Washington, DC: Resources for the Future, 1990a, pp. 27–96; Michael Hazilla and Raymond J. Kopp. "Social Cost of Environmental Quality Regulations: A General Equilibrium Analysis." *Journal of Political Economy* 98(4), 1990, pp. 853–73; A. Myrick Freeman III. *Air and Water Pollution Control: A Benefit-Cost Assessment*. New York: John Wiley & Sons, 1982.

benefit (*MSB*) equals the *marginal* social cost (*MSC*) at that point. In fact, only through a marginal analysis can the implications of subsequent legislative changes be assessed.

To illustrate this latter point, consider three hypothetical depictions of the 1981 social benefit and cost estimates shown in Figure 11.2(a) through

11.2(c). Costs and benefits in billions of dollars are measured on the vertical axis, and pollution abatement ($A$) associated with air control policy is measured on the horizontal axis. Notice that in all three cases, at the 1981 level of abatement, $A_{1981}$, *TSB* of $37.3 billion is higher than *TSC* of $13.7 billion. What differs across the three diagrams is the location of $A_{1981}$ relative to the efficient level of abatement, $A_e$.

In Figure 11.2(a), $A_{1981}$ is shown as equivalent to the efficient level, $A_e$, the point where the vertical distance between *TSB* and *TSC* is maximized or where the slopes of the two functions are equal. This corresponds to the abatement level that maximizes net benefits to society, or the point where marginal social cost (*MSC*) and marginal social benefit (*MSB*) of abatement are equal. However, it is quite possible that $A_{1981}$ is to the *left* of $A_e$, as is shown in Figure 11.2(b). Such a result would indicate that *too little* abatement has been legislated. Just the opposite case is also possible where *too much* abatement is imposed by law. This alternative is shown in Figure 11.2(c). The point is, without specific *marginal* benefit and cost data, there is no way to know whether or not the regulatory controls in place in 1981 correspond to an efficient level of abatement.

## A Benefit–Cost Analysis of the 1990 Amendments

In an excellent and very readable article, Portney (1990b) extends and updates his benefit–cost analysis to assess the 1990 Amendments. In particular, he assigns estimated benefits and costs to each of the three major sets of provisions of the 1990 law: those for acidic deposition (Title IV), for urban air pollution (Titles II and V), and for hazardous air pollutants (Title III). There are two major differences between this analysis and the one Portney conducted for the earlier period. First, in this study *marginal* costs and benefits are examined as opposed to *total* costs and benefits. This use of marginal values allows for a determination of whether the *additional* controls imposed by the new amendments are allocatively efficient. Second, this study is a "seat-of-the-pants" evaluation, as Portney puts it, because only *explicit* private costs are considered. His defense is simply that such nonrigorous analyses are typically what are used in practice.

**Marginal Costs and Benefits.** To facilitate the discussion, we present Portney's estimates of marginal benefits and costs in Table 11.8, which we assume are points lying on the true marginal social benefit (*MSB*) and marginal social cost (*MSC*) curves.[16] The table lists the reported values in 1990 dollars for the three sets of provisions as well as for the aggregate of all three. For ease of comparison to the values Portney derived for the pre-1990 period, the magnitudes also are stated in 1984 dollars in parentheses.

---

[16] Recall from Chapters 8 and 9 that technically these values are *incremental* as opposed to *marginal*, since the magnitudes represent a discrete change from one policy initiative to another.

| TABLE 11.8 | ESTIMATED ANNUAL MARGINAL COSTS AND BENEFITS OF THE 1990 CLEAN AIR ACT AMENDMENTS |
|---|---|

**Stated in billions of 1990 dollars**
**(1984 dollars given in parentheses)**

|  | Acidic Deposition | Urban Air Quality | Hazardous Air Pollutants | Aggregate Range | Aggregate Point Estimate |
|---|---|---|---|---|---|
| Marginal costs | $4 ($3.2) | $19–$22 ($15.1–$17.5) | $6–$10 ($4.8–$7.9) | $29–$36 ($23.1–$28.6) | $32 ($25.4) |
| Marginal benefits | $2–$9 ($1.6–$7.2) | $4–$12 ($3.2–$9.5) | $0–$4 ($0–$3.2) | $6–$25 ($4.8–$19.9) | $14 ($11.1) |

SOURCE: Drawn from Paul R. Portney. "Economics and the Clean Air Act." *Journal of Economic Perspectives 4(4)*, Fall 1990b, pp. 173–81.

Notice that most of the estimates are reported as a range of values, since there is some amount of guesswork involved.

Overall, Portney suggests that abatement linked to the 1990 Amendments should yield a marginal social benefit (*MSB*) somewhere in the range of $6 to $25 billion annually, with most of it due to urban air quality improvements. Portney also offers a rough point estimate for *MSB* of $14 billion, which is $11.1 billion in 1984 dollars. The comparable estimate for marginal social cost (*MSC*) is $29 to $36 billion annually, or $23.1 to $28.6 billion in 1984 dollars. Again, the majority of costs are attributable to urban air quality controls. A point estimate for *MSC* to correspond to the benefit side is $32 billion, or $25.4 billion in 1984 dollars. From a relative perspective, the $25.4-billion cost estimate suggests that the 1990 Amendments are expected to be very costly, particularly in light of the fact that the *total* social costs of U.S. policy as of 1981 were estimated to be only $13.7 billion.

**Benefit–Cost Comparison.** Based on these estimates, one possible conclusion is that the 1990 Amendments overregulate society, since *MSC* far outweighs *MSB*.[17] This relationship holds even if we conservatively compare the low end of the range for *MSC* ($29 billion) with the upper end of the range for *MSB* ($25 billion), giving an excess of $4 billion in nominal terms. On the other hand, the excess could be as much as $30 billion, if we

---

[17] There is, however, an important caveat. If, for example, Portney's marginal cost estimates are *not* reflective of least-cost decisions, meaning they lie *above* the true *MSC* curve, then the appropriate conclusion is that the 1990 Amendments are not being implemented in a cost-effective manner. If this is the case, the efficiency of the abatement level being achieved by the 1990 law is indeterminant.

use the high end of the range for *MSC* ($36 billion) with the low end of the range for *MSB* ($6 billion).

To further illustrate this important result, Figure 11.3 presents two graphical models of these estimates expressed in 1984 dollars. The first in panel (a) depicts the relationship between *MSC* and *MSB*. Notice that the hypothetical abatement level corresponding to the 1990 Amendments, $A_{1990}$, is located to the *right* of the efficient abatement level, $A_e$. It follows, therefore, that society would be better off with less regulation, which translates to a movement on the graph from $A_{1990}$ to $A_e$.

The model in panel (b) illustrates these same results using an approximation of the *TSC* and *TSB* as of 1990. To obtain the estimate for *TSC*, we add the estimated *MSC* for the 1990 law in 1984 dollars, $25.4 billion, to Portney's earlier estimate of *TSC* for 1981 measured in 1984 dollars, $13.7 billion. This yields an estimate for the 1990 *TSC* of $39.1 billion.

| | |
|---|---|
| *TSC* effective 1981: | $ 13.7 billion |
| + *MSC* for 1990 Amendments: | + 25.4 billion |
| *TSC* effective 1990: | $ 39.1 billion |

Similarly, to derive an approximation of *TSB* from all air quality controls in effect as of 1990, the estimated *MSB* for the 1990 Amendments, $11.1 billion, is added to Freeman's estimate of *TSB*, $37.3 billion, to get an approximation for the *TSB* as of 1990 at $48.4 billion.

| | |
|---|---|
| *TSB* effective 1978: | $ 37.3 billion |
| + *MSB* for 1990 Amendments: | + 11.1 billion |
| *TSB* effective 1990: | $ 48.4 billion |

These values for *TSB* and *TSC* are shown in the diagram corresponding to $A_{1990}$. Notice that while *TSB* exceeds *TSC*, the associated abatement level is nonetheless in excess of the efficient level, $A_e$.

The implication of these findings is that by implementing the 1990 Amendments, the U.S. government has overregulated the private sector to achieve cleaner air. Overallocation of resources to implement this legislation means that resources are being underallocated toward other uses. There are many who agree with this conclusion, arguing, for example, that the allocation of government spending among environmental problems is disproportionate to the associated risks. A common outcry is aimed at the relatively small amount of federal monies devoted to reducing the risks of such hazards as radon and tobacco smoke, which are known health hazards. For example, an article in the business press, citing EPA data, points out that while radon is responsible for some 5,000 to 20,000 deaths per year, only about $100 million is spent annually to fight the problem. These

| FIGURE 11.3 | ANALYZING THE MARGINAL SOCIAL COST (*MSC*) AND MARGINAL SOCIAL BENEFIT (*MSB*) ASSOCIATED WITH THE 1990 CLEAN AIR ACT AMENDMENTS |

According to Portney's estimates, the *MSC* associated with the 1990 amendments outweighs the *MSB*. Thus the *MSC* is above the *MSB* at $A_{1990}$. Notice that $A_{1990}$ is higher than the efficient abatement level, $A_e$, where *MSB* intersects with *MSC*. This implies that society would be better off with less regulation, which translates to a movement from $A_{1990}$ to $A_e$.

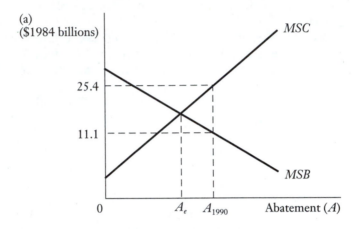

This model shows the estimated values of *TSB* and *TSC* associated with the hypothetical abatement level established by the 1990 Amendments, $A_{1990}$. Although *TSB* exceeds *TSC* at this point, $A_{1990}$ is higher than the efficient abatement level, $A_e$. Just as in the upper diagram, this model implies that the 1990 Amendments overregulate the private sector to achieve cleaner air.

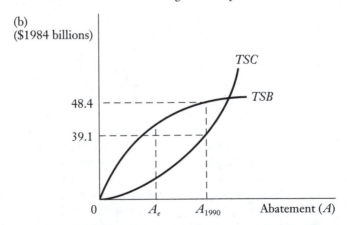

SOURCE: Values derived from Paul R. Portney. "Economics and the Clean Air Act." *Journal of Economic Perspectives* 4(4), Fall 1990b, pp. 173–81; Paul R. Portney. "Air Pollution Policy." In Paul R. Portney, ed., *Public Policies for Environmental Protection*. Washington, DC: Resources for the Future, 1990a, pp. 27–96.

statistics are troubling when compared to the $1.2 billion being spent on global warming, to which zero deaths are attributed.[18] But as we stated at the outset, benefit–cost analysis of environmental issues is *not* an exact science. These values are just estimates, and the scientific evidence on most if not all environmental problems is incomplete.

Taken in this context, Portney's research should be recognized for what it is, *and* for what it is not. While it is validated by some existing data as well as the work of other researchers, it is nonetheless a series of estimates and guesses, albeit educated ones. There are no hard-and-fast conclusions that can be drawn from such preliminary results. Rather, more advanced research, using new data as they become available, is necessary to make a more concrete determination about the efficiency implications of the 1990 Amendments.[19]

# A Benefit–Cost Analysis of the Air Quality Standards

Perhaps the most important contribution of Portney's findings is that they motivate the need for further investigation of the Clean Air Act. To that end, we conduct a benefit–cost analysis of the standards established through this legislation, focusing on the *efficiency* implications of two specific issues: (1) the *absence of cost considerations* in setting the standards; and (2) the *uniformity* of the standards. The *equity* implications of the Clean Air Act are discussed in Application 11.3. Although equity considerations are not the mainstay of economic analysis, they have taken on increasing importance in U.S. environmental policy making. President Clinton's 1994 signing of Executive Order 12898 directs all federal agencies to make environmental justice part of their missions.[20]

## Absence of Cost Considerations in the Standard-Setting Process

**Setting the National Ambient Air Quality Standards (NAAQS).** From an efficiency perspective, a common criticism of both the primary and secondary NAAQS is that they are motivated solely by the anticipated benefits from protecting public health and welfare with no mention of the economic feasibility of doing so. Effectively, this means that costs, including implicit costs, are not to be explicitly considered. Such an omission is particularly problematic for the primary standards for health, which are to include a *"margin of safety."* This wording suggests that there is some level

---

[18] See Main (May 20, 1991).

[19] For a recent benefit–cost analysis of the Clean Air Act, see U.S. Environmental Protection Agency, Office of Air and Radiation. *The Benefits and Costs of the Clean Air Act, 1970 to 1990.* Washington, DC: October 1997. This can be accessed at **www.epa.gov/airprogm/oar/sect812/ index.html.**

[20] This executive order can be accessed at **www.npr.gov/library/direct/orders/264a.html.**

APPLICATION 11.3

## The Inequities of Air Pollution—Who Suffers More?

While efficiency criteria are the mainstay of economic analyses, an evaluation of any public policy also must consider issues of equity. Does the policy correct for any preexisting inequities across population groups? Does its implementation affect all segments of society in the same way? These sorts of questions are particularly relevant to an assessment of national air quality policy. Consider the difference in air quality between rural and urban communities or between attainment and nonattainment areas. And while these differences seem to be strictly regional in orientation, it turns out that they translate to inequities across income, ethnic, and racial population groups.

The linkage is simple. Much of the racial- and ethnic-based differences in air pollution exposure arise because a high proportion of minorities live in urban centers, where the ambient air is dirtier than in suburban and rural areas. In fact, some 63 percent of the nation's air-polluting facilities are located in urban areas. Given these residential differences, it is not surprising that certain minority groups are at relatively greater risk to the health hazards associated with exposure to urban air pollution.

The graphic below presents results of a study that examined the proportion of Hispanic, Asian/Pacific, African American, White, and Native American people living in areas of reduced air quality. Other analyses also find evidence of these environmental inequities. For example, Brajer and Hall (1992) examine the distribution of income, ethnic, and racial groups affected by exposure to ozone and fine particulate matter in the South Coast Air Basin of California. The results show a positive correlation between particulate matter exposure and the percentage of lower-income families as well as with the percentage of African Americans and Hispanics. Similar results are found for ozone exposure, although some of the correlations are statistically weaker.

So what is being done about the problem? In the United States, the EPA formed an Environmental Equity Workgroup in 1990 to assess the evidence about risk to minority and low-income groups and to consider appropriate responses to any inequities it identifies. (Its findings are given in a formal report titled *Environmental Equity: Reducing Risk for All Communities* issued in June 1992.) In 1994, the EPA also established its Office of Environmental Justice. In the same year, President Clinton issued Executive Order 12898, *Federal Actions to Address Environmental Justice in Minority Populations and Low-Income Populations*. This directive requires agencies to develop strategies that incorporate environmental justice into their operations.

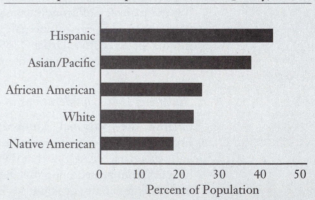

**U.S. Populations Exposed to Poor Air Quality, 1993**

SOURCE: Fred Seitz and Christine Plepys. *Monitoring Air Quality in Healthy People 2000.* Statistical Notes No. 9. Hyattsville, MD: National Center for Health Statistics, 1995, as cited in Council on Environmental Quality, *Environmental Quality, 25th Anniversary Report.* Washington, DC: U.S. Government Printing Office, 1997, Figure 6.1, p. 111.

SOURCES: U.S. Environmental Protection Agency, Office of Policy, Planning, and Evaluation. *Environmental Equity: Reducing Risk for All Communities.* Washington, DC, June 1992; Council on Environmental Quality, *Environmental Quality, 25th Anniversary Report.* Washington, DC: U.S. Government Printing Office, 1997; D. R. Wernette and L. A. Nieves. "Breathing Polluted Air." *EPA Journal* 18(1), March/April 1992, pp. 16–17; Victor Brajer and Jane V. Hall. "Recent Evidence on the Distribution of Air Pollution Effects." *Contemporary Policy Issues,* April 1992, pp. 63–71.

of pollution that will not cause any harm to public health. But is there a pollution level that does not harm at least one individual? Probably not. So, without the balance of cost considerations, the law seems to suggest setting the primary standards for criteria pollutants at zero. Although such an extreme was not Congress' intent, the law does not provide appropriate guidelines to set the NAAQS at an efficient level.[21]

**Setting the National Emission Standards for Hazardous Air Pollutants (NESHAP).**  An analogous argument has been made about the NESHAP as originally defined in the Clean Air Act. Recall from our prior discussion that the United States had made little progress in controlling air toxics prior to the changes made in the 1990 Amendments. To a great extent, this lack of progress was the result of using a **benefit-based decision rule** to control these substances. Specifically, for any identified air toxic the EPA was required to set a standard that "*. . . provides an ample margin of safety to protect the public health . . .*"[22] It is difficult to conceptualize what an "*ample margin of safety*" might be for substances like carcinogens, which pose a threat even at low emission levels. Again, since the law did not allow for any consideration of costs, taken literally it seemed to be calling for the setting of the NESHAP at zero emission levels. Such a radical decision would have had serious consequences for American industry, since many of these substances are critical to industrial processes. Recognizing the problem, the EPA was reticent to identify a substance as a hazardous air pollutant, and little was done to control these dangerous toxics for many years.[23]

Through the 1980s, there was some controversy about the identification and subsequent standard setting for air toxics, particularly for carcinogens. One suggestion was to allow for economic feasibility in the standard-setting process, a solution supported by then EPA administrator, William Ruckelshaus. Opponents argued that such an objective approach was inappropriate for dealing with matters as delicate as human health.

Attempting to settle the debate, researchers tried to assess the efficiency implications of air toxic controls. One such investigation presents a collection of case studies that uses benefit–cost analysis to assess proposed uniform standards known as "Best Available Technology" (*BAT*) standards to control air toxics.[24] Three substances form the basis of the investigation: benzene, coke oven emissions, and acrylonitrile.[25] For benzene, the study cites an annual control cost of $2.6 million to achieve a benefit of 0.4 lives saved per year from reduced exposure. These findings imply that for the *BAT* controls on benzene to be efficient, the value of a statistical life would

**benefit-based decision rule**  A guideline to improve society's well-being with no allowance for a balancing of the associated costs.

---

[21] This discussion is elaborated in Burtraw and Portney (1991) and Portney (1990a).

[22] See Clean Air Act, Sec.112.(b)(1)(B).

[23] National Commission on Air Quality (March 1981), pp. 76–77.

[24] See Haigh, Harrison, and Nichols (1984).

[25] Acrylonitrile is a feedstock used in chemical production to produce such commodities as clothing, automobile hoses, and plastic pipe.

have to be \$6.5 million (i.e., \$2.6/0.4). For coke oven emissions and acrylonitrile emissions the comparable values would have to be \$2.3 million and \$145 million, respectively. Hence, the researchers show that, based on a generally accepted value of \$1 million for a statistical life saved, all three control policies would fail a customary benefit–cost test.

Today, U.S. regulation of hazardous air pollutants is better defined, thanks to the 1990 Amendments. All air toxics subject to federal controls are identified explicitly in the law, and the EPA has been charged with the responsibility of setting emission standards for these within a 10-year time frame. Furthermore, although the Clean Air Act continues to require that the standards protect public health and the environment, it also allows for the costs of achieving these standards to be considered—an important step toward efficiency in the setting of the NESHAP.

### Uniformity of the National Ambient Air Quality Standards (NAAQS)

A critical observation to make about the NAAQS is that, since they are nationally based, they ignore any regional-specific cost or benefit differences associated with meeting them. All nonattainment regions must meet the same uniform standards regardless of such differences as existing pollution levels, access to technology, demographics, and traffic patterns. Yet the marginal costs and benefits of reducing pollution to the same level across these highly diverse regions will likely be quite dissimilar. This likely explains why some regions met the legislated deadlines with relative ease, while others continue to struggle with compliance. Thus, while the shift to federally mandated standards was intended to strengthen U.S. policy, it nonetheless contributed to the inefficiency that typically arises with a command-and-control approach.

One legislative change that allowed for some regional-specific differences is the recognition of PSD areas and the use of existing air quality in those regions as the relevant standard. This policy reform effectively elevates the standard for PSD areas above the NAAQS applicable to nonattainment areas. The relevant issue is whether this particular use of differentiated standards represents an efficient allocation of resources across both types of regions.[26] Some economists question the wisdom of assigning more resources to already clean areas in order to achieve a higher standard of air quality.[27] To investigate this issue, we use benefit–cost analysis in a simple economic model.

**Benefit–Cost Analysis of Higher PSD Standards.** To justify the relatively higher standards in PSD areas economically, the associated *MSC* and *MSB* of abatement for these regions must intersect at a higher level of

---

[26] In order for the differentiated abatement levels to be efficient, it must be the case that the efficient level of abatement in a PSD area is higher than that in a nonattainment area.

[27] See Portney (1990a), pp. 78–79.

FIGURE 11.4 ### ECONOMIC MODELING OF HIGHER AIR QUALITY STANDARDS IN PSD AREAS RELATIVE TO NONATTAINMENT AREAS

The graphs show three possible scenarios under which the use of higher standards in PSD areas relative to nonattainment areas would be efficient. In panel (a), $MSB_{PSD} = MSB_{NON}$. In this case, the efficient abatement level in the PSD area, $A_{PSD}$, would be higher than the efficient level in a nonattainment area, $A_{NON}$, only if $MSC_{PSD}$ is *lower* than $MSC_{NON}$. In panel (b), $MSC_{NON} = MSC_{PSD}$. Here, efficiency holds only if $MSB_{PSD}$ is *above* $MSB_{NON}$. Finally, in panel (c), both the $MSC$ and $MSB$ curves are unique to each area. Under this assumption, one way efficiency results is if the following conditions hold: (1) $MSB_{PSD}$ is *below* $MSB_{NON}$; (2) $MSC_{PSD}$ is *below* $MSC_{NON}$; and (3) the vertical distance between the $MSC$ curves is sufficiently *greater* than that between the $MSB$ functions to support $A_{PSD}$ being greater than $A_{NON}$.

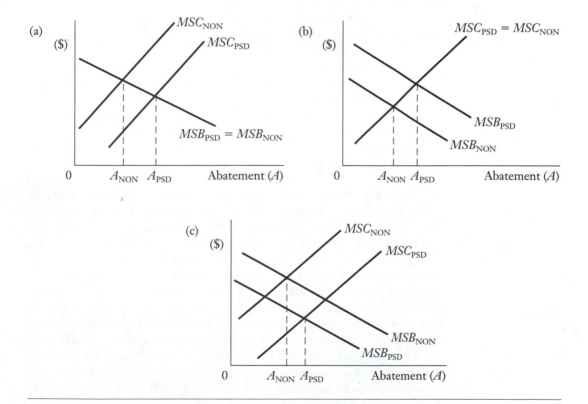

abatement than the comparable intersection for nonattainment areas. For this to occur, there must be certain differences in either or both of the $MSC$ and $MSB$ across the two types of regions. In Figure 11.4, we analyze three possible scenarios under which the use of different standards across PSD and nonattainment areas would be efficient. The marginal cost and benefit curves for a representative PSD area are labeled as $MSC_{PSD}$ and $MSB_{PSD}$, and those for a nonattainment area as $MSC_{NON}$ and $MSB_{NON}$.

In panel (a), the $MSB$ functions are identical across the two types of areas; that is, $MSB_{PSD} = MSB_{NON}$ at all abatement levels ($A$). If this relationship holds, the efficient abatement level in the PSD area, $A_{PSD}$, would be higher than the efficient level in a nonattainment area, $A_{NON}$, only if $MSC_{PSD}$ is *lower* than $MSC_{NON}$. In panel (b), the opposite set of conditions is modeled with the $MSC$ functions drawn as identical curves. Here, efficiency holds only if $MSB_{PSD}$ is *above* $MSB_{NON}$. Finally, in panel (c), both the $MSC$ and $MSB$ curves are allowed to be unique to each area. Under this latter assumption, one way that efficiency results is if the following three conditions hold: (1) $MSB_{PSD}$ is *below* $MSB_{NON}$; (2) $MSC_{PSD}$ is *below* $MSC_{NON}$; and (3) the vertical distance between the $MSC$ curves is sufficiently *greater* than that between the $MSB$ functions to support the relative position of $A_{PSD}$ and $A_{NON}$.[28]

So far what we have illustrated is that the use of relatively higher standards for PSD areas *can* be efficient, but only under certain conditions. Now we need to consider the logic of each scenario based on the expected relationship between the respective marginal costs and benefits for the two areas. For context, think of the differences between nonattainment areas and the most stringently controlled PSD areas, which are Class I. Recall that these include national parks and wilderness regions. One reason these areas have cleaner air is that they are less populated and less industrialized than their nonattainment counterparts. How might these conditions affect the $MSB$ and $MSC$?

On the cost side, it is reasonable to expect that $MSC_{PSD}$ is lower than $MSC_{NON}$, since there are fewer polluting sources to control in PSD regions. By itself, this assertion suggests that the model in panel (b) of Figure 11.4 is not a likely representation of actual conditions. Now consider the benefit side. The primary benefits of maintaining higher air quality in PSD areas are nonhealth gains, such as enhanced recreational uses, aesthetic improvements, and protection of the ecology. In contrast, the major benefits of cleaning up the more populated nonattainment areas are improvements in human health. Since health improvements are generally valued more at the margin than nonhealth gains, $MSB_{NON}$ is likely higher at all abatement levels than is $MSB_{PSD}$. Based on this hypothesis, the model shown in panel (a) appears to be inaccurate. Taking these assumed benefit differences into account along with the expected cost differences, the model in panel (c) appears to be more accurate than either (a) or (b). But recall that for this model to support the efficiency criterion, several conditions have to hold. Hence all we can conclude is that the higher standards in the cleaner PSD areas *may* be justifiable on efficiency grounds under certain economic circumstances.

---

[28]Other scenarios are possible under which both the $MSC$ and $MSB$ curves are allowed to be unique and the $A_{PSD}$ is higher than $A_{NON}$. To see this, try modeling a case different from the one shown in panel (c).

Another reform that acknowledges regional-specific differences was the reclassification of nonattainment areas for ozone, carbon monoxide, and particulate matter enacted within the 1990 Amendments. By imposing progressively more stringent controls on the dirtiest of these areas, these revisions may have improved efficiency. Again, this issue can be examined through benefit–cost analysis.

**Benefit–Cost Analysis of Progressively Regulated Nonattainment Areas.** To give our analysis context, we consider two of the new classifications for nonattainment ozone areas—"marginal" at the cleaner end of the continuum and "extreme" at the other. Now we can apply benefit–cost analysis to examine the efficiency of strengthening regulatory controls in extreme ozone areas.

Since the United States is imposing more stringent regulations on extreme ozone regions, the *MSC* in extreme regions will necessarily be higher than the *MSC* in marginal ozone regions at all levels of abatement. Hence, in order for the use of different control methods to make sense from an economic perspective, it must be the case that the *MSB* at the existing level of abatement in extreme regions must be greater than the *MSB* at the current abatement level in marginal regions.[29] As long as this is correct, we can argue that the higher incremental costs of more stringent regulations are at least to some extent justified by higher incremental benefits.

# Conclusions

U.S. air quality policy has evolved considerably over the past several decades. Legislative initiatives and the infrastructure to implement them have become more extensive and more complex. Indeed, the 1990 Clean Air Act Amendments are far more comprehensive than any U.S. environmental legislation enacted to date. Today, there is a massive network of agencies and interagencies working toward the objective of improving national air quality. In some sense, such an evolution is not surprising. Air pollution is a difficult problem, and the sheer size of the United States means that air quality controls must accommodate a variety of meteorological, geographical, and economic conditions.

Despite the numerous revisions and new initiatives, U.S. legislation continues to be based primarily on a command-and-control approach evidenced largely by the use of uniform standards to define national air quality. The problem is that such an approach is not likely to achieve an efficient solution to the nation's air pollution problems. In fact, benefit–cost analysis suggests that clean air policy initiatives have been more costly to society

---

[29] If the *MSB* curves are the same for both regions, this relative difference will necessarily hold, since the abatement level in extreme regions is by definition lower than that in marginal regions. If the two curves are distinct, then it must be the case that the *MSB* in extreme regions lies everywhere above the *MSB* in marginal regions.

than necessary. Similar conclusions follow from a qualitative evaluation of the standard-setting process. From an economic perspective, uniform standards are a troubling element of U.S. air legislation. Likewise, the absence of cost considerations in establishing these standards defies time-tested economic theory.

Of course, there are no simple answers, nor can there be any sweeping conclusions without careful reservations. Air quality issues involve many intangibles that are difficult to quantify. Moreover, many of the nation's new clean air policies have not been fully implemented, so part of the assessment must rely on estimated projections. Nonetheless, the analytical process guided by economic theory provides a way to better understand the motivation and economic implications of the Clean Air Act and to set more realistic expectations about achieving the nation's air quality objectives.

## Summary

- There were no federal air pollution laws until 1955 when the Air Pollution Control Act was passed and no comprehensive legislation until the Clean Air Act of 1963. The 1970 Clean Air Act Amendments marked dramatic policy changes in the United States, followed by still more amendments in 1977.

- On November 15, 1990, President Bush signed into law extensive changes in U.S. air quality control policy in the form of the 1990 Clean Air Act Amendments.

- Two groups of air pollutants have been identified as those causing the greatest damage to outdoor air quality—criteria pollutants and hazardous air pollutants.

- The six criteria pollutants are particulate matter, sulfur dioxide, carbon monoxide, nitrogen dioxide, tropospheric ozone, and lead. An initial list of 189 hazardous air pollutants is identified in the 1990 Clean Air Act Amendments.

- Established by the EPA, the National Ambient Air Quality Standards (NAAQS) state the maximum allowable concentrations of criteria air pollutants that may be emitted from stationary or mobile sources into the outside air.

- Primary NAAQS are standards set to protect public health, with some margin of safety. Secondary NAAQS are intended to protect public welfare.

- For the hazardous air pollutants, National Emission Standards for Hazardous Air Pollutants (NESHAP) are established for every major source of one or more of the listed hazardous air pollutants.

- Coordination of air quality control policy between federal and state governments is formalized through the State Implementation Plan (SIP). An SIP is an EPA-approved procedure outlining how a state intends to implement, monitor, and enforce the NAAQS and the NESHAP.

- There are currently 247 air quality control regions (AQCRs) defined in the United States. These are classified into nonattainment areas and PSD areas. In the 1990 Clean Air Act Amendments, new classifications are established for certain of the nonattainment areas.

- The research of Paul Portney suggests that the total social benefits of U.S. clean air legislation as of 1981 outweigh the total social costs. In a more current study, Portney finds that the 1990 Amendments may abate pollution beyond the efficient level.

- The NAAQS ignore regional-specific cost or benefit differences associated with meeting them. This uniformity suggests an inefficient allocation of resources across the AQCRs.

- The primary and secondary NAAQS are motivated solely by anticipated benefits from protecting public health and welfare, meaning that costs are not explicitly considered.

- The historical lack of progress in setting the NESHAP was the result of using a benefit-based decision rule. The 1990 Amendments have improved air toxics regulation by identifying substances to be controlled in the law and by revising the standard setting to allow for costs to be considered.

- The higher standards in the cleaner PSD areas *may* be justifiable on efficiency grounds under certain economic conditions.

- The use of progressively more stringent controls on the dirtiest nonattainment regions may have improved resource allocation, if the marginal benefit of abatement in these regions is higher than in cleaner nonattainment areas.

# Key Concepts

natural pollutants
anthropogenic pollutants
criteria documents
criteria pollutants
hazardous air pollutants
stationary source
mobile source

National Ambient Air Quality
    Standards (NAAQS)
primary NAAQS
secondary NAAQS
National Emission Standards for
    Hazardous Air Pollutants
    (NESHAP)

maximum achievable control
   technology (MACT)
State Implementation Plan (SIP)
Air Quality Control Regions
   (AQCR)

prevention of significant
   deterioration (PSD) areas
nonattainment areas
benefit-based decision rule

# Review Questions

1. If you were responsible for setting the NAAQS for lead, what key determinants would you consider if the standard were established to meet the efficiency criterion? Be sure to itemize separately the benefits and costs associated with your decision.

2. Using the efficiency criterion, carefully analyze the problem faced by the EPA in identifying hazardous air pollutants prior to the 1990 Amendments.

3. a. Briefly explain the significance of Prevention of Significant Deterioration (PSD) areas to the setting of air quality standards.
   b. From an economic perspective, explain the paradox associated with setting higher standards in PSD areas relative to nonattainment areas. Show how an inefficient result may arise using an *MSB–MSC* model.

4. Briefly summarize Portney's overall assessment of the 1990 Clean Air Act Amendments and discuss the major implications of these findings for society.

5. Refer back to Table 11.8 for the marginal benefit and cost estimates of the 1990 Clean Air Act Amendments. Conduct an individual benefit–cost analysis for each of the three major components of the amendments, namely acidic deposition, urban air quality, and hazardous air pollutants. What do you conclude?

6. Visit the site of EPA's Green Book: Nonattainment Areas for Criteria Pollutants, which can be accessed at **www.epa.gov/oar/oaqps/ greenbk**, and use the data to investigate which AQCRs in your state have nonattainment status for each of the criteria pollutants. Summarize your findings.

# Additional Readings

Aeppel, Timothy. "Clean Air Act Triggers Backlash as Its Focus Shifts to Driving Habits." *The Wall Street Journal*, January 25, 1995, pp. A1, A10.

Anderson, J. W. "Revising the Air Quality Standards: A Briefing Paper on the Proposed NAAQS for PM and $O_3$." Washington, DC: Resources for the Future, February 1997.

Brannigan, Martha. "CAT Scan May Soon 'Map' Air Pollution." *The Wall Street Journal*, November 10, 1994, p. B7.

*EPA Journal* 18(1), "Environmental Protection—Has It Been Fair?" March/April 1992.

Freeman, A. Myrick, III. "Air and Water Pollution Policy." In Paul R. Portney, ed., *Current Issues in U.S. Environmental Policy.* Baltimore: Johns Hopkins University Press, 1978.

Hall, Jane V. "Air Quality in Developing Countries." *Contemporary Economic Policy* 13(2), April 1995, pp. 77–85.

Hall, Jane V., and Amy L. Walton. "A Case Study in Pollution Markets: Dismal Science vs. Dismal Reality." *Contemporary Economic Policy* 14(2), April 1996, pp. 67–78.

Koch, Gayle S., and Paul R. Ammann. "Current Trends in Federal and State Regulation of Hazardous Air Pollutants." *Journal of Environmental Regulation* 4(1), Autumn 1994, pp. 25–41.

Krupnick, Alan J., and J. W. Anderson. "Revising the Ozone Standard." *Resources* 125, Fall 1996.

Solomon, Caleb, and Oscar Suris. "Hot Weather Hurts Efforts to Clean Up Air." *The Wall Street Journal*, July 7, 1994, pp. B1, B6.

Tietenberg, T. H. *Emissions Trading: An Exercise in Reforming Pollution Policy.* Washington DC: Resources for the Future, 1985.

## Related Web Sites

Environmental Issues page at the Organisation for Economic Co-operation and Development — **www.oecd.org/env/**

EPA's Air Pollution Monitoring site — **www.epa.gov/oar/oaqps/montring.html**

EPA's Fact Sheet on the revisions to the NAAQS for PM and Ozone — **ttnwww.rtpnc.epa.gov/naaqsfin/o3pm.htm**

EPA's Green Book: Nonattainment Areas for Criteria Pollutants — **www.epa.gov/oar/oaqps/greenbk**

EPA's Health Effects Notebook for Hazardous Air Pollutants — **www.epa.gov/ttn/uatw/hapindex.html**

EPA's *National Air Quality and Emissions Trends Report, 1996* — **www.epa.gov/oar/aqtrnd96/**

EPA's Office of Air and Radiation report, *The Benefits and Costs of the Clean Air Act, 1970 to 1990* — **www.epa.gov/airprogm/oar/sect812/ index.html**

EPA's *The Plain English Guide to the Clean Air Act* — **www.epa.gov/oar/oaqps/peg_caa/pegcaain.html**

EPA's Unified Air Toxics Web site — **www.epa.gov/ttn/uatw/pollsour.html**

Information on SIPs — **www.epa.gov/oar/oaqps/emission.html#sip**

Overview of the 1990 Clean Air Act Amendments — **www.epa.gov/oar/caa/overview.txt**

| | |
|---|---|
| President Clinton's Executive Order 12898 on environmental justice | **www.npr.gov/library/direct/orders/264a.html** |
| Proposed recommendations of the Grand Canyon Visibility Transport Commission. | **www.nmia.com/~gcvtc/final.html** |
| Section 110 of the Clean Air Act on SIPs | **www.epa.gov/oar/caa/caa110.txt** |
| United Nations Environment Programme (UNEP) | **www.unep.org** |
| U.S. Air Quality Nonattainment Areas | **www.epa.gov/airs/nonattn.html** |
| U.S. NAAQS | **www.epa.gov/airs/criteria.html** |

# Appendix:
# A Reference to Acronyms and Terms
# Used in Air Quality Control Policy

## Environmental Economics Acronyms

| | |
|---|---|
| *TSB* | Total social benefits |
| *TSC* | Total social costs |
| *MSB* | Marginal social benefit |
| *MSC* | Marginal social cost |
| $MSC_{PSD}$ | Marginal social cost of abatement in a PSD area |
| $MSB_{PSD}$ | Marginal social benefit of abatement in a PSD area |
| $MSC_{NON}$ | Marginal social cost of abatement in a nonattainment area |
| $MSB_{NON}$ | Marginal social benefit of abatement in a nonattainment area |

## Environmental Science Terms

| | |
|---|---|
| CO | Carbon monoxide |
| $CO_2$ | Carbon dioxide |
| $mg/m^3$ | Micrograms per cubic meter |
| $mg/m^3$ | Milligrams per cubic meter |
| $NO_x$ | Nitrogen oxides |
| $NO_2$ | Nitrogen dioxide |
| $O_3$ | Ozone |
| Pb | Lead |
| PM | Particulate matter |
| PM-10 | Particulate matter of less than 10 micrograms in diameter |
| ppm | Parts per million |
| $SO_2$ | Sulfur dioxide |
| $SO_x$ | Sulfur oxides |

## Environmental Policy Acronyms

| | |
|---|---|
| AQCR | Air Quality Control Region |
| BAT | Best Available Technology |
| MACT | Maximum Achievable Control Technology |
| NAAQS | National Ambient Air Quality Standards |
| NAPAP | National Acidic Precipitation Assessment Program |
| NESHAP | National Emission Standards for Hazardous Air Pollutants |
| PSD | Prevention of Significant Deterioration |
| SIP | State Implementation Plan |

# 12

# Improving Air Quality: Controlling Mobile and Stationary Sources

Of the two major classes of air pollutants identified by the Clean Air Act, the criteria pollutants are more common. Because they are pervasive, these substances are responsible for most of the air pollution in the world even though they are less dangerous than hazardous air pollutants. The relevant point is that all of society is exposed to the risks of criteria pollutants, which explains why the Clean Air Act places such a strong emphasis on them and why Congress elected to legislate strategies to implement the National Ambient Air Quality Standards (NAAQS). Although the motivation for this decision may be well placed, it turns out that this top-down policy approach has had some adverse consequences—an assertion that will be supported with economic analysis in this chapter.

Starting from a general perspective, we know that the Clean Air Act establishes stringent regulations on both stationary and mobile sources, since both contribute to the release of all six criteria pollutants. This is clear from the emissions data shown in Table 12.1. Although the control instruments applicable to each source group are different, some are commonly motivated. A case in point are controls for urban air pollution, which is caused by the combination and concentration of essentially all the criteria pollutants released from both major source groups.

On the other hand, some air quality problems are more closely linked to particular polluting sources, and these require more specific policy strategies. Look again at Table 12.1 and notice, for example, how mobile sources contribute relatively more to the level of carbon monoxide (CO) emissions, while stationary sources are bigger emitters of sulfur oxides ($SO_x$). Consequently, some control instruments are uniquely motivated by specific emissions and their associated environmental risks. In any case, controlling mobile and stationary sources of criteria pollutants is the means by which

| TABLE 12.1 | ANNUAL CRITERIA POLLUTANT EMISSIONS FOR MOBILE AND STATIONARY SOURCES (THOUSANDS OF SHORT TONS EXCEPT LEAD MEASURED IN SHORT TONS) |
|---|---|

| | 1970 | 1980 | 1990 | 1995 |
|---|---|---|---|---|
| **Particulate Matter (PM-10)** | | | | |
| Stationary | 11,539 | 5,472 | 1,979 | 1,850 |
| Mobile | 666 | 726 | 729 | 697 |
| Miscellaneous | 839 | 852 | 36,267 | 37,925 |
| **Sulfur Oxides (SO$_x$)** | | | | |
| Stationary | 30,557 | 25,198 | 21,585 | 17,715 |
| Mobile | 494 | 696 | 836 | 596 |
| Miscellaneous | 110 | 11 | 14 | 8 |
| **Carbon Monoxide (CO)** | | | | |
| Stationary | 21,531 | 16,552 | 11,978 | 11,399 |
| Mobile | 98,639 | 90,730 | 77,500 | 74,246 |
| Miscellaneous | 7,909 | 8,344 | 11,173 | 6,454 |
| **Nitrogen Oxides (NO$_x$)** | | | | |
| Stationary | 11,036 | 11,917 | 12,233 | 10,858 |
| Mobile | 9,018 | 11,044 | 10,331 | 10,601 |
| Miscellaneous | 330 | 248 | 373 | 228 |
| **Volatile Organic Compounds (VOCs)** | | | | |
| Stationary | 15,032 | 13,912 | 13,558 | 14,061 |
| Mobile | 14,514 | 10,848 | 8,974 | 8,356 |
| Miscellaneous | 1,101 | 1,134 | 1,069 | 446 |
| **Lead (Pb)** | | | | |
| Stationary | 39,171 | 9,448 | 3,778 | 3,407 |
| Mobile | 180,301 | 65,509 | 1,887 | 1,578 |
| Miscellaneous | 0 | 0 | 0 | 0 |

NOTES: For PM-10, fugitive dust emissions were not estimated prior to 1985. In 1995, they represent 92% of the total emissions.
Sums of categories may not equal total due to rounding.

1 short ton = 2,000 pounds.

SOURCE: U.S. Environmental Protection Agency, Office of Air Quality Planning and Standards. *National Air Pollutant Emission Trends, 1900–1995*. Research Triangle Park, NC, October 1996, Tables 5-9, 11 pp. 14–15.

the NAAQS are implemented. Hence, the nation's opportunity to achieve the legislated definition of air quality depends critically on the effectiveness of all federally mandated control instruments—an issue that merits careful investigation and analysis.

To motivate our study of mobile and stationary controls, we begin by discussing urban air pollution, since it is linked to both types of sources. Once done, we begin our analysis of mobile source controls. We investigate current policy based on the 1990 Clean Air Act Amendments, and we present a brief retrospective of what has transpired over time between the government and the American automobile industry. This is followed by an economic analysis that examines the efficiency and cost-effectiveness of U.S. mobile source initiatives. An analogous study follows for stationary sources. Here, an important context will be an environmental problem tied primarily to stationary sources—acidic deposition, more commonly known as acid rain. Of particular interest is an economic evaluation of the market-based program aimed specifically at this problem. An appendix of commonly used acronyms and terms is provided for reference at the end of the chapter.

# Urban Air Pollution: An Important Policy Motivation

Environmentalists as well as policy makers are concerned about the air pollution that characterizes urban centers. In these metropolitan areas, the high concentration of human population, traffic, and industrial activity intensifies the concentration of criteria pollutants and hence increases the environmental risks of exposure. Since a large proportion of the population is exposed to the associated health hazards, increased abatement efforts in cities should yield a higher level of marginal benefit than in rural communities.

## *Measuring U.S. Urban Air Quality*

**Pollutant Standards Index (PSI)** Signifies the worst daily air quality in an urban area over some time period.

To develop a better sense of the magnitude of the problem in the United States, the EPA monitors urban air quality with a particular focus on 23 major urban centers. Over the past several years, the agency has been reporting part of its findings using a **Pollutant Standards Index (PSI).**[1] The PSI value uses daily maximum statistics obtained from a monitoring network on particulate matter (PM-10), sulfur dioxide ($SO_2$), carbon monoxide (CO), ozone ($O_3$), and nitrogen dioxide ($NO_2$) to form a single index number based on the short-term national standards for each substance.[2] The resulting value, ranging from 0 to 500, signifies the worst daily air quality in an urban area over a given time period. A PSI of 100 is considered the standard set by the Clean Air Act. The descriptor words that identify the health effects associated with various ranges of the PSI are as follows:

- 0 to 50:        Good
- 51 to 100:      Moderate

---

[1] The 23 cities include the 10 in which the EPA has regional offices (i.e., Boston, New York, Philadelphia, Atlanta, Chicago, Dallas, Kansas City, Denver, San Francisco, and Seattle), plus 13 other cities, namely Baltimore, Cleveland, Detroit, El Paso, Houston, Los Angeles, Miami, Minneapolis–St. Paul, Phoenix, Pittsburgh, San Diego, St. Louis, and Washington, DC. For more detail on the PSI, visit **www.epa.gov/oar/oaqps/psi.html**.

[2] The only criteria pollutant omitted from the index is lead, since there are no short-term NAAQS for this substance.

- 101 to 199:       Unhealthful

- 200 to 299:       Very unhealthful

- 300 and above:   Hazardous

The PSI and its descriptor are often used by local media to communicate air quality conditions to the general public.

Table 12.2 presents PSI trend data over a 10-year period. The table shows the number of days in a year each city experienced an air quality level that was unhealthful or worse, signified by a PSI of over 100. Notice that for most of the cities, the number of PSI days over 100 was lower in 1994 than in 1990. However, just the opposite occurred for Baltimore, Chicago, Cleveland, Detroit, Minneapolis–St. Paul, St. Louis, and Washington, DC. The data also indicate that the air quality in Los Angeles is far worse than any other major urban area in the sample—a distinction that has persisted for several decades. As early as the 1940s, Los Angeles residents noticed frequent episodes of a brownish haze on the horizon—an awareness that eventually led to nationwide concern about urban air pollution. Today, we know that the brownish haze in Los Angeles and many other metropolitan areas is **urban smog.**

## Urban Smog

Coined from the words *smoke* and *fog*, the word *smog* originally referred to the overall air quality first observed in London at the turn of the century. Used in this context, it refers mainly to the presence of particulate matter and other emissions such as sulfur oxides in the air.[3] Because of Los Angeles' history and its dubious distinction as America's "king of smog," many people erroneously think of this city as the only one facing a severe smog problem. It *is* true that the dense traffic there and the meteorological conditions, make this region particularly vulnerable to smog formation. However, most major cities suffer from the effects of smog. The problem is more pervasive in highly industrialized and heavily populated parts of the world, such as Europe and Japan.

In urban areas, another type of smog can form from a chemical reaction involving several of the criteria pollutants. Scientists refer to this type of smog as **photochemical smog** to distinguish it from the more conventional "smoke and fog" variety. Photochemical smog is formed from certain air pollutants that chemically react in the presence of sunlight (thus the prefix *photo-*), to form entirely new substances. Its principal component is tropospheric ozone ($O_3$), referred to as "ground level ozone." Along with over 100 different compounds, ground level ozone is produced by a chemical reaction of nitrogen oxides ($NO_x$), volatile organic compounds (VOCs) (primarily hydrocarbons), and sunlight. Since the chemical reaction

**photochemical smog** Caused by pollutants that chemically react in sunlight to form new substances; its principal component is ozone ($O_3$).

[3] Pryde (1973), p. 147.

| TABLE 12.2 | TREND DATA FOR MAJOR URBAN AREAS: NUMBER OF PSI DAYS GREATER THAN 100 AT TREND SITES |
| --- | --- |

| MSA | 1985 | 1990 | 1994 |
| --- | --- | --- | --- |
| Atlanta | 9 | 17 | 4 |
| Baltimore | 25 | 12 | 17 |
| Boston | 3 | 1 | 1 |
| Chicago | 9 | 3 | 8 |
| Cleveland | 1 | 2 | 4 |
| Dallas | 27 | 8 | 1 |
| Denver | 38 | 9 | 2 |
| Detroit | 2 | 3 | 8 |
| El Paso | 32 | 27 | 10 |
| Houston | 64 | 61 | 29 |
| Kansas City | 3 | 2 | 0 |
| Los Angeles | 208 | 178 | 136 |
| Miami | 5 | 1 | 0 |
| Minneapolis–St.Paul | 14 | 1 | 3 |
| New York | 65 | 18 | 8 |
| Philadelphia | 31 | 14 | 6 |
| Phoenix | 88 | 9 | 7 |
| Pittsburgh | 9 | 11 | 2 |
| San Diego | 88 | 60 | 16 |
| San Francisco | 5 | 1 | 0 |
| Seattle | 25 | 5 | 0 |
| St. Louis | 10 | 8 | 11 |
| Washington, DC | 17 | 5 | 7 |
| Subtotal | 778 | 456 | 280 |
| Other Sites | 878 | 552 | 333 |
| **Total** | 1,656 | 1,008 | 613 |

NOTES: PSI is the Pollutant Standards Index, a dimensionless number ranging from 0 to 500 converted from daily monitoring data for PM-10, $SO_2$, CO, $O_3$, and $NO_2$ based on their short-term NAAQS, Federal Episode Criteria, and Significant Harm Levels. (Lead is excluded because it has no short-term NAAQS.)

MSA is a Metropolitan Statistical Area.

Data are reported from trend sites, that is, those for which there is sufficient historical data to be used for trends.

SOURCE: U.S. Environmental Protection Agency, Office of Air Quality Planning and Standards. *National Air Quality and Emissions Trends Report, 1994*. Research Triangle Park, NC, October 1995, Table A-13, pp. A-23–A-24.

is stimulated by sun and temperature, peak ozone levels are observed in the warmer seasons of the year. In most parts of the United States, the ozone season is from May to October. In warmer regions such as the South and Southwest, ozone levels might be elevated for the entire year.[4]

Both mobile and stationary sources contribute to photochemical smog formation, since both emit $NO_x$ and VOCs. Transportation sources emit-

---

[4]For more on urban smog, visit **www.epa.gov/oar/oaqps/peg_caa/pegcaa03.html#topic3a**.

## Mexico City's Serious Smog Problem

Mexico City faces an ongoing battle to reduce its air pollution problem, said to be the worst in the world. At points in time, its ozone and carbon monoxide levels have been measured at almost four times the acceptable level by U.S. standards. The smog in this famous capital city is so severe that the future of many of its historic buildings, statues, and monuments is seriously threatened. Workers are unable to keep up with the continual degradation of the city's buildings, some of which are centuries old. The city's historian, Jorge Hernandez, laments the lost detail on Mexico City's treasured statues that can never be replaced.

Officials are taking steps to reverse some of the damage. A primary target is the automobile, allegedly responsible for two-thirds of the smog problem. Such a statistic is not surprising given that some 3 million drivers operate vehicles averaging 10 years of age. In an attempt to rid the city of the aging automobile population, new car buyers must turn in an old one—a requirement started in 1993. To mitigate the problem in the future, automobile manufacturers in Mexico made a commitment to begin installing catalytic converters on their new vehicles, but residents demanded more immediate action.

In response, Mexico City officials ordered the installation of pollution abatement devices on all taxicabs and small buses. This mandate may extend to private citizens as part of the license renewal process. Needless to say, this official stance has sparked the entrepreneurial spirit in literally hundreds of firms, submitting prototypes of pollution devices for the city's approval. Another mandate begun in 1990 requires that every car in the city be prohibited from the streets one day each week. Under this plan, each automobile is assigned a colored sticker corresponding to the particular day of the week on which driving is banned. The city's billboards herald which color corresponds to which day, and teams of enforcers work the intersections to make certain the mandate is followed. Violators are fined 30 days of minimum wages, or approximately $120.

In 1997, forest fires so worsened the city's already poor air quality that officials had to ban half of the 3 million automobiles from roadways and urge the city's 60,000 factories to cut back production by 33 percent. According to one official, these stringent measures have had a substantial economic impact, estimated to cost $8 million per day for lost production and reduced labor hours. Added to these economic costs were associated health costs of some $3.5 million per day.

SOURCES: William Cormier. "Smog Eats Mexico City's Monuments." *The Brockton Enterprise.* November 23, 1992; Stephen Baker. "Mexico's Motorists Meet the Smog Patrol." *Business Week.* June 25, 1990, p. 100; Jonathan Marshall. "How Ecology Is Tied to Mexico Trade Pact." *San Francisco Chronicle.* February 25, 1992, p. A8; Reuters. "Mexico's Bad Air Exacts Financial Toll, Official Says." *Boston Globe*, May 30, 1998, p. A5.

ting the largest amounts of these substances are ordinary highway vehicles, particularly those fueled by gasoline. Among stationary sources, fossil-fueled power stations are the primary emitters of $NO_x$, while oil refineries, gas stations, and chemical manufacturing plants are major sources of VOCs.

It is important to recognize that in urban centers, officials are more concerned with emissions from transportation sources because of traffic congestion. In Mexico City, for example, local officials are implementing drastic controls on mobile sources, including a program that prohibits the use of every automobile for one day per week on a rotating basis. Application 12.1 discusses the air quality conditions faced by Mexico's smoggy capital city and officials' attempts to find a solution.

| TABLE 12.3 | NATIONAL EMISSIONS ESTIMATES FOR MOBILE SOURCES BY MAJOR CATEGORY (THOUSANDS OF SHORT TONS PER YEAR EXCEPT LEAD IN SHORT TONS) |

| | PM | $SO_x$ | CO | $NO_x$ | VOCs[a] | Pb |
|---|---|---|---|---|---|---|
| **Gasoline-Powered Highway Vehicles** | | | | | | |
| 1970 | 307 | 180 | 87,313 | 5,714 | 12,706 | 171,961[b] |
| 1975 | 294 | 215 | 82,189 | 6,504 | 10,194 | 130,206[b] |
| 1980 | 189 | 218 | 76,888 | 6,128 | 8,577 | 62,189[b] |
| 1985 | 134 | 211 | 76,126 | 5,666 | 9,006 | 15,978[b] |
| 1990 | 107 | 213 | 61,516 | 5,113 | 6,524 | 1,690[b] |
| 1995 | 104 | 224 | 57,156 | 5,583 | 5,778 | 1,387 |
| **Diesel-Powered Highway Vehicles** | | | | | | |
| 1970 | 136 | 231 | 721 | 1,676 | 266 | |
| 1975 | 177 | 288 | 945 | 2,141 | 351 | |
| 1980 | 208 | 303 | 1,161 | 2,493 | 402 | |
| 1985 | 229 | 311 | 1,261 | 2,423 | 370 | |
| 1990 | 250 | 358 | 1,342 | 2,375 | 330 | |
| 1995 | 200 | 80 | 1,468 | 2,022 | 326 | |
| **Other Mobile Sources[c]** | | | | | | |
| 1970 | 223 | 83 | 10,605 | 1,628 | 1,542 | 8,340[d] |
| 1975 | 256 | 99 | 11,462 | 1,879 | 1,676 | 5,012[d] |
| 1980 | 329 | 175 | 12,681 | 2,423 | 1,869 | 3,320[d] |
| 1985 | 368 | 208 | 13,706 | 2,734 | 2,008 | 229[d] |
| 1990 | 372 | 265 | 14,642 | 2,843 | 2,120 | 197[d] |
| 1995 | 393 | 292 | 15,622 | 2,996 | 2,252 | 191[d] |

NOTES: 1 short ton = 2,000 pounds.

[a] VOC emissions are used to measure the formation of ozone, $O_3$.

[b] Data shown for Pb are for *all* highway vehicles.

[c] Other mobile sources are nonroad gasoline, nonroad diesel, aircraft, railroads, and marine vessels.

[d] Data shown for Pb are for *all* off-highway vehicles.

SOURCE: U.S. Environmental Protection Agency, Office of Air Quality Planning and Standards, *National Air Pollutant Emission Trends, 1900–1995.* Research Triangle Park, NC, October 1996, Tables A1–A6, pp. A-2–A-27.

# Controlling Mobile Sources

Of all the transportation vehicles, the primary focus of U.S. policy is highway vehicles such as passenger cars and trucks. As the trend data in Table 12.3 show, these polluting sources, particularly those that are gasoline powered, emit the largest quantity of nearly every criteria pollutant.[5] These

[5] As noted in the table, the emissions of volatile organic compounds (VOCs) are used as a proxy measure of ground level ozone formation. More information on automobile emissions can be found at **www.epa.gov/ OMSWWW/05-autos.htm**.

## The "Big Three" Form a Research Consortium in the 1990s

Stiffer requirements for auto emissions in the 1990 Clean Air Act amendments and under current California law are partly responsible for the formation of a 1990s version of an emissions control research consortium comprising the three largest U.S. automakers—General Motors, Ford, and Chrysler. A similar arrangement formed in 1953 and a related cross-licensing agreement ultimately were dissolved by a 1969 antitrust suit settled through a consent decree. Interestingly, the provisions of that consent decree, which prohibited cooperation for any technological research in emissions controls, expired in 1987.

Of course, times have changed from the 1950s when General Motors, Ford, and Chrysler enjoyed unquestionable dominance of the automobile industry. Their control of the market in that era was in large part responsible for the legal action against the former research consortium. Government officials had reason to believe that this earlier research effort was another delay tactic made possible through implicit collusion. Now, in the 1990s, the "Big Three" face pressure from foreign producers and as a result control a much less commanding market share. Imports currently account for some 30 percent of all U.S. new car sales, up from a 0.4 percent share in the post–World War II period. That fact, coupled with a pro-business political atmosphere, makes the 1990s consortium an unlikely target for antitrust officials. In fact, the U.S. government is now supporting collaborative research efforts, validating that support through legislation passed in 1984 by Congress. For their part, GM, Ford, and Chrysler argue that their cooperative effort not only will help achieve environmental policy objectives but also will strengthen their position against foreign competition.

The research effort, named USCAR (United States Council for Automobile Research) is one of eight such agreements among the automakers. It is aimed at investigating a variety of technologies to develop cleaner-running automobiles as well as cleaner fuels. For an up-to-date perspective on the outcome of this research effort, visit **www.uscar.org/index.html**.

SOURCES: Krystal Miller. "Big 3 to Cooperate on Efforts to Meet Clean-Air Rules." *The Wall Street Journal*, June 9, 1992, p. B9; Walter Adams and James W. Brock. "The Automobile Industry." In Walter Adams, ed., *The Structure of American Industry*. New York: Macmillan, 1990.

data explain the policy focus on the manufacture of these vehicles and the increasing number of initiatives aimed at developing alternative fuels. For its part, the American automobile industry has begun to take a more aggressive position toward reducing motor vehicle pollution, not only because of government controls, but also to accommodate environmentally conscious consumers. In 1992, the "Big Three" formed a research consortium to develop cleaner-running automobiles, a cooperative effort discussed in Application 12.2.

Such public and private initiatives were unheard of as recently as 20 years ago. The evolution of U.S. controls on motor vehicles underscores the inherent problems associated with regulation of a major industrial sector—in this case, the U.S. auto industry. Scientific evidence tying the automobile to the formation of smog has existed since the early 1950s, but no federal mandate to control auto emissions was legislated until 1965. And it was not until 1970 that emission limits appeared within the law itself.

## A Brief Retrospective on Motor Vehicle Emission Controls[6]

By most accounts, national legislation on motor vehicle emissions was slow to start in the United States. In 1963, the nation passed into law the Clean Air Act, the first extensive set of air quality controls. Notably absent from its provisions was any direct regulation of automobile emissions. This was a startling omission given that California had passed new laws that same year to do exactly that. In contrast to California's activism, the Clean Air Act of 1963 took a much more cautious approach, giving virtually no power to federal officials to control mobile sources directly. It was not until 1965 when the Clean Air Act was first amended that federal controls on mobile sources were strengthened, calling for uniform emission standards. Somewhat ironically, this transition was motivated in large part by the historically uncooperative automobile industry. The reason was an economic one. Automakers had an incentive to lobby for *national* controls, since they wanted to avoid the costly alternative of having to meet state-specific standards. The 1965 law set maximum emissions for new automobiles starting with the 1968 model year, but for only two of the major pollutants—carbon monoxide and hydrocarbons.

Mobile source controls in the 1970 Amendments were precedent setting in that new car emission standards were stated explicitly in the statutes themselves and were extremely stringent. In retrospect, most argue that achieving them was not feasible with available technology. Emissions of carbon monoxide and hydrocarbons were to be reduced by 90 percent by the 1975 model year from their 1970 levels, with comparable reductions for nitrogen oxide emissions by the 1976 model year from their 1971 level. These standards were to be applicable over the entire useful life of the vehicle—a requirement that placed even more pressure on the automobile industry. Manufacturers had to guarantee their emission control systems for this entire period, not only to the initial buyer, but to every subsequent purchaser as well. Predictably, Detroit's auto makers sought extensions to the legislated deadlines and adjustments to the targeted emission levels. Ultimately, the compliance dates originally set for 1975 and 1976 were postponed for five years.

All told, the early years of mobile source controls were marked by a series of extensions and a chronicle of delays. As the power struggle between Washington and Detroit continued, society grew increasingly impatient with the lack of progress. Washington officials knew that federal policy on motor vehicle emissions was in need of major revision.

## Current U.S. Controls on Motor Vehicles and Fuels

Attempting to correct errors of the past, the 1990 Clean Air Act Amendments strengthen U.S. controls over motor vehicle emissions and fuels. In

---

[6]To read more about this history, see "Milestones in Auto Emissions Control" at **www.epa.gov/ OMSWWW/12-miles.htm**.

addition to tougher command-and-control regulations, the new laws also incorporate incentives to encourage technological development of cleaner-running vehicles and cleaner alternative fuels. Among the more salient features of the new law are:

- Emission reductions for cars and trucks
- Onboard pollution control systems for conventional motor vehicles
- Fuel quality controls
- Initiatives to develop clean fuel vehicles

A brief summary of each of these initiatives follows.[7]

**Emission Reductions for Motor Vehicles.**   The 1990 Amendments impose tougher regulations on tailpipe emissions from all types of highway vehicles. More refined than under existing law, the new standards have two tiers. The first refers to the initial five years, or 50,000 miles of use, and the second establishes less stringent standards for the remainder of the vehicle's useful life redefined at 10 years, or 100,000 miles. Beyond this extension of a car's economic life, the new emissions limits are implemented much as they have been in the past—uniformly applicable to every new model car.

**Onboard Pollution Control Systems for Light-Duty Vehicles.**   To control refueling emissions, the 1990 law requires onboard vapor recovery systems to be installed on new light-duty vehicles. Other provisions call for emission control diagnostic systems on all light-duty vehicles and trucks starting with the 1994 model year. At minimum, these systems must be able to accurately identify a failure in the vehicle's catalytic converter and oxygen sensor over its useful life.

**reformulated gasoline** Newly developed fuels that emit less hydrocarbons, carbon monoxide, and toxics than conventional gasoline.

**oxygenated fuel** Formulations with enhanced oxygen content to allow for more complete combustion and hence a reduction in CO emissions.

**Fuel Quality Controls.**   Just as vehicles are more stringently regulated under the 1990 law, so too are fuels and fuel additives. For example, after December 31, 1995, any fuel containing lead or lead additives was prohibited for highway use. Other provisions require the use of newly developed cleaner fuels in certain of the nonattainment areas. For instance, reformulated gasoline must be used in some ozone nonattainment regions and oxygenated fuel in designated carbon monoxide nonattainment areas. **Reformulated gasoline** refers to formulations that emit less hydrocarbons, carbon monoxide, and toxics than conventional gasoline.[8] **Oxygenated fuel** contains more oxygen to allow for more complete combustion and a reduction in carbon monoxide emissions.

---

[7] See **www.epa.gov/oar/oaqps/peg_caa/pegcaa04.html** for an online description of Clean Air Act initiatives aimed at mobile sources.

[8] For further information, see "Reformulated Gasoline and Vehicle Performance" at **www.epa.gov/OMSWWW/rfgvehpf.htm**.

# Changing Fuels for America's Automobiles: The Pros and Cons

Two characteristics of petroleum-based fuels are linked to air pollution—its *burning efficiency* and its *volatility*. When fuels burn inefficiently, carbon monoxide (CO) emissions are produced as a by-product of combustion. This problem is more prevalent in cold weather and is exacerbated when fuels are burned in poorly maintained engines. As efficiency improves, carbon dioxide ($CO_2$) emissions are formed instead. A fuel's volatility, or its capacity to evaporate, is also important to air pollution since evaporation releases toxic vapors into the air. Fuel volatility arises from the presence of volatile organic compounds (VOCs), which are added to enhance a fuel's octane rating or antiknock properties. The higher the volatility of gasoline, the more VOC emissions are released into the atmosphere.

The 1990 Clean Air Act Amendments explicitly call for the use of several types of "cleaner fuels" under certain well-defined conditions. These are broadly classified into three groups: **oxygenated fuels, reformulated gasoline,** and **clean alternative fuels.**

**Oxygenated Fuels.** The U.S. oxygenated fuels program is aimed at reducing carbon monoxide (CO) emissions and therefore is scheduled for use in CO nonattainment areas. Fuel additives provide the oxygen content needed to enhance fuel efficiency and allow for more complete combustion. Fuel prices are expected to increase by a few cents per gallon as a result.

**Reformulated Gasoline.** Launched in 1995, the reformulated gasoline program is applicable to regions facing severe ozone problems. Aimed specifically at fuel volatility and toxicity, reformulated fuel must contain at minimum 2 percent oxygen and at maximum 1 percent benzene. Standards for this fuel require specific reductions in hydrocarbon and toxic emissions.

**Clean Alternative Fuels.** Clean alternative fuels may include reformulated gasoline or other alternatives in place of the more conventional petroleum-based products. These alternatives include ethanol ("grain alcohol"), methanol ("wood alcohol"), compressed natural gas, propane (liquified petroleum gas), and electricity. The table below summarizes the major advantages and disadvantages of these fuels based on information provided by the EPA.

| Fuel | Advantages | Disadvantages |
|---|---|---|
| Ethanol | Excellent automotive fuel<br>Very low emissions of ozone-forming hydrocarbons and toxics<br>Made from renewable sources<br>Can be domestically produced | High fuel cost<br>Somewhat lower vehicle range |
| Methanol | Excellent automotive fuel<br>Very low emissions of ozone-forming hydrocarbons and toxics<br>Can be made from a variety of feedstocks, including renewables | Fuel initially would be imported<br>Somewhat lower vehicle range<br>Possible increase in $NO_x$<br>Lower cold-weather performance<br>High levels of formaldehyde emissions |
| Natural Gas | Very low emissions of ozone-forming hydrocarbons, toxics and CO<br>Can be made from a variety of feedstocks, including renewables<br>Excellent fuel especially for fleet vehicles | Higher vehicle cost<br>Lower vehicle range<br>Less convenient refueling |
| Propane | Cheaper than gasoline today<br>Most widely available clean fuel today<br>Somewhat lower emissions of ozone-forming hydrocarbons and toxics<br>Excellent fuel, especially for fleet vehicles | Cost will rise with demand<br>Limited supply<br>No energy security or trade balance benefits |
| Reformulated Gasoline | Can be used in all cars without changing fuel distribution system<br>Somewhat lower emissions of ozone-forming hydrocarbons and toxics | Somewhat higher fuel cost |
| Electricity | Potential for zero vehicle emissions<br>Power plant emissions easier to control<br>Can recharge at night when power demand is low | Current technology is limited<br>Higher vehicle cost<br>Lower vehicle performance<br>Lower vehicle range<br>Less convenient refueling |

SOURCES: U.S. Environmental Protection Agency, Office of Mobile Sources. "Clean Fuels: An Overview." Fact Sheet OMS-6, Ann Arbor, MI, January 1993a; U.S. Environmental Protection Agency, Office of Mobile Sources. "Vehicle Fuels and the 1990 Clean Air Act." Fact Sheet OMS-13, Ann Arbor, MI, January 1993b; Art Kinsman. "Fueling the Future." *AAA World*, April 1992; Joseph D. Younger. "Cleaner, 'Greener' Gasoline?" *AAA World*, November/December 1992.

To encourage compliance with these new fuel laws, market-based incentives are used. Marketable credits are issued for fuels that exceed legal requirements. These credits can be used by the recipient or transferred to another individual in the same nonattainment area.

**clean fuel vehicle**
A vehicle certified to meet stringent emission standards.

**Clean Fuel Vehicles.**    Responding further to urban air quality pollution, the 1990 legislation establishes a clean fuel vehicles program. A **clean fuel vehicle** is one that has been certified to meet stringent emission standards for substances such as CO, NO$_x$, PM, and formaldehyde over prescribed time periods. For designated ozone and carbon monoxide nonattainment areas, states must set up programs for the adoption of clean fuel vehicles by owners or operators of fleets of more than 10 vehicles. These programs must be phased in starting with the 1998 model year. At this point, a fixed percentage of all new fleet vehicles bought in each area must be clean fuel vehicles and must use **clean alternative fuels.** These are any fuels, such as methanol, ethanol, or other alcohols, or any power sources, including electricity, used in a clean fuel vehicle. Application 12.3 on the facing page presents the pros and cons of using clean fuels to reduce air pollution.

**clean alternative fuels**    Fuels like methanol, ethanol, or other alcohols, or power sources such as electricity, used in a clean fuel vehicle.

Again, market incentives are integrated into the new provisions. Credits are to be issued to fleet operators or owners who surpass the requirements in the law. They might do this by purchasing clean fuel vehicles in advance of the deadline or by buying more of these vehicles than the law requires. The awarded credits can be held, banked for future use, or traded. They are to be weighted by the emission reduction achieved by each vehicle, which gives the fleet owner a further incentive to go beyond what the law requires.

## Economic Analysis of Mobile Source Controls

Historically, U.S. attempts to control emissions from mobile sources have been frustrated by a litany of problems and delays. In a very real sense, many of the difficulties were predictable, even avoidable. In retrospect, much of the problem was that the law failed to consider the dynamics of the marketplace and the importance of benefit–cost analysis. To provide structure to our evaluation of these issues, we focus our analysis around the following characteristics of mobile source emissions control policy:

- Absence of benefit–cost analysis in setting standards for tailpipe emissions

- Uniformity of auto emissions standards

- Bias against new vehicles

- Implications of clean fuel alternatives

*The Absence of Benefit–Cost Analysis:*
*An Inefficient Decision Rule*

It is an interesting irony that after years of delay in establishing federal limits on auto emissions, the Clean Air Act Amendments of 1970 imposed controls that by most accounts were extraordinarily stringent. Even at that point in legislative history, there was virtually no argument that the stated objectives for emission reductions were ambitious. In part, the stringent controls were a response to accumulating evidence that motor vehicles were a major source of pollution. However, there was also reason to believe that Washington was attempting to take a strong position against the American automobile industry.

Beyond the motivations for tougher standards, the more critical issue is whether the emissions targets were technologically feasible and, if not, whether they were intentionally set beyond what was possible given the existing knowledge base. Most argue that the standards were not attainable and in fact were meant to be *technology-forcing* by design—that is, specifically set to compel the auto industry to find solutions. Such a strategy may have been in order, given the industry's track record to that point. However, most have questioned the government's wisdom in setting emission reductions so far out of reach that manufacturers had a strong case to seek adjustments and postponements.

Just as important is the fact that the implied decision rule used to establish the emissions controls was not supported by benefit–cost analysis. Rather, the standards were set to protect public health and welfare—a purely benefit-based objective. As shown in Figure 12.1, this is linked to abatement activity that maximizes total social benefits, which corresponds to the point where the marginal social benefit ($MSB$) crosses the horizontal axis (i.e., where $MSB = 0$), at $A_0$. Notice that $A_0$ is *higher* than the efficient level, $A_e$, where the marginal social benefit curve intersects the marginal social cost ($MSC$) curve (i.e., where $MSB = MSC$), which implies overregulation.

As it turned out, the 1970 standards were never implemented in their original form. In fact, they were modified considerably. Worse, the haggling over the unrealistic standards between the government and the automobile industry added further to the already long delays. Had the standards been set at levels that accounted for the full extent of the associated costs, it is quite possible that the automobile industry would not have had sufficient support for its lobbying efforts to extend the statutory deadlines. Instead, the lack of efficient decision making left policy makers unarmed for the assault mounted by the automakers. The result? The ultimate burden was borne by society, and the ill-defined decisions of that era accomplished little more than to postpone the provision of cleaner-running vehicles to the marketplace.

FIGURE 12.1 **THE INEFFICIENCY OF A BENEFIT-BASED DECISION RULE ON MOTOR VEHICLE EMISSIONS**

If mobile source standards are set to protect public health and welfare, they represent a purely benefit-based objective. Such an objective calls for abatement activity that maximizes total social benefits, which corresponds to the point where $MSB$ crosses the horizontal axis (i.e., where $MSB = 0$), at $A_0$. Notice that $A_0$ is higher than the efficient level, $A_e$ (i.e., where $MSB = MSC$), which implies overregulation.

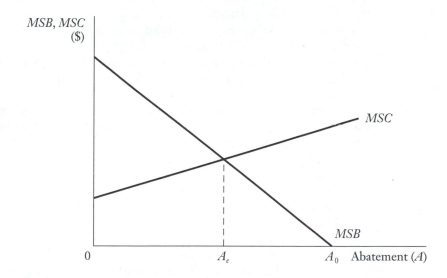

## Uniformity of Auto Emissions Standards

An ongoing problem with U.S. mobile source controls is that with few exceptions the emission standards are applicable "across the board" on every model produced and without regard to where the vehicle will be driven. Another uniform requirement calls for all cars and light-duty trucks starting with 1984 models to meet high-altitude standards, despite the fact that only about 3.5 percent of cars sold in the United States are purchased in high-altitude areas.[9] Ultimately, such an approach needlessly increases the costs of reducing pollution with no offsetting benefit to society.

Disregard for the location where a vehicle is operated overregulates vehicles sold in relatively clean areas and undercontrols those sold in more

[9]Council of Economic Advisers (1982), pp. 145–46; Seskin (1978), p. 91; and White (1982), pp. 67–68. White reports that, according to General Motors, the per unit cost in current dollars of this high-altitude standard is approximately $65 for a gas-powered automobile and $230 for a diesel-powered car.

polluted areas. This is illustrated in Figure 12.2, where we logically assume that the *MSB* of abatement in dirty areas is higher than in clean areas, *ceteris paribus*.[10] Notice that if the standard, $A_s$, is the same for both regions, the dirty area is undercontrolled, since $A_s$ is below the efficient level, $A_e$. The opposite holds in relatively clean areas, where $A_s$ is above the efficient level, $A_e$.

An alternative is to have two sets of standards be administered at the state level based on the degree of pollution in that area. Proponents of this more federalistic approach believe this would yield important cost savings. A 1974 study conducted by the National Academy of Science estimates the costs of a *uniform* 0.4 grams per mile (gpm) standard for $NO_x$ relative to the costs of a *two-tiered* standard, calling for a 0.4 gpm standard in seriously polluted areas (about 37 percent of motor vehicles), and a 3.1 gpm standard in all other areas.[11] The study predicts that a $23-billion savings over the 1975 to 1985 period would have resulted if the two-tiered system had been used.

Similarly, it is argued that the emission controls need not be applicable to every model produced. Substantial savings could be achieved by allowing each producer to meet legislated targets based on *average* emissions of all new cars produced. The benefits based on overall emission reductions would be unchanged, but the costs of compliance would be much lower.[12] The foregone savings help to explain the growth rate of mobile source control costs since the 1970 Amendments, from $1.3 billion ($1986) in 1972 to $7.5 billion ($1986) in 1987.[13]

Current law does allow some exceptions to these uniform standards. Perhaps the most notable is the use of more stringent standards for vehicles sold in California. More recently, other states have followed suit. In December 1994, the EPA approved a plan submitted by clean air officials in 12 eastern states and the District of Columbia (members of the Ozone Transport Commission) to require cars manufactured for their regions to meet California-style emissions standards by 1999.

These regional variances from national requirements have set off a round of debates. The auto industry points to the increased costs of complying with several sets of emissions standards. Others question the wisdom of moving to electric vehicles that have to be fueled by power plants. In some regions like the Northeast, electric power plants are more important contributors to smog than are mobile sources, so the net gain in air quality may not be worth the effort. Furthermore, the technology of electric car engineering is still in its infancy, particularly in addressing the

---

[10] It is not unreasonable in this context to assume that the *MSC* is the same for both regions, since it is referring to abatement of mobile source emissions, and abatement of a mobile source is by definition not specific to a geographical location.

[11] See National Academy of Sciences and National Academy of Engineering (1974).

[12] This is discussed in the economic analysis of mobile source emissions in Council of Economics Advisers (1982), p. 146, which asserts that such an averaging plan could save millions of dollars.

[13] U.S. EPA, Office of Policy, Planning, and Evaluation (December 1990).

FIGURE 12.2 **UNIFORM ABATEMENT STANDARDS ACROSS REGIONS FOR MOBILE SOURCE EMISSION CONTROLS**

Disregard for the location where a vehicle is operated overregulates vehicles sold in relatively clean areas and undercontrols those sold in more polluted areas. Notice that if the standard, $A_s$, is the same for both regions, the dirty area is undercontrolled since $A_s$ is below the efficient level, $A_e$. The opposite holds in relatively clean areas, where $A_s$ is above the efficient level, $A_e$.

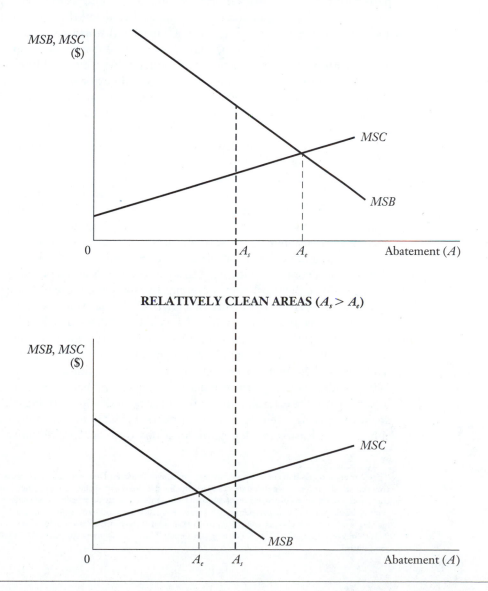

**RELATIVELY DIRTY AREAS ($A_s < A_e$)**

**RELATIVELY CLEAN AREAS ($A_s > A_e$)**

harsher conditions of cold weather climates.[14] What these arguments suggest is that alternatives to uniform emission standards must be well thought out to achieve any significant gain.

### Inherent Bias against New versus Used Automobiles

One of the more troubling dilemmas in environmental law is the inherent bias caused by more stringent controls imposed on *new* polluting sources. This partiality is particularly problematic for motor vehicles, since engine performance as well as sticker price are at issue. As long as there are differences between the regulation of new and used vehicles, there will be price and performance impacts that can create market distortions.

To understand fully how the law can influence market decisions, consider the following scenario, which we model in Figure 12.3. The automobile is a durable good, meaning its economic life extends beyond a single period. Because of this, new and used automobiles are substitutes for one another with the usual relationship between their relative prices. Regulating new car emissions adds to the production costs of those vehicles, shifting the supply curve to the left from $S_1$ to $S_2$. The result is that the higher costs are passed on, at least in part, to consumers, elevating price from $P_1$ to $P_2$. Faced with higher relative prices for new cars, some consumers will purchase a used car or opt to keep a deteriorating one, either of which is likely to be a relatively high emitter of pollutants. We then would observe a shift right in the demand for used cars from $D_1$ to $D_2$. Because the regulation encourages consumers to substitute in favor of used cars, it effectively extends the economic life of cars already on the road. There is also the issue that emission control devices negatively affect a car's acceleration and gas mileage. Thus, the legislation confounds the signaling mechanism of price by diminishing the performance of a relatively higher priced vehicle.

There have been some policy changes that address this dilemma. For example, the 1990 Amendments extend the economic life of the automobile over which emission standards are mandated by increasing the regulatory period from its former five years or 50,000 miles to 10 years or 100,000 miles. Although the standards for the second half of the period are less stringent, the extension to a longer time period helps to reduce the bias against future new vehicles, since most cars on the road ultimately will be subject to at least some degree of emissions control. An alternative idea,

---

[14] Even stronger opposition comes from University of Denver Professor Don Stedman, who argues that all emission standards for automobiles are costly and ineffective. Stedman claims that most auto emissions come from a relatively small proportion of cars with faulty emissions systems or badly tuned engines. These culprits, he claims, can be singled out using his invention called a remote-sensor. According to Stedman, his idea is a better and cheaper control approach than across-the-board rules on tailpipe emissions and fuels (Monaghan, March 10, 1993). For more on remote sensing, visit **www.epa.gov/OMSWWW/15-remot.htm**.

**FIGURE 12.3**

### MODELING THE BIAS AGAINST NEW AUTOMOBILES

Regulating new car emissions adds to the production costs of those vehicles, shifting the supply curve in the new car market to the left from $S_1$ to $S_2$. The result is that the higher costs are passed on, at least in part, to consumers, elevating price from $P_1$ to $P_2$. Faced with higher relative prices for new cars, some consumers will purchase a used car or opt to keep a deteriorating one, either of which is likely to be a relatively high emitter of pollutants. We then would observe a shift right in the demand for used cars from $D_1$ to $D_2$. Because the regulation encourages consumers to substitute in favor of used cars, it effectively extends the economic life of cars already on the road.

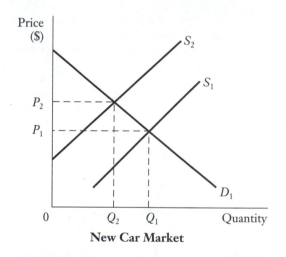

**New Car Market**

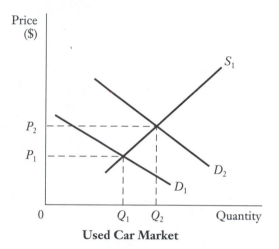

**Used Car Market**

still in the experimental stage, is a program called "Cash for Clunkers." This incentive-based voluntary program, discussed in Application 12.4, allows polluters to earn emissions credits in return for buying older, vintage cars and scrapping them to get these high emitters off the road.

### *Implications of Clean Fuel Alternatives*

Clean fuel provisions in the 1990 Amendments are an extension of technology-based standards, which were formerly directed almost entirely toward engines and emission control systems. Furthermore, the use of more advanced fuel compositions is required only in the dirtier regions of the country. Targeting these areas makes good sense from an economic perspective. The development and use of alternative fuels generates relatively high marginal costs, which aligns with the higher expected marginal benefits that will accrue in the designated nonattainment regions. Hence,

## The "Cash for Clunkers" Program

In March 1992, the United States announced an innovative proposal aimed at encouraging the scrapping of older-model, high-emitting automobiles. This so-called Cash for Clunkers program promotes the issuance of emission reduction credits to firms that purchase and scrap old cars. As in other emissions trading programs, these credits can be applied against legislated reductions imposed on the firm as a stationary source. This voluntary program, now called the Accelerated Retirement of Vehicles Program, ties together controls on stationary sources with those imposed on mobile sources. In fact, President Bush called it "mobile-stationary source trading and emissions control."

To some extent, the national program is based on a prototype experiment put into place in Los Angeles. In 1990, an oil company called Unocal Corp. purchased some 8,400 pre-1971 cars for $700 each over a one-year period and scrapped them. The oil firm estimates that the plan reduced hydrocarbon emissions at an average cost of $7,000 per ton removed. Based on these estimates, it has been suggested that Unocal's approach is cost-effective in a severely polluted area like Los Angeles.

In 1993, the EPA released a document titled *Guidance for the Implementation of Accelerated Retirement of Vehicles Programs.* Through this guidance document, the agency attempts to assist state and local officials with the design and implementation of their own programs. There are several issues that need to be resolved in implementing any such plan. For one thing, some have argued that $700 is not likely to be a sufficient inducement for an individual to give up their used automobile and face the expense of buying a newer car. Responding to this objection, a Unocal official cited a survey it conducted, which showed that 360 of the 800 individuals surveyed did in fact use the $700 to purchase newer and presumably cleaner-running cars. Another potential problem is in determining the price to be paid for these old cars. Related to this issue is controlling the migration of older vehicles from one region to another to seek out the best available price. Finally, there is the matter of how to calculate credits for the purchased vehicles. Should the credits be uniform or should they reflect the expected reduction in pollution per mile over the remaining economic life of the car?

While still in its infancy, the program is capable of providing an incentive to pull high-emitting vehicles off American highways. In fact, according to former acting assistant EPA director Richard Morgenstern, 38 percent of all cars on the road in 1992 were built prior to 1980. These vehicles generated 86 percent of the hydrocarbons and carbon dioxide released by mobile sources into the atmosphere. Appealing to the effectiveness of contrasts, Mr. Morgenstern said:

> "The dirtiest 6 percent of the cars on the road today emit 50 percent of the hydrocarbons. The cleanest 50 percent of cars emit only 3 percent of these hydrocarbons."

SOURCES: *EPA Journal.* "'Cash for Clunkers' to Cut Pollution." *EPA Journal* 18(2), May/June 1992, p. 2; U.S. Environmental Protection Agency, Office of Policy, Planning, and Evaluation. *The United States Experience with Economic Incentives to Control Environmental Pollution.* Washington, DC, July 1992, pp. 7-2–7-3; U.S. Environmental Protection Agency, Office of Air and Radiation, Office of Mobile Sources. *Environmental Fact Sheet: Accelerated Vehicle Retirement Programs.* Washington, DC: December 1997.

this selective legislation follows the fundamental decision rule of benefit–cost analysis, which may approach an efficient solution.

A separate issue is whether the fuel-switching program is a cost-effective way to reduce mobile source emissions. ARCO, the oil company that pioneered the development of reformulated fuel, estimates that it can produce a reformulated gasoline to satisfy the 1990 laws that will cost

## Are Fuel-Based Control Strategies Cost-Effective Solutions?

The 1990 Clean Air Act Amendments call for the use of cleaner fuels to help achieve national air quality objectives. Oxygenated fuels are recommended for use in carbon monoxide (CO) nonattainment areas, particularly in high-altitude regions such as Denver. Despite this national commitment, there is debate about the *cost-effectiveness* of such a fuel-based strategy.

Rowe and colleagues (1990) investigate the use of oxygenated fuels in Denver, an area where the cold temperatures and high altitude make it particularly vulnerable to CO pollution. Rowe and his colleagues form a baseline for their research by estimating the cost per ton of CO reduction in the Denver area from using either of two oxygenated additives, methyl tertiary butyl ether (MTBE) and ethanol. The estimates are based primarily on the incremental costs of blending and distribution, net of the offsetting effect of added octane provided by oxy-additives. Ultimately, they arrive at a statewide total cost for the program's first year of $1 million in 1988 dollars with an effective incremental cost per gallon of fuel of 0.45 cents. Based on an estimated reduction of 10,250 tons of CO for the first year, the program's cost is approximated at $100 per ton of CO reduction. The researchers then modify this regional estimate to be applicable to a national program, adjusting for different prices and market conditions. The result is approximately $300 per ton for the MTBE program and about $590 per ton for ethanol.

With these estimates as a baseline, Rowe and his colleagues consider how these costs per ton compare with three other control alternatives: (1) an enhanced inspection and maintenance program; (2) Denver's Better Air Campaign, which includes a "no drive day" plan in the high CO season; and (3) a trip reduction ordinance, which requires large employers to provide a plan for their workers to reduce the use of single-occupant vehicles. The comparison based on cost per ton of CO removed is:

| | |
|---|---|
| Inspection and maintenance program with 1987 enhancements | $785. |
| Better Air Campaign plan (based only on quantifiable costs): | > $250.* |
| Trip reduction ordinances: | $1,000 to $5,000.** |

*The great majority of costs are not quantifiable; thus, this estimate is highly understated.

**No data on Denver's plan were available, so the estimate is based on the costs of a Phoenix, Arizona, plan.

Using as a major argument the quantifiable costs of the inspection and maintenance program, the study concludes that the use of oxygenated fuel in the Denver area is cost-effective. A similar argument is viable using the other plans as comparisons but with less confidence given the less-than-satisfactory data. While the results are not directly applicable to low-altitude regions, they do offer important support to laws on oxygenated fuel for climates similar to Denver's.

SOURCE: Robert D. Rowe, Michael G. Shelby, Joshua B. Epel, and Ari Michelsen. "Using Oxygenated Fuels to Mitigate Carbon Monoxide Air Pollution: The Case of Denver." *Contemporary Policy Issues* 8, January 1990, pp. 39–53.

consumers 15 cents more per gallon.[15] But is this cost-effective? This question is precisely the issue discussed in Application 12.5, which presents new research evidence on the costs of using oxygenated fuel.

---

[15] Dickerson (January/February 1991).

| TABLE 12.4 | NATIONAL EMISSIONS ESTIMATES FOR STATIONARY SOURCES BY MAJOR CATEGORY (THOUSANDS OF SHORT TONS PER YEAR EXCEPT LEAD IN SHORT TONS) |

| | PM | SO$_x$ | CO | NO$_x$ | VOCs[a] | Pb |
|---|---|---|---|---|---|---|
| **Fuel Combustion** | | | | | | |
| 1970 | 2,871 | 23,456 | 4,632 | 10,061 | 721 | 10,616 |
| 1980 | 2,445 | 21,391 | 7,302 | 11,320 | 1,050 | 4,300 |
| 1990 | 1,076 | 19,599 | 5,063 | 11,484 | 920 | 500 |
| 1995 | 905 | 15,658 | 3,960 | 10,077 | 709 | 493 |
| **Industrial Processes** | | | | | | |
| 1970 | 7,669 | 7,093 | 9,840 | 535 | 10,373 | 26,355 |
| 1980 | 2,754 | 3,774 | 6,950 | 486 | 10,129 | 3,938 |
| 1990 | 604 | 1,945 | 5,174 | 665 | 8,617 | 2,474 |
| 1995 | 632 | 2,015 | 5,608 | 693 | 9,138 | 2,072 |
| **Solid Waste Disposal** | | | | | | |
| 1970 | 999 | 8 | 7,059 | 440 | 1,984 | 2,200 |
| 1980 | 273 | 33 | 2,300 | 111 | 758 | 1,210 |
| 1990 | 242 | 36 | 1,686 | 82 | 2,262 | 804 |
| 1995 | 253 | 37 | 1,766 | 85 | 2,411 | 842 |

NOTE:

[a]VOC emissions are used to measure the formation of ozone, O$_3$.

SOURCE: U.S. Environmental Protection Agency, Office of Air Quality Planning and Standards. *National Air Pollutant Emission Trends, 1900–1995*. Research Triangle Park, NC, October 1996, Tables 5-9, 11 pp. 14–15.

## Controlling Stationary Sources

Stationary sources contribute to the emissions levels of all the criteria pollutants. This source group covers a lot of ground. Included are electric power plants, chemical plants, steel mills, and even residential furnaces. Obviously, certain categories are more important to U.S. control policy than others. Look at the trend data in Table 12.4. Notice how fuel combustion sources, which include fossil-fueled electric power plants, are major contributors of sulfur oxide emissions—the primary cause of acid rain. On the other hand, industrial sources such as petroleum refineries and chemical manufacturers are responsible for most of the VOC emissions. So these stationary sources are important targets for policies aimed at reducing urban smog.

Emissions of all stationary sources are regulated primarily by uniform technology-based standards—indicative of a command-and-control policy approach. In the late 1970s, the EPA did introduce some market-based programs, although these were intended to be subordinate to the ongoing use of standards. For the most part, both the technology-based standards and the market programs are defined and implemented in accordance with two features of stationary sources: the age of the facility—whether it is new or existing; and the location of the facility—whether it is within a prevention of significant deterioration (PSD) area or a nonattainment area. These characteristics form the structural basis for our discussion. To serve as a guideline for what is to follow, refer to Table 12.5 (p. 344) for a summary of the various standards and trading programs that evolved based on these factors.

## Age-Specific Control Differences: New versus Existing Sources

**Defining Technology-Based Emissions Limits.**    In general, the rulings require that facilities constructed or modified after 1970 are to meet more stringent emissions limits than those already in existence. The reasoning was that new or modified stationary sources presumably could integrate the technology needed to meet stringent standards more easily than their older counterparts. Existing facilities would likely face high retrofitting costs, which could hurt local economies. Furthermore, they would eventually deteriorate to the point of needing to be modified or replaced. Hence, over time, the tougher standards would have to be met by *all* stationary sources.

New Source
Performance
Standards (NSPS)
Technology-based
emissions limits es-
tablished for new
stationary sources.

Emissions limits applicable to new and modified stationary sources are called **New Source Performance Standards (NSPS).** According to the Clean Air Act, these are to be technology-based in accordance with the "best system of emission reduction." Such a phrase suggests that the NSPS were meant to be stringent. But in this case, the stringency is tempered somewhat by allowing for costs and energy requirements to be considered as well.[16] Since technological factors are the basis for these limits, the NSPS are allowed to vary across industry categories designated by the EPA. However, each set of industry standards is to be applied *uniformly* across all firms within a given category. Because of the long-term importance of these more stringent controls, Congress established a **dual-control approach,** placing the responsibility for controlling **new or modified stationary sources** with the EPA, and assigning the comparable duties for **existing stationary sources** to state governments.

new or modified
stationary source
A source for which
construction or
modification follows
the publication of
regulations.

existing stationary
source   A source
already present when
regulations have been
published.

**The Bubble Policy.**    In December of 1979, the EPA launched its **bubble policy,** originally conceived as an option for states to use in implementing the national standards for *existing* sources. The intent of this program was to allow a plant to measure emissions of a pollutant, not from each of the release points within the plant, but rather as an *average* of all such points—as if captured within an imaginary bubble. The aim was to offer

bubble policy
Allows a plant to
measure its emissions
as an average of all
emission points ema-
nating from that
plant.

---

[16] However, in practice this cost consideration is meant to imply only that the technology be affordable and not to be used as part of a formal benefit–cost analysis in setting the standards (Portney, 1990a, p. 38).

| **TABLE 12.5** | **TECHNOLOGY-BASED STANDARDS AND MARKET PROGRAMS UNDER THE CLEAN AIR ACT** |
|---|---|

**PSD Areas**
**Classification of Stationary Source**

| Approach | New or Modified Sources | Existing Sources |
|---|---|---|
| Standards | Best Available Control Technology (BACT) | Best Available Retrofit Technology (BART) |
| Market-Based Program | Netting | Bubble Policy |

**BACT** refers to an emission limitation based on the maximum degree of pollution reduction that the permitting authority deems achievable on a case-by-case basis, accounting for energy, environmental, and other economic impacts and costs.

**BART** is applicable only to emissions that might negatively affect visibility in a PSD area and must consider factors such as compliance costs, existing control technology, and the energy and environmental impacts.

**Netting** refers to the use of emissions trading among points within a given source for the same type of pollutant, such that any increase in emissions from a modified source is *exactly matched* by a reduction in emissions from another point within that same source.

The **bubble policy** allows a plant or plant complex to measure its emissions of a single pollutant as an average of all emission points emanating from that plant or complex, as if captured within an imaginary bubble.

**Nonattainment Areas**
**Classification of Stationary Source**

| Approach | New or Modified Sources | Existing Sources |
|---|---|---|
| Standards | Lowest Achievable Emission Rate (LAER) | Reasonably Available Control Technology (RACT) |
| Market-Based Program | Offset Plan | Bubble Policy |

**LAER** refers to an emissions rate that reflects the most stringent emission limitation outlined in a given SIP for the same type of source, or the most stringent limitation achieved in practice for such a source category, whichever is the more stringent.

**RACT** refers to an emissions standard based on the use of technology deemed to be practically available, accounting for technological and economic feasibility, and determined on a case-by-case basis.

An **offset plan** provides for any emissions associated with a new or modified major stationary source to be *more than countered* by the overall reductions achieved by existing sources.

firms flexibility in deciding *how* they could achieve the requisite emissions limits at least cost.

In 1980, the EPA introduced another market-based program called **emissions banking.** Designed to complement the bubble concept, this plan allows a source to accumulate **emission reduction credits** if it abates more than required by law. These credits are then "deposited" through the banking program for future use, establishing the foundation for an emissions market. Emissions banking has been utilized only in a limited way, with only 24 emission banks identified as of 1994.[17]

**emissions banking** Allows a source to accumulate emission reduction credits if it reduces emissions more than required by law and "deposit" these through a banking program.

### *Location-Specific Control Differences: PSD versus Nonattainment Areas*

**Defining Emissions Limits in PSD Areas.**   With the official introduction of prevention of significant deterioration (PSD) areas in 1977, stationary source controls had to be revised to accommodate the change. Since the air quality standard in PSD regions is relatively higher, controls for sources located in these areas had to be made more stringent. However, new facilities in PSD areas would face relatively tougher standards than existing ones. Implemented through a permit procedure, any new or modified source in a PSD area has to meet emissions limits based on what is called the **best available control technology (BACT).** What this means is that a new source has to meet a standard that aligns with the *maximum* degree of pollution reduction available.

**Defining Emissions Limits in Nonattainment Areas.**   Standards for nonattainment areas are relatively less stringent. But just like their PSD counterparts, these sources face different standards based on their age. Existing sources must use **reasonably available control technology (RACT),** which is the least stringent of all the technology-based standards. New or modified sources in these areas must comply with the **lowest achievable emission rate (LAER),** roughly defined as the most stringent emission limit achieved in practice by the same type of source.

**Emissions Trading in PSD Areas.**   To facilitate control in PSD areas, a trading program known as **netting** was developed for use by modified sources.[18] A type of bubble policy, netting allows emissions trading to take place among release points within a facility for the same type of pollutant. Its distinguishing feature is that any added emissions associated with a plant modification must be *exactly matched* by a reduction from somewhere else

**netting**   Developed for PSD areas to allow emissions trading among points within a source for the same type of pollutant, such that any emissions increase due to a modification is matched by a reduction from another point within that same source.

---

[17] Anderson, Lohof, and Carlin (August 1997), p. 6–3. For an interesting and comprehensive discussion on emissions banking and the bubble concept, see Liroff (1986).

[18] Although netting was developed for use in PSD areas, it technically can be used in all areas.

within that same plant. Hence, netting assures that any construction project will have no detrimental effect on the air quality in a PSD area.

**Emissions Trading in Nonattainment Areas.**   In some sense, implementing pollution controls in nonattainment areas must be more strategic. Obviously, there is concern about the environmental impact of allowing new or modified facilities into an area already not meeting the national ambient standards. Yet preventing new construction could potentially worsen air quality, since new plants likely operate more efficiently and cleanly than older ones. In an attempt to achieve the best of both worlds, the 1977 Amendments introduced the **offset plan.** Implemented through a permit procedure, an offset plan assures that emissions from a new or modified source be *more than countered* by the reductions achieved by existing sources. Unlike the bubble policy or netting, the offset plan involves trades between existing and new sources rather than within the same facility or plant complex. To facilitate the plan, an **emissions bank** of accumulated **emission reduction credits** was set up where facilities could deposit and access offsets as needed.

**offset plan**   Developed for nonattainment areas to allow emissions trading between new or modified sources and existing facilities such that releases from the new or modified source are more than countered by reductions achieved by existing sources.

Although the collection of technology-based standards can be confusing, the key points to remember about them are:

- Emissions limits in PSD areas are more stringent than those in nonattainment areas.

- Limits for new sources are more stringent than those for existing sources within both types of areas.[19]

Another important observation is the way in which market incentives are used in the bubble policy, emissions banking, offsets, and netting. Although these programs were intended to be subordinate to the standards, they nonetheless represented a shift toward integrating some economic-based mechanisms into what had been almost exclusively a command-and-control approach. Title IV of the 1990 Clean Air Amendments continues this trend by establishing another type of trading program for stationary sources specifically aimed at the problem of acid rain.

## Controlling Acidic Deposition

**acidic deposition**   Arises when sulfuric and nitric acids mix with other airborne particles and fall to the earth as dry or wet deposits.

Acid rain, or more accurately **acidic deposition,** has been the subject of political and media attention in recent years. Research on the problem has intensified, and both public officials and private citizens have grown

---

[19]Furthermore, although the new source standards for PSD and nonattainment areas (i.e., BACT and LAER, respectively), are supposed to be more stringent than the New Source Performance Standards (NSPS), in practice, the NSPS are generally accepted for either (Portney, 1990a, pp. 37–38).

| TABLE 12.6 | THE PROBLEM OF ACIDIC DEPOSITION: A SUMMARY | |
| --- | --- | --- |
| **Causes** | **Anthropogenic Sources** | **Major Effects** |
| $SO_2$ | Fossil-fuel burning primarily by electric power plants | **Ecological and Forestry Effects**   Acidification of surface waters; localized forest damage |
| $NO_x$ | Fossil-fuel burning primarily by electric power plants and motor vehicles | **Health Effects**   Direct effects include respiratory and cardiovascular problems; some indirect effects possible from increased lead or methylmercury exposure under extreme conditions |
| | | **Aesthetic Effects**   Visibility impairment |
| | | **Property Effects**   Damage to buildings, statues, and monuments |

increasingly cognizant of the implications. As scientific knowledge has grown, so too has the motivation to enact stronger legislation. Effectiveness of policy initiatives is limited by the fact that acid rain is a *regional* air pollution problem, meaning that the source of the contamination is often hundreds of miles from where the detrimental effects are felt. Consequently, some form of federal intervention generally is necessary to control polluters.

**The Problem of Acidic Deposition.**   Acidic deposition occurs when the production of sulfuric and nitric acids mix with other airborne particles and fall to the earth either as dry deposition or as fog, snow, or rain—thus the descriptive phrase, "acid rain." Table 12.6 gives an overview of the causes, sources, and effects of this important regional problem.[20] These acidic compounds result from the chemical reaction of sulfur dioxide ($SO_2$) and nitrogen oxide ($NO_x$) emissions with water vapors and oxidants in the earth's atmosphere.[21] Of the two responsible pollutants, the more significant is $SO_2$. It is formed when the sulfur found naturally in coal or oil is released during combustion and reacts with the oxygen in the atmosphere. Primary generators of $SO_2$ emissions are fossil-fueled electric power plants, refineries, pulp and paper mills, and any sources that burn sulfur-containing coal or oil. According to 1990 estimates, 70 percent of U.S. annual emissions of $SO_2$ are generated by electric power plants, and 92 percent of these are coal-burning plants. By itself, utility coal usage accounts for 85 percent of total coal consumption in the United States.

---

[20]For online information, visit the Web site **www.epa.gov/oar/oaqps/peg_caa/pegcaa05.html**.

[21]An oxidant is any oxidizing agent such as oxygen ($O_2$) or ozone ($O_3$) capable of chemically reacting in the atmosphere to form a new substance.

**The Policy Response: Title IV of the 1990 Amendments.**   Title IV of the 1990 Clean Air Act Amendments is dedicated to a reduction plan for $NO_x$ emissions and an innovative allowance program to decrease $SO_2$ emissions. The reduction plan for $NO_x$ is to be achieved through various performance standards set by the EPA. Ultimately, emissions are to be reduced by 2 million tons from their 1980 level. For $SO_2$, the law establishes a national cap of 8.95 million tons of annual emissions for electric power plants—the major sources of $SO_2$—and a cap of 5.6 million tons for non-utility industrial sources. Both caps are to be met by 2000. This is the first time any national limit has been imposed on a single pollutant. These limits should achieve a 10-million–ton reduction in $SO_2$ emissions below their 1980 level.

**The $SO_2$ Emissions Allowance Program.**[22]   To achieve the $SO_2$ emissions cap, the 1990 law sets up an emissions market that operates through an allocation and transfer system. At the start of the program, the EPA issues **tradeable $SO_2$ emission allowances** or "rights to pollute" to stationary sources, where each allowance permits the release of one ton of $SO_2$. Since no emissions are permitted unless authorized by an allowance, the aggregate number issued by the EPA effectively sets the national limit.[23]

Once the emissions allowances are distributed, they can either be used by the recipient or sold to other sources through a transfer program. This program sets up a market through which allowances can be bought and sold. In May 1992, the first allowance trade was announced between the Tennessee Valley Authority (TVA), a utility operating some 59 coal-fired units, and Wisconsin Power and Light Co., one of the "cleanest" utilities in the country. The transaction involved TVA's purchase of 10,000 allowances at a value of $2.5 to $3 million. The market incentive for the precedent-setting trade is clear once the facts are known. To meet the new federal standards *without* trading, TVA would have to have made an investment in abatement technology estimated at between $750 and $850 million.

An extension of this emissions market is provided through a Special Allowance Reserve, a bank of allowances available for direct sale by the EPA. Since the success of this program depends greatly on external trades, the EPA designated the Chicago Board of Trade (CBOT) to be in charge of running the auctions. Because of its experience, the CBOT can facilitate the exchange of allowances and may reduce the transactions costs of matching up buyers and sellers. Virtually anyone can enter the market for $SO_2$ allowances. In fact, the law specifically states that allowances can

**tradeable $SO_2$ emission allowances**
Permits issued to stationary sources, each allowing the release of one ton of $SO_2$, which can be either held or sold through a transfer program.

---

[22] A good Web site on the U.S. Acid Rain Program that includes a section dedicated to the allowance trading program is **www.epa.gov/acidrain/**.

[23] In Phase I of the plan for the 1995 to 2000 period, each source receives allowances based on the following formula: average fuel usage over the 1985 to 1987 period multiplied by an emission rate of 2.5 pounds of $SO_2$ per million Btu, all divided by 2000. In Phase II, covering the period from 2000 to 2009, the allowance formula is similar except that the emission rate is reduced to 1.2 pounds.

be ". . . *bought, sold and traded by any individual, corporation, or government body.*"[24]

As it turns out, a number of private firms have anticipated the profit opportunities of the newly created pollution market and are competing with the CBOT as allowance brokers. In fact, one of these, called Clean Air Capital Markets, arranged the first $3-million trade between the TVA and Wisconsin Power and Light Co. Thus far, Clean Air Capital has arranged transactions totaling $72 million. Another firm called Cantor Fitzgerald, Inc. has launched a computer-assisted plan to match up long-term exchanges. These entrepreneurial entities are capturing part of CBOT's market, making some question the longevity of CBOT's role in $SO_2$ allowance trading.[25]

# Economic Analysis of Stationary Source Controls

Whether or not the gains of stationary source controls justify the costs can be determined through a benefit-cost analysis. To structure such an investigation, we focus on four aspects of national policy:

- Cost of command-and-control methods relative to market-based incentives
- Uniform technology-based NSPS
- Dual-control approach for new versus existing sources
- Emissions trading policy

## The Relative Cost of Using Command-and-Control Instruments

Because of the absence of benefit–cost balancing in the standard-setting process, it would only be by chance that the resulting stationary source regulations would correspond to those that maximize the net benefits to society. But despite the failure of the standards to meet the efficiency criterion, it is still possible to minimize the cost of meeting them—efficient or not. Unfortunately, the lack of flexibility in a standards-based approach adds significantly to society's costs and offers no incentive to low-cost abaters to clean up beyond the statutory level.

There is a growing body of research that attempts to measure the extent of cost inefficiency associated with command-and-control policy instruments. These studies use computer simulations to model existing conditions in a given region and compare the cost of implementing command-and-control instruments with that of the least-cost alternative.

---

[24] Current data on trading activity of $SO_2$ emissions allowances can be found at EPA's Acid Rain Program, *Emissions Trading and Market Trends* at **www.epa.gov/acidrain/ats/trends.html**.

[25] Taylor (August 24, 1993), and Hong (July 20, 1992).

| TABLE 12.7 | | | | |
|---|---|---|---|---|

## COST EFFECTIVENESS AND AIR QUALITY REGULATION: SOME QUANTITATIVE STUDIES

| Investigators and Year | Command-and-Control Approach | Pollutant Controlled | Geographic Area | Ratio of Command-and-Control Cost to Least Cost |
|---|---|---|---|---|
| Atkinson and Lewis (1974) | SIP regulations | Particulate matter | St. Louis | 6.0 |
| Roach et al. (1981) | SIP regulations | Sulfur dioxide | Four Corners: Utah, Colorado, Arizona, and New Mexico | 4.25 |
| Hahn and Noll (1982) | California emissions standards | Sulfates | Los Angeles | 1.07 |
| McGartland (1984) | SIP regulations | Particulate matter | Baltimore | 4.18 |
| Spofford (1984) | Uniform percentage reduction | Sulfur dioxide Particulate matter | Lower Delaware | 1.78 22.0 |
| Maloney and Yandle (1984) | Uniform percentage reduction | Hydrocarbons | All domestic DuPont plants | 4.15 |
| Krupnick (1986) | Proposed RACT | Nitrogen dioxide | Baltimore | 5.9 |
| Oates, et al. (1989) | Equal proportional treatment | Particulate matter | Baltimore | 4.0 |
| ICF Resources International (1989) | Uniform emission limit | Sulfur dioxide | United States | 5.0 |
| SCAQMD (1992) | Best Available Control Technology | Reactive organic gases and $NO_2$ | Southern California | 1.5 in 1994 1.3 in 1997 |

NOTE: SCAQMD is South Coast Air Quality Management District.

SOURCES: U.S. Environmental Protection Agency, Office of Policy, Planning, and Evaluation. *The United States Experience with Economic Incentives to Control Environmental Pollution*. Washington, DC, July 1992, Table 2-1, pp. 2-3–2-5; T. H. Tietenberg. *Emissions Trading: An Exercise in Reforming Pollution Policy*. Washington, DC: Resources for the Future, 1985; Robert C. Anderson, Andrew Q. Lohof, and Alan Carlin. *The United States Experience with Economic Incentives in Environmental Pollution Control Policy*. Washington, DC: August 1997, Table 3-1, pp. 3-13–3-14; and the original sources cited in the table.

Table 12.7 summarizes a sample of those studies that specifically examine stationary control costs for meeting the National Ambient Air Quality Standards (NAAQS). Each quantifies the cost of using a command-and-control instrument *relative* to the least-cost method. This comparison is expressed as a ratio shown in the last column of the table. Notice the range of results. At the high end, Spofford (1984) found that the costs of using a uniform percentage reduction to meet the particulate matter (PM) standard in the Lower Delaware Valley exceeded the least-cost alternative by a factor of 22. This implies that the costs of using a command-and-control approach are 2,200 percent of what they would be if the policy allowed for equal marginal abatement cost (*MAC*) levels across all polluters in that region. At the other end of the spectrum are the findings of Hahn and Noll (1982). Their ratio of 1.07 suggests that the command-and-control approach is not that far away from the least-cost method. In this case, however, the researchers suggest that their unusual finding may be the result of very stringent controls imposed in Los Angeles by the California control authority with the specific intent of achieving cost-effective standards.

Despite the wide range of values for the cost ratio, in nearly every case the magnitude is significantly greater than one. It is difficult to dispute such a consistent finding that points to the excess costs of using command-and-control instruments to implement the NAAQS. These results suggest that in most instances society should realize important cost savings from a shift to more flexible policy instruments with no reduction in air quality benefits.

### Uniform Technology-Based NSPS

Implicitly, there are two potential problems with the new source performance standards (NSPS). First, they are implemented *uniformly* across all firms in a given category. Second, because the standards are *technology-based*, firms have no flexibility in selecting *how* to meet the national emission limits. Both of these characteristics suggest that cost-effectiveness is not being achieved.

The intent of using uniform emission standards was to prevent regional differences in regulations from affecting new firms' decisions about where to locate. Nonetheless, just as is the case for the uniform emissions limits for new cars, this particular command-and-control approach generally disallows the achievement of a cost-effective outcome. Why? Because the cost-effective solution calls for pollution abatement up to the point where all firms face the same marginal abatement cost (*MAC*), *not* to the point where all firms abate at the same level.

In Figure 12.4, a model of two hypothetical stationary sources, *A* and *B*, is shown with the cost-effectiveness solution indicated where $MAC_A$ intersects $MAC_B$ at $A_0$. (Source *A*'s allocation is measured left to right up to $A_0$, and source *B*'s allocation is measured right to left.) The total cost of abatement, assuming no fixed cost, is shown as the shaded area under the two *MAC*s up to the cost-effective abatement allocation. If instead a uniform standard is used, the abatement allocation across the two firms would force each to abate equally to the point labeled $A_1$.[26] The total cost again would be measured as the area under the two *MAC*s up to the solution

---

[26]$A_1$ represents half of the total abatement standard.

| FIGURE 12.4 | COST-INEFFECTIVENESS OF THE UNIFORM NEW SOURCE PERFORMANCE STANDARD |
|---|---|

The model shows two hypothetical stationary sources, $A$ and $B$, with the cost-effectiveness solution at the point where $MAC_A$ intersects $MAC_B$ at $A_0$. (Source $A$'s allocation is measured left to right up to $A_0$, and source $B$'s allocation is measured right to left.) The total cost of abatement, assuming no fixed cost, is shown as the shaded area under the two $MAC$s up to the cost-effective abatement allocation. If instead a uniform standard is used, the abatement allocation across the two firms would force each to abate equally to the point labeled $A_1$. The total cost would again be measured as the area under the two $MAC$s up to the solution point. But notice that the total cost under the uniform standard approach is higher by the triangular area labeled XYZ.

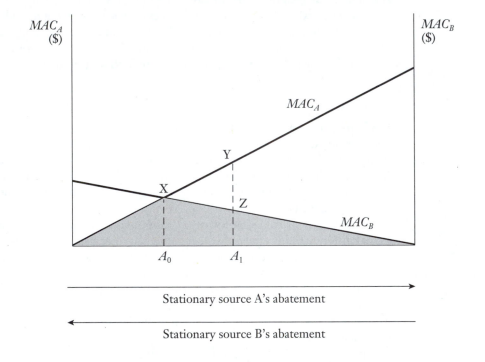

Stationary source A's abatement

Stationary source B's abatement

point. But notice that the total cost under the uniform standard approach is higher by the triangular area labeled XYZ.

Using technology-based NSPS instead of performance-based standards can also produce a result that is not cost-effective. By dictating the type of abatement technology to be used across the board, firms are prevented from finding and using cheaper alternative methods. The result is a waste of scarce economic resources. In fact, two of the "10 Principles for Reinventing Environmental Regulation," released in March 1995 by the

Clinton administration, indicate that environmental regulation is to be performance based.[27] To illustrate the potential problem with using the less flexible technology-based standards, we consider one set of NSPS for coal-burning electric power plants established through the 1977 Amendments to control sulfur dioxide ($SO_2$) emissions—perhaps the most scrutinized set of standards in all of U.S. air quality legislation.

Revisions in the 1977 Amendments included a seemingly innocuous change in the wording of the NSPS:

> "...a standard of performance shall reflect the degree of emission limitation and the *percentage reduction achievable* through application of the best technological system of continuous emissions reduction ... (emphasis added)."

The change to refer to a "percentage reduction achievable" coupled with the specific reference to "the best technological system of continuous emissions reduction" forced coal-burning power plants to install scrubbers to meet the $SO_2$ emissions limit rather than switch to cleaner, low-sulfur coal.[28] The result? The new NSPS created an artificial incentive for coal-burning plants to use high-sulfur fuel with scrubbers, even though substituting low-sulfur fuel would have been a more cost-effective approach.

There is some evidence to support the hypothesis that this technology-forcing revision was costly. A 1986 Congressional Budget Office report presents estimates that the implicit restriction on fuel switching would increase the cost of an 8-million-ton reduction in $SO_2$ emissions by $2.7 billion (in discounted 1985 dollars), and a 10-million-ton reduction by $16.3 billion.[29]

Similar findings were obtained in an independent study conducted by two economists, Lewis J. Perl and Frederick C. Dunbar (1982).[30] Their analysis begins with a baseline estimation of the costs and benefits of $SO_2$ emission reductions based on the former definition of the NSPS under the 1970 Amendments. At that time, power plants could choose either scrubbers or fuel switching to comply with the law. To achieve the reduction of 20.38 million tons called for in the 1970 law, total annual costs would have been $3.3 billion and total benefits would have been $5.4 billion. Hence, had the former NSPS remained in effect, benefits would have exceeded costs by $2.1 billion.

---

[27] See Anderson, Lohof, and Carlin (August 1997), p. 2-1.

[28] The revision elevated the former 1971 standard on $SO_2$ emissions from 1.2 pounds per million Btus of coal consumed to a tougher standard that varied with the sulfur content of the coal. Specifically, for high-sulfur coal the new standard became 1.2 pounds per million Btus of fuel consumed plus a 90-percent emissions reduction, and for low-sulfur coal the limit was 0.6 pounds per million Btus of fuel consumed plus a 70-percent emissions reduction.

[29] U.S. Congress, Congressional Budget Office (CBO) (June 1986), Chapter II.

[30] All of Perl and Dunbar's estimates are expressed in 1980 dollars for the year 1990, when the mandated reductions were to have been achieved.

FIGURE 12.5

## ANALYSIS OF THE NSPS IN THE 1977 CLEAN AIR ACT AMENDMENTS ACCORDING TO PERL AND DUNBAR (1982)

The 1977 NSPS called for a reduction of 23.91 million tons of $SO_2$ emissions to be achieved through the installation of scrubbers. On an incremental basis, notice that to achieve the additional reduction in emissions of 3.53 million tons, costs would rise by $3.75 billion—a unit cost of $1,062 per ton of removed $SO_2$, and benefits would rise by $0.81 billion—a per unit benefit of $229 per ton.

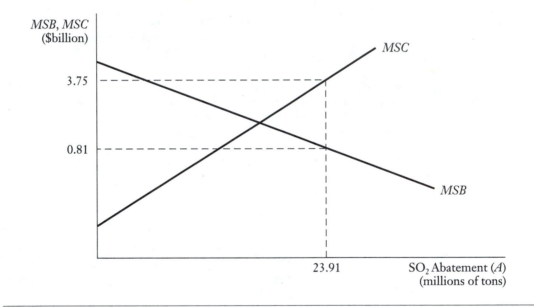

The researchers then repeat the exercise based on the 1977 NSPS, which called for a reduction of 23.91 million tons of $SO_2$ emissions to be achieved through the installation of scrubbers. Under this scenario, they estimated that annual costs would rise to $7.05 billion and benefits would rise to $6.22 billion, so that net benefits would become –$0.83 billion. On an incremental basis, notice that to achieve the additional reduction in emissions, costs would rise by $3.75 billion—a unit cost of $1,062 per ton of removed $SO_2$, and benefits would rise by $0.81 billion—a per unit benefit of $229 per ton. This is illustrated in Figure 12.5. Thus, using benefit–cost analysis, these findings show that the 1977 revision in the NSPS was simply not worth it.

Based on these estimates, it is natural to ask why Congress would force such costly controls on firms. The answer is a complex one, involving political battles, obscure legal interpretations, and special-interest groups. Yet, even a brief review of the facts leaves little doubt that the major force behind these legislative changes was successful lobbying by the United Mine Workers union, a labor group consisting primarily of high-sulfur coal miners. It was in their best interest to limit fuel switching toward low-sulfur coal, leaving high-intensity coal users like electric power plants no choice but to install expensive scrubbers.[31] While the miners' success in saving their jobs did not adversely affect air quality, it *did* elevate abatement costs with no comparable increase in benefits—a clear case of inefficient policy making. (As an interesting postscript, the reference in the law to a "percentage reduction" was omitted in the 1990 Amendments.)

### The Dual-Control Approach and the New Source Bias

The dual-control approach gives states more direct supervision over those firms upon which their economies have come to depend. Yet, despite its apparent logic, such a dual-control system can generate market distortions. There is no reason to expect that state-established controls on existing stationary sources will be the same as those set at the federal level for new or modified sources. As long as there are two sets of standards, firms have both the incentive and the opportunity to avoid the more stringent, and therefore the more costly, of the two. This in turn means that firms' decisions about whether to build a new facility or modify an existing one will be influenced by the legislation. In fact, the logical expectation is that state-determined emissions limits will be relatively more lenient, which suggests that firm decision making will be biased *against* new construction—a true market distortion.

To understand this latter hypothesis, consider that states have an incentive to attract business as a way to create jobs for their constituents and to maintain a healthy tax base to support fiscal spending. States also compete against one another to attract industry. It is generally in a state's best interest to avoid policies that increase firms' operating costs and reduce profits. In this context, states have a political incentive to avoid setting more stringent, and thus more costly, emissions limits that may encourage firms to exit from their jurisdictions and relocate where regulations are more lenient.[32]

What this means for firms is that they can avoid meeting the federally established NSPS simply by maintaining their existing facilities, which would be subject to less stringent state limits. The irony is that the law sets up a disincentive for businesses to build new facilities that would likely operate more efficiently and more cleanly. Hence the controls on existing

---

[31] For more detail, see Ackerman and Hassler (1981). Further evidence of the mining industry's influence on U.S. law is found in Section 125 of the Clean Air Act. These provisions specifically allow government intervention to force the use of locally or regionally available coal to avoid economic disruption in the area.

[32] In practice, there are some limits as to how permissive state laws can be. Recall that under the State Implementation Plan (SIP) each state's standards must be approved by the EPA, so they must conform to the EPA's range of reasonableness.

## ANALYZING THE DUAL-CONTROL APPROACH AND THE NEW SOURCE BIAS: MARGINAL ABATEMENT COST LEVELS FOR NEW VERSUS EXISTING SOURCES

The graph depicts the marginal abatement cost of a hypothetical existing source, $MAC_E$, and the marginal abatement cost of a new stationary source, $MAC_N$. Abatement level $A_{E1}$ represents the more lenient level of a state-determined standard on existing sources, and $A_{N1}$ represents the more stringent controls imposed by the NSPS. The result is not cost-effective because $MAC_{N1}$ corresponding to $A_{N1}$ is higher than $MAC_{E1}$ corresponding to $A_{E1}$. To achieve a cost-effective outcome, the state authority could increase the required abatement level for existing sources to $A_{E2}$ so that $MAC_{E2}$ equals $MAC_{N1}$. Alternatively, the federal control authority could reduce the abatement requirement for new sources until the corresponding marginal abatement cost level equals $MAC_{E1}$.

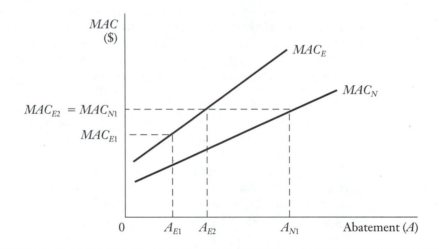

stationary sources are to some extent self-defeating because the disincentive to modernize or replace deteriorating facilities can cause short-term pollution to increase.[33]

From a benefit–cost perspective, the variability in controls for new versus existing stationary sources may cause marginal abatement costs to be higher per ton of pollutant removed in new facilities than in existing ones despite the fact that the associated benefits are identical. This is modeled in Figure 12.6. The diagram shows two $MAC$ curves: that of an existing source, $MAC_E$, and that of a new stationary source, $MAC_N$. Notice that the $MAC_N$ is lower than the $MAC_E$ at every level of abatement to show the

[33] This issue is discussed in Council of Economic Advisers (1982), pp. 144–45.

more advanced control technology available to a new, more modern facility. Now consider the cost implications of two distinct abatement levels— $A_{E1}$, a more lenient level to represent the state-determined standard on existing sources, and $A_{N1}$ to represent the more stringent controls imposed by the NSPS. Notice that $MAC_{N1}$ corresponding to $A_{N1}$ is higher than $MAC_{E1}$ corresponding to $A_{E1}$. Thus, the inconsistency in controls on stationary sources has generated a solution that is not cost-effective.

Theoretically, by altering the emission standard for either existing sources or for new sources, the control authority can achieve a cost-effective abatement solution. For example, if the state official increases the required abatement level for existing sources to $A_{E2}$, $MAC_{E2}$ would equal $MAC_{N1}$. (Alternatively, the federal control authority could reduce the abatement requirement for new sources until the corresponding marginal abatement cost level equals $MAC_{E1}$.) In so doing, the bias against new construction could be eliminated. The outcome would be difficult to realize, however, since the control authority would need detailed information about the control costs for each and every polluting source in its jurisdiction.[34]

### The Economics of Market-Based Trading Programs

While the legislative effort in the United States up through the 1977 Amendments was primarily a command-and-control approach, there were some indications that national policy was beginning to use more market-based instruments to control stationary sources. Perhaps the best example of this trend was the initiation of the EPA's emissions trading program in the mid-1970s implemented through offsets, netting, bubbles, and banking.

**Analysis of Emissions Trading.** To illustrate how the market process operates through these instruments, reconsider the motivations inherent in the offset plan. If Firm A wishes to construct a new plant in a nonattainment area, it might choose to provide the offsetting emissions through one of its own existing plants in the region. Alternatively, it could negotiate the "cost" of having some other firm in the region, Firm B, provide the emission reductions in its place. Firm B has an incentive to provide this service if its costs of doing so are less than what Firm A is willing to pay for it. From an economic perspective, Firm A will "contract out" the task of emission reductions if it is cheaper than performing the task itself. In the end, those firms controlling most of the pollution in a given region will be the ones that can do so more cheaply. Ultimately, all sources will control pollution to the point where the marginal abatement cost of doing so is equal across firms—a cost-effective solution.

---

[34] For a more detailed description of the implications concerning alternative abatement levels for new versus existing sources, the reader is referred to Crandall (1984).

| TABLE 12.8 | EMISSIONS TRADING ACTIVITY |

| Activity | Cost Savings through 1985 ($ millions) | Number of Trades | |
|---|---|---|---|
| | | Internal | External |
| Offsets[a] | — | 1,800 | 200 |
| Bubbles, EPA approved | 300 | 40 | 2 |
| Bubbles, state approved | 135 | 89 | 0 |
| Netting[b] | 525–12,000 | 5,000–12,000 | None |
| Banking | Very small | < 100 | < 20 |

NOTES:

[a]Cost savings are not applicable for offsets, since firms do not avoid any emission reduction under the offset program.

[b]According to the EPA, 1984 is the only year for which detailed data exist for netting transactions. Thus some of the estimates are based on an extrapolation done by Hahn and Hester from the year 1974. For more detail, see U.S. Environmental Protection Agency, Office of Policy, Planning, and Evaluation. *The United States Experience with Economic Incentives to Control Environmental Pollution.* Washington, DC, July 1992.

SOURCES: Drawn from Robert W. Hahn and Gordon L. Hester. "Marketable Permits: Lessons for Theory and Practice." *Ecology Law Quarterly* 16, 1989, pp. 361–406; and Robert W. Hahn. "Economic Prescriptions for Environmental Problems: How the Patient Followed the Doctor's Orders." *Journal of Economic Perspectives* 3(2), Spring 1989, pp. 95–114.

Attempts to quantify the gains of emissions trading have been done by estimating the associated control cost savings. The major findings of two such studies that examine trading activity in the pre-1986 period are presented in Table 12.8. Notice that the activity is delineated according to the four major instruments: offsets, bubbles, netting, and banking. Within each of these categories, the data are further refined to distinguish between trades that are *internal* (i.e., between sources within the same plant), and those that are *external* (i.e., between sources in different facilities). Overall, the results show that trading can be lucrative, with cost savings ranging from $135 million for state-approved bubbles to between $525 million and $12,000 million for netting transactions. The overwhelming majority of trades are internal, which is explained by the inherently higher transactions costs associated with interfirm trades. While in theory banking should help to reduce these costs and foster external trades, the data indicate otherwise. It seems that some other mechanism is needed to bring firms together so that the potential savings can be realized. Such an alternative is evident in the 1990 trading program aimed at acid rain—to date the most ambitious of its kind in U.S. or international legislative history.

**Analysis of the 1990 SO$_2$ Allowance Trading Plan.** Let's consider the cost-effectiveness of the allowance trading established by Title IV of the 1990 Amendments. Polluting sources that can reduce SO$_2$ emissions relatively cheaply will do so and sell off their excess allowances. They have an

| FIGURE 12.7 | COST-EFFECTIVENESS OF THE $SO_2$ ALLOWANCE TRADING PLAN |
|---|---|

Polluting sources that can reduce $SO_2$ emissions relatively cheaply will do so and sell off their excess allowances. They have an incentive to do so as long as their respective *MAC*s are below the market price of an allowance ($P$). In the model shown, the polluter would abate $A_0$ units of $SO_2$. Buyers of allowances or *demanders* are primarily firms unable to match their emissions level to the number of allowances held. For these polluters, abatement is relatively costly, so they will pay for the right to release excess emissions as long as the market price of an allowance ($P$) is below their respective *MAC* levels. On net, buyers and sellers will trade for allowances, and emissions should reach the level where *MAC*s are equal across firms.

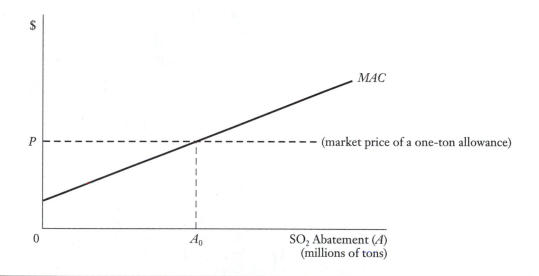

incentive to do so as long as their respective *MAC*s are below the market price of an allowance ($P$), as shown in Figure 12.7. In the model shown, the polluter would abate $A_0$ units of $SO_2$. Excess allowances are an asset to these firms that effectively become *suppliers* in the market for $SO_2$ allowances. The excess can be used either internally to offset emissions at another source within the firm, banked for future use, or sold on the open market. On the other side of the market are buyers of allowances or *demanders*. These are primarily firms unable to match their emissions level to the number of allowances held. For these polluters, abatement is relatively costly, so they will pay for the right to release excess emissions as long as the market price of an allowance ($P$) is below their respective *MAC* levels.

Other potential buyers include brokers and environmental organizations, each of which have different motivations. Brokers are motivated by profit, expecting to resell the allowances for a lucrative rate of return. Environmentalists want to buy allowances and remove them from the market.

On net, buyers and sellers will trade for allowances, and emissions should reach the level where *MAC*s are equal across firms. By creating an "emissions market" and allowing the usual incentives to operate freely, abatement can be accomplished in a cost-effective manner with no compromise to social benefits. Notice that the national emissions limit is achieved, since the number of allowances issued determines the maximum amount of $SO_2$ emissions that may be released. Hence, all the health and ecological benefits of pollution abatement still accrue to society, but the associated costs are lower.

Using information from the results of the second annual spot auction held in March 1994, we can gain a better perspective of how the allowance market operates. On the supply side, the EPA offered 50,000 allowances to be sold to the highest bidders.[35] Private utilities supplied another 58,001 allowances. These were to be sold at various offer prices, ranging from $165 to $550. On the demand side, there were 103 bids submitted for 294,354 allowances. The highest per unit bid was $400, while the lowest was $24. At the close of the auction, all 50,000 EPA-issued allowances had been sold to 37 individual demanders who bid between $150 and $400, for an average of $159. Once the EPA-offered allowances were sold to the highest bidders, the remaining 58,001 allowances were made available for sale. However, none were sold since the remaining bidders were not willing to pay the asking prices.[36]

According to most analysts, the Acid Rain Program has been deemed a success because firms have achieved emission reduction targets at less than 50 percent of the projected cost. Trading, however, has been lower than anticipated, attributable in part to the existence of transaction costs and the fact that many transactions are intra-utility trades (i.e., within the same firm), which are not reported in conventional data. Figure 12.8 shows a comparison of inter-utility to intra-utility trades.

By the beginning of 1997, utilities had traded more than 7 million allowances and bought another 300,000 at the annual auctions. By the end of 1997, the total number of trades had increased to over 15 million.[37] Allowance prices also have shown a sharp rise of late, increasing to $110.36 at

---

[35] The 50,000 allowances are sold in the spot auction for use in the same year unless banked for future use. There are also 100,000 allowances sold in an advance auction for use in the seventh year after the year of sale unless banked for future use.

[36] U.S. EPA, Office of Communications, Education, and Public Affairs (March 29, 1994).

[37] Anderson, Lohof, and Carlin (August 1997), pp. 6–17; U.S. Environmental Protection Agency, Acid Rain Program. *Emissions Trading and Market Trends*, **www.epa.gov/acidrain/ats/trends.html**, updated January 1998.

FIGURE 12.8

## A COMPARISON OF INTRA-UTILITY AND INTER-UTILITY SO₂ ALLOWANCE TRADES

**Allowances Transferred within Organizations
(Utilities or Groups of Utilities)
3/94–12/97**

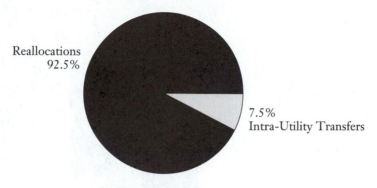

Reallocations
92.5%

7.5%
Intra-Utility Transfers

*34.1 Million Allowances*

**Allowances Transferred between Organizations
3/94–12/97**

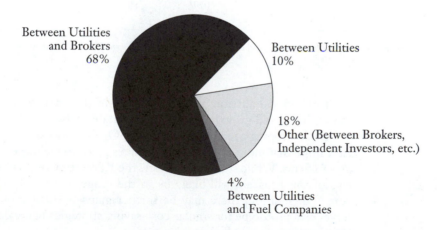

Between Utilities
and Brokers
68%

Between Utilities
10%

18%
Other (Between Brokers,
Independent Investors, etc.)

4%
Between Utilities
and Fuel Companies

*15.1 Million Allowances*

SOURCE: U.S. Environmental Protection Agency, Acid Rain Program. *Emissions Trading and Market Trends*, **www.epa.gov/acidrain/ats/trends.html**, updated January 1998.

| FIGURE 12.9 | TREND DATA ON SO$_2$ ALLOWANCE INTER-UTILITY ALLOWANCE TRADING |
| --- | --- |

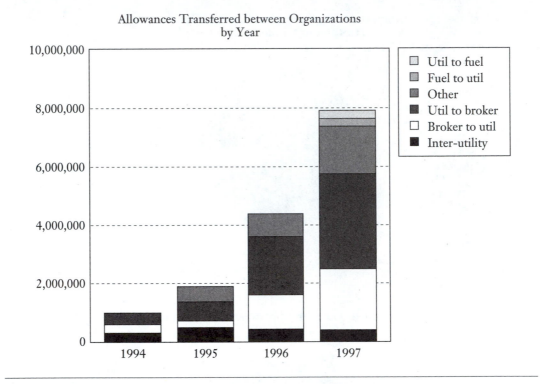

Allowances Transferred between Organizations
by Year

SOURCE: U.S. Environmental Protection Agency, Acid Rain Program. *Emissions Trading and Market Trends*, **www.epa.gov/acidrain/ats/trends.html**, updated January 1998.

the 1997 annual auction, up from $68.14 in the prior year. Figure 12.9 shows the overall growth of inter-utility trades between 1994 and 1997.[38]

By developing a national market for SO$_2$ allowances, Congress and the EPA hope that more trading activity takes place to yield greater cost savings to firms. While still in its infancy, the EPA estimates that the cost savings of this program will likely be in the range of $0.7 to $1 billion per year.[39] In addition, there may be further gains as this national program serves as a prototype for similar cost-saving strategies being developed by state environmental officials.

---

[38] For a recent analysis of SO$_2$ allowance trading, see Schmalensee, Joskow, Ellerman, Montero, and Bailey (Summer 1998), or Stavins (Summer 1998).

[39] 56 *Federal Register* (FR) 63097, December 3, 1991.

One example is a Massachusetts plan called MassIMPACT that allows emissions trading for several types of pollutants. Launched in 1994, this program is touted as the first state program of its kind in the United States. On the West Coast, California's South Coast Air Quality Management District developed what it calls the Regional Clean Air Incentives Market (RECLAIM) program. Also started in 1994, this program uses a bubble-type approach whereby polluters are issued tradeable permits for releases of sulfur oxides, nitrogen oxides, and reactive organic gases. Trading among polluters is to be allowed under prespecified rules. California officials anticipate a savings in annual compliance costs of $437 million.[40] Other states with active emissions trading programs include Delaware, Illinois, Michigan, New Jersey, and Texas.[41]

# Conclusions

Current U.S. air quality policy is ambitious and complex, implemented primarily through a comprehensive set of controls on mobile and stationary sources. There is no doubt that the trend toward integrating more market-based initiatives is a landmark in legislative history. Evidence is accumulating that market instruments are a more cost-effective means to achieve air quality than command-and-control policies. Of course, some of the newer programs such as the allowance trading program for sulfur dioxide are still too new to evaluate. But the anecdotal evidence seems to suggest that these policies will have some measure of success.

Other aspects of existing air control policy are less satisfying and continue to be debated. The dual-control approach to setting standards for stationary sources is one example of how government policy can create market distortions. Another is the regulatory bias against new cars inadvertently caused by the nation's policy on mobile source emissions. All of this means that, as a nation, we still have much to learn—about air quality and about policy instruments that work effectively to protect it. As we have come to discover, policy development and appraisal are ongoing processes. In the context of air quality controls, the simple truth is that it is extremely difficult to assess exactly what has been accomplished through all the revisions of the past several decades. Even more difficult is to project the success of the 1990 Amendments, which will not be fully implemented until

---

[40]Allen (January 8, 1993); Allen (September 29, 1993); U.S. EPA, Office of Policy, Planning, and Evaluation (July 1992), pp. 7-1–7-2.

[41]For information on any state market-based program, visit **www.epa.gov/OMSWWW/market.htm**, and click on Directory of Air Quality Economic Incentive Programs: On-Line Database. From there, find the menu of options, and click on the one labeled "By Program Location."

2005. In the interim, the United States must continue to make policy adjustments and respond to the challenge of achieving both its air quality objectives *and* economic prosperity.

# Summary

- In metropolitan areas, the concentration of human population, traffic patterns, and industrial activity intensifies the concentration of criteria pollutants and hence increases the environmental risks of exposure. The EPA prepares trend statistics for major urban centers and reports part of its findings using a Pollutant Standards Index (PSI).

- In urban areas, photochemical smog can form from a chemical reaction involving several of the criteria pollutants. The principal component of photochemical smog is "ground level" or tropospheric ozone. Ozone's precursors, $NO_x$ and VOCs, are emitted by both mobile sources and stationary sources.

- The Clean Air Act of 1963 gave virtually no power to federal officials to control mobile source emissions. It was not until the 1970 Amendments that emission standards for new automobiles were explicitly stated in the law.

- The 1990 Amendments strengthen federal control over motor vehicle emissions and fuels. The new law also incorporates market-based incentives to encourage development of cleaner-running vehicles and alternative fuels.

- The stringent controls on mobile sources established by the Clean Air Act Amendments of 1970 may have been purposefully unrealistic to force technology development by the automobile industry. The implied decision rule used to establish the controls was benefit-based, set to protect public health and welfare.

- The uniformity of the national emission standards for automobiles inflates the costs of reducing pollution with no added benefit to society.

- Different controls on new versus used motor vehicles affects relative prices and engine performance, which creates market distortions. Since new and used cars are substitutes, tougher regulations on new vehicles can bias buying decisions in favor of used cars.

- The use of reformulated fuels and oxygenated fuels is being called for in the nation's dirtiest regions, where they can yield the most benefit to society.

- Standards applicable to new stationary sources are called New Source Performance Standards (NSPS). The EPA is in charge of controlling new or modified sources, while states set standards for existing facilities.

- In 1979, the EPA initiated the bubble policy for stationary sources and launched its emissions banking program in 1980.

- In PSD areas, standards for any proposed new or modified source are to be based on the best available control technology (BACT). Existing facilities releasing emissions that might impair visibility in PSD areas are required to install best available retrofit technology (BART).

- In nonattainment areas, existing sources must use at minimum reasonably available control technology (RACT). New or modified sources must comply with the lowest achievable emission rate (LAER).

- To facilitate control in PSD areas, netting was developed for use by modified sources. For nonattainment areas, the permit program includes trading for new or modified sources through an offset plan.

- Acidic deposition is caused by the reaction of $SO_2$ and $NO_x$ emissions with water vapors and oxidants in the earth's atmosphere. These chemical reactions form sulfuric and nitric acids, which mix with other airborne particles and fall to the earth as dry or wet deposition.

- To control acidic deposition, Title IV of the 1990 Amendments is dedicated to a reduction plan for $NO_x$ emissions and an allowance program to reduce $SO_2$ emissions.

- Once emission allowances for $SO_2$ are issued, they may be exchanged through an allowance market. Small banks of allowances are available for direct sale by the EPA or through annual auctions supervised by the Chicago Board of Trade.

- The New Source Performance Standards (NSPS) are implemented uniformly across all firms in a given category and are technology-based. As a result, firms have no flexibility to find the least-cost method of achieving them.

- Under the dual-control system, state-determined limits will likely be more lenient. Thus, firms can avoid meeting the NSPS by maintaining existing plants instead of building new ones.

- The EPA's Emissions Trading Program can yield a cost-effective solution, since sources abate to the point where the *MAC* of doing so is equal across firms.

## Key Concepts

| | |
|---|---|
| Pollutant Standards Index (PSI) | new or modified stationary sources |
| photochemical smog | existing stationary sources |
| reformulated gasoline | bubble policy |
| oxygenated fuel | emissions banking |
| clean fuel vehicle | netting |
| clean alternative fuels | offset plan |
| New Source Performance | acidic deposition |
|    Standards (NSPS) | tradeable $SO_2$ emission allowances |

## Review Questions

1. In the 1990 Clean Air Act Amendments, Congress and the EPA rely on the automobile industry to develop a "cleaner" automobile. At the same time, the government imposes a relatively minor federal tax on gasoline.
   a. Do you see any problem with the implicit signals the federal government is sending to the American auto manufacturer and to American car drivers through these policies? Briefly discuss.
   b. Formulate a hypothetical economic policy to motivate automobile manufacturers to advance the technology of cleaner motor vehicles.

2. Refer back to the discussion of a two-tiered system of automobile emissions standards studied by the National Academy of Science. Use a graph to model this system and illustrate how the cost savings are achieved.

3. New source bias may exist for either stationary or mobile sources. Select one of these and briefly discuss why this bias leads to a solution that is *not* cost-effective. What policies would you implement to eliminate this bias?

4. Distinguish between the technology-based emission standards, RACT and LAER, used to control stationary sources.

5. a. Carefully explain how economic theory supports: (i) the bubble policy; and (ii) the emission allowance program for sulfur dioxide.
   b. Other than these two programs, briefly summarize any two U.S. policies that use market incentives to control air pollution.

6. a. Using the results presented in Table 12.8 explain why transactions costs are so important in explaining the success or failure of the EPA's bubble program.
   b. How would you devise a program that minimizes the transactions costs of bringing polluters together so that they could effectively equalize the level of their individual *MACs*?

7. In July 1997, the EPA announced new air quality standards for small (2.5 micrometers in diameter) particulate matter referred to as PM-2.5.

Steel mills are major sources of these smaller particles, and therefore must find ways to abate. To analyze the implications, consider the following hypothetical model of two steel plants, one owned by Bethlehem Steel ($B$) and one by National Steel ($N$), both located in Pittsburgh.

$$\text{Bethlehem:} \quad MAC_B = 1.2A_B \qquad \text{National:} \quad MAC_N = 0.3A_N$$
$$TAC_B = 0.6A_B^2 \qquad\qquad\qquad TAC_N = 0.15A_N^2$$

Assume each plant emits 40 units of PM-2.5 for a total of 80 units. In order for the Pittsburgh area to meet the new standard, the EPA determines that the combined abatement for both plants must total 30 units.

a. If the new abatement standard is implemented *uniformly* across the two firms, find the total cost of abatement.

b. Find the *cost-effective* solution and illustrate graphically, labeling all curves, intercepts, and relevant intersections. Calculate the associated cost savings.

# Additional Readings

Carey, John. "We Can Fight Smog without Breaking the Bank." *Business Week*, October 3, 1994, pp. 128–29.

Feldman, Stephen L., and Robert K. Raufer. *Emissions Trading and Acid Rain: Implementing a Market Approach to Pollution Control.* Totowa, NJ: Rowman and Littlefield, 1987.

Hahn, Robert W., and Gordon L. Hester. "Where Did All the Markets Go? An Analysis of EPA's Emissions Trading Program." *Yale Journal on Regulation* 6(109), 1989, pp. 109–53.

Hall, Jane V., and Amy L. Walton. "A Case Study in Pollution Markets: Dismal Science vs. Dismal Reality." *Contemporary Economic Policy* 14(2), April 1996, pp. 67–78.

Hubbard, Thomas N. "Using Inspection and Maintenance Programs to Regulate Vehicle Emissions." *Contemporary Economic Policy* 15(2), April 1997, pp. 52–62.

Klaassen, Ger, and Andries Nentjes. "Creating Markets for Air Pollution in Europe and the USA." *Environmental and Resource Economics* 10, September 1997, pp. 125–46.

Kruger, Joseph, and Melanie Dean. "Looking Back on SO$_2$ Trading: What's Good for the Environment Is Good for the Market." *Public Utilities Fortnightly*, August 1997, pp. 30–37.

Krupnick, Alan J., and Paul R. Portney. "Controlling Urban Air Pollution: A Benefit–Cost Assessment." *Science* 252, April 26. 1991, pp. 522–28.

Lareau, Thomas J. "The Economics of Alternative Fuel Use: Substituting Methanol for Gasoline." *Contemporary Policy Issues* 8, October 1990, pp. 138–52.

National Acid Precipitation Assessment Program. *1992 Report to Congress.* Washington, DC: U.S. Government Printing Office, June 1993.

Rusco, Frank W., and W. David Walls. "Vehicular Emissions and Control Policies in Hong Kong." *Contemporary Economic Policy* 13(1), January 1995, pp. 50–61.

Tietenberg, T. H. *Emissions Trading: An Exercise in Reforming Pollution Policy.* Washington, DC: Resources for the Future, 1985.

Toman, Michael A. (Ed.). *Pollution Abatement Strategies in Central and Eastern Europe.* Washington, DC: Resources for the Future, 1994.

United Nations Environment Programme and the World Health Organization. "Air Pollution in the World's Megacities." *Environment* 36(2), March 1994, pp. 4–13, 25–37.

U.S. Environmental Protection Agency. *United States/Canada Air Quality Agreement—Progress Report.* Washington, DC, March 1992.

Woodruff, David, Larry Armstrong, and John Carey. "Electric Cars: Will They Work and Who Will Buy Them?" *Business Week*, May 30, 1994, pp. 104–14.

## Related Web Sites

Description of the major
Clean Air Act initiatives
aimed at mobile sources                    www.epa.gov/oar/oaqps/peg_caa/pegcaa04.html

Discussion paper, "The Costs
and Benefits of Reducing
Acid Rain" by Dallas Burtraw,
Alan J.Krupnick, Erin
Mansur, David Austin, and
Deirdre Farrell, July 1997                  www.rff.org/disc_papers/abstracts/9731.htm

EPA's Acid Rain Program                     www.epa.gov/acidrain

EPA's Acid Rain Program,
*Emissions Trading and Market
Trends*                                     www.epa.gov/acidrain/ats/trends.html

EPA's Concerned Citizens and
Consumer Information site                   www.epa.gov/OMSWWW/consumer.htm

EPA's fact sheet, "Automobile
Emissions: An Overview"                     www.epa.gov/OMSWWW/05-autos.htm

EPA's Market Incentives
Resource Center                             www.epa.gov/OMSWWW/market.htm

EPA's *Measuring Air Quality:
The Pollutant Standards Index*              www.epa.gov/oar/oaqps/psi.html

EPA's fact sheet, "Milestones
in Auto Emissions Control"                  www.epa.gov/OMSWWW/12-miles.htm

EPA's fact sheet, "Remote
Sensing: A Supplemental
Tool for Vehicle Emission
Control"                                    www.epa.gov/OMSWWW/15-remot.htm

Information on urban smog                   www.epa.gov/oar/oaqps/peg_caa/pegcaa03.html#topic3a

Overview of acid rain          **www.epa.gov/oar/oaqps/peg_caa/pegcaa05.html**

Reformulated Gasoline and
Vehicle Performance          **www.epa.gov/OMSWWW/rfgvehpf.htm**

United States Council for
Automobile Research
(USCAR)          **www.uscar.org/index.html**

# Appendix:
# A Reference to Acronyms and Terms
# Used in Air Quality Control Policy

### Environmental Economics Acroyms

| | |
|---|---|
| $MAC$ | Marginal abatement cost |
| $MAC_E$ | Marginal abatement cost for an existing stationary source |
| $MAC_N$ | Marginal abatement cost for a new stationary source |
| $MSB$ | Marginal social benefit |
| $MSC$ | Marginal social cost |

### Environmental Science Terms

| | |
|---|---|
| CO | Carbon monoxide |
| $CO_2$ | Carbon dioxide |
| gpm | Grams per mile |
| $NO_x$ | Nitrogen oxides |
| $NO_2$ | Nitrogen dioxide |
| $O_2$ | Oxygen |
| $O_3$ | Ozone |
| Pb | Lead |
| PM | Particulate matter |
| PM-10 | Particulate matter of less than 10 micrograms in diameter |
| $SO_2$ | Sulfur dioxide |
| SOx | Sulfur oxides |
| VOC | Volatile organic compound |

### Environmental Policy Acronyms

| | |
|---|---|
| BACT | Best available control technology |
| BART | Best available retrofit technology |
| LAER | Lowest achievable emission rate |
| NAAQS | National Ambient Air Quality Standards |
| NSPS | New Source Performance Standards |
| PSD | Prevention of significant deterioration |
| PSI | Pollutant Standards Index |
| RACT | Reasonably available control technology |
| RECLAIM | Regional Clean Air Incentives Market |
| SIP | State Implementation Plan |

# 13

# *Global Air Quality:*
# *Policies for Ozone Depletion*
# *and Global Warming*

While most air pollutants produce localized effects, others have more far-reaching implications. Such is the case for contaminants that alter atmospheric conditions, posing a risk that is geographically without bound and generating a free-ridership problem that crosses national boundaries. Of course, the effects can vary by degree across different locations. But since the associated damage is widespread, and since the source cannot be linked to a specific site or region, this air quality problem is termed *global* air pollution. Controlling global air pollution is a unique policy challenge, since solutions must be developed not only through domestic initiatives but also through international treaties and programs.

In this chapter, we investigate the principal issues associated with global air pollution by studying **ozone depletion** and **global warming.** In each case, we consider theories about the causes and sources of the respective atmospheric disturbance and the available evidence to support these theories. Using this as a fundamental basis, we then explore the major policy responses that have been set in motion in the United States and other nations along with proposals for alternatives. Ultimately, our objective is to evaluate the effectiveness of existing and proposed policy responses economically, given what we know about the origin of the problem and the associated risks. As in the last two chapters, there is a reference list of acronyms and terms in an appendix to the chapter.

# The Problem of Ozone Depletion

**ozone layer** Ozone present in the stratosphere that protects the earth from ultraviolet radiation.

Starting in the 1950s, scientists began measuring the earth's **ozone layer,** specifically the ozone present in the stratosphere—the layer of the atmosphere lying between 7 and 25 miles above the earth's surface. The effort was motivated by more than scientific curiosity. Stratospheric ozone protects the earth from ultraviolet radiation. Some variability in the depth of the ozone layer was assumed normal, including an observed thinning above Antarctica during the southern spring. This would generally fill back in by November each year. However, in the early 1980s, scientists became concerned when this thinning was found to be increasing in size and persisting into December. In 1985, an "ozone hole" the size of North America was discovered over Antarctica. It was then that world attention was drawn in earnest to the problem of **ozone depletion** and the pollutants responsible for the damage.[1]

**ozone depletion** Thinning of the ozone layer originally observed as an "ozone hole" over Antarctica.

While all of the implications are not known with certainty, there are some consequences of increased ultraviolet radiation about which there seems to be some agreement. Scientists tell us that rising levels of ultraviolet radiation can alter delicate ecosystems, diminish human immune systems, and increase the risk of skin cancer. The National Academy of Sciences estimates that 10,000 more cases of skin cancer per year would result for every 1-percent decline in stratospheric ozone.

## Searching for the Causes of Ozone Depletion

Research scientists debate about the principal cause of the "ozone hole" extending approximately 9 million square miles over the Antarctic.[2] While no one theory has been able to explain the extent of ozone depletion fully, scientists agree that the presence of **chlorofluorocarbons (CFCs)** in the atmosphere is the most likely explanation—a theory originally advanced in 1974 by F. Sherwood Rowland and Mario Molina, two University of California researchers. The pair won the Nobel Prize in chemistry for this theory in 1995.

**chlorofluorocarbons (CFCs)** A family of chemicals that scientists believe contributes to ozone depletion.

CFCs are a family of chemicals commonly used in refrigeration, air-conditioning, packaging, insulation, and as aerosol propellants. These are sometimes referred to by their trade names, Freon and Styrofoam. In fact, the energy crisis in the 1970s was responsible for an even greater usage of CFCs as foaming agents in the production of home insulation. The rise of the fast-food industry was also a contributing factor to intensified CFC use, as polymer foams were utilized to produce disposable cups and food containers.[3] These long-lived compounds are not destroyed in the lower atmosphere and therefore are able to drift up into the stratosphere, where their

---

[1] For the published report, see Farman, Gardiner, and Shanklin (1985).

[2] A smaller hole over the Arctic is also under investigation.

[3] Kemp (1990), pp. 127–28.

| FIGURE 13.1 | CUMULATIVE PRODUCTION OF CFCs: 1958–1994 |

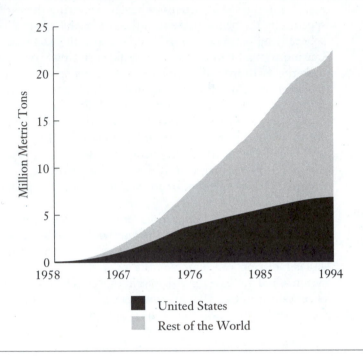

**United States**

**Rest of the World**

NOTE: Data shown refer to CFC-11 and CFC-12.

SOURCE: U.S. International Trade Commission. *Synthetic Organic Chemicals, United States Production and Sales.* Washington, DC, U.S. Government Printing Office, annual.

chlorine components destroy ozone. And because of their long atmospheric lifetimes, CFCs released today affect the ozone layer for decades to come.

Another major group of ozone depleters are halons, also characterized as having long atmospheric lifetimes. Prior to government controls, these substances were becoming increasingly important in the production of fire extinguishants. While their use is not as widespread as CFCs, halons are known to have a higher potency for ozone depletion than their chlorine-containing counterparts.

Despite the lack of hard evidence at the time, the United States opted to ban the use of CFCs in most aerosol sprays in 1978, and other countries followed suit. However, other uses of these ozone depleters were not controlled, and little effort was aimed at finding substitutes. As a result, domestic and international CFC use continued to grow. Data on *cumulative* CFC production are given in Figure 13.1. As these data suggest, there was little question that a stronger policy position was needed on those factors contributing to ozone depletion.[4]

[4]For more information on the science of ozone depletion, visit **www.epa.gov/ozone/science/ science.html**.

# Controlling Ozone Depletion

As a global air pollution problem, ozone depletion cannot be controlled without an integrated international effort. More formally, think of this environmental problem as an externality with *transboundary* implications. The 1990 Clean Air Act Amendments specifically call for the president to enter into international agreements that encourage joint research on ozone depletion and to establish regulations consistent with those in the United States. While not without political implications, a number of international agreements and multilateral treaties have been executed or are on the negotiating table. A brief summary of the most significant of these follows.[5]

## *International Agreements to Control Ozone Depletion*

In 1987, 24 countries as well as the European Community Commission signed the Montreal Protocol on Substances that Deplete the Ozone Layer. Among the signatories were the major producers of CFCs. This landmark agreement called for a 50-percent reduction of CFC consumption and production, a target that was to be achieved gradually up through the turn of the century. To achieve this objective, each party to the protocol was responsible for designing and implementing an effective control program in accordance with the agreed-upon deadlines.

In 1990, some 59 countries executed the London Amendments to the Protocol. These amendments, which strengthened the worldwide commitment to protecting the ozone layer, were in direct response to reports that ozone depletion might be more severe than originally believed. The new agreement outlined a full phaseout plan aimed at eliminating ozone-depleting substances such as methyl chloroform, fully halogenated chlorofluorocarbons, and carbon tetrachloride between 1995 and 2005. Later, at the 1992 Copenhagen Conference, these phaseout deadlines were advanced to 1996. Table 13.1 offers a summary of how these phaseout agreements have evolved over time. As of 1997, more than 160 countries joined in this international effort and ratified the treaty. Collectively, these nations represent over 96 percent of the world's usage of CFCs and more than 85 percent of the world population.[6] Most recently, the treaty signatories met in Montreal to formulate what is being called the Montreal Amendments.

A market approach was also part of the international effort to protect the ozone layer. Specifically, production and consumption allowances were issued to the protocol participants, and transfers were permitted under certain guidelines. To assure that the phaseouts were achieved, trading was conditioned upon revision of each country's aggregate production limits to levels lower than what would have occurred without the transfers.

---

[5] Much of the subsequent discussion is drawn from Council on Environmental Quality (March 1992, January 1993, and 1997).

[6] Dumanoski (November 26, 1992).

| TABLE 13.1 | INTERNATIONAL AGREEMENTS FOR PHASEOUT OF OZONE DEPLETERS | | |
|---|---|---|---|
| Substance | 1987 Montreal Protocol | 1990 London Amendments | 1992 Copenhagen Conference |
| CFCs | 50% cut by 2000 (5 types covered) | Phaseout by 2000 (15 types covered) | Phaseout by 1996 (15 types covered) |
| Carbon tetrachloride (a solvent used in CFC production) | No controls | Phaseout by 2000 | Phaseout by 1996 |
| Halons | Freeze at 1986 levels in 1992 | Phaseout by 2000 | Phaseout in 1994 |
| HCFCs (CFC substitutes) | No controls | Phaseout by 2040 | Freeze in 1996; phaseout by 2020 |
| Methyl bromide (pesticide) | No controls | No controls | Freeze in 1995 at 1991 levels; phaseout by 2010 |
| Methyl chloroform (solvent) | No controls | Phaseout by 2005 | Phaseout by 1996 |

SOURCES: Council on Environmental Quality. *Environmental Quality, 23rd Annual Report.* Washington, DC: U.S. Government Printing Office, January 1993, p. 139; UN Environment Program cited in Dianne Dumanoski. "Nations Act to Speed Phaseout of Ozone-depleting Chemicals." *Boston Globe*, November 26, 1992.

Ongoing negotiations are aimed at encouraging more nations to ratify the protocol's amendments. Some countries have been hesitant to participate because of the high costs of converting production technology to eliminate the use of ozone-depleting substances. This is particularly problematic for developing nations. In response to these real concerns, a three-year Interim Multilateral Fund of $160 million was established in 1990 by the protocol participants to assist developing countries in transitioning toward the requisite CFC-replacement technologies. There is also a provision to allow a 10-year grace period for these countries.

Support for developing nations, such as China and India, is crucial to the success of the global initiative. As these nations evolve economically, their increased need for refrigeration (and the associated use of ozone-depleting substances), coupled with their large populations have serious implications for the earth's ozone layer. Indeed, the parties to the protocol agreed to increase the Multilateral Fund to $240 million if China and India signed the agreement, committing the incremental amount directly to these two countries. In June 1991, China did agree to sign, and in June 1992,

India did as well.[7] To better understand the importance of gaining the cooperation of developing nations, consider the following. Given India's expected growth rate, refrigerator consumption in that nation is predicted to rise to nearly 80 million units by the year 2010. This is a dramatic increase from its 1989 level of only 6 million.[8] Without cooperation and commitment that extends beyond national borders, the problem of ozone depletion cannot be resolved.

For its part, the United States has charged the EPA with formulating and implementing a domestic control policy to meet the protocol's phaseout schedule. We next investigate the fundamentals of U.S. policy on ozone depletion with a particular emphasis on the market-based instruments that are integral to achieving both national and international objectives.

### U.S. Policy to Control Ozone Depletion

The 1990 Clean Air Act Amendments significantly strengthened U.S. policy on ozone-depleting substances. Title VI of these amendments is dedicated to protecting the ozone layer. Chief among its rulings are those that define how ozone-depleting substances are to be identified and those that establish a plan to phase them out of usage. These provisions must comply with the nation's commitment to the protocol.[9]

Congress charged the EPA with the responsibility of publishing a complete list of all ozone-depleting substances, including those already identified in the 1990 Amendments. This list distinguishes between Class I and Class II substances, where Class I refers to those having a greater potential for damage.

**ozone depletion potential (ODP)**
A numerical score that signifies a substance's potential for destroying stratospheric ozone relative to CFC-11.

Each listed substance is assigned a numerical value signifying its **ozone depletion potential (ODP)** relative to chlorofluorocarbon-11 (CFC-11). For each substance class, specific phaseout schedules are outlined, which state the maximum amount that can be produced or consumed each year through the phaseout period. Table 13.2 gives the phaseout dates for U.S. production of all ozone-depleting substances.

Recognizing the industry's dependence on CFCs, the 1990 Amendments include provisions to establish a mandatory national recycling program for Class I and II substances, with the intent that recycled refrigerants could be used as substitutes for virgin materials. A related set of provisions calls for federal programs and research aimed at finding safe alternatives to

---

[7] In 1992, the fund became permanent and has continued to grow. For example, a budget of $510 million was approved for the 1994 to 1996 period. To learn more about the fund, visit the site at the United Nations Environment Programme, **www.uneple.org/ozat/aboutus/mf.html**.

[8] World Resources Institute (1992a), pp. 152–53.

[9] Other provisions deal with safety requirements such as the proper handling of refrigerants in servicing motor vehicle air conditioners and the safe use and disposal of listed substances during the servicing or disposal of appliances and refrigeration equipment. Strict labeling regulations are also mandated.

| TABLE 13.2 | PHASEOUT OF U.S. PRODUCTION OF OZONE-DEPLETING SUBSTANCES |
| --- | --- |

| Name | End of U.S. Production |
| --- | --- |
| CFCs | January 1, 1996 |
| Halons | January 1, 1994 |
| Carbon tetrachloride | January 1, 1996 |
| Methyl chloroform | January 1, 1996 |
| HCFC (hydro CFCs) | January 1, 2003* |

NOTE: Production of the HCFCs with the most severe ozone-destroying effects will end by January 1, 2003; production of the rest of the HCFCs will end by January 1, 2030.

SOURCE: U.S. Environmental Protection Agency, Office of Air Quality Planning and Standards. *The Plain English Guide to the Clean Air Act.* "Repairing the Ozone Layer," **www.epa.gov/oar/oaqps/ peg_caa/pegcaa06.html**.

identified ozone depleters.[10] There were also two legislated instruments that explicitly used market incentives to eliminate ozone-depleting substances. These were an **excise tax** and a **marketable allowance system.**

**excise tax on ozone depleters** An escalating tax on the production of ozone-depleting substances.

**An Excise Tax on Ozone Depleters.** One market-based instrument used to control ozone depletion was an escalating **excise tax** on the production for sale of ozone-depleting substances. This tax was enacted by Congress in 1990. The tax rate per pound was a base dollar amount multiplied by the chemical's ozone-depletion potential (ODP), where the base amount was higher for each successive year in the phaseout schedule. The tax was initially set at $1.37 per pound, and by 1995, it had increased to $5.35 per pound. From an economic perspective, notice that such a tax elevated the effective price of ozone depleters and thus motivated a reduction in quantity demanded.

**allowance market for ozone-depleting chemicals** A system that allows firms to produce or import ozone depleters only if they hold an appropriate number of tradeable allowances.

**An Allowance Market for Ozone-Depleting Chemicals.** The other major market instrument used under U.S. policy was an allowance system for ozone-depleting substances. The underlying premise was that firms were allowed to produce or import the substances only if they held an appropriate number of allowances. Each allowance authorized a one-time release of some amount of the substance based on its ODP.[11] In the aggregate, the number of baseline allowances was set to freeze domestic production

[10] See Sec. 608 and Sec. 612 of the 1990 Amendments as well as Lee (May/June 1992) for a discussion of these and other provisions in Title VI of the Clean Air Act related to ozone depletion. For direct information about the legislation itself, visit **www.epa.gov/ozone/title6/usregs.html**.

[11] For example, CFC-11 and CFC-12 each have an ozone-depletion potential (ODP) of 1.0, whereas CFC-113 has an ODP of 0.8. Using these ODPs as weights, 100 allowances could be used either to produce 100 tons of CFC-11 or CFC-12 or 125 tons of CFC-113. Notice how this weighting system gives firms more flexibility in terms of how they comply with the law.

of ozone-depleting substances at their 1986 levels. Given the large number of potential buyers for these allowances, the EPA chose to allocate them only to the largest domestic consumers and producers. Over time, the number of available allowances was gradually reduced and eventually brought to zero.

In the interim, market exchanges of allowances were permitted under strict guidelines—even with firms in other signatory nations of the protocol. Transfers were of two types—trades with other parties and interpollutant transfers. Interpollutant transfers are exchanges of production of one substance in a given year for production of another in that same year, using a weighting scheme based on the ozone-depletion values. The proviso for allowance transfers was that trading had to yield greater reductions in annual production or consumption than would have occurred without the transfers.

The policy move toward the allowance system preceded the 1990 Amendments and followed only after years of study and analysis by policy officials. Following the 1978 ban of CFCs in all so-called nonessential aerosols, the EPA began investigating the feasibility of further controls on the ozone-depleting substances. In an EPA-commissioned study conducted by the Rand Corporation, three alternative control approaches were analyzed: a technology-based command-and-control approach, a fixed emission charge, and a tradeable emission permit system.[12] Each approach was modeled to achieve a given level of reductions over a 10-year period so that the accumulated costs of each plan could be compared. The study showed that the permit system achieved the desired reductions in the most cost-effective manner. Specifically, the costs for this more flexible market-based approach were estimated to be $94.7 million versus $107.8 million for the fixed emission charge, and $185.3 million for the technology-based controls.

Given the long life of ozone depleters, the EPA considered the regulatory implications over an even longer time period—out to 2075. As part of its Regulatory Impact Analysis (RIA), the EPA conducted a benefit–cost study of a formal phaseout plan.[13] The agency's benefit assessment assigned a value to the damages that would be prevented by controlling these substances. These included health effects associated with increased exposure to ultraviolet radiation and nonhealth effects like reduced crop yields, rising sea levels, and property damage.[14] In total, the EPA estimated that accumulated damages would be approximately $6.5 trillion by 2075.[15]

---

[12] Palmer et al. (1980).

[13] For more detail, see U.S. EPA, Stratospheric Protection Program, Office of Air and Radiation (December 1987).

[14] In addition to destroying stratospheric ozone, CFCs have been identified as so-called greenhouse gases —a fact we will address later in the chapter. Hence, some of the effects identified in the RIA are associated with the contribution of CFCs to global warming.

[15] Cogan (1988), p. 88.

| TABLE 13.3 | VALUE OF CFCs TO AMERICAN INDUSTRY |
|---|---|

| Usage | Value of Products and Services |
|---|---|
| Refrigeration | $ 6.0 billion |
| Air-conditioning | $10.9 billion |
| Mobile air-conditioning | $ 2.0 billion |
| Plastic foams | $ 2.0 billion |
| Cleaning agents | Valued in $ billions |
| Food freezants | $ 400 million |
| Sterilants | $ 100 million |

SOURCE: Drawn from Alliance for Responsible CFC Policy. *Montreal Protocol: A Briefing Book*. Rosslyn, VA: Alliance for Responsible CFC Policy, December 1986.

On the cost side, a value had to be assigned to all anticipated market disruptions that would arise from a proposed phaseout plan. Some 84 distinct use categories for CFCs were analyzed—the two largest being mobile air-conditioning and refrigeration.[16] All told, the EPA's estimate of control costs associated with a phaseout plan was $27 billion through 2075. To get a sense of how this dollar amount might be shared among various CFC-dependent products and services, see Table 13.3. While these costs are significant, they pale in comparison to the dollar value of damages that would result if the United States took no action at all. Consequently, U.S. regulations to control ozone-depleting substances were announced in August 1988, less than one year after the signing of the Montreal Protocol.[17]

## An Economic Analysis of U.S. Policy on Ozone Depletion

Critical to U.S. policy on ozone-depleting substances was the market-based allowance system for producers of these chemicals. Starting from a fundamental economic premise, this program should have approached a more cost-effective solution. Since trades were permitted among those firms holding allowances, those best able to find substitutes for the controlled chemicals would have done so and sold their allowances to less efficient producers. Because the number of allowances was controlled by the government and declined over time, the objective of gradually eliminating the substances was not impeded. Yet, the provision for trading acted as the

---

[16] To provide some sense of the pervasive use of CFCs at the time, consider the following. In 1985, 90 million cars and light duty trucks used 120 million pounds of CFCs in their air conditioning units. Another 95 million pounds were used in over 100 million refrigerators, 30 million freezers, 180,000 refrigerated trucks, and hundreds of thousands of food service businesses. In all, approximately 660 million pounds of CFCs were consumed during 1985 (Cogan 1988, p. 15).

[17] See 53 *Federal Register* 30598.

FIGURE 13.2

## PRICE ADJUSTMENTS OF CFCs
## AND CFC SUBSTITUTES

As the phaseout plan advanced, there was reduced availability of CFCs. This is illustrated in panel (a) by the shift left of the supply of CFCs, which elevated their price. As this occurred, the demand for CFC substitutes rose, as shown in panel (b). Prices of substitutes were relatively high at the outset. But this price differential diminished as technological advance and government support of that innovation brought about cost declines for substitutes, which in turn shifted the supply curve to the right as shown in panel (b).

**(a)**

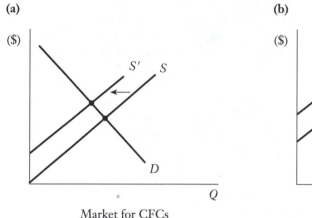

Market for CFCs

**(b)**

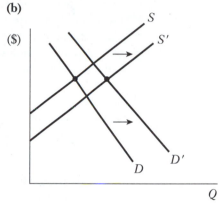

Market for CFC Substitutes

incentive for the development of substitutes by those firms that could do so at least cost.

Because U.S. policy was implemented through such a market-oriented instrument, its progress was observed through the price mechanism. The prices of CFCs and other ozone-depleting chemicals signaled the impact of the phaseout and the underlying market adjustments. As the phaseout plan advanced, there was reduced availability of CFCs. This is illustrated in Figure 13.2(a) by the shift left of the supply of CFCs, which elevated their prices. Manufacturers of CFC-dependent products faced higher production costs as a result and passed at least some of this cost increase on to consumers. So buyers of commodities such as refrigerators and auto air-conditioning units paid higher prices over time.[18] Also, as CFC prices increased, the demand for CFC substitutes rose, as shown in Figure 13.2(b).

---

[18] Of course, the ultimate change in price depended on the elasticity of demand for these products, which in turn depended on the availability of substitutes. The more substitutes there are for a given product, the more elastic or responsive consumers will be to changes in the price of that product. Since there are few good substitutes for refrigerators, we would expect demand to be price inelastic. Hence, much of the cost increase from the phaseout plan was likely passed on to refrigerator buyers.

One consequence of these events was the evolution of a black market for CFCs. This developed in large part because the phaseout dates established by industrialized nations preceded those set by developing nations.[19]

Because costs and prices were allowed to move naturally, the usual incentives encouraged a market adjustment to the observed industry declines and price changes. Theoretically, two opposing reactions were possible. On the one hand, firms may have perceived a profit advantage in developing ozone-friendly substitute products. Recall that such a market reaction was explicitly supported by U.S. policy on developing safe alternatives. Prices of CFC substitutes were relatively high at the outset. For example, the 1987 price of CFC-12, commonly used in automobile air-conditioning units, was approximately $0.50 per pound, while a substitute, HFC-134a, was estimated to be $3 per pound.[20] However, this price differential diminished as technological advance and government support of that innovation brought about cost declines for substitutes, which in turn shifted the supply curve to the right. This is shown in Figure 13.2(b). Application 13.1 illustrates how industry responded to the market incentives brought about by these changes.

A second possibility is that the relatively small number of firms possessing allowances gained some measure of market power and price control. These firms could have enjoyed above-normal profits at society's expense and made little if any movement toward providing alternative solutions to the marketplace. This explains why some opponents of the allowance plan argued that the EPA compromised its intended cost-effective plan by issuing the valuable "rights" only to a select few. One possible solution would have been to transfer any excess profit to the government, which in turn could redistribute the windfall in a more effective and equitable manner. Such a safeguard was actually implemented in 1990 when Congress approved the escalating excise tax on ozone-depleting chemicals. Notice how a redistribution of income was achieved when fiscal spending was funded by the tax revenues collected from producers of CFCs and other such substances.

In another step to lower the costs associated with the phaseout, the 1990 Amendments called for a national recycling program for CFCs used in refrigeration and air conditioners. Consider the economics of this approach. By making recycled substances available in the market, firms reduce their demand for virgin compounds to produce more ozone-depleting products. Furthermore, firms that depend on these substances can use recycled materials beyond the phaseout deadlines, thus avoiding costly retrofitting until substitutes are developed and made available for sale.[21]

---

[19] For further discussion on this issue, see Arnst (1997), Arnst and McWilliams (1997), and Council on Environmental Quality (1997), p. 202.

[20] Putnam, Hayes, and Bartlett, Inc. (1987).

[21] Lee (May/June 1992).

## Searching for Alternatives to CFCs: The Corporate Response

Private efforts to respond to the phaseout plan on CFC production and consumption were the subject of much attention from Capitol Hill to Wall Street. Some of the nation's largest corporate entities had to make major adjustments in the way they did business or suffer the consequences. In 1988, DuPont announced its plans to voluntarily halt all production of CFCs by the year 2000, a segment of its business that generates revenues of $750 million per year. As of 1990, the conglomerate had allocated $170 million to research aimed at developing substitutes for ozone depleters and reportedly committed up to $1 billion to continue that effort. Notwithstanding the importance of these ventures, only the naive would view these actions as corporate altruism. There is no question that firms recognize the value of an environmentally conscious image and the financial retribution that befalls a careless decision. In a speech delivered in London titled "Corporate Environmentalism," DuPont's CEO Edgar Woolard argued:

"Avoiding environmental incidents remains the single greatest imperative facing industry today."

Beyond aggressive efforts on the production side of the house, industrial consumers of CFCs also exerted a measure of influence. Most made dramatic cuts in consumption of CFCs and pushed hard for the development of viable alternatives to make up the difference. Over a two-year period, IBM reduced its CFC consumption by approximately 31 percent and announced a complete halt in usage by 1993. The automobile industry, already a major player in air pollution issues, is in need of an alternative to CFCs. Of the 355 to 425 million pounds of CFCs produced in 1991, approximately 20 percent was used as a refrigerant in motor vehicle air-conditioning units.

Fortunately, the market responded. The statutory deadline for phasing out most ozone-depleting substances was the end of 1995. Spurred by the entrepreneurial spirit, the effort of research teams paid big dividends. Coming to market are usable and less environmentally harmful alternatives. For example, many 1993 cars were equipped with a redesigned air-conditioning unit that uses a hydrofluorocarbon by the trade name of "R-134a." This is the successor to the ozone-depleting refrigerant "R-12," also known as Freon. The new compound contains no chlorine, greatly diminishing its adverse effect on the earth's protective ozone layer.

Still more innovative advances have been brought to market, some aimed at replacing aerosol propellants. Recent innovations use new packaging with flexible pouches to house the product, surrounded by a mass of compressed air. There is no doubt that the best and fastest innovators stand to gain substantially in the movement away from ozone-depleting substances.

SOURCES: David Kirkpatrick. "Environmentalism: The New Crusade." *Fortune*, February 12, 1990, pp. 44–52; Emily T. Smith, Vicki Cahan, Naomi Freundlich, James E. Ellis, and Joseph Weber. "The Greening of Corporate America: 'Sometimes You Find That the Public Has Spoken and You Get On with It.'" *Business Week*, April 23, 1990, pp. 96–103; Emily T. Smith. "Developments to Watch: Aerosol Cans That Run on Compressed-Air Power." *Business Week*, June 12, 1989; Consumer Reports. "Greener Cooling." *Consumer Reports*, March 1993, p. 133; AAA World. "CFC-Free A/C." *AAA World*, March/April 1993, p. 23.

Overall, the use of the tradeable allowance plan along with the excise tax, the recycling program, and the safe alternatives policy achieved the phaseout objectives in a more cost-effective manner. Such a control program was less disruptive than an immediate ban on production, which would have affected virtually every segment of society with no time to make proper adjustments.

# The Problem of Greenhouse Gases and Global Warming

**greenhouse gases (GHGs)** Gases collectively responsible for the absorption process that naturally warms the earth.

A source of controversy is the predicted climate response to the increasing production of what are termed **"greenhouse gases (GHGs)."** On the agenda of the 1992 Rio Summit, the issue of accumulating greenhouse gases and the associated predictions of global warming is one that continues to be debated. In fact, during 1997, the international community formulated the Kyoto Protocol, which continues the climate change initiative first discussed in Rio. The scientific community is not at all in agreement about this complex phenomenon. Because of the uncertainty, national and international policy responses to this hypothesized global air pollution problem have been tentative at best.

## *Understanding the Potential Problem*

**global warming** Caused by sunlight hitting the earth's surface and radiating back into the atmosphere where its absorption by GHGs heats the atmosphere and warms the earth's surface.

The premise of **global warming** is based on the following accepted scientific facts. Sunlight, passing through the atmosphere, hits the surface of the earth and is radiated back into the atmosphere where it is absorbed by naturally present gases such as carbon dioxide ($CO_2$). This absorption process heats the atmosphere and warms the earth's surface. This is somewhat like a greenhouse that allows sunlight through the glass exterior but prevents the heated air from escaping back outside—thus the phrase, "greenhouse effect." This natural phenomenon is responsible for the existence of life on earth as we know it. Without the so-called greenhouse gases, the earth's temperature would be some 30 to 40 degrees Celsius cooler.

There are about 20 such gases collectively responsible for this warming phenomenon. The primary ones are carbon dioxide ($CO_2$), methane ($CH_4$), chlorofluorocarbons (CFCs), nitrous oxide ($N_2O$), and tropospheric ozone ($O_3$), all of which arise from a number of different sources. Look at Table 13.4, which itemizes the primary anthropogenic sources of each and gives estimates of their proportionate contribution to global warming. Since the presence of these gases affects the earth's temperature, any significant disruption to their natural levels would have climatological impacts. A study conducted by the National Academy of Sciences in 1979 predicts that a doubling of $CO_2$ would generate a rise in the earth's temperature of 1.5 to 4.5 degrees Celsius (or 2 to 8 degrees Fahrenheit).[22] Climate changes in turn would alter the distribution and productivity of agricultural regions, weather conditions, and the level of the earth's seas. Although there is a consensus about the linkage between rising levels of $CO_2$ and temperature change, there is great uncertainty about the timing and magnitude of the outcome.

---

[22] This estimate was later supported in 1985 by a number of other organizations, namely the World Meteorological Organization, the United Nations Environment Programme, and the International Council of Scientific Unions. See National Research Council (1979) cited in U.S. EPA, Office of Policy, Planning and Evaluation, Office of Research and Development (December 1989).

| TABLE 13.4 | GREENHOUSE GASES AND THEIR CONTRIBUTION TO GLOBAL WARMING |

| Greenhouse Gas (GHG) | Proportionate Effect | Major Sources |
|---|---|---|
| Carbon dioxide ($CO_2$) | 61% | Burning of fossil fuels and deforestation |
| Methane ($CH_4$) | 15% | Various agricultural and biological activities, including decomposition at landfills |
| Chlorofluorocarbons (CFCs) | 12% | Aerosol propellants, refrigerants, and various industrial activities |
| Nitrous oxides ($N_2O$) | 4% | Fertilizers, fossil fuel burning |
| Other (ozone [$O_3$], Halons, water vapor, particles) | 8% | Chemical reactions from combustion |

SOURCE: J. T. Houghton, G. J. Jenkins, and J. J. Ephraums, eds. *Climate Change: The IPCC Scientific Assessment.* Report prepared for the Intergovernmental Panel on Climate Change by Working Group I. Cambridge, England: Cambridge University Press, 1990, as reported in Timothy E. Wirth and John Heinz. *Project 88—Round II Incentives for Action: Designing Market-Based Environmental Strategies.* Washington, DC: May 1991, Table 2-1, p. 16.

Although scientists estimate that there have been a number of cooling and warming cycles throughout the earth's history, current concern about a warming trend stems from the rising anthropogenic production of the most prevalent GHG, which is $CO_2$. $CO_2$ is a by-product of fossil fuel combustion, which is basic to the production of energy that supports most industrial activities. Accumulating $CO_2$ is exacerbated by widespread deforestation such as the burning of tropical rain forests. As plant life is destroyed, there is less photosynthesis taking place—a process that absorbs $CO_2$ from the atmosphere naturally. On these basic facts, most scientists seem to agree. Many also agree that the magnitude of increased levels of atmospheric $CO_2$ is likely to be substantial—estimated to grow to twice the level of preindustrial times by the year 2050. Table 13.5 gives an overview of the growth and projected trend of atmospheric concentrations of $CO_2$ and the other primary GHGs. However, predicting the *effect* of this trend on the environment is very difficult.

### Scientific Uncertainty

While there is some consensus that rising amounts of $CO_2$ will change the earth's climate, the real dilemma is that no one knows with certainty the timing or the extent of the outcome, in part because there are many factors to consider. Not the least of these is the influence of other GHGs that play a role in this complex process. Increasing amounts of methane, nitrous

| TABLE 13.5 | GROWTH OF GREENHOUSE GAS CONCENTRATIONS |

| | Atmospheric Concentration | | Projected Concentration |
|---|---|---|---|
| Gas | Pre-1850 | 1987 | Mid-21st Century |
| $CO_2$ | 275.00 ppmv | 348.00 ppmv | 400.00–550.00 ppmv |
| $CH_4$ | 0.70 ppmv | 1.70 ppmv | 1.80–3.20 ppmv |
| $N_2O$ | 0.29 ppmv | 0.34 ppmv | 0.35–0.40 ppmv |
| CFC-11 | 0 | 0.22 ppbv[a] | 0.20–0.60 ppbv |
| CFC-12 | 0 | 0.39 ppbv[a] | 0.50–1.10 ppbv |
| $O_3$ | 0% to 25% lower than present day | 10.00–100.00 ppbv[b] | 15% to 50% higher than present day |

NOTES: ppmv = parts per million by volume; 1 ppmv = 0.0001% of the atmosphere.

ppbv = parts per billion by volume; 1 ppbv = 0.001 ppmv.

[a]Estimated value given is for 1986.

[b]Estimated value given is for 1985.

SOURCES: U.S. Environmental Protection Agency, Office of Policy, Planning, and Evaluation, Office of Research and Development. *The Potential Effects of Global Climate Change on the United States.* Washington, DC, December 1989, Table 2-1, p. 13, citing Ramanathan (1988), and Lashof and Tirpak (1989).

oxides, and CFCs are cause for concern because they are believed to be more damaging than $CO_2$, even though they are present in lower amounts.[23]

Even more problematic to scientific predictions are the so-called feedback effects that can either lessen or intensify the warming phenomenon. For example, volcanic dust acts to filter the sun's warming rays, which would counter some of the influence of accumulating GHGs. Similarly, scientists argue that sulfur particles in the air can have a cooling effect on the earth. On the other side of the ledger is the role of the oceans and forests, which are **carbon sinks** or major absorbers of $CO_2$. But this capacity likely will be diminished by higher temperatures thus intensifying the warming effect. Even cloud cover is a factor to be considered, although the qualitative impact is uncertain. Clouds contribute directly to the greenhouse effect, but they may also have an even stronger cooling influence because of their ability to reflect sunlight back into space.[24] The nature and amount of cloud cover is itself affected in complex ways by climate changes. So,

**carbon sinks**
Natural absorbers of $CO_2$ such as forests and oceans.

---

[23]Kemp (1990), pp. 154–55, and Kerr (May 16, 1997).

[24]Ramanathan et al. (1989).

depending on *how* the earth's cloud cover changes with climate variations, the net outcome will be different.[25] Since so little is known with certainty, scientific research is ongoing in an attempt to settle at least some of the controversy.

## Predicting the Potential Effects of Global Warming

Since the science of global warming is itself the subject of debate, it is not surprising that there is a symmetrical lack of substantive information on what the eventual outcome of accumulated GHGs might be. Nonetheless, through the use of computer simulation models and laboratory experimentation, researchers have been able to assimilate some information about the presumed implications. By way of example, Table 13.6 presents a summary of expert predictions assembled by the National Academy of Sciences in 1987 about the estimated climate responses to increased GHGs in the atmosphere. Notice that the predictions span a broad range of expected outcomes.

A more comprehensive study was conducted by the EPA at the request of Congress in 1987. The agency's findings culminated in a December 1989 report.[26] Estimates include predictions about forest ranges, biodiversity, the earth's sea levels, agricultural productivity, water and air quality, and health risks. There are also regional-specific effects estimated by the study.

Rising sea levels are considered to be one of the more probable outcomes of global warming, arising from thermal expansion of the earth's waters and melting of ice glaciers. Estimated changes range from an increase of 0.5 meters to as much as 2.0 meters (or 1.5 to 7 feet) by the year 2100. One of the studies conducted as part of the EPA investigation estimates that a one-meter rise could destroy 26 to 66 percent of the 13,145 square miles of U.S. coastal wetlands. Other changes include erosion of coastal regions, flooding, and storm surges.[27]

Agricultural changes are particularly difficult to predict, in large part because of the uncertainty of the agricultural system. Even absent the influence of global warming, crop yields are sensitive to weather, insect damage, and soil conditions, none of which can be predicted with certainty. Nonetheless, scientific predictions attempt to identify both gains and losses to the world's agricultural production.

---

[25] U.S. EPA, Office of Policy, Planning, and Evaluation, Office of Research and Development (December 1989), pp. 17–18.

[26] U.S. EPA, Office of Policy, Planning and Evaluation, Office of Research and Development (December 1989).

[27] The specific estimates for wetlands loss were conducted by Park et al. (1989), participants in a contributing project to the EPA study. Other national studies are also ongoing. For example, research conducted by the Canadian government is presented in an annual report produced by Environment Canada, *Understanding CO$_2$ and Climate*. Ottawa: Atmospheric Environment Service.

| TABLE 13.6 |
|---|

## PREDICTIONS OF CLIMATE RESPONSE ACCORDING TO AN EXPERT PANEL

The following gives a summary of the conclusions of an expert panel convened by the National Academy of Sciences on the possible climate responses to increased levels of greenhouse gases. For detail, the full report should be consulted.

| Climate Response | Definition | Prediction |
|---|---|---|
| Large stratospheric cooling | Increased levels of $CO_2$ and other trace gases combined with reduced heating from diminished ozone will cause a significant temperature reduction in the upper stratosphere. | Virtually certain |
| Global mean surface warming | If the level of $CO_2$ doubles, global mean surface warming over the long term is predicted to be between 1.5 to 4.5 degrees C. | Very probable |
| Global mean precipitation increase | The heating of the earth's surface will cause elevated evaporation and, therefore, greater global mean precipitation, although some regions may actually have diminished rainfall. | Very probable |
| Reduction of sea ice | As the earth's temperature increases, the warmer temperature will cause melting of sea ice. | Very probable |
| Polar winter surface warming | The air at the polar surface may warm as much as three times the global average due to the reduction in sea ice. | Very probable |
| Summer continental dryness/warming | Several, but not all, studies show that summer continental dryness will result, primarily from earlier termination of winter storms. | Likely in the long term |
| Rise in global mean sea level | An elevated mean sea level is considered probable due to the thermal expansion of the seas and the melting of ice. | Probable |

SOURCE: National Research Council. *Current Issues in Atmospheric Change.* Washington, DC: National Academy Press, 1987 as cited in U.S. Environmental Protection Agency, Office of Policy, Planning, and Evaluation, Office of Research and Development. *The Potential Effects of Global Climate Change on the United States.* Washington, DC, December 1989, p. xxvi.

On the plus side, there is some evidence to support the possibility of a beneficial fertilization effect from increased levels of $CO_2$, since it is a necessary component of photosynthesis. In fact, some believe that present levels of $CO_2$ are suboptimal, so a rise in temperature could be beneficial.[28] Furthermore, certain parts of the world would profit from the northward

---

[28] Wittwer (1984).

shift of viable agricultural land predicted to occur with a warming trend. For example, the former Soviet Union and Canada would likely gain valuable agricultural land, and some existing agricultural regions would enjoy extended growing seasons and enhanced productivity. Of course, some areas that currently support grain production may suffer serious losses should this shift occur. Examples include farming regions in the former Soviet Union, the midwestern part of the United States, and wheat-growing sections of Canada.[29] Ultimately, such changes could have serious implications for trade patterns among nations and overall food supplies.

Other effects such as changes in ecosystems are also the subject of research. For example, there is concern about the ability of plants and animals to adjust at the same rate as a relatively fast-changing climate. Scientists are concerned that ecosystems may be detrimentally affected and that some species may even die off in the process.

Scientific predictions about the effects of global warming are not at all conclusive. There is disagreement about which of the conjectured events may occur, the degree of impact, and the timing of any associated outcome. Even with sophisticated modeling techniques, forecasts are based on many assumptions, the accuracy of which directly affects the precision of the prediction. So the research continues. In the interim, policy makers must decide how to respond to rising $CO_2$ levels when there is much uncertainty about the implications.

# The Policy Response to Global Warming

Setting policy in response to accumulating GHGs is a difficult problem for two reasons. First, as discussed, the concept of global warming is complex, and little is known with certainty. Second, because both the source of the problem and the predicted effects are global in scope, any effective policy solution relies on international agreement. Many nations contribute significantly to the aggregate level of GHG emissions. The top 10 national emitters are shown in Figure 13.3.

### The International Response

At the 1992 Rio Summit, global climate change was an important agenda item for the many national representatives who gathered at the 12-day worldwide conference. Among the major agreements produced at the summit was the U.N. Framework Convention on Climate Change (UNFCCC),

---

[29]Kemp (1990), p. 157.

FIGURE 13.3

## TOP 10 NATIONAL EMITTERS OF GREENHOUSE GASES

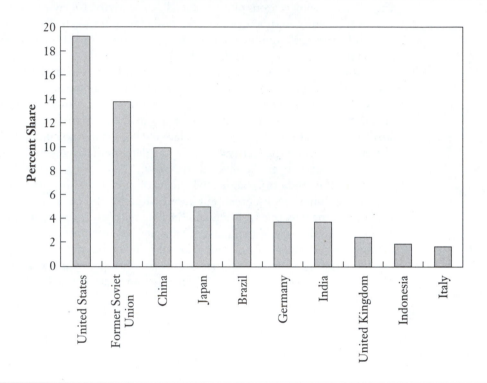

NOTE: The data show the percent share of the increase in the atmosphere's warming potential based on 1991 emissions levels and show the highest ranking emitters.

SOURCE: From *World Resources 1994–1995: A Guide to the Global Environment* by World Resources Institute. Copyright © 1994 by World Resources Institute. Used by permission of Oxford University Press, Inc.

which deals with global warming and other air quality issues. Among its major provisions are:

- Countries must implement national strategies to limit GHG emissions with the objective of reducing emissions to their 1990 levels by 2000.

- The treaty accommodates differences in political and economic conditions among nations by avoiding uniform emission targets and timetables for only one GHG.

- Signatories are encouraged to recognize climate change in the formulation of economic, social, and environmental policies.

- Industrialized nations will assist developing countries in obtaining data and in limiting emissions.

- Countries will elevate public awareness of climate change through education and training.

- Nations will participate in a continuing international research effort.

The convention was to become effective following the ratification by 50 nations. In October 1992, the United States became the first industrialized country, and the fourth overall, to do so following a unanimous vote by the U.S. Senate.[30] By the close of 1993, the requisite number of nations had ratified the treaty, and it became legally binding in March 1994. Following ratification, certain of the signatories were required to develop a **National Action Plan (NAP)** for their respective countries. A NAP includes a specific description of a nation's policy prescription to control GHGs and its estimated target level of emissions for the future. NAPs are to be reviewed by the Conference of Parties (COP)—the ruling body of the Framework Convention, and the participants are then bound by specific requirements of the treaty.[31]

**National Action Plan (NAP)**
A nation's policy to control GHGs and a statement of its target emissions level for the future.

In December of 1997, a COP was held in Kyoto, Japan. The goal of this meeting was to reach an agreement or protocol that would address the issue of GHG emissions after the year 2000. A key outcome of the Kyoto meeting was the establishment of binding emissions targets for developed nations. For example, by 2008 to 2012, the European Union is to achieve a limit that is 8 percent below its 1990 level, the U.S. limit is to be 7 percent below, and Japan's 6 percent below. These will become effective only after 55 nations have ratified the agreement. Achieving these limits will be accomplished through emissions trading within two blocs—one among the European nations called the "European Bubble," and another called the "Umbrella Group" that includes Australia, Canada, New Zealand, Russia, and the United States. Further details of the agreement, including its market-based approach, were discussed during a November 1998 meeting in Buenos Aires.[32]

## The U.S. Response

Subsequent to the ratification of the U.N. Framework Convention, President Clinton announced his program for reducing national emissions of

---

[30] Council on Environmental Quality (January 1993), pp. 142–43.

[31] World Resources Institute (1994b), p. 202.

[32] Fialka (December 11, 1997). For an excellent overview of the Kyoto Protocol, see Susan R. Fletcher (1997). "Global Climate Change Treaty: Summary of the Kyoto Protocol." Washington, DC: National Institute for the Environment, December 22, 1997, which is available online at **www.cnie.org/nle/clim-3.html**.

GHGs to 1990 levels by 2000. This program relied primarily on voluntarism, a cooperative effort between industry and government termed "partnerships for progress." The objectives were to advance technologies aimed at improving energy efficiency and to develop markets for sources of renewable energy. Among the voluntary steps of the Clinton proposal were outreach programs to train contractors on how to build more energy-efficient homes and a plan to encourage investment in hydroelectric power plants. Such an approach is not new to U.S. energy-saving efforts. The same sort of cooperative spirit is the fundamental premise of an EPA program called "Green Lights" discussed in Application 13.2.[33]

In October 1997, President Clinton devised a new climate change proposal. Its key components are:

- Binding emissions targets

- A $5-billion program of tax cuts and R & D for new technologies

- Industry-by-industry consultations on how to reduce emissions and rewards for early actions

- A requirement that developing countries must participate in addressing climate change

- The use of domestic and international emissions trading systems after 10 years of experience with other incentives and federal efforts[34]

### Investigating Market-Based Policy Options

An economic policy response to global warming would use market-based instruments to reduce the accumulation of GHGs, primarily $CO_2$. Many such initiatives have been proposed in the economic literature. These are designed to correct the market failure aspect of global warming. Anthropogenic emissions of GHGs are a **negative externality.** The effects of these gases are not captured within the market transaction and therefore are borne by society. To correct the problem, policy instruments must internalize the externality so that the market participants absorb the cost of the damages. Two types of market-based controls that have been proposed both in domestic and international policy forums are a **pollution charge** and a **tradeable permit system.**[35]

**pollution charge**
A fee that varies with the amount of pollutants released.

**Pollution Charge.**   The use of some type of **pollution charge** to reduce $CO_2$ emissions has received a fair amount of attention in both domestic and

---

[33] Associated Press (October 19, 1993a); Beamish (October 18, 1993).

[34] *President Clinton's Climate Change Proposal*, October 22, 1997, **www.whitehouse.gov/Initiatives/Climate/proposal.html**.

[35] For an excellent discussion of a variety of proposals aimed at reducing greenhouse gases, see Wirth and Heinz (1991), Chapter 2.

## The EPA's "Green Lights Program"

Cooperation between the public and private sectors is the hallmark of the "Green Lights Program," an energy-saving plan launched by the EPA in 1991. One of several voluntary programs, this one urges the corporate sector and lower levels of government to invest in energy-efficient lighting, but only if it is profitable to do so *and* if lighting quality is improved or at least maintained at existing levels.

Just how important is the Green Lights Program to a cleaner atmosphere? According to EPA reports, lighting accounts for about 25 percent of U.S. electricity consumption. And every kilowatt-hour of electricity saved prevents the release of 1.5 pounds of carbon dioxide ($CO_2$) emissions, 5.8 grams of sulfur dioxide ($SO_2$), and 2.5 grams of nitrogen oxides ($NO_x$). In fact, if energy-efficient lighting were used wherever it was profitable to do so, U.S. electricity demand would be reduced by over 10 percent, resulting in reductions of these emissions by 4 to 7 percent. An even more impressive statistic is that the decrease in $CO_2$ emissions would be equivalent to reducing the number of cars on the road by 42 million—about one-third of the total.

Organizations that sign a partnership agreement with the EPA, or a *Memorandum of Understanding* as it is called, make a formal commitment to survey and upgrade 90 percent of their domestic facilities within five years. For its part, the EPA agrees to provide technical support services and training to its partners. There are now over 2,500 participants in the program, including 1,374 corporate partners, 81 utilities, and 249 state and local government partners. In the aggregate, these participants have made a commitment involving more than 5 billion square feet of facility space—a total that is equivalent to one out of every 14 commercial buildings.

The anticipated changes in the environment from the Green Lights Program and other similar plans sponsored by the Department of Energy are shown in the table below.

|  | Green Lights: 1992 | Green Lights: 2000 |
| --- | --- | --- |
| **Commitment** | 2.8 billion square feet | 24 to 60 billion square feet |
| **Expected Results** | | |
| Energy savings | 12.4 billion kWh/yr. | 104 to 226 billion kWh/yr. |
| Carbon emissions avoided | 2.3 million metric tons | 22 to 55 million metric tons |
| Sulfur dioxide emissions avoided* | 0.0675 million metric tons | 1.3 million metric tons |
| Savings in electricity bills** | $870 million | $7 to $15.8 billion |

NOTES:

kWh = kilowatt-hour

*Due to the trading allowances for sulfur dioxide introduced in the 1990 Amendments, these emission reductions may be in the form of allowance credits, expected to be worth $300 to $1,000 per ton.

**Values based on a price of 7.0 cents/kWh.

Programs such as this one operate on the premise that the private sector will cooperate to help improve the environment as long as their market-based objectives are not undermined. The EPA is winning support for its Green Lights Program and other energy-efficient plans by illustrating to potential participants that they can contribute to a cleaner environment and at the same time reduce operating costs and enhance profitability. The EPA argues that using more efficient lighting technologies is expected to yield an internal rate of return of 20 to 30 percent on average.

SOURCES: U.S. Environmental Protection Agency, Office of Air and Radiation. "The Climate is Right for Action: Voluntary Programs to Reduce Greenhouse Gas Emissions." Washington, DC, October 1992; U.S. Environmental Protection Agency, Office of Air and Radiation. "Green Lights Program: The First Year." Washington, DC, February 1992; U.S. Environmental Protection Agency. "Green Lights Program," **www.epa.gov/greenlights.html**; Council on Environmental Quality. *Environmental Quality 25th Anniversary Report.* Washington, DC: U.S. Government Printing Office, 1997, p. 218.

international policy discussions. However, the specific form of the charge has been the subject of debate. In general, three types of product charges have been proposed as possible candidates: a gasoline tax, a Btu tax, and a carbon tax.

**gasoline tax** A per unit tax levied on each gallon of gasoline consumed.

- A **gasoline tax** is a per unit tax levied on each gallon of gasoline consumed.

**Btu tax** A per unit charge based on the energy content of fuel measured in British thermal units (Btu).

- A **Btu tax** is a per unit charge based on the energy or heat content of fuel measured in British thermal units (Btu).

**carbon tax** A per unit charge based on the carbon content of fuel.

- A **carbon tax** is a per unit charge based on the carbon content of fuel.

**corrective tax** A tax aimed at rectifying a market failure and improving resource allocation.

Unlike taxes on income or consumption that generate market distortions, these are referred to as **corrective taxes** since they are aimed at internalizing a negative externality and hence correcting a market failure. By design, these taxes should *reduce* market inefficiency. In addition, all three are revenue-generating, an attribute that is sometimes used to promote this type of policy in the face of rising national deficits.[36] Beyond these common characteristics, these taxes differ in terms of their applicability, ease of implementation, and overall effectiveness in achieving environmental objectives.

**tradeable permit system for GHG emissions** Based on the issuance of marketable permits, where each allows the release of some amount of GHGs.

**Tradeable Permit System.** An alternative market instrument to control global warming is a **tradeable permit system for GHG emissions**—precisely the approach outlined by the Kyoto agreement. The United States has experience with such instruments, using domestic trading of sulfur dioxide permits to mitigate acid rain as well as national and international trading of CFC permits to combat ozone depletion. Conceptually, the design of a GHG emissions market would follow those already in place. However, the implementation of this permit program on an international scale would be far more difficult to accomplish.

While these and other market-based proposals have appeal, there are also drawbacks that must be considered. Evaluating the pros and cons is facilitated through economic analysis, using the criterion of efficiency and the decision rule of maximizing net benefits.

# Economic Analysis of Global Warming Control Policies

Ideally, environmental policy should achieve an efficient allocation of resources—where net benefits are maximized or equivalently where the

---

[36]Interestingly, however, there are those who believe environmental taxes should be revenue neutral, so that the motivation and the outcome are exclusively oriented in favor of environmental quality. See, for example, OECD (1989a), pp. 13–14.

marginal social benefit from implementing policy is exactly offset by the marginal social cost. While assessing benefits is always the more difficult process, it is particularly so for global warming because of the gray areas that weaken scientific predictions. Hence, before we can analyze specific policy proposals, we need to first consider the dilemma of estimating the potential benefits from *any* initiative designed to control climate change.

### Estimating the Benefits of Controlling Global Warming: Two Opposing Views

To illustrate how benefit assessment is at the root of the global warming policy dilemma, we consider the findings of two research efforts—each arriving at a very different conclusion. The first estimates short- and long-term expected benefits as reported in a recent publication by the Organisation of Economic Co-operation and Development (OECD) in Paris. The second is a published commentary on the *relative* benefits of climate change control policy authored by economist Wilfred Beckerman.

**Short- and Long-Term Expected Benefits: A Report from the OECD.** A recent report prepared as part of the activity of the OECD Environment Committee includes some new estimates of the expected benefits from controlling global warming. These are presented as estimated damages associated with climate change.[37] Some of the projections for the U.S. economy are given in Table 13.7. Notice that two columns of dollar values are given. The first gives damage estimates from the more conventional prediction of a temperature rise of 2.5 degrees Celsius, while the second presents estimates based on a temperature rise of 10 degrees Celsius over a very long term. According to this report, the benefits of controlling global warming based on conventional climate change predictions would be $61.6 billion (or approximately 1.1 percent of GDP), and as high as $338.6 billion (or at least 6 percent of GDP), over the very long run of 250 to 300 years.

**An Assessment of Relative Benefits: A Study by Beckerman.** In a published article, economist Wilfred Beckerman argues that not only are the damages from global warming difficult to assess, but even if the most dire predictions are correct, most are not sufficient to warrant the high costs of avoidance.[38] Beckerman cites a 1988 EPA report that estimates the net effect of global warming on U.S. agriculture to be within a range between a net gain of $10 billion and a net loss of $10 billion. While the media often focus on the potential for financial loss, a net gain is actually possible, since some parts of the nation will enjoy longer growing seasons, enhanced by increased precipitation and the fertilization of increased carbon dioxide ($CO_2$) concentrations. At the other extreme, even if the maximum estimated

---

[37] Cline (1992).

[38] Beckerman (1990).

| TABLE 13.7 | ESTIMATED EFFECTS OF GLOBAL WARMING ON THE U.S. ECONOMY |

**Annual Damage to U.S. Economy**
**(billions of dollars at 1990 prices)**

| Major Damage | 2.5 Degrees C | 10 Degrees C Very Long Term Warming |
|---|---|---|
| Agriculture | $17.5 | $95.0 |
| Forest loss | 3.3 | 7.0 |
| Species loss | 4.0 | 16.0 |
| Sea level rise | | 35.0 |
| Dykes, levees | 1.2 | |
| Wetlands losses | 4.1 | |
| Drylands losses | 1.7 | |
| Electricity requirements | 11.7 | 67.0 |
| Nonelectric heating | −1.3 | −4.0 |
| Human morbidity | 5.8 | 33.0 |
| Migration | 0.5 | 2.8 |
| Hurricanes | 0.8 | 6.4 |
| Leisure activities | 1.7 | 4.0 |
| Water supply | 7.0 | 56.0 |
| Urban infrastructure | 0.1 | 0.6 |
| Tropospheric ozone | 3.5 | 19.8 |
| **Total** | **$61.6** | **$338.6** |

SOURCE: William R. Cline. "Global Warming: Estimating the Economic Benefits of Abatement." In Organisation for Economic Co-operation and Development, *Global Warming: The Benefits of Emission Abatement.* Paris: OECD, 1992, p. 55, Table 5. Reprinted with permission.

loss of $10 billion is incurred, Beckerman points out that this is only about 0.2 percent of U.S. GDP. Furthermore, these estimates ignore the gains from the inevitable progression of agricultural technology advances, genetic engineering, and the like, all of which would likely counter any losses from global warming.

In sum, Beckerman argues that we should be very cautious about proceeding with any policy initiative to significantly reduce $CO_2$ emissions. He argues strongly that the costs associated with a 50-percent reduction in $CO_2$ emissions called for by most environmentalists would far outweigh the expected benefits. Such a massive reduction would likely increase energy prices by 400 to 500 percent. To burden society with such a high cost should be undertaken only with a full understanding of what the reduction will ultimately gain. In this case, it is not at all clear that the gain, measured in terms of reduced damages, would offset the expected costs.

The implications of the OECD report and Beckerman's analysis are quite different, even though both share the same perspective—that benefit assessment is critical to developing policy aimed at global warming. Beckerman argues that the associated benefits do not appear to outweigh the social costs. However, the research reported by the OECD suggests that *long-term* benefits might be more relevant to this particular environmental problem. If this time element is considered, policy development might take a very different direction. Taken together, the two analyses suggest the need for more research. In the interim, studies such as these explain the challenge policy makers face in deciding how to respond to this environmental issue.

Recognizing this challenge, economists strongly promote market-based policies designed to consider the benefits and costs of government controls. Although there are many types of instruments that use market forces to operate, all of them can be motivated by modeling the cause of global warming, rising GHG emissions, as a market failure.

### An Economic Model of the Market Failure

To simplify our analysis and give it context, we focus on the release of $CO_2$—the most prevalent GHG, arising primarily from the production of electricity. Figure 13.4 illustrates a hypothetical market for electricity generation, which consists of two groups of electric power plants—one using fossil fuels that generate $CO_2$ emissions and the other using alternative fuel technologies such as solar, wind, or nuclear power. Panel (a) depicts the marginal private cost of fossil fuel users ($MPC_F$) and the associated marginal social cost ($MSC_F$). $MSC_F$, by definition, is the vertical sum of the $MPC_F$ and the marginal external cost ($MEC_F$) of electricity production. Thus, $MEC_F$ is implicitly shown as the vertical distance between $MSC_F$ and $MPC_F$, and represents the cost of health and property damages associated with $CO_2$ emissions. Panel (b) shows the marginal social cost of alternative fuel users, ($MSC_A$). For simplicity, it is assumed that this segment of the market does not generate any negative externalities. Thus, $MSC_A$ is exactly equal to $MPC_A$. Panel (c) presents the aggregate market for electricity shown with a hypothetical demand curve ($D$) measuring the marginal social benefit of electricity usage ($MSB$) and two distinct supply curves, ($S_p$) and ($S_s$). The $S_p$ is the private market supply of electricity found as the horizontal sum of $MPC_F$ and $MPC_A$, while $S_s$ is the social market supply found as the horizontal sum of $MSC_F$ and $MSC_A$.

In the absence of $CO_2$ emission controls, equilibrium is determined by the intersection of market demand, $D$, and *private* market supply, $S_p$. Thus,

| FIGURE 13.4 | MODELING THE NEGATIVE EXTERNALITY OF GHG EMISSIONS ASSOCIATED WITH ELECTRICITY GENERATION |

In the absence of $CO_2$ emission controls, the competitive equilibrium is determined by the intersection of market demand, $D$, and *private* market supply, $S_p$ (i.e., the horizontal sum of $MPC_F$ and $MPC_A$), yielding a market quantity and price of $Q_c$ and $P_c$ respectively. At $P_c$, fossil fuel utilities supply $Q_{F1}$, while alternative fuel users supply a much smaller amount, $Q_{A1}$. The efficient equilibrium is determined by market demand, ($D$), and the *social* market supply, $S_s$ (i.e., the horizontal sum of $MSC_F$ and $MSC_A$).The resulting efficient price, $P_e$, is higher than $P_c$ because demanders are now paying the full cost of their consumption activity. At $P_e$, the efficient quantity of electricity is $Q_e$, which represents the correct mix of production using fossil and alternative fuels. Fossil fuel–based production has declined from $Q_{F1}$ to $Q_{F2}$, reducing the emissions of $CO_2$, and alternative fuel–based production has increased from $Q_{A1}$ to $Q_{A2}$.

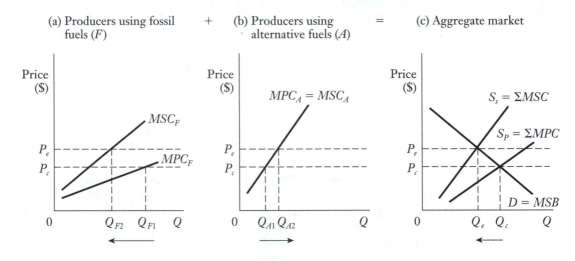

(a) Producers using fossil fuels ($F$)     +     (b) Producers using alternative fuels ($A$)     =     (c) Aggregate market

the competitive equilibrium quantity and price are $Q_c$ and $P_c$ respectively. At $P_c$, fossil fuel utilities are willing to supply $Q_{F1}$, while the alternative fuel users supply a much smaller amount, $Q_{A1}$.[39] Notice that fossil fuel users can supply most of the electricity to the market at price $P_c$ because their $MPC_F$ is relatively low. Without policy controls, these utilities do not consider the external costs of their $CO_2$ emissions, so private market incentives

[39] While the market segments modeled in Figure 13.2 are hypothetical, it is interesting to note that as of 1996 approximately 72 percent of electricity generated in the United States was produced by burning carbon-based fuels. See U.S. Energy Information Administration, U.S. Department of Energy, at **www.eia.doe.gov/cneaf/electricity/epa/fig01.html**.

allocate too many resources to their production processes and too few to alternative fuel users. Consequently, $P_c$ is sending a false signal about how to efficiently allocate productive inputs, and the market fails.

To correct the market failure, the external cost of fossil fuel emissions must be brought into the market transaction. As shown in panel (c), this means that market price must be determined by market demand, $D$, and the *social* market supply, $S_s$, which includes both external and private costs. Notice that the efficient equilibrium price, $P_e$, is higher than what the private market determines because electricity demanders are now paying the full cost of their consumption activity. That is, the per unit price, $P_e$, paid for electricity is exactly equal to the marginal social cost incurred to produce it.[40] At this higher price level, the quantity of electricity has been reduced to its efficient level, $Q_e$. This new price level corrects the mix of fossil and alternative fuels used to produce electricity. At $P_e$, fossil fuel–based production appropriately has declined from $Q_{F1}$ to $Q_{F2}$, effectively reducing the emissions of $CO_2$. At the same time, the higher price provides an incentive to alternative fuel users to supply more electricity, shown as the increase from $Q_{A1}$ to $Q_{A2}$.

Although the above discussion is hypothetical, it turns out that some utility regulators are beginning to examine the notion of **externality regulation.** Application 13.3 explains some of these efforts along with a discussion of the pitfalls that may be encountered as utilities are forced to bear the full cost of their production activity. Other policy instruments employ the same pricing mechanism in a more general context, such as a pollution charge and a tradeable permit system, which were introduced earlier. These now can be analyzed in the context of this model.

### Evaluating Market-Based Policies[41]

**An Analysis of Pollution Charges.** As discussed, a pollution charge can be implemented in the form of a **gasoline tax,** a **Btu tax,** or a **carbon tax.** All these instruments attempt to attach a price to the negative externality of anthropogenic GHG emissions, but each uses a different basis for the tax. This in turn suggests that the implications vary as well.

Because gasoline is a carbon-based fuel, its combustion produces $CO_2$ as a by-product. By levying a tax on gasoline, its effective market price will increase, discouraging consumption and encouraging the use of cleaner

---

[40] It is important to note that the socially desirable level of electricity production, $Q_e$, still includes some fossil fuel–based production, meaning that $CO_2$ emissions are not totally eliminated. However, they are reduced to the level that society believes is acceptable based on the trade-off between the marginal social benefit of electricity usage and the marginal social cost.

[41] For an interesting overview of market-based policies on global warming, see Larry Parker. "Global Climate Change: Market-Based Strategies to Reduce Greenhouse Gases." Washington, DC: Committee for the National Institute for the Environment." March 9, 1998, available online at **www.cnie.org/nle/ clim-5.html**.

## Environmental Least-Cost Planning:
## Utilities Learn the Economics of Pricing Pollution

Until recently, utilities used what is called **least-cost planning** when seeking regulatory approval for a new power source. This approach involves a determination of prospective costs of a proposed power plant to justify its approval by regulators. Such an evaluative assessment is flawed in that it fails to consider the external costs to society of the pollution generated by the new source. Consequently, proposals involving fossil fuel burning plants would almost always get the nod of approval, since coal and oil are cheaper than more environmentally friendly, alternative power sources.

Recently, some state regulators have begun to revise this format to use what is being called **environmental least-cost planning,** a procedure aimed at internalizing the negative externality of pollution. How? Exactly the way economic theory suggests—by pricing pollution. Under this revised method, the regulator's cost assessment must include some measure of the external cost associated with the proposed facility's expected emissions. New York was the first state to initiate this form of **externalities regulation,** with Massachusetts second in line.

Of course, the changeover is not without its share of problems—the main one being exactly *how* to set the price of pollution. In Massachusetts, the regulators assign the following costs to some of the more common emissions:

| Emissions | External Cost per Ton |
|---|---|
| Sulfur dioxide ($SO_2$) | $1,700 |
| Carbon dioxide ($CO_2$) | 24 |
| Nitrogen oxides ($NO_x$) | 7,200 |

Some of these "price tags" are based on estimated costs of controlling pollution. For example, the external cost per ton of $CO_2$ emissions is based on the cost of planting enough trees to rid the atmosphere of that amount of $CO_2$.

These prices have met with some resistance, particularly from the utilities themselves, many of which believe the costs are too high. Other opponents argue that the *basis* of the price estimates is faulty. Among this opposing group is Robert Stavins, an economist at Harvard University. He argues that the cost should be based on a collection of factors that define the *effects* of the pollution, such as health damage and degradation of property values, rather than the cost of controlling it.

In any case, these price tags on pollution dramatically increase the relative costs of a power source dependent on fossil fuels compared to one that uses wind or solar power. If the bottom line shows that proposed plants powered by alternative fuel sources are less costly from society's perspective, despite the higher market prices for these fuels, regulators will force utilities to select these environmentally safer alternatives. Ultimately, these higher fuel costs will be reflected in the prices charged to electricity consumers. Hence, the cost to reduce pollution will be shared by the utility and the consumer—precisely where it belongs, internal to the market transaction. An added benefit is that the elevated price of electricity should encourage conservation by consumers. Moreover, utilities will have an incentive to implement demand-side policies, such as efficient-lighting programs, to reduce demand and lessen the need for new power sources.

SOURCES: Scott Allen. "Polluting Power Plants to Pay Price." *Boston Globe*, November 12, 1992; Joan O'C. Hamilton and Geoffrey Smith. "Making Clean Energy Sweeter to Utilities." *Business Week*, July 15, 1991.

alternative fuels. As fewer gallons of gasoline are burned, less $CO_2$ is emitted into the atmosphere.[42]

In the United States, gasoline taxes already are being collected by state and federal governments, so an increase in the tax rate to bring about a reduction in carbon emissions would be relatively easy to implement. The major drawback from an environmental perspective is that the tax has limited applicability. It targets only polluting sources using gasoline—relatively minor emitters of $CO_2$, and ignores more significant sources that burn other fossil fuels like oil and coal. Furthermore, it imposes a disproportionate burden on some segments of the economy, such as rural communities that lack good public transportation systems and certain industries such as interstate trucking firms. Hence, the broader-based carbon tax or the Btu tax is often proposed as a superior alternative. Application 13.4 presents an analysis of the Clinton version of the Btu tax originally proposed in 1993.

While the Btu tax and the carbon tax each use a slightly different tax base, the general purpose of each is the same—to encourage fuel-switching and conservation by elevating fuel prices. Of the two, the carbon tax is more specific, since it targets only carbon-based fuels. In fact, it is considered to be the more relevant form of taxation to mitigate $CO_2$ emissions, since the carbon content of fuel and carbon emissions are generally proportional to one another. Effectively, the carbon tax changes *relative* fuel prices, and theoretically could elevate the price of fossil fuel by the marginal cost of the environmental damage caused by its combustion. In the context of Figure 13.4 panel (a), the tax amount should equal the vertical distance between $MPC_F$ and the $MSC_F$ for fossil fuel users, measured at the efficient output level, $Q_{F2}$. Such a per unit charge would successfully internalize the external costs associated with the burning of fossil fuels.

In practice, the carbon tax is being used in Finland, the Netherlands, Norway, and Sweden.[43] In the United States, the EPA has studied this tax as part of its investigation of alternative control options. The agency has estimated that a tax of $5 per ton of carbon would reduce $CO_2$ emissions by approximately 1 to 4 percent by the year 2000 with revenues of $7 to $10 billion per year. By increasing the tax to $25 per ton, emissions would decline by some 8 to 17 percent, and revenues would be between $38 and $50 billion per year.[44] In addition, a carbon tax would increase the effective

---

[42] To the extent that the gasoline tax reduces the consumption of gasoline, other harmful emissions such as nitrogen oxides ($NO_x$) and volatile organic compounds (VOCs) will also be reduced, helping to mitigate other air quality problems such as urban smog.

[43] For more information on various international pollution charges aimed at greenhouse gases, the reader should consult the following: Anderson, Lohof, and Carlin (August 1997); U.S. Environmental Protection Agency, Office of Policy, Planning, and Evaluation (July 1992); or Organisation for Economic Cooperation and Development (1989a and 1991).

[44] These estimates are provided in U.S. Environmental Protection Agency, Office of Policy Planning and Evaluation (March 1991), p. 3-5.

## The Btu Tax: A Market-Based Energy Proposal

One economic instrument that can be used to reduce GHGs is the Btu tax. A type of **product charge,** the Btu tax is so named because it taxes the energy content of fuels measured in British thermal units (Btu). If levied on all types of fuels, the Btu tax encourages energy conservation across the board by elevating the prices of all fuels. If levied only on fossil fuels, the Btu tax acts much like a carbon tax, raising the relative price of fossil fuels to discourage their use and mitigate the effects of global warming caused by carbon dioxide ($CO_2$) emissions.

In 1993, the Btu tax became national news when President Clinton introduced it as part of his economic package. The Clinton version of this tax was initially proposed as a levy of 25.7 cents per million British thermal units (mmBtu) on natural gas, coal, nuclear power, and crude oil for the first year of implementation, with an *additional* charge on crude oil of 34.2 cents per mmBtu to be phased in thereafter. The motivation of the energy tax was obvious—to encourage conservation and to generate revenues to reduce the deficit. On a relative basis, the price differential against crude oil was meant to lessen U.S. dependence on foreign oil supplies. To see the price effects more clearly, the estimated change in various fuel prices associated with the Clinton Btu tax proposal are given below:

| Energy Source | Tax-Induced Price Increase |
|---|---|
| Gasoline | 7.5 cents per gallon |
| Natural gas | 26.3 cents per 1,000 cubic feet |
| Home heating oil | 3.6 cents per gallon |
| Coal | $5.57 per ton |
| Nuclear and hydro power | $2.66 per 1,000 kilowatts |

SOURCE: U.S. Treasury Department.

However well intended, Clinton's energy tax proposal received mixed reviews. Not surprisingly, the sharpest criticism came from utilities and major organizations like the American Petroleum Institute who objected to the price implications and to the government's interference in the marketplace. Beyond this general resistance, there were also objections from certain parts of the country like New England, a region heavily dependent on oil for home heating. Congressional representatives from that region opposed the elevated tax on crude oil from an equity perspective, asserting that their constituents would bear a higher than average burden from the tax.

Responding to some of these arguments and other lobbying efforts, the proposal was revised to eliminate the additional levy on oil. Nonetheless, although the general motivation of the Clinton Btu tax was to elevate energy prices to encourage conservation by Americans, it met stiff political opposition and never materialized as a policy instrument.

SOURCES: Michael Kranish. "Energy Tax Plan Changes Sought." *Boston Globe*, February 19, 1993; Rick Wartzman. "Administration Alters Proposal for Energy Tax." *The Wall Street Journal*, April 2, 1993.

price of crude oil, leading to a reduction in oil imports and less dependence on foreign oil sources.

**Evaluating a Tradeable Permit System.** One of the more critical aspects of the Kyoto Protocol is a GHG tradeable permit system for developed nations. While the details of this arrangement have not yet been decided, any such agreement specifies a worldwide emissions limit and allocates a predetermined number of permits to each national participant. Each country will likely be responsible for the initial distribution of permits to sources within its own borders and the oversight of any trading among those sources. Countries able to reduce emissions below the amount initially allowed by agreement could sell their excess permits to the highest bidding country. Just as in the trading of $SO_2$ allowances and CFC permits, the trading of GHG permits can lead to a cost-effective solution. Nations and individual sources best able to reduce emissions would do so, while those that could not achieve the needed reductions would buy the permits. If the system operates efficiently, the price of the permit should be the dollar value of the external cost associated with the emissions. Again, as shown in Figure 13.4(a), this price should equal the vertical distance between $MSC_F$ and $MPC_F$.

While conceptually appealing, the tradeable permit system does have operational problems. For one thing, arriving at an international agreement is complex, since global warming is expected to have varying impacts on different parts of the world. In fact, some nations stand to gain economically. To persuade these countries to agree to an emissions limit is difficult. Another problem is setting the initial allowance allocations for each nation. Matters of population, expected economic growth, and existing emission levels are just some of the relevant considerations. For example, if existing emission levels were used as the cap, this would severely limit the growth of developing nations. This explains why developing nations are not expected to participate in the trading outlined by the Kyoto Protocol. Still another dilemma is how to monitor emissions of the national participants, particularly if reforestation were allowed as a means to earn emissions credits.[45] This type of globally based program unfortunately lends itself to the public goods problem of free-ridership. So, despite the potential for a cost-effective solution, there are many tough issues to be resolved.

## Conclusions

Formulating sound policy in response to global air pollution is a major undertaking. Scientific knowledge about atmospheric disturbances and the associated implications is still limited, particularly for global warming. As long as the extent of environmental risk is unknown, the benefits of corrective policy initiatives are likewise indeterminate. Consequently, public officials are unable to justify the social costs of policy controls with reliable information about the comparable benefits.

Even when the knowledge base is stronger, such as for ozone depletion, policy development is still complicated by the global nature of the

---

[45] Satellite monitoring would likely have to be implemented if reforestation were part of any such program. See Wirth and Heinz (1991) pp. 18–22 and U.S. Environmental Protection Agency, Office of Policy, Planning, and Evaluation (March 1991), pp. 3-7–3-10

problem. A successful resolution depends critically on international commitment, supported in turn by domestic initiatives. On this front, there have been several achievements. Examples include the Montreal Protocol and its subsequent amendments and more recently the ratification of the U.N. Framework Convention and the Kyoto Protocol. Nonetheless, there are still important issues to be worked out, not the least of which is how to gain the cooperation of developing nations. These countries lack the financial resources and the technology to innovate around the causes of global air pollution. Yet, their cooperation is critical given the expected rate of industrial and economic growth in these nations and the associated ramifications for the environment.

Despite the difficulties, there has been progress in recognizing the relevant issues, acknowledging the unknowns, and investigating alternative solutions. Furthermore, scientific research is ongoing in the hope of reaching a general consensus about the implications of global air pollution. That policy development has been tentative—particularly in responding to the threat of global warming—is recognition of how important a balancing of benefits and costs is to that process.

# Summary

- Ozone depletion refers to damage to the earth's stratospheric ozone layer caused by certain pollutants.

- Scientists agree that the presence of chlorofluorocarbons (CFCs) in the atmosphere is the most likely explanation for ozone depletion. CFCs are a family of chemicals commonly used in refrigeration, air-conditioning, packaging, insulation, and as aerosol propellants.

- The Montreal Protocol of 1987, subsequently revised through the 1990 London Amendments and the 1992 Copenhagen Conference, is an international agreement aimed specifically at the problem of ozone depletion. The agreements called for a full phaseout plan of CFCs, methyl chloroform, fully halogenated chlorofluorocarbons, and carbon tetrachloride by 1996.

- Title VI of the 1990 Amendments is dedicated to protecting the earth's ozone layer. Two legislated instruments that used market incentives to achieve the commitment to eliminate the production and consumption of ozone-depleting substances were an excise tax and a marketable allowance system.

- The excise tax was levied on the production for sale of ozone-depleting substances. The tax rate was a base dollar amount multiplied by the chemical's ozone depletion potential (ODP), where the base amount was higher for each successive year in the phaseout schedule.

- Under the marketable allowance system, firms could produce or import ozone depleters only if they held allowances or "rights" to do so. Over time, the number of available allowances was gradually reduced and eventually brought to zero. Allowance exchanges were permitted under strict guidelines.

- The prices of CFCs and other ozone-depleting chemicals signaled the impact of the phaseout and the underlying market adjustments. The excise tax helped to counter the accumulation of excess profits to firms holding the limited number of allowances.

- Global warming, or the "greenhouse effect," is caused by sunlight hitting the earth's surface and radiating back into the atmosphere, where it is absorbed by naturally present greenhouse gases (GHGs) such as carbon dioxide ($CO_2$). This process heats the atmosphere and warms the earth's surface. Any significant disruption to the natural levels of GHGs would have climatological impacts.

- The accumulation of $CO_2$ arises from fossil fuel combustion and widespread deforestation. The resulting global warming is predicted to affect forest ranges, biodiversity, sea levels, agricultural productivity, water and air quality, and human health. The timing and the magnitude of these effects are uncertain.

- One agreement generated at the Rio Summit was the U.N. Climate Change Convention, which became legally binding in March 1994.

- In December of 1997, a Conference of Parties (COP) was held in Kyoto, Japan. A key outcome of the Kyoto meeting was the establishment of binding emissions targets for developed nations.

- Subsequent to the ratification of the U.N. Framework Convention, President Clinton announced his program for reducing national emissions of GHGs to 1990 levels by the year 2000. The program relied primarily on voluntarism.

- In October 1997, President Clinton devised a new climate change proposal, the elements of which include binding emissions targets, a $5-billion program of tax cuts and R & D for new technologies, and the use of domestic and international emissions trading systems.

- Market-based instruments have been proposed as strategic options to help mitigate the effects of global warming. Among these are a pollution charge and a tradeable permit system.

- Benefit assessment is critical to developing policy to control global warming. Economists promote market-based policies designed to consider both the benefits and costs of government controls.

- The environmental problem of global warming can be illustrated by modeling accumulating GHG emissions as a negative externality. To correct the market failure, the external cost must be brought into the market transaction.

- A common type of pollution charge is the gasoline tax. Its applicability is limited, since it targets relatively minor emitters of $CO_2$.

- The carbon tax targets only fossil fuels and more directly taxes the cause of the pollution.

- The Btu tax is a charge based on the energy content of a fuel. Because it is broader based, it shifts the tax burden more equally across the economy.

- An alternative market-based proposal to combat global warming is the use of an international market for permits to emit GHGs, an approach adopted under the Kyoto Protocol.

## Key Concepts

| | |
|---|---|
| ozone layer | carbon sinks |
| ozone depletion | National Action Plan (NAP) |
| chlorofluorocarbons (CFCs) | pollution charge |
| ozone depletion potential (ODP) | gasoline tax |
| excise tax on ozone depleters | Btu tax |
| allowance market for ozone- | carbon tax |
|    depleting chemicals | corrective tax |
| greenhouse gases (GHGs) | tradeable permit system for GHG |
| global warming |    emissions |

## Review Questions

1. By restricting CFC production, the Montreal Protocol and U.S. regulations have increased the price of CFCs. Assume your employer is a major CFC producer. Present an economic argument either for or against the restrictions.

2. Other than financial assistance, how might industrialized countries help developing countries to control ozone depletion?

3. Consider the distributional effects of agricultural productivity due to global warming. Discuss some of the ramifications of this outcome with regard to regional economies, national economies, and world trade.

4. a. Why is it that a carbon tax is preferred to either a Btu tax or the gasoline tax when the objective is to reduce carbon dioxide ($CO_2$) emissions?

   b. Instead of enacting a carbon tax, assume Congress decides to provide tax incentives to noncarbon-based energy sources, such as solar and wind power. Would this instrument be cost-effective in reducing $CO_2$ emissions?

   c. Now suppose that the government chooses to initiate tax incentives (e.g., a tax credit) for these energy alternatives along with the carbon tax. Would this be a more socially optimal solution? Explain briefly.

5. During the 1970s, domestic oil prices rose sharply due to supply restrictions initiated by the OPEC nations. As prices rose, Congress instituted tax incentives for homeowners to substitute away from oil as a heating fuel and move toward alternative sources like solar energy. During the 1980s, these incentives were eliminated. What was the underlying motivation of implementing the tax incentives in the first place? Why did Congress remove them?

# Additional Readings

Barthold, Thomas A. "Issues in the Design of Environmental Excise Taxes." *Journal of Economic Perspectives* 8(1), Winter 1994, pp. 133–51.

Benarde, Melvin A. *Global Warning . . . Global Warming.* New York: John Wiley & Sons, 1992.

Benedick, Richard Elliot. *Ozone Diplomacy: New Directions in Safeguarding the Planet.* Cambridge, MA: Harvard University Press, 1991.

Carey, John, and Catherine Arnst. "Greenhouse Gases: The Cost of Cutting Back." *Business Week*, December 8, 1997, pp. 64–66.

Choucri, Nazli, ed., *Global Accord: Environmental Challenges and International Responses.* Cambridge, MA: The MIT Press, 1993.

Gibbs, W. Wayt. "The Treaty That Worked—Almost." *Scientific American*, September 1995, pp. 19–20.

*Journal of Economic Perspectives* 7(4). "Symposia on Global Climate Change," Fall 1993.

Manne, Alan, and Richard Richels. *Buying Greenhouse Insurance: The Economic Costs of $CO_2$ Emission Limits.* Cambridge, MA: The MIT Press, 1992.

Morgenstern, Richard D. "Environmental Taxes: Is There a Double Dividend?" *Environment* 38(3), April 1996, pp. 16–20, 32–34.

Muller, Frank. "Mitigating Climate Change: The Case for Energy Taxes." *Environment* 38(2), March 1996, pp. 13–20, 36–43.

Nordhaus, William D. "To Slow or Not to Slow: The Economics of the Greenhouse Effect." *The Economic Journal* 101, July 1991, pp. 920–37.

Roberts, Paul Craig. "What's Flying Out the Ozone Hole? Billions of Dollars." *Business Week*, June 13, 1994, p. 22.

———. "Warning: The Greens May Be Hazardous to Our Economy." *Business Week*, September 29, 1997, p. 22.

Schmalensee, Richard, Thomas M. Stoker, and Ruth A. Judson. "World Carbon Dioxide Emissions: 1950–2050." *The Review of Economics and Statistics* (80), February 1998, pp. 15–27.

Shapiro, Michael, and Ellen Warhit. "Marketable Permits: The Case of Chlorofluorocarbons." *Natural Resources Journal* (23), July 1983, pp. 577–91.

Stipp, David. "Science Says the Heat Is on." *Fortune*, December 8, 1997, pp. 126–29.

Toman, Michael A. "A Framework for Climate Change Policy." *Resources* (127), Spring 1997.

## Related Web Sites

| | |
|---|---|
| Article by Larry Parker on market instruments for global warming | **www.cnie.org/nle/clim-5.html** |
| Article by Susan Fletcher on the Kyoto Protocol | **www.cnie.org/nle/clim-3.html** |
| Benefits of the CFC Phaseout | **www.epa.gov/ozone/geninfo/benefits.html** |
| EPA's Green Lights Program | **www.epa.gov/greenlights.html** |
| EPA's site on global warming | **www.epa.gov/globalwarming/** |
| EPA's *The Plain English Guide to the Clean Air Act.* "Repairing the Ozone Layer" | **www.epa.gov/oar/oaqps/peg_caa/pegcaa06.html** |
| Information on the Multilateral Fund | **www.unepie.org/ozat/aboutus/mf.html** |
| Information on Title VI of the Clean Air Act on ozone depletion | **www.epa.gov/ozone/title6/usregs.html** |
| Latest phase out schedule under the Montreal Protocol | **www.unepie.org/ozat/protocol/countdow.html** |
| Ozone Depletion Glossary | **www.epa.gov/ozone/defns.html** |
| Ozone Secretariat at the United Nations Environment Programme | **www.unep.org/unep/secretar/ozone** |
| *President Clinton's Climate Change Proposal* | **www.whitehouse.gov/Initiatives/Climate/proposal.html** |
| Science of ozone depletion | **www.epa.gov/ozone/science/science.html** |

Secretariat at the United
Nations Framework Conven-
tion on Climate Change          **www.unfccc.de/homep.htm**

U.S. accelerated phaseout of
ozone-depleting substances      **www.epa.gov/ozone/title6/phaseout/accfact.html**

# Appendix:
# A Reference to Acronyms and Terms
# in Global Air Quality Control Policy

### Environmental Economics Acronyms

| | |
|---|---|
| $MPC_F$ | Marginal private cost of fossil fuel users |
| $MSC_F$ | Marginal social cost of fossil fuel users |
| $MEC_F$ | Marginal external cost of fossil fuel users |
| $MSC_A$ | Marginal social cost of alternative fuel users |
| $MPC_A$ | Marginal private cost of alternative fuel users |

### Environmental Science Terms

| | |
|---|---|
| Btu | British thermal unit |
| CFCs | Chlorofluorocarbons |
| CFC-11 | Chlorofluorocarbon-11 |
| $CO_2$ | Carbon dioxide |
| GHG | Greenhouse gas |
| GWP | Global warming potential |
| mmBtu | Million British thermal units |
| $CH_4$ | Methane |
| $N_2O$ | Nitrous oxide |
| $NO_x$ | Nitrogen oxides |
| $O_3$ | Ozone |
| ODP | Ozone depletion potential |
| ppbv | Parts per billion by volume |
| ppmv | Parts per million by volume |
| $SO_2$ | Sulfur dioxide |
| VOC | Volatile organic compound |

### Environmental Policy Acronyms

| | |
|---|---|
| COP | Conference of Parties |
| NAP | National Action Plan |
| RIA | Regulatory Impact Analysis |
| UNFCCC | U.N. Framework Convention on Climate Change |

# V

# *The Case of Water*

Water is so much a part of what we are and where we live, it is generally taken for granted. Satellite photographs of earth are convincing evidence of the predominance of water on our planet, covering over 70 percent of its surface. Over half of the three-mile-deep outer layer of the earth is water. All biological organisms depend on water for life—to transport nutrients, to regulate temperature, and to support virtually all biochemical systems that sustain life.[1] Ironically, the abundance of water on earth disguises the fact that *usable* water is scarce, and as a result efforts to conserve and protect this natural resource have been less than adequate.

While most of the earth is covered by water, much of it is seawater and hence unusable for drinking and crop irrigation. A recent review of accumulated scientific research puts the estimate of fresh water on the planet at less than 1/30th of the earth's entire supply, and very little of this amount is contained in lakes and streams. Most of our fresh water supply—some 77 percent, according to estimates—is trapped in ice and snow. Another 22 percent lies beneath the earth's surface, and most of this (about two-thirds) is not accessible absent prohibitive costs.[2] Finally, of what fresh water *is* available and accessible, much of it has been damaged by pollution.

Population growth and industrial development have placed competing demands on water resources. Fortunately, nature provides a powerful mechanism that regularly replenishes water supplies. Yet despite this restorative process, our water supply is not unlimited. Some parts of the world face severe water shortages, and virtually everywhere on earth, industrial activity, improper waste disposal, and human carelessness have damaged lakes and streams and contaminated accessible groundwater supplies.

The dependence of all forms of life on this scarce resource demands that society understand the risks of water pollution and take appropriate action to minimize those risks. However, since water pollution is an externality, corrective action must come about through government intervention. In the United States, water quality control policy has taken decades to develop and,

---

[1] Lyklema and van Hylckama (1988).
[2] United Nations (1978) as cited in White (1988).

by most accounts, still has much to accomplish. Most argue that national policy is in need of significant reform, though there is disagreement about what revisions should be made and how to implement them. What *is* clear is that water quality laws have not been consistently effective. Although there have been successes, there are still water bodies in decline and there are continuing threats to some drinking water supplies. Furthermore, it appears that national policy objectives are not efficient and that many control instruments in use are not cost-effective.

In this module, we undertake a collection of important tasks: to understand how water resources are threatened by contamination, to examine policy initiatives aimed at the problem, and to analyze the outcome using economic criteria. We begin our study in Chapter 14, which provides a broad overview of the Clean Water Act. Chapter 15 focuses on the primary control instruments used to achieve clean water goals. In Chapter 16, we shift our attention to the Safe Drinking Water Act and the standards used to protect human health.

# 14

# Defining Water Quality: The U.S. Clean Water Act

Water is a classic example of a common property resource characterized by the absence of property rights. Unless government intervenes, water supplies will likely be overused and contaminated. In the United States, controls on water quality have a long history dating back to the turn of the century, and remarkably, certain of these early laws are still on the books. Of course, much has happened in water quality legislation over the past hundred years or so, and the evolution continues.

Effective water policy depends on a careful appraisal of existing water quality conditions, the setting of appropriate objectives, and the design of effective instruments to bring the two together. As we have learned in previous chapters, these tasks depend on good risk assessment techniques and sound risk management practices. In the case of water policy formulation, however, many problems have impeded risk analysis. Assessing the extent of water pollution has been hampered by inadequate monitoring systems. National objectives have not always been properly motivated by benefit and cost considerations, and even when they have, reliable estimates have been hard to come by. Furthermore, some policy instruments have been guided more by public and political pressures than by sound environmental management practices. As a consequence, resources have been misallocated, and society has had unrealistic expectations about what federal policy can accomplish.

Beyond these procedural difficulties are the natural complexities of water resources, which present a further challenge to policy makers. Water supplies are heterogeneous, with different chemical, biological, and ecological attributes. They also serve different functions—an important factor in policy decisions. Consider how quality controls on water used for drinking have to be much more stringent than those applied to waters used only for navigation. Geographical location, including proximity to urban or industrial centers, affects the usage of water resources and their vulnerability to contamination. These differences suggest that policy objectives and control instruments must be sensitive to the variations caused by nature and by human activity. Adding to the challenge is a complex, natural cycle that links together water resources, land, and the atmosphere. This interdependence suggests the need for an integrated approach that acknowledges the transmedia implications. Taken together, these issues add up to an ambitious policy agenda—one we begin to investigate in this chapter.

As a preface to our analysis of water quality policy, we present a general overview of water resources and the sources of contamination that threaten them. This discussion helps to motivate our subsequent investigation of how U.S. policy to protect these resources has evolved to the present day. We then focus on national policy goals under the Clean Water Act and how standards are used to define water quality for the nation. A two-part policy analysis follows. The first is an evaluation of the standard-setting process. The second is a benefit–cost analysis of U.S. water quality initiatives that uses the economic analytical tools we have developed previously. At the end of the chapter is an appendix of acronyms and terms for reference.

## Understanding Water Resources for Policy Development

### *Identifying Water Resources and Their Interdependence*

Most of us are cognizant of the fact that water is a significant component of the surface of the earth and its underlying geological layers. In fact, policy specifically addresses two major categories of water resources, **surface water** and **groundwater.**

**surface water**
Bodies of water open to the earth's atmosphere as well as springs, wells, or other collectors directly influenced by surface water.

- **Surface water** refers to all bodies of water that are open to the earth's atmosphere, such as rivers, lakes, oceans, and streams, and also springs, wells, or other collectors that are directly influenced by surface water.

**groundwater** Fresh water beneath the earth's surface, generally in aquifers.

- **Groundwater** refers to the fresh water located beneath the earth's surface, generally in what are called aquifers, which are underground geological formations that supply wells and springs.

Setting policy to protect and maintain these resources is a major undertaking because these water supplies are so vast and because they are remarkably heterogeneous.

Surface waters represent a highly diverse group of water bodies that support distinct ecological systems, serve different uses, and often face dissimilar sources of pollution. Because of these differences, policy makers

| TABLE 14.1 | SURFACE WATERS OF THE EARTH |
|---|---|
| **Open Ocean Waters** | Open ocean waters are the deep waters beyond the continental shelf and those waters over the continental shelf that are not measurably affected by the input of freshwater from rivers. |
| **Ocean Coastal Waters** | Ocean coastal waters refer to the saltwaters along ocean shorelines, which are less enclosed and more influenced by oceanic processes than estuaries and generally lie over the continental shelf within the territorial sea. |
| **Estuaries** | Estuaries are regions of interaction between rivers and nearshore ocean waters, where tidal action and river flow mix fresh and saltwater together. Estuaries include bays, mouths of rivers, salt marshes, and lagoons. |
| **Inland Waters** | Inland waters are bodies of fresh water, including rivers, streams, lakes, and reservoirs. |
| **Wetlands** | Wetlands refer to areas that are saturated by surface or groundwater with vegetation adapted for life under those soil conditions. These regions are transitional between aquatic and terrestrial ecosystems and include swamps, bogs, fens, marshes, and estuaries. |

SOURCES: U.S. Congress, Office of Technology Assessment. *Wastes in Marine Environments.* Washington, DC: U.S. Government Printing Office, 1987, p. 4; U.S. Environmental Protection Agency, Office of Communications, Education, and Public Affairs. *Terms of Environment, Glossary, Abbreviations and Acronyms.* Washington, DC, September 1992.

in the United States categorize surface waters into the following groups: **open ocean waters, ocean coastal waters, estuaries, inland waters,** and **wetlands,** each of which is described in Table 14.1. Although national policy is aimed at protecting all of these waters, specific policy instruments and programs are often aimed at one of these categories.

Groundwater is an enormous resource—by volume over 50 times the annual flow of the earth's surface waters. It is of critical importance, since it is available at virtually every point on earth and because it is the *only* reliable source for many arid and semi-arid regions of the world.[1]

**hydrological cycle**
Explains the natural movement of water from the atmosphere to the surface, beneath the ground, and back into the atmosphere.

Adding to the complexity of water supplies is the interdependence of all water resources—a phenomenon explained by the **hydrological cycle.** This cycle models the natural movement of water from the earth's atmosphere to the surface and beneath the ground, and back into the atmosphere through a series of natural processes.[2] This model is depicted in Figure 14.1, which shows how the earth's water supply is continuously in motion to replenish itself. Notice that the hydrological cycle illustrates the natural process that joins together the waters on the earth's surface, those below the ground, and the water vapor in the atmosphere. It also communicates an important message about the ramifications of water contamination. The earth's atmosphere and its water supplies are remarkably interdependent.

---

[1] For more detail, see Heath (1988).

[2] For a complete discussion of this important water cycle, see U.S. Congress, Office of Technology Assessment (1988).

FIGURE 14.1

## THE HYDROLOGICAL CYCLE

Groundwater and surface water are linked together by the **hydrological cycle.** Water is transported from the atmosphere to the surface of the earth through **precipitation.** Some precipitation never reaches the earth's surface but instead is **evaporated** back up into the atmosphere as water vapor or clouds. Some of it settles on trees and plants where it is absorbed and later returned to the atmosphere through the process of **transpiration.** Water landing on buildings and other man-made structures is also evaporated.

The precipitation that *does* reach the earth's surface can take a number of routes from the point called the **watershed** or the **drainage basin.** It can collect in pools where it is later evaporated. It also might flow over the surface where it is collected in lakes and streams, a process known as **runoff.** From there, it may evaporate, soak into the ground through the process of **infiltration,** or flow into the oceans where some portion of it is evaporated. Finally, precipitation may infiltrate the ground directly and flow into soil and rock formations into the water table where it is collected within an aquifer—a process called **percolation.**

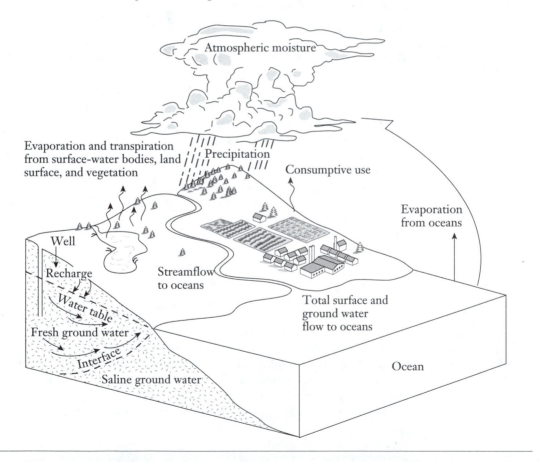

SOURCE: Council on Environmental Quality. *Environmental Trends.* Washington, DC: U.S. Government Printing Office, 1989, p. 21.

Pollutants that damage a river or stream can easily be carried to nearby groundwater supplies, and contaminants in the atmosphere can damage surface waters through precipitation.[3] Hence, while surface water and groundwater are in a practical sense distinct water supplies, potential threats to one can have implications for the other because of the hydrological cycle that ties them together.

### Targeting Water Quality Policy

Both surface water and groundwater resources are vulnerable to contamination from a wide variety of sources—some more obvious than others. In fact, most people tend to think only of the discharges from industrial facilities and power plants as the primary sources of water pollution. However, water resources are contaminated by many other sources that are more obscure but nonetheless serious. Conventionally, the source categories of water pollution are characterized as **point sources** and **nonpoint sources.**

**point source** Any single identifiable source of pollution such as a fixed location or facility from which contaminants are discharged.

- A **point source** is any single identifiable source of pollution such as a fixed location or facility from which contaminants are discharged.

- A **nonpoint source** is one that cannot be identified accurately and degrades a water body in a diffuse, indirect way over a relatively broad area.

**nonpoint source** A source of pollution that cannot be identified accurately and degrades a water body in a diffuse, indirect way over a relatively broad area.

As a group, point sources cover a lot of ground, so policy instruments often distinguish among the following categories:

- **Publicly owned treatment works (POTWs)** that treat wastewaters flowing through sewer systems

- **Industrial facilities** such as private factories, mills, or other physical plants

- **Combined sewer systems** that carry both sewage and storm water runoff to waste treatment plants

Nonpoint sources by definition are difficult to identify, and hence difficult to control. Examples are land runoff (such as from farms, urban areas, construction sites, and mines), septic systems, landfills, spills, and atmospheric deposition. Only recently have government authorities begun to address these less obvious polluting sources. Hence, control efforts are still in the early stages of development. As an example, Application 14.1 discusses how the Chesapeake Bay has been polluted by both nonpoint and point sources and what is being done to save this important natural resource.

---

[3] Recall from Chapter 12 that sulfur dioxide ($SO_2$) and nitrogen oxide ($NO_x$) emissions contribute to acid rain, which in turn damages lakes and other surface waters.

# Deterioration and Restoration of the Chesapeake Bay

For more than 20 years, the Chesapeake Bay was deteriorating. This popular U.S. estuary—the largest in North America—suffered serious stress from a barrage of polluting sources. Among them were sewage treatment plants, atmospheric deposition, urban and rural runoff, and industrial dischargers. The vulnerability of this majestic water body is explained partly by the large number of major rivers that flow into the bay from Maryland, Virginia, West Virginia, Pennsylvania, and Delaware. Furthermore, its geographical location within the boundaries of Maryland and Virginia is such that it does not benefit from the cleansing forces of the open ocean.

The bay receives an enormous amount of nutrients and suspended solids. Most originate from municipal treatment plants and agricultural runoff, entering from upstream sources. The major effects are declines in submerged vegetation and severe eutrophication—the gradual aging process during which a water body evolves into a marsh and eventually disappears. Because the eutrophication is extreme, hypoxia—a serious depletion of dissolved oxygen—is common in the bay. This condition has been blamed for fish kills that are both ecologically and commercially devastating. Other contaminants such as heavy metals and organic substances are linked to industrial and municipal pipelines as well as urban and rural runoff.

One of the more dramatic consequences of the Chesapeake's contamination is the decline in its productivity. Commercial fishing from this large estuary has always been prolific even when measured on a national scale. In 1985, for example, most of the 815 million pounds of fish caught in Virginia and Maryland came from the bay's waters. For that year, this catch accounted for 13 percent of the national total and was valued at almost $124 million. National attention was drawn immediately to observations that the bay's bountiful marine life was being threatened by pollution. In the past two decades, oyster production has fallen by 99 percent. Severe reductions also have been observed in such species as striped bass, white perch, and the blueback herring.

Official response to the bay's decline began in the 1970s. A seven-year study completed in 1983 reported on the major causes and sources of the deterioration. Later that year, the Chesapeake Bay Agreement was signed by the EPA, Maryland, Virginia, Pennsylvania, the District of Columbia, and the Chesapeake Bay Commission. This historic document authorized the Restoration and Protection Plan—the oldest estuarine program in the United States. It is a cooperative agreement among the signatories to clean up the bay and restore its productivity. In 1987, the program was made a part of the provisions of the Water Quality Act, and a new, more specific agreement was drafted and signed. In 1991, still another in the series of Chesapeake Bay documents was executed—this one aimed at accelerating the restoration efforts to assure progress toward meeting the program's objectives.

These efforts have not gone unrewarded. Since 1985, a 19-percent reduction in the bay's phosphorus levels has been observed along with a 5-percent drop in its nitrogen content. Submerged vegetation has begun to return to the shorelines, and the population of striped bass is showing signs of increase.

SOURCES: U.S. Environmental Protection Agency, Office of Water. *National Water Quality Inventory: 1994 Report to Congress.* Washington, DC, December 1995, pp. 330–31; U.S. Environmental Protection Agency, Office of Communications, Education, and Public Affairs. *Securing Our Legacy: An EPA Progress Report 1989–1991.* Washington, DC, April, 1992, pp. 32–33; U.S. Congress, Office of Technology Assessment. *Wastes in Marine Environments.* Washington, DC: U.S. Government Printing Office, 1987, pp. 21–22, 100–08, 157–64; U.S. Environmental Protection Agency. *Environmental Progress and Challenges: EPA's Update.* Washington, DC, August 1988, p. 66.

*Setting the Policy Agenda*

Recognizing the complexity of water resources and their vulnerability to pollution, policy makers have a comprehensive agenda of what must be accomplished through specific initiatives. In the United States, there is a three-part goal for clean and safe water as follows:

- All Americans will have drinking water that is clean and safe to drink.

- Effective protection of America's rivers, lakes, wetlands, aquifers, and coastal and ocean waters will sustain fish, plants, and wildlife, as well as recreational, subsistence, and economic activities.

- Watersheds and their aquatic ecosystems will be restored and protected to improve human health, enhance water quality, reduce flooding, and provide habitat for wildlife.[4]

These themes communicate that water quality is important not only to protect human health but also to protect the ecology and to assure that all uses of water are maintained. Therefore, we should expect water quality to be defined broadly in the law and pollution controls to be instituted from a wide range of perspectives. Indeed, there are many different laws and special programs aimed at water pollution, although the most comprehensive is the Clean Water Act. To get a sense of how the federal government became involved in clean water legislation and how today's policy position developed, consider the following evolution of U.S. water quality policy.

## Water Quality Legislation in the United States: An Overview

Similar to the development of U.S. air policy, government controls on water quality date back to the late 1800s. In the early days, these rulings were aimed solely at protecting human health and were unsophisticated by today's standards. Over time, the legislation evolved into a fairly complex set of laws to protect not only human health, but also the natural condition of the earth's water resources and the aquatic life they support. A summary of the evolution is given in Table 14.2, which serves as an outline for the following discussion.[5]

---

[4] U.S. EPA, Office of the Chief Financial Officer (September 1997), p. 28. This goal is presented in the document titled *EPA Strategic Plan*, which can be accessed online at **www.epa.gov/ocfopage/plantoc.htm**.

[5] Much of the following is drawn from Adler, Landman, and Cameron (1993), pp. 5–10; Freeman (1990), pp. 97–108; and Freeman (1978), pp. 45–53. For an online summary of major legislative milestones, see **www.epa.gov/OWOW/cwa/timeline.html**.

| TABLE 14.2 | EVOLUTION OF U.S. WATER QUALITY LAWS |
|---|---|

| Legislative Act | Major Provisions |
|---|---|
| Rivers and Harbor Act of 1899 | Prohibits the discharge of refuse into all U.S. navigable waters without a permit. |
| Water Pollution Control Act of 1948 | Called for the federal government to conduct research, implement surveys to study contamination, provide loans to municipalities for construction of POTWs. |
| Water Pollution Control Act Amendments of 1956 | Authorized state governments to set criteria to define water quality; strengthened federal government's role; established a grant program to subsidize construction of POTWs; instituted the enforcement conference. |
| Water Quality Act of 1965 | Required states to establish ambient water quality standards, devise implementation plans, issue permits to satisfy standards, and set up a monitoring and enforcement program. |
| The Marine Protection, Research, and Sanctuaries Act | Regulates ocean dumping of materials that may harm health, the marine ecology, or the economic potential of the oceans; also acts as the domestic instrument that implements the international agreement called the London Dumping Convention. |
| Federal Water Pollution Control Act of 1972 | Shifted the primary responsibility for water quality controls from the states to the federal government; established the first set of national goals for water quality; authorized EPA to establish technology-based effluent standards. |
| Clean Water Act of 1977 | Postponed compliance deadlines for meeting the effluent standards; established new treatment standards for wastes sent to POTWs; strengthened controls on toxic pollutants. |
| Water Quality Act of 1987 | Established federal subsidies to states for loans to finance POTW construction; required states to set up programs for nonpoint polluting sources. |

SOURCES: Robert W. Adler, Jessica C. Landman, and Diane M. Cameron. *The Clean Water Act: 20 Years Later.* Washington, DC: Island Press, 1993, pp. 5–10; A. Myrick Freeman III. "Water Pollution Policy." In Paul R. Portney, ed., *Public Policies for Environmental Protection.* Washington, DC: Resources for the Future, 1990, pp. 97–108; A. Myrick Freeman III. "Air and Water Pollution Policy." In Paul R. Portney, ed., *Current Issues in U.S. Environmental Policy.* Baltimore, MD.: Johns Hopkins University Press for Resources for the Future, 1978, pp. 45–53.

## Early U.S. Water Quality Laws

The evolution of U.S. water quality laws began with the Rivers and Harbor Act of 1899. Technically still in force, this legislation prohibits the discharge of refuse into all U.S. navigable waters. Federal legislation on water pollution per se originated nearly half a century later with the Water Pollution Control Act of 1948. Up until this time, water pollution control laws had been enacted by state and local governments. Much like the first national law on air quality control, the role of the federal government in the 1948 act was limited—apparently for the same reason. There was a reluctance to bring federal intervention into what had been perceived as the responsibility of the states. The 1948 act did, however, introduce a federal loan program to assist municipalities in the construction of publicly owned treatment works (POTWs)—a program that was to have long-term ramifications.[6] In fact, the 1956 amendments to this act converted the loan plan to an outright grant program whereby the U.S. government would subsidize up to 55 percent of POTW construction costs. Aside from this revision, however, national water quality legislation remained weak.

Attempting to address the deficiencies, Congress passed the Water Quality Act of 1965. For the first time, the law itemized specifically what state authorities were to accomplish with some provision for federal oversight. Chief among these responsibilities were setting standards, devising implementation plans to meet those standards, and issuing permits. While seemingly well-defined, the new provisions met with failure. Why? State governments were ill prepared and poorly motivated for the important tasks assigned to them. A major obstacle was that states were unable to translate water quality standards into discharge limits. Such a procedure calls for advanced and costly modeling techniques that state governments simply were unable to orchestrate. They also had difficulty identifying which dischargers were responsible for a water body not meeting the standards, so they had little leverage in enforcing the law. There was also an incentive problem, since states recognized that stringent discharge limits would discourage industry from locating in their jurisdictions.[7] Finally, there was a lack of consistency in how standards were set and enforced across the nation due to state-specific differences in resources and technological expertise. In sum, it was apparent that further reform was needed.

### Evolving toward Today's Policy Position

Responding to the continuing decline in national water quality and recognizing the failure of delegating virtually all control to state authorities, Congress passed two major pieces of water control legislation in 1972. One was the Marine Protection, Research, and Sanctuaries Act (MPRSA) whose primary objective was to regulate ocean dumping. Application 14.2 presents a discussion of this and other legislation protecting ocean waters. The other major law enacted in 1972 was the Federal Water Pollution Control Act (FWPCA)—considered to be a milestone in the evolution of U.S. water quality legislation. In fact, much of what guides U.S. policy today originated with this act.

It was through the FWPCA that primary responsibility for water quality shifted from the states to the federal government. National goals were defined for the first time, including one calling for the elimination of all

---

[6] We will analyze the POTW grant program in the next chapter.

[7] Notice how this incentive problem arises—just as it does in states' development of implementation plans to control air pollution.

## U.S. Policy to Protect Ocean Waters

Deliberate ocean dumping and accidental oil spills are two problems that require special mandates. So Congress passed legislation specifically to protect oceans and coastal waters. Two of these are the Marine Protection, Research, and Sanctuaries Act (MPRSA), and the Oil Pollution Act of 1990 (OPA).

### The Marine Protection, Research, and Sanctuaries Act (MPRSA)

In 1972, Congress passed the Marine Protection, Research, and Sanctuaries Act (MPRSA), also known as the Ocean Dumping Act. Its major purpose is to regulate ocean dumping of materials that may harm human health, the marine ecology, or the economic potential of the oceans. This act is also the domestic instrument that implements the rulings of the London Dumping Convention, an international agreement on ocean dumping to which the United States is a party. Under the MPRSA, dumping of certain materials is explicitly prohibited, such as radiological, chemical, and biological warfare agents; high-level radioactive wastes; and medical waste. The dumping of other wastes such as dredged materials is controlled through permitting. The MPRSA also authorizes the secretary of commerce to designate certain areas of the marine environment as National Marine Sanctuaries. To learn about these areas, visit **www.sanctuaries.nos.noaa.gov/welcome.html**.

In 1988, the Ocean Dumping Ban Act was enacted by Congress to amend the MPRSA. Among its mandates is a ruling to end the dumping of sewage sludge and industrial waste by the close of 1991. It also regulates garbage barges and makes it unlawful for medical wastes to be disposed of in any coastal or navigable U.S. waters.

### Oil Pollution Act of 1990 (OPA)

Oil spills from tanker accidents or offshore oil drilling platforms have made headlines worldwide. Perhaps the best known spill in U.S. waters is that of the *Exxon Valdez* on March 24, 1989. The environmental and economic damages of this accident were substantial, estimated in the several billions of dollars. In the aftermath, Congress recognized the need to pass additional legislation to control and respond to oil spills. In 1990, it enacted the Oil Pollution Act (OPA), which amends provisions in the Clean Water Act to institute tougher controls on oil spills. One section of this act is dedicated to the Prince William Sound region where the *Valdez* incident occurred. The rest is aimed at controlling and preventing the threat of oil pollution to all marine environments.

Under the OPA, a National Contingency Plan is established to provide for effective action to remove oil and hazardous substance discharges. To execute this plan, the act instituted a National Planning and Response System activated in part by response teams formed by the U.S. Coast Guard. Other provisions in the OPA identify those parties responsible for removal costs, damages to natural resources and property, associated loss of profits or earning capacity, and costs of providing public services. Congress also recognized the need to develop preventive initiatives. Among these are provisions to strengthen the standards for obtaining licenses, certificates of registry, and merchant mariners' documents and to clarify the basis under which these may be suspended or revoked. There are also rulings aimed at improving the construction of ocean-going vessels.

SOURCES: Marine Protection, Research, and Sanctuaries Act; Oil Pollution Act of 1990; U.S. Environmental Protection Agency, Office of Water. *Marine and Estuarine Protection: Programs and Activities.* Washington, DC, February 1989; Council on Environmental Quality. *Environmental Quality, 23rd Annual Report.* Washington, DC: U.S. Government Printing Office, January 1993, pp. 34–35.

polluting discharges by 1985. New technology-based effluent limitations were to be set within one year by the EPA as the primary instruments of U.S. water quality control.[8] The federal cost share of sewage treatment construction was increased to 75 percent, and a National Commission on Water Quality was formed to monitor policy effectiveness and to study any economic and technological implications. But it soon became apparent that the new law was overly ambitious, falling far short of its objectives. When the newly established commission issued its first report in 1976, it stated that 20 percent of dischargers likely would not meet the first phase of compliance with the effluent limits, which had been targeted for 1977.[9] In fact, the EPA had not even defined all of the standards by that date, despite the one-year deadline. Citing hundreds of pending legal cases challenging the EPA-mandated limits and attempting to explain the observed lack of progress, the commission's report and recommendations prompted another round of revisions eventually enacted as the Clean Water Act (CWA) of 1977.

Making much needed midcourse corrections, the CWA of 1977 extended the compliance deadlines for meeting the effluent limitations. It also strengthened the law on toxic water pollutants. Still more extensions and revisions followed when the act later came up for reauthorization—these in the form of the Water Quality Act of 1987.[10] The 1987 act authorized more federal monies to support POTW construction. It also required states to establish programs aimed at nonpoint polluting sources and authorized federal funding of $400 million to support that effort.

The most recent reauthorization of the Clean Water Act began under the 102nd Congress with many hearings held by the Senate and House in 1991. The review process ignited intense discussion among Senate members, the EPA, and administration officials. In the interim, no analogous bill was introduced in the House of Representatives. An accumulation of disagreements so delayed the procedures that it soon became clear that the 102nd Congress would not complete the process. Similar debate continued through the next three sessions of Congress, leaving the reauthorization unresolved to date.[11] In the interim, a Clean Water Action Plan was developed by the Department of Agriculture, the EPA, and other federal agencies. This plan acts as the core of President Clinton's Clean Water Initiative and is discussed in Application 14.3.[12]

---

[8] In the next chapter, we will investigate how these effluent limits are defined and conduct an economic analysis of their effectiveness.

[9] National Commission on Water Quality (March 1976).

[10] Though this act officially changed the title of U.S. legislation, we will follow convention and refer to this legislation as the Clean Water Act.

[11] For more on the reauthorization process, see Knopman and Smith (1993), and Adler (1993).

[12] The Clean Water Action Plan can be accessed directly at **www.epa.gov/cleanwater/action/toc.html**.

# The Clean Water Action Plan

In February 1998, the U.S. Department of Agriculture and the EPA submitted the new Clean Water Action Plan to the Clinton administration. It would form the core of President Clinton's Clean Water Act Initiative.

The Action Plan is formulated around the following four tools to achieve water quality objectives:

- **A Watershed Approach**
  This Action Plan envisions a new, collaborative effort by federal, state, tribal, and local governments; the public; and the private sector to restore and sustain the health of watersheds in the nation. The watershed approach is the key to setting priorities and taking action to clean up rivers, lakes, and coastal waters.

- **Strong Federal and State Standards**
  This Action Plan calls for federal, state, and tribal agencies to revise standards where needed and make existing programs more effective. Effective standards are key to protecting public health, preventing polluted runoff, and ensuring accountability.

- **Natural Resource Stewardship**
  Most of the land in the nation's watersheds is cropland, pasture, rangeland, or forests, and most of the water that ends up in rivers, lakes, and coastal waters falls on these lands first. Clean water depends on the conservation and stewardship of these natural resources. This Action Plan calls on federal natural resource and conservation agencies to apply their collective resources and technical expertise to state and local watershed restoration and protection.

- **Informed Citizens and Officials**
  Clear, accurate, and timely information is the foundation of a sound and accountable water quality program. Informed citizens and officials make better decisions about their watersheds. This Action Plan calls on federal agencies to improve the information available to the public, governments, and others about the health of their watersheds and the safety of their beaches, drinking water, and fish.

The Action Plan also identifies 10 principles to guide the nation's effort to restore and protect America's waters. These are:

1. Strong Clean Water Standards
2. Clean Water: Healthy People
3. Watershed Management
4. Restore Watersheds Not Meeting Clean Water Goals
5. Build Bridges between Water Quality and Natural Resource Programs
6. Respond to Growth Pressures on Sensitive Coastal Waters
7. Prevent Polluted Runoff
8. Stewardship of Federal Lands and Resources
9. Improve Water Information and Citizens' Right to Know
10. Ensure Compliance and Protect All Citizens Fairly

SOURCE: U.S. Department of Agriculture and the U.S. Environmental Protection Agency. *Clean Water Action Plan: Restoring and Protecting America's Waters.* EPA-840-R-98-001, Washington, DC: 1998.

| TABLE 14.3 | OBJECTIVES AND POLICY GOALS OF THE U.S. CLEAN WATER ACT |

The objective of this Act is to restore and maintain the chemical, physical, and biological integrity of the Nation's waters. In order to achieve this objective it is hereby declared that, consistent with the provisions of this Act—

(1) it is the national goal that the discharge of pollutants into the navigable waters be eliminated by 1985;

(2) it is the national goal that wherever attainable, an interim goal of water quality which provides for the protection and propagation of fish, shellfish, and wildlife and provides for recreation in and on the water be achieved by July 1, 1983;

(3) it is the national policy that the discharge of toxic pollutants in toxic amounts be prohibited;

(4) it is the national policy that Federal financial assistance be provided to construct publicly owned waste treatment works;

(5) it is the national policy that areawide waste treatment management planning processes be developed and implemented to assure adequate control of sources of pollutants in each state;

(6) it is the national policy that a major research and demonstration effort be made to develop technology necessary to eliminate the discharge of pollutants into the navigable waters, waters of the contiguous zone, and the oceans; and

(7) it is the national policy that programs for the control of nonpoint sources of pollution be developed and implemented in an expeditious manner so as to enable the goals of this Act to be met through the control of both point and nonpoint sources of pollution.

SOURCE: Clean Water Act (Federal Water Pollution Control Act) as amended, Sec. 101(a).

## Policy Objectives under the Clean Water Act

In the United States as in many industrialized nations, there are many laws aimed at protecting water quality, some directed solely at ocean waters, some at drinking water, and some at specific water bodies.[13] Of these, none is more comprehensive than the Clean Water Act. While its provisions are not consistently stringent for all water resources and for all polluting sources, they *do* cover both ground and surface water, and they address both point and nonpoint sources of contamination. To understand the far-reaching intent of this major act, look at Table 14.3 which lists the national goals for water quality enacted by Congress. Of these, the three considered most important are those numbered (1) through (3) referred to as the **"zero**

[13] In Chapter 16, we will analyze U.S. policy to protect drinking water with a particular emphasis on the Safe Drinking Water Act.

discharge goal," the **"fishable–swimmable goal,"** and the **"no toxics in toxic amounts goal,"** respectively. These are implemented primarily through the technology-based effluent limits as well as the three approaches outlined in the fourth, fifth, and sixth goals stated in the act. These approaches address funding for POTW construction, areawide waste treatment management, and research and development, respectively. The seventh goal, which calls for the development of nonpoint source pollution programs, was added with the Water Quality Act of 1987.

### The Zero Discharge Goal

**zero discharge goal**
A U.S. objective calling for the elimination of all polluting effluents into navigable waters.

The **zero discharge goal** called for the elimination of all polluting effluents into navigable waters by 1985. The objective was ambitious. It was motivated by the ineffectiveness of states' control efforts prior to 1972 and by evidence that had been accumulating about the deterioration of U.S. water resources. For example, in 1969 the buildup of oil and industrial wastes in Ohio's Cuyahoga River caused it to literally catch fire. Two years later, a report of Ralph Nader's investigation of U.S. water quality titled *Water Wasteland* cited incident after incident of damage to U.S. waters caused by pollution.[14] Believing there was a need for a strong government response with a fixed deadline, the zero discharge goal was written into law.

### The Fishable–Swimmable Goal

**fishable–swimmable goal** An interim U.S. objective requiring that surface waters be capable of supporting recreational activities and the propagation of fish and wildlife.

The **fishable–swimmable goal** was written as an interim objective to be met until the zero discharge goal could be achieved. According to this objective, surface waters were to be capable of supporting recreational activities and the propagation of fish and wildlife by 1983. In so doing, this goal established a *baseline* level of water quality across all states and set a fixed deadline of July 1, 1983 by which the baseline would be achieved.

### No Toxics in Toxic Amounts

**no toxics in toxic amounts goal** A U.S. goal prohibiting the release of toxic substances in toxic amounts into all water resources.

The **"no toxics in toxic amounts" goal** is a national policy prohibiting the release of toxic substances in toxic amounts into all water resources. Singling out toxic pollutants responded to the observation of increasing numbers of water bodies contaminated by dangerous chemicals. Throughout the 1960s and 1970s chemical use had been on the rise. The discovery of new synthetic chemicals during that period added uncertainty to the potential threat.

These three goals were intended to be the guiding principles for achieving and maintaining water quality throughout the United States. In truth, none of these objectives were met by the stated deadlines nor have they since been achieved, though they are still the ultimate targets of policy initiatives.

---

[14] Zwick and Benstock (1971), as cited in Adler et al. (1993), pp. 5–6.

# The Ecological and Economic Impacts of Oil Tanker Spills

All too often, the media report on another oil tanker that has run aground, spilling its hazardous cargo into surrounding ocean waters. As recently as January 1996, a barge off the coast of Rhode Island made national headlines—this one releasing over 700,000 gallons of heating oil into the ocean and damaging some of the region's renowned beaches. The largest spill in history involved 97 million gallons when two tankers collided in 1979 off the coast of Trinidad and Tobago. In the United States, the most damaging spill occurred in March 1989 when the *Exxon Valdez* ran aground in Alaskan waters, and 11 million gallons of oil poured into Prince William Sound.

In January 1993, the second of two major oil spills within five weeks of one another made world headlines. Both occurred off the coast of the European continent. The first involved a Greek oil tanker named the *Aegean Sea* that ran aground in stormy seas off the coast of Spain in December 1992. The tanker split in two and dumped 23 million gallons of oil into the northwestern port of La Coruna. Early damage reports placed a dollar value of $50 million on the destruction. The second incident involved the Liberian-registered tanker *Braer*, carrying 26 million gallons of light crude oil. The 18-year-old vessel lost power just south of the Shetland Islands in the North Sea and ran aground along the rocky coastline. Preliminary damage reports estimate the cost in the hundreds of millions of dollars.

In the aftermath of these accidents, society must contend with the environmental damage and the economic losses. Birds, fish, sea otters, and other marine life are killed or found coated with oil, struggling to survive. Coastlines are contaminated as the crude oil makes its way to shore. Some of the losses have market implications, such as regional economic losses in tourism and the destruction of commercially valued fish and shellfish. Even more difficult to assess are damages based on the existence value of the ecology—the ocean itself, the marine life it supports, and natural coastlines.

No one can accurately determine the numbers of birds, fish, and sea mammals destroyed as a result of these accidents. Even if this were possible, there is the daunting problem of assigning a dollar value to ecological quality and biological life. Nonetheless, analysts attempt to assess and monetize these damages along with other market effects. In the *Exxon Valdez* case, between 3,500 and 5,500 sea otters were destroyed. An estimated 30,000 sea birds also were killed—among them the nation's prized bald eagle. Including these losses, dollar damages attributable to the *Valdez* incident have been estimated in the billions of dollars.

SOURCES: Matt Bai and Scott Allen. "Oil Spill Spreads Off Rhode Island Coast." *Boston Globe*, January 21, 1996, pp. 1, 24; William Miller. "Oil Spill Threatens North Sea Wildlife." *Boston Globe*, January 6, 1993; Associated Press. "Updating Previous Big Spills." *Boston Globe*, January 6, 1993, p. 6; William E. Schmidt. "Aground, Tanker Spills Oil on Shetland." *New York Times*, January 6, 1993, p. A3; Peter H. Raven, Linda R. Berg, and George B. Johnson. *Environment*. New York: Saunders College Publishing; Harcourt Brace Jovanovich College Publishers, 1993, pp. 15, 197.

## Identifying Pollutants under the Clean Water Act

Water can be polluted at virtually any point in the hydrological cycle and by many different contaminants. The contamination can arise either deliberately through illegal waste disposal or accidentally, such as when oil tankers spill their cargo into the oceans—a problem discussed in Application 14.4. Many pollutants are responsible for degrading the earth's water supplies, ranging from excess plant nutrients to synthetic toxics. A list of the major categories of water pollutants is given in Table 14.4.

| TABLE 14.4 | MAJOR CATEGORIES OF WATER POLUTANTS |
|---|---|

| Category | Description | Examples |
|---|---|---|
| Plant nutrients | Substances that promote the growth of aquatic plant life; high levels of nutrients in a water body indicate enrichment or eutrophication, which is the fertilization of a water body. | Nitrate and phosphate compounds |
| Sediment and other suspended solids | Small particles of solid pollutants suspended in water bodies, which resist removal by conventional means. | Organic and inorganic particles, including soil and silt |
| Pathogens | Microorganisms that can cause disease in humans, animals, and plants. | Bacteria, viruses, parasites |
| Inorganic chemicals | Chemical substances of mineral origin that are not of basic carbon structure. | Acids, road salt |
| Heavy metals | Metallic elements with high atomic weights that tend to accumulate in the food chain. | Mercury, chromium, cadmium, arsenic, lead |
| Organic compounds | Synthetics and animal or plant-produced substances containing primarily carbon, hydrogen, nitrogen, or oxygen. | Pesticides, plastics, oil, gasoline, detergents |
| Thermal modification | Elevated temperature of water bodies caused by the discharge of heated water from industrial processes and electricity generation. | Heated water |
| Radioactive substances | Substances that emit ionizing radiation during decay. | Radioisotopes |

SOURCES: U.S. Environmental Protection Agency, Office of Communications, Education, and Public Affairs. *Terms of Environment, Glossary, Abbreviation and Acronyms*. Washington, DC, September 1992; Peter H. Raven, Linda R. Berg, and George B. Johnson. *Environment*. New York: Saunders College Publishing; Harcourt Brace Jovanovich College Publishers, 1993.

Introduced in the Clean Water Act of 1977, three categories of pollutants are relevant to national law. These are: **toxic pollutants, conventional pollutants,** and **nonconventional pollutants.** These classifications came about to allow for tougher controls on toxic contaminants. As we will investigate in the next chapter, these play a role in how the technology-based effluent limits are implemented.

**toxic pollutant** A contaminant which upon exposure will cause death, disease, abnormalities, or physiological malfunctions.

**conventional pollutant** An identified pollutant that is well understood by scientists.

- A **toxic pollutant** refers to a contaminant which upon exposure will cause death, disease, behavioral abnormalities, genetic mutations, or physiological malfunctions in biological organisms or their offspring.

- A **conventional pollutant** is an identified pollutant that is well understood by scientists and may be in the form of organic waste, sediment, acid, bacteria, viruses, nutrients, oil and grease, or heat.

**nonconventional pollutant** A default category for pollutants not identified as toxic or conventional.

- A **nonconventional pollutant** is the default category for those pollutants not identified as toxic or conventional.

Classifying a pollutant as toxic is based on its degradability (i.e., its ability to break down into a less complex form), persistence (i.e., how long it remains in the environment), the presence of affected organisms and their importance, and the nature and the degree of effect of the pollutant on such organisms. Among the 65 toxic compounds and families of compounds listed in the Clean Water Act are such substances as benzene, chloroform, lead, mercury, and arsenic. This list translates into 126 individual toxic substances referred to as **priority pollutants.** Conventional pollutants include suspended solids, those classified as biological oxygen demanding (BOD),[15] fecal coliform, and pH.[16]

# Defining Water Quality: Standard Setting under the Clean Water Act

**receiving water quality standards** State-established standards defined by use designation and water quality criteria.

As originally required under the Water Quality Act of 1965, surface water quality is defined by **receiving water quality standards.** These state-established standards have two distinct components:

- **Use designation** for the water body
- **Water quality criteria** to sustain the designated uses

**use designation** Component of receiving water quality standards that identifies the intended purposes of a water body.

The **use designation** identifies the intended purposes of a water body such as for irrigation or shellfishing. The **water quality criteria** give the biological and chemical water attributes necessary to sustain or achieve these designated uses, including a *maximum concentration of pollutants* allowed.

## Use Designation[17]

**water quality criteria** Component of receiving water quality standards that gives the biological and chemical attributes necessary to sustain or achieve designated uses.

States are authorized to decide the designated beneficial uses for all intrastate water bodies, subject to EPA approval. Among the uses they should consider are public water supplies, propagation of fish and wildlife, recreational activities, and agricultural purposes, as shown in Table 14.5. At minimum, designated uses must be sufficient to support swimming and some fishing in order to be consistent with the national fishable–swimmable goal. Furthermore, adoption of waste transport or waste assimilation as a designated use is specifically prohibited. This latter ruling refers directly to

---

[15] This refers to the amount of oxygen needed by microorganisms to decompose organic compounds.

[16] See CWA, Sec. 307.(a)(1) on toxic pollutants and Sec. 304.(a)(4) on conventional pollutants; and U.S. EPA, Office of Water Regulations and Standards (September 1988), p. 9.

[17] The following is drawn from 40 CFR 131.10 Designation of Uses and U.S. EPA, Office of Water (March 1994).

| TABLE 14.5 | INDIVIDUAL BENEFICIAL USES FOR WATERBODIES AS RECOMMENDED BY THE EPA |
| --- | --- |

| Use | Description |
| --- | --- |
| Aquatic life support | The waterbody provides suitable habitat for survival and reproduction of desirable fish, shellfish, and other aquatic organisms. |
| Fish consumption | The waterbody supports a population of fish free from contamination that could pose a human health risk to consumers. |
| Shellfish harvesting | The waterbody supports a population of shellfish free from toxicants and pathogens that could pose a human health risk to consumers. |
| Drinking water supply | The waterbody can supply safe drinking water with conventional treatment. |
| Primary contact recreation-swimming | People can swim in the waterbody without risk of adverse human health effects (such as catching waterborne diseases from raw sewage contamination). |
| Secondary contact recreation | People can perform activities on the water (such as canoeing) without risk of adverse human health effects from occasional contact with the water. |
| Agriculture | The water quality is suitable for irrigating fields or watering livestock. |

SOURCE: U.S. Environmental Protection Agency, Office of Water. *National Water Quality Inventory: 1992 Report to Congress.* Washington, DC, March 1994, p. ES-3.

the assertion that pollution dilution is not a viable substitute for waste treatment.[18]

**use–support status**
A classification of a water body based on a state's assessment of its present condition relative to what is needed to maintain its designated uses.

**Use–Support Status.** Periodically, state authorities must determine the **use–support status** of a water body by assessing its present condition and comparing it with what is needed to maintain its designated uses. One of five classifications is assigned to characterize use–support status of surface waters. As described in Table 14.6, these classifications are: **fully supporting, threatened, partially supporting, not supporting,** and **not attainable.** States' findings on use–support status are submitted to the EPA, analyzed, and reported to Congress as part of a biennial National Water Quality Inventory required by the Clean Water Act.[19]

## *Water Quality Criteria*[20]

To assure that designated uses are achieved and maintained, states must either establish **water quality criteria** subject to EPA approval or adopt

---

[18] U.S. Congress, Congressional Research Service (1972), as cited in Adler (1993), p. 159; and Van Putten and Jackson (1986).

[19] For an online summary of the 1996 National Water Quality Inventory, visit **www.epa.gov/OW/ resources/brochure/broch2.html**.

[20] The following is drawn from 40 CFR 131.11 Criteria; CWA, Sec.303; and U.S. EPA, Office of Water Regulations and Standards (September 1988), pp. 8–11.

| TABLE 14.6 | CLASSIFICATIONS OF USE–SUPPORT FOR U.S. SURFACE WATER QUALITY | |
|---|---|---|

| Use–Support Level | Water Quality Condition | Definition |
|---|---|---|
| Fully supporting | Good | Water quality meets designated use criteria. |
| Threatened | Good | Water quality supports designated uses now but may not in the future unless action is taken. |
| Partially supporting | Fair (impaired) | Water quality fails to meet designated use criteria at times. |
| Not supporting | Poor (impaired) | Water quality frequently fails to meet designated use criteria. |
| Not attainable | Poor | The state, tribe, or other jurisdiction has performed a use-attainability study and demonstrated that use support is not attainable due to one of six biological, chemical, physical, or economic/social conditions specified in the *Code of Federal Regulations*. |

SOURCE: U.S. Environmental Protection Agency, Office of Water. *National Water Quality Inventory: 1994 Report to Congress.* Washington, DC, December 1995, Table ES-1, p. ES-5.

**numeric criteria**
Stated as concentrations of chemicals or pollutants allowed in water expressed in micrograms per liter ($\mu$g/L).

**narrative criteria**
Expressed in concise, qualitative statements.

**biocriteria** Expressed in broad statements about the condition of an aquatic system, typically based on the findings of biomonitoring procedures.

criteria set by the EPA itself. The EPA is responsible for developing and publishing criteria that reflect the most current scientific knowledge on all identifiable effects of pollution on health, aquatic life, and welfare. These criteria are pollutant-specific and may be expressed as **numeric criteria, narrative criteria,** or **biocriteria.**

- **Numeric criteria** are stated as concentrations of chemicals or pollutants allowed in water expressed in micrograms per liter ($\mu$g/L).

- **Narrative criteria** are expressed in concise, qualitative statements, typically in a "free from" format, such as "free from toxic pollutants in toxic amounts."

- **Biocriteria** are expressed as broad statements about the overall condition of an aquatic system, typically based on the findings of biomonitoring procedures.

All criteria must have a sound scientific basis, and if there are multiple uses designated for a water body, the criteria must be set to support the most sensitive use.

## Analysis of Receiving Water Quality Standards

The **receiving water quality standards** are a critical element of U.S. water quality policy because they are linked directly to the nation's objectives, particularly the fishable–swimmable goal. However, the process of establishing these standards has been problematic as has their reliance on the effluent limitations for implementation.

### Administrative Problems in Establishing Water Quality Criteria

A major source of contention is the poor performance of both the EPA and state officials in defining water quality criteria, particularly those for toxics. The EPA has been criticized for not having developed all the criteria documents needed to support states' use designations. Because of this and other related problems, states have missed important deadlines. According to the EPA, the delay is due mainly to insufficient resources to develop the data and to conduct the analyses. Consequently, the agency has had to rely on results obtained from or published by the scientific community, which lengthens the process considerably.[21]

These long delays have taken their toll on states' participation in the standard-setting process. According to EPA regional and state officials, part of the hesitancy is that some states question the scientific validity of the data or the analyses that form the basis of the criteria documents. There is also concern about the outdated information being used by the agency. Some states have indicated that effluent limits based on defined criteria are far too stringent, with some more restrictive than states' drinking water standards for the same pollutants. In other instances, the limits are set below detectable levels, complicating states' compliance efforts.[22]

There is also dispute about how federal policy identifies the most dangerous water pollutants. Government officials at the EPA and at the state level argue that the 126 identified priority pollutants do not constitute a comprehensive list of the most dangerous toxic contaminants. The EPA acknowledges that criteria are needed for many nonpriority pollutants that potentially cause serious health effects. Hence, it may be that the law is overregulating priority pollutants at the direct expense of underregulating more common and perhaps more dangerous contaminants.[23]

### Absence of Benefit–Cost Analysis in Setting the Standards

When the states were called upon to establish receiving water quality standards, the law allowed them to specify different standards for each interstate water body within their jurisdictions. It was implied that they could use an evaluation of benefits and costs in setting these standards, but they were *not* required by law to do so.[24] Of course, the use designation had to

---

[21] U.S. GAO (July 1991), p. 29.

[22] U.S. GAO (July 1991), pp. 30–31.

[23] U.S. GAO (July 1991), pp. 17, 29. For a detailed discussion of the inadequacies in the water quality standard-setting process, see Adler et al. (1993), Chapter 4.

[24] Freeman (1990), p. 102.

be consistent with national goals, indicating at minimum a water quality level to support fishing and swimming—a goal that was *solely* benefit-based with no consideration given for economic costs.

Even in states' reports to the EPA on use–support status, benefit–cost assessment is not being done, even though the law calls for such an analysis. According to the Clean Water Act, states are called upon to submit a biennial water quality report in which they must identify waters that have met the fishable–swimmable use designation. This report is supposed to include estimates of the associated costs and benefits of that achievement. The reference in the law is as follows:

> "Each State shall prepare and submit . . . a report which shall include . . . an estimate of (i) the environmental impact, (ii) the economic and social costs necessary to achieve the objective of this Act in such state, (iii) the economic and social benefits of such achievement, and (iv) an estimate of the date of such achievement. . ."

Despite this requirement, most states report only physical, chemical, and biological changes in water quality and estimated changes in physical loadings from point and nonpoint sources. Only a few use models that translate these data into economic activities such as commercial fishing, and even fewer attempt to monetize the results. According to a recent report to Congress,

> "None of the States and Territories reporting on their water quality programs attempted to describe the full extent of economic benefits and costs associated with progress made in improving and protecting water quality conditions."[25]

Most information on the benefits and costs of water quality improvements is limited to the results of research studies focusing on a single location or a specific water body. A case in point is an academic study of the benefits of water quality improvements to marine sportfishing along the East Coast. For a closer look at this study, which is being supported by the EPA, see Application 14.5. Efforts such as these may advance researchers' understanding about how best to measure water quality benefits on a comprehensive scale. In the interim, state officials are a long way from assessing the benefit categories recommended by the EPA, which are shown in Table 14.7. Even if data collection and assessment methods improve, there is currently no explicit mandate to assure that the benefit–cost decision rule is used to define water quality standards. Hence, there is no assurance that water pollution abatement will be set at an efficient level.

---

[25] U.S. EPA, Office of Water (March 1994), p. 18.

## How Much Is Cleaner Water Worth to Marine Sportfishing?

Most water quality research focuses on a particular water body or region as the context of their analysis. Such is the case for a University of Maryland study supported by the EPA, which is analyzing the coastal region that extends from New York to south Florida (excluding the Florida Keys). The selection is motivated by the economic activity being studied—marine sportfishing. Some 80 percent of all East coast marine sportfishing takes place in the area targeted by the study. Furthermore, the region is one where there are active pollution control initiatives in place as well as management plans for recreational fisheries.

The objective of this university research is to develop a database and a procedure that can be used to estimate the economic value of two related factors: access to marine sportfishing and changes in the "catch rate" of various species, where catch rate is the average number of fish caught per fishing trip at a given site. The link between these two factors and economic benefits is a logical one. Water quality policy reform can improve the catch rate, which will in turn affect fishermen's decisions about where to fish, what species they fish for, whether they fish from the shore or from a boat (called the "fishing mode"), and even how often they go fishing. By measuring these changes in fishermen's behavior, researchers can make the link to a monetized benefit measure of improved fishing conditions that can be achieved through tougher pollution controls.

To determine catch rates, the analysis uses survey data collected by the National Marine Fisheries Service. Three broad categories of catch rates are defined by type of fish: big game fish (e.g., marlin and tuna), small game fish (e.g., bluefish and mackerel), and bottom fish (e.g., snapper and grouper). Thus far, three different benefit estimates have been calculated:

- A 20-percent increase in the catch rate of small game fish for both fishing modes at all sites would increase the average benefit of each fishing trip by $0.33.

- A 20-percent increase in the catch rate of bottom fish by boat would increase the average benefit per trip by $1.27.

- A 20-percent increase in the catch rate of large game fish would yield an increase in benefits of $1.56 per trip.

By publishing a detailed report of their findings, the university hopes their study will lay the ground work for other regional analyses. In addition, the model developed by the research will be capable of assessing interregional impacts, such as how changes in fishing conditions in Florida can affect fishing activity in the Chesapeake Bay region.

SOURCE: U.S. Environmental Protection Agency, Office of Water. *National Water Quality Inventory: 1990 Report to Congress*. Washington, DC, April 1992a, p. 164.

### *Lack of Consistency with the Technology-Based Effluent Limitations*

Another problem with the standard-setting procedure relates to the use of federally mandated effluent limitations to achieve the states' receiving water quality standards. The source of contention is that the link between the water quality standards and the effluent limitations is blurred at best. Why?

| TABLE 14.7 | CLASSIFICATION OF ECONOMIC BENEFITS OF WATER QUALITY RECOMMENDED BY THE EPA |
|---|---|

### Intrinsic Benefits

**No Current Use by the Individual**

| Community benefits: | Biocentric satisfaction of knowing that an ecological community is sustained for its own sake. |
|---|---|
| Existence benefits: | Vicarious enjoyment from the knowledge that others are using the resource. Stewardship interest in providing an opportunity for others to use the resource in the future. |

**Potential Future Use by the Individual**

| Option benefits: | Interest in securing an option to participate in an activity or use the resource at some point in the future. |
|---|---|

### Current Benefits

**Indirect Use by the Individual**

| Aesthetic benefits: | Conditions enhance the characteristics of current adjoining fixed amenities, such as lakeside property. |
|---|---|
| Recreational benefits: | Conditions enhance the characteristics of current adjoining transitory activities, such as hiking and photography. |
| Structural ecosystem benefits: | Conditions maintain the functional ecosystem processes, such as stable climate and purification of land, air, and water. |

**Direct Use by the Individual**

| Recreational benefits: | Conditions enhance the characteristics of current water-contact activities, such as boating, swimming, and fishing. |
|---|---|
| Commercial benefits: | Conditions enhance the characteristics of current production processes and activities. |

**Other Uses**

| Extractive commercial uses: | Production processes where water is a medium for other goods (e.g., commercial fishing, medical industries). |
|---|---|
| Commercial navigation: | Examples include dams, canals, and ports. |
| Agricultural irrigation: | Water used as an input to production of crops. |
| Industrial processes: | Water itself is used as an input to production (e.g., processing, cooling, and steam generation). |
| Municipal water: | Water used for drinking, washing, and fire protection. |

SOURCE: Adapted from Research Triangle Institute. *Benefit–Cost Assessment Handbook for Water Programs, Volume 1*, prepared for the EPA, Economic Analysis Division, April 1993, Figure 3-1, p. 3-2 as cited in U.S. Environmental Protection Agency, Office of Water. *National Water Quality Inventory: 1990 Report to Congress*. Washington, DC, April 1992a, Figure 12-1, p. 167.

Because each is motivated differently—the standards by water *usage* and the effluent limits by *technology*. Since the effluent limits are technology-based, they are motivated by what is practical or feasible rather than by benefit–cost analysis or environmental criteria. The intent was to avoid the problem states had encountered of estimating the relationship between a predetermined water quality level and the pollution reduction needed to achieve it. However, it is precisely this relationship that is needed to map the effluent limits to the water quality standards.

Since the technological limits are applied uniformly within defined groups of point sources, they do not account for varying conditions across water bodies or for the different uses of water bodies designated by states. So, even if all dischargers met the effluent limits, there is no guarantee that water quality as the states have defined it would be achieved. In fact, it is precisely because of this possibility that the law requires states to identify those waters for which the effluent limitations are insufficient. Officially, these waters are to be labeled as "water quality limited" and placed in a priority ranking. More stringent controls must then be established.[26] These additional rulings are necessary because the policy instrument—the effluent limitation, is not properly linked to the objective—the water quality standard.

Many factors are responsible for the observed delays and inconsistencies in the standard-setting process. Yet, virtually all are characteristic of a command-and-control approach to environmental policy. The Clean Water Act lacks incentive mechanisms to encourage support and compliance from state governments and from the polluting sources themselves. Such an approach must instead rely on layers of regulations that become difficult to implement, monitor, and enforce.

## Benefit–Cost Analysis of U.S. Water Quality Control Policy

Water quality is a goal about which there is little debate—at least from a qualitative perspective. The issue is not a zero–one option of whether or not this objective is worth pursuing, but rather to determine the *extent* to which water contamination should be controlled. As is always the case in environmental policy, the question is, "How clean is clean?" Once this fundamental question has been addressed, a secondary issue is to evaluate *how* this goal, however defined, is to be achieved. Both issues are complex, but they can be addressed with considerable objectivity using benefit–cost analysis and the efficiency criterion. Relying on the careful work of well-respected environmental economists, we can examine the evidence and draw some qualitative, albeit guarded, conclusions.[27]

---

[26] See CWA, Sec. 303.(d)(1)(A) and U.S. GAO (January 1989), pp. 2–3.

[27] To review a recent benefit–cost analysis of water policy, see U.S. Environmental Protection Agency, Office of Water. *Clean Water Act Initiative: Analysis of Costs and Benefits*. Washington, DC: 1994.

*Benefit–Cost Analysis of the FWPCA of 1972*

The enactment of the Federal Water Pollution Control Act (FWPCA) of 1972 marked a major shift in U.S. policy toward stronger controls administered by the federal government. Because of its importance in the development of U.S. policy, the FWPCA has been a common subject of analysis—not all of it with favorable results. Part of the criticism is that overall water quality did not improve significantly as a result of the 1972 reforms. However, a review of water quality trend data is insufficient evidence to evaluate the effectiveness of federal policy. First, it is not valid to assume that an observed favorable trend is entirely the result of regulatory controls. Water quality is influenced by other factors, such as use intensity, population growth, and industrial development. Second, even if the trend data *were* indicative of improved water quality and could be attributed to policy, these improvements or benefits must be considered along with the costs society incurred to achieve them.

While a number of studies have estimated and monetized the benefits of improved water quality, these analyses typically focus on a specific water body or a particular region. Furthermore, some examine only a single aspect of water quality such as recreational use or the value to the commercial fishing industry.[28] Only one analysis has been done that attempts to synthesize the findings of existing research to arrive at a comprehensive benefit measure of improved water quality attributable to the FWPCA of 1972. This landmark study was conducted by A. Myrick Freeman, III, in 1979 for the Council on Environmental Quality and later revised in 1982.[29] An overview of Freeman's findings follows, with all values expressed in 1984 dollars.

**Estimating the Benefits of the FWPCA of 1972.** To arrive at a dollar value of the total social benefits (*TSB*) associated with the FWPCA of 1972, Freeman surveyed the findings of about 20 existing empirical studies. As shown in Table 14.8, he classified the benefit measures into four categories: (1) recreational use, (2) nonuser benefits, (3) commercial uses, and (4) diversionary uses. Adjusting for differences in price levels, Freeman arrived at an estimate of annual *TSB* for 1985 of between $5.7 and $27.7 billion, with a point estimate of $14.0 billion.[30] This magnitude can be interpreted as the annual benefit of achieving the effluent limitations established by the 1972 legislation.

**Estimating the Costs of the FWPCA of 1972.** To estimate the comparable costs associated with the FWPCA, Freeman examined two sets of

---

[28] A survey of some of these studies is found in Cropper and Oates (1992), particularly Section IV.

[29] Freeman (December 1979) and (1982).

[30] The 1985 date is linked to the goals of the FWPCA, specifically that all polluting discharges were to be eliminated by that year.

| TABLE 14.8 | MONETIZED ANNUAL BENEFITS OF THE FWPCA AS OF 1985 ($1984 BILLIONS) |
|---|---|

| Category | Range | Point Estimate |
|---|---|---|
| **Recreation** | | |
| Freshwater fishing | $0.7–2.1 | $ 1.5 |
| Marine sports fishing | 0.1–4.5 | 1.5 |
| Boating | 1.5–3.0 | 2.2 |
| Swimming | 0.3–3.0 | 1.5 |
| Waterfowl hunting | 0.0–0.5 | 0.2 |
| Subtotal | $2.6–13.1 | $ 6.9 |
| **Nonuser Benefits** | | |
| Aesthetics, ecology, property value | $0.7–5.9 | $ 1.8 |
| **Commercial Fisheries** | $0.6–1.8 | $ 1.2 |
| **Diversionary Uses** | | |
| Drinking water/health | $0.0–3.0 | $ 1.5 |
| Municipal treatment costs | 0.9–1.8 | 1.3 |
| Households | 0.2–0.7 | 0.4 |
| Industrial supplies | 0.7–1.4 | 0.9 |
| Subtotal | $1.8–6.9 | $ 4.1 |
| **Total** | $5.7–27.7 | $14.0 |

NOTES: Estimates are originally presented in Freeman (1982) in 1978 dollars. They have been converted to 1984 dollars using the implicit price deflator.

SOURCE: A. Myrick Freeman III. *Air and Water Pollution Control: A Benefit–Cost Assessment.* New York: John Wiley & Sons, 1982, Table 8-3, p. 161 and Table 9-1, p. 170. Copyright © (1982, John Wiley & Sons, Inc.) Reprinted by permission of John Wiley & Sons, Inc.

estimates—one provided by the Council on Environmental Quality (CEQ) and one by the EPA.[31] The CEQ data use EPA estimates of the engineering costs of complying with the 1972 act absent the additional spending associated with the 1977 Amendments. According to these data, the average annual costs over the 1979 to 1988 period are about $23.2 billion. The EPA data are based on legislative requirements as of December 1982 and therefore include *some* of the costs incurred by the 1977 revisions. These estimates show that the average annual costs are $30.8 billion. Freeman drew from both sources and arrived at an estimate of total social costs (*TSC*) in 1985 of between $25 and $30 billion with a midpoint of $27.5 billion.

**Benefit–Cost Comparison.**    Now consider a comparison of Freeman's estimates, assuming they reflect the true benefits and costs to society. The

---

[31] Council on Environmental Quality (1980b); Freeman (1982); and U.S. Environmental Protection Agency (1984a), Table 3, pp. 15–16, as cited in Freeman (1990), pp. 125–26.

range of values for *TSB* is between $5.7 and $27.7 billion, while the comparable *TSC* estimate is between $25.0 and $30.0 billion. Notice that the two sets of values overlap by only a small amount. We also can examine the relationship between Freeman's point estimate of *TSB*, $14.0 billion, and the midpoint of his *TSC* estimate range, $27.5 billion. In this case, the *TSC* of water quality control as of 1985 exceeds the associated *TSB*—a finding that indicates an unfavorable outcome. This result is illustrated in Figure 14.2(a). Notice that at the abatement level associated with U.S. regulations as of 1985, $A_{1985}$, *TSC* is higher than *TSB*. Also note that $A_{1985}$ is above the efficient level, $A_e$, where net benefits are maximized.

The comparable marginal analysis is shown in Figure 14.2(b), where $A_e$ corresponds to the point where the marginal social cost (*MSC*) curve intersects the marginal social benefit (*MSB*) curve. Notice that at $A_{1985}$, *MSC* exceeds *MSB*, and that this abatement level is to the *right* of $A_e$.

If Freeman's estimates are reasonable, the findings suggest that as of 1985, the United States was overregulating water quality. The marginal benefit to society was not justified by the marginal cost incurred, and too many resources were allocated to water quality controls. This result is symptomatic of any number of problems. It could be that some of the water quality standards were too stringent, forcing an abatement level that was too expensive for the benefits received. Alternatively, the standards could have been set appropriately but the instruments used to implement them such as the permitting system or the effluent limits were not cost-effective.[32]

As in any empirical study, there are always caveats attached to the conclusions. In a recent publication, Freeman (1990) points out several reservations about the values used to support his conclusions. First, the EPA's cost estimates include expenditures associated with the added 1977 controls on toxics, though the associated gains are not captured in the benefit estimate. Second, he argues that the cost estimates suffer from the usual biases associated with the engineering approach.[33] Freeman suggests that the cost values are likely inflated, since they do not allow for the potential of more cost-effective decisions at the firm level or cost savings due to technological advances.

An independent commentary on Freeman's work argues further that the benefit estimate would likely be higher if existence and option values were included.[34] Although Freeman *does* attempt to include some valuation of "nonuser benefits," the estimate for this category is highly uncertain because of the methods used in the underlying studies upon which it is based.[35]

---

[32] If this were the case, then the cost estimates lie *above* the true *MSC*.

[33] Recall from Chapter 9 some of the reservations about using this approach, including uncertainty about price movements, availability of raw materials, and energy costs in future time periods.

[34] Howe (1991), p. 15.

[35] Freeman (December 1979), pp. 161–62. Look back at Table 14.8. Notice that although the estimated range for this category is within a range of $0.7 billion and $5.9 billion, Freeman uses a conservative point estimate of $1.8 billion.

| FIGURE 14.2 | BENEFIT–COST ANALYSIS OF THE U.S. FWPCA OF 1972 AS OF 1985 |

This model is based on Freeman's estimates of the total social costs (*TSC*) and total social benefits (*TSB*) as of 1985 based on regulations given in the FWPCA of 1972. As the diagram shows, *TSC* > *TSB* in 1985, and abatement level $A_{1985}$ is above the efficient level, $A_e$, where net benefits are maximized.

**Total Social Benefits and Total Social Costs**

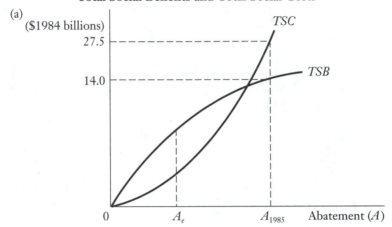

This model shows the comparable relationships to Figure 14.2(a), using marginal analysis. Notice that $A_e$ in this depiction corresponds to the point where the marginal social cost (*MSC*) curve intersects the marginal social benefit (*MSB*) curve. In 1985, at abatement level $A_{1985}$, *MSC* > *MSB*. Notice that $A_{1985}$ is to the right of $A_e$, suggesting that U.S. policy in effect at that time overregulated water quality.

**Marginal Social Benefit and Marginal Social Cost**

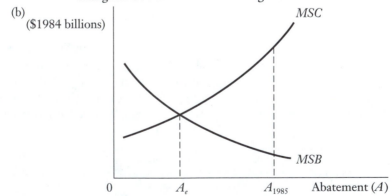

SOURCE: Values depicted based on A. Myrick Freeman III. *Air and Water Pollution Control: A Benefit-Cost Assessment.* New York: John Wiley & Sons, 1982, Table 8-3, p. 161 and Table 9-1, p. 170. Copyright © (1982, John Wiley & Sons, Inc.). Reprinted by permission of John Wiley & Sons, Inc.

Recognizing the potential inaccuracies while defending his overall conclusion, Freeman argues that, even with a 20-percent *upward* adjustment to the benefit estimate and a 20-percent *reduction* in the cost values, the data still suggest an inefficient outcome.[36]

Freeman's work, though not without limitations, is a valuable analysis in that it draws attention to the potential inefficiencies of the 1972 legislation. Taken in the context of the subsequent revisions to this legislation, we need to consider whether the post-1972 reforms accomplished much in terms of improving the efficiency of water quality policy. To examine this question, we next consider the benefits and costs of U.S. water pollution policy in a more current period.

### Advances in Benefit–Cost Analysis of U.S. Water Quality Policy

**An Updated Benefit Estimate of U.S. Water Quality Controls.**  Assessing benefits continues to be the most difficult task in benefit–cost analysis of environmental policy. Nonetheless, there have been advances in the methods used to estimate environmental benefits. One in particular is the use of the Contingent Valuation Method (CVM) touted for its ability to capture existence value as well as user value of environmental resources.

A study conducted by researchers at Resources for the Future in Washington, DC, uses the CVM approach to estimate the value of water quality improvements associated with U.S. regulations.[37] The researchers, Carson and Mitchell, surveyed individuals across the United States in 1983, asking them to assign a dollar value to the minimum levels of water quality specified in the Clean Water Act, that is, for boatable, fishable, and swimmable surface waters. As indicated in Table 14.9, usable responses helped to form a preliminary nationwide estimate of the total social benefits (*TSB*) of water quality at $29.2 billion per year. All values are expressed in 1990 dollars. The authors then combine this estimate with elements of Freeman's earlier findings that were not captured by their survey and arrive at an adjusted value of $39.1 billion. Notice that this estimate is considerably higher than what Freeman found, which is $20.1 billion in 1990 dollars when adjusted for inflation and number of households.[38] A final modification is made to adjust for changes in the number of households, the general price level, real

---

[36] Freeman also discusses the difficulty of attempting to assess the overall benefit of water quality control given the heterogeneity of surface waters and the sensitivity of water quality indicators to sampling locations and time. He further points out that the benefit estimates used in his analysis measure only the gains from controls on point sources even though many bodies of water are seriously impaired by nonpoint sources (Freeman, December 1979, pp. ix–x).

[37] See Carson and Mitchell (1993). To review the CVM, see the analysis presented in Chapter 8.

[38] Carson and Mitchell explain that the difference is due to the broader measure of water quality improvement considered in their analysis. Recall that Freeman measures the benefit of achieving the effluent limitations, whereas Carson and Mitchell measure the benefit of achieving the swimmable goal. It is also possible that their estimate is higher because the CVM approach captures the existence value of clean water.

| TABLE 14.9 | BENEFIT ESTIMATES OF WATER QUALITY IMPROVEMENTS: A CONTINGENT VALUATION STUDY (EXPRESSED IN 1990 DOLLARS) |

### Survey Results of Contingent Valuation Study

| Water Quality | Estimated Willingness to Pay (average per person per year in $1990) |
|---|---|
| Boatable | $106. |
| Fishable | 80. |
| Swimmable | 89. |
| Total | $275. |

### Preliminary Estimate of Annual Economic Benefits Based on Survey Results

Economic Benefit to Achieve Swimmable Water Quality from Baseline of Nonboatable Quality:

| Range | $24–$45 billion |
|---|---|
| Point Estimate | $29.2 billion |

### Adjusted Estimate of Annual Economic Benefits of Clean Water

| Adjusted to add benefits of commercial usage and marine recreational activities from Freeman (1982): | $39.1 billion |
|---|---|
| Scaling for increases in real income and changes in attitude about water pollution from 1983 to 1990: | $46.7 billion |

SOURCE: Drawn from Richard T. Carson and Robert Cameron Mitchell. "The Value of Clean Water: The Public's Willingness to Pay for Boatable, Fishable, and Swimmable Water." *Water Resources Research* 29(7), July 1993, pp. 2445–54.

income, and attitudes about water pollution up to 1990. Their final estimate of *TSB* is $46.7 billion per year as of 1990. This magnitude represents the value of improving water quality from a baseline of nonboatable to swimmable water quality.

**Comparable Costs of U.S. Water Quality Controls.** For comparison to Carson and Mitchell's benefit assessment, we can consider cost estimates from a number of government sources. One comprehensive data source is the EPA, whose estimates of annualized costs of water quality control are shown in Table 14.10. Notice that the EPA data show a projected annual cost in 1990 of $50.6 billion. Carson and Mitchell cite the most recently available cost data from the Department of Commerce, which indicate that

| TABLE 14.10 | EPA Cost Estimates of Water Quality and Drinking Water Control (Billions of 1990 Dollars[a]) |
|---|---|

| Program | Year | | | | |
|---|---|---|---|---|---|
| | 1980 | 1987 | 1990 | 1995 | 2000 |
| Water quality[b] | $27.2 | $41.0 | $46.3 | $57.5 | $68.7 |
| Drinking water | 2.4 | 3.7 | 4.3 | 6.4 | 7.9 |
| Total[c] | $29.5 | $44.7 | $50.6 | $63.8 | $76.4 |

NOTES:

[a] Estimates are originally given by the EPA in 1986 dollars; they have been adjusted to 1990 dollars using the CPI.

[b] Water quality costs are those pursuant to the Clean Water Act as amended in 1987 and the Marine Protection, Sanctuaries and Research Act of 1972.

[c] Some totals do not agree with components shown due to rounding.

SOURCE: U.S. Environmental Protection Agency, Office of Policy, Planning, and Evaluation. *Environmental Investments: The Cost of a Clean Environment.* Washington, DC, December 1990, Table 2-1, pp. 2-2–2-3.

1988 annual costs of U.S. water quality control are approximately $37.3 billion expressed in 1990 dollars.[39] To be conservative, we use both of these sources and assume that annualized total social costs (*TSC*) for 1990 are somewhere in the range of $37.3 to $50.6 billion or about $44.0 billion as a midpoint estimate.[40]

**An Updated Benefit–Cost Comparison for U.S. Water Control Policies.** We next compare the *relative* values of the *TSB* and *TSC* estimates. In so doing, we observe that the *TSB* of $46.7 billion is slightly higher than the comparable *TSC* estimate of $44.0 billion. However, Carson and Mitchell suggest that costs are likely to rise above benefits in the future because of the spending needed to bring all surface waters up to the swimmable level. In any case, the comparison of *total* magnitudes as of 1990 does not indicate whether the associated abatement level is efficient. As Figure 14.3 illustrates, the efficient abatement level occurs where net benefits are maximized at point $A_e$, the point where *TSB* exceeds *TSC* by the greatest distance. Given the available estimates for 1990, we can conclude only that the associated abatement level lies somewhere between 0 and $A_1$ where *TSB* is above *TSC*. However, there is no reason to assume that this level coincides with $A_e$.

[39] Bratton and Rutledge (1990), pp. 32–38, as cited in Carson and Mitchell (1993).

[40] While these cost estimates are quite comprehensive and include costs to *all* economic sectors, they do *not* capture the true social costs of water quality control because implicit costs are not included.

| FIGURE 14.3 | BENEFIT–COST ANALYSIS OF U.S. POST-1972 WATER QUALITY POLICY: TOTAL SOCIAL BENEFITS AND TOTAL SOCIAL COSTS |
|---|---|

The efficient abatement level occurs where net benefits are maximized at point $A_e$, the point where *TSB* exceeds *TSC* by the greatest vertical distance. Based on available estimates for 1990, the abatement level for post-1972 U.S. regulations lies somewhere between 0 and $A_1$, where *TSB* is everywhere above *TSC*. Note, however, that there is no reason to assume that it coincides with point $A_e$.

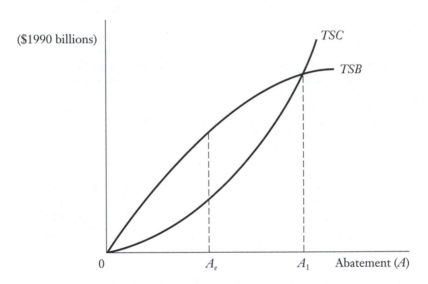

To determine whether or not this is the case, we need to compare marginal social cost (*MSC*) and marginal social benefit (*MSB*) as of 1990. Although these magnitudes are not directly available, a rough approximation is possible by comparing *incremental* costs and *incremental* benefits over a relevant time period as long as the magnitudes are measured in constant dollars. In this context, the appropriate comparison is the incremental costs and benefits between 1985 and 1990, using Freeman's estimates for 1985 and Carson and Mitchell's for 1990. After converting all estimates to 1990 dollars, these incremental values are as follows:

**Incremental Control Costs for 1985–1990:**

| | |
|---|---|
| 1990 Control Costs (EPA and Dept. of Commerce) | $44.0 billion |
| − 1985 Control Costs (Freeman) | 34.6 billion |
| Incremental Costs | $ 9.4 billion |

| FIGURE 14.4 | BENEFIT–COST ANALYSIS OF U.S. WATER CONTROL POLICY FOR THE 1985–1990 PERIOD: MARGINAL SOCIAL COST AND MARGINAL SOCIAL BENEFIT |
|---|---|

In this model, incremental costs for the 1985 to 1990 period are shown using the conventional marginal social cost (*MSC*) curve with an analogous interpretation on the benefit side. Notice that the 1990 abatement level, $A_{1990}$, occurs at a point *below* the efficient level, $A_e$, where *MSC* intersects *MSB*.

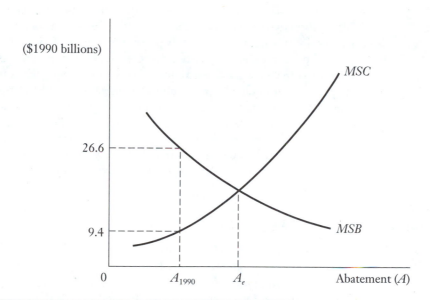

**Incremental Benefits for 1985–1990:**

| | |
|---|---|
| 1990 Benefits (Carson and Mitchell) | $46.7 billion |
| − 1985 Benefits (Freeman) | 20.1 billion[41] |
| Incremental Benefits | $26.6 billion |

These calculations communicate an important result. Since the incremental benefits are greater than the incremental costs, there is reason to believe that the post-1972 revisions to U.S. water legislation have not achieved an efficient abatement level. This result is illustrated in Figure 14.4, where incremental costs are shown using the conventional marginal social cost (*MSC*) curve with an analogous interpretation on the benefit side. Notice

---

[41] As noted above, this magnitude is the value of Freeman's estimate after being adjusted by Carson and Mitchell for number of households and inflation.

that the 1990 abatement level, $A_{1990}$, is *lower* than the efficient level, $A_e$, where *MSC* intersects *MSB*. This suggests that more stringent controls on polluting sources may be justified.

This assessment is an interesting one, but it is based on crude calculations. For one thing, as Carson and Mitchell assert, most U.S. waters are at a level above the nonboatable quality baseline assumed in the benefit estimate. Hence, costs to achieve swimmable quality are lower than they would be if all water bodies were actually at the baseline level. Furthermore, the calculations implicitly assume that the values between 1985 and 1990 are directly comparable, which is not the case on the benefit side. Because the 1990 benefit assessment is determined by the Contingent Valuation Method, it is a more comprehensive estimate than Freeman's because it includes some measure of existence value. Consequently, Freeman's estimate of $20.1 billion likely undervalues benefits for the 1985 period, which in turn means that incremental benefits are likely biased upward. It can be argued, however, that existence values in 1985 would not be large enough to change the *qualitative* result. In any case, until more accurate data are available, the conclusion that current U.S. regulations underallocate resources to water quality control is a tentative one at best.

# Conclusions

The water on earth has some natural capacity to replenish itself through the hydrological cycle. Likewise, water bodies have some ability to assimilate certain of the pollutants they receive. However, there is a limit to nature's restorative powers. Furthermore, the hydrological cycle that contributes to the restoration process is also the mechanism that can spread contamination. Water pollution is pervasive, and virtually every form of human activity and many natural processes contribute to the problem.

Although water pollution *is* widespread, society has come to recognize the problem and has begun to take action. In the United States, water quality legislation has been expanded and strengthened over the past several decades. This evolution coupled with what are unquestionably ambitious national objectives would seem to suggest that policy officials have made a concerted effort to respond to the country's water pollution problems. Despite these assertions, most argue that whatever legislative progress *has* been realized, it has happened at too slow a pace. There have been missed deadlines both in establishing effluent limitations and in setting the receiving water quality standards.

Even without the delays that admittedly have slowed the process, economic analyses suggest that the end result may not be an efficient solution. If this *is* the case, valuable resources are not being employed in their best possible use, and society is paying for the misallocation. Accepting that we cannot change the past, the real question is whether the nation can learn from its mistakes. There is still much to be done in revising existing policy and establishing new initiatives—a realization that is an integral part of Congress' recent deliberations to reauthorize the Clean Water Act.

An important motivation in moving national policy forward will be for Congress to consider how much progress has been made toward reaching national water quality objectives and at what measure of costs. Once done, it must determine how much of any realized improvement can realistically be attributed to existing policy. Finally, constructive revisions must be proposed, and feasible options formulated as needed. In the next chapter, we will examine the control instruments currently used to achieve national objectives—in a very real sense a textbook exposition of what U.S. policy makers are now undertaking as they continue to develop water quality policy for the nation.

## Summary

- The earth's water supply comes from two major sources, surface water and groundwater.

- Surface water and groundwater are linked together by the hydrological cycle, a model that explains the movement of water from the earth's atmosphere to the surface and back into the atmosphere.

- The two primary source categories of water pollution are point sources and nonpoint sources.

- Federal legislation on water pollution began with the Water Pollution Control Act of 1948. Provisions in the Water Quality Act of 1965 were the first to itemize states responsibilities in pollution control with some provision for federal oversight.

- In 1972, Congress passed the Marine Protection, Research, and Sanctuaries Act (MPRSA) to regulate ocean dumping. It also enacted the Federal Water Pollution Control Act (FWPCA), which shifted primary responsibility from states to the federal government. Further amendments were accomplished through the Clean Water Act (CWA) of 1977 and the Water Quality Act of 1987.

- The three most important objectives of the Clean Water Act are the zero discharge goal, the fishable–swimmable goal, and the no toxics in toxic amounts goal.

- U.S. law distinguishes among three categories of pollutants: toxic pollutants, conventional pollutants, and nonconventional pollutants.

- Surface water quality is defined in the Clean Water Act by receiving water quality standards. These standards assign a use designation for each water body and identify water quality criteria necessary to sustain designated uses.

- State authorities determine the use–support status of a water body by assessing its present condition and comparing it with what is needed to maintain its designated uses.

- One problem with the receiving water quality standards is that the EPA has not developed all the needed criteria documents to support states' use designations. Another is that states are not required by law to use a benefit–cost evaluation to establish these standards. Also, the link between receiving water quality standards and effluent limits is unclear since each is motivated differently—one by usage and the other by technology.

- According to a benefit–cost analysis of the Federal Water Pollution Control Act, the total social costs of regulatory control as of 1985 exceed the associated total social benefits. This suggests that too many resources were being allocated to water quality controls at that time.

- A more recent analysis, which used the Contingent Valuation Method to estimate benefits, found that as of 1990, the total social benefits of U.S. controls exceeded total social costs.

- Over the 1985 to 1990 period, estimates indicate that the incremental benefits exceeded incremental costs by $17.2 billion, suggesting that current legislation may underregulate polluting sources.

## Key Concepts

| | |
|---|---|
| surface water | toxic pollutants |
| groundwater | conventional pollutants |
| hydrological cycle | nonconventional pollutants |
| point source | receiving water quality standards |
| nonpoint source | use designation |
| zero discharge goal | water quality criteria |
| technology-based effluent limitations | use–support status |
| | numeric criteria |
| fishable–swimmable goal | narrative criteria |
| no toxics in toxic amounts goal | biocriteria |

# Review Questions

1. Use the concept of the hydrological cycle to explain how contamination of surface waters can also cause degradation of groundwater.

2. Refer to the Application on the Chesapeake Bay. Discuss both the natural and man-made conditions that are most responsible for the degradation of this water body.

3. Nutrients and pesticides are prevalent causes of water pollution. From an economic perspective, analyze why more has not been done to control agricultural runoff, the major source of these contaminants.

4. Identify two significant trends that characterize the evolution of U.S. water quality policy up through the 1987 Water Quality Act.

5. Using economic analysis, comment on the following statement: "The Clean Water Act's zero discharge goal was doomed from the beginning."

6. a. Discuss the major difficulties associated with estimating the benefits of water pollution abatement.
   b. Propose a policy approach which would promote states' use of benefit–cost analysis in setting and evaluating standards.

7. Reconsider the benefit–cost analyses of U.S. clean water policy offered by Freeman and by Carson and Mitchell. Are their different conclusions justified from a policy perspective? Why or why not? Are the respective estimation methods used by these researchers a factor in your assessment? Explain.

8. Consider the following benefit and cost relationships for mercury abatement ($A$).

$$MSB = 30 - 0.3A \qquad MSC = 16 + 0.2A$$
$$TSB = 30A - 0.15A^2 \qquad TSC = 16A + 0.1A^2,$$

where $A$ is the percentage of mercury abatement and dollar values are in millions.
   a. Suppose the mercury abatement level was set at 20 percent for 1997. Are net benefits positive or negative?
   b. On the basis of the efficiency criterion, should controls on mercury be tightened or relaxed? Support your response with specific calculations.

9. Visit the Web site at **www.epa.gov/OW/resources/9698/locate2. html**, and select a state in the nation. Write a one-page summary of

the surface and groundwater quality in that state. Provide some policy suggestions to improve water quality levels. Be specific.

## Additional Reading

Browner, Carol M. "The Administration's Proposals: We Must Embrace a Watershed Approach." *EPA Journal* (20)1–2, Summer 1994, pp. 6–9.

Dahl, T. E. *Wetlands Losses in the United States: 1780's to 1980's.* Washington, DC: U.S. Department of the Interior and U.S. Fish and Wildlife Service, 1990.

Knopman, Debra S., and Richard A. Smith. "20 Years of the Clean Water Act: Has U.S. Water Quality Improved?" *Environment* 35(1), January/February 1993, pp. 17–20, 34–41.

Newman, Alan. "A Blueprint for Water Quality." *Environmental Science and Technology* 27(2), 1993, pp. 223–25.

Rogers, Peter. *America's Waters.* Cambridge, MA: MIT Press, 1993.

Satchell, Michael. "Rape of the Oceans." *U.S. News and World Report*, June 22, 1992, pp. 64–68, 70–71, 75.

U.S. Environmental Protection Agency, Office of Water. *The Quality of Our Nation's Water: 1990.* Washington, DC, June 1992.

U.S. General Accounting Office. *Water Pollution: Improved Coordination Needed to Clean Up the Great Lakes.* Washington, DC, September 1990.

World Health Organization. "Health Hazards of Water Pollution." In David H. Speidel, Lon C. Ruedisili, and Allen F. Agnew, eds., *Perspectives on Water: Uses and Abuses.* New York: Oxford University Press, 1988.

## Related Web Sites

| | |
|---|---|
| Clean Water Action Plan | **www.epa.gov/cleanwater/action/toc.html** |
| Clinton's Clean Water Act Initiative | **www.cleanwater.gov** |
| EPA's Office of Water | **www.epa.gov/OW/** |
| *EPA Strategic Plan* | **www.epa.gov/ocfopage/plantoc.htm** |
| Legislative milestones in water protection | **www.epa.gov/OWOW/cwa/timeline.html** |
| National Marine Sanctuaries Program | **www.sanctuaries.nos.noaa.gov/welcome.html** |
| National Ocean Conference | **www.yoto98.noaa.gov/oceanc/index.html** |
| Report Brochure for the National Water Quality Inventory: 1996 Report to Congress | **www.epa.gov/OW/resources/brochure/broch2.html** |
| State Reports on Water Quality | **www.epa.gov/OW/resources/9698/locate2.html** |

# Appendix:
# A Reference to Acronyms and Terms
# in Water Quality Control Policy

### Environmental Economics Acronyms

| | |
|---|---|
| CVM | Contingent Valuation Method |
| *TSB* | Total social benefits |
| *TSC* | Total social costs |
| *MSB* | Marginal social benefit |
| *MSC* | Marginal social cost |

### Environmental Science Terms

| | |
|---|---|
| BOD | Biological oxygen demand |
| $\mu$g/L | Micrograms per liter |

### Environmental Policy Acronyms

| | |
|---|---|
| CWA | Clean Water Act |
| CEQ | Council on Environmental Quality |
| FWPCA | Federal Water Pollution Control Act |
| MPRSA | Marine Protection, Research, and Sanctuaries Act |
| OPA | Oil Pollution Act of 1990 |
| POTWs | Publicly owned treatment works |

# 15

---

# *Improving Water Quality: Controlling Point and Nonpoint Sources*

---

As we discussed in the last chapter, U.S. water policy has a fairly long history and one that has been characterized by a series of significant revisions. Yet few would debate the need for further reform. While there has been measurable improvement in U.S. water quality, some waterbodies continue to deteriorate, and most are still threatened by contamination—particularly the pollution from nonpoint sources. Furthermore, there is concern about certain of the policy instruments in use. A common criticism is an overreliance on uniform technology-based limits and a lack of economic incentives to get the job done. An investigation of these and other issues form the agenda for this chapter.

Our analysis will cover the following aspects of U.S. water quality policy:

- Effluent limitations and permits to control point sources

- Grant program for publicly owned treatment works (POTWs)

- Nonpoint source control policy

In each case, we present an overview of the control approach followed by an analytical evaluation. Where appropriate, the evaluation will be based on the economic criteria of efficiency and cost-effectiveness. We conclude the chapter with a discussion of several market-based instruments to achieve water quality, some of which are already in use on a limited scale. An appendix of acronyms and terms is provided at the end of the chapter for reference.

# Controlling Point Sources: Effluent Limitations

As evidence began to mount in the 1960s and early 1970s that U.S. waters were deteriorating, Congress realized that federal legislation needed a major overhaul. The result was a command-and-control policy dominated by uniform pollution standards—a response not unlike the initial reaction to America's air quality problems.

## An Overview of the Effluent Limits and National Permits

**technology-based effluent limitations** Standards to control discharges from point sources based primarily on technological capability.

Instituted through the Federal Water Pollution Control Act (FWPCA) of 1972, **technology-based effluent limitations** are the primary control instruments through which U.S. water quality objectives are to be achieved. Following a command-and-control approach, these standards limit the amount of contaminants that may be released into surface waters by point sources. As technology advances, these EPA-established regulations are to be revised to identify available control measures and practices. Over time, the intent is for effluents to be completely eliminated to meet the zero discharge goal.

All point sources are subject to these end-of-pipe effluent limits, which vary by the type of polluting source, the age of the facility, and sometimes by the contaminant released. For example, publicly owned treatment works (POTWs) must meet a special set of secondary treatment standards based on "best practicable control technology."[1] For *indirect* dischargers who release their effluents to these facilities, standards are established for the amount of pretreatment that must be done. Still other types of technology-based limits are defined for industrial dischargers who release their wastes *directly* into surface waters. A summary of the different technology-based effluent limits is given in Table 15.1, though the distinctions are sometimes more apparent than real. Note also that, although there are different standards for different types of polluting sources, they are applicable *uniformly* to all individual polluters within each designated category.

**National Pollutant Discharge Elimination System (NPDES)** A federally mandated permit system used to control effluent releases from direct industrial dischargers and POTWs.

Once determined, pollution limits for direct industrial dischargers and for POTWs are communicated through a permitting system called the **National Pollutant Discharge Elimination System (NPDES)** administered by the EPA. In simplest terms, this system prohibits any *direct* discharges into navigable waters without an NPDES permit.[2] These permits state precisely what the effluent limitations are as well as the requirements for monitoring and reporting. Though the EPA bears the overall responsibility of

---

[1] Secondary treatment refers to the second step in the waste treatment process in which bacteria consume the organic elements of waste.

[2] Permits are *not* required for indirect dischargers whose effluents are released to permitted POTWs. More information on the NPDES program can be found at **www.epa.gov/owmitnet/gen2.htm**.

| TABLE 15.1 | A SUMMARY OF EFFLUENT LIMITS SPECIFIED IN THE CLEAN WATER ACT |
| --- | --- |

| Standard | Polluting Source | Pollutant |
| --- | --- | --- |
| Best practicable technology currently available (BPT) (phased out; replaced by BAT and BCT) | Direct industrial dischargers | EPA-specified water pollutants |
| Best available technology economically achievable (BAT) | Direct industrial dischargers (existing sources) | Toxic and nonconventional pollutants |
| Best conventional control technology (BCT) | Direct industrial dischargers (existing sources) | Conventional pollutants |
| Best available demonstrated control technology (BADCT) | Direct industrial dischargers (new sources) | Toxic, conventional, and non-conventional pollutants |
| Pretreatment standards | Indirect industrial dischargers (existing and new sources) | Pollutants not susceptible to POTW treatment or potentially damaging to POTW operations |
| Secondary treatment standards | POTWs | Oxygen-demanding substances and suspended solids |

the program, states may administer NPDES permits as long as certain federal requirements are satisfied. Currently, 40 states have assumed this responsibility.[3]

Defining effluent limits for direct industrial dischargers is a monumental task, since they must reflect technological differences across industry groups such as steel mills, pesticide manufacturers, and fertilizer manufacturers. In fact, recall from the previous chapter that problems associated with these standards caused serious delays that slowed the nation's progress toward achieving its water quality objectives. For these and other reasons, these standards have been the subject of the most criticism by policy analysts, and hence we examine them more closely.

### Technology-Based Effluent Limitations for Direct Industrial Dischargers

While many factors are considered in setting the effluent limits for commercial facilities, the most important is the technological capability of each industry, meaning what *can* be achieved by using certain pollution control

---

[3] Council on Environmental Quality (January 1993), p. 230; Anderson, Lohof, and Carlin (August 1997), p. 4-3.

**best available demonstrated control technology (BADCT)** Technological basis for effluent limits applicable to new, direct industrial dischargers.

**best available technology economically achievable (BAT)** Technological basis for effluent limits applicable to existing, direct industrial dischargers of nonconventional and toxic pollutants.

**best conventional control technology (BCT)** Technological basis for effluent limits applicable to existing, direct industrial dischargers of conventional pollutants.

equipment. Because of this, these standards are called **technology-based effluent limitations.** However, polluting sources are allowed to choose the means by which the limit is achieved. This means that these effluent limitations are more accurately termed **performance-based standards.** These industry-specific standards are further delineated by the age of the polluting source, much as is done for air quality standards, with differences outlined between new and existing sources.

According to the Clean Water Act, a new source is one whose construction was begun *after* proposed regulations have been announced. For *new* industrial point sources, the effluent limitations are more stringent than those for existing sources, based on what the law calls **best available demonstrated control technology (BADCT).** In fact, wherever practical the BADCT limits are to explicitly prohibit effluent discharges.

For *existing* sources, two types of limits are applicable based on the type of pollutant released: **best available technology economically achievable (BAT)** standards for controlling nonconventional and toxic pollutants and **best conventional control technology (BCT)** standards, which are applicable to conventional pollutants.[4] These are considered minimum or baseline controls, allowing for more stringent standards to be used if needed to achieve the desired water quality for a particular waterbody. In setting the BAT standards, the "best available technology" for each industry is determined by a number of factors, including processes used, costs, energy requirements, and any impact on the environment beyond water quality. The determinants for the BCT standards add a consideration for the "reasonableness of the relationship" between the associated benefits and costs.

## Analysis of Effluent Limitations on Point Sources

The command-and-control approach to U.S. water quality policy has been the subject of some debate. Much of the criticism has been lodged against the technology-based effluent limits, which have been blamed for the lack of progress achieved by U.S. policy. Among the recognized problems are:

- Delays in establishing the standards

- Vague statutory definitions

- Meeting the zero discharge goal

- Lack of economic decision rules

---

[4] The BAT and BCT standards replaced the **best practicable technology currently available (BPT)** standards originally mandated in the 1972 Federal Water Pollution Control Act. The BPT standards are still applicable in a few instances, but these too will be replaced eventually.

These problems contribute to an inefficient solution to the U.S. water pollution problem. Even accepting the inefficiency, there is also strong evidence to suggest that the effluent limitations are not cost-effective.

## Administrative Delays

Under the 1972 law, industrial point sources were to have achieved an initial phase of compliance with the BPT standards by 1977 followed by a second phase calling for attainment of the BAT standards by 1983. As it turned out, neither of these deadlines were met, with much of the blame pointed at the EPA. Although the agency was to have determined all the BPT standards within one year of the act's enactment, it failed by a wide margin. While the one-year time frame may have been overly ambitious, it is harder to defend why the EPA had not defined all the BPT standards by 1977—the date by which polluters were to have achieved compliance with them. In any case, the first phase deadline had to be postponed to 1983. The second phase was not only delayed but also redefined through a new set of standards for conventional pollutants—the BCT standards, with the BAT standards retained specifically for toxics and nonconventional pollutants.

Over the past 20 years, the EPA's track record has been slow in developing and revising effluent guidelines—the basis for the federal limitations. Reportedly, there are still many industrial categories not covered by guidelines, and some that have been established are seriously out of date. Such delays are worrisome for toxic effluents, which pose relatively high environmental risks. The potential inequity of these risks is discussed in Application 15.1. Of the 51 sets of guidelines issued for point source categories, 35 are aimed specifically at toxics. However, 19 of these have not been revised in more than five years, and 9 of these 19 were established back in the 1970s.[5] What caused such delays? Part of the answer lies in how the standards were originally defined in the law.

## Imprecise and Inconsistent Definitions

**water quality–related limitations**
Modified effluent limits to be met if the desired water quality level is not being achieved, even if polluting sources are already satisfying the technology-based limits.

A fundamental problem with the effluent limitations is that they are not aligned with the nation's objectives. The basis of the standards is what is technologically feasible for each group of polluting sources—*not* what is necessary to achieve water quality. In fact, the potential inadequacy of these standards is implied by the statutes themselves. Modifications to the effluent limits are allowed in the form of **water quality–related limitations.** These are to be met by every polluting source if the desired level of water quality is not being achieved—even if a source is already satisfying the technology-based limits. While this may seem reasonable, it nonetheless speaks to the deficiency of the effluent limits. The very fact that modifications might be

---

[5] U.S. General Accounting Office (GAO) (July 1991), p. 27.

# Toxic Fish Consumption: Are the Risks Equitable?

There are two distinct motivations that affect an individual's decision to fish and consume the catch. One is purely recreational—fishing for sport. The other is subsistence—a means to sustain a regular food supply. Individuals engaging in either or both types of fishing are at greater risk of exposure to water pollution than the general population. It is true that those who fish purely for pleasure can minimize their risk by traveling to less polluted waters or by electing not to consume their catch. However, those who rely on fish and shellfish as part of their regular diet have limited options and therefore bear the highest relative risk of exposure to contaminated waters.

Researchers have tried to identify which population groups are most vulnerable to toxic contamination through fish consumption. Some studies suggest a relationship between race or ethnic origin and per capita fish consumption. For example, survey data indicate that people of color consume more fish than the rest of the population. Other studies find that Asians and African Americans eat more seafood than Caucasians. It is also the case that certain Native Americans comprise one of the largest subsistence fishing communities in the United States. Unfortunately, research on this latter group of Americans has been frustrated by a lack of data. The problem is that most studies use a sample of only *licensed* fishermen. Such data do not include *reservation-based* Native Americans because, according to treaty rights, these individuals do not have to obtain a state fishing license.

To illustrate the risk implications of such consumption differences, we consider the findings from a recent survey study of Detroit residents. According to this investigation, the average daily fish consumption across the entire sample is 18.3 grams per person per day. This statistic by itself is disconcerting, since the standard used in the state of Michigan to regulate point source toxic releases is based on a much lower consumption rate of 6.5 grams per person per day. However, the equity implications are even more troubling. The highest consumption rate across all defined population groups is for off-reservation Native Americans, estimated at 24.3 grams per person per day. The comparable statistics for African Americans, other minorities, and whites, are 20.3, 19.8, and 17.9, respectively. These data suggest that the risk of exposure to contaminated waters is not shared equally across population groups. Even worse, the extent of the inequality may be far greater than the estimates imply, since reservation-based Native Americans are unavoidably excluded from the analysis.

If researchers could determine the cause of the relatively high consumption rate for Native Americans, it might be possible to make inferences about the on-reservation population. It is true that some tribes have a cultural tradition of fishing-based economies, but it is also believed that Native Americans living on reservations depend on subsistence fishing for economic reasons. If this hypothesis is correct, then both cultural and economic factors play a role in fish consumption rates. Thus, it may be the case that reservation-based Native Americans consume fish at a higher rate than the available data suggest and therefore face a high health risk from toxic exposure.

SOURCES: Patrick C. West. "Invitation to Poison? Detroit Minorities and Toxic Fish Consumption from the Detroit River." In Bunyan Bryant and Paul Mohai, eds., *The Proceedings of the Michigan Conference on Race and the Incidence of Environmental Hazards*, 1992, as cited in Adler et al., 1993, p. 57; Patrick C. West. "Health Concerns for Fish-Eating Tribes? Government Assumptions Are Much Too Low." *EPA Journal* 18(1), March/April 1992, pp. 15–16; U.S. Environmental Protection Agency, Office of Communications, Education, and Public Affairs. "Federal Actions Address Environmental Justice." *EPA Activities Update*, Washington, DC: February 22, 1994a; Associated Press. "EPA: Fish Aren't Safe to Eat from 46 Waterways." *Brockton Enterprise*, November 20, 1992.

needed calls into question the characterization of these technology-based limitations as "best." The law acknowledges that these so-called best standards might not be sufficient to achieve water quality and further requires that some polluting sources abate beyond what has been determined as the "best conventional" or "best practicable" technology.

Still more problems arise in attempting to establish and implement these limitations for designated categories of point sources. While the use of technology-based limits appears to be an objective and scientific approach to standard setting, the law does not identify clearly what level of technology is appropriate. Phrases like "best practicable," "best available," and "best conventional" are not exact terms. Without more careful guidelines and objective decision rules, officials are left with the difficult task of trying to *infer* what these terms mean and how to implement them in practice.[6]

### Meeting the Zero Discharge Goal

In retrospect, the zero discharge goal established in 1972 was overly ambitious. Furthermore, its call for the complete elimination of water polluting effluents is likely an inefficient objective. Nonetheless, it was the target set by Congress under federal law.[7] The Clean Water Act also requires the EPA to review existing standards and successively advance them toward a zero limit as new technology becomes available. Yet, the EPA's effort in this regard has been something less than satisfactory. In the past 20 years, there have been only a few instances—among them onshore oil and gas wells—where this limit has been imposed. Although there is no comprehensive way to determine which of the effluent guidelines *should* have been moved to a zero discharge limit, there are indications that this may have been the case in certain instances. One example is the set of effluent standards for the organic chemicals, plastics, and synthetic fibers industry. Although the EPA knew that certain industrial plants had the capacity to achieve the zero discharge goal, it did not impose a zero effluent limit. The Natural Resources Defense Council challenged the EPA's position. Yet even after a federal appeals court required the agency to reassess its decision, the EPA did not change its ruling. Instead, it defended its position on the basis of differences across plants and its lack of resources to further investigate.[8]

### The Absence of Economic Decision Rules

Economists and other policy analysts are quick to point out the absence of economic decision rules in guiding the specification of the BAT and BCT

---

[6] CWA, Sec. 302; Freeman (1990), pp. 106–107.

[7] For a more detailed discussion of the zero discharge goal, see Van Putten and Jackson (1986).

[8] Adler, Landman, and Cameron (1993), pp. 143–44.

standards. To understand the implications of this deficiency, consider the following observations:

- The law does not mandate that the standards be set to maximize net benefits, which prevents the attainment of an efficient level of abatement.

- The standards are applied uniformly across dischargers within identified industrial groups, which impedes a cost-effective outcome.

**Lack of an Efficiency Criterion.**   The Clean Water Act allows for many factors to be considered in setting the BAT and BCT standards beyond technological feasibility, including economic consequences. However, the provisions do little more than list the relevant factors, offering no guidance as to how they are to be used in decision making. This is problematic, since the determinants itemized in the law are many, and they cross over from engineering and scientific criteria to economic considerations.

In the definition of the BCT standards for conventional pollutants, there is a troubling lack of precision in the reference to benefits and costs. According to law, officials are to consider the "... *reasonableness of the relationship between the costs of attaining a reduction in effluents and the effluent reduction benefits derived. . . .*" This is a far cry from setting abatement levels at the point where marginal benefits and costs are equal. Absent from the BAT standards is any reference to economic benefits. For these limits, which are applicable to toxics, only the cost of achieving the mandated effluent reduction is among the list of determinants.

Without congressional guidelines as to how all determinants, including economic ones, are to be measured and weighted relative to one another, the standards are left to discretion and subjective judgment. The result? Many disagreements and legal battles have ensued among industrial sources, government officials, and environmental groups, delaying the process on which much of the force of the law depends.[9] Beyond these general problems is the absence of any opportunity for the BAT standards to achieve an efficient level of abatement and only a very remote one for the BCT limits.

**Cost-Ineffective Decision Making.**   As we have discussed in previous chapters, in instances where the law prevents the use of the efficiency criterion, a "second-best" economic solution is to select cost-effective policy instruments to achieve an objective. Cost-effectiveness requires that abatement levels be set to achieve equal marginal abatement cost ($MAC$) levels across all polluters. However, under the Clean Water Act, the *uniformity* of

---

[9]Freeman (1978), p. 55.

| TABLE 15.2 | COST-EFFECTIVENESS OF MARKET-BASED CONTROLS: SOME QUANTITATIVE STUDIES |

| Investigators and Year | Command-and-Control Approach | Geographic Area | Ratio of Command-and-Control Cost to Least-Cost |
|---|---|---|---|
| Johnson (1967) | Equal Proportional Treatment | Delaware Estuary | 3.13 at 2 mg/l DO 1.62 at 3 mg/l DO 1.43 at 4 mg/l DO |
| O'Neil (1980) | Equal Proportional Treatment | Lower Fox River, WI | 2.29 at 2 mg/l DO 1.71 at 4 mg/l DO 1.45 at 6.2 mg/l DO |
| Eheart et al. (1983) | Equal Proportional Treatment | Willamette River, OR | 1.12 at 4.8 mg/l DO 1.19 at 7.5 mg/l DO |
| Eheart et al. (1983) | Equal Proportional Treatment | Delaware Estuary in PA, DL, and NJ | 3.00 at 3 mg/l DO 2.92 at 3.6 mg/l DO |
| Eheart et al. (1983) | Equal Proportional Treatment | Upper Hudson River, NY | 1.54 at 5.1 mg/l DO 1.62 at 5.9 mg/l DO |
| Eheart et al. (1983) | Equal Proportional Treatment | Mohawk River, NY | 1.22 at 6.8 mg/l DO |

NOTES:

DO = dissolved oxygen

mg/l = milligrams per liter

SOURCES: U.S. Environmental Protection Agency, Office of Policy, Planning and Evaluation. *The United States Experience with Economic Incentives to Control Environmental Pollution.* Washington, DC, July 1992, Table 2-1, p. 2-3–2-5, citing Tietenberg (1985) and the original sources given in the table.

the effluent limits likely prevents such an outcome. Although the law allows the limitations to be industry-specific, the associated effluent reductions must be achieved by all polluting sources within each industry group—regardless of firm-level differences in resource availability or technological expertise. If all dischargers must achieve the same standard, the only way the *MAC*s would be equivalent across polluters is if these polluting sources were identical. Since this clearly is not the case, the standards impose higher costs to society than are necessary.

Just how significant is the problem? Unfortunately, there is no research that provides a comprehensive answer to this question. However, some economic studies have attempted to quantify the cost implications of command-and-control instruments for specific waterbodies. Table 15.2 summarizes the findings of some of these. Each analysis determines a ratio of the cost of implementing a command-and-control approach to that of the least-cost market-based method. In each case, the ratio is significantly greater than 1, meaning that the command-and-control approach is relatively more costly than the use of economic incentives.

Underlying the problem of uniform standards is the lack of a reward system for efficient abaters to reduce effluents beyond legal limits. In fact, it has been argued that the structure of the effluent limits acts as a market *disincentive* for technological innovation.[10] Based on the law, if a discharger were to develop a new technology to reduce effluents more efficiently, the limits would be tightened based on the innovative discovery. This response would impose higher abatement costs on *all* effluent dischargers, including the innovating entity. Furthermore, since the limits are used to establish performance-based rather than technology-based standards, the law would not require polluters to employ the new technology. Thus, there is no market opportunity and hence no monetary reward for new innovation. The result is that most dischargers tend to employ the same technology used to set the limits in the first place, even though they are not required to do so. The rationale is to avoid the potential of an official compliance inquiry that might arise if an alternative technology were used.

## Waste Treatment Management and the POTW Program

An important and sometimes controversial aspect of the Clean Water Act is the federal funding authorized by Congress to support the construction of publicly owned treatment works (POTWs). POTWs are potentially significant sources of water contamination. Among the pollutants released by these facilities are pesticides, heavy metals, viruses, and bacteria. Unless municipal waste water is properly treated, the associated pollution threatens ground and surface water drinking supplies, aquatic life, recreational opportunities, and the overall health and stability of ecosystems. Responding to the potential risks, the Clean Water Act requires POTWs to satisfy technology-based secondary treatment standards and calls for federal appropriations to support this mandate. In fact, the fourth policy goal of the act specifically states:

> ". . . it is the national policy that Federal financial assistance be provided to construct publicly owned waste treatment works."

Investment in this program has been significant with a total federal outlay of $56 billion through fiscal year 1992.[11]

---

[10] Freeman (1978), p. 57.

[11] U.S. EPA, Office of Water (March 1994), p. 231.

## *The Pre-1987 Federal Grant Program*

**federal grant program** Provided major funding from the federal government for a share of the construction costs of POTWs.

Prior to 1987, one titled section of the Clean Water Act was devoted to waste treatment management. The voluminous and highly detailed set of provisions outlined the **federal grant program** for the construction of POTWs throughout the nation. Administered by the EPA, the program authorized billions of dollars of federal monies to municipalities each year, starting in 1973 with $5 billion and ending in 1990 with $1.2 billion. The federal share of construction costs was set at a maximum of 75 percent until 1984, when it was reduced to 55 percent.

## *Shift to the State Revolving Fund (SRF) Program in 1987*

**State Revolving Fund (SRF) program** Establishes state lending programs to support POTW construction and other projects.

As part of the 1987 Clean Water Act reauthorization, capitalization grants to each state are authorized to establish a revolving fund for water pollution projects. States are to provide 20 percent in matching funds to support the effort. This **State Revolving Fund (SRF) program,** which replaced the federal grants, is targeted to provide loans for POTW construction as well as for other environmental projects. Currently, every state and Puerto Rico has established an SRF program. Approximately $16 billion has been appropriated for this plan through 1995.[12]

# Analysis of the POTW Funding Program

Most understand the motivation of the federal subsidy of POTW construction, given the potential health and ecological threat of inadequate waste treatment. Yet the issue is not whether the intent of the program is well-founded but rather whether federal subsidies are an effective instrument to improve national water quality. To organize a study of this important component of U.S. water quality regulation, we consider three primary questions:

1. What is the relationship between the allocation of federal monies and any observed improvement in waste treatment across the United States?

2. To what extent is efficiency served in the federal aid plan, and what incentives or disincentives are present?

3. What are the equity implications in terms of who actually pays for this funding?

---

[12] U.S. EPA, Office of Water (January 1995) as cited in Anderson, Lohof, and Carlin (August 1997), p. 7-35. For more detail on the SRF program, visit **www.epa.gov/owm/finan.htm**.

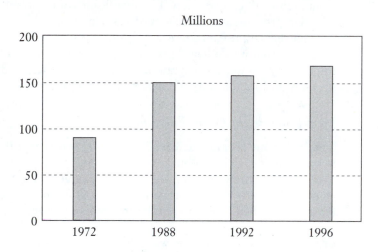

**FIGURE 15.1**  **U.S POPULATION SERVED BY MODERN SEWAGE FACILITIES**

Millions

SOURCE: U.S. Environmental Protection Agency, Office of Water. *The Clean Water State Revolving Fund: Financing America's Environmental Infrastructure—A Report of Progress.* Washington, DC: January 1995, pp. 6–14.

### *Assessing the Accomplishments Attributable to Federal Subsidies*

To argue that federal subsidies have been effective because municipal waste treatment has progressed measurably is falsely motivated. The problem is that such an argument implicitly assumes that the federal program is fully responsible for any observed improvement. In fact, there is evidence to suggest that this is not true at all.

It *is* true that an increasing proportion of the population is served by facilities using at least secondary treatment. In 1960, of all people served by a wastewater facility this proportion was only 4 percent. By 1980, the proportion rose to 73 percent. As of 1988, 138 million Americans were being served by at least secondary treatment—an 85-percent increase over 1977. More recent data show that as of 1996, over 150 million Americans were being served by modern waste treatment facilities, as indicated in Figure 15.1.[13] Yet, research shows that the majority of federal grant monies only *displaced* local funds that would have been allocated to POTW construction had the national program not been in place.

A 1984 empirical study found the rate of fund displacement to be 67 percent, meaning that every additional dollar of federal money *permanently*

---

[13] Council on Environmental Quality (1982), Table A-61, p. 295, as cited in Freeman (1990), p. 136; U.S. EPA (December 1990a), p. 2, U.S. EPA, Office of Water (January 1995) as cited in Anderson, Lohof, and Carlin (August 1997), Figure 7-3, p. 7-36.

displaced 67 cents of municipal spending on POTW construction.[14] This means that roughly two-thirds of every dollar in federal grant money acted only as a *substitute* for local funding with only a third as *incremental* investment in POTW construction. The significance of this result is that the observed improvement in wastewater treatment cannot be attributed fully to the grant program. Since only a portion of the federal monies was incremental to what would have been spent at the local level, only a fraction of the improved water quality can be linked to the federal aid program. See Application 15.2 for more on this important observation.

### Inefficiencies in the Grant Program

That the grant program achieved something less than a dollar-for-dollar improvement is an important realization, but it is only part of the story. It turns out that the well-intended plan was plagued by a number of inefficiencies. One was that the original program as established in 1972 did not assure that federal funds were allocated where incremental benefits were expected to be highest, such as in areas suffering from the worst pollution problems. This misallocation was not addressed until Congress passed the 1977 amendments, which required states to establish priority lists of facilities most in need of financial assistance.

Another problem is that the federal aid package was directed toward proper *construction* of new POTWs, yet lacked any provision to encourage *maintenance* and *operation* of these facilities once they had been built. In the 1970s, the EPA's annual inspections of POTWs revealed that only about 30 to 50 percent were operating satisfactorily. Similar findings were reported by the U.S. General Accounting Office (GAO).[15]

Most if not all of the grant program's inefficiencies were due to one important void—a lack of incentives. Fundamental to the program's design was the share of costs to be absorbed by the federal government. Recall this was set at a 75-percent maximum until 1984. Such a large proportion shifted most of the spending away from local governments, leaving them little incentive to minimize costs in the building of treatment facilities. In fact, with the addition of special aid from federal and state governments, some municipalities had to raise as little as 5 percent of the overall construction costs. Consequently, some POTWs are larger and more elaborate than necessary, motivated by a desire to attract industry and promote growth. Such excess capacity is a waste of economic resources and has been blamed for the observed poor operating performance of certain facilities.[16]

Responding to such inefficiencies, the U.S. government made several changes to the program. Grant awards were cut to $2.4 billion per year

---

[14] Jondrow and Levy (1984), p. 176.

[15] See Council on Environmental Quality (1976), p. 18, and U.S. EPA (November 1974), p. 16 reported in U.S. EPA (1975), p. IV-37.

[16] U.S. Congressional Budget Office (CBO) (1985a), pp. ix, 12.

## The POTW Grant Program: Displacement of Local Funding

In a 1984 empirical study, two researchers named Jondrow and Levy reported some interesting findings about the U.S. government's POTW grant program. Their investigation shows that every additional dollar of federal grants awarded *permanently* displaced 67 cents of municipal spending. The analysis further estimates that 28 cents of every dollar of unspent federal budget authority *temporarily* displaced (i.e., postponed) local expenditures on POTW construction. This latter form of displacement is associated mainly with the early phase of the federal program. At that point, local authorities had an incentive to delay expenditures while the federal program was getting under way or while awaiting federal approval of a proposed project.

According to Jondrow and Levy, these estimates translate to the following dollar values for 1973 at the start of the POTW grant program:

$1.05 billion in federal grants
− $714 million of municipal expenditures *permanently* displaced

$346 million
− $1.4 billion of municipal expenditure *temporarily* displaced

($1.06 billion) net addition to POTW construction

Based on these calculations, the total displacement of municipal spending on sewer treatment in 1973 was approximately 200 percent. Thus, the federal program actually caused a *reduction* in overall funding for POTW construction of over $1 billion. According to the researchers, the high proportion of displacement in 1973 is explained mainly by the large amount of temporary displacement that is more likely to occur in the initial stages of the program. Hence, this displacement would be expected to decline as the program became more established. In fact, conducting an analogous exercise for 1980, Jondrow and Levy find that temporary displacement was much lower for the period. Nonetheless, total displacement was still a significant amount, estimated to be $2.5 billion or 64 percent of the total grant expenditures for that year.

Related statistics bear out the findings of Jondrow and Levy. According to a report conducted by the Congressional Budget Office, the $18-billion federal grant program authorized in 1972 marked a major shift of the financial burden for POTW construction from local governments to the federal level. Over the 1970 to 1977 period, the annual federal outlay under the grant program rose from $0.5 to $6.0 billion with average local spending falling from $4.0 billion to $1.5 billion.

Collectively, these data suggest that the POTW grant program did not contribute dollar for dollar to improvements in U.S. water quality. Given the enormous financial investment in the program, this conclusion cannot be taken lightly. In simplest terms, this outcome is a classic case of misallocated resources. One can only hypothesize about the loss in environmental quality that could have been achieved had these billions of dollars been spent more wisely.

SOURCES: James Jondrow and Robert A. Levy. "The Displacement of Local Spending for Pollution Control by Federal Construction Grants." *American Economic Review* 74(2), 1984, pp. 174–178; U.S. Congressional Budget Office (CBO). *Efficient Investments in Wastewater Treatment Plants*. Washington, DC: U.S. Government Printing Office, 1985a, p. 4.

through 1985—a significant reduction from the range in prior years of $4 billion to $6 billion. Starting in 1985, the federal cost share was reduced to 55 percent. Tighter restrictions on grant authorizations were instituted, such as limiting funds to servicing the needs of existing rather than projected population levels. This latter revision was an attempt to discourage the deliberate construction of excess capacity as a way to promote local economic growth.[17] Finally, the Water Quality Act of 1987 altered the basic premise of the program from outright construction aid to funding for state-administered revolving loans.

Notice that these changes shift more of the cost burden back to local governments. In so doing, municipalities must become more self-sufficient in developing revenue sources to fund wastewater treatment and therefore should make more cost-effective decisions. Furthermore, concern for higher sewer fees prompts local residents to take a more active role in assuring that local officials carefully consider costs. According to a statistical analysis done by the U.S. Congressional Budget Office (CBO), increases in the lifetime local cost share of up to about 50 to 60 percent *do* lead to efficiency improvements measured in terms of declines in lifetime unit costs.[18] Finally, by placing responsibility closer to the funded project, decisions can better reflect state and local needs.

### Equity Implications

Beyond the efficiency issues, there are also equity considerations associated with the POTW program. Some municipalities had not yet been funded when the grant program was eliminated, placing a relatively higher cost burden on those communities. The inequity is greater for smaller, rural communities that are unable to take advantage of scale economies. The shift to the State Revolving Fund (SRF) program may have provided some measure of offset, however, since state-managed loans can be tailored through interest rates or grace periods to accommodate lower income or wealth levels of certain local communities.[19]

On a broader scale, there is evidence that the grant program did provide for a more equitable tax burden across the national population. A 1980 study showed that federal cost-sharing reduces the burden imposed on the lowest income families from 0.6 to 0.4 percent of family income and increases the comparable burden of highest income families from 0.3 to 0.8 percent.[20] It is not yet apparent as to how the allocation of the tax burden has been affected by the shift to the SRF program.

---

[17] See U.S. CBO (1985a), p. 3. For more on the inherent incentive toward excess capacity, see Freeman (1978), pp. 63-64.

[18] For more detail on this study, consult U.S. CBO (1985a), Chapter II.

[19] U.S. CBO (1985a), pp. 54, 59-60.

[20] Gianessi and Peskin (1980).

# Controlling Nonpoint Sources[21]

In 1987, the federal government added a seventh policy goal calling for the development of programs to control nonpoint polluting sources.

> "... it is the national policy that programs for the control of nonpoint sources of pollution be developed and implemented in an expeditious manner so as to enable the goals of this Act to be met through the control of both point and nonpoint sources of pollution."

**Nonpoint Source Management Program** A three-stage, state-implemented plan aimed at nonpoint source pollution.

This addition to the national list of objectives was in response to the growing awareness that these diffuse sources are major contributors to surface water and groundwater pollution. Enacted officially as Section 319 of the Water Quality Act of 1987, the **Nonpoint Source Management Program** was launched as a three-stage plan to be implemented by states with federal approval and financial assistance. The first step of the program calls for states to prepare assessment reports in which they identify waters that cannot achieve or maintain water quality standards without some action taken toward nonpoint sources. They must also identify categories of nonpoint sources or specific point sources responsible for the problem.[22] In the second stage, states must develop management programs in which they designate **best management practices (BMP)** to reduce pollution from every identified category, subcategory, or individual nonpoint source, taking into account the impact on groundwater resources. As of 1992, 51 states and territories have full EPA approval of their management programs. The final step calls for implementation of these programs over a multiyear time period.

**best management practices (BMP)** Strategies other than effluent limitations to reduce pollution from nonpoint sources.

To support states' efforts, federal grants are available for up to 60 percent of the total costs incurred. Through fiscal year 1996, federal appropriations totaled over $470 million.[23] In 1991, the EPA issued final guidance on how these funds are to be awarded and managed. This guidance encourages states to focus on high-priority activities, such as dealing with high-risk nonpoint problems, promoting comprehensive watershed management, and protecting sensitive and ecologically significant waters such as wetlands, estuaries, and scenic rivers. In 1989, the EPA developed its *Nonpoint Source Agenda for the Future* to help define national goals for nonpoint source pollution and to find appropriate mechanisms to achieve them. Application 15.3 has more on this national agenda.

---

[21] The following is drawn from CWA, Sec. 319. Nonpoint Source Management Programs and U.S. EPA, Office of Water (March 1994), pp. 247–48. For online information about the EPA's Nonpoint Source Pollution Control Program, visit **www.epa.gov/OWOW/NPS/**.

[22] A summary of these reports was published by the EPA in 1992 in *Managing Nonpoint Source Pollution*.

[23] Council on Environmental Quality (1997), p. 236.

# The EPA's *Nonpoint Source Agenda for the Future*

To help define objectives for nonpoint source programs and ways to implement them, the EPA drafted a *Nonpoint Source Agenda for the Future* in 1989. This agenda outlines a comprehensive approach to controlling nonpoint sources and achieving the policy goals of the Clean Water Act. Working with state and local governments, the EPA hopes to eliminate what it perceives to be significant barriers that hinder successful implementation of nonpoint source control programs. To date, three such barriers have been identified:

- Inadequate public awareness of the nonpoint pollution problem
- Inadequate knowledge or transfer of knowledge of successful solutions to nonpoint pollution
- Inadequate incentives to correct nonpoint source pollution

The identification of these barriers gives the agenda direction and helps to establish priorities for state governments and local authorities. Implementation is to be carried out through five themes that characterize the agenda and hence the EPA's overall objectives. What follows is a brief description of each theme.

### Themes of the *Nonpoint Source Agenda for the Future*

| | |
|---|---|
| **Public Awareness:** | To help states and local governments educate the public about the effects of nonpoint source pollution. |
| **Successful Solutions:** | To assist state and local governments by establishing information networks to communicate feasible solutions to existing problems and strategies to avoid future problems. |
| **Economic Forces:** | To provide financial incentives to prevent or reduce nonpoint source pollution and to eliminate any that encourage environmentally damaging activities. |
| **Regulatory Solutions:** | To assist states and localities in developing regulatory solutions through the use of a clearinghouse and information transfer workshops. |
| **Good Science:** | To develop scientific criteria and monitoring protocols that can be used to evaluate nonpoint source pollution and establish sound control programs at the state and local levels. |

Through this comprehensive agenda, the EPA hopes to provide the national leadership needed for state and local governments to identify, solve, and prevent the significant problem of nonpoint source water pollution.

SOURCES: U.S. Environmental Protection Agency, Office of Water. *National Water Quality Inventory: 1990 Report to Congress.* Washington, DC, April 1992a, p. 149; U.S. Environmental Protection Agency, Office of Water. *Managing Nonpoint Source Pollution.* Washington, DC, January 1992, pp. 7–10.

# Analysis of Controls on Nonpoint Sources

There is no debate that the emphasis of water pollution control in the United States has been on point sources. Through 1987, policy officials focused their energies on developing standards, issuing permits, and monitoring these more visible and obvious sources of contamination. Over time, it became increasingly apparent that these efforts were insufficient. Nonpoint source pollution from land runoff and atmospheric deposition was continuing to threaten surface water and groundwater supplies, and existing policy was simply not designed to deal with it. In 1994, EPA Administrator Carol Browner characterized the extent of the problem as follows:

> "The single greatest remaining threat to America's rivers, lakes, and estuaries is polluted runoff, sometimes called nonpoint source pollution. Silt, pesticides, fertilizer, and other pollutants are carried off farms, suburban lawns, industrial plants, and city streets into waterbodies whenever it rains."[24]

Since the 1987 provisions delegate much of the implementation to state governments, we need to consider the reasonableness of this decision. What are the pros and cons? We also must evaluate what the federal government is doing vis-à-vis what is needed to support states' efforts.[25]

## Delegating Control to the States: The Pros

One factor in support of delegating nonpoint source control to state governments is the variability of nonpoint source pollution. Not only are these sources difficult to identify and isolate, but the extent of the associated damage is unpredictable. A major source of the problem is land runoff from farms, city streets, mines, construction sites, and so on. Because runoff is influenced by precipitation, the resulting contamination is affected by many exogenous factors such as weather, geological patterns, and soil conditions. Not only are these factors uncontrollable, but they also vary considerably from location to location. Logically, the use of broad-based, uniform controls is likely to be ineffective and difficult to implement. In a 1984 report on nonpoint source pollution, the EPA acknowledged this point:

> "Flexible, site-specific, and source-specific decision making is the key to effective control of nonpoint sources. Site-specific decisions must consider the nature of the watershed, the nature of the

---

[24] Browner (Summer 1994), p. 6.

[25] Much of the following is drawn from U.S. GAO (October 1990), Chapter 2. Another comprehensive examination of policy on nonpoint source pollution is U.S. EPA, Office of Policy, Planning and Evaluation (June 29, 1992). A review of the EPA's 12 findings in this source is given in Adler et al. (1993), pp. 188–89.

waterbody, the nature of the nonpoint source(s), the use impairment caused by the nonpoint source(s), and the range of management practices available to control nonpoint source pollution."[26]

Another factor influencing the coordination of effort between state and federal authorities is the relationship between nonpoint source pollution and land use practices. Land use practices include such activities as agriculture, mining, forestry, and urban development, all of which historically have been controlled by local governments. It therefore becomes a politically sensitive issue when the federal government sets policy that dictates how a state or local community is to use its own land resources. A good example is environmental policy affecting forestry—an industry that can harm the ecology but also often sustains local or regional economies. In some sense, the 1987 nonpoint source program attempts to address the interests of both sides by giving states the major responsibility of policy design and implementation, while assigning oversight to the EPA through its review of states' assessments and programs.

### Delegating Control to the States: The Cons

Although there is some logic to controlling nonpoint pollution close to the source, state governments often lack information to carry out their responsibilities. Data on the extent of water contamination are inadequate, due in large part to ineffective monitoring systems. Though the Clean Water Act requires states to assess surface waters and report the findings every two years, the law does not specify what proportion of these waters is to be included in the biennial review.[27]

Adding to the dilemma is the fact that most state assessment data are collected from monitoring systems designed to detect point source pollution, which do not give an accurate picture of the damage from nonpoint sources. Insufficient monitoring data not only hinders environmental assessment but also impedes the evaluation of states' management programs and their designation of best management practices (BMP). Without good monitoring systems, changes in contaminant levels cannot be properly measured. Hence, incentives to propose new plans or revisions to existing ones are limited at best.

Finally, there is always the potential problem of inconsistent pollution controls when state governments are in charge of policy implementation. Such inconsistencies are problematic since water contamination in one state can flow downstream into another state's jurisdiction. Anticipating this possibility, Congress did provide for intervention by the EPA to arrange for interstate management conferences. If a state's waterbody is not meeting

---

[26] U.S. EPA (1984b), pp. xiii–xiv.

[27] U.S. GAO (July 1991), pp. 21–22.

standards due to nonpoint sources in another jurisdiction, that state can petition the EPA to arrange a conference to solve the problem.

## Analyzing the Federal Role in Nonpoint Source Controls

Although states have the primary responsibility for implementing nonpoint source controls, they require support from the federal government on a number of fronts. The problem is that policy resources dedicated to water quality have long been focused on point sources, and consequently some adjustments must be made at the federal level. To illustrate, we consider two areas in need of attention:

- Allocation of resources between point and nonpoint source pollution policy
- Coordination of nonpoint source programs with other federal programs

**Resource Allocation.**    Because of the historic emphasis on point source water pollution, federal funds are needed to fill information voids about nonpoint source pollution. For example, states need water quality criteria to develop standards suited to these diffuse sources of impairment. Unfortunately, the EPA's experience with establishing criteria for point source pollutants is not directly applicable, so the task is expected to be very time-intensive. Similarly, efforts must be made to improve the nation's monitoring technologies, or "protocols" as they are called. Here again, the work to date has focused on measuring contaminants released by point sources. It now must be extended to establishing better protocols aimed at the more complex problem of nonpoint source pollution. Attending to these needs will require substantial resources.

Table 15.3 shows the relative spending on point versus nonpoint source pollution control for selected years starting in 1972 and projected through 2000. The data clearly indicate the national emphasis on point source control. Notice also that the *proportion* of total spending dedicated to nonpoint source pollution shows a decline from 6.2 percent in 1972 to a projected 1.7 percent in 2000. Part of the reason is that the EPA is charged with much greater responsibility for controlling point sources. However, there are two other observations that are more difficult to explain. First, the EPA has not been aggressive in using the funds that *have* been authorized by Congress for nonpoint sources. Through 1991, the EPA had requested only $22 million of the $400 million approved for Section 319 programs, and through 1993 the accumulated requests totaled $200 million. Second, the proportion of funding across the two types of sources is *not* supported by relative risk analysis. A recent study showed that while health risks from point and nonpoint source pollution are comparable, nonpoint sources pose

| TABLE 15.3 | ANNUALIZED EXPENDITURES ON POINT VERSUS NONPOINT SOURCE POLLUTION CONTROL ($1986 MILLIONS) |
|---|---|

| | Year | | | | |
|---|---|---|---|---|---|
| **Program** | **1972** | **1980** | **1987** | **1995** | **2000** |
| Point Source | $8,543 (93.8%) | $22,116 (97.2%) | $33,642 (97.7%) | $47,300 (98.1%) | $56,604 (98.3%) |
| Nonpoint Source | 567 (6.2%) | 647 (2.8%) | 779 (2.3%) | 893 (1.9%) | 959 (1.7%) |
| Water Quality Total[a] | $9,110 (100%) | $22,763 (100%) | $34,421 (100%) | $48,194 (100%) | $57,563 (100%) |

NOTES: Relative proportions are given in parentheses.

[a] Total excludes expenditures on drinking water controls.

SOURCE: U.S. Environmental Protection Agency, Office of Policy, Planning, and Evaluation. *Environmental Investments: The Cost of a Clean Environment*. Washington, DC, December 1990, Table 3-3, p. 3-3.

a much greater risk to ecosystems.[28] As discussed in previous chapters, policy controls do not always follow scientific findings on actual risk but instead are based on public perceptions of risk. Hence, there is a need to improve public awareness about nonpoint source pollution—one of the themes of the EPA's *Nonpoint Source Agenda for the Future* discussed previously.

**Coordination with Other National Programs.** Another issue to be resolved at the federal level is the conflict between water quality objectives and other regulations. This becomes an issue for government programs supporting industries like agriculture and forestry, which are major contributors to nonpoint source pollution. Consider, for example, the agricultural commodity programs operated by the U.S. Department of Agriculture (USDA). These programs are designed to stabilize and support crop prices, which in turn protects the incomes of the nation's farmers. Over two-thirds of U.S. croplands are enrolled in these programs. To operationalize the price protection, an acreage base is established for a given program crop along with a crop yield based on that acreage, both of which are determined from historical values. Farmers participating in this program cannot plant crops other than the so-called program crop, nor can they plant more

---

[28] The issue of funding priorities between point and nonpoint sources is discussed in U.S. GAO (October 1990), pp. 49–53; and Adler et al. (1993), p. 256. Findings on relative risks between the two sources are given in U.S. EPA (August 1989).

than their base acreage in that crop. While such supply restrictions help to maintain crop prices, they also promote practices that can lead to water pollution.

A case in point is the incentive for farmers to specialize in certain program crops, since benefits are based on historical production levels. The problem is that repeated plantings of the same crop year after year depletes the soil and makes plantings more vulnerable to pests. Consequently, farmers tend to rely more on agrichemicals such as fertilizers and pesticides, both of which contribute to agricultural runoff—a problem responsible for the contamination of 50 to 70 percent of assessed U.S. surface waters.[29] Recognizing the conflict, the EPA and the USDA have begun to coordinate the Nonpoint Source Management Program with the USDA's projects. There have even been some arrangements for personnel sharing between the two—an initiative that has brought both agencies new insights that are proving valuable to their respective programs.[30]

# Proposals for Reform: Using the Market

On balance, federal officials have been slow to react to the inefficiency and cost-ineffectiveness of U.S. water quality policy. There are, however, indications that this trend might be changing. Following the lead of several European countries, the United States is beginning to consider the potential cost savings of using market-based approaches to water quality policy. In fact, some local governments are currently experimenting with these types of incentive-based policy tools. To analyze these economic instruments, we consider two market approaches to point source pollution control: effluent fees and tradeable effluent permits. We then extend the analysis to the more complex case of nonpoint source control by studying product charges and effluent reduction trading within a "bubble."

**volume-based effluent fee** Based on the quantity of pollution discharged.

**pollutant-based effluent fee** Based on the degree of harm associated with the contaminant being released.

## Market Approaches to Point Source Pollution

**Effluent Fees.** As discussed in Chapter 5, an **effluent fee** is a charge based on the discharge of pollution. In order for an effluent charge to provide an incentive for pollution reduction, it must be based on either the volume or the type of effluent released. For example, a **volume-based** fee is imposed on a per unit basis so that polluters pay higher amounts for larger quantities of discharges. Similarly, to discourage the release of more damaging effluents like those containing toxics, the fee should be **pollutant-based,**

---

[29] U.S. GAO (October 1990), pp. 15–17.

[30] For further information, consult U.S. GAO (October 1990), Chapter 4. A related discussion is given in Harrington, Krupnick, and Peskin (1985).

**APPLICATION 15.4**

## Germany's Effluent Charge System

Like most advanced countries, Germany experienced substantial economic growth and industrialization during the 1960s. By the early 1970s, this surge of development had taken its toll on Germany's natural environment, particularly its water resources. In some regions, the contamination was so severe it was impeding customary uses of some waterbodies.

Germany's first line of defense was to create the Cabinet Committee for Environmental Protection, which it established in 1971. By design, this body was responsible for coordinating all environmental activities at the federal level of government. In one of its first official documents, the committee advocated the use of market-based instruments. Among its recommendations was the implementation of an effluent charge to help restore Germany's water quality. As proposed, this charge was to be levied on every discharger in an amount equal to the *incremental* damages caused by its effluents—precisely the kind of solution economists endorse.

Response to the committee's recommendation for an effluent charge was mixed. Support came from some international organizations such as the Organisation for Economic Co-operation and Development (OECD) and the 1972 World Environmental Conference sponsored by the United Nations. However, the Länder (i.e., all the states of the Federal Republic of Germany) opposed the shift to an economic approach. Instead, they supported a more moderate transition with an *integration* of market-based instruments into the country's existing command-and-control structure. There was also strong opposition from most of Germany's industrial sector. Ultimately, a revised initiative was imposed, which integrated an effluent charge system into Germany's existing command-and-control regulatory framework.

In September 1976, the German government passed the Effluent Charge Law, which combined a discharge fee with a permit structure similar to the U.S. system. Implemented in 1981, the new law requires each German state to levy an effluent charge on all direct dischargers of such pollutants as settleable solids, mercury, and cadmium. One of the unique elements of this landmark legislation is a market-based incentive that reduces a polluter's charge liability if it complies with federally mandated minimum standards. Studies indicate that this incentive has had its intended qualitative effect—at least in some German cities and towns. Some municipalities and industrial dischargers claim that this aspect of the new law was the primary motivation for their increased investment in waste treatment.

From a financial perspective, the effluent charge adds to government revenues. There is also anecdotal evidence that this instrument can provide significant cost savings. Germany's Council of Experts on Environmental Questions claims that an effluent charge can achieve a given level of water quality for about 33 percent less than if uniform standards were used. Finally, there are indications that the effluent charge may stimulate innovation in pollution abatement. According to the OECD, Germany's clean water technology market has grown considerably and is now the largest segment of its environmental protection market nationwide.

SOURCES: Gardner M. Brown Jr. and Ralph W. Johnson, "Pollution Control by Effluent Charges: It Works in the Federal Republic of Germany, Why Not in the U.S." *Natural Resources Journal* 24, October 1984, pp. 929–66; and J. B. Opschoor and Has B. Vos. *Economic Instruments for Environmental Protection.* Paris: Organisation for Economic Co-operation and Development, 1989.

meaning it is higher for discharges containing more harmful substances. Countries such as Australia, Belgium, France, Germany, and Spain have instituted effluent charges to control water contamination.[31] Application 15.4

---

[31] Organisation for Economic Co-operation and Development (1994), p. 68. For a summary of certain of these effluent charge systems, see Hahn (1989).

FIGURE 15.2

## COST-EFFECTIVENESS OF A PER UNIT EFFLUENT FEE

Suppose the government sets a per unit effluent fee for releases of some toxic water pollutant. The decisions of two hypothetical firms are shown below, each facing different *MAC* curves but the same marginal effluent fee (*MEF*). Firm 1 faces $MAC_1$ and abates $A_1$ units of effluent, and Firm 2 faces $MAC_2$ and abates $A_2$ units. Although the individual abatement levels are different, the associated *MAC* incurred by each firm is the same.

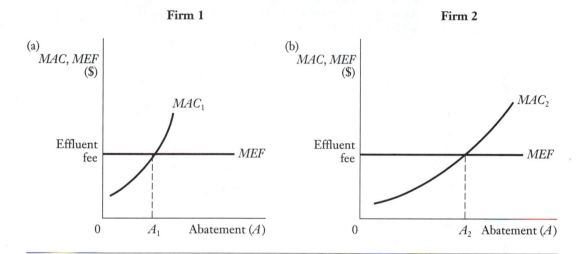

discusses Germany's experience with this market-based instrument. World-wide use of effluent fees is still somewhat limited. There are complications in setting the level of the fee, and because of the complexity, administrative costs can be prohibitive.[32]

To illustrate these issues, suppose the government sets a per unit effluent fee for releases of some toxic water pollutant. The outcome would be that each polluting source would abate up to the point where its marginal abatement cost (*MAC*) equaled the fee. Since all *MAC*s would be equal, the effluent charge would yield a cost-effective solution. This is shown in Figure 15.2 for two hypothetical firms, each facing different *MAC* curves but the same marginal effluent fee (*MEF*). Firm 1 faces $MAC_1$ and abates $A_1$ units of effluent, and Firm 2 faces $MAC_2$ and abates $A_2$ units. Although the abatement amounts are different, the associated level of *MAC* for each firm is the same.

---

[32] Several economists have examined the advantages and limitations of effluent fees or taxes. Examples include Rose-Ackerman (1973, 1977) and Herzog (1976), each of whom gives the basic framework of an effluent charge approach with discussion of its real-world limitations. Russell (1979) discusses the major considerations in designing an effluent charge system.

| FIGURE 15.3 | **INEFFICIENCY OF A NATIONAL PER UNIT EFFLUENT FEE** |

In the model below, the *MSC* is the same for two regions, but there are different *MSB* curves—$MSB_{low}$ in a low population area and $MSB_{high}$ in a high or densely populated area. If the per unit effluent fee is set at *MEF*, each region will abate $A_o$ units. Notice that $A_o$ is above the efficient level for the sparsely populated region, $A_{low}$, and below the efficient level for the densely populated region, $A_{high}$. If the objective were to achieve efficiency at the regional level, regulatory officials would have to establish a unique effluent fee for every location corresponding to the abatement level where the respective *MSB* and *MSC* were equal.

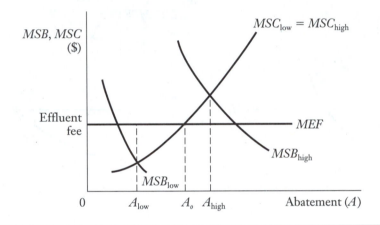

Recognize, however, that the combined abatement level achieved by all firms would not be efficient unless the marginal social cost of abatement (*MSC*) (i.e., the horizontal sum of all the individual *MAC*s ($MAC_{mkt}$) plus the government's marginal cost of monitoring and enforcement (*MCE*), were equal to the associated marginal social benefit of abatement (*MSB*). Identifying the *MSB* and the *MSC* in practice is very difficult, and the costs of collecting the necessary data would likely be prohibitive. Even if this task were somehow accomplished, the solution would be efficient only in the aggregate and *not* for the specific waterbodies affected. Unless the marginal benefits and costs at each pollution site were identical, the fee would not yield a waterbody-specific efficient outcome. For example, the fee would effectively overregulate polluters in regions where the associated marginal benefits of abatement were relatively low, such as in sparsely populated locations, and would underregulate polluters where the conditions were reversed, holding all else constant.

Such an outcome is shown in Figure 15.3, where it is assumed for simplicity that the *MSC* is the same for two regions, but there are different

*MSB* curves—$MSB_{low}$ in a low population area and $MSB_{high}$ in a high population area. If the per unit effluent fee is set at *MEF*, each region will abate $A_0$ units. Notice, however, that $A_0$ is *above* the efficient level for the sparsely populated region, $A_{low}$, and *below* the efficient level for the densely populated region, $A_{high}$. Hence, if the objective were to achieve efficiency at the regional level, regulatory officials would have to impose a unique effluent fee for every location corresponding to the abatement level where the respective *MSB* and *MSC* are equal. The data required to implement such a complex plan coupled with the sophisticated monitoring needed would make this approach highly impractical—at least on a national scale. However, there are opportunities for states to institute such programs, and in fact some have begun to do so. Officials in a number of states like Florida, Connecticut, and New York have instituted volume-based fees, while California, Indiana, Louisiana and others have set fees that vary with volume and toxicity.[33] A similar approach is being used by some POTWs.[34] These initiatives are extensions of the permit fees implemented through the National Pollutant Discharge Elimination System (NPDES). Normally, these charges are independent of the type or amount of effluent being discharged. Thus, the associated *MEF* is zero, offering no incentive for polluting sources to abate.[35]

**tradeable effluent permit market**
The exchange of "rights to pollute" among polluting sources.

**Tradeable Effluent Permits.** An alternative economic instrument is the establishment of a **tradeable effluent permit market.** This could be implemented using the existing NPDES, by issuing each permit as a set of tradeable, per unit "rights to pollute." As discussed in Chapter 5, there are potential gains from trading as long as *MAC*s differ across polluting sources. If a discharger does not need to release all the effluents allowed, it can hold the excess rights for future use or sell them to other dischargers. If it needs to release more than allowed by law, it must either abate more or buy the rights it needs from polluters holding an excess. Low-cost abaters will have excess rights, which they would be willing to sell at any price greater than or equal to their *MAC*. High-cost abaters would be willing to buy these as long as the selling price is less than or equal to their own *MAC*. Market forces will establish a price for permits such that all firms abate to the point where the associated level of *MAC* is equal across firms—a cost-effective solution.

---

[33] Duhl (December 1993), p. 10.

[34] For POTWs, incentive effects appear to occur only for pollutant-based charges and not for those tied to volume. See Sims (1977) as cited in U.S. EPA, Office of Policy, Planning, and Evaluation (July 1992), p. 3–2. To date, there has been no comprehensive study of the incentive effects associated with analogous charges set through the NPDES.

[35] The EPA's Office of Policy, Planning, and Evaluation launched a project to devise a sliding scale fee system based on the toxicity of discharges in the states for which the agency writes NPDES permits. The revenues received under the new system would be held in a Water Pollution Trust Fund. Part of the monies would be used to cover administrative costs, with the remainder distributed to states for initiating pollution prevention practices. See U.S. GAO (July 1991), p. 39.

| TABLE 15.4 | EXAMPLES OF POINT-TO-POINT TRADEABLE EFFLUENT PERMIT MARKETS |
|---|---|

| State | Waterbody | Pollutant |
|---|---|---|
| Wisconsin | Fox River | biological oxygen demand, nutrients |
| California | South San Francisco Bay | copper |
| Colorado | Cherry Creek | phosphorus |
| Florida | Tampa Bay | nitrogen, total suspended solids |

SOURCE: U.S. Environmental Protection Agency, Office of Water. *Effluent Trading in Watersheds Policy Statement*, **www.epa.gov/ OWOW/watershed/tradetbl.html**, last updated January 5, 1998.

Table 15.4 lists some of the applications of point-to-point tradeable effluent permit markets, including a frequently cited program designed to clean up the Fox River. In 1981, Wisconsin officials instituted this plan for one type of pollutant being released to the Fox River.[36] The initial allocation of permitted discharges was based on historical data and was valid for a five-year period. Officials expected that unequal *MAC*s among polluting sources would provide the impetus for active trading of effluent reduction credits. One researcher estimated that this market could potentially yield a cost savings of about $7 million. However, the savings have not materialized, since only one trade has taken place.[37] Why? Several conditions may justify the absence of trading in this case. For one thing, participants in the program still had to meet the federally established technology-based effluent limits. Since such standards constrain independent decision making, they likely limit the incentive mechanism of the trading program. Furthermore, two of the major classes of dischargers involved, namely pulp and paper mills and municipal waste treatment plants, do not operate in competitive markets, which also dampens market forces. Finally, the key participants in the program did not fully support the plan, further limiting its potential for success.[38] These observations suggest that market conditions and existing regulatory constraints must be considered in the design of a successful trading program.

### Market Approaches to Nonpoint Source Pollution

Using a market approach to reduce nonpoint source pollution is more complex because the problem itself is more difficult to identify. The dilemma

---

[36] The pollutant group targeted by the program are so-called BOD-based effluents. BOD stands for biological oxygen demand, which measures the amount of oxygen needed by microorganisms to decompose organic compounds. Hence, as the waste level in a waterbody rises, the BOD measure rises as well.

[37] U.S. EPA, Office of Policy, Planning, and Evaluation (July 1992), p. 5-15, citing O'Neil et al. (1983) on the cost-savings estimation.

[38] Hahn (1989).

becomes apparent if we reconsider a pricing instrument like an effluent fee in this context. Implemention is problematic, since land runoff and atmospheric deposition arise from a number of sources. Since the contribution of each polluting source is indeterminate, an effluent fee cannot be implemented fairly—at least not in the usual sense. If policy makers were to impose a uniform fee on all known contributors to a runoff problem, the result would be inequitable. The fees would be passed on to consumers of the goods produced at these sites through higher prices, and those individuals would bear most of the costs. However, the benefits of the reduced runoff would accrue primarily to individuals located near the waterway.[39] Because of these difficulties, an indirect approach can be used such as a product charge levied on the commodity whose usage adds to a known runoff problem.

**product charge**
Fee added to the price of a pollution-generating product based on its quantity or some attribute responsible for pollution.

**Product Charge.**    An often cited example of using a **product charge** to control runoff is the use of a fertilizer tax. Since agricultural runoff is a major contributor of nonpoint source pollution, such a market instrument appears to have merit. Imposing a tax on fertilizer causes its effective price to rise, which in turn should reduce the quantity demanded. In theory, the optimal tax is one that covers the marginal external costs associated with fertilizer use in the production of agricultural products. In practice, however, the operative issue is whether the demand response to the elevated effective price is sufficient to measurably reduce the runoff problem.

As of 1994, 46 states had imposed such a tax, but the rates apparently were too low to have much of an effect on fertilizer consumption. Tax rates range from less than $1.00 to $4.00 per ton—a very small proportion of the product's price, which is anywhere from $60 to $200 per ton. With taxes levied at no higher than a 2.5 percent rate, and usually much lower than that, the decline in consumption has been negligible.[40] Even if the rates were elevated, the effect on quantity demanded would likely not be sufficient to significantly mitigate the associated pollution problem. Since fertilizer is an important input in crop production, its demand is likely to be price inelastic. In fact, studies of the use of such fees in Europe show that even with a tax rate of 50 percent, fertilizer usage is not significantly reduced.[41] Ultimately, the incremental benefit of these taxes tends to be not in the decline in fertilizer use but in the associated revenues that can be used to enhance environmental protection and fund research. Some $14 million are raised each year from these taxes in the United States.[42]

---

[39] Harrington et al. (1985). For a more in-depth analysis of the efficiency and equity considerations of nonpoint source controls in the agricultural sector, see Spurlock and Clifton (1982).

[40] Anderson, Lohof, and Carlin (August 1997), p. 4-21, citing the Fertilizer Institute; U.S. EPA, Office of Policy, Planning, and Evaluation (July 1992), p. 3-5.

[41] U.S. EPA, Office of Water (January 1992), p. 196.

[42] U.S. EPA, Office of Policy, Planning, and Evaluation (July 1992), p. 3-5. For a discussion of some specific usage of such product charges, see U.S. EPA, Office of Water (January 1992), pp. 196–97.

**effluent reduction trading policy** A market approach whereby an abatement objective is established for a watershed and sources are allowed to negotiate trades for "rights to pollute."

**effluent reduction credits** Tradeable permits issued to a polluting source if it discharges a lower level of effluents than what is allowed by law.

**effluent allowances** Tradeable permits issued up front to a polluting source that give it the right to release effluents in the future.

**Effluent Reduction Trading within a "Bubble."** An alternative market-based approach to nonpoint source pollution is the use of an **effluent reduction trading policy** within a "bubble" (sometimes called a "bowl" to signify its use for a watershed). The premise is exactly the same as what underlies a bubble to control air pollution. In simple terms, an overall abatement objective is established for a watershed, and then each polluting source is assigned an effluent limit. Once done, these sources are allowed to negotiate trades among themselves for "rights to pollute" issued as **effluent reduction credits** or **effluent allowances.**[43] **Effluent reduction credits** are issued if a polluter discharges *less* than what is permitted by law. **Effluent allowances** are issued up front and give the polluter the right to release pollution in the future.[44] Polluting sources have an incentive to trade as long as their *MAC*s are not equal at current abatement levels. Ultimately, the market will establish a price for each allowance or credit such that all polluters abate to the point where their respective *MAC* levels are equal. This approach has been used to allow trading between point and nonpoint source polluters and between nonpoint sources, as shown in Table 15.5.[45] In theory, such trades should bring about efficiency gains, since abatement costs are typically much higher for point sources than they are for nonpoint sources. Perhaps the most frequently cited example of a point–nonpoint trading program is one designed to clean up the Dillon Reservoir.[46]

The Dillon Reservoir is an important resource to Colorado, since it supplies Denver residents with more than half of their water supply. Over time, residential and industrial development in the area caused a serious pollution problem. The reservoir was receiving significant amounts of phosphorus, which was contributing to its decline. Officials tracked the damaging discharges and determined that over half was coming from nonpoint sources. The remainder was coming from 4 municipal treatment plants, 16 small treatment plants, and an industrial facility. Although these point sources were being controlled by discharge limits, they faced substantial marginal costs in trying to achieve them. More importantly, the large municipal treatment facilities faced much higher marginal abatement costs than the nonpoint sources in the watershed. The Dillon Reservoir problem was a textbook case of unequal marginal abatement costs across

---

[43] While still in the planning stage, the EPA is currently drafting a framework for effluent trading in watersheds. This policy proposal is in direct response to President Clinton's *Reinventing Environmental Regulations* (March 1995). To read more about this proposal, visit **www.epa.gov/OWOW/watershed/framwork. html**.

[44] Students may wish to review the distinction between credits and allowances, which was introduced in Chapter 5.

[45] Case studies on some of these projects can be viewed online at **www.epa.gov/OWOW/ watershed/ hotlink.htm**.

[46] See Hall and Howett (1994) for more on the Tar-Pamlico basin project. See U.S. EPA, Office of Policy, Planning, and Evaluation (July 1992), pp. 5-15 and 5-16 for more on the Dillon Reservoir project, from which much of the following discussion is drawn.

| TABLE 15.5 | EXAMPLES OF POINT-TO-NONPOINT AND NONPOINT-TO-NONPOINT TRADEABLE EFFLUENT PERMIT MARKETS | | |

| State | Waterbody | Pollutant | Type of Trading |
|---|---|---|---|
| Colorado | Dillon Reservoir | phosphorus | point-to-nonpoint nonpoint-to-nonpoint |
| Colorado | Boulder Creek | ammonia, nutrients | point-to-nonpoint |
| Colorado | Chatfield Basin | phosphorus | point-to-nonpoint |
| Maryland | Wicomico River | phosphorus | point-to-nonpoint |
| New York | Long Island Sound | dissolved oxygen | point-to-nonpoint |
| North Carolina | Tar-Pamlico Basin | nitrogen, phosphorus | point-to-nonpoint |
| Ohio | Honey Creek Watershed | phosphorus | point-to-nonpoint |
| Tennessee | Boone Reservoir | nutrients | point-to-nonpoint |
| Washington | Chehalis River Basin | biological oxygen demand | point-to-nonpoint |

SOURCE: U.S. Environmental Protection Agency, Office of Water. *Effluent Trading in Watersheds Policy Statement*, **www.epa.gov/ OWOW/watershed/tradetbl.html**, last updated January 5, 1998.

polluting sources where cost savings could be realized through a trading scheme.[47] With the EPA's support, officials in the area instituted a point/ nonpoint source trading program. Initial allocations of phosphorous discharge limits were set, and trades were allowed between point and nonpoint sources on a 2-to-1 ratio.[48]

Despite the classic conditions at the Dillon Reservoir, active trading has been minimal. There are, however, some logical explanations for this outcome. For one thing, point sources in the Dillon area have become more efficient abaters over time. As they have, their abatement costs have declined, which in turn lessens their incentive to trade for pollution rights. Also, the region's economic development has begun to slow down, which necessarily lessens the amount of discharges and hence the need for market trades. Finally, the 2-to-1 trading ratio, while well intentioned, discourages trading, since point sources are allowed only 1 unit of effluent for

---

[47] An EPA study suggests that there was a potential for over $1 million in cost savings. See Elmore et al. (1984) cited in Harrington et al. (1985). For a discussion of why these savings might not be realized, see Hahn (1989).

[48] A trading ratio of 2 means that point sources are allowed 1 unit of effluent for every 2 they purchase from nonpoint sources. A ratio greater than 1 favors point source reductions and discourages trades. Conversely, a ratio less than 1 favors reductions by nonpoint sources and encourages trades. For an analysis of these ratios and an overview of point/nonpoint source trading, see Letson (1992). A more rigorous study is given by Malik, Letson, and Crutchfield (1993).

every 2 credits they buy. Interestingly, it is reported that a few trades have been proposed between nonpoint sources at the Dillon Reservoir region, an outcome that was not anticipated by the program planners.[49] It is still too soon to predict the long-term success of such trading programs, since they are still relatively new. In any case, the experiences at the Dillon Reservoir may be valuable to other officials planning to establish similar markets.

# Conclusions

An ongoing source of debate is the nation's dependence on a command-and-control approach to achieving water quality and the methods it uses to guide critical decisions. Since 1972, U.S. water control policy has been rooted in the use of technology-based effluent limitations. There have been documented delays in setting these limits, which in turn have slowed states' efforts in achieving receiving water quality standards. Beyond the time problem, there is a lack of guidance in the law as to how the technological and economic determinants of these limits are to be considered relative to one another. An efficient abatement level is not likely, given the absence of any mandate to use benefit–cost analysis in defining these standards. Furthermore, because the effluent standards are applied uniformly within major groups of polluters, a cost-effective solution is also unlikely.

Another costly policy decision has been the federal funding of POTW construction. Studies show that these funds have served primarily to displace rather than supplement local spending, suggesting that observed improvements in waste treatment are not directly attributable to the billions of dollars spent at the federal level for this program. In addition, by removing much of the cost burden from municipalities, local officials had little incentive to make cost-conscious decisions in building waste treatment facilities. Policy makers have recognized the problem and revised the law in an attempt to restore the incentive mechanisms removed by the long-term grant program.

Beyond this dependence on command-and-control instruments, there are gaps in the overall policy approach. Nonpoint polluting sources such as agricultural and urban runoff are major contributors to water contamination, and the United States has only begun to address this highly complex issue. The 1987 amendments initiated the Nonpoint Source Management Program, but this program cannot succeed unless resources are allocated to improving monitoring technologies and to advancing the knowledge base about nonpoint source pollution.

---

[49] U.S. EPA, Office of Policy, Planning, and Evaluation (July 1992), pp. 5-15 and 5-16. The reader should consult Harrington et al. (1985), particularly pp. 29–30, for a clear explanation as to why trading might be more likely among nonpoint sources and other determinants of trading activity.

In the past, the federal government virtually ignored market incentives in implementing water quality regulations. Economic instruments such as effluent fees and permit trading programs may be viable alternatives to the nation's current standards-based approach. Perhaps the use of economic incentives will bring about significant costs savings and cleaner water for the nation. Clearly, U.S. water quality policy development has been and continues to be an evolutionary process. Environmental controls must be continuously evaluated and revised to reflect new technologies, changes in natural conditions, and innovative proposals for better solutions.

# Summary

- Point sources are subject to end-of-pipe effluent limits that vary by the type of polluting source, the age of the facility, and sometimes by the type of contaminant released.

- Effluent limits for direct industrial dischargers and for publicly owned treatment works (POTWs) are communicated through the National Pollutant Discharge Elimination System (NPDES).

- For new industrial point sources, the effluent limitations are more stringent than those for existing sources.

- For existing industrial point sources, two types of limits are applicable based on the type of pollutant released. These are best available technology economically achievable (BAT) standards for controlling nonconventional and toxic pollutants and best conventional control technology (BCT) standards for conventional pollutants.

- There have been delays in developing and revising the guidelines that serve as a basis for the effluent limitations. It is also the case that these limitations are not aligned with U.S. objectives, since they are based on what is technologically feasible rather than what is needed to achieve water quality. The EPA is also criticized for not imposing zero effluent limits where achievable in accordance with the nation's zero discharge goal.

- The Clean Water Act does not mandate that the BAT and BCT standards be set to maximize net benefits, which prevents an efficient solution. Furthermore, they are applied uniformly across dischargers within identified groups, which disallows a cost-effective outcome.

- Prior to the 1987 revisions, one titled section of the Clean Water Act outlined the federal grant program for the construction of POTWs. In 1987, a new section in the law authorized capitalization grants to states for setting up a revolving fund for various projects.

- One criticism of the POTW grant program is that the majority of federal monies only displaced local funding for new construction. Furthermore, federal aid was aimed only at construction of POTWs, with no provisions to assure proper operation and maintenance of these facilities. An economic issue is that the federal cost share shifted most of the expenditures away from local governments, leaving them little incentive to minimize costs.

- Under the Nonpoint Source Management Program initiated in 1987, states must prepare assessment reports in which they identify waters unable to achieve quality standards without controls on nonpoint sources. They also must develop management programs in which they designate best management practices (BMP) to reduce pollution from identified nonpoint sources.

- One factor supporting states' responsibility for nonpoint sources is the location-specific nature of nonpoint source pollution. Another is the political sensitivity of federal controls on land use. On the opposite side are information deficiencies that hinder state governments' ability to carry out their responsibilities. There is also the potential problem of inconsistent control efforts, which become problematic when contamination flows downstream across jurisdictions.

- At the federal level, far less funding has been allocated to nonpoint source pollution than to point source contamination. There have also been conflicts between water quality objectives and the goals of other regulations and programs, such as those directed by the USDA.

- The United States is beginning to consider the potential cost savings of using market-based approaches to water quality policy. Some local governments are experimenting with these types of incentive-based policy tools.

- An effluent charge can be based either upon the volume or the type of effluent released. Countries such as Australia, Belgium, France, Germany, and Spain have instituted effluent charges to control water contamination.

- Tradeable effluent permit markets could be implemented using the existing NPDES by issuing the permit as a set of tradeable, per unit "rights to pollute." Potential gains from trading exist as long as marginal abatement costs differ across polluting sources.

- Product charges can be levied on a commodity whose usage adds to a known runoff problem, such as fertilizers that contribute to agricultural runoff. An alternative is the use of an effluent reduction trading policy within a "bubble," which has been used to allow trading between point and nonpoint sources.

# Key Concepts

technology-based effluent
   limitations

National Pollutant Discharge
   Elimination System (NPDES)

best available demonstrated control
   technology (BADCT)

best available technology
   economically achievable (BAT)

best conventional control
   technology (BCT)

water quality–related limitations

federal grant program

State Revolving Fund (SRF)
   Program

Nonpoint Source Management
   Program

best management practices (BMP)

volume-based effluent fee

pollutant-based effluent fee

tradeable effluent permit market

product charge

effluent reduction trading policy

effluent reduction credits

effluent allowances

# Review Questions

1. a. Evaluate the use of "technological attainability" as the primary determinant of the effluent limitations.
   b. Economically analyze the use of *uniform* technology-based effluent limitations.

2. Discuss the incentive/disincentive implications of the federal assistance programs for POTW construction.

3. As an alternative to standards, one policy proposal is the use of permit trading between point sources of water pollution. Give the major reason why this is advantageous: (a) from an economic perspective; and (b) from an environmental perspective.

4. According to EPA Administrator Carol Browner,

   "We've done the easy part of controlling pollution at the end of the pipeline. For the first time ever, we are tackling the hard part—the control of polluted runoff, which is the biggest remaining barrier we face in keeping the nation's waters clean."[50]

   Working as part of the EPA's team, your assignment is to give a clear, objective presentation of a market-based approach to reduce nonpoint source pollution. Include in your discussion the theoretical issues and any practical concerns that must be addressed prior to implementing your proposal.

---

[50]U.S. EPA, Office of Communications, Education, and Public Affairs (February 22, 1994b).

5. a. To help fight the problem of nonpoint source pollution associated with agricultural runoff, your state is contemplating charging an annual fee of $500 to every seller of pesticides. If this fee is to achieve an efficient solution, state specifically according to externality theory (a) what the $500 fee must represent; and (b) in which market.
   b. Illustrate graphically, labeling where and how the fee is imposed.

## Additional Readings

Downing, Donna, and Stuart Sessions. "Innovative Water Quality-Based Permitting: A Policy Perspective." *Journal of Water Pollution Control Federation* 57(5), May 1985, pp. 358–65.

Joeres, Erhard F., and Martin H. David, eds. *Buying a Better Environment: Cost-Effective Regulation through Permit Trading.* Madison, WI: University of Wisconsin Press, 1983.

Knopman, Debra S., and Richard A. Smith. "20 Years of the Clean Water Act: Has U.S. Water Quality Improved?" *Environment* 35(1), January/February 1993, pp. 17–20, 34–41.

Krupnick, Alan J. "Reducing Bay Nutrients: An Economic Perspective." *Maryland Law Review* 47, 1988, pp. 452–80.

Magat, Wesley A., and W. Kip Viscusi. "Effectiveness of the EPA's Regulatory Enforcement: The Case of Industrial Effluent Standards." *Journal of Law and Economics* 33, October 1990, pp. 331–60.

Oates, Wallace E., and Dianna L. Strassmann. "Effluent Fees and Market Structure." *Journal of Public Economics* 24, 1984, pp. 29–46.

O'Neil, William B. "The Regulation of Water Pollution Permit Trading Under Conditions of Varying Streamflow and Temperature." In E. Joeres and M. David, eds. *Buying a Better Environment: Cost-Effective Regulation through Permit Trading.* Madison, WI: University of Wisconsin Press, 1983, pp. 219–31.

Smith, Stephen. "Green Taxes and Charges: Policy Practices in Britain and Germany." Institute for Fiscal Studies, November 1995.

U.S. Environmental Protection Agency. Office of Water. *The Clean Water State Revolving Fund and the Clean Water Action Plan.* Washington, DC: March 1998.

U.S. General Accounting Office. *Water Pollution: Improved Monitoring and Enforcement Needed for Toxic Pollutants Entering Sewers.* Washington, DC, April 1989.

## Related Web Sites

| | |
|---|---|
| Case Studies of Trading Programs | **www.epa.gov/OWOW/watershed/hotlink.htm** |
| EPA's *Draft Framework for Watershed-Based Trading* | **www.epa.gov/OWOW/watershed/framwork.html** |
| EPA's *Effluent Trading in Watersheds Policy Statement* | **www.epa.gov/OWOW/watershed/tradetbl.html** |
| NPDES permit program | **www.epa.gov/owmitnet/gen2.htm** |

Nonpoint Source Pollution
Control Program                 **www.epa.gov/OWOW/NPS/**

Overview of Watershed Trading    **www.epa.gov/OWOW/watershed/trading.htm**

State Revolving Fund (SRF) Program  **www.epa.gov/owm/finan.htm**

# Appendix:
# A Reference to Acronyms and Terms
# in Water Quality Control Policy

### Environmental Economics Acronyms

| | |
|---|---|
| $MAC$ | Marginal abatement cost of a single polluter |
| $MAC_{mkt}$ | Marginal abatement cost of all polluters |
| $MCE$ | Marginal cost of enforcement |
| $MEF$ | Marginal effluent fee |
| $MSB$ | Marginal social benefit of abatement |
| $MSB_{low}$ | Marginal social benefit of abatement in an area with a low population |
| $MSB_{high}$ | Marginal social benefit of abatement in an area with a high population |
| $MSC$ | Marginal social cost of abatement |

### Environmental Science Terms

| | |
|---|---|
| BOD | Biological oxygen demand |
| DO | Dissolved oxygen |
| mg/L | Milligrams per liter |

### Environmental Policy Acronyms

| | |
|---|---|
| BADCT | Best available demonstrated control technology |
| BAT | Best available technology economically achievable |
| BCT | Best conventional control technology |
| BMP | Best management practices |
| BPT | Best practicable technology currently available |
| FWPCA | Federal Water Pollution Control Act |
| NPDES | National Pollutant Discharge Elimination System |
| POTWs | Publicly owned treatment works |
| SRF | State Revolving Fund |

# 16

# *Protecting Drinking Water: The U.S. Safe Drinking Water Act*

In 1993, 400,000 residents of Milwaukee, Wisconsin, became ill from a waterborne disease that was transmitted through the city's drinking water. Ultimately, more than 40 people lost their lives. Beyond the human suffering, an estimated sum of $37 million in wages and productivity was lost. How could a city's water supplies become so polluted? What went wrong? There are several theories—human error, aging facilities, illegal discharges, and monitoring failures among them. Another is that the disease outbreak was a result of poorly defined federal controls. The claim is that regulations divert attention and resources to lower-priority problems, which in this case caused officials to miss the warning signs of the contamination.[1] Whatever the reason, the Milwaukee incident sparked national concern about the potential for similar problems across America. It also triggered skepticism and criticism of U.S. drinking water policy. What regulations are in place to protect drinking water supplies? How effective is this part of U.S. water quality control policy?

Drinking water supplies depend on ground and surface water resources, both of which are protected by the Clean Water Act. However, this act requires a level of water quality to support aquatic life and recreational uses—a level that calls for far less stringent standards than those necessary to support safe drinking. Furthermore, although the Clean Water Act is comprehensive, its protection of groundwater resources is limited. Groundwater is the source of drinking water for half of the U.S. population and for 95 percent of rural Americans.[2] Hence, regulations beyond those in the

---

[1] Smith (Summer 1994).

[2] U.S. EPA (August 1988), p. 52.

Clean Water Act are necessary to minimize the risks of contaminated drinking water.

In this chapter, we focus on the nation's drinking water policy, which is governed by the Safe Drinking Water Act. Like the Clean Water Act, this legislation is based primarily on a standards-based, command-and-control policy approach—a characteristic we evaluate from an economic perspective. Our investigation is timely because this law has recently been reauthorized and amended by Congress. We begin with a brief review of the origin and evolution of drinking water standards and laws. From this point, we discuss the objectives of the Safe Drinking Water Act and the standards used to define drinking water quality for the nation. Once done, we analyze the federal standard-setting process, the performance of state and local governments in meeting these standards, and the cost implications for society. We then consider the economics of pricing water supplies. Once again, an appendix of acronyms and terms is provided at the end of the chapter.

## The Evolution of U.S. Safe Drinking Water Legislation

Throughout the early history of the United States, deaths caused by diseases such as cholera and typhoid fever were not uncommon. For many years, no one realized that these diseases were caused by bacteria living in water supplies used for drinking. It was not until 1854 that an epidemiologist named Dr. John Snow linked cholera to contaminated water. Another 30 years passed before specific bacteria were identified as the cause of waterborne disease. Armed with this evidence, the federal government enacted the Interstate Quarantine Act of 1893. As Table 16.1 shows, this was the first federal law in the evolution of U.S. drinking water controls. This act authorized the surgeon general to issue regulations to prevent the spread of disease from any foreign country to the United States or from one state to another. In 1912, the first water-related regulation was passed—a ruling that outlawed the use of a common drinking cup on interstate carriers.[3]

### Setting Standards to Protect Drinking Water

Recognizing that banning common drinking cups was of little value if the water itself was contaminated, federal authorities passed the Public Health Service Act of 1912—the first U.S. law to specifically call for drinking water health standards. As authorized, these standards were limited in scope—targeting only contaminants capable of spreading communicable waterborne diseases. Hence, in 1914, the Public Health Service set *bacteriological* standards for drinking water. Recognizing the potential health risks of other types of substances, the standards were expanded in 1925 to

---

[3] McDermott (1973) as cited in Larson (1989).

| TABLE 16.1 | EVOLUTION OF U.S. DRINKING WATER LEGISLATION |
|---|---|

| Legislation | Major Provisions |
|---|---|
| Interstate Quarantine Act of 1893 | Authorized the surgeon general to issue regulations to prevent the spread of disease; led to the first U.S. water regulation passed in 1912 prohibiting the use of a common drinking cup on interstate carriers. |
| Public Health Service Act of 1912 | Provided for the U.S. Public Health Service to set bacteriological standards for drinking water. |
| Revisions to Public Health Standards in 1925, 1942, 1946, 1962 | Strengthened existing standards; required more stringent testing procedures; established maximum allowable concentrations for certain substances. |
| Safe Drinking Water Act of 1974 | Authorized the EPA to establish drinking water standards; controlled underground injection activities and protected sole-source aquifers. |
| Safe Drinking Water Amendments of 1986 | Accelerated procedures for the standard-setting process; provided greater protection of groundwater sources of drinking water; banned the use of lead in public drinking water systems. |
| Safe Drinking Water Amendments of 1996 | Integrates risk assessment and benefit–cost analysis into standard-setting procedures; authorizes a $1 billion per year Drinking Water State Revolving Fund; promotes prevention through source water protection and better management. |

SOURCES: Charles D. Larson. "Historical Development of the National Primary Drinking Water Regulations." In Edward J. Calabrese, Charles E. Gilbert, and Harris Pastides, eds., *Safe Drinking Water Act: Amendments, Regulations, and Standards.* Chelsea, MI: Lewis Publishers, 1989, pp. 3–15; H. McDermott. "Federal Drinking Water Standards—Past, Present, and Future." *Water Well Journal* 27(12), 1973, pp. 29–35; Andrew A. Dzurik. *Water Resources Planning.* Savage, MD: Rowman & Littlefield Publishers, 1990; U.S. Congress, Office of Technology Assessment (OTA). *Protecting the Nation's Groundwater from Contamination.* Vol. I., Washington, DC: U.S. Government Printing Office, October 1984, Chapter 3, pp. 64–75; Sidney M. Wolf. *Pollution Law Handbook: A Guide to Federal Environmental Laws.* New York: Quorom Books, 1988, Chapter 4, pp. 133–37; 1996 U.S. Congress. *Safe Drinking Water Act Amendments,* Public Law 104-182, 104th Congress, approved August 6, 1996.

consider chemical characteristics like lead and copper. Over the next several decades, more revisions followed, each time adding more structure to the law and strengthening existing standards and controls.[4]

In the 1960s, there was a turn of events that was to change the direction of U.S. drinking water policy. In 1963, the Public Health Service formed an advisory committee to evaluate the existing drinking water standards and make appropriate recommendations. In 1967, the committee recommended that toxic contaminants be addressed—an advisory that *would* have led to limits on such chemicals as chlordane and DDT. However, it was argued that setting standards on toxics went beyond the jurisdiction of the Public Health Service, whose authority was limited to controlling communicable disease. Although the responsibility may have been misplaced, the

---

[4]McDermott (1973) as cited in Larson (1989); Dzurik (1990), p. 61.

concern was appropriate. Chemical usage was on the rise, pesticides were being detected in groundwater supplies, and the general public was becoming alarmed. A federal committee was formed in 1969 to evaluate the 1962 standards and make recommendations. It completed its work in 1971—one year after the EPA had been established. The newly established agency reviewed the committee's report, which ultimately became the cornerstone of new regulations. These were issued under the Safe Drinking Water Act (SDWA) of 1974 at which point the responsibility of protecting drinking water shifted from the Public Health Service to the EPA.[5]

### The Safe Drinking Water Act (SDWA) of 1974[6]

Capitalizing on the broader jurisdiction of the EPA, the Safe Drinking Water Act (SDWA) was aimed at protecting drinking water from *any* contaminant that could threaten human health or welfare—not just bacteria responsible for communicable disease. Primary standards were to be established for organic and inorganic chemicals, radionuclides, and microorganisms identified as having adverse effects on public health. Secondary standards, which were actually just guidelines, were to be defined to protect welfare by controlling such characteristics as taste and odor.

Not unlike other early environmental laws, the SDWA of 1974 was not without problems that ultimately caused major delays. It originally called for interim health standards to be set within 180 days. These were to be revised through a coordinated effort between the EPA and the National Academy of Science (NAS), at which time they would become final regulations. These regulations were to establish pollution limits called maximum contaminant levels (MCLs) that the NAS believed would protect human health. The complex procedures coupled with the EPA's alleged lack of initiative delayed the process considerably. In fact, by the mid-1980s, relatively few contaminants had been regulated by the EPA, and most interim standards still had not been revised. These procedural problems and uneven compliance by public water utilities led to the 1986 Amendments.

### The Safe Drinking Water Amendments of 1986

The 1986 Amendments expanded federal controls on drinking water and corrected some of the failings of the original SDWA. To accelerate procedures for the standard-setting process, maximum contaminant levels (MCLs) were required for a list of 83 contaminants according to a strict timetable over the 1987 to 1989 period. Responding to growing concerns about lead contamination, the amendments prohibited all future use of lead pipe and solder in public drinking-water systems, now known as the "lead

---

[5] Larson (1989).

[6] Drawn from U.S. Congress, Office of Technology Assessment (OTA) (October 1984), Vol. I., Chapter 1, pp. 8–9, Chapter 3, pp. 64–75; Wolf (1988), Chapter 4, pp. 133–37.

ban." Other revisions attempted to provide better protection of underground drinking water supplies.

Although the SDWA of 1986 addressed some important concerns, most agreed that further changes were needed. Numerous proposals for reform were discussed as part of the most recent reauthorization of this act. Ultimately, Congress passed the SDWA Amendments of 1996—the law currently in force.

### The Safe Drinking Water Act Amendments of 1996[7]

**Drinking Water State Revolving Fund (DWSRF)**
Authorizes $1 billion per year from 1994 to 2003 to finance infrastructure improvements

In an attempt to correct existing problems with the nation's safe drinking water legislation, President Clinton signed into law the 1996 SDWA Amendments on August 6, 1996. An important element of this legislation is the establishment of a **Drinking Water State Revolving Fund (DWSRF)**. Recognizing the success of the POTW State Revolving Fund program, Congress initiated a similar plan for drinking water as part of these new amendments. This fund is authorized for $1 billion per year for the 1994 to 2003 period to finance infrastructure improvements.[8] Another important change addresses standard-setting procedures. The new amendments repeal the provisions that required the EPA to design and implement standards for 25 additional contaminants every 3 years. Replacing these rulings is a new requirement that drinking water standards be based on sound risk assessment and benefit–cost analysis. In fact, the law specifically states:

> ". . . in considering the appropriate level of regulation for contaminants in drinking water, risk assessment, based on sound and objective science, and benefit–cost analysis are important analytical tools for improving the efficiency and effectiveness of drinking water regulations to protect human health."

This represents a significant revision, integrating an economic decision rule into the standard-setting process. There are also new provisions promoting prevention through better management and source water protection rather than relying solely on remediation.

## Objectives of the Safe Drinking Water Act

Interestingly, the SDWA has no statutory objectives per se. However, according to the House of Representatives, the primary purpose of the act is:

---

[7] For online information on the implementation of the SDWA Amendments of 1996, which is in progress, visit **www.epa.gov/OGWDW/sdwa/sdwa.html**.

[8] To learn more about the DWSRF, visit **www.epa.gov/OGWDW/dwsrf.html**.

"... to assure that water supply systems serving the public meet minimum national standards for protection of public health."

To accomplish this goal, the SDWA of 1974 authorized three key directives:

- To establish drinking water health standards applicable to public water systems

- To control underground injection activities that may threaten drinking water[9]

- To protect **sole-source aquifers** (i.e., those that are the only source of drinking water for a given area)[10]

The 1986 Amendments added another directive—

- To protect groundwater supplies used for drinking

**sole-source aquifers**
Underground geological formations containing groundwater that are the only supply of drinking water for a given area.

It is important to have some perspective about how these directives relate to those of other U.S. water quality laws. Compared to the Clean Water Act, which has a comprehensive span of control, notice that the Safe Drinking Water Act (SDWA) is more focused. Its aim is to define, monitor, and enforce whatever standards are needed to assure that water drawn from the tap is safe for human consumption.[11] First of all, note the phrase "drawn from the tap," suggesting that bottled water is *not* regulated through the SDWA. Assuring the potability of this water falls within the jurisdiction of the Food and Drug Administration—a matter discussed in Application 16.1. Second, it is important to realize that the goals of the SDWA are not independent of the Clean Water Act, which controls *all* water resources including those used for drinking. Since the rulings of the Clean Water Act are not stringent enough to assure the safety of drinking water, the SDWA imposes the tougher standards needed to assure potability. However, it does rely implicitly on the Clean Water Act to achieve a baseline level of water quality and to control the effluents of polluting sources.

Finally, the groundwater protection added in 1986 is indicative of the fragmentary U.S. approach to controlling groundwater contamination. There are many statutes implemented by different government agencies aimed at this important natural resource—arguably an ineffective approach

---

[9] This directive controls various underground wells, such as those used to inject wastes or fluids from oil production into the ground, to assure that these materials do not contaminate underground drinking water supplies.

[10] U.S. Congress, OTA (October 1984), Vol. I., Chapter 3, pp. 73–75, citing U.S. House of Representatives (1974) on p. 74.

[11] For more information about water drawn from the tap, consult **www.epa.gov/OGWDW/wot/wot. html**.

## Who Regulates the Quality of Bottled Water?

By 1995, sales of bottled drinking water had grown into a thriving $3 billion market. To a large extent, these impressive revenues reflect consumers' uncertainty about the quality of public drinking water. Some are concerned about aesthetic issues, and others about more serious threats like lead contamination. Whatever the cause, the response of many consumers is to substitute bottled water for tap water.

Implicit in households' decisions to buy bottled water is the assumption that this substitute commodity is of higher quality than tap water. For this assumption to be valid, it must be the case that bottled water is subject to more stringent standards than is public drinking water or that suppliers of bottled water are closer to compliance with some set of universal standards than their public counterparts. Are either of these scenarios correct? To answer this question, we need to compare the regulations affecting private and public drinking water supplies.

To begin, the two types of water supplies are controlled by different entities. Public drinking water supplies are controlled by the Safe Drinking Water Act through standards administered by the EPA and state authorities. Bottled water quality falls within the jurisdiction of the Food and Drug Administration (FDA). The reason is that bottled water is considered a "food," and as such is part of the FDA's charge.

To assure consumer safety, the FDA requires that bottled water products be produced in compliance with FDA Good Manufacturing Practices. All products must be clean and safe for human consumption, and must be processed and distributed under sanitary conditions. Furthermore, according to a 1978 agreement, the FDA must adopt the EPA's public drinking water standards for bottled water. The FDA also has its own standards, dealing with aesthetics and health concerns. As a further precaution, domestic bottled water producers who distribute their products interstate are subject to periodic, unannounced site inspections by the FDA and by state health officials. There is also some measure of self-regulation within the industry.

What does all of this mean to the consumer? It is true that there are federal and state regulations in place to protect the quality of bottled water, and indeed there is consensus that bottled water is safe for human consumption. However, there is no reason to assume that it is *safer* to drink than ordinary tap water, since the same health standards are applicable to both.

Beyond this issue, there is also debate about whether bottled water is being unfairly or deceptively marketed. For example, it has been alleged that some bottled water is nothing more than ordinary tap water. Yet, its price can be as much as 1,000 times higher than the price of public water supplies. Further allegations have been made about misleading information about the characteristics or sources of bottled water products. To address these problems, the FDA established new labeling requirements for bottled water that will provide consistency to such designations as "mineral," "distilled," or "sterile" and will require the identification of bottled water drawn from municipal supplies. Truth-in-labeling is not a new concept, but its application to the increasingly popular bottled water industry may be long overdue.

SOURCES: U.S. Environmental Protection Agency, Office of Drinking Water. *Bottled Water: Helpful Facts and Information.* Washington, DC (undated); Sue Kirchhoff. "FDA Proposes Bottled Water Measure Up to Tap Standards." *Boston Globe*, January 1, 1993; U.S. Environmental Protection Agency. *Bottled Water Fact Sheet*, Washington, DC: March, 1991; R. Lee Sullivan. "Snob Water." *Forbes*, August 14, 1995, p. 192.

| FIGURE 16.1 | GROUND WATER CONTAMINANTS PRIORITIZED BY STATES |
|---|---|

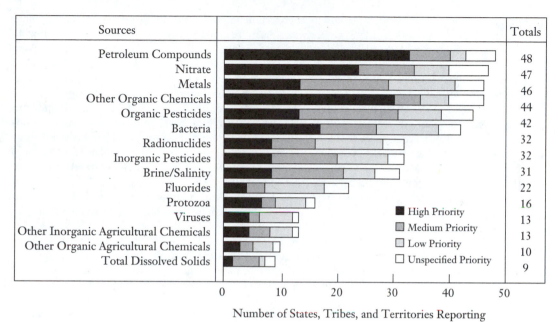

| Sources | | Totals |
|---|---|---|
| Petroleum Compounds | | 48 |
| Nitrate | | 47 |
| Metals | | 46 |
| Other Organic Chemicals | | 44 |
| Organic Pesticides | | 42 |
| Bacteria | | 42 |
| Radionuclides | | 32 |
| Inorganic Pesticides | | 32 |
| Brine/Salinity | | 31 |
| Fluorides | | 22 |
| Protozoa | | 16 |
| Viruses | | 13 |
| Other Inorganic Agricultural Chemicals | | 13 |
| Other Organic Agricultural Chemicals | | 10 |
| Total Dissolved Solids | | 9 |

Legend: ■ High Priority ▦ Medium Priority ☐ Low Priority ☐ Unspecified Priority

Number of States, Tribes, and Territories Reporting

SOURCE: 1994 Section 305(b) reports submitted by States, Tribes, and Territories, as presented in U.S. Environmental Protection Agency, Office of Water (December 1995), Figure 6.6, p. 108.

with no unified oversight.[12] This outcome evolved from the false belief that groundwater was naturally protected from contamination because of its location within layers of soil and rock. In the 1970s, this assumption was called into question when pesticides were discovered in U.S. groundwater supplies. Since then, every state in the nation has discovered some amount of pollutants in its groundwater.[13] The most commonly observed groundwater contaminants as of 1994 are shown in Figure 16.1. Public concern prompted a call for more aggressive legislative controls, and existing laws were amended in an attempt to address the problem. However, no single legislative act has ever been passed whose main objective is to protect groundwater resources.[14]

---

[12] Among the laws with some provisions to protect groundwater are: the Comprehensive Environmental Response, Compensation, and Liability Act, the Federal Insecticide, Fungicide, and Rodenticide Act, the Resource Conservation and Recovery Act, and the Toxic Substances Control Act. For more detail on this important issue, the reader should consult U.S. Congress, OTA (October 1984), Vol. I., Chapter 3.

[13] U.S. EPA, Office of Pesticides and Toxic Substances (October 1991), pp. 1–2; U.S. Congress, OTA (October 1984), Vol. I., p. 3.

[14] U.S. Congress, OTA (October 1984), Vol. I., pp. 63, 73–75.

**APPLICATION 16.2**

## Pesticides and Other Agrichemicals in U.S. Groundwater

Surveys conducted by federal, state, and local governments in the late 1970s revealed some troubling statistics about the pollution of U.S. groundwater. As more contamination was discovered, monitoring efforts intensified as did research endeavors to determine the magnitude of the problem. Recognizing a need to assimilate the accumulating data, the EPA established the Pesticides in Ground-Water Data Base using information gathered from some 150 monitoring studies. In 1988, the agency published the results in the *Interim Ground-Water Data Base Report.* One of its findings was that 46 different pesticides had been found in the groundwater supplies of 26 states—all of which were believed attributable to conventional agricultural activities. Although the database was valuable in generally assessing the problem, it nonetheless was a collection of information gleaned from diverse sources. Hence, the EPA saw the need to establish a nationally sponsored baseline of groundwater contamination data from which to monitor progress over time. It was this recognition that motivated the National Pesticide Survey of Drinking Water Wells conducted between 1988 and 1990.

The national survey analyzed samples from 1,349 drinking water wells across all 50 states. In November of 1990, the agency released the survey's Phase I report, which asserted that approximately 10.4 percent of the community wells and 4.2 percent of the private wells in the sample had a detectable amount of at least one pesticide. Based on these sample data, the EPA inferred that nearly 10,000 community drinking wells and about 446,000 private domestic wells in the United States were contaminated by at least one pesticide. The Survey Report went on to indicate, however, that less than 1 percent of private wells and no community drinking water wells had contamination levels high enough to threaten human health.

Phase II of the EPA's survey report was completed in 1992 and is a statistical analysis of the findings in Phase I. A number of statistical associations were identified, including a link between pesticide contamination and agricultural activity. The analysis also found that the transport of chemicals to well water is affected by numerous factors, including precipitation and the proximity of surface waters to drinking water wells.

Overall, the EPA contends that while pesticide contamination of groundwater exists, most of the nation's supplies are relatively "safe," at least in the short term. In those local areas where this is not the case, the EPA asserts that every effort must be made to address the problem and the associated health risks. The agency does acknowledge, however, that detectable levels of pesticides in well water on a widespread scale may suggest a threat to groundwater quality in the long run. In this regard, the survey data establish the baseline needed to help monitor changes in contaminant levels over time. This trend data should be useful in formulating policy initiatives and designing national strategies to protect U.S. groundwater supplies.

SOURCES: U.S. Environmental Protection Agency, Office of Pesticides and Toxic Substances. *Pesticides in Drinking-Water Wells.* Washington, DC: September 1990; U.S. Environmental Protection Agency, Office of Pesticides and Toxic Substances. *Pesticides and Ground-Water Strategy.* Washington, DC, October, 1991; U.S. Environmental Protection Agency, Office of Water, Office of Pesticides and Toxic Substances. *National Pesticide Survey: Update and Summary of Phase II Results.* Washington, DC, Winter 1992.

### Pollutants Controlled under the Safe Drinking Water Act

The Safe Drinking Water Act controls *all* types of contaminants that may threaten human health and not just those linked to communicable disease. Its rulings refer to "contaminants" as any physical, biological, or radiological substances in water. The 1986 Amendments were much more specific, listing 83 contaminants for which drinking water standards are to be set, with new contaminants to be drawn from a list of **priority contaminants** devised by an advisory group, published, and updated regularly.

The following are among the criteria for selecting **priority contaminants:**

**priority contaminants** Pollutants for which drinking water standards are to be established based on specific criteria.

- The contaminant must be known or expected to occur in a public water system.

- The contaminant may have an expected adverse effect on human health.

Consideration of which substances are identified on the priority list shall include but not be limited to contaminants identified in the Comprehensive Environmental Response, Compensation, and Liability Act (also known as Superfund), and pesticides registered under the Federal Insecticide, Fungicide, and Rodenticide Act. More on the problem of pesticides and other agricultural chemicals in drinking water is given in Application 16.2.

Still more changes came with the 1996 Amendments, calling for risk assessment and benefit–cost analysis to govern which contaminants are to be regulated and the standard-setting process itself. In addition to developing new rules and guidance for priority contaminants, a new infrastructure also is being established for future decisions called the **National Contaminant Occurrence Database (NCOD).** This is to be a collection of data on both regulated and unregulated contaminants that may occur in U.S. public water systems. The purpose of the NCOD is to facilitate identification and selection of contaminants to be controlled in the future.[15]

## Setting Standards to Define Safe Drinking Water

The most important directive of the SDWA is to set standards that define drinking water quality for the nation. Under the law, there are two types of standards: **primary standards** to protect human health; and **secondary standards** to protect public welfare.[16] The distinction is an important one, both in how each is defined and how each is implemented.

### Establishing National Primary Drinking Water Regulations

The emphasis of the SDWA is clearly on the primary or health standards for drinking water. These are applicable only to public water systems and

---

[15] For further information, see **www.epa.gov/OGWDW/standard/pp/ncodpp.html**.

[16] There is consistency between the meaning of the primary and secondary drinking water standards and that of the primary and secondary ambient air quality standards in the United States.

are to be implemented *uniformly* throughout the country. More formally, these standards are called **National Primary Drinking Water Regulations (NPDWR)**. Each regulation consists of three parts:

- **Maximum contaminant level goal (MCLG)**
- **Maximum contaminant level (MCL)**
- **Best available technology (BAT)** for public water supply treatment[17]

**National Primary Drinking Water Regulations (NPDWR)** Health standards for public drinking water supplies implemented uniformly.

**Setting the Goal: The MCLG.** One of the key elements of a primary drinking water regulation is the **maximum contaminant level goal (MCLG)**. This defines the level of a pollutant at which no known or expected adverse health effects occur, allowing for an adequate margin of safety. MCLGs are based on data obtained in the risk assessment process discussed in Chapter 7. Of particular relevance is the evidence on carcinogenicity of water contaminants. The MCLG for known or probable carcinogens is zero, meaning that no amount of such a contaminant is allowed in public drinking water. For any substance that is not a carcinogen, the MCLG is set according to the established reference dose (RfD) for that contaminant. Recall that an RfD is an estimate of the amount of a pollutant to which humans can be exposed over a lifetime without harm.[18] The key point to remember is that the MCLG is *not* an enforceable standard. Instead, it serves as a target or objective toward which the primary standard is to be aimed.

**maximum contaminant level goal (MCLG)** Component of an NPDWR that defines the level of a pollutant at which no known or expected adverse health effects occur, allowing for a margin of safety.

**Setting the Standard: The MCL.** Once the target or MCLG is established, the primary standard is set. The primary standard gives the **maximum contaminant level (MCL)** allowed in drinking water. It is to be set as close to the MCLG as is feasible, where feasibility is defined through the BAT technology. More formally, an MCL is the highest permissible level of a contaminant in water delivered to any user of a public system. It is expressed as an **action level** measured in milligrams per liter (mg/L). Unlike the MCLGs, the MCLs are federally enforceable. Determination of the MCLs was changed by the 1996 Amendments. Specifically, the new law requires a published determination as to whether the benefits of the MCL are justified by the cost. Table 16.2 lists the MCLs for selected contaminants and their associated health effects.[19]

**maximum contaminant level (MCL)** Component of an NPDWR that states the highest permissible level of a contaminant in water delivered to any user of a public system.

**action level** Manner in which MCLs are expressed, generally measured in milligrams per liter.

---

[17] Each regulation must also outline requirements for monitoring, reporting, and public notification. U.S. EPA, Office of Water (May 1992).

[18] As discussed in Chapter 7, an RfD is expressed in milligrams of a pollutant per body weight per day.

[19] For a complete listing of contaminants and their standards, visit **www.epa.gov/OGWDW/wot/appa. html**.

| TABLE 16.2 | NATIONAL PRIMARY DRINKING WATER STANDARDS FOR SELECTED CONTAMINANTS |
|------------|----|

| Contaminant | MCL[a] (mg/L) | Health Effects |
|-------------|---------------|----------------|
| **Organic Chemicals** | | |
| Atrazine | 0.003 | reproductive and cardiac effects |
| Benzene | 0.005 | cancer risk |
| Carbon tetrachloride | 0.005 | cancer risk |
| Chlordane | 0.002 | cancer risk |
| Heptachlor | 0.0004 | cancer risk |
| Styrene | 0.1 | liver, nervous system effects |
| Vinyl Chloride | 0.002 | cancer risk |
| **Inorganic Chemicals** | | |
| Arsenic[b] | 0.05 | dermal and nervous system toxicity effects |
| Asbestos | 7 MFL[c] | benign tumors |
| Cadmium | 0.005 | kidney damage |
| Fluoride[b] | 4 | skeletal damage |
| Lead | 0.015 | central and peripheral nervous system damage; kidney damage |
| Mercury | 0.002 | kidney, nervous system damage |
| **Radionuclides** | | |
| Beta particle and Photon activity | 4 mrem/yr[d] | cancer risk |
| Radium 226/228 | 5 pCi/L[e] | bone cancer risk |
| Radon | 300 pCi/L[e] | cancer risk |
| **Microbiological** | | |
| Turbidity | 0.5–1.0 NTU[f] | interferes with disinfection |
| Legionella | TT[g] | Legionnaire's disease (pneumonia), Pontiac fever |
| Viruses | TT[g] | gastroenteritis |

NOTES:

[a]MCLs are measured in milligrams per liter (mg/L) unless otherwise noted.

[b]MCL is currently under review.

[c]MFL = million fibers per liter, with fiber length > 10 microns.

[d]mrem/yr = millirem or 1/1,000 rem per year.

[e]pCi/L = picocuries per liter.

[f]NTU = nephelometric turbidity unit.

[g]TT means treatment technique requirement in effect.

SOURCES: U.S. Environmental Protection Agency, Office of Ground Water and Drinking Water. *Water on Tap: A Consumer's Guide to the Nation's Drinking Water*. "Appendix A: National Primary Drinking Water Standards." Washington, DC: July 1997; U.S. Environmental Protection Agency, Office of Water. *Fact Sheet: National Primary Drinking Water Standards*. Washington, DC, August 1991; U.S. Environmental Protection Agency, Office of Water. *Drinking Water Regulations and Health Advisories*. Washington, DC, April 1992b.

## Strengthening Controls on Lead Contamination of Water Supplies

In 1991, the EPA tightened the lead standard for drinking water to a maximum contaminant level (MCL) of 0.015 mg/L. Announcing the new standard, then EPA Administrator William K. Reilly stated,

> "Today's action will reduce lead exposure for approximately 130 million people . . . We estimate approximately 600,000 children will have their blood lead content brought below our level of concern because of these standards."

According to the EPA's initial 1992 survey based on test data from 6,400 large water systems, approximately 13 percent did not meet the new lead standard. Of those cities with populations greater than 50,000, the following were found to have the highest lead content in their public drinking water supplies:

| City | Lead Levels (parts per billion [ppb]) |
|---|---|
| Charleston, South Carolina | 165 |
| Utica, New York | 160 |
| Newton, Massachusetts | 123 |
| Columbia, South Carolina | 114 |
| Medford, Massachusetts | 113 |
| Chicopee, Massachusetts | 110 |
| Yonkers, New York | 110 |
| Waltham, Massachusetts | 76 |
| Brookline, Massachusetts | 72 |
| Taylor, Michigan | 69 |

The EPA estimates that only about 1 percent of water systems with elevated lead levels will have to treat source waters. The reason is that most of the lead content in drinking water comes from the public water delivery system and not the water supply itself. The contamination arises from corrosion of lead pipe service lines and plumbing solder. The "lead ban," which was legislated as part of the Safe Drinking Water Amendments of 1986, prohibits the future use of lead pipes, solder, or flux. Nonetheless, some older homes built before 1930 have lead waterpipes, and some newer homes built before the lead ban was enacted have copper pipes joined with lead-based solder. Consequently, in areas with a highly corrosive water supply, lead can leach out of these pipes or solder joints, contaminating the water that reaches residents. To combat this problem, treatment technologies have been developed to reduce water corrosivity. Congress also added more controls by passing the Lead Contamination Control Act of 1988, which calls for the repair or removal of water coolers that are not lead-free and bans the future sale and manufacture of these potential sources of contamination.

Beyond these comprehensive measures, the EPA is also using a public education program to communicate simple procedures households can follow to reduce their risk of lead exposure. The EPA advisory recommends that all tap water be allowed to run for about a minute before using it for cooking or drinking as a means to flush out any lead sediment from pipes. For homes in areas where the new action level is exceeded, further precautions are recommended, such as running tap water for several minutes before using and avoiding the use of hot tap water for drinking or cooking. These precautionary measures coupled with the strengthened federal regulations should lessen considerably the risk of lead exposure that threatens human health.

SOURCES: U.S. Environmental Protection Agency, Office of Communications and Public Affairs. "EPA Tightens Standards for Lead in Drinking Water." *Environmental News*, Washington, DC, May 7, 1991; Timothy Noah. "EPA Finds Unsafe Lead Levels in Water." *The Wall Street Journal*, May 12, 1993; U.S. Environmental Protection Agency, Office of Water. *Lead Contamination Control Act*. Washington, DC, July 1988.

**best available technology (BAT)**
Treatment technology that makes attainment of the MCL feasible, taking cost considerations into account.

**Defining Treatment Technologies.** The law requires that each national primary drinking water regulation identify the treatment technology that makes attainment of the MCL feasible. This is characterized as the **best available technology (BAT)** observed under field conditions, taking account of cost considerations. Since this technology is not a requirement per se, the primary water quality regulations are more accurately characterized as performance-based standards.

### Current Status of the National Primary Drinking Water Regulations (NPDWRs)

As of 1998, NPDWRs have been announced for 8 volatile organic chemicals, 57 synthetic organic chemicals and inorganic chemicals, fluoride, coliform and other microbiological contaminants, and lead and copper.[20] All standards are to be reviewed at least once every five years and must be amended whenever enhanced health protection is possible through changes in technology, treatment, or other means. For example, more stringent primary standards for lead in drinking water were announced by the EPA in 1991. As a consequence, public water supplies in many U.S. communities now exceed the lead action level. For more on the implications of this outcome, see Application 16.3 on the facing page.

### Establishing National Secondary Drinking Water Regulations

**secondary maximum contaminant levels (SMCLs)**
National standards for drinking water that serve as guidelines to protect public welfare.

Protection of public welfare is the statutory objective of secondary drinking water standards. More to the point, these standards deal with contaminants that so impair aesthetics and other nonhealth-threatening characteristics like odor and taste that a substantial number of individuals may be forced to discontinue use of the public water system. Referred to as **secondary maximum contaminant levels (SMCLs),** these standards serve as guidelines to protect public welfare and are *not* enforceable by the federal government. Furthermore, unlike the primary standards, the secondary standards are not uniform, since they may vary with geographic or other conditions. Table 16.3 (p. 500) gives the U.S. SMCLs as of 1998 and the associated effects of each listed contaminant.

## Analysis of U.S. Safe Drinking Water Policy

Because the SDWA Amendments of 1996 have not yet been fully implemented, we conduct some elements of our analysis based on the pre-1996

---

[20] U.S. EPA, Office of Water. "Phase V Rule: Fact Sheet" (May 1992).

| TABLE 16.3 | U.S. SECONDARY MAXIMUM CONTAMINANT LEVELS (SMCLs) |
|---|---|

| Substance | SMCL (mg/L)[a] | Contaminant Effects |
|---|---|---|
| Aluminum | 0.05 to 0.2 | discoloration |
| Chloride | 250 | taste; pipe corrosion |
| Color | 15 color units | aesthetic |
| Copper | 1.0 | taste; staining of porcelain |
| Corrosivity | noncorrosive | aesthetic and health related (corrosive water can leach pipe materials, like lead, into water) |
| Fluoride[b] | 2.0 | dental fluorosis (brownish discoloration of the teeth) |
| Foaming agents | 0.5 | aesthetic |
| Iron | 0.3 | taste; staining of laundry |
| Manganese | 0.05 | taste; staining of laundry |
| Odor | 3 threshold odor numbers | aesthetic |
| pH | 6.5–8.5 | water is too corrosive |
| Silver | 0.10 | argyria (discoloration of the skin) |
| Sulfate | 250 | taste; laxative effects |
| Total dissolved solids | 500 | taste; possible relation between low hardness and cardiovascular disease; indicator of corrosivity (related to lead levels in water); can damage plumbing and limit effectiveness of soaps and detergents |
| Zinc | 5 | taste |

NOTES:

[a] SMCLs are expressed in mg/L unless otherwise noted.

[b] Indicates under review.

SOURCES: U.S. Environmental Protection Agency, Office of Water. *Drinking Water Regulations and Health Advisories.* Washington, DC, April 1992b; U.S. Environmental Protection Agency, Office of Water. "Is Your Drinking Water Safe?" Washington, DC, December 1991; U.S. Environmental Protection Agency, Office of Ground Water and Drinking Water. "Current Drinking Water Standards," last revised September 21, 1998, **www.epa.gov/OGWDW/wot/appa.html**.

regulations. This also helps to explain the motivation behind some of the revisions in the new law.

Prior to the 1996 Amendments, several aspects of the Safe Drinking Water Act were criticized by environmental economists and policy analysts, particularly in light of reported incidents of contaminated drinking water supplies. One important concern centered around the standard-setting process at the federal level and the potentially inefficient outcome it generates.

Were contaminant levels being properly determined? And if not, what were the ramifications? Another key issue was the subpar performance at the state and local levels in meeting the standards and maintaining adequate treatment facilities. Was the less-than-satisfactory track record the result of ill-defined standards, poor enforcement procedures, inadequate resources, or some combination of factors? To begin, let's consider the standard-setting process that forms the fundamental basis of the Safe Drinking Water Act.

## The Federal Role: Setting the Standards

The statutory goals of the Safe Drinking Water Act (SDWA), that is, the maximum contaminant level goals (MCLGs), are defined as the level of a pollutant at which no adverse human health effects occur with a "margin of safety." Allowing for an adequate margin of safety seems to suggest a contaminant level where *no* individual would be harmed. Given the variability of human sensitivities, this seems to imply that at least some MCLGs must be set at zero. Notice that there is no mention of feasibility or cost considerations in setting these goals. They are purely benefit-based.

Since the maximum contaminant levels (MCLs) are aimed at these goals, they too were benefit-based prior to the 1996 Amendments. Although the MCLs are to consider "feasibility" defined through technological availability, there was no legal requirement that the associated marginal costs of achieving the standard be balanced with the expected marginal gains. As is the case with any such regulation, the absence of an explicit balancing of costs and benefits at the margin means that efficiency is not being used to regulate drinking water. And given the language of the MCLG, there was potential for overregulation of some contaminants and inflated costs before the 1996 Amendments.

Consider the graph in Figure 16.2 that models the total social health benefits (*TSB*) and total social costs (*TSC*) of abating some hypothetical drinking water contaminant beyond the efficient level. If the MCL is set to maximize social health benefits, the resulting abatement level is $A_1$, corresponding to the point where the *TSB* curve reaches its highest level. In this case, $A_1$ is *above* the efficient level of abatement, $A_e$. Hence, the benefit-based standard would overregulate this contaminant, imposing unnecessarily high costs on society.

All of this explains the importance of a paragraph in the 1996 Amendments specifying precisely how the MCLs are to be determined. According to this paragraph, at the time a new NPDWR is proposed, the EPA must publish a determination identifying whether or not the benefits of the MCL justify the costs. Effectively, this means that the EPA must develop a new regulatory impact analysis (RIA) framework for any proposed NPDWR.

FIGURE 16.2

## THE INEFFICIENCY OF BENEFIT-BASED PRIMARY DRINKING WATER STANDARDS

The model illustrates the relationship between the total social health benefits (*TSB*) and total social costs (*TSC*) of abating some hypothetical drinking water contaminant beyond the efficient level. If the maximum contaminant level (MCL) is set to maximize social health benefits, the resulting abatement level is $A_1$, corresponding to the point where the *TSB* curve reaches its highest level. In this case, $A_1$ is *above* the efficient level of abatement, $A_e$. Hence, the benefit-based standard would overregulate this contaminant, imposing unnecessarily high costs on society.

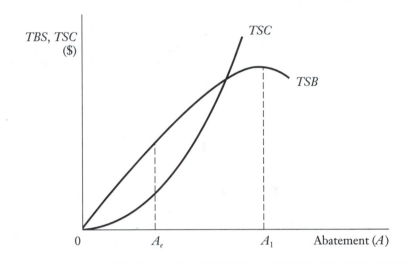

The benefit–cost analysis is to be based on specific health risk reduction and cost analysis used in risk assessment for any proposed MCL.[21]

**The Cost Implications.** A recent analysis of U.S. water quality policy cites the dramatic rise in treatment costs that have come about since the SDWA was enacted. Forecasts indicate that the typical American household will face a 50-percent increase in these costs by 2000.[22] Much of the increase in regulatory costs is due to the more stringent requirements called for in the 1986 Amendments. According to estimates based on analyses done in late 1986 and early 1987, the annual costs of implementing these amendments are about $2.5 billion. The full breakdown of this magnitude by ruling and by type of cost is given in Table 16.4. A more recent

---

[21] To learn more about the EPA's development of economic considerations in setting drinking water standards, visit **www.epa.gov/OGWDW/ria/riadoc.html**.

[22] See Howe (1991), p. 15, citing *U.S. Water News* (January 1991), p. 10.

| TABLE 16.4 | ESTIMATED ANNUAL COSTS TO WATER SYSTEMS UNDER THE SDWA AMENDMENTS OF 1986 ($1986 MILLIONS)[a] |
|---|---|

| Rule | Number of Systems Affected | Annualized Capital/O & M Costs[b] | Average Annual Monitoring Cost | Total Annual Compliance Cost |
|---|---|---|---|---|
| Volatile organic chemicals | 1,824 | $  32.7 | $ 23.1 | $   55.8 |
| Filtration | 10,228 | 511.6 | 17.1 | 528.6 |
| Total coliforms | 200,183 | 0 | 75.2 | 75.2 |
| Synthetic organic chemicals | 2,284 | 45.4 | 32.2 | 77.5 |
| Inorganic chemicals | 1,896 | 123.2 | 12.4 | 135.6 |
| Lead/copper corrosion control | 43,927 | 302.2 | 32.9 | 335.2 |
| Radionuclides | 22,867 | 790.3 | 2.6 | 792.9 |
| Disinfection | 103,354 | 474.8 | 12.8 | 487.7 |
| Total | c | $2,280.2 | $208.3 | $2,488.5 |

NOTES:

[a]Most estimates presented result from regulatory and economic analyses conducted by the EPA in late 1986 and early 1987. Dollars are rounded to the nearest 100,000.

[b]Figures in this column include the estimated annualized costs over 20 years at a 10-percent discount rate and one year of annual operation and maintenance (O & M) expenses.

[c]The number of water systems affected cannot be added together because some systems will be affected by multiple rules.

SOURCE: U.S. General Accounting Office. *Drinking Water: Compliance Problems Undermine EPA Program as New Challenges Emerge.* Washington, DC, June 1990, Table 4.1, p. 53.

**Regulatory Impact Analysis (RIA)**
Required under Executive Order 12291 that called for information about the potential benefits and costs associated with a "major" federal regulation.

report projects annualized control costs through the year 2000. These estimates are shown in Table 16.5 and assume full implementation of the SDWA prior to the 1996 Amendments. Notice how real costs are expected to rise over time—an outcome that may impede the EPA's ability to implement the law. The financial burden that these regulations place on state and local authorities is an important concern, particularly since many public water systems are already unable to comply with the law due to resource limitations.

What these findings imply is that both social costs and benefits are important considerations in the regulatory process. The premise is rooted in economic theory and recommended in President Clinton's Executive Order 12866 and previously in Executive Order 12291 issued by President Reagan. Under both presidential directives, the benefits and costs associated with a major regulatory action must be assessed and made public. Establishing or revising primary drinking water standards is an example of a government action subject to this requirement. In 1991, when the lead standard was revised, Reagan's Executive Order was in force, so the estimated benefits and costs were presented within a **Regulatory Impact Analysis (RIA).** We next consider the key results of this mandated benefit–cost analysis.

| TABLE 16.5 | TREND DATA AND PROJECTIONS ON CONTROL COSTS FOR SAFE DRINKING WATER |
| --- | --- |

| Year | Annualized Control Costs[a] ($1986 millions)[a] |
| --- | --- |
| 1986 | $2,979. |
| 1987 | 3,111. |
| 1988 | 3,250. |
| 1989 | 3,415. |
| 1990 | 3,587. |
| 1991 | 3,926. |
| 1992 | 4,319. |
| 1993 | 4,586. |
| 1994 | 4,917. |
| 1995 | 5,350. |
| 1996 | 5,684. |
| 1997 | 5,949. |
| 1998 | 6,264. |
| 1999 | 6,491. |
| 2000 | 6,571. |

NOTE:

[a] These cost data assume full implementation at a 7-percent discount rate.

SOURCE: Drawn from U.S. Environmental Protection Agency, Office of Policy, Planning, and Evaluation. *Environmental Investments: The Cost of a Clean Environment, A Summary*. Washington, DC, December 1990, Table 2-1, pp. 2-2–2-3.

### The Regulatory Impact Analysis (RIA) for the New Lead Standard in Drinking Water[23]

In June 1991, the EPA announced a maximum contaminant level goal (MCLG) for lead of zero and a more stringent maximum contaminant level (MCL) of 0.015 mg/L. This new primary standard lowered the allowable lead level in drinking water from its former limit of 50 parts per billion (ppb) to 15 ppb measured at any point in a public water distribution system. Regulations for water treatment were also instituted to assure that the new action level would be met. Taken together, these regulations were expected to have a substantial financial impact on the regulated community— in excess of $100 million per year. Hence, by law, the new rulings were subject to Executive Order 12291 and had to be accompanied by a Regulatory Impact Analysis (RIA) with a full description of the associated benefits and costs. Table 16.6 provides the detail.

---

[23] The following is drawn from U.S. EPA, Office of Ground Water and Drinking Water (May 1991), and U.S. *Federal Register*, Vol. 56, No. 110 (June 7, 1991); Rules and Regulations.

| TABLE 16.6 | ESTIMATED BENEFITS AND COSTS OF THE NEW LEAD STANDARD: RESULTS FROM THE RIA |
| --- | --- |

### Incremental Benefits

**Health Benefits**
**Descriptive Assessment:**

Reduction in the exposure of about 130 million people to lead in drinking water.

Reduction in the blood lead level of an additional 570,000 children to below 10 micrograms per deciliter.

**Monetized Annualized Value**
**(based on avoided medical costs):**

| From corrosion control and source water treatment: | $2.8 to $4.3 billion per year |
| From replacement of lead service lines: | $70 to $240 million per year |

**Material Benefits**
**Descriptive Assessment:**

Reduced damages to public water system pipelines, which extends pipe life and minimizes leakage.

Reduced damages to customers, such as less leakage, extended life of water-using appliances, less staining of clothing and water fixtures, and fewer repairs.

**Monetized Annualized Value:**

| Accruing to households and water systems: | $500 million per year |

**Annualized Benefits:** **$3.4 to $5.0 billion per year**

### Incremental Costs

**Treatment, Implementation, Education Costs**
**Descriptive Assessment:**

Source water treatment; corrosion control treatment; lead-line replacement; public education; monitoring costs; state implementation impacts.

**Monetized Annualized Value:**

| Treatment costs: | $390 to $680 million |
| Monitoring costs: | $ 40 million |
| Education costs: | $ 30 million |
| State implementation costs: | $ 40 million |

**Annualized Costs:** **$500 to $790 million per year**

### Net Benefits

**Annualized Net Benefits:** **$2.9 to $4.2 billion per year**

NOTES: Annualized costs for source water treatment, corrosion control, and lead-line replacement were derived from total capital costs, which were estimated to be between $2.9 and $7.7 billion.

SOURCES: U.S. Environmental Protection Agency, Office of Ground Water and Drinking Water. *Fact Sheet: National Primary Drinking Water Regulations for Lead and Copper.* Washington, DC, May 1991; U.S. *Federal Register,* Vol. 56, No. 110 (June 7, 1991); Rules and Regulations.

**Incremental Benefits of the New Lead Standard.**   According to the RIA, the expected incremental benefits of the tougher lead standard include reductions in damages to health and to materials. For health benefits, the qualitative assessment was described as a reduction in the exposure of 130 million people to lead in drinking water and a reduction in the blood lead level of an additional 570,000 children to below 10 micrograms per deciliter. To monetize these benefits, they were translated into avoided medical costs and estimated as within a range of $2.87 and $4.54 billion annually. Incremental material benefits were described as accruing to both public water facilities and to private households. These include such gains as longer pipe life, reduced leakages, extended life of water-using appliances, and fewer repairs. The estimated value of these benefits was $500 million per year. Combining these values, the aggregate incremental benefits associated with tightening the lead standard in drinking water were estimated at between $3.4 and 5.0 billion per year.

**Incremental Costs of the New Lead Standard.**   On the cost side, the RIA itemized annual expenditures for treatment, monitoring, education, and implementation is as shown in Table 16.6. The highest costs were assessed for treatment procedures at between $390 and $680 million per year. In the aggregate, the incremental costs of implementing the new lead action level were estimated at between $500 and $790 million per year.

**Net Benefits of the New Lead Standard.**   Based on the benefit and cost estimates, the EPA determined that the annualized net benefits of tightening the standard for lead in drinking water were between $2.9 and $4.2 billion. Although these findings did not dictate the new action level, they did communicate in economic terms the net gain to society associated with the regulatory decision.

### The State and Local Role: Compliance and Enforcement

Since the Safe Drinking Water Act relies heavily on a command-and-control approach, its success depends critically on sound monitoring and enforcement procedures that assure compliance with the primary standards. Public water systems are required periodically to sample water supplies, test them in an approved laboratory, and report the data to state authorities. In turn, these data are to be analyzed to determine if the system is meeting its monitoring responsibilities and if it is complying with the national standards. States are responsible for enforcement if any violations are noted, giving priority to those systems designated as "significant non-compliers (SNC)."[24] The EPA must step in if the state does not properly enforce the law.

---

[24] The classification as an SNC is based on either the frequency of violations or the severity of the violations, such as the extent to which a system exceeds the MCL. See U.S. General Accounting Office (GAO) (June 1990), p. 14.

Although these procedures may seem to be in order, an investigation conducted by the U.S. General Accounting Office (GAO) found that the extent of compliance by public water systems had been overstated by the EPA.[25] Part of the problem lies in the EPA's classification of SNCs versus "other non-compliers." The classification system was put into place to focus scarce resources on the worst offenders. However, according to the GAO, the SNC criteria are such that many serious violators are not being confronted. Deficiencies were identified at every level of government, specifically the local water system, the state, and the EPA. Problems were discovered in the sampling and testing procedures conducted by community water systems. The GAO also found that states were not consistently reporting violations to the EPA. Since the EPA's data management system relies on state tracking systems for compliance information, its reporting of these data is sometimes inaccurate and overstated.

Another failing in the process is the inadequate enforcement action taken by both state authorities and the EPA, despite the added stringency provided by the 1986 Amendments. In its review of enforcement procedures in six states, the GAO found that states took timely and appropriate action in only 24 of the 95 SNC violations committed by 75 public water systems. Most notable was the observation that many SNCs remained in noncompliance for several years. In fact, 46 of the SNC cases reviewed, or nearly half, had met the SNC criteria for more than four years.

Why is the compliance record so poor? Some of the reasons are procedural, having to do with how states and the EPA respond to violations of federal law. However, even if these administrative issues were corrected, there would still be unresolved compliance issues due to both technological and economic considerations. A recent analysis done by the Natural Resources Defense Council reports that severely outmoded treatment facilities and failing water distribution systems characterize the majority of public water systems across the nation.[26] These technological problems are exacerbated by the absence of watershed protection approaches, which forces an overreliance on treatment techniques. With regard to economic considerations, the GAO argues that the SDWA imposes what it calls "staggering costs" on public water systems faced with contamination problems. This is particularly true for small systems that are unable to finance the costs of corrective action and to compete for external funding. Of the 75 systems examined by the GAO, two-thirds served 500 or fewer people, and 87 percent served 3,300 or less.[27] This economic dilemma is worse in those cases where water prices are set below cost.

The funding problem helps to explain the motivation for the State Revolving Fund (SRF) authorized by the 1996 Amendments. Among the

---

[25] U.S. GAO (June 1990).

[26] Cohen and Olson (March 1994).

[27] U.S. GAO (June 1990), p. 46.

fund's objectives are to finance infrastructure improvements, to assist small and disadvantaged communities, and to encourage pollution prevention as a means to ensure safe drinking water.[28] In retrospect, it seems that a balancing of benefits and costs may have avoided some of the costing difficulties public officials face. Another likely explanation is the lack of economically sound pricing practices for drinking water supplies—an issue we examine more closely.

## Economic Principles in Pricing Water Supplies

At all levels of government, the costs of implementing the SDWA present a challenge. Not only are these costs inflated because of inefficient decision making, but in many communities they are not properly reflected in the pricing of water supplies. Basic economic theory illustrates that resources are misallocated if the price of a good or service is not equal to the associated marginal social cost of production. In this context, society's marginal cost of *current* water usage includes the explicit costs incurred by water supply facilities plus the opportunity costs of forgone *future* consumption. All too often, water is priced at a fixed rate that is independent of use and therefore independent of rising marginal costs. The result is overconsumption. If present consumption is higher than its allocatively efficient level, future supplies will be adversely affected. The 1996 Amendments recognize the importance of efficient water use and explicitly require the EPA to establish guidelines to encourage water conservation.[29]

### *An International Comparison*

An international comparison of water consumption patterns reveals two very interesting findings. First, U.S. per capita consumption is higher than most nations around the world. For example, in 1990, the average American consumed approximately 2,161 cubic meters of water. Contrast this with the same statistic for Canada, which is reported at about 1,500 cubic meters, or for all of Europe, estimated at 750 cubic meters.[30] A second important observation is that water prices vary considerably across countries as shown in Figure 16.3. Notice how European countries face much higher prices for water than the United States and Canada. And it is the European nations that have much lower consumption rates than their North American counterparts. Of course, this outcome is precisely what the Law of

---

[28] U.S. EPA, Office of Water, Office of Ground Water and Drinking Water. *Drinking Water State Revolving Fund*, last revised 6/23/98, **www.epa.gov/OGWDW/dwsrf.html**.

[29] To learn more about the guidelines for water conservation plans as required under the new amendments, visit **www.epa.gov/owmitnet/genwave.htm**.

[30] World Resources Institute (1992b), p. 102.

**FIGURE 16.3**

**INTERNATIONAL WATER PRICES:**
**A COMPARISON ACROSS SELECTED**
**INDUSTRIALIZED COUNTRIES (1989)**

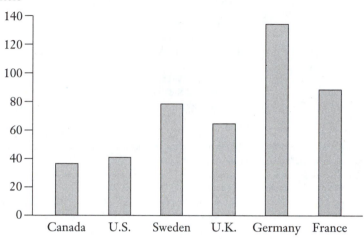

Cents per 1,000 liters

NOTE: Excludes cost of sewage treaatment.

SOURCE: "International Water Prices, 1989" chart, from *1992 Information Please Environmental Almanac.* Copyright © 1991 by World Resources Institute. Reprinted by permission of Houghton Mifflin Company. All rights reserved.

Demand predicts—that higher prices are associated with lower quantities consumed. What these data convey is that water use *is* price sensitive—an important observation given that some locations in the United States employ pricing policies that actually encourage inefficient water use. By examining these pricing practices in more detail, we can identify the inherent weaknesses and consider some economically sound alternatives.

### Pricing Practices of U.S. Water Utilities

**flat fee pricing scheme** Pricing water supplies such that the fee is independent of water use.

**uniform rate pricing structure** Pricing water supplies to charge more for higher water usage at a constant rate.

Table 16.7 provides data on the actual pricing practices of water utilities based on a 1995 survey of community water systems.[31] Notice that a considerable percentage use a **flat fee pricing scheme,** which refers to pricing that is independent of water use. Such an approach would be efficient only if the associated marginal costs were zero. Nearly half employ a **uniform rate (or flat rate) pricing structure,** which *does* charge more for higher usage but at a constant rate. This structure would be efficient only if

---

[31] U.S. EPA, Office of Water, Office of Ground Water and Drinking Water. January 1997, p. 15.

| TABLE 16.7 | PERCENTAGE USE OF VARIOUS PRICING STRUCTURES |

| Pricing | Percentage of Community Water Systems |
|---|---|
| Uniform rate | 49.0 |
| Declining block | 16.0 |
| Increasing block | 11.0 |
| Peak period | 0.9 |
| Separate flat fee | 15.3 |
| Combined flat fee | 10.0 |
| Other | 8.2 |

NOTES: Percentages do not sum to 100% because some systems used more than one rate structure.

Uniform rate: A price that is a fixed amount per unit of water used.

Declining block: A pricing scheme designed such that the per unit price declines as water use increases. Units are typically referred to as blocks, where each block represents a specific quantity of water.

Increasing block: A pricing scheme designed such that the per unit price increases as water use increases.

Flat fee: A fixed fee paid monthly or annually which is independent of actual water use.

SOURCE: U.S. Environmental Protection Agency, Office of Water, Office of Ground Water and Drinking Water. *Community Water Systems Survey, Volume I. Overview*. Washington, DC, January 1997, p. 15.

marginal costs were constant and equal to the uniform rate being charged. Neither of these pricing structures reflect the rising marginal social costs of water provision, and thus they act as a disincentive for consumers to economize on water usage.

The other major pricing methods represented in the table are the **declining block** and **increasing block** pricing structures. Each of these allows for changes in per unit prices for different "blocks" of consumption levels, but obviously each works in the opposite direction of the other. Both pricing structures are illustrated graphically in Figure 16.4. Since they are motivated differently, we need to examine them more closely and consider how each affects water usage.

**declining block pricing structure**
Pricing scheme that allows the per unit price of different "blocks" or quantities of water to decline as usage increases.

**Declining Block Pricing Structure.** Referring back to the data in Table 16.7, the **declining block** structure is used by 16 percent of the surveyed water systems. Its usage appears to have its basis in the typical utility's cost structure. Throughout the United States, most water utilities tend to have high fixed costs and relatively low variable costs.[32] In an attempt to recover these high fixed costs, some utilities encourage higher consumption levels with declining block pricing as shown in Figure 16.4(a). In so doing, they

[32] U.S. EPA, Office of Policy, Planning, and Evaluation (March 1991), pp. 4–7

FIGURE 16.4 · **ALTERNATIVE PRICING STRUCTURES OF WATER**

The declining block pricing structure is one form of water pricing. In the United States, most water utilities incur relatively low variable costs but high fixed costs. In an attempt to recover these fixed costs, utilities use declining block pricing to encourage higher consumption levels. In so doing, they are able to exploit available scale economies and incur lower average costs. From society's vantage point, this pricing scheme is inefficient because utilities are incorrectly using an average cost pricing framework as opposed to a marginal cost pricing framework.

**(a)** · · **Declining Block Structure**

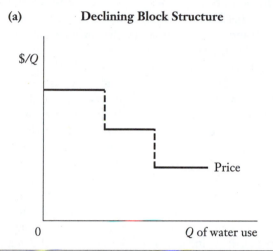

An increasing block pricing structure calls for a higher per unit price as water consumption increases. This provides an economic incentive for more conservative water usage. Benefit–cost analysis is implicitly reflected in this approach. As each additional block of water is used, higher marginal costs are considered along with the marginal benefits of consumption.

**(b)** **Increasing Block Structure**

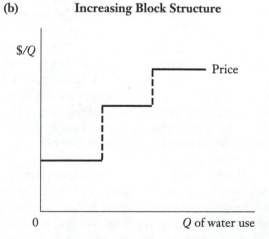

can exploit available scale economies and incur lower average costs. From the utility's perspective, the declining block price structure has merit. But from society's point of view, the pricing scheme is inefficient. Although this inefficiency arises for several reasons, the major culprit is that suppliers are incorrectly using average cost pricing as opposed to a marginal cost pricing framework.

**Increasing Block Pricing Structure.**   Looking again at Table 16.7, notice that one of the least common pricing practices (aside from pricing linked to peak periods) is **increasing block pricing.** As illustrated in Figure 16.4(b), the customer pays a higher per unit price as water consumption increases—a practice that provides an economic incentive for more conservative water usage. Notice how benefit–cost analysis is implicitly reflected in this approach. As each additional block of water is used, higher marginal costs are considered along with the marginal benefits of consumption. Of course, unless the increasing price blocks accurately reflect society's marginal cost, the result will not be efficient. Also, there are implementation costs to be considered in instituting this pricing structure, since metering is necessary to track usage. This factor explains why some smaller utilities favor a uniform rate system despite its inherent inefficiencies.

Based on this fundamental analysis, it is argued that the EPA and other government authorities should attempt to structure water pricing to reflect the associated marginal cost to society. A further consideration is to find ways to make such a pricing scheme financially feasible for all types of water utilities, including smaller facilities. Although this would be a challenging undertaking, it could make a measurable difference in both current and future water quality.

**increasing block pricing structure**
Pricing scheme whereby the per unit price of different "blocks" of water increases as water use increases.

# Conclusions

For more than 20 years, the Safe Drinking Water Act has been the legislation responsible for protecting human health from contaminated tap water. Like most environmental laws, this one has been the subject of debate and criticism—even more so as it recently came up for reauthorization before the U.S. Congress. Confidence in national drinking water policy has weakened in recent years. Right or wrong, most Americans had been fairly complacent about the quality of tap water. However, reports such as the EPA's 1992 survey on lead levels and the 1993 Milwaukee incident have made both private citizens and public officials question the effectiveness of U.S. drinking water policy.

Prior to the 1996 Amendments, the structure of the SDWA was markedly simple—a direct application of the command-and-control approach. It established contaminant limits designed to assure that public water supplies were safe for human consumption and relied on state and local authorities to make certain that these standards were met. From an economic perspective, such an approach is flawed. The standards were benefit-based, with no requirement for a balancing of marginal benefits and costs. Furthermore, there were no incentives to encourage compliance or to stimulate technological advance to meet the standards in a cost-effective manner. Instead, achieving safe drinking water relied on constant monitoring and enforcement—procedures that are difficult and costly to implement.

The recently enacted SDWA Amendments of 1996 address some of these shortcomings. A major set of revisions deals with integrating risk assessment and benefit–cost analysis into the setting of drinking water standards. This is a major shift away from the strict command-and-control approach that characterized this legislation until now. There is also a new Drinking Water State Revolving Fund (DWSRF), which is aimed at helping states and local communities improve the infrastructure needed to ensure clean drinking water supplies. Another important reform is the integration of preventive programs to protect and manage sources of drinking water supplies.

Because water resources are so diverse and at the same time interconnected, policy formulation is not straightforward, nor is the revision process. Both the Clean Water Act and the Safe Drinking Water Act continue to be rooted strongly in the command-and-control approach with standards providing the legislative muscle. But there has been some integration of market-based incentives into this policy structure and gradual changes to launch initiatives to *prevent* water contamination and lessen the dependence on end-of-pipe treatment. These are nontrivial revisions, as are the problems confronting the nation at this phase of its water quality policy development.

# Summary

- The Interstate Quarantine Act of 1893 was the first federal law in the evolution of U.S. drinking water standards. The Public Health Service Act of 1912 called for standards to prevent the spread of communicable waterborne diseases. These were set in 1914 and revised over the next several decades.

- The Safe Drinking Water Act of 1974 (SDWA) was aimed at protecting drinking water from any contaminant that could threaten human health or welfare. It established primary standards to protect human health and secondary standards to protect welfare.

- The 1986 Amendments expanded federal controls on drinking water and corrected some of the failings of the original SDWA.

- The 1996 Amendments were signed into law on August 6, 1996. Among the chief revisions are the integration of risk assessment and benefit–cost analysis into standard-setting, a new Drinking Water State Revolving Fund (DWSRF) to improve infrastructure, and efforts to encourage prevention through better management and source water protection.

- The primary purpose of the Safe Drinking Water Act is to assure that public water systems meet minimum standards to protect human health.

- The 1986 Amendments identified 83 contaminants for which drinking water standards were to be set.

- Under U.S. law, there are National Primary Drinking Water Regulations (NPDWRs) aimed at protecting human health. Each regulation consists of a maximum contaminant level goal (MCLG), a maximum contaminant level (MCL), and a specification of the best available technology (BAT) for public water supply treatment.

- The MCLG defines the level of a pollutant at which no known or expected adverse health effects occur, allowing for an adequate margin of safety.

- The MCL is the highest permissible level of a contaminant in water delivered to any user of a public system. Determination of the MCLs was changed by the 1996 Amendments such that a published determination must be made as to whether the benefits of the MCL are justified by the cost.

- The BAT represents the feasible treatment technology capable of meeting the standard, taking account of cost considerations.

- Secondary Drinking Water Regulations establish secondary maximum contaminant levels (SMCLs) for pollutants that impair aesthetics and other characteristics like odor and taste. These are nonenforceable federal guidelines aimed at protecting public welfare.

- Enforcement of the primary drinking water standards is shared between the EPA and state governments. The major responsibility is assigned to state governments, provided that certain criteria are met.

- Prior to the 1996 Amendments, the Safe Drinking Water Act (SDWA) did not call for a balancing of benefits and costs in setting the maximum contaminant levels (MCLs). Hence, efficiency was not being used to regulate drinking water quality.

- Important revisions in the 1996 Amendments specify how the MCLs are to be determined. At the time a new NPDWR is proposed, the EPA must publish a determination identifying whether or not the benefits of the MCL justify the costs.

- According to a government study, the extent of compliance by public water systems has been overstated by the EPA, and enforcement action has been inadequate.

- Many U.S. communities use improper pricing practices of water supplies, such as a flat fee, uniform rate, or declining block structure, none of which account for rising marginal costs. The result is overconsumption of water resources.

## Key Concepts

Drinking Water State Revolving Fund (DWSRF)

sole-source aquifers

priority contaminants

National Primary Drinking Water Regulations (NPDWR)

maximum contaminant level goal (MCLG)

maximum contaminant level (MCL)

action level

best available technology (BAT)

secondary maximum contaminant level (SMCL)

Regulatory Impact Analysis (RIA)

flat fee pricing scheme

uniform rate pricing structure

declining block pricing structure

increasing block pricing structure

## Review Questions

1. In what ways did the Safe Drinking Water Act Amendments of 1986 best address the shortcomings in the law? In what ways did it fail?

2. a. Explain the practical difference between the MCLG and the MCL.
   b. Draw the relationship of marginal social benefit and marginal social cost for the MCLG for lead, assuming it is set at an efficient level. Intuitively explain your model.

3. Support or refute Congress' decision to make the secondary drinking water standards *not* enforceable by the federal government.

4. According to the EPA, uncontrolled disposal of pesticide residues and containers contributes significantly to groundwater contamination and hence threatens drinking water supplies. Design and evaluate a deposit/refund system for pesticide containers.

5. Determine the water pricing structure that is used in your hometown. Using the criterion of allocative efficiency, defend the current practice or propose an alternative pricing structure.

## Additional Readings

Dziegielewski, Benedykt, and Duane D. Baumann. "Tapping Alternatives: The Benefits of Managing Urban Water Demands." *Environment* 34(9), November 1992, pp. 6–11, 35–41.

Dzurik, Andrew A. *Water Resources Planning.* Savage, MD: Rowman & Littlefield Publishers, 1990.

Ferguson, Tim W. "Socialized Water." *Forbes,* March 11, 1996.

Gordon, Wendy. "Federal Protection of Ground Water." In David H. Speidel, Lon C. Ruedisili, and Allen F. Agnew, eds. *Perspectives on Water: Uses and Abuses.* New York: Oxford University Press, 1988, pp. 326–29.

Howitt, Richard E., Dean E. Mann, and H. J. Vaux, Jr. "The Economics of Water Allocation." In Ernest A. Engelbert with Ann Foley Scheuring, eds. *Competition for California Water.* Berkeley, CA: University of California Press, 1982, pp. 136–62.

MacLeish, William H. "Water, Water, Everywhere, How Many Drops to Drink?" *World Monitor,* December 1990, pp. 54–58.

Mazari, Marisa. "Potential for Groundwater Contamination in Mexico City." *Environmental Science and Technology* 27(5), 1993, pp. 794–802.

Mohl, Bruce. "Testing the Water." *Boston Globe,* February 26, 1996.

Newman, Alan. "A Blueprint for Water Quality." *Environmental Science and Technology* 27(2), 1993, pp. 223–25.

Tomsho, Robert. "Cities Reclaim Waste Water for Drinking." *The Wall Street Journal,* August 8, 1994, pp. B1, B6.

Waxman, Henry. "Amending the Safe Drinking Water Act: View from Congress." *EPA Journal 20(1–2),* Summer 1994, pp. 32–33.

World Health Organization. "Health Hazards of Water Pollution." In David H. Speidel, Lon C. Ruedisili, and Allen F. Agnew, eds. *Perspectives on Water: Uses and Abuses.* New York: Oxford University Press, 1988.

## Related Web Sites

| | |
|---|---|
| Current drinking water standards | **www.epa.gov/OGWDW/wot/appa.html** |
| Drinking Water Regulations and Guidance | **www.epa.gov/OGWDW/regs.html** |
| Drinking Water and Health Fact Sheets | **www.epa.gov/OGWDW/hfacts.html** |
| Drinking Water State Revolving Fund (DWSRF) | **www.epa.gov/OGWDW/dwsrf.html** |
| Economic Considerations in Drinking Water Standard Setting | **www.epa.gov/OGWDW/ria/riadoc.html** |
| EPA's *Community Water Systems Survey, Volume I* | **www.epa.gov/ogwdw000/cwssvr.html** |
| EPA's *Water on Tap: A Consumer's Guide to the Nation's Drinking Water* | **www.epa.gov/OGWDW/wot/wot.html** |

| | |
|---|---|
| Implementation of the SDWA Amendments of 1996 | **www.epa.gov/OGWDW/sdwa/sdwa.html** |
| National Drinking Water Contaminant Occurrence Database | **www.epa.gov/OGWDW/standard/pp/ncodpp.html** |
| Water Efficiency—General Information | **www.epa.gov/owmitnet/genwave.htm** |

# Appendix:
# A Reference to Acronyms and Terms
# in Drinking Water Quality Control

### Environmental Economics Acronyms

| | |
|---|---|
| *TSB* | Total social benefits |
| *TSC* | Total social costs |

### Environmental Science Terms

| | |
|---|---|
| mg/L | Milligrams per liter |
| ppb | Parts per billion |
| RfD | Reference dose |

### Environment Policy Acronyms

| | |
|---|---|
| BAT | Best available technology |
| DWSRF | Drinking Water State Revolving Fund |
| MCL | Maximum contaminant level |
| MCLG | Maximum contaminant level goal |
| NAS | National Academy of Science |
| NCOD | National Contaminant Occurrence Database |
| RIA | Regulatory Impact Analysis |
| SDWA | Safe Drinking Water Act |
| SMCL | Secondary maximum contaminant level |
| SNC | Significant noncompliers |

# VI

## *The Case of Solid Wastes and Toxic Substances*

In 1978, the state of New York urged 1,000 families to leave their homes and ordered an emergency evacuation of 240 others, all residents of a Niagara Falls community known as Love Canal. Built on a site that 30 years earlier had been a chemical dumping ground, the ill-fated Love Canal was eventually declared a disaster area by President Carter. In 1982, the residents of Times Beach, Missouri learned that their groundwater and soil contained dangerously high levels of dioxins, the result of contaminated road oil that had been used in the town 11 years earlier. Times Beach was completely evacuated. In 1987, what came to be known as the "garbage barge" hauled some 3,100 tons of New York's trash for months in the Gulf of Mexico and the Caribbean, searching for a place to deposit its decaying and foul-smelling cargo. These events and countless others awakened society to the potential risks of solid waste pollution and exposure to toxic chemicals.

The extent of these problems is not completely known, and efficient solutions appear to be just as elusive. Not only are *current* waste generation and disposal practices at issue, but also the damages caused by waste mismanagement of the *past*. In a broad sense, there are two interrelated issues to be addressed: excess waste generation and the use of toxic substances that eventually become part of the waste stream. Chemicals leaking from buried waste and mismanaged disposal sites have caused serious damage to human health and the ecology, some of it irreparable. Less severe, but nonetheless cause for concern, is the growth rate of municipal trash generation—millions of tons of bottles, cans, food scraps, and the like. In many communities, residents and public officials are still searching for cost-effective ways to collect and dispose of the accumulating heap. What makes these problems all the more troubling is that the environmental damage cuts across all media—land, water, and air.

Policy development aimed at solid waste pollution got a late start in the United States, and most argue that current legislation is inadequate. In the 1960s and 1970s, U.S. environmental policy was firmly focused on controlling air and water pollution, but little in the way of substantive federal legislation was passed during this period to manage and reduce the solid waste stream. Why this lack of initiative? For one thing, population centers had remained fairly compact for a long time and seemingly were able to manage the wastes being generated. Managing solid wastes was viewed as a local responsibility and not one that required national action. Furthermore, the problems associated with the treatment and disposal of chemical wastes, particularly synthetics, did not accelerate until the 1970s.[1] Regardless of the logic of these explanations, there is one root cause that underlies all of them. Society failed to recognize the significance of solid waste as an environmental and health risk. The result? Policy makers are having to play catch-up with a problem that, at least until recently, has been advancing in magnitude and severity.

In this module, we assess this environmental and social dilemma and analyze the solutions brought forth by government. In Chapter 17, we focus on hazardous waste pollution—the risks it poses to society and the federal legislation designed to minimize those risks. Chapter 18 examines the challenges of managing nonhazardous wastes and the policy efforts of both the federal and lower levels of government. Our focus shifts in Chapter 19, where we analyze federal laws aimed at controlling pesticides and other toxic substances *before* they are introduced into commerce and eventually enter the waste stream. Not unlike our analyses of air and water degradation, the tools of economic analysis are used throughout to assess government's effectiveness in responding to environmental risks.

---

[1] U.S. EPA, Office of Solid Waste and Emergency Response (October 1985).

# 17

# Managing Hazardous Solid Waste and Waste Sites

An official order to evacuate homes and businesses following the discovery of a hazardous waste leak is a chilling reminder of the potential risks of solid waste pollution. All too often, there are accounts of strange odors emanating from basements, tainted water supplies, or health symptoms for which doctors have no diagnosis—reports that are eventually linked to a waste accident or cover-up from years past. Once-thriving communities in the United States like Love Canal, New York, and Times Beach, Missouri, actually became ghost towns because of the toxic effects of hazardous waste. Why did the problem reach such a level before something was done?

By the time federal policies were formulated in the United States, the nation was already suffering from the ill effects of mismanaged hazardous wastes that had been accumulating for decades. At the same time, the growth rate of the waste stream was rising due to urban development, industrialization, population growth, and increasing chemical usage. There was also a glaring lack of information about the magnitude of the problem. In fact, some argue that we still do not have a complete picture of the extent and severity of solid waste pollution in this country. What we *do* know is that the damage extends to all environmental media, which means that the effects are widespread, difficult to control, and costly to society. Accepting this characterization, it should not be surprising to learn that there are several major legislative acts aimed at the dilemma. While some deal with the damage from *past* mismanagement, others attempt to control the *present* solid waste stream.

Investigating this multidimensional control approach is the objective of this chapter. Our aim is to explain the policy position of the United States in dealing with hazardous waste. The operative issue is whether or not existing policy is effective and if not, whether there are viable alternatives that should be implemented. We begin with an overview of the hazardous waste problem and a brief discussion of how the federal response evolved. We then focus on the two major U.S. laws aimed at hazardous waste—the Resource Conservation and Recovery Act (RCRA) and Superfund. Here, the goal is to explain the overall intent and structure of these laws so that they can be analyzed from an economic perspective. An appendix of acronyms is provided for reference at the end of the chapter.

# Characterizing the Hazardous Waste Problem[1]

**hazardous solid wastes** Any unwanted materials or refuse capable of posing a substantial threat to health or the ecology.

**Hazardous solid wastes** are any unwanted materials or refuse capable of posing a substantial threat to health or the environment. A diverse range of substances fall into this broad category, so it is useful to consider the hazardous constituents of wastes as part of subgroups like pesticides and synthetic chemicals as listed in Table 17.1. Notice from the table that these substances serve important functions in productive activity. Often, the properties that make them useful in production are precisely those that make them dangerous to society once they enter the **waste stream.** The **waste stream** refers to the series of events starting with waste **generation** and proceeding though the **transportation, storage, treatment,** and **disposal** of these materials.[2] Environmental and health risks arise both because of excess generation and improper management of these materials once they enter the waste stream.

**waste stream** Series of events starting with waste generation and including transportation, storage, treatment, and disposal of solid wastes.

## *The Magnitude and Source of the Problem*

In the United States, estimates of annual hazardous waste generation range anywhere from 250 to 500 million tons. This translates to about 1 ton per person annually.[3] Nations everywhere must deal with the risks of accumulating hazardous wastes. In Canada, for example, the reported annual level of hazardous wastes is 3.63 million tons, or about 0.14 tons per person, and in Italy, the level is estimated at 4.01 million tons, or 0.07 tons per person.[4] Third-world countries also are confronting the problem as they evolve into more industrialized economies. These developing nations also

---

[1] Following the literature and government data reporting, we have omitted from this discussion any reference to medical wastes and radioactive wastes.

[2] To read more about the waste stream, visit **www.epa.gov/epaoswer/osw/index.htm**.

[3] McCarthy and Reisch (1987) and U.S. Congress, Office of Technology Assessment (OTA) (1983) as cited in Wirth and Heinz (1991), p. 43. These values are based on that portion of hazardous wastes controlled by U.S. waste regulations. Absent this qualifier, the grand total is estimated to be 1.3 billion tons per year, of which 75 percent is controlled by the Clean Water Act.

[4] Direct international comparisons cannot be made with precision given differences in definitions and estimating methods across nations. The statistics cited are drawn from selected data in World Resources Institute (1993), "Country Comparisons," pp. 333–640.

**TABLE 17.1**      TYPES OF HAZARDOUS SUBSTANCES

**Acids and Bases**

Description:  Acids are characterized as having a low pH between 0 and 6, and bases as having a high pH between 8 and 14. Highly acidic or basic substances are corrosive. In the waste stream, discarded acids and bases can corrode the containers in which they are stored and leach into land and nearby waterways.

Uses:  Acids and bases are frequently used in processes such as plating procedures and metal stripping.

**Heavy Metals**

Description:  Heavy metals include lead, arsenic, cadmium, barium, copper, and mercury. They are highly toxic and do not readily break down in the human body.

Uses:  These metals possess properties that are useful in plating and production processes and in numerous commodities. Some have special properties, such as copper, which is an excellent conductor of electricity and is highly resistant to corrosion.

**Reactives**

Description:  Reactives are substances that behave violently when combined with air or water. Included are explosives and flammables. Common examples are petroleum or natural gas by-products. The instability of reactive substances makes them potentially harmful in the waste stream.

Uses:  Reactives are useful in certain industrial processes. For example, laboratories use these chemicals to accelerate a reaction, and plastics manufacturing uses them to speed up polymerization to harden plastic.

**Synthetic Organic Chemicals**

Description:  Synthetic organic chemicals are man-made substances that are hydrocarbon based, some created from relatively new processes like chemical splicing and molecular engineering. Two important subcategories of synthetic organic chemicals are solvents and pesticides.

Uses:  Many synthetics are highly resistant in use, making them valuable to industrial applications. Polychlorinated biphenyls (PCBs) were formerly used as insulators in transformers because of their resistance to heat and electrical charges.[a]

**Solvents**

Description:  Solvents are liquids that can dissolve or disperse one or more substances. Examples include ethylene, benzene, pyridine, and acetone.

Uses:  Solvents are used for a variety of industrial processes, such as degreasing, stripping, cleaning, and thinning procedures.

**Pesticides**

Description:  Pesticides are used to prevent, destroy, or repel any unwanted form of plant or animal life. These include insecticides, rodenticides, herbicides, and fungicides. Some are highly resistant, which allows them to persist in the environment for a long time without the need for frequent reapplication. Some are nearly insoluble in water, making their use as insecticides on crops resistant to rainfall. Many are acutely toxic.

Uses:  These substances are used mainly in agriculture but also in such industries as textiles, paper, and wood production treatment.

NOTE:
[a] The highly toxic nature of PCBs led eventually to a 1976 ban on their manufacture, processing, distribution, and use in the United States, except in completely enclosed electrical equipment.

SOURCES: Drawn from Russell W. Phifer and William R. McTigue, Jr. *Handbook of Hazardous Waste Management.* Chelsea, MI: Lewis Publishers, 1988, Chapter 3; Samuel S. Epstein, M.D., Lester O. Brown, and Carl Pope. *Hazardous Waste in America.* San Francisco: Sierra Club Books, 1982, pp. 14–26; U.S. Environmental Protection Agency. *Meeting the Environmental Challenge: EPA's Review of Progress and New Directions in Environmental Protection.* Washington, DC, December 1990a, p. 120.

| TABLE 17.2 | ENVIRONMENTAL DEGRADATION AT U.S. HAZARDOUS WASTE SITES AS OF 1991 |

| Reported Impacts | Percent of Sites Affected[a] |
| --- | --- |
| Groundwater | 85.2 |
| Drinking water | 73.1 |
| Soil | 72.1 |
| Surface water | 50.4 |
| Air | 26.0 |
| Vegetation | 10.5 |
| Animal life | 7.8 |
| Human health | 6.6 |

NOTE:

[a]Sites included in the report are those designated by the United States as on its National Priorities List, that is, those that pose the greatest threat to human health and the ecology.

SOURCE: Council on Environmental Quality. *Environmental Quality, 22nd Annual Report.* Washington, DC: U.S. Government Printing Office, March 1992, Table 90, p. 338, citing U.S. Environmental Protection Agency, *Superfund NPL Characterization Project: National Results.* Washington, DC, 1991.

have to contend with wastes deliberately dumped inside their borders by firms from advanced countries seeking to avoid the costs of and regulatory constraints on disposal.[5] There is no doubt that the problem of hazardous waste exists worldwide, and there is no question that there are serious risks in ignoring it.

All environmental media—the atmosphere, ground and surface waters, and soil—are vulnerable to hazardous waste contamination. Ocean pollution, soil contamination, disease, fish kills, and livestock loss are among the potential damages. The health and ecological effects can be severe and long-term, particularly from exposure to persistent pollutants like PCBs and DDT that bioaccumulate in the environment. As shown in Table 17.2, water and soil contamination are the most prevalent type of damage linked to hazardous waste sites. Contamination of drinking water can occur when rainwater absorbs pollutants as it runs through disposal sites. The resulting leachate can pollute ground and surface waters—damage that is costly and sometimes impossible to rectify. Surrounding soil can be polluted in the same way. Food crops grown in such contaminated soil absorb pollutants that are later ingested by humans and animals. Particularly vulnerable are households living near hazardous waste sites. One of the most often cited cases of an entire community affected by the contamination is Love Canal, New York. A brief account of the story is given in Application 17.1.

Just who is responsible for generating all these toxic waste materials? It turns out that every sector of the economy—households, industry,

---

[5]Kharbanda and Stallworthy (1990), p. 105.

## The Hazardous Waste Site Called Love Canal

In the late 1880s, an entrepreneur named William T. Love began excavating a canal that would connect the upper and lower ends of the Niagara River in upper New York State. Envisioned as the future site of a major industrial complex, the Love Canal project was designed to make use of the enormous supply of hydroelectric power that would be provided naturally by the 280-foot drop between the two ends of the river. Before the plan was finished, alternating current (AC) was developed, and the once futuristic Love Canal project lost its appeal. Love's visionary complex was never finished, but one segment of the partially constructed canal remained. It simply filled with water, and for a time was used for swimming.

In the 1940s, Hooker Chemical and Plastics Corporation, through agreement with the canal's owner, began using the site to dump chemical wastes. Ultimately buying the canal to use as a dump site, Hooker discarded over 21,000 tons of chemicals into the Love Canal between 1942 and 1952. Among the toxic wastes were benzene derivatives, dioxins, and trichlorophenol (TCPs) contaminated with a highly potent carcinogenic substance called TCDD. According to one source, TCDD is so lethal that less than 3 ounces could kill all the residents of New York City (Epstein et al., 1982, p. 93).

Some years later, the postwar construction boom that characterized America in the 1950s prompted the city of Niagara Falls to condemn the properties surrounding the canal to make room for a new school and a residential area. In 1953, Hooker signed the canal over to the city for $1 in exchange for a release from any liability for damage associated with the dump site. Despite the danger, the canal was filled in, and construction proceeded. The school opened in 1955, and hundreds of homes were built.

Buyers of the new homes were unaware of the chemical dump site. Soon after moving in, they began to complain about fumes coming from the former dump site and chemical burns their children got from playing in nearby fields. Lawns and gardens refused to grow, and pools of black liquid began to surface in backyards. In the mid-1970s, the same black sludge started to seep into basements after heavy rains. Finally, in 1977 after numerous complaints, the city called in a consultant. The findings confirmed the residents' worse fears—toxic chemicals had leached from the canal and contaminated the ground and surface water.

One resident named Lois Gibbs took action, suspecting that her son's history of health problems might have been caused by the chemical leaks. What followed was a complex and bitter struggle for Gibbs and the other Love Canal residents. Despite mounting evidence, the state's response to the problem was less than adequate. Gibbs and the other residents formed the Love Canal Homeowners Association, Inc. and took matters into their own hands. Every level of government eventually became involved along with public agencies, health officials, researchers, and the media. In 1979, the Department of Justice filed a series of lawsuits against Hooker Chemical, the city of Niagara Falls, the city's board of education, and the Niagara County Health Department. In May 1980, President Carter declared Love Canal a disaster area, and that summer $15 million in grants and loans was offered to New York to purchase new homes for the relocated families.

SOURCES: Samuel S. Epstein, M.D., Lester O. Brown, and Carl Pope. *Hazardous Waste in America*. San Francisco: Sierra Club Books, 1982, Chapter 5; Lois Marie Gibbs. *Love Canal: My Story*. Albany: State University of New York Press, 1982; Melanie L. Griffin. "The Legacy of Love Canal." *Sierra*, January/February 1988, pp. 26–28.

government, and institutions—contributes to the hazardous waste stream.[6] While none of these sources should be ignored, there is no question that

---

[6]For example, U.S. households dispose of an estimated 385 million gallons of used motor oil each year— literally 35 times more oil than the *Valdez* spilled into Alaskan waters in 1989.

| TABLE 17.3 | HAZARDOUS WASTE GENERATION IN THE UNITED STATES BY MAJOR INDUSTRY[a] |
| --- | --- |

| Industry | Percentage of Hazardous Waste Generation |
| --- | --- |
| Chemical | 79.0 |
| Petroleum refinery | 7.0 |
| Transportation equipment | 1.0 |
| Fabricated metals | 1.0 |
| Primary metals | 1.0 |
| Electrical equipment | 0.4 |
| National security | 0.4 |
| Other | 9.0 |

NOTE:

[a]Excludes radioactive wastes.

SOURCE: U.S. Environmental Protection Agency. *Environmental Progress and Challenges: EPA's Update*. Washington, DC, August 1988, p. 80, Figure L-2, from U.S. Environmental Protection Agency, Office of Solid Waste. *National Screening Survey of Hazardous Waste Treatment, Storage, Disposal, and Recycling Facilities*. Washington, DC.

most hazardous wastes are generated by industry. In the United States, 99 percent of industrial hazardous wastes comes from so-called large-quantity generators, those producing over 2,200 pounds per month. Another 1 million tons per year are added by small-quantity generators, producing between 220 and 2,200 pounds per month. This latter group includes such diverse entities as biological laboratories, automobile repair shops, dry cleaners, greenhouses, art museums, and exterminators. As shown in Table 17.3, the chemical and petroleum industries are responsible for generating most of the hazardous waste in the United States, with 79 percent attributable to the former. The distribution is also skewed geographically, with the eastern, midwestern, and southern United States producing more than the western and Rocky Mountain regions.[7]

From an economic perspective, any adverse effects associated with the use and disposal of hazardous substances are negative externalities. Hence, policy is needed to regulate markets where the problem arises and internalize the external costs. In the United States, the early development of solid waste policy was anything but aggressive. Most argue that this segment of environmental legislative history should be characterized as having been reactive—even passive at times. This lack of spirited attention to solid waste problems by federal officials was matched by the same absence in the private sector. The environmentalism of the 1960s was preoccupied with fouled rivers and streams, urban smog, and threatened wildlife, paying little attention to the accumulating trash and the risks of chemical wastes.[8]

---

[7]U.S. EPA (August 1988), p. 80.

[8]One important exception was the 1962 work of Rachel Carson, *Silent Spring*, which warned of the risks of pesticide chemicals.

# The Evolution of U.S. Solid Waste Policy

It is often suggested that the U.S. government did virtually nothing in the way of controlling solid wastes until *after* the Love Canal saga made national news in the late 1970s. This suggestion on face value is erroneous. The primary piece of federal legislation on solid wastes, the Resource Conservation and Recovery Act, had been passed by Congress two years *prior* to that infamous event. Furthermore, the draft version of the Superfund legislation dealing with abandoned and uncontrolled hazardous waste sites had been completed in October of 1978—only two months after the nation first learned about Love Canal and well before the related publicity that continued into 1980.[9] The point is that the United States *did* have a national policy agenda on solid waste in the 1970s, but the legislation had passed with little scrutiny and was not fully responsive to the magnitude of the problem. Hence, while Love Canal was not the catalyst for introducing federal solid waste legislation, this event and others like it motivated public officials and private citizens to give the matter more attention. Several federal laws and amendments speak to this evolution as shown in Table 17.4 (p. 528). An overview of the chronology that ties together these laws and their primary objectives follows.

### Federal Recognition of the Solid Waste Problem

U.S. policy on waste control originated with the Solid Waste Disposal Act (SWDA) passed in 1965. Its primary objectives were to provide financial assistance to state and local governments for planning waste management programs and to initiate a national research plan aimed at finding better disposal methods. In 1970, this seminal waste legislation was amended by the Resource Recovery Act. More significant in intent, this act marked a slight shift in emphasis from disposal to conservation by encouraging recycling and technological development to reduce waste generation. However, the emphasis continued to be on *nonhazardous* waste and the use of land disposal in local communities.[10]

### Developing Policy to Control the Risks of Hazardous Wastes

**"cradle-to-grave" management system**
A command-and-control approach to regulating hazardous solid wastes through every stage of the waste stream.

In 1976, the Resource Conservation and Recovery Act (RCRA) was passed by Congress as amendments to the original Solid Waste Disposal Act. The hallmark of RCRA was a distinct set of regulations within the act that established a **"cradle-to-grave" management system** for controlling hazardous wastes. The metaphor refers to a policy strategy for controlling, managing, and tracking these wastes throughout every stage of the waste

---

[9] Landy et al. (1990), p. 140.

[10] U.S. EPA, Office of Solid Waste and Emergency Response (October 1985).

| TABLE 17.4 | OVERVIEW OF U.S. LEGISLATION ON HAZARDOUS SOLID WASTES |
|---|---|
| **Legislative Act** | **Major Provisions** |
| Solid Waste Disposal Act (SWDA) of 1965 | Provided financial assistance to state and local governments in planning solid waste disposal programs; initiated a national research plan aimed at finding better waste disposal methods. |
| Resource Recovery Act of 1970 | Encouraged recycling and technological controls to reduce waste at the generation point; continued to promote land disposal of wastes in local communities and to emphasize nonhazardous solid waste. |
| Resource Conservation and Recovery Act (RCRA) of 1976 | Represented the first U.S. official position on hazardous waste control; established a "cradle-to-grave" management system for hazardous waste; delegated the administration of nonhazardous waste primarily to state governments. |
| The Hazardous and Solid Waste Amendments of 1984 | Reauthorized RCRA and broadened federal control; shifted emphasis from land disposal to waste reduction and toward improved treatment technologies for hazardous wastes; elevated the standards for hazardous waste facilities. |
| Comprehensive Environmental Response, Compensation, and Liability Act (CERCLA) of 1980 (known as Superfund) | Called for the preparation of a national inventory of hazardous waste site information from which to identify sites posing the greatest threat to health and the ecology; placed these sites on the National Priorities List (NPL); designated a fund of $1.6 billion to clean up NPL sites and pay for associated damages. |
| Superfund Amendments and Reauthorization Act (SARA) of 1986 | Reauthorized CERCLA; increased the fund to $8.5 billion to be financed primarily from feedstock taxes; called for federal action on 375 sites within a five-year period; promoted permanent cleanup technologies. |

SOURCES: Sidney M. Wolf. *Pollution Law Handbook: A Guide to Federal Environmental Laws.* New York: Quorum Books, 1988, Chapters 6, 7; U.S. Environmental Protection Agency, Office of Solid Waste and Emergency Response, *The New RCRA Fact Book*, Washington, DC, October 1985; Resource Conservation and Recovery Act of 1976; Hazardous and Solid Waste Amendments of 1984; Comprehensive Environmental Response, Compensation, and Liability Act of 1980; Superfund Amendments and Reauthorization Act of 1986.

cycle, as shown in Figure 17.1. A separate set of provisions delegated the administration of nonhazardous waste primarily to state governments.[11]

Congress reauthorized and strengthened RCRA through the Hazardous and Solid Waste Amendments of 1984.[12] The new provisions reinforced the evolving policy shift away from land disposal and toward waste

---

[11] The provisions applicable to hazardous waste are given in Subtitle C of RCRA. Online information dealing with Subtitle C can be found at **www.epa.gov/epaoswer/osw/hazwaste.htm**. In the next chapter, we will investigate and analyze the rulings in Subtitle D of RCRA aimed at nonhazardous, municipal solid wastes.

[12] Despite the change in title, conventional practice is to use the acronym RCRA to refer to this legislation.

| FIGURE 17.1 | THE "CRADLE-TO-GRAVE" MANAGEMENT SYSTEM UNDER RCRA: CONTROLLING, MANAGING, AND TRACKING THE HAZARDOUS WASTE STREAM |
|---|---|

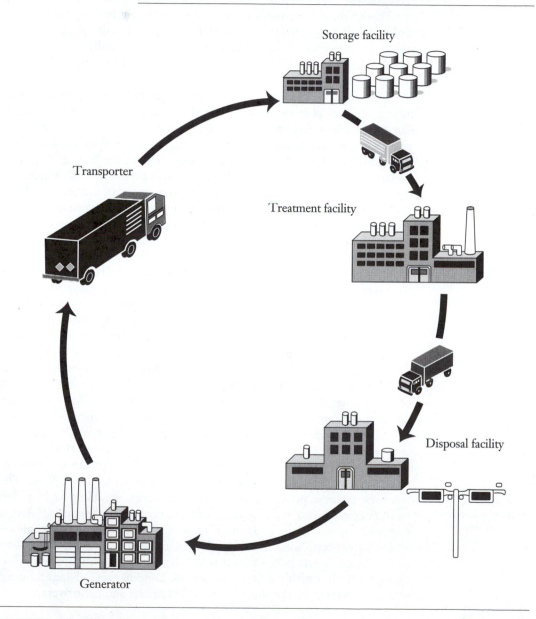

SOURCE: U.S. Environmental Protection Agency, Office of Solid Waste. *Solving the Hazardous Waste Problem: EPA's RCRA Program.* Washington, DC, November 1986, p. 11.

reduction efforts and better treatment technologies. Standards for hazardous waste facilities were strengthened with new safety requirements such as groundwater monitoring equipment and leachate collection systems. Control was broadened by adding two groups of facilities to those regulated under RCRA—owners and operators of certain underground storage tanks and all small quantity waste generators. Stringent rulings were imposed on underground storage tanks that house potentially dangerous substances. Application 17.2 has more on the potential risks of underground storage tanks.

Beyond RCRA's controls on *current* solid waste management, guidelines and financial support were needed to address the damages caused by *past* contamination and to clean up abandoned and uncontrolled hazardous waste sites. On the heels of the Love Canal dilemma, the Comprehensive Environmental Response, Compensation, and Liability Act (CERCLA), or Superfund as it is more commonly known, was passed in 1980. Under this law, the federal government was authorized to clean up contaminated sites and to recover damages from parties identified as responsible. Past and present owners of hazardous waste site facilities were required to notify the EPA of conditions at these sites by 1981. This baseline information along with data collected on an ongoing basis would comprise a national inventory of hazardous waste sites called the **Comprehensive Environmental Response, Compensation, and Liability Information System (CERCLIS).** This system is used to identify those sites posing the greatest threat to human health and the ecology—a classification referred to as the National Priorities List (NPL). The first "Superfund" of $1.6 billion was established to finance the cleanup of priority sites and to pay for damages.

**Comprehensive Environmental Response, Compensation, and Liability Information System (CERCLIS)**
A national inventory of hazardous waste site data.

As it turned out, CERCLA was a national failure on two counts. First, the $1.6 billion Superfund was used to remediate only eight of the thousands of contaminated sites across the nation.[13] Second, according to the U.S. General Accounting Office (GAO), the CERCLIS inventory did not assess the full magnitude of the problem as was its intended purpose.[14] These failures were the primary motivation for the revision and reauthorization of CERCLA through the Superfund Amendments and Reauthorization Act (SARA) passed in 1986. SARA raised the Superfund to $8.5 billion. This was to be financed primarily from **feedstock taxes,** including $2.75 billion from a petroleum tax and $1.4 billion from a tax on raw chemicals.[15] An important reform was the promotion of *permanent* cleanup technologies to replace short-term solutions of burying toxic wastes or transferring them from one site to another. Another was a requirement to initiate federal action on 375 sites within a five-year period. Despite these changes, Superfund continues to be the source of political debate and controversy.

**feedstock taxes**
Taxes levied on raw materials used as productive inputs.

---

[13] Wolf (1988), p. 227.

[14] U.S. General Accounting Office (GAO) (December 1987), pp. 2–3.

[15] Prior to their expiration at the end of 1995, these taxes raised some $1.5 billion per year (Reisch, 1998).

## Hazardous Wastes from Leaking Underground Storage Tanks

Current estimates indicate there are over 5 million underground storage tanks containing petroleum products or other hazardous substances in the United States. About 2 million of these are regulated under RCRA. The practice of burying storage tanks was done as a safety measure to prevent fires. Ironically, these tanks now have become the source of a serious environmental hazard. Some 400,000 of the underground storage tanks in the United States are believed to be leaking—a number expected to rise in the future. These tanks are so large, even a pinhole can lead to a serious waste problem. About 49 percent of the regulated storage tanks in the United States are filled with petroleum and owned by gasoline stations, with another 47 percent owned by industries that store petroleum for their own use, such as airports, farms, golf courses, and firms with large trucking fleets. The remaining 4 percent are filled with other chemicals stored for industrial use.

A major source of concern is that the inventory of buried tanks is aging, making leakages more likely and increasingly so as time goes on. It turns out that many of these tanks were placed in the ground in the 1950s and 1960s during the oil boom of that era. Studies have indicated that about one-third of fuel storage tanks in the United States are over 20 years old or of unknown age. Unfortunately, many of these older vessels were constructed of bare steel, making them vulnerable to corrosion. Adding to the dilemma are all the abandoned storage tanks left by defunct gas stations that failed during the OPEC crisis of the 1970s. In these cases, it is feared that the tanks may not have been closed properly. Since so much time has passed, determining ownership and responsibility for any discovered leaks is difficult at best.

According to the EPA, the primary cause of leaks is corrosion of steel tanks. Other important causes are spills and overfills. Spills occur when the hose that delivers the contents is pulled from the entry pipe before it has completely drained, and overfills result from trying to add more product than the tank can hold. Piping failures and loose fittings for attachments such as pumps and vent lines can also be the cause of leakages.

Leaks from underground storage tanks or their piping can contaminate groundwater and soil, poison crops, cause fires or explosions, and harm human health. Human exposure can occur through direct contact with contaminated soil or water or via inhalation of toxic emissions. Aside from breathing dangerous vapors released into a nearby building, inhalation also can occur during showering with contaminated water when volatile components are released.

SOURCES: U.S. Environmental Protection Agency. *Environmental Progress and Challenges: EPA's Update.* Washington, DC, August 1988, pp. 102–05; U.S. Environmental Protection Agency. *Meeting the Environmental Challenge: EPA's Review of Progress and New Directions in Environmental Protection.* Washington, DC, December 1990a, p. 16; U.S. Environmental Protection Agency, Office of Solid Waste and Emergency Response. *Leaking Underground Storage Tanks and Health: Understanding Health Risks from Petroleum Contamination.* Washington, DC, January 1992.

In February 1994, the Clinton administration announced its proposal for major changes in the Superfund program. In an attempt to cut the program's high costs and to accelerate procedures, Clinton's plan called for limitations on the liability of responsible parties, more flexible cleanup standards, and an $8.1-billion trust fund to cover disputed liability claims.[16]

---

[16]U.S. EPA, Office of Communications, Education, and Public Affairs (February 22, 1994c); Regan, Weber, Roush, and Kelly (April 25, 1994).

The proposal, like many others dealing with environmental issues, never made it through the 103rd Congress. And to date, no decision has been made by Congress regarding the reauthorization of Superfund.[17]

# Controlling Hazardous Wastes: RCRA[18]

**source reduction**
Preventive strategies to reduce the quantity and toxicity of hazardous wastes at the point of generation.

**waste management**
Control strategies to reduce the quantity and toxicity of hazardous wastes at every stage of the waste stream.

To minimize the risks of hazardous waste pollution, efforts must be made to reduce the quantity and toxicity of the waste stream. Most agree that two general approaches are needed to achieve these broad-based objectives. The first is **source reduction,** a preventive strategy aimed at the generation stage. The second is to undertake sound **waste management** practices to control those wastes that cannot be eliminated. While RCRA's objectives make a general reference to preventive strategies, there is little question that management of the waste stream is the primary emphasis. A command-and-control framework characterizes the implementation plan, just as is true for clean air and water initiatives.

Primary responsibility for controlling hazardous wastes is assigned to the federal government—mainly through the EPA. However, Congress provided little guidance as to *how* the agency should design and implement its newly drafted policy position effected by the 1976 RCRA. This absence of legislative muscle is often blamed for what became long delays in launching the program and in deflecting opposition from those most affected by the new regulations. Just as critical to the policy challenge was the uncertainty about the extent of hazardous waste pollution. Absent the obvious sources that had become national news, no one—not even major federal agencies—had a complete picture of the problem. The EPA's response was to devise a command-and-control approach intended to give structure to what must have seemed little more than ordered chaos.

## The "Cradle-to-Grave" Management Approach[19]

The RCRA program emerged as the **"cradle-to-grave" management system**—a multipronged, command-and-control approach to regulating hazardous waste. Its four major components are:

- **Identification** of hazardous wastes
- **National manifest system** for tracking and monitoring the movement of wastes

---

[17] To read more about this reauthorization process during the 105th Congress, see Reisch (1998), which can be accessed online at **www.cnie.org/nle/waste-17.html.**

[18] For more information on RCRA, visit **www.epa.gov/epaoswer/osw/basifact.htm.**

[19] Much of the following is drawn from U.S. EPA, Office of Solid Waste (November 1986).

- **Permit system** for **treatment, storage, and disposal facilities (TSDFs)**
- Development of **standards** for TSDFs[20]

**characteristic wastes** Hazardous wastes identified as those exhibiting certain characteristics that imply a substantial risk.

**Identification of Hazardous Wastes.**[21]   A fundamental element of the management system is a procedure for identifying wastes considered to be hazardous and therefore subject to federal regulations. The rules are highly detailed, since an error of omission would allow a dangerous material to escape federal control. Essentially, a waste is considered hazardous under the law if it falls into a defined category. One category is called **characteristic wastes**—those with characteristics or attributes that imply a substantial risk. In the United States, these attributes are ignitability, corrosivity, reactivity, and toxicity. Another category is a set of **listed wastes**—those pre-identified by the EPA as having met certain criteria such as the presence of toxic or carcinogenic constituents. Using these categories, waste generators are responsible for determining which of their wastes are hazardous and assuring that these are managed in compliance with federal law.

**listed wastes** Hazardous wastes that have been pre-identified by government as having met specific criteria.

**The National Manifest System for Tracking Wastes.**   If a generator chooses to transfer any hazardous wastes offsite for treatment, storage, or disposal, that movement is tracked by the **national manifest system.** Once the wastes are ready for transport, the generator must prepare a document called a **manifest** that identifies the hazardous material and all the parties responsible for its movement. The document remains with the shipment from the point of generation through to its final disposal. The objective is clear—to assure that dangerous waste materials are accounted for through every phase of the waste cycle, reducing the opportunity for illegal dumping.

**manifest** A document used to identify hazardous waste materials and all parties responsible for its movement from generation to disposal.

**The Permit System.**   While the tracking system monitors the *location* of hazardous waste, a **permitting system** controls its management at the **treatment, storage, and disposal facilities (TSDFs).**[22] Every TSDF must obtain a permit to operate. The permitting process is stringently controlled, since its purpose is to ensure that TSDFs meet federal **standards,** many of which are aimed at protecting groundwater from waste contamination.

**permitting system** A control approach that authorizes the activities of TSDFs according to pre-defined standards.

**Standards.**   Two sets of standards control the waste management practices of TSDFs. **General regulatory standards** apply to *all* types of TSDFs

---

[20] U.S. Congress, OTA (1983), Chapter 7.

[21] See 40 CFR Part 261, Identification and Listing of Hazardous Waste.

[22] For basic information on the activities of TSDFs, visit **www.epa.gov/epaoswer/osw/tsd.htm**. To learn more about the permitting of hazardous wastes, see **www.epa.gov/epaoswer/hazwaste/permit/prmtguid.htm**.

and control generic functions like inspections, emergency plans, and participation in the manifest program. There are also **technical regulatory standards** that outline procedures and equipment requirements for specific types of waste facilities. For example, storage facilities must follow careful procedures to avoid leakages into the surrounding environment. Disposal sites must use technologies such as cover systems, liners, and leakage-detection systems.

Although these four components of the "cradle-to-grave" system provided controls over the hazardous waste stream, the program was inadequate in one important respect—it did not indicate nor even suggest a hierarchy of preferred methods for managing these wastes. This omission meant that virtually nothing was being done to slow the overuse of land at the disposal stage.[23] From a broader perspective, it also meant that national policy was not supporting preventive strategies to reduce the *size* of the hazardous waste stream. Responding to this inadequacy, Congress passed the Hazardous and Solid Waste Amendments of 1984. Unlike their predecessor, these amendments outline in detail how hazardous wastes are to be controlled and explicitly set forth restrictions on land disposal. In so doing, the law prioritizes hazardous waste treatment technologies, which is intended to provide an incentive for source reduction and hence prevention of hazardous waste pollution.

### Moving toward Pollution Prevention

Several references in the 1984 Amendments speak to the policy shift away from land disposal and toward preventive solutions. The law's general provisions were revised to include the following mandate:

> ". . . reliance on land disposal should be minimized or eliminated, and land disposal, particularly landfill and surface impoundment, should be the least favored method for managing hazardous wastes . . ."

Other rulings specifically prohibit land disposal of untreated hazardous wastes except under certain conditions. These controls are intended to encourage facilities to find alternatives that prevent pollution. To reinforce the emphasis on prevention, the 1984 law added the following to RCRA's statement of objectives:

> "The Congress hereby declares it to be the national policy of the United States, that, wherever feasible, the generation of hazardous waste is to be reduced or eliminated as expeditiously as possible."

---

[23] For more detail, see Fortuna and Lennett (1987), Chapter 9.

# Analysis of U.S. Hazardous Waste Policy

The nation's "cradle-to-grave" management system is a classic example of a command-and-control policy approach. As such, it lacks incentives, which decreases the likelihood of an efficient or cost-effective outcome. To investigate this hypothesis, we consider the following aspects of the RCRA program:

- Identification of hazardous waste
- Standard-setting process
- Manifest system
- 1984 land restrictions

### Risk-Based, Uniform Rules of Identification

Central to RCRA's control approach is the identification of hazardous wastes. Two elements of this process merit consideration. One is the absence of risk–benefit analysis in defining the identifying categories, and the other is the uniformity in how these categories are implemented.

To begin, the law requires that hazardous waste be identified according to characteristics and criteria that are risk-based. Although the rulings attempt to identify the risks of exposure to hazardous waste accurately, they include no provision for balancing these risks with the benefits provided by these materials before they enter the waste stream. That being the case, all wastes satisfying these criteria are regulated with the same stringency regardless of how they originated. Consequently, a waste material associated with a product that is vital in use is treated under the law in exactly the same way as one generated from an output of relatively low value to society.[24]

Another problem is that the identifying criteria are applied *uniformly*. There are no qualifiers to allow for differences in the degree of toxicity across various waste constituents. Effectively, the procedure sets up a zero–one decision-making process that translates to a set of uniform standards. If a waste falls into one of the predefined categories, it is hazardous; if not, it is nonhazardous by default. Also, the law does not allow for any flexibility in determining how much of a given substance poses a hazard to society. Yet there can be wide variation in the risk of exposure to the same quantity of different hazardous substances.[25] From an economic perspective, ignoring this variation is allocatively inefficient. Since there are known differences in risk across hazardous waste constituents, it is also true that

---

[24] It is interesting to note that certain wastes are exempt from this identification process, such as those associated with the production of crude oil and natural gas. The importance of these products suggests that a risk–benefit assessment may have been used to justify these exemptions. It is also true that the initial RCRA was passed during a period of great uncertainty about U.S. oil supplies.

[25] For more detail, see U.S. Congress, OTA (1983), Chapter 6.

the marginal benefits of abating these constituents are different. If marginal abatement costs are the same, society's welfare could be improved by allocating more resources to abating relatively high-risk substances and fewer to those posing a lower risk. Yet there is no provision in the law for such flexibility.

### Benefit-Based, Uniform Standards

RCRA controls hazardous waste management primarily through standards imposed on the generators, transporters, and treatment, storage, and disposal facilities (TSDFs). According to the law, these standards are to be established *"as may be necessary to protect human health and the environment."*[26] Such a mandate clearly defines the standard-setting process as benefit-based with no consideration for economic costs. The lack of cost considerations is particularly problematic for standards with long-run implications. Examples include the technical standards for TSDFs relating to groundwater monitoring, closure, and post-closure procedures. Standards on post-closure procedures guide a facility's activities for 30 years after a facility is closed. The purpose is to prevent active hazardous waste facilities from becoming problem sites after they cease operation—undoubtedly a response to the nation's concerns with abandoned and uncontrolled sites. Although the intent seems to be well motivated, the long-term nature of these standards assures that compliance costs will be significant. Yet costs are not allowed to influence the standard-setting process.[27] As long as this is the case, the standards so fundamental to federal policy will not likely be set to achieve allocative efficiency.

Another criticism of the standards-based approach is that with few exceptions, it offers states no flexibility in how they administer RCRA's hazardous waste program. While state officials can submit their own plans, these are approved only if they are equivalent to the national program or consistent with those applicable in other states.[28] There is virtually no provision for site-specific differences—either in the facilities themselves or in the types of wastes they handle. The lack of consideration for such differences means that the criterion of cost-effectiveness will not likely be met.

### Failures of the Manifest System

One of the more prominent elements of RCRA's "cradle-to-grave" approach is the manifest system. Congress' intent in establishing this elaborate tracking procedure was to deter illegal disposal and reduce the adverse effects associated with such practices.[29] The system is a definitive command-and-control instrument. There are no incentives, no pricing mechanisms,

---

[26] RCRA, Sec. 3004.(a).

[27] See 45 *Federal Register* 33, 159-60 as cited in U.S. Congress, OTA (1983), pp. 283–85.

[28] RCRA Sec. 3006.(b).

[29] U.S. GAO (February 22, 1985), p. 3.

and no options. It was a no-nonsense response to a tough problem, and in that sense the approach was understandable, albeit inefficient. Why? Because its objective is solely benefit-based—to halt the damage caused by mismanaged hazardous wastes. Characteristic of the RCRA program, economic considerations play no role in its design or implementation.

Beyond the efficiency implications, a more fundamental issue is the effectiveness of the manifest plan. It turns out that despite its elaborate design, the tracking system has not been a major factor in controlling hazardous wastes because of its limited scope. For all its complexity, the tracking system applies only to wastes that are transported off-site by the generator. According to estimates, these represent only 4 to 5 percent of the nation's hazardous waste stream. Most large firms manage wastes on their own premises. It is smaller businesses, particularly those in crowded urban areas that rely on other facilities to treat and dispose of their wastes.[30] It *is* true that this proportion should increase over time due to the 1984 revision to make small quantity generators subject to RCRA. Nonetheless, it is expected to remain a small fraction of the total hazardous waste stream.[31]

Finally, the high compliance costs associated with the tracking program sets up the potential for a perverse outcome. To understand this claim, consider the following. Hazardous waste generators that typically rely on off-site facilities have three options available to them:

- Legally dispose of their wastes by complying with the manifest system

- Attempt to evade the law and illegally discard their wastes

- Reduce the amount of wastes they generate

Assuming that generators wish to maximize profits, they must consider the *relative* costs of these options in their decision making. When the United States instituted the manifest system, it elevated the costs of legal disposal, making both source reduction *and* illegal disposal relatively cheaper and hence more attractive options from a profitability perspective. The key question is—which of the two options will firms pursue? While there is some anecdotal evidence that "midnight dumping" has diminished since RCRA was passed, there is no definitive answer to this critical question.[32] Until such evidence is available, there is no reason to dismiss the possibility that this well-intended program might promote the very practice it sought to deter—illegal hazardous waste disposal.

From nearly every perspective, RCRA's track record during its early years was less than impressive. There were major delays in implementation,

---

[30] Wirth and Heinz (1991), p. 47; U.S. EPA, Office of Solid Waste (November 1986), p. 9.

[31] Assuming these smaller entities would use off-site facilities instead of absorbing the cost of obtaining an on-site permit, the U.S. Congressional Budget Office (CBO) estimated that the amount of waste managed off-site should rise from about 4 percent in 1983 to 10 percent by 1990 (U.S. CBO, 1985b), p. 50.

[32] Wirth and Heinz (1991), p. 47.

more than a few policy reversals, several potential loopholes, and many questions about its effectiveness. These observations were largely responsible for Congress' enactment of the hard-hitting 1984 Amendments. Attempting to solve a litany of problems, these amendments continue to rely on command-and-control policy instruments. There is still a glaring absence of economic incentives in the law, though the land restrictions may have been an exception.

## Market Implications of the 1984 Land Restrictions

As the nation's hazardous waste program was evolving in the late 1970s, it became apparent that existing policy was doing nothing to halt the overuse of land disposal. One reason why landfilling had become so prevalent was that it was cheaper than other disposal options. This differential is due in part to more significant scale economies for landfilling relative to alternative practices, particularly waste incineration. For example, large-sized landfills face unit costs of $23 to $49 per metric ton, while large incineration facilities incur much higher unit costs of $80 per ton.[33] The problem is that these values are *private* costs and do not account for the external costs of environmental damages. If these latter costs were internalized, prices would be higher and any misallocation corrected. An appropriate economic solution would be to use a pricing instrument that captures the social costs of all hazardous waste services. In 1984, policy makers chose instead to use a command-and-control approach—a restriction on landfilling. This policy decision *does* have economic consequences, though the net effect is not clear-cut.

Restricting the land disposal of hazardous waste elevates the costs of providing these services, which should be reflected in higher prices to waste generators. Just as in our analysis of the manifest system, we need to ask how generators are likely to respond. As profit-maximizers, they would consider the relative costs of all available options. Again, they could reduce the amount of waste they generate or they could maintain their waste level and seek an alternative waste management practice. The difference here is that alternative waste management does not necessarily mean illegal disposal. Waste generators could use less landfilling by employing a treatment method like incineration to reduce the volume of wastes to be disposed of. Although the options are complex, we can gain some insight by modeling the two *legal* options facing the waste generator:

- Substituting treatment for disposal

- Using preventive strategies to achieve source reduction

By way of illustration, we use incineration as the representative treatment method.

---

[33] U.S. EPA (March 1, 1984), as cited in Hahn (1988), pp. 201–230.

| FIGURE 17.2 | THE IMPACT OF LAND RESTRICTIONS UNDER RCRA'S 1984 AMENDMENTS |
|---|---|

The higher costs of the 1984 land restrictions shift up the *MPC* and *MSC* for land disposal, decreasing the private market solution from $L_0$ to $L_1$. Because production is lower, the external costs are smaller as well, declining from area *abc* to area *def*. If the waste generator uses less landfilling because it pursues source reduction, the net result of the 1984 rulings is an improvement for society measured by this external cost reduction. However, if the generator does not reduce its level of wastes, then the decrease in land disposal must have been achieved by using some alternative practice, such as incineration. Increased use of incineration is shown as a shift right of *MSB* in that market, which increases equilibrium output from $I_0$ to $I_1$. As a result, external costs in this market increase from area *ghi* to area *gjk*. Unless the decline in external costs in the landfilling market outweighs the increase in the incineration market, the 1984 land restrictions would achieve no net reduction in the external costs borne by society.

**(a) Market for Land Disposal Services**

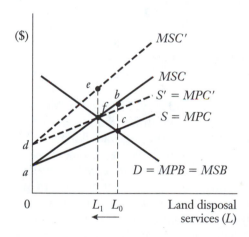

**(b) Market for Incineration Services**

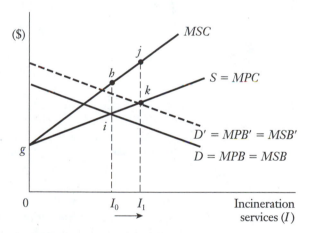

**Pre-1984 Market Equilibrium.** The two relevant markets are shown in Figure 17.2—land disposal in panel (a) and incineration in panel (b). Marginal private benefit (*MPB*) curves represent the decisions of waste generators, which are identical to marginal social benefit (*MSB*) functions, assuming no consumption externalities. On the supply side, marginal private cost (*MPC*) curves denote the decision making of the respective waste service facilities. The *MPCs* are distinct from the marginal social cost (*MSC*) curves to indicate that negative externalities are associated with production in each market, with each marginal external cost (*MEC*) implied by the vertical distance between each pair of *MPC* and *MSC* curves. Prior to the 1984 land restrictions, private equilibrium in each market is determined by the intersection of *MPC* and *MPB*. In the landfill market, the pre-1984 equilibrium output level is $L_0$. The total measure of external costs associated with that output level is the area between *MPC* and *MSC* up to that point, or triangular area *abc*. In the incinerator market, the initial equilibrium output level is $I_0$ and area *ghi* represents the analogous measure of external costs in that market.

**Post-1984 Market Equilibrium.**   Now consider the effect of the 1984 land restrictions. These rulings lead to higher operating costs in the land disposal market. In Figure 17.2(a), *MPC* shifts up to *MPC′*, and *MSC* rises by the same amount to *MSC′*. The result is a decline in landfill use from $L_0$ to $L_1$. Because production is lower, the associated external costs are smaller as well, declining to area *def*. Notice that the land restrictions do not eliminate the market inefficiency, since there is nothing in these rulings that causes external costs to be internalized by the market participants. It *is* the case, however, that the total external costs associated with land disposal have declined. Hence, if waste generators use less landfilling because they pursue source reduction, the 1984 rulings should reduce the health and ecological damages caused by hazardous wastes, holding all else constant. However, if generators do *not* reduce their level of wastes, then the decrease in land disposal must have been achieved by using some alternative waste management practice. Assuming the alternative is the use of incineration, we need to consider how the effects in that market affect the net result.

   Increased use of incineration is shown in Figure 17.2(b) as a shift right of *MSB* to *MSB′*, which increases private equilibrium output from $I_0$ to $I_1$. This outcome was predicted by the U.S. Congressional Budget Office (CBO), which forecasted that the 1984 restrictions would increase the quantity of waste incinerated from 2.7 million metric tons (MMT) in 1983 to more than 11 MMT by 1990.[34] Notice, however, that at the higher equilibrium level, external costs have increased to area *gjk*. What can we conclude from this observation? Unless the decline in external costs in the landfilling market outweighs the increase in the incineration market, the 1984 land restrictions would achieve no net reduction in the external costs borne by society.

   Obviously, a key issue is to determine the extent to which source reduction is undertaken in response to the 1984 RCRA land rulings. The outcome is difficult to predict. In part, the problem is that there are many factors that influence a firm's decision to reduce waste—an issue discussed in Application 17.3.[35] Despite the inherent difficulties, the CBO conducted an

---

[34] U.S. CBO (1985b), Table 14, p. 49.

[35] There are also other changes in the 1984 Amendments that confound the outcome. One of these is the increase in demand for all off-site waste services, which is expected to occur as a result of expanding RCRA's span of control to include small quantity waste generators. This increase in demand would add still more pressure on rising prices of disposal services.

## INFORM's Study of Industrial Source Reduction Activities

What motivates a firm to reduce its waste generation? Once the decision is made, how do firms determine the best course of action? Answers to questions like these are usually known only to industry insiders and corporate decision makers. Fortunately, independent research on these issues has recently been conducted by INFORM, a nonprofit organization located in New York. The results of this 10-year effort provide new evidence on what factors determine industry's efforts to engage in **source reduction** activities.

To better understand the motives of source reduction and the eventual outcome, INFORM used a case study approach to examine pollution prevention strategies and the results achieved by a sample of 29 highly diverse organic chemical plants. An initial survey was conducted during 1985. A follow-up study was later undertaken to document changes instituted between 1985 and 1990 by the 27 plants that had remained in operation. To assure a representative depiction of the industry, the sample of plants was drawn from three states: California, New Jersey, and Ohio. Similarly, INFORM made certain to include different types of facilities distinguished by such characteristics as size, degree of centralization, type of production process, and output produced.

INFORM's analysis revealed important information about what motivates source reduction activities. The most commonly reported reason for initiating a source reduction action was given as the costs and overall problems of waste disposal. The increasing burden of regulation was the second most common response and appears to be an increasingly important factor in these decisions based on the five-year trend. Other determinants cited by the survey participants were liability issues, process costs, worker safety, and community relations.

INFORM's comprehensive case study approach also reported on the eventual outcome of the plants' source reduction actions. The 1985 survey found that all activities yielded a waste reduction of approximately 7 million pounds per year. A dramatic improvement was documented for 1990—a combined reduction in wastes for all activities of 180 million pounds per year. More insight can be gained by examining other data from INFORM's 1990 report that quantify the effectiveness of source reduction.

| Factor | Amount |
|---|---|
| Average reduction | 68 percent |
| Average increase in product yields | 6.8 percent |
| Average quantity reduced/activity/year | 2,405,621 lbs |
| Total quantity reduced during the study period | 180,421,596 lbs |
| Average dollars saved/activity/year | $484,616 |
| Total dollars saved during the study period | $28,592,367 |
| Average dollars spent/activity | $946,612 |
| Total dollars spent during the study period | $48,277,197 |
| Average payback period | 12.2 months* |
| Average length of time to implement | 8.8 months |

NOTE:

*This average payback period is based on only those activities where both dollars spent and dollars saved were reported. Also, the three highest figures for the payback period (i.e., 88, 70, and 48 years) were excluded because they were much higher than other values reported.

SOURCE: U.S. Environmental Protection Agency, Office of Pollution Prevention. *Pollution Prevention 1991: Progress on Reducing Industrial Pollutants*, Washington DC, October 1991, pp. 63–66.

TABLE 17.5 CHANGES IN WASTE GENERATION BY INDUSTRY ASSOCIATED WITH THE 1984 RCRA AMENDMENTS (THOUSANDS OF METRIC TONS)

| Industry | Quantity in 1983 | Quantity in 1990 No Waste Reduction[a] | Quantity in 1990 with Waste Reduction[b] |
|---|---|---|---|
| Chemicals and allied products | 127,245 | 136,678 | 115,167 |
| Primary metals | 47,704 | 49,597 | 41,611 |
| Petroleum and coal products | 31,358 | 29,213 | 25,526 |
| Fabricated metal products | 25,364 | 25,493 | 11,820 |
| Rubber and plastic products | 14,600 | 17,954 | 17,252 |
| Miscellaneous manufacturing | 5,614 | 5,856 | 5,001 |
| Nonelectrical machinery | 4,859 | 5,717 | 4,831 |
| Transportation equipment | 2,977 | 3,243 | 2,781 |
| Motor freight transportation | 2,160 | 2,160 | 1,836 |
| Electrical and electronic machinery | 1,929 | 2,313 | 1,557 |
| Wood preserving | 1,739 | 2,095 | 1,743 |
| Drum reconditioners | 45 | 45 | 16 |
| **Total** | 265,595 | 280,364 | 229,141 |
| Percent change from 1983 | — | +5.6 | −13.7 |

NOTES:

[a] Assumes no waste reduction efforts by industry in response to the 1984 RCRA Amendments. Projection of waste levels in 1990 based on growth in industrial output levels forecasted by the CBO generation model. Decreases in waste quantities therefore result from declining levels of industrial and waste-producing activities.

[b] Assumes waste-reduction efforts by industry.

SOURCE: U.S. Congress, U.S. Congressional Budget Office. *Hazardous Waste Management: Recent Changes and Policy Alternatives.* Washington, DC: U.S. Government Printing Office, 1985b, Table 13, p. 48.

analysis of how the 1984 RCRA Amendments might be expected to affect waste generation levels. Table 17.5 presents the CBO's industry-specific estimates of pre- and post-1984 waste generation both with and without source reduction. If industries undertake no waste reduction, aggregate hazardous waste generation is estimated to increase from 265,595 thousands of metric tons in 1983 to as much as 280,364 in 1990—roughly a 5.6 percent increase. At the other extreme is the best possible outcome, which assumes sufficient incentives to encourage waste reduction. In this case, aggregate waste generation is estimated to *decline* by about 14 percent between 1983 and 1990, even allowing for waste growth associated with higher production levels.[36]

---

[36] U.S. CBO (1985b), Table 13, p. 48.

| TABLE 17.6 | ESTIMATED CHANGE OF ANNUAL COSTS FOR HAZARDOUS WASTE MANAGEMENT FOR 1983 AND 1990 ($ 1983 MILLIONS) |
|---|---|

| Industry | 1983 Cost[a] | 1990 Cost No Waste Reduction | 1990 Cost with Waste Reduction | Percentage Change with Waste Reduction |
|---|---|---|---|---|
| Chemicals and allied products | $1,544 | $3,122 | $2,283 | 48% |
| Primary metals | 1,243 | 2,302 | 1,661 | 34 |
| Fabricated metal products | 899 | 1,191 | 735 | −18 |
| Rubber and plastic products | 798 | 2,026 | 1,771 | 122 |
| Miscellaneous manufacturing | 267 | 356 | 308 | 15 |
| Nonelectrical machinery | 254 | 324 | 279 | 10 |
| Motor freight transportation | 229 | 247 | 247 | 8 |
| Transportation equipment | 191 | 360 | 286 | 50 |
| Electrical and electronic machinery | 156 | 237 | 163 | 4 |
| Petroleum and coal products | 136 | 940 | 634 | 366 |
| Wood preserving | 56 | 91 | 61 | 9 |
| Drum reconditioners | 6 | 6 | 2 | −67 |
| Total | $5,779 | $11,201 | $8,429 | |
| Incremental change from 1983 | — | +$ 5,422 | +$2,650 | |
| Percent change from 1983 | — | +93.8% | +45.9% | |

NOTE:

[a] Assumes full compliance with RCRA before the 1984 Amendments.

SOURCE: U.S. Congressional Budget Office. *Hazardous Waste Management: Recent Changes and Policy Alternatives.* Washington, DC: U.S. Government Printing Office, 1985b, Table 15, p. 51.

Table 17.6 presents the estimated costs associated with these waste generation magnitudes. With no waste reduction activity, aggregate costs rise from $5,779 million in 1983 to $11,201 million in 1990, measured in 1983 dollars—nearly a doubling of real expenditures to comply with the new regulations. If these estimates are reasonable, it is likely that firms will initiate waste reduction activities. If so, under the most favorable assumptions, the CBO estimates that the increase in 1990 compliance costs will be limited to about $2.7 billion.[37] These findings suggest that at least one aspect of U.S. hazardous waste policy—the land restrictions—may provide

---

[37] The dollar expenditures would increase even with the decline in generation because of more stringent requirements for treatment and disposal methods in the 1984 Amendments. U.S. CBO (1985b), Table 15, pp. 50–51.

an economic incentive to help achieve the national goal of reducing hazardous waste generation. Absent this single element of the law, U.S. policy relies on a command-and-control approach that fails to achieve either efficiency or cost-effectiveness. This is a disconcerting observation, particularly since other nations and even some state governments have used market instruments successfully to help control hazardous waste pollution.

### Market Instruments in Hazardous Waste Control Policy

Market instruments attempt to use the price mechanism to make polluters confront the full costs of their actions and respond accordingly. Since there are significant risks associated with hazardous waste pollution, the external costs can be enormous. Hence, if price were somehow made to reflect these costs, polluters—or in this context hazardous waste generators—would have a powerful incentive to engage in source reduction activities.

**pollution charge**
Fee charged to the polluter that varies with the amount of contaminants released.

**waste-end charge**
Fee implemented at the time of disposal based on the quantity of waste generated.

A conventional market approach to waste control policy is the use of a **pollution charge**, which can be implemented as a **waste-end charge**. A waste-end charge is so named because it is effected at the time of disposal based on the quantity of waste generated. This type of economic instrument is used internationally. For example, Australia, Austria, Denmark, France, and Germany are among the nations that charge a tax on waste disposal based on what is sent to processors like landfills and incinerators. Another application of a waste-end charge is to charge a fee on hazardous wastes—a practice followed by Australia, Austria, Belgium, and Finland.[38] In each case, the waste-end charge elevates the effective price of waste management services. If the charge is high enough, it should *discourage* waste generation and *encourage* source reduction.

One of the more successful international uses of such a market instrument is one that was designed and implemented by the German State of Baden-Württemberg. Officials there have employed a variable rate charge on hazardous waste and are monitoring its effect on waste generation. What they have observed is that this pricing mechanism does appear to be high enough to encourage waste reduction.[39] In the United States, similar economic approaches have been employed by state governments in designing and implementing their hazardous waste programs—an issue discussed in Application 17.4. Despite the international evidence and the experience of state governments, federal hazardous waste policy has employed no analogous market instruments to date.

---

[38] OECD (1994), pp. 63–65.

[39] OECD (1989a), OECD (1991), and *Landesabfallabgabengesetz*, Article 4, as cited in U.S. EPA, Office of Policy, Planning, and Evaluation (July 1992), p. 9-1.

## Using the Market to Control Hazardous Wastes

Although the feedstock tax imposed under CERCLA may appear to have been motivated by the incentives of a product charge, its true intent was to provide a reliable source of funds for the nation's remediation program. Beyond this revenue-raising initiative, the use of a tax to reduce hazardous waste generation remains exclusive to state governments. While some states had introduced waste levies before the Superfund tax was effected, most imposed their own version of a pollution charge after the feedstock tax became law. Typically, this instrument was implemented as a **waste-end charge.**

As of 1990, 31 states actively tax hazardous wastes at or beyond the point of generation. Technically, such a waste-end charge is imposed to encourage waste reduction. However, this motivation is not universally apparent. In fact, revenue-raising appears to be the overriding influence in some instances. Many states use the revenues to finance monitoring costs or cleanup expenditures at sites where damages have occurred. Some add the waste tax revenues to their general funds, forcing environmental needs to compete for these funds along with all other state programs.

The characteristics of these market instruments vary considerably from state to state. Some states impose the tax directly on the generator at the first stage of the waste stream. Others levy the charge at the postgeneration phase by taxing the facility operator, such as a storage or treatment facility. Revenue motivations aside, taxing the generator offers a stronger incentive for waste reduction than does imposing the charge on a facility engaged in treatment, storage, or disposal. Some levy higher taxes on landfilling than on incineration, which should discourage land disposal.

The rate of the tax also differs widely. As of 1990, the rate of tax imposed by Vermont and California was more than $100 per ton for land disposal. Six other states levy a tax that is greater than $50 per ton. Across all states, including those using no tax, the average rate was $21 per ton. More refined data would show even more state-specific differences, such as varying rate schedules based on waste characteristics like the type of waste and/or whether the waste was generated outside state boundaries. And some states allow an exemption for on-site disposal. If these differences properly reflect local economic and environmental conditions, the use of a hazardous waste tax at the state level may be far superior than any uniform charge imposed at the national level.

SOURCES: Robert C. Anderson, Andrew Q. Lohof (Resource Consulting Associates), and Alan Carlin (U.S. Environmental Protection Agency, Office of Economy and Environment, Office of Policy, Planning and Evaluation). *The United States Experience with Economic Incentives in Environmental Pollution Control Policy.* Washington, DC: August 1997, Chapter 4; U.S. Congressional Budget Office as reported in U.S. Congress, U.S. Congressional Budget Office. *Hazardous Waste Management: Recent Changes and Policy Alternatives.* Washington, DC: U.S. Government Printing Office, 1985b, p. 82; U.S. Congress, U.S. Congressional Budget Office, Office of Technology Assessment (OTA), Statement of Joel S. Hirschhorn for the Hearing Record, Senate Committee on Environment and Public Works, 98:2 (September 10, 1984); Craig E. Reese. "State Taxation of Hazardous Materials." *Oil and Gas Tax Quarterly* 33, 1985, pp. 502–26.

## Managing Uncontrolled Hazardous Waste Sites: CERCLA

By most accounts, the Comprehensive Environmental Response, Compensation, and Liability Act of 1980 (CERCLA), more commonly known as Superfund, is considered a landmark legislative act because its intent is solely remedial rather than preventive. Despite its precedent-setting intent and a $1.6-billion fund, the 1980 law failed to execute on its commitments.

The 1986 Amendments attempted to address these failures, but many problems still remain. To understand why, we need to investigate the basic elements of this important national policy.

### Response and Cleanup

Superfund gives the federal government broad authority to respond whenever there is a release or the threat of a release of a hazardous substance, which it identifies as:[40]

- One that has been so designated under any of the following: the Water Pollution Control Act; the Solid Waste Disposal Act; the Federal Water Pollution Control Act; the Clean Air Act; and the Toxic Substances Control Act; and

- One that may present substantial danger to health, welfare, or the environment when released.[41]

Notification of any release exceeding amounts specified in the law (1 pound unless stated otherwise), is to be made to the National Response Center (NRC). Failure to do so is punishable by fine or imprisonment. To implement these response actions, a comprehensive set of regulations was established called the **National Contingency Plan (NCP).**[42] The NCP outlines the procedures to put Superfund into action, a summary of which is given in Table 17.7. By Executive Order, response activities are delegated to the EPA and are to be carried out through removal actions or remedial actions.

**National Contingency Plan (NCP)** Set of regulations that outlines official response actions to a release or the threat of a release of a hazardous substance.

**removal actions** Official responses to a hazardous substance release aimed at restoring immediate control.

**Removal Actions.**   Removal actions are responses aimed at restoring immediate control to a release site. An example is an emergency cleanup of a chemical spill at a waste site or at the scene of an accident involving a transporter of hazardous chemicals. Depending on conditions, the removal action may include barricading a contaminated site, providing temporary drinking water supplies or shelter to nearby residents, or securing hazardous waste containers. These activities are undertaken only as short-term measures.[43]

**remedial actions** Official responses to a hazardous substance release aimed at achieving a more permanent solution.

**Remedial Actions.**   Remedial actions are long-term responses aimed at finding a more permanent solution to a release site. Several steps are

---

[40] CERCLA, Sec. 101(14) and Sec. 102(a).

[41] Since these descriptions are purposefully comprehensive, CERCLA *does* itemize certain exclusions, among them petroleum, natural gas, natural gas liquids, liquefied natural gas, or synthetic gas usable for fuel.

[42] Visit **www.epa.gov/superfund/whatissf/sfproces.htm** to learn more about the actual steps involved in a Superfund site cleanup.

[43] U.S. EPA (August 1987); U.S. EPA, Office of Solid Waste and Emergency Response (May 1992).

| TABLE 17.7 | THE NATIONAL CONTINGENCY PLAN: PHASES OF RESPONSE ACTIONS |
|---|---|

| Phase | Response Action |
|---|---|
| **Phase I:** Site Discovery and Notification | Report the release to the National Response Center (NRC) and the affected state. |
| **Phase II:** Preliminary Assessment | Determine the nature, extent, and source of the release and the magnitude of the hazard using available data; make recommendation for further action. |
| **Phase III:** Immediate Removal Action | Implement appropriate immediate removal action such as measuring and sampling, removing hazardous substances from site, restraining spread of release, preventing access to site, controlling the source of release, recommending evaluation of threatened population, or any other emergency measures. |
| **Phase IV:** Site Evaluation and Determination of Appropriate Response Level | Conduct site evaluation; collect data; determine amount, type, and location of hazardous substances and potential for migration; determine appropriate response level; recommend site for immediate removal, planned removal, National Priorities List (NPL) remedial action candidate, or no further action. |
| **Phase V:** Planned Removal | Determine if site qualifies for planned removal; take appropriate response action to reduce or eliminate risk; action is completed when serious risk is abated *or* 6 months/$1 million limit is reached. |
| **Phase VI:** Remedial Action | Evaluate NPL sites and determine appropriate remedy as follows: conduct preliminary assessment; take initial remedial action if needed; perform remedial investigation; assess alternatives; determine appropriate extent of remedy from alternatives; proceed with chosen action if state assurances and contribution requirements are met and if fund-financing is approved. |
| **Phase VII:** Cost Recovery and Documentation | Complete documentation of government response action. |

SOURCE: Drawn from U.S. Congress, Office of Technology Assessment (OTA). *Technologies and Management Strategies for Hazardous Waste Control.* Washington, DC: U.S. Government Printing Office, 1983, Chapter 7, Table 57, pp. 306–07.

**National Priorities List (NPL)** A classification of hazardous waste sites posing the greatest threat to health and the ecology.

involved, making the process very time-intensive. Following the official identification of a problem, called site discovery, a complete assessment is made of all available information, and an inspection is ordered to sample soil, ground and surface water, and to document the site layout. The findings ultimately are evaluated using a risk ranking system that assigns a numerical score to a site based on its inherent risks. If the site receives a 28.50 score or higher out of a 100-point maximum, it is placed on the **National Priorities List (NPL).**[44] As of 1997, 1,405 sites were listed on the NPL.

[44] U.S. EPA, Office of Emergency and Remedial Response (June 1992), p. 9. To view an online listing by state of NPL sites, visit **www.epa.gov/superfund/sites/npl/npl.htm.**

Only if a site is listed on the NPL can remedial actions be undertaken by the federal government. The rest are relegated to state and local officials for an appropriate response.

Once a site is placed on the NPL, a feasibility study is done, which involves a complete examination of the site and an appraisal of available cleanup options. This can take from 18 to 30 months and can cost up to $1 million. The action plan selected and support for the decision are documented and used in efforts to recover funding from parties responsible for the release. Design work follows to adapt the action plan to the specific attributes of the site. This stage takes another 12 to 18 months and adds another $1 million on average to the tally. Finally, the actual site cleanup or remedial action begins. On average, the total cost is $25 million per site and can take years to accomplish. Because the costs of remedial action are so high and the damage so extensive, there are more sites needing cleanup than there are funds available. The EPA uses a prioritization strategy whereby the agency's headquarters and its regional offices arrive at a consensus as to which sites are most in need of attention.[45]

### Compensation, Liability, and Enforcement

Superfund gives the EPA authority to force those parties responsible for a hazardous substance release to correct the problem and pay for the damage. This is accomplished either through an administrative order or by bringing a civil action against the responsible party. According to current law, so-called **potentially responsible parties (PRPs)** include any existing or former owner or operator of a hazardous waste facility as well as those involved, however remotely, in the disposal, treatment, or transport of hazardous substances to the contaminated site. The extent of the financial accountability is similarly extensive—to include all costs of removal or remedial action and any damages to natural resources or human health.[46] From an economic perspective, the intent is to force guilty parties to internalize the externality of whatever market transaction contributed to the release.

**potentially responsible parties (PRPs)**
Any current or former owner or operator of a hazardous waste facility and all those involved in the disposal, treatment, or transport of hazardous substances to the contaminated site.

### Emergency Planning

Title III of the Superfund Amendments and Reauthorization Act of 1986 is a free-standing piece of legislation known as the Emergency Planning and Community Right-to-Know Act. The purpose of this act is to inform citizens about the existence and potential release of hazardous substances and to provide a planning system for emergencies. To develop the planning

---

[45] U.S. EPA, Office of Solid Waste and Emergency Response (May 1992), p. 6; U.S. EPA, Office of Emergency and Remedial Response (June 1992), pp. 10–12.

[46] CERCLA, Sec. 107.(a).

system, each state government must devise and implement a comprehensive plan to deal with a hazardous substance release.

A related objective of Title III is to keep the public informed about the production of hazardous substances and their discharge into the environment. To accomplish this goal, Title III has a number of reporting requirements. One of these calls for annual toxic chemical release reports from facilities that manufacture, process, or use specific chemicals in an amount that exceeds a mandated threshold. Data from these reports are used to compile the **Toxics Release Inventory (TRI),** a national database about releases of hazardous substances.[47] All data are published annually by the EPA and are available to the general public. Currently, information is collected on more than 600 chemicals and 28 chemical categories.

**Toxics Release Inventory (TRI)**
National database that gives information about hazardous substances released into the environment.

## An Analysis of Superfund

In concept, the Comprehensive Environmental Response, Compensation, and Liability Act (CERCLA) is the most unusual of all U.S. environmental laws. Unlike RCRA and other environmental legislation like the Clean Air Act, Superfund is not a regulatory program. Rather, its aim is to clean up the damage at uncontrolled or abandoned hazardous waste sites, using liability standards to identify the so-called potentially responsible parties and make them pay for their actions.[48] While the overall intent is beyond reproach, the implementation has produced mixed results.

### Assessing Superfund's Performance

By most accounts, Superfund's Remedial Program has moved at a snail's pace. Table 17.8 gives data on identified CERCLIS and NPL sites for the 1980 to 1994 period and the number of sites removed each year. As of 1994, only 64 NPL sites had been removed out of the 1,355 identified NPL sites. Further, it is argued that even the small number of removed sites is an inflated measure of Superfund's progress, since the EPA has not in all cases properly addressed the potential of recurring problems.[49] This argument relates to the selection of an appropriate risk management strategy for dealing with these sites. If benefit–cost analysis guided the decision making, the high costs of cleanup would be used to determine how far remedial actions should go in cleaning up a site. Opponents of such an approach argue that the associated risks of a hazardous release should be reduced to zero or close to it, implying that a pure risk standard ought to be employed. Both

---

[47] More information about the TRI can be found at **www.epa.gov/opptintr/tri/**.

[48] For an interesting discussion of how CERCLA is part of an important trend in U.S. environmental policy, see Humphrey and Paddock (1990).

[49] See U.S. Congress, OTA (1985).

| TABLE 17.8 | CERCLIS AND NPL SITES, 1980–1994 |

| | Sites Listed | | Sites Removed |
| | CERCLIS | NPL | NPL |
| Year | (number, cumulative) | | (number per year) |
| --- | --- | --- | --- |
| 1980–1986 | 25,200 | 901 | 13 |
| 1987 | 27,600 | 964 | 0 |
| 1988 | 30,000 | 1,194 | 4 |
| 1989 | 31,900 | 1,254 | 11 |
| 1990 | 33,600 | 1,236 | 1 |
| 1991 | 34,200 | 1,245 | 9 |
| 1992 | 36,400 | 1,275 | 2 |
| 1993 | 37,500 | 1,320 | 11 |
| 1994 | 38,600 | 1,355 | 13 |

NOTES: Number of CERCLIS sites has been rounded.

Number of NPL sites represents the cumulative total of proposed, final, and deleted NPL sites as of the end of each fiscal year.

SOURCE: CERCLIS, Office of Emergency and Remedial Response, *Federal Register* notices through September 30, 1994, as cited in U.S. Environmental Protection Agency, Office of Emergency and Remedial Response. *Progress Toward Implementing Superfund, Fiscal Year 1994; Report to Congress.* Washington, DC: undated.

arguments are firmly entrenched in the issue of "how clean is clean?" Until this is resolved, significant amounts of resources may be wasted.

## What's Wrong with Superfund?

Superfund's lack of success cannot be blamed on any single factor. There are many reasons that explain its generally disappointing track record, all of which tend to fall into two major categories. The first is the lack of information about the extent of the problem, both at the outset of the program and throughout its implementation. The second source of failure is linked to the structure of the program and the absence of incentives to advance the remediation process.

**Information Problems.**[50] The EPA faces many problems in dealing with the aftermath of decades of careless dumping. A major obstacle is that the agency had to start at ground zero with very little data on the extent of the nation's hazardous waste site problem. As information first began to accumulate, the EPA learned that the problem was far worse than it had anticipated. There is also a strong contention that all the significant problems

---

[50] Much of the following is drawn from U.S. GAO (December 1987), Table 2.1, p. 14, Chapter 3; and U.S. EPA (March 1987) cited on p. 22 of this GAO report.

still have not been identified. At issue is to determine how much of this information gap is within the EPA's control.

A major criticism of the Superfund program is that there has been insufficient federal control, direction, and financial support for state programs aimed at identifying potential Superfund sites. While all states are required under RCRA to submit an inventory of any sites ever used for hazardous waste disposal, the methods used to comply with this requirement are not consistent. Furthermore, there is a lack of initiative in how states identify sites in need of remedial action, relying mainly on private citizens' complaints. The EPA has been criticized for not providing sufficient guidance or funding to rectify this problem, choosing to allocate its budget solely to cleanup activities

Inadequate state reporting is only part of the problem. According to the U.S. General Accounting Office (GAO), there are other data gaps caused by the EPA's regional offices not properly aggregating state-reported data. In a 1987 study of site identification in five states, the GAO found that over 800 sites were missing from the CERCLIS inventory, and some of these are believed severe enough to qualify for the NPL. Of the 232 sites that the GAO could identify, 83 percent were reported by states but not listed by the appropriate EPA regional office. The GAO estimates that the true number of CERCLIS sites is in the range of 130,340 to 425,380—markedly different from the 27,507 that were officially listed in the study year.

Beyond these data problems, there is also a lack of knowledge about the most effective technologies to accomplish the complex cleanup task. The many phases of remedial action are time-intensive and costly. Presumably, experience will help to shorten the time horizon. In the interim, the EPA is continuing its cleanup efforts and at the same time pursuing cost recovery settlements from responsible parties to help defray Superfund's enormous expense.

**Lack of Incentives.**　　Like the provisions of RCRA, the Superfund legislation is distinguished by the conspicuous absence of market mechanisms. Even the feedstock taxes used to fund the $8.5 billion Superfund are aimed mainly at raising revenues rather than encouraging decisions to improve the environment. Since these taxes are levied on oil and certain raw chemicals, it may seem as if they are product charges aimed at deterring the use of these hazardous substances. However, Congress' decision to target these materials was motivated by the need for a substantial and fairly reliable tax base from which to collect much-needed revenues.[51] Despite the statutory label of "environmental taxes," these levies offer little incentive to diminish hazardous waste pollution.

---

[51] SARA added another revenue source in 1986, calling for a new tax based on a mandated percentage of corporate income. U.S. EPA, Office of Policy, Planning, and Evaluation (July 1992), p. 3-5; CERCLA, Title II; and SARA, Part VII, Sec. 59A.

Other incentive issues arise in how liability is established under Superfund. In the law itself as well as in how the courts have inferred Congress' intent, the determination of who is responsible for damages and to what extent is all-encompassing and unyielding. Motivated by the knowledge that the $8.5-billion fund would not be nearly enough to pay for the massive cleanup, Congress and the courts use whatever legislative and judicial muscle necessary to impose the "polluter-pays principle." While the intent was to achieve swift action against the guilty parties and advance the remediation process, the plan backfires because it sets up an unexpected and perverse incentive.

The problem is rooted in how the law identifies a potentially responsible party (PRP) and in how the liability is defined. In establishing legal responsibility, the courts use the concepts of strict liability and joint and several liability.[52] **Strict liability** means that individuals can be held liable even if negligence is not proven. **Joint and several liability** means that a single party found liable for damages can be held responsible for *all* associated costs even if that party's actual contribution to the damages is minimal.[53] The use of such tough legal standards was intended to save the government the complex and time-intensive process of proving negligence and then determining what proportion of costs each PRP must pay.[54] There was also the expectation that the use of joint and several liability would encourage an identified PRP to name all other responsible parties at a given site.

Unfortunately, these expectations proved to be off the mark. Recognizing the potential to be held accountable for *all* costs at a named waste site, few PRPs were willing to come forward with information. Furthermore, because joint and several liability assigns the entire costs of cleanup to a single party, there was a strong financial incentive for a liable party to use delay tactics or to incur the relatively lower costs of litigation to fight the charges.[55] As a consequence, the well-intended legal standards have led to long delays and a diversion of resources from cleanup to litigation proceedings. In fact, a 1985 study puts the estimate of legal expenses at about 55 percent of the total dollars expended on remediation.[56]

**strict liability**
Legal standard that identifies individuals as responsible for damages even if negligence is not proven.

**joint and several liability** Legal standard that identifies a single party as responsible for all damages even if that party's contribution to the damages is minimal.

---

[52] Interestingly, these legal concepts are *not* written into Superfund's provisions. They were initially in the bill submitted before Congress, but were removed as part of an agreement between the House of Representatives and the Senate before signing it into law. However, the courts took the initiative, and reinstated these notions based on what they perceived to be Congress' intent (Mazmanian and Morell, 1992, p. 36).

[53] It is also true that the use of these liability standards under Superfund extends well beyond what is imposed under traditional common law. For example, causality does not have to be shown to establish liability under Superfund, as is the case under common law. Hence, there is no need to show proof that a defendant's wastes are those that caused the damage. All that is necessary is evidence that the defendant is a PRP. See Anderson (1989), pp. 427–32 for more detail.

[54] For an interesting article that discusses the issue of cost allocation in detail, see Butler, Schneider, Hall, and Burton (1993).

[55] Mazmanian and Morell (1992), pp. 36–37.

[56] Light (1985), p. 10205.

As a matter of record, in 1994 EPA Administrator Carol Browner stated the following about the need for Superfund reform:

> "Although the clock ran out on Superfund reauthorization this year, a broad-based coalition for reform was established. That coalition, ranging from corporation to small businesses to environmentalists, developed a vital blueprinting for change . . . One in four Americans live within four miles of a Superfund toxic waste site and many businesses, particularly small businesses, are still unfairly burdened—ultimately change is essential."[57]

# Conclusions

Most would agree that U.S. hazardous waste policy has broadened and strengthened considerably over the past two decades. As the evolution continues, we observe public officials beginning to integrate preventive initiatives into the overall policy solution. By addressing the generation of hazardous waste *before* it becomes a problem, the nation can avoid some of the associated health and ecological risks, not to mention the high costs of correcting the degradation. Yet in spite of these favorable assessments and the acknowledgment that some progress has been made, there are still questions about the efficiency and cost-effectiveness of current U.S. policy.

With 20/20 hindsight, it is apparent that the federal government should have acted sooner to respond to the risks of hazardous waste pollution. But such an assessment assumes full information—a luxury the United States clearly did not have. Confronted with tough problems, a marked lack of data, and a very angry constituency, Congress sought policy instruments that they thought would be direct, uncompromising, and capable of achieving a swift resolution. Given this motivation, it is not surprising that the major laws on hazardous solid waste are couched within a command-and-control framework. Understanding this motivation, however, does not change the fact that such a policy approach came at some measure of sacrifice—a loss of efficiency and cost-effectiveness. Exacerbating the problem, many of Congress' intentions were not carried out as planned. Not only did most of the initiatives lack incentive mechanisms, many were also set in motion without a full understanding of the extent of the problem. As such, they were destined for failure. Such was the fate of the Superfund legislation, a unique body of law that continues to be a source of contention among government officials, industry, and private citizens.

Midcourse corrections might save the nation considerable expense in executing its policy missions and could restore the level of environmental

---

[57] U.S. EPA, Office of Communications, Education and Public Affairs (October 17, 1994).

risk to an acceptable level more quickly. The strategy has to be directed both at repairing the damage from the past and seeking ways to reduce and more efficiently manage the present waste stream. Congress must decide a new course of action to reauthorize the Superfund law. If nothing else, policy makers seem to have recognized the need for reform and the importance of using risk management strategies in all environmental initiatives—even in the absence of extensive information. Such an awareness may be significant to what appears to be a critical phase in the evolution of U.S. hazardous waste policy.

# Summary

- Hazardous solid wastes are any unwanted materials or refuse capable of posing a substantial threat to health or the environment.

- Estimates of annual generation of hazardous waste in the United States range from 250 to 500 million tons. Industry is responsible for the largest proportion. Chemical producers generate about 79 percent of all the hazardous wastes in the United States.

- U.S. policy on solid wastes originated with the Solid Waste Disposal Act (SWDA) enacted in 1965. This act was amended in 1970 by the Resource Recovery Act and later by the Resource Conservation and Recovery Act (RCRA) in 1976.

- RCRA represented the nation's first official policy position on hazardous waste control. Congress reauthorized and strengthened RCRA through The Hazardous and Solid Waste Amendments of 1984.

- The Comprehensive Environmental Response, Compensation, and Liability Act (CERCLA), or Superfund, was passed in 1980. This act was aimed at identifying and cleaning up the nation's worst, inactive hazardous waste sites and to recover damages from responsible parties.

- CERCLA was revised in 1986 through the Superfund Amendments and Reauthorization Act (SARA), which brought the Superfund budget up to $8.5 billion.

- Under RCRA, a command-and-control hazardous waste program was devised, commonly referred to as the "cradle-to-grave" management approach. Its four components are: (1) the identification and listing of hazardous waste; (2) a national manifest system; (3) a permit system for treatment, storage, and disposal facilities (TSDFs); and (4) the setting of standards for these facilities.

- One problem with RCRA is that the characteristics and criteria used to identify hazardous waste are risk-based with no provision to consider the benefits of these materials before they enter the waste stream. Another problem is that the identifying categories are applied uniformly with no qualifiers to allow for differences in the degree of toxicity across various waste constituents or differences in quantity.

- The standards applicable to TSDFs are benefit-based with no consideration for economic costs. Hence, it is not likely that allocative efficiency will be achieved. Furthermore, with few exceptions, the standards are applied uniformly. There is virtually no provision for site-specific differences, likely disallowing a cost-effective solution.

- The manifest system is a command-and-control instrument that is benefit-based in motivation. Economic considerations played no role in its design or implementation. It has not been a major factor in reducing risk because of its limited scope.

- The land restrictions imposed with the 1984 Amendments caused land disposal facilities to face higher unit costs and elevate their prices. In response, generators could either initiate waste reduction or alter their waste management practices. Although these rulings may reduce the external costs borne by society, inefficiency is not eliminated.

- One market-based approach to hazardous waste management is a waste-end charge levied at the time of disposal.

- Under CERCLA, the federal government can undertake a response action whenever there is an actual or potential release of a hazardous substance that may present imminent danger to public health or welfare. The National Contingency Plan (NCP) outlines procedures to implement these activities either as removal actions or remedial actions.

- Title III of SARA is a free-standing piece of legislation known as the Emergency Planning and Community Right-to-Know Act. Its purpose is to inform citizens about potential releases of hazardous substances and to provide a planning system for emergencies. One of its reporting requirements calls for data that are used to form the Toxics Release Inventory.

- Superfund's provisions have produced mixed results. One problem is the lack of information about the extent of the problem. The second source of failure is the lack of incentives to enhance the remediation process. The use of strict liability and joint and several liability has led to delays and the diversion of resources from cleanup to litigation proceedings.

## Key Concepts

| | |
|---|---|
| hazardous solid wastes | manifest |
| waste stream | permitting system |
| "cradle-to-grave" management system | pollution charge |
| | waste-end charge |
| Comprehensive Environmental Response, Compensation, and Liability Information System (CERCLIS) | National Contingency Plan (NCP) |
| | removal actions |
| | remedial actions |
| feedstock taxes | National Priorities List (NPL) |
| source reduction | potentially responsible parties (PRPs) |
| waste management | |
| characteristic wastes | Toxics Release Inventory (TRI) |
| listed wastes | strict liability |
| | joint and several liability |

## Review Questions

1. Consider the various provisions in RCRA that discourage land-based waste disposal. Identify and explain one aspect of the law that is command-and-control in approach and one that is incentive-based.

2. Propose an alternative method of identifying hazardous waste that is more efficient than the one mandated under RCRA without compromising the objective of risk reduction. Support your proposal with a well-defined risk management strategy.

3. Use benefit–cost analysis to evaluate the Superfund remedial action program qualitatively.

4. Recommend an incentive-based reform that would improve states' identification of hazardous waste sites.

5. a. An ongoing debate about the Superfund program is the determination of the optimal abatement level, characterized as the "how clean is clean" problem. Choose one of the risk management strategies and propose how it might be used to resolve this issue.
   b. In your view, why has there been no movement to initiate such a proposal?

## Additional Readings

Been, Vicki. "Unpopular Neighbors: Are Dumps and Landfills Sited Equitably?" *RFF Newsletter*, April 1994.

Dower, Roger C. "Hazardous Wastes." In Paul R. Portney, ed., *Public Policies for Environmental Protection*. Washington, DC: Resources for the Future, 1990, pp. 151–94.

Fortuna, Richard C., and David J. Lennett. *Hazardous Waste Regulation: The New Era.* New York: McGraw-Hill, 1987.

Friedland, Steven I. "The New Hazardous Waste Management System: Regulation of Wastes or Wasted Regulation?" *Harvard Environmental Law Review* 5(71), 1981, pp. 89–129.

Gerrard, Michael B. *Whose Backyard, Whose Risk.* Cambridge, MA: MIT Press, 1994.

Harper, Richard K., and Stephen C. Adams. "CERCLA and Deep Pockets: Market Responses to the Superfund Program." *Contemporary Economic Issues* 14(1), January 1996, pp. 107–15.

Hoffman, Andrew J. "An Uneasy Rebirth at Love Canal." *Environment* 37(2), March 1995, pp. 4–9, 25–31.

Hong, Peter, and Michele Green. "The Toxic Mess Called Superfund," *Business Week*, May 11, 1992, pp. 32–34.

Kunreuther, Howard, and Ruth Patrick. "Managing the Risks of Hazardous Waste." *Environment* 33(3), April 1991, pp. 13–15, 31–36.

Landy, Marc K., Marc J. Roberts, and Stephen R. Thomas. *The Environmental Protection Agency: Asking the Wrong Questions.* New York: Oxford University Press, 1990.

Levenson, Howard. "Wasting Away: Policies to Reduce Trash Toxicity and Quantity." *Environment* 32(2), March 1990, pp. 10–15, 31–36.

National Academy of Sciences. *Reducing Hazardous Waste Generation: An Evaluation and a Call for Action.* Washington, DC: National Academy Press, 1985.

Ritter, Don. "Challenging Current Environmental Standards." *Environment* 37(2), March 1995, pp. 11–12.

U.S. Congress, Office of Technology Assessment (OTA). *Serious Reduction of Hazardous Waste.* Washington, DC: U.S. Government Printing Office, September 1986.

U.S. Environmental Protection Agency, Office of Solid Waste and Emergency Response. *RCRA Environmental Indicators: FY 1991 Progress Report and Implementation Plan for the Future.* Washington, DC, January 1992.

# Related Web Sites

| | |
|---|---|
| Activities of TSDFs | **www.epa.gov/epaoswer/osw/tsd.htm** |
| Dates and events at Love Canal | **www.essential.org/cchw/lovcanal/lcdates.html** |
| EPA's *The Hazardous Waste Permitting Process: A Citizen's Guide* | **www.epa.gov/epaoswer/hazwaste/permit/prmtguid.htm** |
| Facts about waste and RCRA | **www.epa.gov/epaoswer/osw/basifact.htm** |
| Facts on the waste stream | **www.epa.gov/epaoswer/osw/index.htm** |
| Hazardous Waste Data | **www.epa.gov/epaoswer/hazwaste/data** |
| Information on Subtitle C of RCRA | **www.epa.gov/epaoswer/osw/hazwaste.htm** |
| Information on Superfund | **www.epa.gov/superfund/index.htm** |

| | |
|---|---|
| Information on the Toxics Release Inventory (TRI) | **www.epa.gov/opptintr/tri/** |
| Listing and Maps of NPL sites by state | **www.epa.gov/superfund/sites/npl/npl.htm** |
| "Superfund Reauthorization Issues in the 105th Congress" by Mark Reisch (1998) | **www.cnie.org/nle/waste-17.html** |
| Superfund site cleanup process | **www.epa.gov/superfund/whatissf/sfproces.htm** |

# Appendix: A Reference to Acronyms in Hazardous Waste Policy Control

### Environmental Economics Acronyms

| | |
|---|---|
| *MPB* | Marginal private benefit |
| *MSB* | Marginal social benefit |
| *MEC* | Marginal external cost |
| *MPC* | Marginal private cost |
| *MSC* | Marginal social cost |

### Environmental Science Acronyms

| | |
|---|---|
| MMT | millions of metric tons |

### Environmental Policy Acronyms

| | |
|---|---|
| CERCLA | Comprehensive Environmental Response, Compensation, and Liability Act |
| CERCLIS | Comprehensive Environmental Response, Compensation, and Liability Information System |
| NCP | National Contingency Plan |
| NPL | National Priorities List |
| NRC | National Response Center |
| PRP | Potentially responsible party |
| RCRA | Resource Conservation and Recovery Act |
| SARA | Superfund Amendments and Reauthorization Act |
| SWDA | Solid Waste Disposal Act |
| TSDFs | Treatment, storage, and disposal facilities |

# 18

## *Managing Municipal Solid Waste*

**municipal solid waste (MSW)** Nonhazardous wastes disposed of by local communities.

Every local community has to deal with collecting and disposing of what most of us offhandedly call trash. **Municipal solid waste (MSW),** as it is more formally termed, is the collection of cans, bottles, food scraps, newspapers, lawn clippings, and old furniture that characterizes everyday living. How could such a mundane matter as everyday trash become an issue? Mainly because society has seen it as exactly that—a routine part of living that merits no particular attention. As long as the unsightly pile of old newspapers and garbage leaves the street corner, most citizens give the matter little thought—that is, until some public official proposes a new landfill site on the next block. The typical reaction is a negative one—dubbed the "not in my backyard," or "NIMBY," syndrome. This response coupled with the growth trend in municipal waste generation and an aging disposal system have left many communities with a difficult problem.

As part of the nonhazardous waste stream, municipal solid wastes pose no *direct* threat to human, animal, or plant life. Nonetheless, there are risks to society and the ecology if too much is generated or if it is improperly managed. Like many other countries around the world, the United States has depended on landfills to dispose of its MSW. Unsanitary conditions at these sites can contaminate water and soil with disease-spreading bacteria. A more serious risk is the release of toxic substances into the environment. Toxic contamination can arise from natural decomposition processes or the presence of household or industrial hazardous substances mixed in with municipal refuse. There is also the risk of atmospheric pollution caused by gases released from waste decomposition or from the incomplete combustion of incinerated wastes.

Given the potential damages, public policies are needed to control waste management practices, to find ways to recover and reuse waste materials, and to develop new technologies. In the United States, much of the responsibility for these policies is delegated to state and local governments with some measure of federal oversight. Such an approach allows for more flexibility in devising waste management programs than is the case for hazardous waste controls. In some communities, innovative policies have been developed to deal with MSW, including the use of market instruments to achieve environmental goals.

In this chapter, we consider the risks of MSW pollution and analyze the policy response to these risks. To understand the motivation of government programs and regulations, we begin by characterizing the generation and composition of this waste stream. Here, we use international comparisons to provide context to our discussion of U.S. data. Once done, we outline the delegation of responsibilities between federal and state governments given by the Resource Conservation and Recovery Act (RCRA). We then present a market model of MSW management services and explore potential sources of inefficiency. This discussion prepares the way for an economic analysis of various market instruments used by state and local governments to manage the MSW stream.

## Characterizing Municipal Solid Waste[1]

### Observing a Trend

Many U.S. communities have been observing an increase in the size of the MSW stream, a phenomenon that is only partly linked to population growth. As shown in Table 18.1, per capita generation rates are also rising, suggesting that the characterization of Americans as a "disposable society" may be well placed. Built-in product obsolescence, persuasive advertising that encourages excessive consumption, and reliance on prepared and therefore heavily packaged food products are all contributing factors. Despite this apparent growth trend in MSW generation, the development of better waste management practices has lagged behind.

For years, the United States and most European countries have depended primarily on landfills to dispose of MSW, a practice that at least for a time seemed a reasonable solution. In the 1980s, reports of a "capacity crisis" warned that many municipal landfills were running out of space and others were being closed for improper waste management practices. More recently, counter arguments have emerged stating that the so-called capacity crisis in the United States was exaggerated, occurring in only certain locations. These reports point out that the rash of dump closings has involved mainly small sites, and that increased recycling, and a greater use of waste incineration have contributed to what is now a surplus of landfill space in some areas. Indeed, some communities have been able to negotiate lower

---

[1] To access the most recent update of the characterization of municipal solid waste in the United States, visit **www.epa.gov/epaoswer/non-hw/muncpl/**.

| TABLE 18.1 | TREND DATA ON U.S. ANNUAL MSW GENERATION FROM 1960 TO 1995 BY WEIGHT | | | | |
|---|---|---|---|---|---|
| **Year** | **1960** | **1970** | **1980** | **1990** | **1995** |
| Total MSW generated by weight (millions of tons) | 88.1 | 121.1 | 151.6 | 197.3 | 208.1 |
| Total population (thousands) | 179,979 | 203,984 | 227,255 | 249,402 | 262,755 |
| Per capita MSW (pounds per day) | 2.68 | 3.25 | 3.66 | 4.33 | 4.34 |

SOURCE: U.S. Environmental Protection Agency, Office of Solid Waste and Emergency Response. *Characterization of Municipal Solid Waste in the United States: 1996 Update.* Washington, DC, May 1997, Table 1, p. 28 and Table 49, p. 142.

contract prices with trash management firms, suggesting that the reported glut in disposal capacity may be real—at least in some regions. Yet some major waste companies continue to argue that landfill space is declining.

In either case, there is no debate that the MSW disposal system in the United States is aging. According to a recent report from the Congressional Office of Technology Assessment, 70 percent of MSW landfills in the United States began operation before 1980. Many lack proper controls such as waterproof cover systems, suitable liners to prevent leaching, or leachate collection systems. The absence of well-engineered controls creates a potential for serious environmental problems, such as methane gas explosions, the accumulation of bacteria, and contamination to ground and surface waters. These concerns are exacerbated when even small proportions of hazardous waste are mixed in with the nonhazardous materials.[2]

## The Composition of MSW in the United States

To get a sense of what comprises MSW in the United States, we can examine its composition both by the types of products being discarded and the kinds of materials entering the waste stream. The designated **product groups** are durable goods (e.g., appliances, furniture, and tires), nondurable goods (e.g., magazines, clothing, motor oil, batteries, and household cleansers), packaging and containers, food, and yard trimmings. Figure 18.1(a) gives the relative proportions by weight of these product groups based on the 208 million tons of MSW generated in 1995. Notice that packaging and containers account for over a third of this total, or

**product groups**
Categories of products in the MSW stream identified as durable goods, nondurable goods, packaging and containers, food, and yard trimmings.

---

[2] U.S. Congress, Office of Technology Assessment (OTA) (1989), p. 284.

| FIGURE 18.1 | PROPORTION BY WEIGHT OF PRODUCTS AND MATERIALS GENERATED IN U.S. MUNICIPAL SOLID WASTE IN 1995 |

**(a) Proportion by Weight of Products Generated in U.S. Municipal Solid Waste in 1995**

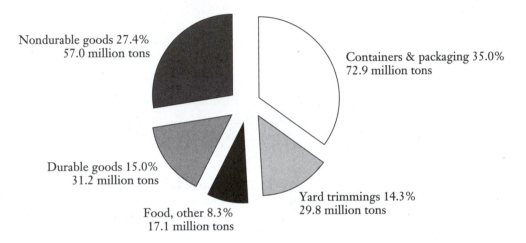

Nondurable goods 27.4%
57.0 million tons

Containers & packaging 35.0%
72.9 million tons

Durable goods 15.0%
31.2 million tons

Food, other 8.3%
17.1 million tons

Yard trimmings 14.3%
29.8 million tons

**(b) Proportion by Weight of Materials Generated in U.S. Municipal Solid Waste in 1995**

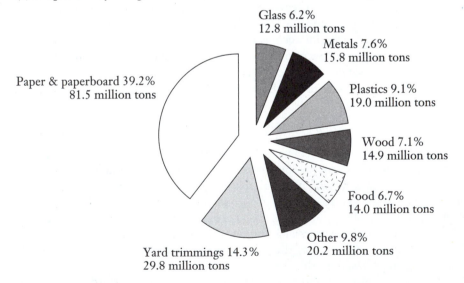

Glass 6.2%
12.8 million tons

Metals 7.6%
15.8 million tons

Paper & paperboard 39.2%
81.5 million tons

Plastics 9.1%
19.0 million tons

Wood 7.1%
14.9 million tons

Food 6.7%
14.0 million tons

Other 9.8%
20.2 million tons

Yard trimmings 14.3%
29.8 million tons

SOURCE: U.S. Environmental Protection Agency, Office of Solid Waste and Emergency Response. *Characterization of Municipal Solid Waste in the United States: 1996 Update*. Washington, DC, May 1997, Figure ES-1, p. 5; Figure ES-2, p. 7.

**materials groups**
Categories of materials in the MSW stream identified as paper and paperboard, yard waste, food, glass, metals, plastics, textiles, rubber, and wood.

72.9 million tons. The **materials groups** identified in MSW are paper and paperboard, yard waste, food waste, glass, metals, plastics, textiles, rubber, and wood. Proportions by weight for these categories are shown in Figure 18.1(b). According to these data, paper and paperboard represent the largest proportion by weight of discarded materials in 1995, accounting for 39.2 percent of the total.[3]

Composition data by materials convey information about how manufacturing decisions ultimately affect waste accumulation. Table 18.2 (p. 564) gives trend data on the materials content of the nation's MSW for the 1960 to 1995 period. Notice that the generation of paper and paperboard has grown fairly steadily over time, rising from 30 million tons, or 34 percent of the total in 1960, to 81.5 million tons, or 39.2 percent in 1995. Paper wastes are procyclical, meaning that the amount varies directly with the economic business cycle. This explains why the total weight of paper wastes in 1975, a recession year, is less than it was in 1970. The fastest growing segment of MSW in the United States is plastics, which has risen steadily from 0.4 million tons in 1960 to 19.0 million tons in 1995. This growth rate is just as impressive when viewed on a proportionate basis, at less than 1 percent of 1960's total MSW by weight to over 9 percent of the total in 1995. These data explain why there has been a surge of interest in recycling plastics, an issue discussed in Application 18.1 (p. 565). Recovery rates for plastics and the other components of MSW as of 1995 are shown in Figure 18.2 (p. 566).

### International Comparisons

Proper management of the MSW stream is a universal objective. Table 18.3 (p. 567) shows per capita MSW generation (measured in pounds per day) for the top 50 waste-generating nations in the world. Notice that the major industrialized nations and the oil-producing countries are at the upper end of MSW generation rates. What is also apparent from the data is that Americans are among the highest MSW generators in the world.[4] Notice how the U.S. data compares with other industrialized nations such as Germany and Japan. For example, Japan's per capita rate of 2.0 pales in comparison to the U.S. statistic. Some of the international differences are attributable to the amount of packaging used by producers. For example, in 1988, it was estimated that the average American generated some 463 pounds of packaging waste. Citizens of both the European Community and Japan are said to have produced at least 25 percent *less* than that amount.[5]

---

[3] U.S. EPA, Office of Solid Waste and Emergency Response (May 1997).

[4] These data have been compiled by World Resources Institute based on available country statistics. Because they are intended to provide a broad international comparison of waste generation rates, they are drawn from a number of sources and are based on methods and assumptions that are not necessarily the same as those used to prepare national data. Hence, these statistics, which are undated, are not directly comparable to domestically compiled data such as those reported by the EPA for the United States.

[5] McCarthy (Winter/Spring 1993).

TABLE 18.2

## TREND DATA ON MSW GENERATED IN THE UNITED STATES: 1960–1995 BY MATERIALS

| | Millions of Tons[a] | | | | | | | |
| --- | --- | --- | --- | --- | --- | --- | --- | --- |
| | 1960 | 1965 | 1970 | 1975 | 1980 | 1985 | 1990 | 1995 |
| **Materials in Products** | | | | | | | | |
| Paper and paperboard | 30.0 | 38.0 | 44.3 | 43.0 | 55.2 | 61.5 | 72.7 | 81.5 |
| Glass | 6.7 | 8.7 | 12.7 | 13.5 | 15.1 | 13.2 | 13.1 | 12.8 |
| Metals | 10.8 | 11.1 | 13.8 | 14.3 | 15.5 | 14.2 | 16.6 | 15.9 |
| Plastics | 0.4 | 1.4 | 2.9 | 4.5 | 6.8 | 11.6 | 17.1 | 19.0 |
| Rubber and leather | 1.8 | 2.6 | 3.0 | 3.9 | 4.2 | 3.8 | 5.8 | 6.0 |
| Textiles | 1.8 | 1.9 | 2.0 | 2.2 | 2.5 | 2.8 | 5.8 | 7.4 |
| Wood | 3.0 | 3.5 | 3.7 | 4.4 | 7.0 | 8.2 | 11.9 | 14.9 |
| Other[b] | 0.1 | 0.3 | 0.8 | 1.7 | 2.5 | 3.4 | 3.2 | 3.6 |
| Subtotal—Materials in products | 54.6 | 67.5 | 83.3 | 87.5 | 108.9 | 118.7 | 146.2 | 161.1 |
| **Other Wastes** | | | | | | | | |
| Food wastes | 12.2 | 12.7 | 12.8 | 13.4 | 13.0 | 13.2 | 13.2 | 14.0 |
| Yard trimmings | 20.0 | 21.6 | 23.2 | 25.2 | 27.5 | 30.0 | 35.0 | 29.8 |
| Miscellaneous inorganic wastes[c] | 1.3 | 1.6 | 1.8 | 2.0 | 2.3 | 2.5 | 2.9 | 3.2 |
| Subtotal—Other wastes | 33.5 | 35.9 | 37.8 | 40.6 | 42.8 | 45.7 | 51.1 | 46.9 |
| **Total MSW Generated by Weight** | 88.1 | 103.4 | 121.1 | 128.1 | 151.6 | 164.4 | 197.3 | 208.1 |

| | Percent of Total[a] | | | | | | | |
| --- | --- | --- | --- | --- | --- | --- | --- | --- |
| | 1960 | 1965 | 1970 | 1975 | 1980 | 1985 | 1990 | 1995 |
| **Materials in Products** | | | | | | | | |
| Paper and paperboard | 34.0 | 36.8 | 36.6 | 33.6 | 36.4 | 37.4 | 36.9 | 39.2 |
| Glass | 7.6 | 8.4 | 10.5 | 10.5 | 10.0 | 8.0 | 6.6 | 6.2 |
| Metals | 12.3 | 10.7 | 11.4 | 11.2 | 10.2 | 8.6 | 8.4 | 7.6 |
| Plastics | 0.4 | 1.4 | 2.4 | 3.5 | 4.5 | 7.1 | 8.7 | 9.1 |
| Rubber and leather | 2.1 | 2.5 | 2.5 | 3.0 | 2.8 | 2.3 | 2.9 | 2.9 |
| Textiles | 2.0 | 1.8 | 1.7 | 1.7 | 1.7 | 1.7 | 2.9 | 3.6 |
| Wood | 3.4 | 3.4 | 3.1 | 3.4 | 4.6 | 5.0 | 6.0 | 7.1 |
| Other[b] | 0.1 | 0.3 | 0.6 | 1.3 | 1.7 | 2.1 | 1.6 | 1.7 |
| Subtotal—Materials in products | 62.0 | 65.3 | 68.8 | 68.3 | 71.8 | 72.2 | 74.1 | 77.4 |
| **Other Wastes** | | | | | | | | |
| Food wastes | 13.8 | 12.3 | 10.6 | 10.5 | 8.6 | 8.0 | 6.7 | 6.7 |
| Yard trimmings | 22.7 | 20.9 | 19.2 | 19.7 | 18.1 | 18.2 | 17.7 | 14.3 |
| Miscellaneous inorganic wastes[c] | 1.5 | 1.5 | 1.5 | 1.6 | 1.5 | 1.5 | 1.5 | 1.5 |
| Subtotal—Other wastes | 38.0 | 34.7 | 31.2 | 31.7 | 28.2 | 27.8 | 25.9 | 22.6 |

NOTES:

[a] The sum of any given column may not add to total due to rounding.

[b] The category "Other" in products is primarily associated with disposable diapers. Also included are electrolytes and other materials in lead-acid batteries not classified as plastics or metals.

[c] Miscellaneous inorganic wastes includes such materials as soil, stones, and bits of concrete.

SOURCES: U.S. Environmental Protection Agency, Office of Solid Waste and Emergency Response. *Characterization of Municipal Solid Waste in the United States: 1992 Update.* Washington, DC, July 1992a, Table 1, p. 2-2; U.S. Environmental Protection Agency, Office of Solid Waste and Emergency Response. *Characterization of Municipal Solid Waste in the United States: 1996 Update.* Washington, DC, May 1997, Table 1, p. 28.

APPLICATION 18.1

# The Facts on Recycling Plastics

Over the past three decades, plastic use in the United States has risen by over 10 percent per year, which translates to a substantial growth rate of plastic wastes. Relative to the total MSW stream, plastic wastes represent 9.1 percent of the total by weight, but by volume, they account for a much higher proportion. Containers and packaging are by far the largest proportion of plastic wastes, representing 7.7 million tons in the United States in 1995, or nearly 41 percent of the plastics waste stream.

Beyond the sheer quantity of plastic wastes, these materials can also endanger the environment. According to the EPA, most of the wastes collected during harbor surveys and beach cleanups are plastics. In addition to the aesthetic degradation of such littering, disposal of plastics in surface waters threatens virtually all forms of marine life. Plastics also contain such additives as colorants, stabilizers, and plasticizers, some of which include toxics like cadmium and lead. Reportedly, 28 percent of the cadmium and 2 percent of the lead found in MSW arise from plastics.

Exacerbating the problem, the recovery rate for plastic wastes in the United States has been poor. In 1985, only 0.1 million tons or less than 1 percent of all plastic wastes generated, was recovered. In 1995, the figure rose to 1 million tons, or roughly 5.3 percent of the total. Why is the overall recovery rate for plastics so poor? The bottom line is that recycled plastics have to compete with virgin materials. And for any recycled product to be competitive, all three steps in the recycling process—collection, separation of materials, and manufacture of new products—must be executed efficiently.

One of the key issues in producing recycled plastic is the resin content. Plastics are made from a variety of different types of resins. Currently, there appear to be sizable and lucrative markets for products made from single resins but not for commodities produced from mixed plastics, which command a lower market value. The problem is, even though many products are made of only a single resin, all of these end up together in the waste stream. To achieve a homogeneous collection of a particular resin, different kinds of plastics have to be identified and separated after collection—a costly step in the recycling process. An important problem is that plastic wastes often are not easily identified, even by experts.

Hence, in order for plastic waste recovery rates to improve, cost-effective methods must be developed to more easily identify different types of plastics and to more readily separate them into batches of single resins. Until these technologies are developed, recycling will continue to focus on easily recognizable plastic wastes that accumulate in large amounts. This explains why soft drink bottles and milk containers currently account for the greatest majority of recycled plastic. It also explains why many packaging manufacturers have begun to label their containers with a recycling symbol and a code number that identifies the resins that were used.

SOURCES: Resource Integration Systems, Ltd., and Waste Matters Consulting, Portland, OR. *Decisionmaker's Guide to Recycling Plastics*. Prepared for the Oregon Department of Environmental Quality Solid Waste Reduction and Recycling Section and U.S. EPA, Region X, Solid Waste Program. December 1990, pp. 7–9; U.S. Environmental Protection Agency, Office of Solid Waste and Emergency Response. *EPA's Report to Congress on Methods to Manage and Control Plastic Wastes*. Washington, DC, February 1990; U.S. Environmental Protection Agency, Office of Solid Waste and Emergency Response. *Characterization of Municipal Solid Waste in the United States: 1992 Update*. Washington, DC: U.S. EPA, July 1992a, Tables 1 and 2, pp. 2–2, 2–3, and Table 7, p. 2-12; U.S. Environmental Protection Agency, Office of Solid Waste and Emergency Response. *Characterization of Municipal Solid Waste in the United States: 1996 Update*. Washington, DC: U.S. EPA, May 1997, Table 1, p. 28, Table 7, pp. 40–41.

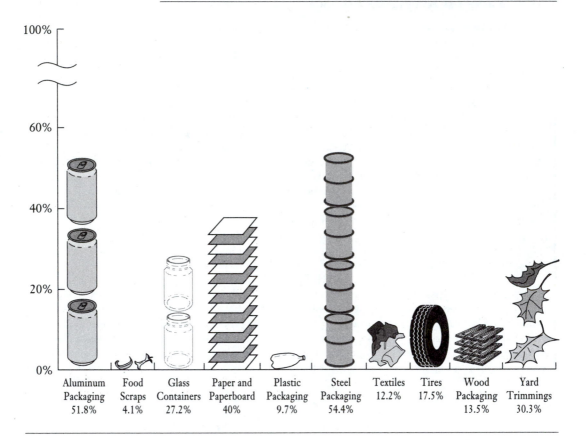

FIGURE 18.2 **RECOVERY RATES FOR MAJOR COMPONENTS OF U.S. MUNICIPAL SOLID WASTE IN 1995**

SOURCE: U.S. Environmental Protection Agency, Office of Solid Waste and Emergency Response. *Environmental Fact Sheet*, "Recycling Municipal Solid Waste: 1995 Facts and Figures." Washington, DC, #EPA/530-F-97-015, April 1997.

These variations may also reflect cultural preferences, environmental awareness, economic conditions, or government regulations. Of course, statistical comparisons across nations are not totally reliable. Estimation methods and even the definitions used for MSW are often different. Nonetheless, even assuming some measure of inaccuracy, the United States is clearly at the high end of worldwide MSW generation rates.

There is also considerable variability in recycling rates across nations. In the United States, the national MSW recycling rate for 1995 was 27 percent.[6] Japan and many European countries have practiced recycling for

---

[6]To learn more about recycling in the United States, visit **www.epa.gov/epaoswer/non-hw/recycle/index.htm**.

| TABLE 18.3 | | | | | |
|---|---|---|---|---|---|

### INTERNATIONAL DATA ON MUNICIPAL SOLID WASTE GENERATION: THE TOP 50 NATIONS RANKED BY PER CAPITA GENERATION RATES

| Country | Waste (lbs. per capita per day) | Rank | Country | Waste (lbs. per capita per day) | Rank |
|---|---|---|---|---|---|
| Australia | 4.2 | 1 | Spain | 1.9 | 26 |
| New Zealand | 4.0 | 2 | Germany | 1.8 | 27 |
| France | 4.0 | 3 | Iceland | 1.8 | 28 |
| Canada | 3.7 | 4 | Hungary | 1.6 | 29 |
| United States | 3.3 | 5 | Greece | 1.5 | 30 |
| Norway | 2.9 | 6 | Italy | 1.5 | 31 |
| Netherlands | 2.6 | 7 | Portugal | 1.5 | 32 |
| Denmark | 2.6 | 8 | Soviet Union (former) | 1.3 | 33 |
| Finland | 2.4 | 9 | Czechoslovakia | 1.3 | 34 |
| Bahrain | 2.4 | 10 | Albania | 1.3 | 35 |
| United Arab Emirates | 2.4 | 11 | Bulgaria | 1.3 | 36 |
| Saudi Arabia | 2.4 | 12 | Austria | 1.3 | 37 |
| Kuwait | 2.4 | 13 | Poland | 1.3 | 38 |
| Oman | 2.4 | 14 | Romania | 1.3 | 39 |
| Israel | 2.4 | 15 | Indonesia | 1.3 | 40 |
| Qatar | 2.4 | 16 | Columbia | 1.2 | 41 |
| Iraq | 2.4 | 17 | Guatemala | 1.1 | 42 |
| Luxembourg | 2.2 | 18 | Liberia | 1.1 | 43 |
| Switzerland | 2.2 | 19 | Cote d'Ivoire | 1.1 | 44 |
| United Kingdom | 2.2 | 20 | Malta | 1.1 | 45 |
| Belgium | 2.0 | 21 | Gabon | 1.1 | 46 |
| Sweden | 2.0 | 22 | Kenya | 1.1 | 47 |
| Japan | 2.0 | 23 | Trinidad and Tobago | 1.1 | 48 |
| Ireland | 2.0 | 24 | Cape Verde | 1.1 | 49 |
| Singapore | 1.9 | 25 | Mozambique | 1.1 | 50 |

SOURCE: "Municipal Solid Waste (top 50)," from *1993 Information Please Environmental Almanac.* Copyright © 1992 by World Resources Institute. Reprinted by permission of Houghton Mifflin Company. All rights reserved.

much longer than the United States, and their national averages reflect their experience. Japan in particular is touted as the nation with the highest national recycling rate for municipal wastes, quoted by most as being above 50 percent. Other nations with land constraints similar to Japan's such as the Netherlands also recycle about half of their local solid wastes.[7] Again, direct international data comparisons must be adjusted for political, cultural, economic, and demographic distinctions that affect the recyclability of manufactured products and the effectiveness of recycling programs.

---

[7] Kharbanda and Stallworthy (1990), pp. 148–51.

# The Policy Response: An Overview

As mentioned in the previous chapter, there is a set of provisions within the Resource Conservation and Recovery Act (RCRA) that apply to nonhazardous waste, including MSW.[8] For the most part, the responsibility of nonhazardous waste management is assigned to states with supervision and support provided by the federal government. This delegation of authority implies that policy makers view MSW controls as a responsibility best undertaken close to the source. Not every community faces the same problems, and even among those that do, the degree of environmental risk can vary considerably across localities. Factors such as town population, age of a landfill, and the proximity of ground and surface water sources to landfills are among the conditions affecting the outcome.

## States' Responsibilities

According to RCRA, states are to develop their own waste management plans, but these must meet certain federal requirements. For example, state plans must include provisions to close or upgrade existing open dumps and to prohibit the establishment of new ones. They also must require that nonhazardous wastes either be used for resource recovery or be properly disposed of such as in a sanitary landfill. Some flexibility is allowed to account for state- or regional-specific factors that may affect the MSW stream, such as the industry profile in the area, the local availability of markets for recovered material, and population density.

RCRA also requires states to establish whatever regulatory powers they need to comply with the law. Typically, states pass their own legislation to meet federal requirements and to fulfill their responsibilities as outlined in their state plans. Some have used incentive-based approaches such as providing grant monies for their cities and towns to set up waste management programs. Others have passed laws calling for local governments to set up recycling plans. One example is New Jersey's 1987 recycling law, discussed in Application 18.2. Some have passed more stringent laws *mandating* that local governments and disposal facilities recycle—among them, Connecticut, Oregon, Rhode Island, Washington, and Wisconsin.[9]

In further support of such efforts, in October 1991 President Bush signed Executive Order 12780, titled the Federal Recycling and Procurement Policy. This directive required all federal agencies to step up their recycling efforts and to foster the development of markets for recycled products.[10] With a similar intent, President Clinton issued Executive

---

[8] These provisions are given in Subtitle D of RCRA. For online information on this section of the law, visit **www.epa.gov/epaoswer/osw/non-hw.htm**.

[9] U.S. EPA, Office of Solid Waste and Emergency Response (November 1989), pp. 16–17.

[10] Council on Environmental Quality (March 1992), pp. 112–14.

**APPLICATION 18.2**

## State Recycling Goals: New Jersey's Solid Waste Initiative

Following the lead of states like Oregon and Rhode Island, New Jersey enacted a mandatory recycling law in 1987. The legislation calls for a statewide recycling rate of 15 percent for the first year and a 25 percent rate for each year thereafter, with an ultimate objective of 65 percent by 2000. To implement the law, all of New Jersey's 21 counties had to develop and submit a recycling plan as part of their solid waste plans. The law specifies that at least three materials must be recycled. While it does not mandate what these three must be, it is generally assumed that they will be newspapers, aluminum cans, and glass containers.

The statewide recycling efforts are to be financed by a $1.50-per-ton facilities surcharge, which officials estimate will generate approximately $12 million in revenues each year. These funds will be allocated to the program participants. While this revenue-sharing provides some incentive for counties and municipalities to participate in the program, New Jersey authorities took further steps to assure the program's success. For example, several incentive mechanisms were established, including a 50 percent tax credit for industries purchasing new recycling equipment. There is also a requirement that 45 percent of the state's paper purchases be spent on recycled paper to promote markets for recyclables. In addition, authorities have established an infrastructure throughout the state with recycling coordinators positioned within each county and municipality to develop and implement local recycling plans and to communicate important information to program participants.

Despite the complexities of orchestrating a recycling program in a state with a 7.5 million population and 567 municipalities, New Jersey has enjoyed remarkable success thus far. During 1989, just two years after the recycling law went into effect, about 20 percent of its residential and commercial solid waste and almost 39 percent of its entire solid waste stream were being recycled—wastes that would have found their way to New Jersey's limited landfills were it not for the 1987 law. With a 1996 recycling rate of 45 percent, New Jersey seems to be making progress toward its goal of 65 percent by 2000.

SOURCES: U.S. Environmental Protection Agency, Office of Solid Waste. *Recycling Works! State and Local Solutions to Solid Waste Management Problems*, Washington, DC, January 1989, pp. 20–22; National Solid Wastes Management Association (NSWMA). *Recycling in the States: Mid-Year Update 1990*. Washington, DC: NSWMA, 1990; Jenny M. Heumann. "State Recycling Programs: A Waste Reduction Emphasis." *Waste Age*, August 1997.

Order 12873 in October 1993 titled On Federal Acquisition, Recycling and Waste Reduction. It too is aimed at promoting recycling and the use of recycled products. While these responses are positive, they fall short of what some other nations are doing. For example, in the same year that President Bush signed his Executive Order, Germany passed a new ordinance that is much more aggressive in its approach toward recycling, as Application 18.3 explains.

### Federal Responsibilities

Based on RCRA's provisions for nonhazardous wastes, the federal government must provide financial and technical assistance to states in designing and implementing their waste management plans. It also must encourage

## Germany's Green Dot Program

A commonly cited example of a national recycling plan is Germany's packaging ordinance. According to one press report, this 1991 law is the most ambitious recycling program in the world. The progressive mandate set recycling targets of 72 percent of glass, tinplate, and aluminum and 64 percent of cardboard, paper, plastic, and composites to be met by July 1, 1995. To achieve these ambitious objectives, Germany's ordinance stipulates that industry is to be responsible for the collection and recycling of all its packaging. If businesses' efforts fail to meet the statutory targets, the German government will institute costly deposits on essentially all packaging.

Responding to these tough requirements, firms have collaborated to form a private, nonprofit company, called Duales System Deutschland (DSD) (meaning a dual system), to provide collection and recycling services to consumers. Through its network, DSD assures that used packaging will be collected and sent to a proper recycling facility. To facilitate the collection phase, DSD distributes yellow bins and bags for all packaging waste other than glass containers, which continue to be collected via drop-off plans already in place.

Of course, such an undertaking does not come cheap. DSD's start-up costs have been estimated to be in the neighborhood of $10 billion, while its operating expenses are expected to be $1 billion per year. To finance these fixed and variable costs, DSD sells to participating companies the right to use a "green dot" on their packages, a symbol that guarantees that the packaging is eligible for the services provided by DSD. The price of a green dot varies with the amount of packaging on each product and its recyclability. At the start of the program, the average price was about one cent per package.

Thus far, reported statistics indicate progress has been made. For example, by April 1992, both domestic- and foreign-based firms had purchased 5,000 licenses for DSD's "green dots" to assure the use of its services for some 40 billion packaging units. Consumers have responded just as vigorously—even more so than was forecasted by analysts. Original predictions were that the Green Dot program would result in the collection of about 100,000 tons of plastics per year, but these estimates were far off the mark. In 1993, German households accumulated nearly four times these projections.

While response to Germany's new ordinance has been favorable, the Green Dot program that supports it is not without problems. DSD lost more than $300 million during its first full year of operation. A further problem involves the potential for fraud in the program. Apparently, some companies are putting the "green dot" symbol on their products without paying for it. In fact, one Duales spokesperson claims that approximately one-third of the green dots that appear on products are fraudulent. Finally, the German government has not yet adjusted its capacity to handle the sharp rise in accumulated recyclables triggered by the new ordinance, and there is concern about its ability to accommodate so rapid a change.

SOURCES: Cynthia Pollock Shea. "Getting Serious in Germany." *EPA Journal* 18(3), July/August 1992, pp. 50–52; Frances Cairncross. "How Europe's Companies Reposition to Recycle." *Harvard Business Review*, March–April, 1992, pp. 34–45; Associated Press. "German Recycling Is Too Successful." *Brockton Enterprise*, July 27, 1993.

states to conserve resources and assist them in finding ways to maximize the use of recoverable resources. The EPA is responsible for establishing minimum criteria for sanitary landfills and other land disposal sites. Approximately 227,000 such facilities are regulated under RCRA.[11] Facilities

[11] U.S. EPA, Office of Solid Waste (November 1986).

not meeting the criteria are considered to be open dumps and must be closed or upgraded in accordance with specific rules.

In September 1991, new regulations were issued to establish tougher standards for land disposal sites starting in 1993. These new rules are to be effective throughout the useful life of a facility plus 30 years after its closure. In addition to the risk reduction provided by these tougher rules, the revisions are expected to encourage source reduction and recycling on a national scale.[12] New regulations were also issued for waste-to-energy incineration facilities. These establish controls on various air emissions and assure proper combustion conditions. These rulings are of special importance, since there are about 150 municipal waste-to-energy facilities currently in operation in the United States.[13] Prior to this time, the EPA had established *guidelines*, but no regulatory controls per se, for MSW incineration facilities.

### The Current Policy Direction

**integrated waste management system**
An EPA initiative to guide state MSW plans that promotes the combined use of source reduction, recycling, combustion, and land disposal ranked in order of preference.

Because states are responsible for their own nonhazardous waste plans, they have the flexibility to develop cost-effective programs. As of 1995, many states have developed bona fide plans, following the EPA's **integrated waste management system.** This system promotes using a combination of techniques and programs aimed at source reduction, recycling, combustion, and land disposal—in that order. To understand how states are responding to this initiative, we need to develop a general market model of MSW services. This provides the analytical tool with which to assess the cost-effectiveness and efficiency of various state programs.

## Modeling the Market for MSW Management Services

In the market for MSW services, the relevant commodity is actually a combination of several distinct activities—the collection, transportation, and disposal of municipal solid waste. Based on this output definition, we model the market for MSW services in Figure 18.3, using some hypothetical demand ($D$) or marginal private benefit ($MPB$) curve and some supply ($S$) or marginal private cost ($MPC$) curve. Together, these curves determine the competitive equilibrium price or fee for MSW services, $P_c$ and the equilibrium quantity, $Q_c$.

---

[12] U.S. EPA, Office of Solid Waste and Emergency Response (November 1989), pp. 18–19 and pp. 108–09; Council on Environmental Quality (March 1992), pp. 112–13.

[13] Council on Environmental Quality (January 1993), p. 134.

| FIGURE 18.3 | THE MARKET FOR MUNICIPAL SOLID WASTE SERVICES |

This model illustrates the market for MSW management services. The hypothetical demand or *MPB* curve and the supply or *MPC* curve determine the competitive equilibrium price of MSW services, $P_c$, and the equilibrium quantity, $Q_c$. The impact of Congress' decision to tighten federal controls on landfill disposal causes the *MPC* to shift upward to *MPC'* elevating equilibrium price to $P_c'$ and causing a decline in quantity to $Q_c'$. The decrease in quantity of MSW services may mean that generators are using a source reduction strategy. It might also be the case that the generation rate is the same but generators are recycling more of their wastes. Finally, they might be maintaining the same generation rate *and* the same recycling rate but be engaging in illegal disposal to get rid of some of their wastes.

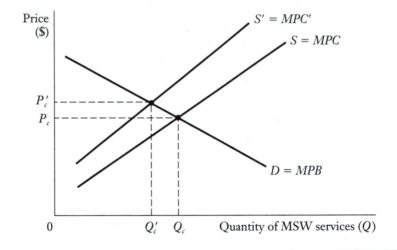

### The Supply of MSW Services

The supply side of the MSW services market represents the production decisions of private firms under contract with cities and towns or those of municipalities that provide these services directly to the community. In this market, the costs of production reflect the expenses of operating a fleet of disposal trucks, managing an approved landfill or incinerator, and labor. Under the usual assumptions about production and diminishing returns, the *MPC* exhibits a positive slope. Among the nonprice factors affecting supply in this market are land availability and government regulation.

Consider, for example, the impact of Congress' decision to tighten federal controls on landfill disposal. These tougher standards led to the closing of several hundred landfills that were unable to meet the law's new requirements. This outcome along with the NIMBY syndrome limited the

**tipping fees** Prices
charged for disposing
of wastes in a facility
such as a landfill.

availability of landfill space in some locations. As a result, landfill prices, or
**tipping fees** as they are called, have risen. As Figure 18.3 shows, this outcome is modeled as an upward shift of *MPC*, which causes an increase in
price to $P_c'$ and a decline in equilibrium quantity to $Q_c'$.

### The Demand for MSW Services

The demand side of this market represents the purchasing decisions of
MSW generators. In this context, the quantity response to changes in price
takes on an important meaning about how wastes are managed. To understand this, reconsider the decline in quantity from $Q_c$ to $Q_c'$ due to the
regulation-induced price increase described in Figure 18.3. How might
generators change their behavior to achieve this reduction in quantity?
One possibility is that they use a source reduction strategy and produce less
trash. Another is that they generate the same amount of trash but demand
less services because they recycle. Finally, they might maintain the same
generation rate *and* the same recycling rate, but engage in illegal disposal
to avoid the higher price of MSW services.[14] Which of these options is
chosen depends on their availability to the generator and the prices of these
options relative to the price of MSW services. Recognizing the natural
market response of demanders to higher-priced MSW services, a local community can encourage recycling by offering a cost-effective program to its
residents.[15] In the absence of such a program, some generators may be motivated to dispose of their wastes illegally.

The demand, or *MPB*, for municipal waste services also responds to
certain nonprice changes. For example, more affluent individuals tend to
generate larger amounts of trash, since they purchase more products and
replace them more frequently. Thus, demand for MSW services likely
would shift to the right as the income of a community rises, holding all else
constant. Another nonprice determinant of demand is tastes and preferences. As generators become more environmentally responsible, we would
expect their demand for these services to decline as they adjust their purchases toward products with less packaging. In sum, waste generators in
each community likely face a uniquely shaped demand curve that responds
somewhat predictably to both price and nonprice changes.

If actual MSW markets behaved in accordance with this model *and* if
there were no externalities, we could conclude that MSW markets achieve
an efficient solution where $MPC = MPB$. However, it turns out that these

---

[14] Jenkins (1993), pp. 4–6.

[15] Recent data indicate that the design and implementation of recycling programs produce varying effects
on disposal reduction and on local budgets. According to a study conducted by Franklin Associates, curbside recycling generates high costs that do not appear to be justified by the associated benefits. Nationally,
this type of recycling plan is estimated to lower disposal by only 2.5 percent compared to more conventional drop-off programs that achieve a 4.5-percent decrease. See Bailey (October 4, 1994).

conditions typically are violated in actual MSW markets. The resulting resource misallocation is an important issue that merits further investigation.

### Resource Misallocation in the Market for MSW Services

There are two distinct problems that arise in most MSW services markets, and both are associated with the supply side of the market.

- Pricing of MSW services does not properly reflect the rising $MPC$ associated with increases in production levels.

- Production of MSW services gives rise to negative externalities.

**Flat Fee Pricing of MSW Services.** In most communities, suppliers charge a **fixed fee** per household or commercial establishment for MSW services. Since the fee is the same regardless of the quantity of waste generated at each location, this type of pricing scheme is known as a **flat fee pricing system.** Notice that the waste generator is charged nothing for any additional containers of trash beyond the first one, which means that the price does not reflect rising $MPC$. Demanders effectively pay a *marginal* price of zero, and hence have no incentive to reduce wastes. More formally, the market price under this scenario is being determined *as if* the $MPC$ is zero. This phenomenon is illustrated in Figure 18.4, where the $MPC$ is shown coincident with the horizontal axis. Notice that under such a scenario, the market equilibrates where $MPC = MPB = 0$ at $Q_0$. Compared to the competitive equilibrium, too many resources are being allocated to MSW services. In communities where MSW services are publicly provided, the price mechanism is further dampened because the fee is not explicitly communicated but rather collected through property taxes. But whether these services are publicly or privately provided, the use of a fixed fee has serious efficiency implications.[16]

**fixed fee or flat fee pricing system**
Pricing MSW services independent of the quantity of waste generated.

**Negative Externalities.** Even if waste generators are charged a fee equal to the $MPC$, there still may be a resource misallocation if production of MSW services gives rise to negative externalities. Such an outcome is not uncommon in waste management markets. For example, Application 18.4 (p. 576) reports on the negative externalities associated with tire disposal and a new technology that may help reduce these effects. In the MSW services market, external costs may be due to groundwater contamination, air pollution from incineration, or impairment of aesthetics. As we have illustrated in other contexts, such a production externality is captured by a marginal external cost ($MEC$) curve, which must be added to the $MPC$ to identify the marginal social cost ($MSC$) of producing the good. Assuming no externalities on the demand side, the marginal social benefit ($MSB$) of

---

[16]Wirth and Heinz (1991), pp. 48–49.

| FIGURE 18.4 | MODELING A FIXED FEE SYSTEM FOR MSW SERVICES |

In most communities, a **fixed fee** per household or per commercial establishment is charged for MSW services. Since the fee is the same regardless of the quantity of waste generated at each location, this type of pricing scheme is also known as a **flat fee pricing system.** The waste generator is charged nothing for any additional containers of trash beyond the first one, which means that the price does not reflect rising *MPC*. Instead, demanders are effectively paying a *marginal* price of zero, and hence have no incentive to reduce wastes. More formally, the market price under this scenario is being determined *as if* the *MPC* is zero or coincident with the horizontal axis. Under such a scenario the market equilibrates where $MPC = MPB = 0$, at $Q_0$. Compared to the competitive equilibrium, too many resources are being allocated to MSW services.

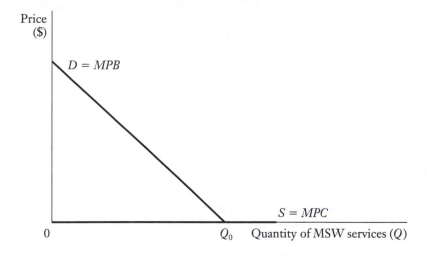

consumption is the same as the *MPB* function. The efficient solution is determined where the *MSC* equals the *MSB* as illustrated in Figure 18.5 (p. 577). (To avoid confounding the effect of the externality with that of charging a fixed fee, we show the *MPC* as a positively sloped curve.) Notice that the efficient output level is $Q_e$, which is *lower* than the private market outcome, $Q_c$.

To summarize, we observe that private MSW markets typically do not yield an efficient outcome. The use of fixed fees distorts the signaling mechanism of price, effectively removing the incentive to economize on trash generation. The private market's disregard for external costs leads to a further distortion. Singularly or in combination, these factors contribute to an overallocation of resources to waste services and an overproduction of municipal trash. Is there any solution to these problems? Actually, a number of pricing schemes can be used to correct the inefficiency.

**APPLICATION 18.4**

# Garbage or Resource? The Case of Scrap Tires

One person's trash is another person's treasure—an appropriate commentary on the market for recyclables. Some solid waste can be returned to productive use, provided there is an active market for the recycled material. Encouraging waste generators to recycle is important, but it is only part of the story. Recycling sets up a reliable supply of inputs that presumably can be used in the production of some new commodity. However, in order for this market to be viable, there must be a healthy demand side of buyers willing and able to purchase these recycled materials at the going market price. If not, society can expect a trade-off of one problem for another—a waste heap for a glut of unwanted recycled materials.

An interesting case is the market for scrap tires. Current estimates place the total number of discarded tires at approximately 3 billion—a nontrivial disposal problem that is increasing at the rate of 242 million per year in the United States alone. Furthermore, fewer than 7 percent of scrap tires are recycled into alternative products like asphalt pavement, car mats, mud guards, and playground swings. Another 5 percent are exported, only 11 percent are incinerated for fuel value by pulp and paper mills, power plants, and cement factories, and the remaining 78 percent end up in stockpiles, landfills, and illegal disposal sites.

Given the enormous supply of used tires, there is a powerful incentive to find some productive use for this burdensome contribution to the solid waste stream. Most experts agree that the use of scrapped tires as an energy source makes good sense from an energy efficiency standpoint. Their heat value exceeds that of coal, at about 12,000 to 16,000 Btus per pound. However, environmental and economic factors have been major stumbling blocks to expanding the use of scrap tires for energy recovery. Because of both air quality and aesthetic impairment, there is resistance to siting an energy facility that is dependent on scrap tires for fuel. Until recently, most tire-to-energy technologies have been relatively dirty, resulting in atmospheric emissions that are unacceptable. But a new patented technology held by a New Mexico firm—Titan Technologies—appears to hold promise.

Titan's newly developed process bakes 6-inch squares of tire chips instead of burning whole tires or tire shreds. According to company officials, the process uses a closed system of catalytic drums and requires relatively low temperatures—about 450 degrees Fahrenheit. The result is a conversion process that yields by-products much less damaging to the environment. Furthermore, Titan operates on a large scale—much larger than conventional waste-to-energy facilities. Exploiting scale economies allows Titan to achieve lower unit costs and market its energy at a competitive price. This "buy-back rate" is critical to the viability of this particular waste-to-energy market. Currently, unit costs of production are so high that buy-back rates are competitive only in certain regional markets like the Northeast and California, where competing energy supplies are expensive. Finding ways to lower unit costs means that tire-to-energy production may be able to service a national market. If this economic feasibility is established, demand for scrap tires should be stimulated, and the environmental hazard markedly reduced.

SOURCES: Robert Metz. "N.M. Firm Is Ready to Roll Into the Tire Recycling Industry." *Boston Globe*, December 28, 1993, p. 34; U.S. Environmental Protection Agency, Office of Solid Waste and Emergency Response. *Summary of Markets for Scrap Tires*, Washington, DC, October 1991; U.S. Environmental Protection Agency, Office of Policy, Planning, and Evaluation. *Economic Incentives: Options for Environmental Protection*, Washington, DC, March 1991, pp. 2-13–2-15.

| FIGURE 18.5 | **ALLOCATIVE INEFFICIENCY IN PRIVATE** |
| --- | --- |
| | **MARKETS FOR MSW SERVICES:** |
| | **THE PRESENCE OF A NEGATIVE EXTERNALITY** |

A resource misallocation may arise if production of MSW services gives rise to a negative externality. The external costs might be due to groundwater contamination, air pollution from incineration, or impairment of aesthetics. Such a production externality is captured by a marginal external cost ($MEC$) curve, which must be added to the $MPC$ to identify the marginal social cost ($MSC$) of producing the good. Assuming no externalities on the demand side, the marginal social benefit ($MSB$) function is the same as the $MPB$. The efficient solution is determined where the $MSC$ equals the $MSB$. Notice that the efficient output level occurs at $Q_e$, which is *lower* than the private market outcome, $Q_c$.

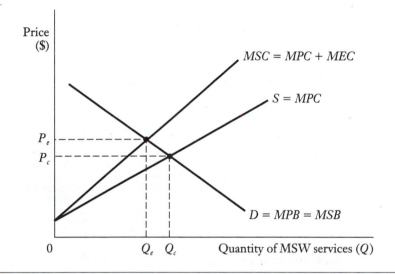

## A Market Approach to MSW Policy[17]

In recent years, some communities have begun to institute market-based policies aimed at reducing the problems associated with MSW. Of interest are three approaches that directly exploit the signaling mechanism of price. These are **back-** or **waste-end charges, front-end** or **retail disposal charges,** and **deposit/refund systems.**

[17] Much of the following is drawn from Wirth and Heinz (1991), pp. 48–65, Jenkins (1993), and U.S. EPA, Office of Solid Waste and Emergency Response (February 1991).

| FIGURE 18.6 | MODELING A WASTE-END CHARGE TO RESTORE EFFICIENCY IN THE MARKET FOR MSW SERVICES |
|---|---|

This model illustrates how a **waste-end charge** can be implemented to achieve efficiency in the market for MSW services. Because such a charge varies with the quantity of waste, it avoids the market distortion caused by a flat fee pricing scheme. To achieve efficiency, the waste-end charge must be set to cover the *MSC* at the efficient equilibrium, where *MSB* is exactly equal to *MSC*. In the model shown below, the appropriate per unit fee would be set equal to $P_e$.

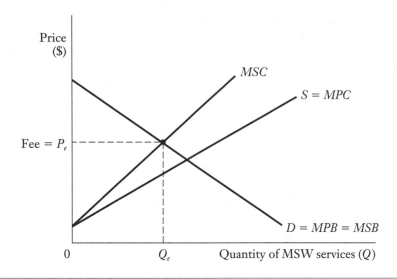

## Back-End or Waste-End Charges

**back-end** or **waste-end charge** Fee implemented at the time of disposal based on the quantity of waste generated.

**unit pricing scheme** Common designation for the use of a waste-end charge.

**flat rate pricing** Unit pricing scheme that charges the same price for each additional unit of waste.

As discussed in the previous chapter, a **waste-end charge** is so named because it is implemented at the time of disposal based on the quantity of waste generated. Because such a charge varies with the quantity of waste, it avoids the market distortion caused by a flat fee pricing scheme. To achieve efficiency, the waste-end charge must be set to cover the *MSC* at the efficient equilibrium. This solution is illustrated in Figure 18.6, with the appropriate per unit fee shown as $P_e$. Notice that this fee is a *price per unit of waste* to be paid by all generators, which is very different from charging a *price per household* as is done under a flat fee system.

In practice, programs that use waste-end charges are called **unit pricing schemes** to indicate that prices for MSW services are charged on a per-unit-of-waste basis. The units may be measured either by weight or by volume generated, though the latter is more commonly used at the present time. The same price can be charged for each unit, called **flat rate pricing,**

**variable rate pricing**
Unit pricing scheme that charges a different price for each additional unit of waste.

or the price can vary, called **variable rate pricing**.[18] Perhaps the best known example of a community having implemented unit pricing is the city of Seattle. In fact, Seattle's program has come to be the prototype upon which other communities have modeled their own MSW unit pricing plans. The program is implemented by having each MSW generator register with the city for the number and volume of trash containers it expects to use in a week. Based on the registration, a fee is calculated using a schedule of volume-based prices.[19]

By moving from a fixed fee schedule to a unit pricing program, two important market incentives are restored. First, unit pricing communicates to generators that increased waste services are associated with a nonzero marginal cost of production, ideally the marginal social cost.[20] Effectively, this provides an incentive to economize on waste generation by using a source reduction strategy. Second, by elevating the price of collection and disposal, the *relative* price of alternative approaches declines. Given that recycling and disposal are substitute activities, the change in relative prices may encourage more recycling, which means less disposal. There are also favorable equity implications, since unit pricing does not force small MSW generators to subsidize larger ones, as is the case with a flat fee system.[21] Finally, while there is the theoretical possibility that unit pricing may encourage illegal disposal, there is little evidence that this activity is increasing dramatically in communities where such programs are in use.[22]

Beyond these theoretical arguments, there is a fair amount of anecdotal and empirical evidence that unit pricing is a viable policy instrument. For example, Seattle officials have observed that trash disposal in landfills has declined since unit pricing was introduced. In the early 1980s, the typical single-family residence was disposing about three and one-half 30-gallon receptacles each week. In 1988, 60 percent of the city's households had subscribed to one 32-gallon container per week, and this proportion rose to 87 percent a year later.[23] An analysis of the experience of Tacoma, Washington, which has instituted a program similar to Seattle's, shows that a 10-percent increase in fees resulted in a 2-percent decline in waste disposal.[24] More formal evidence is presented by Robin Jenkins (1993) who

---

[18] To learn about the unit pricing scheme used in a particular community, visit **www.epa.gov/epaoswer/non-hw/payt/comm.htm**.

[19] Seattle uses a schedule of bimonthly fees based on trash can capacity. For 1988, these were reported as follows: $10.70 for a 19-gallon can; $13.75 for a 32-gallon can; $22.75 for a 60-gallon can; and $31.75 for a 90-gallon can. See Seattle Solid Waste Utility (1988), as cited in Wirth and Heinz (1991), pp. 50–51.

[20] According to Jenkins (1993), p. 90, Seattle's fees do not cover the marginal external cost of MSW services.

[21] Furthermore, concerns about the regressiveness of unit pricing is being handled by Seattle and other communities by allowing special rates for low-income groups or senior citizens. See, for example, Wirth and Heinz (1991), p. 51 and U.S. EPA, Office of Solid Waste and Emergency Response (February 1991).

[22] See U.S. EPA (September 1990), cited in Wirth and Heinz (1991), p. 52, and Goldberg (February 1990), pp. 98–104, cited in U.S. EPA, Office of Policy, Planning, and Evaluation (March 1991), p. 2-9.

[23] Seattle Solid Waste Utility (1991), as cited in Wirth and Heinz (1991), p. 51.

[24] See Goddard (1990), as cited in Wirth and Heinz (1991), p. 51.

conducted a rather extensive statistical study on unit pricing. The results show that the effect of switching from a fixed fee to a volume-based fee of 50 cents per container is a decrease in waste per person per day of 0.2 pounds. This translates to an estimated decline of 3,650 tons per year for a community of 100,000 people or 18,250 tons annually for a community of 500,000 people.

As the evidence accumulates, more and more communities are following Seattle's lead and moving to unit pricing programs. Current estimates indicate that over 3,400 communities in 37 states are using this form of MSW pricing.[25] In fact, some local authorities have enhanced the prototype to improve its efficiency. For example, one of the problems with Seattle's "per-can" pricing plan is that the preregistered number of receptacles on which the fee is based is not always an accurate forecast of actual trash generation. Consequently, generators can be charged a full rate even if some receptacles are half full or not used at all. Recognizing this potential inefficiency, some communities have instituted more flexible programs whereby generators purchase stickers for receptacles of various sizes. Then, they *choose* how many receptacles they need each period and simply apply the prepaid stickers to the receptacles used.[26] Application 18.5 discusses this **"bag-and-tag" approach,** which has met with some success in Perkasie, Pennsylvania.

**"bag-and-tag" approach** Unit pricing scheme implemented by selling tags to be applied to waste receptacles of various sizes.

### Front-End or Retail Disposal Charges

**front-end** or **retail disposal charge** Fee levied on a product at the point of sale designed to encourage source reduction.

An alternative pricing scheme aimed at the MSW problem is the use of a **retail disposal charge.** In contrast to a waste-end charge imposed on *wastes* at the point of *disposal*, a retail disposal charge is levied on *products* at the point of *sale*. Since such a charge is instituted at the pregeneration stage, its objective is to encourage pollution prevention through source reduction.[27] This includes motivating manufacturers to seek out product designs and packaging that are more environmentally responsible.

From a practical perspective, local conditions tend to dictate when a retail disposal charge might be more appropriate than a waste-end charge. For example, a waste-end pricing scheme should be coordinated with a recycling program to deter illegal disposal. Hence, if a community has not instituted such a plan, a better option might be to use a front-end charge. A similar argument applies to communities where there is a predominance of

---

[25] See Skumatz (March 21, 1996), as cited in Anderson, Lohof, and Carlin (August 1997), p. 4-10.

[26] Wirth and Heinz (1991), p. 51.

[27] While source reduction is also possible from using unit pricing, it is not assured. All that can be said with certainty is that unit pricing schemes encourage a decline of waste *disposal*. But this may be achieved through an increase in recycling with no change in the waste generation rate. Conversely, front-end or retail disposal charges directly encourage a decline in waste *generation* by reducing the quantity demanded of a product *before* it enters the waste stream.

## "Bag-and-Tag" Systems: An Alternative to Seattle's Per-Can Pricing Scheme

Although the city of Seattle has received national acclaim for its innovative unit pricing waste program, the market-based plan has not been without problems. One in particular is that per-can pricing schemes are based on residents' *forecasts* of their waste generation rate, which may or may not be accurate. As a result, some generators end up paying for disposal services on a full can of trash even if it is half empty or not used at all. This potential inefficiency has prompted some communities to design modified versions of the Seattle prototype, called "bag-and-tag" systems.

Under these "bag-and-tag" plans, the advantages of unit pricing are maintained, but residents have the flexibility to assure that they pay only for the wastes they generate. One way these systems are implemented is by providing collection and disposal services only to trash placed in specially designated containers sold by the municipality. Program participants purchase in advance a supply of these trash bags, typically available in various sizes and priced accordingly. In each collection period, residents use only as many of the prepaid trash bags as they need. A variation of the system operates from the same premise except that stickers or tags are sold by the municipality, and these are then affixed to residents' own trash containers. In either case, the inefficiency of the per-can pricing plan is resolved while maintaining the advantages of unit pricing.

In the late 1980s, High Bridge, New Jersey, instituted a tag pricing system, charging residents an annual fee for 52 stickers. An annual charge per household was set, which covered the program's administrative costs plus the disposal cost of one container per week for each household. Restrictions on maximum weight and volume are imposed on a per-sticker basis. To provide greater flexibility to residents, additional stickers can be purchased from the town or traded between low-use and high-use residents.

At about the same time as High Bridge got its plan under way, the town of Perkasie, Pennsylvania began selling town-issued trash bags to implement its unit pricing program. To distinguish between low- and high-waste generators, Perkasie uses a differential charge based on bag size. A 20-pound trash bag commands a price of $0.80, while the larger 40-pound container is sold for $1.50. All of Perkasie's trash bags have a "tree logo" to distinguish them from receptacles used by nonparticipants. Like the High Bridge plan, residents pay for services only on the quantity of waste generated in a given period and not on a predetermined and likely inaccurate forecast.

Preliminary estimates of waste reduction under each program are impressive. For example, in its first 10 months of operation, High Bridge officials reported a 24-percent decrease in waste tonnage. An even greater decline of 40 percent was observed after Perkasie's first full year of operation.

SOURCES: Timothy E. Wirth and John Heinz. *Project 88—Round II Incentives for Action: Designing Market-Based Environmental Strategies.* Washington, DC, May 1991, pp. 49–53; U.S. Environmental Protection Agency, Office of Policy, Planning, and Evaluation. *Economic Incentives: Options for Environmental Protection*, Washington, DC, March 1991, pp. 2.7–2.12; Timothy Tregarthen. "Garbage by the Bag: Perkasie Acts on Solid Waste." *The Margin*, September/October 1989, p. 17.

multiunit residences, making waste-end fees difficult to implement. Finally, a front-end charge can be used to complement a waste-end charge system to discourage the use of products that yield large amounts of waste or wastes that pose a particular threat to health or the environment. Examples include products like motor oil, batteries, and automobile tires.

---

| FIGURE 18.7 | MODELING A RETAIL DISPOSAL CHARGE TO CORRECT A CONSUMPTION EXTERNALITY: THE MARKET FOR HOUSEHOLD BATTERIES |

The disposal of batteries poses an environmental risk to society because they are made with heavy metals like mercury or cadmium. Battery consumers do not consider the external effects, so the *MPB* effectively overstates the true marginal benefits of consumption. This means that the *MSB* is actually *below* the *MPB*. In the absence of government intervention, equilibrium output is $Q_c$, determined where *MPB* intersects *MPC*. The efficient output level is lower, determined by the intersection of *MSC* and *MSB* or $Q_e$. (For simplicity, we assume that no production externalities exist, so *MSC* = *MPC*.) To correct the inefficiency, government can impose a retail disposal charge on batteries at the point of sale equal to the difference between *MSB* and *MPB* at $Q_e$. We can model the imposition of the charge as a shift up of *MSC* by distance *xy*, resulting in an effective price to the consumer of $P_R$.

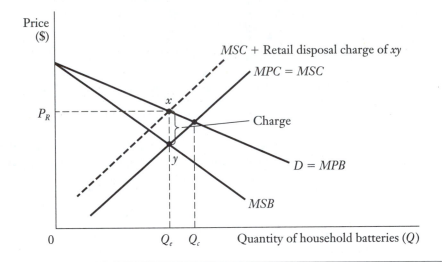

To better understand the environmental and economic consequences of retail disposal charges, consider the market for household batteries. Batteries are made with heavy metals like mercury or cadmium, so their disposal poses an environmental risk to society. Battery consumers do not consider the external effects, so the *MPB* effectively overstates the true marginal benefits of consumption. This means that the *MSB* is actually *below* the *MPB*, as shown in Figure 18.7.[28] In the absence of government

---

[28] The externality is not modeled as an *MEC* added to the *MPC* because in this case it is *not* associated with the production side of the market. Rather, the externality arises from consumption or the demand side. Hence, the externality must be *deducted* from the *MPB* curve to show that the true benefits to society, the *MSB*, are reduced by the amount of the environmental damage. For a more rigorous and detailed analysis of this type of externality, the interested reader is referred to Tresch (1981).

intervention, equilibrium output is determined where *MPB* equals *MPC* or $Q_c$. However, the efficient output level is lower, determined by the intersection of *MSC* and *MSB* or $Q_e$. (For simplicity, we assume that no production externalities exist, so *MSC* = *MPC*.) To correct the inefficiency, government can impose a retail disposal charge on batteries at the point of sale equal to the difference between *MSB* and *MPB* at $Q_e$. In Figure 18.7, we model the imposition of the charge as a shift up of the *MSC* by distance xy, resulting in an effective price to the consumer of $P_R$.[29]

Retail disposal charges are being used both internationally and domestically. For example, Finland and Norway have imposed these charges on products packaged in nonreturnable containers. The specific aim of these fees is incentive-based—to encourage consumers to move away from such commodities and substitute those that have returnable and reusable containers. Sweden also uses retail disposal charges for a number of products, including batteries made of cadmium, lead, or mercury. While part of the objective is to diminish the damage caused by disposal of these products, the charge is also being used to generate revenue.[30] Domestically, retail disposal charges are imposed on a multitude of products by many state governments. Table 18.4 (p. 584) lists some common applications. Most of the target products and materials are those expected to generate high external costs. For example, Maine imposes a $5-charge on major appliances, and Louisiana charges $2 for each tire sold.

### Deposit/Refund Systems

**deposit/refund system** Two-part pricing scheme that imposes an up-front charge for potential damages caused by improper waste disposal that is reimbursed at the end of the product cycle if proper action is taken to avoid those damages.

An alternative market instrument that can mitigate MSW pollution is a **deposit/refund system,** which is actually a two-part pricing scheme. It imposes an up-front charge for potential damages caused by improper disposal, and it allows for a refund of that charge at the end of the product cycle if the consumer takes proper action to avoid those damages. Typically, the consumer must return the product or its container for recycling or safe disposal. The formal model of this system was presented in detail in Chapter 5, so it is not repeated here. More relevant to this discussion is the conceptual relationship between this instrument and the other two pricing schemes. Notice that the deposit is imposed at the time of purchase exactly like a retail disposal charge. The refund attempts to reduce disposal and encourage recycling much like a waste-end charge.[31]

---

[29] It matters not whether the retail disposal charge is levied on the seller or the buyer of the product, since economic incidence (i.e., the party who ultimately bears the burden of the fee) is not determined by statutory incidence (i.e., the party who is initially charged the fee). For more detail, the reader can consult any good principles of microeconomics text.

[30] See Organisation for Economic Co-operation and Development (1994), pp. 70–82 and Organisation for Economic Co-operation and Development (1989a), pp. 55–66. It is sometimes argued that the revenue objective tied to retail disposal charges is more important than the incentive goal, since the resulting difference in price is not sufficient to affect purchasing decisions. This is sometimes cited as a drawback of these types of pricing instruments.

[31] See research by Fullerton and Kinnaman (1995) relating to this issue.

| TABLE 18.4 | EXAMPLES OF STATE RETAIL DISPOSAL TAXES EFFECTIVE 1990–1991 | |
|---|---|---|
| **State** | **Waste** | **Amount of Tax** |
| California | Tires | $0.25 |
| Florida | Multiple materials | $0.01 per package |
| Louisiana | Tires | $2.00 |
| Maine | Tires | $1.00 |
| | Major appliances | $5.00 |
| Nebraska | Multiple materials | 0.015 percent of sales |
| New Jersey | Multiple materials | 0.0225 percent of sales |
| North Carolina | Tires | 1 percent of price |
| Oklahoma | Tires | $1.00 |
| Oregon | Tires | $0.50 |
| Rhode Island | Beverages | Wholesale tax of $0.04 per case |
| | Multiple materials | Sales tax exemption on biodegradable returnable items |
| Tennessee | Beverages | 6 percent of soda receipts and $0.50 per barrel of beer |
| Utah | Tires | $1.00–$2.00 |
| Virginia | Tires | $0.50 |
| | Beverages | 0.06 percent of sales |
| Washington | Tires | $1.00 |
| | Multiple materials | 0.015 percent of sales |
| Wisconsin | Tires | $2.00 |

SOURCE: Drawn from Tellus Institute, Boston, MA, 1991, as cited in Frank Ackerman, "Taxing the Trash Away." *Environment*, June 1992, pp. 2–5 and 43. Reprinted with permission of Frank Ackerman.

This innovative economic instrument has gained acceptance both domestically and internationally. In the United States, deposit/refund systems are aimed primarily at beverage containers and lead-acid batteries, as Table 18.5 indicates. Similar applications are quite common in other countries as well. For example, Australia, Canada, Denmark, Finland, Germany, Norway, Sweden, and Portugal are among the nations that use deposit/refund systems for beverage containers. Some nations have gone a step further or at least are investigating the prospect. Greece, Norway, and Sweden have introduced a deposit/refund mechanism on car hulks. New car buyers pay a deposit at the time of purchase and in some cases receive a

| TABLE 18.5 | EXAMPLES OF STATE DEPOSIT/REFUND PROGRAMS EFFECTIVE 1990–1991 |
|---|---|

| State | Product | Amount of Deposit |
|---|---|---|
| California | Beverage | $0.02 |
| Connecticut | Beverage | $0.05 |
| | Batteries | $5.00 |
| Delaware | Beverage | $0.05 |
| Iowa | Beverage | $0.05 |
| Massachusetts | Beverage | $0.05 |
| Maine | Batteries | $1.00 |
| | Beverage | $0.03–$0.05 |
| Michigan | Beverage | $0.05 |
| New York | Beverage | $0.05 |
| Oregon | Beverage | $0.02–$0.20 |
| Vermont | Beverage | $0.05 |
| Washington | Batteries | $5.00 |

SOURCE: Drawn from Tellus Institute, Boston, MA, 1991, as cited in Frank Ackerman, "Taxing the Trash Away." *Environment*, June 1992, pp. 2–5 and 43. Reprinted with permission of Frank Ackerman.

larger refund if the automobile is returned to a designated recovery site when it is no longer wanted.[32] Similarly, the United States is contemplating a broader use of deposit/refunds for such commodities as lubricating oil, industrial solvents, and pesticide or fertilizer containers.

# Conclusions

Municipal solid wastes—the simple by-products of production and consumption—have become a local public issue in communities everywhere. Today, most agree that former claims of a landfill crisis were exaggerated. Even the famous "garbage barge" story of 1987 has been explained as the result of a botched business deal. Nonetheless, the world was listening and in the absence of 20/20 hindsight responded to what it heard. Private citizens began to change their behavior—avoiding products with excess

---

[32] Organisation for Economic Co-operation and Development (1994), pp. 82–86, and Organisation for Economic Co-operation and Development (1989a), pp. 82–88.

packaging and participating in local recycling programs, and they turned to government for broader solutions.

In retrospect, many argue that people responded to false signals—a crisis that did not exist and unfounded predictions of doom and gloom. This assertion is probably true, at least to a point. However, it is wrong to conclude that there were no solid waste issues to resolve and no environmental risks to manage. Open dumps *had* become a health hazard, and most of society had been ignorant of the potential problems of excess waste generation and poor waste management practices. Having said this, a more relevant question is whether the response itself—both by private citizens and by government, however motivated, was and is appropriate.

In the United States, Congress passed laws to restrict the use of land for waste disposal and to replace the nation's open dumps with modern, sanitary landfills. It then delegated the responsibility for devising local waste management programs to the states, encouraging plans that promoted waste reduction and recycling. The land restrictions and the landfill rulings added costs to local waste management, and some states responded with market instruments that reflected these costs.

What was the result of these policy moves? At this stage, the most accurate assessment is that these efforts have yielded mixed results. Some waste generators are pursuing source reduction activities, while others are illegally disposing of their wastes. Some states and local governments have developed successful, cost-effective recycling centers, while others are struggling with expensive curbside programs that have placed a heavy tax burden on their residents. Add to this the series of debates about the viability of markets for recycled materials. Netting it out, these observations imply that municipal waste policies are still evolving, and public officials at all levels of government need to consider some needed reforms. Much can be learned from observing market responses to regulatory decisions and revisions. Rising prices for waste disposal and gluts of recycled materials are important signals to policy makers about how and where to make strategic changes. If these signals are not ignored, future policy should approach more efficient and cost-effective solutions to the problem of municipal solid waste.

## Summary

- In 1990, containers and packaging accounted for the highest proportion by weight of all discarded products in the U.S. municipal solid waste (MSW) stream. The fastest growing segment of MSW in the United States is plastics.

- Internationally, the major industrialized nations are among the highest MSW generators. Some of the international differences are attributable to the amount of packaging used by producers, cultural preferences, environmental awareness, economic conditions, or government regulations.

- One set of provisions in the Resource Conservation and Recovery Act (RCRA) is concerned with the management of nonhazardous wastes, including the MSW stream. For the most part, this section of the law assigns the responsibility of nonhazardous waste management to states with supervision and support provided by the federal government.

- Under RCRA, states are required to develop their own waste management plans, but these must meet certain requirements to receive federal approval. They also must establish whatever regulatory powers they need to comply with RCRA, such as enacting legislation to meet federal requirements.

- The federal government must provide financial and technical assistance to states in designing and implementing their waste management plans. The EPA must establish minimum criteria for sanitary landfills and other land disposal sites.

- The EPA actively encourages state authorities to use an integrated waste management system, which promotes source reduction, recycling, combustion, and land disposal, in that order.

- Resources are misallocated in private MSW services markets that use a flat fee pricing system, which charges a fixed fee per household. The inefficiency occurs because the constant price does not properly reflect rising *MPC* and because production of MSW services gives rise to a negative externality.

- A waste-end charge is implemented at the time of disposal based on the quantity of waste generated. In practice, programs using waste-end charges are referred to as unit pricing schemes to indicate that prices for MSW services are charged on a per-unit-of-waste basis.

- Retail disposal charges are levied on the product at the point of sale. Since this charge is imposed at the pregeneration stage, its objective is to encourage pollution prevention through source reduction.

- A deposit/refund system imposes an up-front charge for potential damages caused by improper disposal and allows for a refund of that charge at the end of the product cycle if the consumer takes proper action to avoid those damages.

# Key Concepts

| | |
|---|---|
| municipal solid waste (MSW) | back- or waste-end charges |
| product groups | unit pricing scheme |
| materials groups | flat rate pricing |
| integrated waste management system | variable rate pricing |
| | "bag-and-tag" approach |
| tipping fees | front-end or retail disposal charge |
| fixed fee or flat fee pricing system | deposit/refund system |

# Review Questions

1. a. Summarize a specific municipal solid waste problem in your hometown or one that recently has been reported in the media. Use the specific stages of the waste stream in your discussion.

   b. What policies have been proposed or implemented to address the problem you describe? Analyze these policies from an economic perspective.

2. Using what you have learned about market-based incentives, suggest a policy initiative that would discourage land disposal in the United States.

3. Refer to Application 18.2, which addresses New Jersey's recycling program. Identify which elements of the program are command-and-control in approach and which are market based.

4. Using the information in Application 18.3, compare Germany's Green Dot program to U.S. national initiatives on recycling. In your view, which is likely to be more effective in the long run? Explain.

5. Diagram a general model of MSW management services. Show the simultaneous effect of the federal restrictions on landfills *and* rising consumer awareness of the benefits of "green packaging." Assuming a private competitive market, predict the effect on the price and quantity of MSW services.

6. Consider the following model of a hypothetical market for MSW management services:

$$MPB = 25 - 2Q$$
$$MPC = 4 + Q$$
$$MEC = 0.5Q,$$

where $Q$ is the number of trash containers per household per month.

    a. Quantitatively determine the effect of the resource misallocation due to:

      (i)  the presence of the negative externality.

      (ii)  the use of a flat fee pricing system in the presence of a negative externality.

    b. Support your answer to part (a) with a graphical model.

    c. Determine the dollar value of a waste-end charge that would restore efficiency to this market. Explain your answer intuitively.

7.  a. Contrast the Seattle per-can pricing program with Perkasie's "bag-and-tag" approach both from an environmental and an economic perspective.

    b. Why might weight-based unit pricing for MSW management be more advantageous than volume-based programs?

# Additional Readings

Bailey, Jeff. "Curbside Recycling Soothes the Soul, but Cost Is High." *The Wall Street Journal*, January 19, 1995.

Boerner, Christopher, and Kenneth Chilton. "False Economy: The Folly of Demand-Side Recycling." *Environment* 36(1), January/February 1994, pp. 6–15, 32–33.

Callan, Scott J., and Janet M. Thomas. "The Impact of State and Local Policies on the Recycling Effort." *Eastern Economic Journal* 23(4). Fall 1997, pp. 411–23.

Daley, Beth. "Illegal Disposal of Trash Spreads." *Boston Globe*, March 6, 1994.

Erwin, Lewis, and L. Hall Healey, Jr. *Packaging and Solid Waste: Management Strategies.* New York: AMACOM, 1990.

Fullerton, Don, and Thomas C. Kinnaman. "Household Responses to Pricing Garbage by the Bag." *American Economic Review* 86(4), September 1996, pp. 971–84.

Judge, R., and A. Becker. "Motivating Recycling: A Marginal Cost Analysis." *Contemporary Policy Issues* XI(3), July 1993, pp. 58–68.

Martin, Mary. "Truly Fashionable Recycling: Plastic Bottles Get New Life as Polyester Fiber." *Boston Globe*, March 3, 1994.

Miranda, Marie Lynn, Jess W. Everett, Daniel Blume, and Barbeau A. Roy, Jr. "Market-Based Incentives and Residential Municipal Solid Waste." *Journal of Policy Analysis and Management* 13(4), Fall 1994, pp. 681–98.

Miranda, Marie Lynn, and Joseph E. Aldy. "Unit Pricing of Residential Municipal Solid Waste: Lessons from Nine Case Study Communities." *Journal of Environmental Management* 52, January 1998, pp. 79–93.

Platt, Brenda A., Neil Seldman, Bernd Granke, and Bernd Mayer. *Garbage in Europe: Technologies, Economics, and Trends.* Washington, DC: Institute for Local Self-Reliance, May 1988.

Repetto, Robert, Roger C. Dower, Robin Jenkins, and Jacqueline Geoghegan. *Green Fees: How a Tax Shift Can Work for the Environment and the Economy.* Washington, DC: World Resources Institute, 1992.

Thompson, Claudia. *Recycled Papers.* Cambridge, MA: MIT Press, 1992.

## Related Web Sites

| | |
|---|---|
| Characterization of municipal solid waste in the United States | **www.epa.gov/epaoswer/non-hw/muncpl/** |
| Germany's Green Dot Program | **www.green-dot.com/e/home/home.htm** |
| Information on recycling in the United States | **www.epa.gov/epaoswer/non-hw/recycle/index.htm** |
| Information on Subtitle D of RCRA | **www.epa.gov/epaoswer/osw/non-hw.htm** |
| National Solid Wastes Management Association | **www.envasns.org/nswma/** |
| Unit pricing scheme by community | **www.epa.gov/epaoswer/non-hw/payt/comm.htm** |

# 19

# Controlling Toxic Chemicals: Production, Use, and Disposal

Toxic substances are extensively regulated in the United States. Air toxics, for example, are controlled under the Clean Air Act. The discharge of hazardous pollutants into waterways is governed by the Clean Water Act, and the Resource Conservation and Recovery Act (RCRA) regulates the hazardous solid waste stream. Notice how all these federal laws deal with the *release* of toxics into the environment. In this chapter, we study legislation aimed at controlling chemical substances *before* they become residuals and enter the waste stream—when they are formulated and produced.

Approximately 5 percent of the U.S. economy is engaged in the production of chemicals and allied products. Over 65,000 chemical substances are produced in this country, with more than 1,000 new ones introduced each year.[1] While this increasing reliance on chemicals has added to the variety, durability, and usefulness of products available to society, there has also been a cost. Certain of these chemicals, such as polychlorinated biphenyls (PCBs) and the pesticide dichloro-diphenyl-trichloroethane (DDT), pose a threat to human health and ecosystems. In some cases the risks are not fully understood until long after the damage has been done.

Recognizing the potential risks of chemical usage and the impact of toxic residuals in the waste stream, Congress passed the Federal Insecticide, Fungicide, and Rodenticide Act (FIFRA) and the Toxic Substances Control Act (TSCA). These two laws, each from a different vantage point, control the production, distribution, and consumption of pesticides and other chemicals. By instituting controls before these substances are introduced into commerce, those that pose an unacceptable risk can be restricted in

---

[1] U.S. EPA (August 1988), p. 126.

use or even banned. In so doing, the toxicity of the hazardous waste stream should be abated and the associated environmental risks reduced. Notice that this approach is preemptive because it eliminates the need to treat and dispose of some amount of hazardous residuals. The underlying premise is that the waste stream is part of a larger cycle that originates with the design and development of products. Hence, regulating hazardous substances at the pregeneration phase of the waste stream is an effective way to prevent pollution.

In this chapter, our objectives are to understand the intent of FIFRA and TSCA, to analyze their implementation, and to evaluate their effectiveness using economic criteria and decision rules. To organize our investigation, we begin with an overview of the Federal Insecticide, Fungicide, and Rodenticide Act (FIFRA)—its evolution and its current regulatory structure. Following this presentation, we conduct an analysis of this act and its overall control approach. An analogous treatment is used to study the Toxic Substances Control Act (TSCA). At the conclusion of these two parallel discussions, we conduct a comprehensive analysis of U.S. policies on solid waste and toxic substances that have been the focus of this module. Risk–benefit analysis is the primary approach used in this summary evaluation. An appendix of acronyms is provided at the end of the chapter.

# An Overview of U.S. Pesticide Controls: FIFRA

*A Brief Retrospective*[2]

Congress enacted the Federal Insecticide, Fungicide, and Rodenticide Act (FIFRA) in 1947 and charged the Department of Agriculture with its administration. Its primary aim was to regulate pesticide labeling to protect against fraudulent products. In 1970, the newly established EPA assumed responsibility for FIFRA, and two years later Congress passed amendments to the act. These amendments changed virtually every aspect of the original law, shifting its focus to health and environmental protection. A key revision was the requirement for registration of new pesticides and the reevaluation and reregistration of those already on the market. Pesticide registration continues to be the chief regulatory instrument of federal controls on pesticides.

Over time, further revisions were made. Part of the reform has been to require more sophisticated test data from registrants to determine if better safeguards are needed in labeling, packaging, or formulations. Not unlike other major policies, U.S. pesticide initiatives have sometimes proven to be overly ambitious. In fact, of the approximately 600 pesticides needing reregistration under FIFRA, the EPA had issued **registration standards** for

---

[2]The following section is drawn from U.S. EPA, Office of Pesticides and Toxic Substances (December 1988); U.S. EPA (August 1988), pp. 113–19; and Wolf (1988), p. 154. For an online review of FIFRA, visit **www.law.cornell.edu/uscode/7/ch6.html**.

only about 185 of them by the late 1980s. These standards are important as each includes a review of available data, a listing of information needed for reregistration, and a statement of the current regulatory position on the pesticide.

In 1988, Congress passed the FIFRA Amendments—the set of rulings currently in force. These revisions improved registration and reregistration procedures and authorized a fee system to help pay for the reregistration process. The amendments also strengthened the EPA's control over the storage, transportation, and disposal of pesticides, including labeling of both the pesticide and its container. Added to the EPA's responsibilities was to regulate the use, disposal, refill, and reuse of pesticide containers. Congress also rescinded one of the agency's responsibilities—that of accepting stocks of suspended and canceled pesticides and disposing of them at the government's expense. Instead, the EPA can require registrants and distributors to handle a recall. Application 19.1 (p. 594) reports on the disposal dilemma that arose following the U.S. cancellation of ethylene dibromide (EDB) in 1984.[3]

## Controlling New Pesticides through Registration

**pesticide registration** Formal listing of a pesticide with the EPA that must be approved based on a risk–benefit analysis before it can be sold or distributed.

**risk–benefit analysis** Decision rule that assesses the risks of an environmental hazard along with the benefits of not regulating that hazard.

A major objective of FIFRA is to require the **registration** of all pesticides *before* they can be distributed or sold.[4] Registration is subject to EPA approval based on a **risk–benefit analysis.** The EPA must assure that the benefits of using the substance outweigh the associated health and ecological risks. Hence, the law implicitly identifies those pesticides associated with unreasonable adverse effects by denying their registration. Based on the law, a pesticide may not be registered if:

- its composition does not warrant its proposed claims;

- its labeling does not comply with the law;

- it will not perform its intended function without causing unreasonable adverse effects on the environment; *or*

- it cannot be used in widespread practice without generating unreasonable adverse environmental effects.

Since FIFRA's original enactment in 1947, over 50,000 pesticides have been registered for use in the United States—most before their risks were fully understood.[5] Advances in risk assessment are helping officials reduce the

---

[3] For a listing of banned and severely restricted pesticides, visit **www.epa.gov/oppfead1/ international/ piclist.htm**.

[4] For online information on pesticide registration, visit **www.epa.gov/pesticides/chemreg.htm**.

[5] U.S. EPA (August 1988), p. 115. Today, there are about 25,000 formulated products registered for use in the United States. See U.S. EPA, Office of Pesticides and Toxic Substances (May 1991), p. 2.

## Pesticide Cancellation: The Case of Ethylene Dibromide

In 1948, a new pesticide was introduced to commercial markets—ethylene dibromide (EDB). Its effectiveness was borne out by its extensive use on fruits, vegetables, and stored grain. Over 35 years later, it was learned that EDB caused cancer in laboratory animals and was found to be linked to soil and groundwater contamination. In 1984, the EPA halted most uses of the product. All supplies of the toxic EDB immediately became unusable and unwanted material—effectively becoming part of the hazardous waste stream. Since the EDB cancellation predated the 1988 FIFRA Amendments, the EPA was bound by law to dispose of any of the unused pesticide if requested to do so. It also had to compensate users and manufacturers for any costs incurred from the emergency action.

As a consequence of the cancellation, the EPA was left with a huge stockpile of EDB wastes and no known method of safe disposal. Pending a decision as to how the disposal would be accomplished, the pesticide was held in storage. In 1986, an ominous discovery was made—drums filled with EDB in a Missouri warehouse were found to be leaking. News of the incident alerted the general public to the serious problems of pesticide waste disposal.

The EPA had planned to neutralize the EDB stock through a chemical process that had been tested only in laboratories, but the plan had been delayed by mechanical problems. When the agency attempted to remove the EDB from the leaking drums, which by that time had begun to corrode, toxic vapor emissions were discharged into the atmosphere. The EPA spent $1.5 million before it determined that the chemical treatment it had been considering for EDB was not viable for all formulations. It then looked into incineration that could somehow accommodate the corrosivity of the substance. That option was expected to cost between $6 million and $8 million. As of 1990, all stocks of EDB had finally been disposed of.

In terms of understanding the risks of managing pesticide wastes, there are likely no clearer examples than those that arise when pesticides are canceled on a mass scale. In addition to the EDB suspension, the United States has had to deal with two other emergency cancellations—one for 2,4,5-T/silvex and another for dinoseb. As of 1990, the EPA was still in the process of disposing of dinoseb, an herbicide and crop desiccant it banned in 1986. Expected disposal costs for this pesticide have been estimated at over $100 million. Beyond these emergency actions, the United States has canceled the registrations of 34 pesticides and halted the use of 60 toxic, inert ingredients in pesticide formulations as of 1990. Although the EPA no longer must accept supplies of suspended and canceled pesticides, registrants and distributors have to be prepared to handle a recall. The potential difficulties of finding safe disposal methods for canceled pesticides and the risks of interim storage underscore the importance of risk assessment within the registration process and the need to develop safer, less toxic substitutes.

SOURCES: U.S. Environmental Protection Agency. *Environmental Progress and Challenges: EPA's Update.* Washington, DC, August 1988, pp. 128–33, 118; U.S. Environmental Protection Agency. *Meeting the Environmental Challenge: EPA's Review of Progress and New Directions in Environmental Protection.* Washington, DC, December 1990a, pp. 18–20.

**pesticide tolerances**
Legal limits on the amount of pesticide remaining as a residue on raw agricultural products or in processed foods.

probability of making uninformed registration decisions and prevent the use of any pesticide posing an unreasonable risk to society.

At the time of registration, the EPA also sets legal limits or **tolerances** on the amount of a pesticide that may remain as a *residue* on raw or processed food without causing an unacceptable health risk. In effect, the registration acts as a license for use, and the tolerances specify the conditions under which that use is approved. Tolerances for most foods are enforced by the Food and Drug Administration (FDA) according to the provisions of the Federal Food, Drug, and Cosmetic Act (FFDCA).

Rulings in both FIFRA and FFDCA have been amended by the Food Quality Protection Act (FQPA) of 1996. Signed by President Clinton on August 3, 1996, the new law sets a single standard for both laws, requiring that all tolerances be "safe." Under the law, safety refers to *"a reasonable certainty that no harm will result from aggregate exposure."* By imposing one standard, the FQPA eliminates an inconsistency problem posed by one of the provisions of the FFDCA known as the Delaney Clause, which is discussed in Application 19.2 (p. 596).[6]

### Controlling Existing Pesticides through Reregistration

**pesticide reregistration** Formal reevaluation of a previously licensed pesticide already on the market.

One of the more important aspects of the 1988 FIFRA Amendments are the rulings dealing with the **reregistration** of previously licensed pesticides. As a result of the reevaluation process, many unsafe pesticides have been restricted in use or banned. Examples include agricultural uses of chlordane and virtually all uses of DDT and ethylene dibromide (EDB). As harmful chemicals like these are restricted or eliminated, industries and consumers must find alternative, and presumably less toxic, pesticides. Consequently, some amount of hazardous pollution should be prevented instead of having to be remediated after the fact.

In 1988, approximately 600 groups of pesticide active ingredients were targeted for reregistration. Thus far, registration standards have been issued on less than a third of these.[7] The process is a major undertaking, and the 1988 amendments were intended to accelerate what had been an inordinately slow procedure. To expedite the process, deadlines were imposed for the series of tasks needed to complete the reregistration procedure. These tasks are described in a five-phase approach, which is detailed in Table 19.1 (p. 597).[8]

Based on original estimates, the nine-year reregistration process should cost about $250 million. Are these high costs worth the effort? The fact is, controlling pesticides poses a tough problem for policy makers and for society as a whole. As a group of substances, pesticides can contribute positively to agriculture and other industries. Yet exposure to these substances can harm the ecology and cause serious health problems like cancer, birth defects, and neurological impairments. Both sets of factors need to be considered in a risk–benefit analysis. Hence, the $250-million expense to

---

[6] Council on Environmental Quality (1997), pp. 94–96; Kimm (January/February/March 1993). To read more about the FQPA of 1996, visit **www.epa.gov/oppfead1/fqpa/**.

[7] The 194 registration standards that have been issued represent approximately 350 active ingredients that account for 85 to 90 percent of the volume of pesticides used in the country. U.S. EPA, Office of Pesticides and Toxic Substances (May 1991), p. 4.

[8] U.S. EPA, Office of Pesticides and Toxic Substances (June 1991).

## Solving the Delaney Clause Dilemma

The Delaney Clause was perhaps the most controversial piece of environmental legislation ever passed in the United States. Named after its sponsor, former U.S. Representative James Joseph Delaney of New York, the 1958 law effectively banned the use of any food additive found to cause cancer—no matter how negligible the degree of risk was. Under Section 409 of FFDCA dealing with processed foods, pesticide residues are considered food additives. Hence, the Delaney Clause directly affected the use of pesticides based on the residue that remained after processing. As it turned out, the provision had even more far-reaching implications because the EPA elected to coordinate its decisions on pesticide residues in raw food with those applicable to processed foods. In fact, in a federal appeals court decision in July 1992, it was ruled that the EPA could not allow any pesticide residues in processed food that exceeded what was allowed on raw food if the pesticide posed *any* measure of carcinogenic risk—no matter how small.

Some of the controversy associated with the Delaney Clause arose because of a statute in Section 409 called the "flow-through" provision. In essence, this provision said that processed foods would be considered safe if the residues remaining were not in excess of what had been established for raw foods under Section 408. Because of the relationship between these two sections in the FFDCA, the EPA coordinated its policies on setting tolerances for residues on raw food with those applicable to processed foods. Through this "coordination policy," the EPA would not approve the use of a pesticide for raw foods under Section 408, if this use could have resulted in a violation under Section 409 for processed foods.

A problem arose because some pesticides concentrate during processing, and the resulting concentration could have caused the remaining residue to exceed the approved tolerance level for raw foods. If so, the pesticide then became subject to separate approval under Section 409 and the Delaney Clause. Thus, if the pesticide was associated with even the smallest measure of carcinogenic risk, its use was banned. It was prohibited from use not only for processed food, but because of EPA's "coordination policy," for raw food as well.

This coordination policy came under fire because of the inconsistencies it caused. Tolerance levels under Section 408 were to be set using risk–benefit analysis, but those under Section 409, because of the Delaney Clause, were risk-based. Furthermore, pesticides with negligible carcinogenic risks would be banned from use if they concentrated during processing, yet pesticides with higher carcinogenic risks could have been used on raw foods because if they did not concentrate during processing, they did not require a Section 409 ruling.

The Food Quality Protection Act (FQPA) of 1996 solved the paradox by amending both FIFRA and FFDCA. First, it establishes a single standard applicable to both raw and processed food, avoiding the use of different decision rules under two laws. Second, it defines safety to include all risks—not just carcinogenic risks. After decades of debate and controversy, the Delaney dilemma seems to have been resolved.

SOURCES: Victor J. Kimm. "The Delaney Clause Dilemma." *EPA Journal*, January/February/March 1993; Council on Environmental Quality. *Environmental Quality, 23rd Annual Report*. Washington, DC: U.S. Government Printing Office, January 1993, p. 87, Table 100, p. 424; Council on Environmental Quality. *Environmental Quality 25th Anniversary Report*. Washington, DC: U.S. Government Printing Office, 1997, pp. 94–96.

| TABLE 19.1 | THE FIVE-PHASE REREGISTRATION PROCESS UNDER THE 1988 FIFRA AMENDMENTS | |
|---|---|---|
| **Phase** | **Timetable** | **Description** |
| **Phase I** | | |
| Listing of active ingredients | 10 months from enactment | The EPA publishes lists of pesticide active ingredients that are subject to reregistration and inquires whether registrants intend to seek registration. |
| **Phase II** | | |
| Declaration of intent and identification of studies | Completed in 1990 | Registrants are to respond to EPA requests and to identify any missing or inadequate scientific studies needed to satisfy data requirements under the revised law. The first installment of the reregistration fee is due. |
| **Phase III** | | |
| Summarization of studies | Completed in October 1990 | Registrants must summarize existing studies to expedite EPA's review process, commit to generate or share the cost of generating new data if studies are not available, and pay the final installment of the reregistration fee. |
| **Phase IV** | | |
| EPA review and data call-ins | Completed in July 1992 | The EPA must complete its review of registrants' submissions under Phase II and III and issue whatever requirements are necessary to complete all data requirements. |
| **Phase V** | | |
| Reregistration decisions | To be completed in 1997 | The EPA conducts a comprehensive investigation of all data submitted and decides whether to reregister the pesticide. |

SOURCES: Federal Environmental Pesticide Control Act, Sec. 4; U.S. EPA, Office of Pesticides and Toxic Substances. *For Your Information: Pesticide Reregistration.* Washington, DC, June 1991.

administer the reregistration process may be warranted if it facilitates government's ability to conduct such an analysis and properly manage whatever risks are justified by the associated social benefits.

# Analysis of FIFRA

## *Risk–Benefit Analysis under FIFRA*

No pesticide may be distributed or sold unless it has been registered with the EPA, and registration is denied for any substance associated with *"unreasonable adverse effects on the environment."* Thus, the statutory definition of this phrase implicitly identifies the standard used to evaluate pesticides.

> "The term 'unreasonable adverse effects on the environment' means any unreasonable risk to man or the environment, taking into account the economic, social, and environmental costs and benefits of the use of any pesticide."[9]

Notice that, unlike most U.S. environmental laws, FIFRA explicitly calls for a consideration of the costs and benefits of pesticide use in determining unreasonable risk. This clearly suggests the need for risk–benefit analysis. That is, the risks of using a pesticide measured in terms of health and ecological effects should be weighed against the associated benefits such as increased crop yields.

It turns out, however, that risks are the dominant factor in the EPA's registration decisions. For *new* pesticides, risks are evaluated from data on health and environmental effects submitted by manufacturers as part of the registration application. Hence, the onus of proving that risks are not "unreasonable" lies with the producer. If risks are found to be negligible, the EPA generally assumes that benefits exist based on the manufacturer's willingness to absorb the high cost of registration. If risks are found to be greater than negligible, the manufacturer typically has to formulate a risk reduction strategy or show that the benefits exceed the risks.[10] When the EPA conducts a special review of an *existing* pesticide, a formal benefit analysis is done. In these instances, benefits are measured by determining biological effects, such as changes in agricultural yields, and then these effects are monetized.

## Problems in Risk Assessment

At least in principle, the nation's approach to pesticide control appears to have merit. So, why is U.S. pesticide policy the subject of intense debate? Probably the best answer is that there is much uncertainty about the associated risks despite the widespread exposure. Many scientists question the EPA's methods of assessing pesticide risks. Some argue that the risks are underestimated, citing the agency's lack of attention to inert ingredients or the cumulative effects from using multiple pesticides in combination. Others assert that the opposite is true, claiming that findings from animal bioassays overstate the potential harm to humans. The EPA contends that it has neither the staff nor the financial resources to undertake a complete reevaluation of all pesticides in use, even if there were consensus about appropriate risk assessment procedures. Beyond these issues, there is also

---

[9] FIFRA, Sec. 2.(bb).

[10] Generally, manufacturers try to reduce the risks or withdraw the registration application. U.S. General Accounting Office (GAO) (March 1991), pp. 3, 9.

concern about how tougher pesticide controls would affect agricultural productivity. Without viable pesticide substitutes, there could be serious implications for world food supplies.

### A New Policy Direction

In 1993, a report by the National Academy of Sciences (NAS) triggered what appears to be a major shift in U.S. pesticide policy and perhaps a resolution to some of the questions. What the NAS found was that children are not being sufficiently protected from pesticides risks by U.S. policy. At the core of this assessment is that the smaller size of children and their diets make them more vulnerable to pesticide risks. Almost immediately, the Clinton administration announced its intention to develop a new pesticide plan—a joint effort by the EPA, the FDA, and the Department of Agriculture. Ultimately called the Pesticide Environmental Stewardship Program, the plan's major objective is to reduce pesticide use—not just regulate it. The goal is to promote **Integrated Pest Management (IPM)**—a collection of methods to foster more selective use of pesticides and greater reliance on natural deterrents. In support of this objective is an incentive-based proposal to encourage chemical manufacturers to develop alternative products.[11]

**Integrated Pest Management (IPM)**
A combination of control methods aimed at encouraging more selective use of pesticides and greater reliance on natural deterrents.

# An Overview of U.S. Legislation on Toxic Substances: TSCA

### The Policy Response to Chemical Risks[12]

Chemicals are an integral part of modern society and represent a major industry in the U.S. economy. Used properly, most of these substances contribute positively to the quality of life. Yet exposure to chemicals can pose significant risks to society. Unfortunately, some of the health risks of chemical exposure, particularly long-term and permanent effects, were not known until *after* these substances had been introduced into commerce and had become widely used.[13] Responding to the problem, Congress enacted the Toxic Substances Control Act (TSCA) in 1976. One of the act's primary

---

[11] U.S. EPA, Office of Pesticide Programs. "Pesticide Environmental Stewardship Program," **www.epa. gov/oppbppd1/PESP/**; Associated Press (September 21, 1993). For a discussion of other incentives to reduce pesticide use, see Williams (May/June 1992).

[12] Much of the following discussion is drawn from U.S. EPA, Office of Toxic Substances (June 1987), pp. 2–8 and U.S. EPA (August 1988), pp. 112–27. For online information on TSCA, see **www.law.cornell.edu/ uscode/15/ch53.html**.

[13] An important example is the chemical group polychlorinated biphenyls (PCBs), substances formerly used as insulators in electrical transformers and as lubricants and dye carriers in paints, inks, and dyes. The toxicity of PCBs was not known until after these substances had leaked into the environment and began to accumulate in the tissues of animals and fish, thereby entering the food chain. The discovery led to a 1976 ban on their manufacture, processing, distribution, and use in the United States, except in completely enclosed electrical equipment (U.S. EPA, August 1988, p. 120).

objectives is to identify and control chemical substances that present a risk to health or the environment *before* they are introduced into commerce. By confronting the environmental and health risks of chemicals at the pre-manufacture stage, the government has an opportunity to prevent pollution rather than having to correct problems after the fact. TSCA also provides a way to monitor the risks of chemicals already on the market and to take action as needed. Since so little was known about most of the chemical substances in use, Congress also authorized the compilation of an inventory of all chemicals commercially produced or processed in the United States between 1975 and 1979. Using data collected from manufacturers and importers, the government published the first **TSCA inventory** in 1979, which contained information on more than 62,000 chemicals.

**TSCA inventory** Database of all chemicals commercially produced or processed in the United States.

TSCA gives the EPA authority to gather information on chemical risks from producers, to require testing on existing chemicals, and to review most newly introduced chemicals before they are manufactured and made available for use on a broad scale. Depending on its findings, the EPA takes appropriate action. The regulatory response can range from requiring warnings during production and distribution to banning the chemical's manufacture. Risk controls may be imposed at any stage in the chemical's life cycle, including its manufacture, processing, distribution in commerce, usage, and disposal.

To avoid the inefficiency and potential inconsistency of dual controls, TSCA acknowledges and accounts for the mandates of other laws dealing with toxic substances and the agencies that implement them. Some of these are listed in Table 19.2. Under the law, the EPA is to coordinate its control activities with those of other agencies such as the Food and Drug Administration (FDA), the U.S. Department of Agriculture (USDA), and the Occupational Safety and Health Administration (OSHA). As a chemical risk is discovered, the EPA must consider whether other agencies have investigated that risk, and if so, it must determine if existing laws adequately address the problem. In fact, the EPA must use other laws it administers to reduce risk, such as the Clean Water Act, the Clean Air Act, and RCRA, *before* implementing TSCA's provisions. Finally, eight product categories are explicitly exempted from TSCA, most of which are regulated under other laws.[14]

### Controlling the Introduction of New Chemicals

Unlike the nation's pesticide law, TSCA does *not* use a registration procedure to control toxic chemical use. Instead, it requires manufacturers to notify the government at least 90 days before they intend to produce or import any **new chemical**—one that is not listed in the national inventory

**new chemical** Any substance not listed in the TSCA inventory of existing chemicals.

---

[14]The eight product groups are tobacco, nuclear material, firearms and ammunition, food, food additives, drugs, cosmetics, and pesticides.

| TABLE 19.2 | SELECTED LAWS GOVERNING THE CONTROL OF SUBSTANCES EXEMPTED UNDER TSCA | |
|---|---|---|

| Legislation | Agency | Substance/Control |
|---|---|---|
| Atomic Energy Act | Nuclear Regulatory Commission | Nuclear waste disposal, nuclear energy production |
| Federal Insecticide, Fungicide, and Rodenticide Act | Environmental Protection Agency | Pesticides |
| Federal Food, Drug, and Cosmetic Act | Food and Drug Administration | Foods, food additives, drug additives, cosmetics |
| Safe Drinking Water Act | Environmental Protection Agency | Controls contaminants in drinking water supplies |
| Occupational Safety and Health Act | Occupational Safety and Health Administration | Controls hazards found in the workplace |
| Clean Air Act | Environmental Protection Agency | Controls the emissions of hazardous air pollutants |
| Clean Water Act | Environmental Protection Agency | Controls the discharge of hazardous pollutants into surface waters |
| Hazardous Materials Transportation Act | Department of Transportation | Regulates the transport of hazardous materials |
| Marine Protection, Research, and Sanctuaries Act | Environmental Protection Agency | Regulates waste disposal at sea |
| Resource Conservation and Recovery Act | Environmental Protection Agency | Regulates hazardous waste generation, storage, transport, treatment, and disposal |
| Comprehensive Environmental Response, Compensation, and Liability Act | Environmental Protection Agency | Provides for cleanup of inactive and abandoned hazardous waste sites |
| Surface Mining Control and Reclamation Act | Department of the Interior | Regulates environmental aspects of mining and reclamation |

SOURCE: U.S. Environmental Protection Agency, Office of Solid Waste. *Solving the Hazardous Waste Problem: EPA's RCRA Program.* Washington, DC, November 1986.

**premanufacture notice (PMN)** Official notification made to the EPA by a chemical producer about its intent to produce or import a new chemical.

of existing chemicals. The notification is made to the EPA via a **premanufacture notice (PMN),** which provides information about the chemical's characteristics, the expected exposure to workers, its intended use, and the health and ecological effects. Upon receipt of the PMN, the EPA has a 90-day review period to evaluate the risks and respond. If the risks are too high or, in the absence of full information, are expected to be too high, the EPA may restrict usage of the chemical permanently or, if more data are needed for a complete risk analysis, temporarily. The determination of unreasonable risk is based on test results of exposure effects such as cancer or birth defects.[15]

Over 24,000 PMNs have been submitted to the EPA since 1979. Of this total, the EPA has restricted or prohibited the production or use of more than 700 chemicals pending further information. Over 800 additional chemicals have been controlled through voluntary agreements with producers, and almost 1,000 have been withdrawn or suspended from the review process by manufacturers in response to EPA concerns. In the aggregate, over 10 percent of the chemicals submitted for review since 1979 have been suspended, restricted, or withdrawn from production or use.[16]

### Controlling Existing Chemicals in Use

Other provisions of TSCA deal with evaluating the risks of over 65,000 chemicals *already* on the market. The law requires manufacturers to notify the EPA if any chemical is found to present a substantial risk to human health or the environment. When this occurs, the EPA's Office of Toxic Substances evaluates the information and takes action, ranging from labeling requirements to outright bans. Between 1980 and 1991, about 5,000 of these notifications were received by the EPA. In more than 550 instances, producers altered their processes to reduce the release of the substances, and the use of the chemical was temporarily or permanently halted. One of the more recent and significant instances of such an action is the three-stage phaseout of asbestos—a harmful substance that was to be completely banned from manufacture, processing, and distribution as of August 25, 1997.[17]

## Analysis of TSCA

### Risk–Benefit Analysis under TSCA

TSCA's statutory objectives are to obtain data on chemical risks and to regulate chemicals posing an "unreasonable risk" to human health or the environment. Interestingly, "unreasonable risk" is not explicitly defined in the law. However, a House of Representatives report sheds some light on what is implied, stating that the determination of "unreasonable risk" involves the following:[18]

---

[15] U.S. EPA, Office of Pollution Prevention (October 1991), p. 142; U.S. EPA, Office of Toxic Substances (June 1987), pp. 3–4. TSCA, Sec. 4.(b)(2)(A).

[16] U.S. EPA, Office of Prevention, Pesticides, and Toxic Substances. "New Chemicals Program," **www.epa.gov/opptintr/newchms/**, last revised June 19, 1998; U.S. EPA, Office of Pollution Prevention (October 1991), p. 142.

[17] U.S. EPA (August 1988), p. 114; *Federal Register* 54:29460–29513 (July 12, 1989), as cited in U.S. EPA, Office of Pollution Prevention (October, 1991), p. 143.

[18] Dominguez (1977), Section 5, p. 5.9.

"...balancing the probability that harm will occur and the magnitude and severity of that harm against the effect of proposed regulatory action on the availability to society of the benefits of the substance or mixture."

Notice how this determination supports the use of risk–benefit analysis in the approval process—just as is the case for pesticides. Like FIFRA, this act empowers the EPA to ban or restrict the use of toxic chemicals that do not pass the risk–benefit test. Such actions should effectively encourage the substitution of alternative, less dangerous substances, which in turn lessens the toxicity of the hazardous waste stream.

A major difference between TSCA and FIFRA is the process used for review of new substances. While FIFRA calls for extensive test data as part of a complex registration process, TSCA requires only a 90-day advance notice of intent to produce a new chemical. Testing is done only upon formal request by the EPA. It has been argued that this regulatory difference properly reflects the relative magnitude of risks between toxic substances and pesticides. Pesticides generally pose a greater risk since they are biologically active. Hence, the more stringent controls and higher costs of introducing a new pesticide into commerce may be justified by the inherently greater risk potential.[19]

### Bias against New Chemical Introductions[20]

A common observation about TSCA's effectiveness is that the EPA has been slow to develop data on *existing* chemicals despite the evidence that such information is critical. Ironically, much of the delay seems to be caused by how TSCA is written, imposing command-and-control procedures that are time-intensive and possibly needless. For example, the EPA literally must write a new regulation each time it wishes to test a chemical substance. Another contributing factor is the agency's current use of a single chemical review process rather than one aimed at a group of similar substances.

Overall, the analysis of *existing* chemicals is complex and bogged down with time-intensive procedures—markedly different from the relatively straightforward rules in place for reviewing *new* substances. The result? Not only do these regulations delay the development of an important database, they also create a bias against the introduction of new chemicals. The government is much more efficient in its testing of new substances than it is for those already on the market. Consequently, chemical producers wishing to avoid such procedures and the associated costs can continue to sell existing and possibly more dangerous substances. Hence, certain of TSCA's

---

[19] Shapiro (1990), pp. 213–14.

[20] Drawn from Shapiro (1990), pp. 223–24, 232–36.

rulings appear to generate the perverse outcome of deterring the development of new, safer chemicals.

### A New Policy Direction[21]

**Product Steward-ship Rulemaking**
Proposal that would require chemical producers to share risk information with their customers and to conduct hazard evaluations on substances in use.

**multimedia, multi-chemical approaches**
Proposed regulatory procedures that would replace existing chemical regulatory actions.

Recognizing the weaknesses in certain of TSCA's provisions, the United States is in the process of revising the TSCA program. Although TSCA's premanufacture rulings for new chemicals have been effective in encouraging substitution of safer chemicals for toxic ones, there has been less success in fostering the same activity for existing chemicals. Among the proposals being considered is a **Product Stewardship Rulemaking.** If effected, the ruling would require chemical producers to share risk information with their customers and to conduct hazard evaluations on the substances their customers use. The anticipated outcome is that manufacturers will be encouraged to find less toxic substitute products when human or ecological exposure is significant.

Proposals such as these are part of an overall plan to revitalize the TSCA program and replace single chemical procedures with **multimedia, multi-chemical approaches.** This change should lessen the procedural difficulties that now hinder the agency's review of existing chemicals. If successful, the bias against new chemical introductions should be reduced or eliminated, and the nation's inventory of chemicals in use can be more efficiently maintained.

# An Economic Analysis of U.S. Solid Waste and Toxics Policy

National policy on toxic chemicals is closely linked to solid waste controls. As we have observed, FIFRA and TSCA attempt to control the production and use of potentially harmful substances *before* they are released into the environment. If such initiatives are successful, there is less risk when these materials enter the waste stream. Given the connection, it is appropriate to evaluate the allocation of resources to both approaches and determine if the allocation makes sense from a risk management perspective. While there are many factors to consider, the major issues can be addressed by examining the evidence on the costs and benefits of these policy efforts.

### Cost Analysis of U.S. Solid Waste and Toxic Control Policies[22]

On the cost side of the issue, much attention has been drawn to the enormous expenditures associated with RCRA and Superfund. Given the complex problems addressed by these laws, high costs are not surprising. The

---

[21] U.S. EPA (December 1990b), as cited in U.S. EPA Office of Pollution Prevention (October, 1991), p. 145.

[22] The following discussion is drawn mainly from U.S. EPA, Office of Policy, Planning, and Evaluation (December 1990).

| TABLE 19.3 | POLLUTION CONTROL COSTS FOR U.S. SOLID WASTE AND CHEMICALS PROGRAMS ($1986 MILLIONS) |

| Program | 1972 | 1980 | 1987 | 1995 (projected) | 2000 (projected) |
|---|---|---|---|---|---|
| RCRA total | $8,436 | $13,612 | $18,409 | $32,468 | $38,055 |
|   Nonhazardous solid waste | 8,436 | 13,612 | 16,683 | 20,338 | 22,302 |
|   Hazardous solid waste | ** | ** | 1,725 | 9,210 | 12,062 |
|   Underground storage tanks | ** | ** | 1 | 2,920 | 3,691 |
| CERCLA (Superfund) | ** | ** | 683 | 4,690 | 8,093 |
| **Solid Waste Total** | $8,436 | $13,612 | $19,092 | $37,158 | $46,148 |
| TSCA | ** | 429 | 365 | 1,119 | 1,234 |
| FIFRA | 92 | 461 | 453 | 1,353 | 1,658 |
| **Chemicals Total** | $ 92 | $ 889 | $ 818 | $ 2,472 | $ 2,892 |

NOTES: All values are in millions of 1986 dollars.

**Means the program was not in existence.

SOURCE: U.S. Environmental Protection Agency, Office of Policy, Planning, and Evaluation. *Environmental Investments: The Cost of a Clean Environment: A Summary*. Washington, DC, December 1990, Table 3-4, p. 3-4; Table 3-5, p. 3-5.

issue is whether or not the costs are justified by the benefits. As we suggested in Chapter 17, the benefit-based approach of both of these laws coupled with the lack of market incentives suggests that the high costs of implementing these laws may not be defensible on economic grounds. To accommodate a broader objective, we now use a different perspective and evaluate these costs *relative* to those associated with TSCA and FIFRA. Ultimately, we want to determine if the comparison makes sense in terms of the social benefits each set of laws is expected to achieve.

Direct costs associated with U.S. solid waste and toxic control policy for selected years are presented in Table 19.3.[23] The dollar values represent costs incurred by *all* economic sectors—the private sector, the EPA, other federal agencies, and state and local governments. All values are expressed in millions of 1986 dollars.[24] Notice there are two major cost categories for solid wastes, those associated with RCRA and those dealing with CERCLA or Superfund. The data for RCRA are further delineated by specific provisions, that is, those for nonhazardous solid waste, those for hazardous waste, and the rulings for underground storage tanks. Cost data on chemical

[23] Since implicit costs are not available, we use the second-best approach of examining explicit or direct costs, recognizing that the magnitude likely undervalues the true social costs.

[24] These pollution control costs are estimates based on full implementation of federal regulations, using survey data on historical expenditures for years up to 1987 and *ex ante* estimates of forthcoming regulations not in place as of 1987.

control policy are separated into those associated with toxic substances under TSCA and those for pesticides governed under FIFRA.

**Solid Waste Control Costs.**    Over the period shown in Table 19.3, the aggregate cost data on solid waste controls exhibit a strong positive trend, rising from approximately $8.4 billion in 1972 to $19.1 billion in 1987—an increase of 126 percent for the 15-year period. Based on projections, this trend is expected to continue at least until the year 2000. For the most part, this general rise in costs reflects the strengthening of the U.S. policy position since the mid-1970s, particularly for hazardous wastes. Consider, for example, the high costs of implementing the "cradle-to-grave" approach mandated by RCRA—a financial commitment that was increased by the rulings of the 1984 Amendments. By 1987, national costs of controlling hazardous wastes had grown to $1.7 billion, and the projections indicate continued growth. These costs are predicted to rise to $12.1 billion by the turn of the century. A similar trend is shown for the costs of regulating underground storage tanks. Notice that expenditures were $1 million in 1987 but are projected to reach nearly $3.7 billion by 2000.

Control costs are also on the rise for nonhazardous waste, though the trend is much more gradual. Federal laws on nonhazardous wastes have been in effect for a longer period of time and have undergone fewer revisions than those governing hazardous wastes. Furthermore, although these costs consistently represent the largest allocation of funding for any solid waste program, the great majority of them are incurred by local governments and private entities with only a small proportion directly linked to federal laws.

Superfund costs pale in comparison to those associated with RCRA, but the growth rate is higher than for any other solid waste program. Looking back at Table 19.3, notice that costs to fully implement the Superfund program in 2000 are expected to reach $8 billion—nearly 12 times the expenditure in 1987. In relative terms, the proportion of total solid waste control costs allocated to Superfund is expected to rise steadily from 3.6 percent in 1987 to a projected 17.5 percent in 2000. There is, however, considerable debate about the accuracy of Superfund cost projections.

Although the EPA's cost estimates for the Superfund program are based on many factors, none of these are certain. One of the key elements affecting the projections is the number of sites to be remediated. The Office of Technology Assessment (OTA) argues that as many as 10,000 sites will be placed on the National Priorities List (NPL)—much higher than the EPA's estimate of 2,000. Based on this projection, the OTA reports that it may take 50 years to clean up the 10,000 sites with aggregate costs reaching as much as $100 billion.[25] Another uncertain data point is the expected cost of

---

[25] U.S. Congress, Office of Technology Assessment (OTA) (1985), p. 3.

cleaning up each site. Such per unit estimates are averages that do not capture the variability across thousands of sites throughout the nation. If the EPA's estimate of $25 million per remedial action is used and if the OTA's projection of 10,000 NPL sites is accurate, aggregate costs could be as high as $250 billion.[26] Finally, there is a common assertion that most Superfund cost projections are undervalued because they typically do not include litigation costs, which are expected to be significant.

**Chemical Control Costs.**   Referring again to Table 19.3, notice that aggregate control costs for both FIFRA and TSCA are much smaller than those incurred for solid wastes. However, they do exhibit a strong growth pattern. Total expenditures show a dramatic increase from $92 million in 1972 to nearly nine times that level, or $818 million, in 1987. Projected costs suggest a considerable growth rate up to 2000.

On a less aggregated level, the growth rate of costs is fairly consistent for the two national programs under TSCA and FIFRA. Control expenditures under TSCA are directly related to the increasing number of pre-manufacture notices (PMNs) received each year. Since 1982, these have averaged over 1,000 per year—much higher than the number submitted in the 1970s and early 1980s. Projections indicate that this increase in new chemical introductions will continue. National controls on pesticides have a much longer history, dating back to 1947. Rising costs to implement FIFRA reflect increasingly tougher laws on registration, reregistration, and safety requirements mandated through recent revisions. The EPA anticipates that private costs will continue to rise as monies are allocated to research and development, cancellations and suspensions of pesticides, and compliance with more stringent farmworker safety and pesticide applicator requirements.

In sum, the costs of U.S. policy on solid waste and toxic substances are significant and rising over time. It is also true that the rate of increase is higher than for any other major environmental program. Based on EPA estimates, total expenditures for solid waste grew by nearly 67 percent from 1985 to 1990 and for chemicals by about 104 percent in the same period. These are much higher than the comparable growth rates for air and water control costs at 19 percent and 28 percent respectively. These observations may mean that standard-setting and the selection of policy instruments to execute solid waste and toxics control have missed the mark—at least from an efficiency perspective. Indeed, this assessment has been suggested by some. However, such an assertion is unwarranted without considering whether these relatively high costs are justified by comparable levels of social benefits.

---

[26] There are many estimates that do not support the EPA's findings. For a summary of some of these projections, consult U.S. Congress, OTA (1985), Table 3-1, p. 62.

### Benefits of U.S. Solid Waste and Toxic Substance Control Policies

As the government launches initiatives to control solid wastes and toxic substances, society's risk of exposure to these hazards should be reduced and the accompanying adverse effects should decline. In theory, the associated benefits can be assessed by measuring and monetizing the reduction in damages to human health and the ecology. Unfortunately, however, no comprehensive benefit analysis has been undertaken for the major U.S. programs on solid wastes and toxics. Even specific benefit measures are lacking. According to one article, of the tens of thousands of chemicals registered with the EPA, health studies have been conducted on only about 10,000, and of these, only about 1,000 have been studied for acute effects.[27] There is an even greater void in formal assessments of ecological benefits. These have particular relevance to Superfund, given its emphasis on compensation for damages to natural resources.[28] Why has so significant an issue escaped the rigors of formal analysis?

Part of the explanation is that national policy on solid waste and toxics is not as well established as air and water quality controls. The United States got a late start in initiating these policies, and there were long delays in implementation once the rulings were in place.[29] Beyond the timing issues, it is also true that certain of the expected benefits of these initiatives are difficult if not impossible to identify. Consider, for example, the manifest program under RCRA. An important expected benefit is the reduction in damages due to a lower incidence of illegal hazardous waste disposal. But it is not possible to measure a decrease in the number of illegal disposals when such activity is not observable. Even those data points that *are* observable are difficult to measure given the sheer magnitude of the relevant variables. There are over 38,500 identified CERCLIS sites, tens of thousands of registered chemicals, over 25,000 pesticide products in use, 5 to 6 million underground storage tanks, 500 hazardous waste land disposal facilities, and thousands of municipal landfills.[30] These statistics help to explain the uncertainty in even defining the extent of the problem, much less assessing the progress achieved by policy.

**comparative risk analysis** Decision rule that evaluates relative risk, also referred to as risk–risk analysis.

**Using Comparative Risk Analysis to Assess Benefits.**   In the absence of quantitative benefit measures, **comparative risk analysis** can be used to gain some insight about expected social benefits. By examining how the risks of exposure to various environmental hazards compare with one another, we can make inferences about the *relative* benefits that accrue to society from regulating these hazards. These qualitative inferences can shed some light on whether or not the associated control costs are justified,

---

[27] Stranahan (February/March 1990).

[28] For more specific information on the nature of ecological risks, see U.S. EPA, Region 5 (May 1991).

[29] Recall that although FIFRA was enacted in 1947, it did not address environmental issues until its revision in 1972.

[30] Williams (May/June 1992); U.S. EPA (August 1988), pp. 52–53.

assuming that risk-based priorities guide the nation's policy agenda. In this context, the objective is to compare the benefits of solid waste policies and those of chemical control policies to alternative mandates by analyzing the risks these regulations attempt to mitigate. Two EPA studies of risk ranking have been conducted in the past several years. The findings of the first investigation titled *Unfinished Business: A Comparative Assessment of Environmental Problems* will be used to support the following analysis.[31]

**EPA's Risk-Ranking Study.**    To conduct the comparative risk study, a task force designated by the EPA defined the universe of environmental issues as a set of 31 problems. For each of these, the team of experts assessed four types of risks: (1) cancer risks; (2) noncancer risks; (3) ecological effects; and (4) welfare effects. The objective was to determine the *relative* risk of each problem within each category. The risk-ranking process was based on available quantitative risk data, subsequent interpretation, and expert judgment. Ultimately, the task force established a priority ranking of environmental problems that could be used to guide national policy. Findings were also compared to an ordinal ranking of the public's perception of environmental risks based on a survey conducted by the Roper Organization. Both the expert ranking and the public's ranking for selected environmental problems are presented in Table 19.4 (p. 610). The overall observations and recommendations of the analysis are given in Table 19.5 (p. 611).

As the risk rankings in Table 19.4 indicate, it appears that the federal government's environmental priorities do not align consistently with the expert risk ranking—an observation that seems to be explained in part by how the general public perceives environmental risk. This observation is described more fully in the list of recommendations given in Table 19.5, specifically item 3. Notice how the task force identifies environmental hazards of high risk where EPA's control efforts are low and hazards of low or medium risk where the comparable effort is high. Every hazard in this latter category is a solid waste issue—active (RCRA) and inactive (Superfund) hazardous waste sites, releases from storage tanks, and municipal nonhazardous wastes. According to this observation, the large amount of resources allocated to solid waste control does not appear to be justified by relative risk analysis. Now, examine the list of environmental hazards in the "high risk/low EPA effort category." Notice that there are several chemical exposure hazards identified in this category—consumer and worker exposure to chemicals, accidental releases of toxics, and "other" pesticide risks. (This latter category includes runoff, leaching, and air deposition associated with the use of pesticides and agricultural chemicals.) The same logic applies to this observation except in the opposite direction. Based on relative risk analysis, it appears that too few resources are being used to control pesticides and other chemicals.

---

[31] U.S. EPA, Office of Policy Analysis, Office of Policy, Planning and Evaluation (February 1987). The conclusions of a follow-up study are reported in U.S. EPA, Science Advisory Board (September 1990).

| TABLE 19.4 | | | | | |
|---|---|---|---|---|---|

**RISK RANKINGS FOR SELECTED ENVIRONMENTAL PROBLEMS**

| Problem | Expert Risk Ranking | | | | Public Risk Ranking |
|---|---|---|---|---|---|
| | Cancer Risk | Noncancer Health Risk | Ecological Effects | Welfare Effects | Overall |
| Active hazardous waste site | 2 | Low | Low | Medium | High |
| Inactive hazardous waste site | 2 | Low | Medium | Medium | High |
| Nonhazardous waste site: municipal | 3 | Medium | Medium | Medium | Not ranked |
| Nonhazardous waste site: industrial | 2 | Medium | Medium | Low | Not ranked |
| Accidental releases of toxics | 4 | High | Medium | Low | High |
| Releases from storage tanks | 3 | Low | Low | Low | Not ranked |
| Pesticide residues | 1 | High | High | Minor | Moderate |
| Other pesticide risks | 2 | Medium | High | Medium | Moderate |
| New toxic chemicals | 2 | Not ranked | Not ranked | Minor | Not ranked |
| Consumer product exposure | 1 | High | Not ranked | Minor | Low |
| Worker chemical exposure | 1 | High | Not ranked | Minor | Moderate |

NOTE: Cancer rankings are on a scale of 1 through 5, with rank 1 being the highest relative risk and rank 5 being a "not assessed" or "no risk" rank.

SOURCE: U.S. Environmental Protection Agency, Office of Policy Analysis, Office of Policy, Planning and Evaluation. *Unfinished Business: A Comparative Assessment of Environmental Problems.* Washington, DC: February 1987.

## Evaluating the Evidence

If we consider the results of the environmental risk analysis along with the national cost data discussed above, we can make three important observations about U.S. policy on solid waste and toxic chemicals:

- There is reason to believe that economic resources are being misallocated across environmental risks.

- National policy appears to be motivated at least in part by public perception of risk.

- Inadequate data and uncertainty limit the policy analysis.

Each of these observations is discussed briefly below.

**Misallocation of Resources.** Given an overall policy objective to reduce environmental risk, the benefits of regulation are appropriately measured

| TABLE 19.5 | GENERAL OBSERVATIONS AND RECOMMENDATIONS BY THE EPA TASK FORCE ON RELATIVE ENVIRONMENTAL RISKS |
|---|---|

1. No environmental problems were ranked consistently "high" or "low" across all four risk types.

2. The project has developed a useful tool to help set priorities.

3. Risks and EPA's current program priorities do not always match. In part, these differences seem to be explainable by public opinion on the seriousness of different environmental problems.

   • Areas of high risk/low EPA effort:
     Radon, indoor air pollution, stratospheric ozone depletion, global warming, accidental releases of toxics, consumer and worker exposure to chemicals, nonpoint sources of water pollution, and "other" pesticide risks.

   • Areas of medium or low risk/high EPA effort:
     Active (RCRA) and inactive (Superfund) hazardous waste sites, releases from storage tanks, and municipal nonhazardous waste.

4. Statutory authorities do not match neatly with risks.

5. National rankings do not necessarily reflect local situations—local analyses are needed.

6. Some chemicals show up as major concerns in multiple problem areas, notably lead, chromium, formaldehyde, solvents, and some pesticides.

7. More research is needed in several areas. The general weakness of exposure data is a special problem because exposure is such an important determinant of risk. In addition, specific data on the different types of risks and environmental problems are often lacking.

8. EPA should now study other areas important to setting priorities.

SOURCE: U.S. Environmental Protection Agency, Office of Policy Analysis, Office of Policy, Planning and Evaluation. *Unfinished Business: A Comparative Assessment of Environmental Problems.* Washington, DC: U.S. Government Printing Office, February 1987, pp. 94–100.

by the risk reduction achieved. Based on benefit–cost analysis, resources should be allocated to balance the incremental benefits, or the reduction in risk, with the incremental costs of achieving them. Yet, the results of the risk-ranking study suggest that the high costs of implementing RCRA and Superfund are not justified by the expected risk reduction, which is low relative to other environmental hazards. Put another way, the comparative risk analysis suggests that resources may be being *overallocated* to solid waste pollution control.[32] Of course, if too many resources are being allocated to solid waste problems, then it must be the case that too few are being used to satisfy other needs. It may be that the misallocation is *between* government and the private sector, meaning that public policies are overfunded. Indeed, this is a common criticism. However, such a broad assertion is difficult to verify at best. What we can consider is how the allocation of resources *among* environmental public policies might be improved, based on the existing distribution between private and public uses.

Reexamine the list of "high risk/low EPA effort" problems identified by the task force in Table 19.5. Of particular relevance to the present investigation are the chemical-related hazards included in this list. The implication is that government should intensify its efforts under TSCA and FIFRA where there is greater opportunity for risk reduction. In fact, of the chemical-related problems in the "high risk/low EPA effort" category, worker exposure to chemicals is tied for first in the cancer risk-ranking and ranked as "high" in the noncancer health risk category. Assuming the risk rankings are accurate, society would gain by transferring some resources away from those hazards where the risks are relatively low and reallocating them toward problems where the risks are higher. In theory, this transfer process should continue until the marginal benefit of reducing risk is the same across all environmental hazards in accordance with the equimarginal principle of optimality.[33]

Although the evidence is far from complete, it seems reasonable to argue that the current standards specified by RCRA and Superfund may have erred on the side of being too stringent and that the controls under TSCA and FIFRA may be too lax. Hence, the costs of achieving these statutory standards cannot likely be justified on economic grounds.

**Public Perception and Policy Making.** Since it appears that allocative efficiency is not governing national priorities on the environment, we ought to consider what might be influencing these decisions. Referring back to Table 19.4, notice that there are major differences between the risk ranking of experts and that of the general public. Furthermore, the intensity of EPA efforts to combat environmental problems is more consistent with public *perception* of risk than it is with *actual* environmental risk. In fact, this

---

[32]There is an important caveat here. As the task force indicates in their final observations, the "low risk/high EPA effort" areas may be indicating that the risks are low *because* of the intensified national effort. If so, some continuance of control efforts may be needed to maintain reduced risk. The issue hinges on whether the marginal benefit of further controls is justified by the marginal costs. In any case, the findings call for further investigation of how national resources are being allocated across competing needs.

[33]Notice that such a reallocation is based on relative rankings of just regulated environmental problems. Hence, the result would optimize the environmental risk reduction possible from government efforts based on a *given* distribution of resources. A general solution could be determined only from a benefit–cost analysis across *all* competing uses and across all economic sectors. Were this empirically possible, one might determine that government uses too many resources for all of its programs as is commonly suggested.

assertion was one of the major conclusions of the EPA report as Table 19.5 indicates.

Consider, for example, the experts' risk ranking of active hazardous waste sites. The experts classify the associated cancer risk in category 2 of 5, adding that fewer than one 100 cases of cancer per year should result nationwide.[34] They also give the problem a low ranking for noncancer risks and for ecological effects. Yet national efforts to control these sites through RCRA is high, and so too is the public perception of the associated risks. A similar argument applies to the mismatch of expert risk ranking for inactive hazardous waste sites relative to the intensity of national effort and the associated costs to control them. Yet again, the public perceives the associated risks as high.

**Limitations of the Risk-Ranking Study.** There are important and, in some cases, disturbing findings associated with the EPA's landmark risk analysis. However, it is critical to understand not only what the study accomplishes but also what its limitations are. As the task force points out in its report, risk assessment data are not complete, and methods for assessing noncancer and ecological risks are not well-defined. There is a need for further research to advance scientific knowledge about environmental hazards and the implications of short- and long-term exposure. In the interim, given the limited data and the scientific uncertainty, evaluations about U.S. policy on solid waste and toxics cannot be made without reservation.

Another qualification of the risk-ranking analysis is that some intangible aspects of risk were not considered. For example, the study did not account for the extent to which certain risks are voluntary, nor did it consider any risks to the existence value of natural resources. Furthermore, the task force acknowledges that its findings were not adjusted for environmental equity. In fact, one of the concluding observations is that national risk rankings are not always indicative of local conditions, and that these must be considered in setting environmental priorities at nonfederal levels of government.[35] Some environmental problems affect certain geographical regions or specific segments of the population more than others. Hence, analyses based on overall or national risks tend to obscure the true implications of these hazards. A case in point is the risk of exposure to hazardous waste facilities—an instance of environmental inequity discussed in Application 19.3 (p. 614).

Even accepting the study's limitations, the risk-ranking analysis strongly suggests the need for further investigation of how the federal government sets priorities for environmental policy initiatives. In the context of solid waste and toxics, it appears that the costs incurred by society to develop and implement comprehensive legislation like RCRA and Superfund relative to those associated with FIFRA and TSCA are not justified

---

[34] U.S. EPA, Office of Policy Analysis, Office of Policy, Planning and Evaluation (February 1987), p. 73.

[35] U.S. EPA, Office of Policy Analysis, Office of Policy, Planning and Evaluation (February 1987), p. 7, 97.

**APPLICATION 19.3**

# Hazardous Waste Sites: Are the Risks Disproportionate?

Unlike the effects of acid rain that can be felt by people living hundreds of miles away from the polluting source, the risks of exposure to hazardous waste tend to be localized. For example, the health effects of groundwater contamination caused by a mismanaged waste site are confined to nearby residents. On that basis alone, we know that these environmental risks are not evenly distributed across the nation. But we need to look beyond this simple observation. The operative issue is to determine if these higher-risk communities are dominated by any racial, ethnic, or income groups. If so, policy officials have to consider how to address the environmental inequity.

In 1990, the EPA formed the Environmental Equity Workgroup to study the evidence on whether certain socioeconomic groups face a disproportionate degree of environmental risk. In 1994, the agency formed the Office of Environmental Justice. Motivating these efforts is the notion that risk-based priorities should guide the direction of U.S. environmental policy. Simply put, society can gain more from environmental policy initiatives if resources are allocated to high-risk regions of the country and high-risk population groups.

As part of its two-year mission, the EPA's workgroup investigated available information on the characteristics of populations living near existing and abandoned hazardous waste facilities. Among other findings, the EPA workgroup discovered that there is a lack of good data on environmental health effects sorted on the basis of socioeconomic factors like race and income. Nonetheless, it did find that minorities and low-income groups appear to have a greater exposure to certain environmental threats, one of which is hazardous waste sites. Why are these groups more strongly represented in areas where these potentially dangerous sites are located? The reasons are complex, but among the determinants are land use decisions, historical residence patterns, and politics.

In its 1992 report, the EPA workgroup referenced a 1983 study conducted by the U.S. General Accounting Office (GAO), which focused on the socioeconomic characteristics of communities near four hazardous waste landfills in eight southeastern states. According to the GAO's findings, three out of four of the landfills cited are located in communities where more than 50 percent of the population is black. At one of these, blacks represent 90 percent of the local population. The income data are also important, indicating a fairly large proportion of the local population living below the poverty level—most of whom are black. In fact, for two of the sites, 100 percent of the families living in poverty are black.

A more recent study was conducted in 1987 by the United Church of Christ to investigate these same issues on a national scale. The results showed that minorities are more likely to live in communities where hazardous waste facilities are located. Specifically, minorities account for over 37 percent of the population in communities where one of the five largest hazardous waste landfills is located or where there is more than one treatment, storage, or disposal facility. This research did not find as strong an association for socioeconomic status as the GAO analysis discovered.

SOURCES: U.S. Environmental Protection Agency, Office of Policy, Planning, and Evaluation. *Environmental Equity: Reducing Risks for All Communities.* Washington DC, June 1992; U.S. General Accounting Office (GAO). *Siting of Hazardous Waste Landfills and Their Correlation with Racial and Economic Status of Surrounding Communities.* Washington, DC, 1983; United Church of Christ Commission for Racial Justice (UCC). *Toxic Wastes and Race in the United States: A National Report on the Racial and Socio-Economic Characteristics of Communities with Hazardous Waste Sites.* UCC, 1987.

by comparative risk analysis. Further research is needed, particularly in benefit assessment, to support and expand upon this hypothesis.

## Conclusions

Recognizing the potential risks of chemical exposure and the enormous costs of remediation efforts, the government has developed legislation aimed at controlling hazardous substances *before* they become a part of the waste stream. Although many legislative acts contribute to this effort, two of the more significant are the Federal Insecticide, Fungicide, and Rodenticide Act (FIFRA) and the Toxic Substances Control Act (TSCA). Both of these are designed to prevent the production and use of substances posing an unacceptable risk to society and to monitor the risks of those that have already been introduced to the marketplace.

Although many pesticides and toxic substances are associated with known health and ecological effects, both can and do contribute to society's well-being. Hence, it is appropriate that decision making under FIFRA and TSCA be guided by risk–benefit analysis. There are, however, practical problems that have hindered the realization of what this strategy can achieve. For example, registration decisions for new pesticides are based on risk data submitted by manufacturers, but benefits are *assumed* to justify those risks based on the registrant's willingness to pay the registration fee. There are similar flaws in the implementation of TSCA, particularly those applicable to chemicals *already* on the market.

New programs are being designed to streamline the implementation of both laws and to integrate more incentives that will encourage the production and use of safer substitutes. The direction is one that fosters pollution prevention to displace some of the reliance on treatment and cleanup. Such a shift in emphasis is supported by comparative risk analysis, particularly in light of the costs to support RCRA and Superfund relative to FIFRA and TSCA. According to this preventive approach, society has to be made to rethink how market decisions ultimately affect the size and toxicity of the waste stream. Firms must adjust how their products are designed, manufactured, and packaged, and households need to modify consumption and consider the external costs of their market decisions. Pollution prevention is an important theme in the ongoing development of environmental policy—one of several issues discussed in our concluding chapter.

## Summary

- Congress enacted the Federal Insecticide, Fungicide, and Rodenticide Act (FIFRA) in 1947. In 1972, Congress passed amendments that shifted the focus of the law to health and environmental protection.

Additional amendments in 1988 were aimed at improving registration and reregistration procedures.

- A major objective of FIFRA is to register all pesticides before they are distributed or sold. Registration is subject to EPA approval based on a risk–benefit analysis. At the time of registration, the EPA must set tolerances on the amount of a pesticide that may remain as a residue on food without causing an unacceptable health risk.

- The dominant factor in pesticide registration decisions is a risk evaluation based on data submitted by manufacturers. If risks are found to be negligible, the EPA assumes that benefits exist based on the manufacturer's willingness to absorb the registration costs.

- The Clinton administration developed a new pesticide program. The goal is to promote Integrated Pest Management (IPM), which fosters selective use of pesticides and greater reliance on natural deterrents.

- In 1976, Congress enacted the Toxic Substances Control Act (TSCA). One of the act's primary objectives is to control chemicals that present a risk to health or the environment before they are introduced into commerce. TSCA also provides for the monitoring and regulation of chemicals already on the market.

- TSCA requires chemical producers to notify the government *before* they intend to produce or import any new chemical, using a premanufacture notice (PMN). The EPA reviews each PMN to evaluate the risks and respond. If the risks are too high, the EPA may restrict usage of the chemical.

- For existing chemicals, TSCA requires manufacturers to notify the EPA if any chemical is found to present a substantial risk to human health or the environment.

- The United States is planning to revise the TSCA program. Among the proposals is a Product Stewardship Rulemaking, which would require chemical producers to share risk information with their customers and to conduct hazard evaluations on the substances customers use. This proposal is part of a plan to replace single chemical procedures with multimedia, multichemical approaches.

- Aggregate cost data on solid waste controls exhibit a strong positive trend between 1972 and 1987, which reflects the strengthening of U.S. policy since the mid-1970s. Aggregate control costs for FIFRA and TSCA are much smaller, but they have increased dramatically over the same period.

- According to an EPA risk-ranking study, federal resources might be *overallocated* to solid waste control and *underallocated* to the regulation of toxic substances and pesticide use. These findings imply that the social costs of RCRA and Superfund relative to those of FIFRA and TSCA may not be justified by comparative risk analysis.

## Key Concepts

pesticide registration
risk–benefit analysis
pesticide tolerances
pesticide reregistration
Integrated Pest Management
  (IPM)
TSCA inventory

new chemical
premanufacture notice (PMN)
Product Stewardship Rulemaking
multimedia, multichemical
  approach
comparative risk analysis

## Review Questions

1. a. Critically compare and contrast the policy approaches of TSCA and FIFRA.
   b. In your view, which of these is more effective in preventing pollution? Explain.

2. Suggest two market-based instruments that would support Clinton's plan for reduced pesticide use. Explain.

3. Reconsider the proposal for Product Stewardship Rulemaking under TSCA. Explain how natural market incentives might encourage compliance with such a ruling. Are there any motivations that operate in the opposite direction? Explain.

4. In 1976, the United States banned the manufacture of PCBs. Propose an alternative policy that would effectively reduce society's exposure to these cancer-causing substances. Support your proposal by discussing two of its strong points. Realistically, why might opponents argue against your idea?

5. a. If you were to plan an empirical study of the benefits of RCRA and Superfund, how would you categorize the primary social benefits?
   b. How, if at all, would your answer differ if you were to do the same type of study for FIFRA and TSCA? Explain.

6. Critically evaluate the EPA's risk-ranking study. Cite one major accomplishment of this analysis and one major failure. Support your answer from a policy perspective.

# Additional Readings

Ely, Clausen. "The Delaney Clause: Point/Counterpoint: An Obscure EPA Policy Is to Blame." *EPA Journal* 19(1), January/February/March 1993, pp. 44–45.

Geyelin, Milo. "Pollution Suits Raise Charges of Racism." *Wall Street Journal*, October 29, 1997, p. B3.

Gutfeld, Rose. "Pesticide Use Would Be Cut Under U.S. Plan." *Wall Street Journal*, June 28, 1993.

Hamilton, James T. "Testing for Environmental Racism: Prejudice, Profits, Political Power?" *Journal of Policy Analysis and Management* 14(1), 1995, pp. 107–32.

Kong, Dolores. "Pesticide Debate About to Resume." *Boston Globe*, September 6, 1993.

Macauley, Molly K., Michael D. Bowes, and Karen L. Palmer. *Using Economic Incentives to Regulate Toxic Substances*. Washington, DC: Resources for the Future, 1992.

Mendeloff, John M. *The Dilemma of Toxic Substance Regulation*. Cambridge, MA: MIT Press, 1988.

Meyerhoff, Al. "The Delaney Clause: Point/Counterpoint: Let's Reform a Failed Food Safety Regime." *EPA Journal* 19(1), January/February/March 1993, pp. 42–43.

Schierow, Linda-Jo. "Risk Analysis and Cost–Benefit Analysis of Environmental Regulations." *Congressional Research Service, Report for Congress*. December 2, 1994.

U.S. Congress. Office of Technology Assessment (OTA). *Green Products by Design: Choices for a Cleaner Environment*. Washington, DC: U.S. Government Printing Office, October 1992.

Weber, Peter. "A Place for Pesticides?" *World Watch*, May/June 1992, pp. 18–25.

Wilson, James D. "Resolving the 'Delaney Paradox.'" *Resources* 123, Fall 1996, pp. 14–17.

# Related Web Sites

| | |
|---|---|
| EPA pesticide programs | **www.epa.gov/pesticides/** |
| Federal Insecticide, Fungicide, and Rodenticide Act (FIFRA) | **www.law.cornell.edu/uscode/7/ch6.html** |
| Food Quality Protection Act (FQPA) of 1996 | **www.epa.gov/oppfead1/fqpa/** |
| Information on Environmental Justice | **www.epa.gov/swerosps/ej/** |
| Information on pesticide registration | **www.epa.gov/pesticides/chemreg.htm** |
| List of banned and severely restricted pesticides | **www.epa.gov/oppfead1/international/piclist.htm** |
| Toxic Substances Control Act (TSCA) | **www.law.cornell.edu/uscode/15/ch53.html** |

# Appendix:
# A Reference to Acronyms in
# Toxic Substances Policy Control

## Environmental Science Acronyms

| | |
|---|---|
| DDT | Dichloro-diphenyl-trichloroethane |
| EDB | Ethylene dibromide |
| PCBs | Polychlorinated biphenyls |

## Environmental Policy Acronyms

| | |
|---|---|
| CERCLA | Comprehensive Environmental Response, Compensation, and Liability Act |
| CERCLIS | Comprehensive Environmental Response, Compensation, and Liability Information System |
| FDA | Food and Drug Administration |
| FFDCA | Federal Food, Drug, and Cosmetic Act |
| FIFRA | Federal Insecticide, Fungicide, and Rodenticide Act |
| FQPA | Food Quality Protection Act |
| GAO | Government Accounting Office |
| IPM | Integrated Pest Management |
| NAS | National Academy of Sciences |
| NPL | National Priorities List |
| OSHA | Occupational Safety and Health Administration |
| OTA | Office of Technology Assessment |
| PMN | Premanufacture notice |
| RCRA | Resource Conservation and Recovery Act |
| TSCA | Toxic Substances Control Act |
| USDA | U.S. Department of Agriculture |

# VII

# *Environmental Management in Transition*

As society learned about environmental damage and the associated risks, it recognized that economic advance and industrialization were largely responsible for the pollution problems it confronted. Such a realization seemed to suggest an unacceptable tradeoff between competing social objectives—economic prosperity and environmental quality. Economic growth is not a goal that many consider to be optional, nor are advances such as air travel, electricity, computer technology, and telecommunications. Nonetheless, most saw the need for policy initiatives that would improve environmental quality and reduce the risk of exposure to hazards like urban smog, polluted rivers and streams, and abandoned hazardous waste sites.

The thrust of the policy response was to use "end-of-pipe" controls on the pollutants released into the environment. Although this approach has yielded some measure of progress, public officials and policy analysts have been concerned about the enormous costs, the unattained policy goals, and the conflict between economic growth and environmental protection. Over time, many revisions have been drafted and numerous new programs launched. Incentives displaced some command-and-control instruments, integrated programs replaced some pollutant- and media-specific initiatives, and prevention has superseded treatment as a waste management option. Taken together, these trends speak to a transition in policy development toward broader, longer-term solutions to environmental damage. The aim is to reconcile the goals of environmental quality and economic prosperity.

In retrospect, it is easy to be critical of what has at times been a painstakingly slow policy development process. But in truth, some of the accomplishments were a direct result of learning—sometimes the hard way—from mistakes and failures. Believing that experience is perhaps the best teacher, we have reason to be optimistic about the direction of environmental policy both nationally and internationally. The wisdom of that experience, coupled with scientific advances and technological innovation, can bring about significant change. Perhaps more importantly, environmental objectives have broadened to consider the future along with the present and to accommodate global interests along with national and local needs. Such is the fundamental premise of sustainable development—a goal to integrate economic prosperity with environmental preservation as a legacy to future generations.

In this final chapter, we examine the strategic approach now evolving in the United States and elsewhere to meet the objective of sustainable development. Although there is much that has yet to be defined, several themes are beginning to emerge. Among them are efforts to advance environmental literacy, a redefinition of policy toward prevention, and the development of cooperative initiatives between the public and private sectors and among nations. Mindful of what has been accomplished and what remains to be done, we explore these themes that characterize what many view as an important transition in environmental management.

# 20

# Strategic Planning for Sustainable Development

Direct regulation of economic activity has characterized much of the evolution of U.S. environmental policy. While this command-and-control approach has contained the problem, most recognize that the nation's reliance on "end-of-pipe" controls does not adequately address the long-term implications of environmental damage. Furthermore, this approach does not accommodate the broader objective of sustainable development—achieving environmental quality *and* economic prosperity.

The comprehensive goal of sustainable development calls for fundamental changes in how society makes market decisions—both in production and consumption. The challenge is to achieve economic prosperity but alter market activity so that natural resources and the environment are protected. Effecting changes of this magnitude calls for a much different policy approach than one that relies on rules and limits—control instruments that often run counter to the polluter's market incentive. If society is going to sustain a long-term commitment to preserving the earth, there has to be a motivation to do so beyond the avoidance of penalties for regulatory noncompliance.

Logically, the motivation should be consistent with economic incentives. The premise is that economic growth and environmental quality can be reinforcing rather than competing objectives. Perceptions must be changed to recognize that resource conservation and pollution abatement can enhance private as well as social interests. Communication must be improved to share information about technologies, inputs, and processes that can protect the environment without diminishing profitability. If successful, cooperation should displace what is sometimes an adversarial position between the public and private sectors of society, and there should be less reliance on costly monitoring and enforcement procedures.

Such a change in direction and attitude calls for a long-term strategic plan that involves all sectors of society. Several broad-based efforts are under way in the United States and elsewhere to begin the process. Among these are initiatives to promote pollution prevention and thus avoid unnecessary and costly abatement and remediation. At the same time, environmental literacy is being advanced—to educate society about the effects of environmental damage and to encourage responsible decision making. Environmental technologies are being developed and an infrastructure established to share these advances throughout the global community. As these and other efforts are taking root, cooperative arrangements are forming between the public and private sectors and among nations that are consistent with the long-term goal of sustainable development.

In this concluding chapter, we explore this transitional phase in environmental policy—both its objectives and its strategic implementation. To understand the motivation of sustainable development, we revisit the materials balance model introduced originally in Chapter 1. Recall that this model illustrates the link between economic activity and the natural environment, which is critical to the achievement of sustainable development. We then study several trends that indicate how environmental policy is being redirected to consider this broader objective. In this part of our analysis, we focus on pollution prevention strategies, international cooperative arrangements, domestic partnerships, and information and technology transfer.

# Sustainable Development

**environmental quality** A reduction in anthropogenic contamination to an "acceptable" level.

Over the past several decades of environmental policy development, the clear focus has been to achieve **environmental quality** by reducing anthropogenic pollution to a level that is "acceptable" to society. Policy makers have struggled with the tough issue of "how clean is clean" and the challenge of devising cost-effective instruments to achieve whatever quality level has been set. Through revisions, political debate, and a growing social consciousness, there has been some progress and a number of shifts in policy development. Yet there has also been an increasing awareness of the need for change more fundamental than periodic revisions of legislative provisions—a redefinition of environmental policy objectives. A consensus is forming that both public and private decision making should be driven by a broader goal that is global in scope and dynamic in perspective. One such goal is **sustainable development**—managing the earth's resources such that their long-term quality and abundance is assured for future generations.[1] To analyze why this transition represents a significant

**sustainable development** Management of the earth's resources such that their long-term quality and abundance is assured for future generations.

---

[1] To learn more about this objective, visit the UN's sustainable development Web site at **www.un.org/esa/sustdev/**.

**FIGURE 20.1**

## REVISITING THE MATERIALS BALANCE MODEL: THE IMPLICATIONS FOR SUSTAINABLE DEVELOPMENT

The materials balance model exemplifies the dynamic relationship between economic activity and nature. Resources flow from nature to an economic system, and by-products or residuals from economic activity represent the return flow back to the environment. Conventional environmental policy uses "end-of-pipe" instruments aimed at controlling the amount of polluting residuals released to the environment. These policies can improve environmental quality in the short run, but they do not adequately address the long-run consequences—the potential for intertemporal trade-offs between one generation and the next. In the long run, society must find ways to reconcile economic growth and environmental quality, which is the underlying premise of sustainable development.

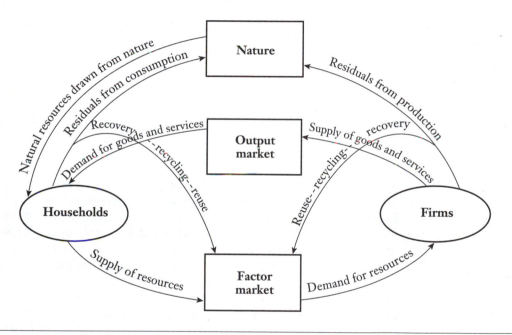

SOURCE: Adapted from Allen V. Kneese, Robert U. Ayres, and Ralph C. D'Arge. *Economics and the Environment: A Materials Balance Approach*. Washington, DC: Resources for the Future, 1970.

**materials balance model** Depiction of the dynamic relationship between economic decision making and the natural environment.

change in environmental policy development, we reintroduce the **materials balance model,** which we studied initially in Chapter 1.

### Revisiting the Materials Balance Model

Figure 20.1 reproduces the **materials balance model,** which exemplifies the dynamic relationship between economic activity and nature. Recall that

FIGURE 20.2

## THE CONVENTIONAL LINEAR
## PERSPECTIVE OF MATERIALS FLOW

The aim of performance- or technology-based standards is to control the amount of polluting residuals released to the environment. Implicit in this approach is a perception that the flow of materials through the economy is *linear*, as illustrated below. As the graphic shows, this view assumes that materials run in *one* direction, entering an economic system as inputs and leaving as wastes or residuals. Hence, the policy focus is on abating contaminating residuals at the end of the flow.

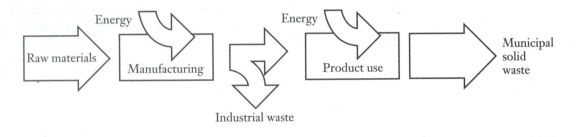

SOURCE: U.S. Congress, Office of Technology Assessment (OTA). *Green Products by Design: Choices for a Cleaner Environment*. Washington, DC: U.S. Government Printing Office, October 1992 as cited in John Gibbons. "Moving Beyond the 'Tech Fix.'" *EPA Journal* 18(4), September/October 1992, p. 31.

this relationship is defined by the flow of resources from nature to an economic system and the return flow of residuals from economic activity back to the environment. Throughout our study of environmental economics, we have focused on the flow of residuals and the potential damages associated with their release to nature. Of primary interest has been an analysis of policy aimed at achieving environmental quality by controlling the size and toxicity of this flow. At this point, we use the materials balance model to explain how these initiatives are short-term and hence inadequate to accommodate the broader aim of sustainable development.

### A Short-Term Policy Approach

As we have discussed throughout the text, the conventional approach of environmental policy is the use of "end-of-pipe" command-and-control instruments to improve **environmental quality.** Relying primarily on performance- or technology-based standards, the aim has been to control the amount of polluting residuals released to the environment *after* they are generated. Implicit in this approach is a perception that the flow of materials through the economy is a linear one, as illustrated in Figure 20.2. As the graphic shows, this view assumes that materials run in *one* direction, entering an economic system as inputs and leaving as wastes or residuals. Hence, policy has focused on abating contaminating residuals at the end of the flow. For example, U.S. clean air policy attempts to control harmful residuals released into the atmosphere, officially termed criteria and hazardous air pollutants. Similarly, national clean water initiatives seek to control toxic, conventional, and nonconventional pollutants released as effluents into waterways. And solid waste policy focuses on managing the hazardous and nonhazardous waste stream, including its final disposal back to nature. Although these policies can improve environmental quality in the short run, they do not adequately address the long-run consequences. To explain why, consider the dynamics of the materials balance model in the context of policy initiatives.

First, nature's capacity to convert matter and energy is limited. Although residuals can be converted to other forms that can flow back into productive use, this process is not without bound. Hence, policy decisions affecting resource use and environmental damage have implications for future generations. Government programs to promote recovery and reuse of residuals shown by the inner flows in Figure 20.1 have helped to delay their release but have not eliminated them. Second, end-of-pipe controls rely mainly on treatment of polluting residuals *after* they are created. Such methods draw resources away from other productive activities—resources that ultimately are added to the residual flow. Third, command-and-control initiatives generally operate at cross-purposes with private market incentives and the broader social goal of economic growth. This observation points to the potential for intertemporal trade-offs between one generation and the next. The pursuit of economic development today can so harm the natural environment as to leave future generations less able to continue that progress. On the other hand, restricting the pursuit of economic gains to protect the environment deprives today's society as well as future generations of a higher standard of living.

What all of this suggests is that environmental policy must consider the long run. The materials balance model reminds us that nature and the circular flow of economic activity are closely linked, and this linkage is a dynamic one. Just as it is foolhardy to pursue economic growth without regard for the environmental implications over time, so too is it irrational to pursue environmental objectives that ignore the future economic consequences. An example of the potential conflict is discussed in Application 20.1 (p. 628), which focuses on the controversy surrounding government subsidies to support the timber industry.

### Moving toward the Long Run: Sustainable Development

Sustainable development is based on the premise that economic growth and environmental quality must be reconciled. Statistical estimates on

APPLICATION 20.1

## The Potential Conflict between Economic Gain and Environmental Quality

One federal subsidy that has been the subject of recent public debate and media attention is the below-cost timber sale program. Administered by the U.S. Forest Service, this program grants companies the right to cut timber on federal lands at reduced costs. Environmentalists believe that this federal program has encouraged the practice of clear-cutting, causing severe soil erosion and threatening ecosystems and the already tenuous future of endangered species. Characterized as the controversy over the plight of the northern spotted owl, the much-publicized debate actually has much broader concerns. Among these is the allegation that federal subsidies foster the use of virgin resources, effectively discouraging the use of recycled materials.

Beyond the environmental implications, the timber subsidy program has also been questioned on economic grounds. In its sale of public timber, the Forest Service is not obligated to recover the federal government's cost of cultivating and marketing the valuable timber. Consequently, although its enormous assets would give it a top-five position in the *Fortune* 500, its pricing policies would classify it as bankrupt in the private sector. In practice, the sale of publicly owned timber is subsidized according to one of three methods: (1) charging a sale price based on the industry's ability to pay versus the timber's market value; (2) assigning a price based solely on the government's cost; or (3) using public funds to finance access roads for harvesting.

Responding to strong arguments on a number of fronts, the Clinton administration suggested the possibility of reducing or even eliminating the timber subsidy program. But the eventual outcome of such a proposal is not entirely predictable. In fact, the EPA has identified several possible scenarios, each of which would have very different impacts on the economy and on national recycling objectives. First, the timber industry might be able to maintain current production levels by reducing other operating costs to counter the effect of the subsidy reduction. As a result, there would be no effect on alternative markets or on the nation's recycling efforts. Second, it could encourage more efficient use of existing supplies and an overall reduction in lumber consumption. Third, the cost effect could precipitate a market shift away from domestic suppliers toward lower-cost foreign producers. Finally, there may be a substitution effect toward other domestic products, including recycled lumber materials.

While no one can forecast the future of the timber subsidy or the related market implications, most observers argue that such programs are in need of reform. Tax preferences such as these, however well intended, create market distortions. In this case, the subsidies embedded in the below-cost timber sales undervalue our nation's forests, setting up an artificial signal to use virgin materials over recycled substitutes. This distortion has serious implications. Overharvesting of national forests jeopardizes the long-term supply of timber, threatens the future of biological species, and endangers the overall quality of the environment.

SOURCES: Timothy E. Wirth and John Heinz. *Project 88—Round II Incentives for Action: Designing Market-Based Environmental Strategies.* Washington, DC: May 1991, pp. 77–86; Randal O'Toole. *Reforming the Forest Service.* Washington, DC: Island Press, 1988; U.S. Congress, Office of Technology Assessment (OTA). *Facing America's Trash: What Next for Municipal Solid Waste?* Washington, DC: U.S. Government Printing Office, 1989, Chapter 5; U.S. Environmental Protection Agency, Office of Policy, Planning, and Evaluation. *Economic Incentives: Options for Environmental Protection,* Washington, DC, March 1991, pp. 5-33–5-39; Michael Kranish. "Clinton Treads into Forests Dispute." *Boston Globe,* April 3, 1993, p. 3.

worldwide population and income growth help to explain why this is important. First, according to one article, per capita income levels have to grow by at least 2 percent per year to reduce world poverty and close the gap between the rich and poor. Second, world population is growing at about 1.7 percent each year, a rate that is expected to decline only very slowly. Collectively, these statistics indicate that economic growth has to be achieved. Hence, to avoid further pollution and natural resource depletion, the associated environmental impact per unit of income must decline at a rate between 3.5 and 4 percent per year.[2] We can generalize the relevant relationship at a point in time as follows:[3]

$$\frac{\text{Environment}}{\text{impact}} = \frac{\text{Income}}{\text{per capita}} \times \frac{\text{Environmental impact}}{\text{per unit of income}} \times \text{Population}$$

Developing countries face more urgent conditions, struggling to advance economically to accommodate a rapidly rising population and at the same time confronted with the environmental contamination that these pursuits have exacerbated. For example, recent projections estimate an annual population growth through 2025 of 4.7 percent for Nigeria, 2.8 percent for Bangladesh, and 1.8 percent for India and Mexico.[4] Higher population necessarily increases the demand for goods and services. If an economy's productive capacity cannot accommodate the population growth, shortages arise and resources are misused in an attempt to compensate for the imbalance.[5]

In the context of the materials balance model, we know that population growth and economic development increase the flow of resources into market activity and the return flow of residuals back to nature. These changes can adversely affect the well-being of future generations if present decision making is not mindful of the long run. Part of the answer is to recognize that the flow of materials through an economy need not be linear. Instead, product design, manufacturing processes, and energy use can be modified so that materials flow through more of a closed system, as shown in Figure 20.3 (p. 630). Notice that this model suggests a much broader approach to environmental protection than controlling residuals *after* they after been generated. This alternative perspective illustrates how economic activity can be altered *throughout* the cycle of production and consumption to achieve a reduction in the associated environmental impact. A potential

---

[2] Nitze (April–June 1993).

[3] This relationship is just an identity, which is more apparent when the equation is rewritten using ratios, as follows:

$$\frac{\text{Environment}}{\text{impact}} = \frac{\text{Income}}{\text{Population}} \times \frac{\text{Environmental impact}}{\text{Income}} \times \text{Population}$$

[4] United Nations Population Division (1993) and International Labour Office (1993) as cited in World Resources Institute (1994b), Table 16.1, pp. 268–69.

[5] For a classic article illuminating the environmental implications of population growth, see Hardin (1968).

<table>
<tr><td>FIGURE 20.3</td></tr>
</table>

## MOVING TOWARD A CLOSED SYSTEM OF MATERIALS FLOW

This model of the materials flow suggests a more comprehensive approach to environmental protection than controlling residuals *after* they have been generated. Instead, this perspective illustrates how economic activity can be altered *throughout* the cycle of production and consumption to reduce the associated environmental impact. Product design, manufacturing processes, and energy use can be modified so that materials flow through more of a closed system.

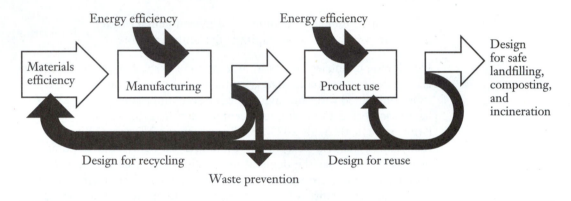

SOURCE: U.S. Congress, Office of Technology Assessment (OTA). *Green Products by Design: Choices for a Cleaner Environment*. Washington, DC: U.S. Government Printing Office, October 1992, as cited in John Gibbons. "Moving Beyond the 'Tech Fix.'" *EPA Journal* 18(4), September/October 1992, p. 31.

**industrial ecosystem** Closed system of manufacturing whereby the wastes of one process are reused as inputs.

outcome of such a strategy is the formation of **industrial ecosystems** whereby residuals from one process are reused as inputs for another.[6] Application 20.2 discusses this concept and reports on several applications of its use in the United States and Denmark.

Sustainable development is an ambitious pursuit. Fundamental to its achievement are changes in how market activity is undertaken within the circular flow and in how environmental policy is drafted. The key is to modify behavior so that economic growth and environmental protection become reinforcing rather than competing goals. Although the needed changes will take time to orchestrate, several initiatives being developed in the United States and elsewhere are moving public and private efforts in this direction.[7] One of these is the promotion of strategies to *prevent* rather than *control* pollution.

---

[6] Frosch (1995) and Frosch and Gallopoulos (1989).

[7] To learn about President Clinton's Council on Sustainable Development, visit **www.whitehouse.gov/ PCSD/**.

# Industrial Ecosystems: When a Bad Becomes a Good

The generation and disposal of production wastes has become a national concern and, as a consequence, the focus of a new manufacturing concept called the industrial ecosystem. This strategic approach to industrial manufacturing arises from the premise that the conventional input–output process can be perceived as a closed system such that the residuals generated from one production process are used as raw inputs for another. This link between processes might occur within a single firm or among several different entities. Overall, the concept is in keeping with the broader concept of sustainable development, which promotes the achievement of both economic growth and environmental preservation. As such, it is directed toward two major objectives. The first is to employ energy and raw materials optimally to assure that each productive input achieves maximum efficiency. The second is to facilitate the reduction of waste material by minimizing the generation of nonreusable wastes that occur as part of the manufacturing function.

Some U.S. firms have already begun to alter their processes so that their wastes can be recycled for use either internally or by other companies. For example, one of ARCO's oil refinery facilities has saved about $2 million per year by selling some of what were formerly hazardous wastes to chemical companies, cement makers, and acid manufacturers. Applying the same general strategy, Dow Chemical has found a way to recover hydrochloric acid, which is then reused internally or sold to other entities. The result is a significant reduction in the release of acid wastes to the environment *and* a $20-million return to Dow. DuPont, the largest chemical manufacturer in the world, found a thriving market for some of its nylon production wastes in the pharmaceuticals and coatings industries.

Obviously, the shift toward "closing the loop" in manufacturing calls for coordination between the industrial participants. Consider the experience of a group of five entities cooperating within a closed manufacturing system in Denmark. The five participants are the city of Kalundborg, a refinery, a power plant, an enzyme plant, and a wallboard manufacturer. Just as the concept suggests, the participants are linking their manufacturing processes together to save resources, energy, and the environment. Three waste by-products are produced by the coal-fired electrical power plant: surplus steam, fly ash, and surplus heat. In a conventional manufacturing environment, these wastes would simply be disposed of. However, as a result of establishing a "closed-loop" manufacturing environment, the surplus steam is sold to the local enzyme plant and the oil refinery for use in their respective manufacturing processes. This arrangement helps to conserve water supplies, which are pumped from a lake seven miles away. Similarly, the surplus heat is sold by the utility to the city of Kalundborg for its heating needs. The fly ash associated with the utility's pollution control equipment is actually a composition of limestone. This is sold to a wallboard manufacturer, which uses it in place of imported gypsum.

Ultimately, innovative systems such as these help in the effort to achieve sustainable development. Arguably, this is a mutually beneficial concept to all participants that also offers important benefits to society as a whole.

SOURCES: Robert A. Frosch and Nicholas E. Gallopoulos. "Strategies for Manufacturing." *Scientific American* 261(3), September 1989, pp. 144–52; Emily T. Smith and David Woodruff. "The Next Trick for Business: Taking a Cue from Nature." *Business Week*, May 11, 1992, pp. 74–75; Stephan Schmidheiny. *Changing Course: A Global Business Perspective on Development and the Environment.* Cambridge, MA: MIT Press, 1992, p. 105.

# Pollution Prevention

There is an old adage that says, *"An ounce of prevention is worth a pound of cure."* This time-honored advice is now being used to help achieve sustainable development. Recent U.S. policy initiatives have begun to emphasize preventive measures that eliminate the release of contaminating residuals and hence avoid having to deal with the associated adverse effects after the fact. According to an EPA directive, **pollution prevention** refers to:

**pollution prevention** Practices that reduce or eliminate the creation of contaminating residuals at the source.

> ". . . the use of materials, processes, or practices that reduce or eliminate the creation of pollutants or wastes at the source. [This] includes practices that reduce the use of hazardous materials, energy, water or other resources, and practices that protect natural resources through conservation or more efficient use."[8]

Based on this definition, pollution prevention promotes a shift from "end-of-pipe" controls to "front-end reduction" strategies. Effectively, this implies that residual generation is a strategic variable and not simply a given to be dealt with after the fact. In the context of the materials balance model, preventive strategies change how economic activity is undertaken so that less contaminating residuals are released to nature.

Strong support for pollution prevention is offered by Barry Commoner, a scientist and director of the Center for Biology of Natural Systems at Queens College. He writes:

> "The impact of a pollutant on the environment can be remedied in two general ways: either the activity that generates the pollutant is changed to eliminate it; or, without altering the activity, a control device is added that traps or destroys the pollutant before it enters the environment . . . The few real improvements have been achieved not by adding controls or concealing pollutants but by simply eliminating them . . . This suggests an addition to the informal environmental laws: If you don't put something into the environment, it isn't there."[9]

Commoner supports his argument with references to such preventive policy initiatives as the elimination of leaded gasoline in the United States and the ban on DDT effected in 1972. Beyond these specific cases, the larger issue is to determine whether pollution prevention can and should be practiced on a broader scale.

---

[8] U.S. EPA (May 13, 1990) as cited in U.S. EPA, Office of Pollution Prevention (October 1991), p. 4.

[9] Commoner (1992), pp. 42–43.

## Moving toward Pollution Prevention: U.S. Laws and Directives

Beginning with the National Environmental Policy Act of 1969 (NEPA), the federal government has attempted to integrate prevention into U.S. environmental legislation. One of the purposes of NEPA is:

> "to promote efforts which will prevent or eliminate damage to the environment and the biosphere."

To formalize pollution prevention as an integral part of U.S. policy, Congress passed the Pollution Prevention Act of 1990.[10] Its provisions outline the *priorities* for national environmental policy as follows:

> "The Congress hereby declares it to be the national policy of the United States that pollution should be prevented or reduced at the source whenever feasible; pollution that cannot be prevented should be recycled in an environmentally safe manner, whenever feasible; pollution that cannot be prevented or recycled should be treated in an environmentally safe manner whenever feasible; and disposal or other release into the environment should be employed only as a last resort and should be conducted in an environmentally safe manner."[11]

Notice that the act ranks pollution prevention as the primary objective with management of residuals as a secondary objective to be achieved through recycling, treatment, and disposal—in that order. Beyond this prioritizing of national initiatives, the act also gives specific directives to guide the promotion of pollution prevention activities in the private and public sectors.

## Strategies to Implement Pollution Prevention

**source reduction** Any practice that lessens the amount of a hazardous substance released into the environment.

**toxic chemical use substitution** Using less harmful chemicals in place of more hazardous substances.

While pollution prevention promotes the reduction of residuals or wastes generated by all segments of society, its emphasis has been on the industrial sector—the major source of hazardous pollution. In fact, two major preventive objectives for industry are **source reduction** and **toxic chemical use substitution. Source reduction** refers to any practice that lessens the amount of a hazardous substance or contaminant that either enters the waste stream or is otherwise released into the environment *before* recycling, treatment, or disposal.[12] **Toxic chemical use substitution** refers

---

[10] For detail on the Pollution Prevention Act, see **www.law.cornell.edu/uscode/42/ch133.html**.

[11] Pollution Prevention Act of 1990, Sec. 6602(b).

[12] Pollution Prevention Act of 1990, Sec. 6603(5)(A).

to the practice of using less harmful chemicals in place of more hazardous substances.[13]

These objectives are supported by several U.S. policy initiatives. For example, source reduction is explicitly listed as the first priority in the EPA's integrated waste management system that guides states' solid waste programs. Also, the Federal Insecticide, Fungicide, and Rodenticide Act (FIFRA) promotes toxic chemical use substitution by empowering the EPA to cancel or restrict the use of any pesticide found to pose an unreasonable risk. In so doing, markets for less harmful pesticides should be created. Similar rulings are given in the Toxic Substances Control Act (TSCA) for nonpesticide chemicals.

A number of techniques have been proposed to help industry achieve the objectives of source reduction and toxic chemical use substitution. Among these are source segregation, raw materials substitution, changes in manufacturing processes, and product substitution.[14] The first of these, **source segregation** refers to any process that keeps hazardous waste from coming in contact with nonhazardous waste. This relatively simple and inexpensive method is widely used by many industries. By keeping the two types of waste materials separate, the accumulation of hazardous waste is not needlessly increased by contaminated nonhazardous waste. These efforts help generators lower their costs of managing wastes and enhance social benefits by reducing the risk of exposure.

Two other methods, **raw materials substitution** and **changes in manufacturing processes,** also hold promise for helping to prevent pollution. Both can be used by industry during the production phase of its operations. By using inputs that generate little or no hazardous waste, the size of the residual flow can be dramatically reduced. Likewise, alternative manufacturing processes can be sought or existing ones altered to generate less hazardous by-products. Finally, **product substitution,** an adjustment made *after* the production phase, refers to the selection of environmentally safe commodities over their potentially polluting substitutes.

**source segregation**
A procedure that keeps hazardous waste from coming in contact with non-hazardous waste.

**raw materials substitution** Using productive inputs that generate little or no hazardous waste.

**changes in manufacturing processes** The use of alternative production methods to generate less hazardous by-products.

**product substitution** Selection of environmentally safe commodities in place of potentially polluting products.

## The Corporate Experience[15]

As environmental regulations strengthened during the 1970s, U.S. corporations realized that increasingly stringent controls would likely follow. Recognizing the trend, some forward-thinking firms decided it would be advantageous to respond in a progressive manner rather than to simply comply with the new mandates. One of the first U.S. companies to adopt

---

[13] U.S. EPA, Office of Pollution Prevention (October 1991), p. 7. Visit **www.epa.gov/opptintr/p2home/aboutp2.htm** for information on the EPA's pollution prevention program.

[14] This discussion is drawn from U.S. EPA, Office of Solid Waste (November 1986), p. 19.

[15] Much of the following is drawn from U.S. EPA, Office of Pollution Prevention (October 1991), Chapter 3; Bringer (1988); and Kelly (November 7, 1994).

this approach was 3M Corporation, launching its "Pollution Prevention Pays Program" in 1975. Through this "3Ps Program" as it is known, the corporate giant designed an employee-based plan aimed at finding ways to reduce the company's pollution while maintaining or improving financial performance. The majority of 3M's prevention strategies are based on technological improvements, such as product reformulation, process modification, recycling, equipment redesign, and waste recovery for resale.

According to corporate officials, the payoffs of 3M's pollution prevention program have been substantial. First, the company has achieved significant reductions in the pollutants it releases into the environment. A recent corporate estimate reports that the program has been responsible for a worldwide reduction in annual releases of about 450,000 tons. In fact, in the first 14 years of the program, 3M claims that its innovative program cut pollution per unit of production in half. Second, the firm asserts that the technological changes it has introduced yielded a financial savings of over $400 million in the first year of the project's operations. Capitalizing on this success, 3M launched a companion program in 1988 called 3P+. Aimed specifically at reducing hydrocarbon emissions, the 3P+ plan calls for a $150-million capital investment that should yield results to surpass the statutory clean air requirements set by both federal and state governments. Thus far, corporate savings from its collective preventive initiatives total more than $700 million.[16]

Following the lead of 3M and other corporate leaders in environmentalism, many other companies have implemented their own pollution prevention programs. By way of example, consider the summary of selected corporate plans given in Table 20.1 along with their objectives and accomplishments. As these examples suggest, many firms seem to have recognized that pollution prevention is not only beneficial to the environment, but good for business as well.[17]

### Economic Analysis of Pollution Prevention

Polluters must determine when preventive approaches should be employed, to what extent, and through which strategy. Economic criteria and their associated decision rules are just as applicable to guiding the use of preventive strategies as they are to any other environmental policy instrument. Whether or not a firm adopts pollution prevention as part of its business strategy will depend to a large extent on its cost relative to other options, such as the use of treatment or abatement technologies. The goal

---

[16]More on 3M's corporate environmental programs can be found at **www.3m.com/profile/envt/index. html**.

[17]Likewise, the public sector is taking action to integrate pollution prevention strategies in its activities. Of particular significance are the initiatives being undertaken by the Department of Defense and the Department of Energy, both of which are discussed in U.S. EPA, Office of Pollution Prevention (October 1991), Chapter 5.

**TABLE 20.1** — CORPORATE PROGRAMS AIMED AT POLLUTION PREVENTION

| Company | Scope | Goals | Accomplishments |
|---|---|---|---|
| **Chevron**<br>Save Money and Reduce Toxics Program (SMART) 1987 | SMART adopts EPA's industrial source reduction, toxic chemical use substitution, and recycling for hazardous and nonhazardous solid wastes. | Reduce hazardous waste generation and recycle.<br><br>Find nontoxic alternatives to toxic materials and processes.<br><br>Devise safer operating procedures to reduce accidental releases.<br><br>Ensure that pollution reductions in one area do not transfer pollution to another. | From 1987 to 1990, Chevron reduced hazardous waste by 60% and saved over $10 million in disposal costs. |
| **Dow**<br>Waste Reduction Always Pays (WRAP)1986 | Industrial source reduction and on-site recycling. | Increase management support for waste reduction activities, establish a recognition and reward system for individual plants, compile waste reduction data.<br><br>Decrease SARA 313 air emissions and toxic air emissions. | SARA 313 overall releases are down from 12,252 tons in 1987 to 9,659 tons in 1989, off-site transfers are down by 15%. Air emissions have decreased by 54% from 1984. |
| **General Electric**<br>Pollution, Waste, and Emissions Reduction Program (POWER) 1989 | Program encompasses all waste streams (e.g., hazardous, nonhazardous, packaging, and ultimate disposal of product) and adopts EPA's hierarchy, which places source reduction first. | Prevent or minimize "the generation or release of waste and pollutants, to the extent technically and economically feasible, throughout the life cycle of the product, including design, production, packaging, and ultimate fate in the environment." | GE Appliances' Louisville plant has reduced its production of hazardous wastewater treatment sludge by 95%. Other GE plants have experienced similar declines in hazardous wastes and air emissions. |
| **Polaroid**<br>Toxic Use and Waste Reduction (TUWR) 1987 | Industrial source reduction and toxic chemical use substitution are priorities followed by recycling and reuse. | Reduce toxic use at the source and waste per unit of production, and emphasize increased recycling of waste materials within the company. | Using 1988 as the base year, the company reported an 11% reduction in toxic use and waste in 1989. |

SOURCE: U.S. Environmental Protection Agency, Office of Pollution Prevention. *Pollution Prevention 1991: Progress on Reducing Industrial Pollutants.* Washington, DC, October 1991, Table 3-2, pp. 45–49.

is to select the least-cost option to achieve cost-effectiveness and enhance profit. Similarly, if the firm determines that pollution prevention *is* a cost-effective option, it must then select among the available strategies to implement it using the cost-effectiveness criterion as a guide. If, for example, the firm can access nontoxic raw materials more cheaply than converting its production processes, it will pursue that strategy.

Given the importance of relative costs in this decision-making process, government can help promote pollution prevention through various means. For example, it can encourage the development of inexpensive non-toxic chemical substitutes and cost-effective production changes perhaps through grants or subsidies. It might also develop ways to enhance the communication of effective pollution prevention strategies to industry. Another approach is for government to assist firms in making accurate cost assessments about pollution prevention strategies. This is precisely the motivation of the Environmental Accounting and Capital Budgeting Project under the EPA's Design for the Environment (DfE) Program. The project is a cooperative effort among government, business, and academia aimed at improving managerial accounting and capital budgeting practices to more fully incorporate environmental considerations. In so doing, the DfE project expects that more businesses will recognize the advantages of using preventive technologies and processes.[18]

Finally, benefit–cost analysis can help determine the extent to which a given preventive strategy should be employed. Qualitatively, we can identify the associated benefits to the firm as abatement cost savings, the avoidance of regulatory penalties for noncompliance, and the gain in revenues associated with presenting an environmentally responsible image to consumers. On the cost side, the firm has to assess the search costs in identifying available options, the administrative costs in analyzing these options, engineering design expenses, and the expenditures to implement the strategy such as retooling or capital investment. To achieve the efficient level at which a pollutant is eliminated, the decision rule is the same as in other contexts. The firm should find the point where the marginal cost of doing so is exactly offset by the marginal benefit.[19]

## International Cooperative Arrangements

Sustainable development is intended to be a global objective, the benefits of which should accrue to all segments of society and to all nations. Because of its intent and its pervasive implications, it calls for a collaborative effort from all stakeholders. In this part of the chapter, we explore representative

---

[18] King and Schaeffer (July–September 1993); U.S. EPA, Office of Pollution Prevention and Toxics (October 1993). Visit **www.epa.gov/opptintr/dfe/** for more on EPA's Design for the Environment Program.

[19] For an economic analysis of pollution prevention and the hierarchy given in the Pollution Prevention Act of 1990, see Helfand (1994).

| TABLE 20.2 | A SUMMARY OF THE RIO SUMMIT'S AGENDA 21 |
| --- | --- |

**Section 1: "Social and Economic Dimensions."**

Includes recommended actions on sustainable development cooperation, poverty, consumption, demographics, health, human settlements, and integration of the environment and development in decision making.

**Section 2: "Conservation and Management of Resources for Development."**

Includes chapters on atmospheric protection, land resources, deforestation, desertification and drought, mountains, agriculture, biological diversity, biotechnology, oceans, freshwater resources, toxic chemicals, hazardous wastes, solid wastes, and radioactive wastes.

**Section 3: "Strengthening the Role of Major Groups"**

Includes ways to increase the participation in sustainable development efforts of major social groups: women, youth, indigenous peoples, nongovernmental organizations, local authorities, trade unions, business and industry, scientific and technological communities, and farmers.

**Section 4: "Means of Implementation."**

Comprises chapters on financial resources; technology transfer, cooperation, and capacity building; science; education; public awareness, and training; institutional arrangements; legal instruments and mechanisms; and information collection, analysis, and dissemination.

SOURCE: Kathy Sessions. "What's in Agenda 21?" *EPA Journal* 19(2), April–June 1993b, p. 14.

examples of international treaties and other types of cooperative agreements. Some we have discussed in other contexts, others are introduced for the first time. What they share is a joining together of national interests to promote some aspect of the dual goals of sustainable development.

### United Nations Conference on Environment and Development (UNCED) [20]

More commonly called the Rio Summit, the U.N. Conference on Environment and Development was a 12-day worldwide forum held in Rio de Janeiro, Brazil in 1992. Thousands of delegates from over 170 nations attended the event to discuss issues and concerns dealing with sustainable development. Among the major documents produced from the summit are *Agenda 21* and the *Rio Declaration*. A brief description of each follows.

*Agenda 21.* This 40-chapter document is a voluntary action plan outlining the course for worldwide progress toward sustainable development. Table 20.2 summarizes its four primary sections collectively intended to guide decision making into the 21st century. Major issues covered within the 900 pages of *Agenda 21* include: financing for developing countries; conservation and sustainable development for forests; prevention and minimi-

---

[20] The following discussion is drawn from Reilly (September–October 1992); Sessions (April–June 1993a), p. 12; and Parson, Haas, and Levy (October 1992).

zation of hazardous and solid wastes; strategies to address ocean pollution and the protection of marine life; international cooperation for technological advance; and risk assessment and management of toxic chemicals. Perhaps the most important achievement of the Rio Summit, *Agenda 21* is the result of two and one-half years of negotiations to reach an international consensus on environmental issues.

***Rio Declaration.*** This document outlines 27 principles to act as guidelines for achieving global environmental quality and economic development. For example, Principle 4 requires that environmental protection be an integral part of development, and Principle 8 calls for a reduction in "*unsustainable patterns of production and consumption.*" Reportedly, the declaration is a compromise from what was originally anticipated. The preparatory meetings were intense, often immersed in seeking a balance among the views of developing and industrialized countries. So fragile was this agreement that it was adopted at Rio without further negotiation for fear that further discussion would jeopardize what was left of the intended Earth Charter.

## International Agreements to Control Transboundary Pollution

Some pollution problems are transboundary, such as acidic deposition, ozone depletion, global warming, and some surface water pollution. Hence, contamination in one nation can travel beyond its borders—a type of international externality. In these cases, formal treaties must be negotiated and agreed to by all affected countries. Within these agreements are often rulings specifically aimed at the distinct problems of developing nations and the need for financial and technical support from their wealthier and more advanced counterparts.

**Montreal Protocol and Amendments.** Originally signed by 24 countries in September of 1987, the Montreal Protocol on Substances that Deplete the Ozone Layer is an important example of international cooperation aimed at environmental protection. Strengthened by the 1990 London Amendments and the 1992 Copenhagen Conference, this treaty is aimed at phasing out CFCs and other ozone-depleting substances. More than 160 countries have ratified the Protocol to date, accounting for over 96 percent of the world's usage of CFCs and more than 85 percent of the world population.[21] Recognizing the special problems of developing nations and at the same time the importance of gaining their support, industrialized countries set up a $160-million Interim Multilateral Fund to assist them in transitioning toward CFC-substitute technologies. They also were given a 10-year grace period to meet the targets of the agreement. An

---

[21] Dumanoski (November 26, 1992).

important accomplishment was the addition of China to the group of signatories in 1991. Its high rate of growth and enormous population mean that its commitment to the protocol is critical. Predictions indicate that China's production of CFCs at 117,000 metric tons in 1991 will more than double by 2000 if demand goes unchecked.[22]

**U.N. Framework Convention on Climate Change.** Adopted by more than 150 nations, including the United States, this convention established a baseline for a global, cooperative response to climate change. In March 1994, the treaty became legally binding following its ratification by the requisite number of 50 countries in 1993. Among the first 10 nations to ratify the agreement was China. It will need strong support from other nations to contain its rising consumption of coal and associated $CO_2$ emissions, predicted to triple over the next 35 years. A key provision, and one that continues to be debated, is a commitment by each signatory to implement a national strategy to limit greenhouse gas (GHG) emissions. Each strategy is to support the common objective of reducing emissions to their 1990 levels by 2000.[23] This provision was the focus of debate at a 1995 meeting of the U.N. Climate Conference in Berlin.

Some participants at the Berlin conference continued to support the commitment, while others argued it is inadequate. Further debate centered around the establishment of specific timetables and emissions targets. Major $CO_2$ generators like Japan and the United States were pressured to make stronger pledges to the climate control treaty, but lobbyists from these countries are concerned about what such commitments might mean to international competitiveness and domestic jobs. The conference produced little more than an agreement to conduct further negotiations called the Berlin Mandate.[24]

In December of 1997, the Kyoto Protocol was formulated. A principal result of the protocol was the setting of binding GHG emission targets for developed nations. These will become effective when 55 nations ratify the agreement. By 2008 to 2012, the United States has committed to reduce GHG emissions by 7 percent below their 1990 levels, and the European Union has agreed to a larger cut of 8 percent. These limits are to be achieved using emissions trading among nations.

**London Dumping Convention (LDC).** Ocean dumping of certain wastes, including radioactive wastes, is prohibited by the Convention on

---

[22] National Environmental Protection Agency (March 1993) as cited in World Resources Institute (1994b), p. 78.

[23] Council on Environmental Quality (January 1993), pp. 142–43; World Resources Institute (1994b), p. 202; Chandler, Makarov, and Dadi (September 1990), p. 125, as cited in World Resources Institute (1994b), p. 78.

[24] Reuters (April 8, 1995).

the Prevention of Marine Pollution by Dumping of Waste and Other Matter, commonly referred to as the London Dumping Convention (LDC). Originally decreed in November 1972, the LDC now has been ratified by 75 nations, including the United States.[25] In fact, all nations that have recently engaged in ocean dumping of radioactive wastes are contracting parties to the LDC. A discussion of some of the recent initiatives brought before the convention is the subject of Application 20.3 (p. 642).

**U.S.–Canada Air Quality Agreement.** In March 1991, an agreement was finalized between the United States and Canada to combat the problem of acid rain and visibility impairment. The agreement calls for each country to commit to national emissions caps on sulfur dioxide ($SO_2$) and nitrogen oxides ($NO_x$). The bilateral provisions also include directives to establish a forum for addressing other transboundary air quality issues. Among these are rulings for each nation to undertake research to improve understanding of their common air pollution problems and stipulations to facilitate a regular flow of information about monitoring, effects of air pollutants, and control methodologies. The U.S. commitment to these concerns is confirmed by the 1990 Clean Air Act Amendments, which refer specifically to Canada's acid rain program. The statutes call for regular reporting to Congress on the $SO_2$ and $NO_x$ emissions of all Canadian provinces participating in Canada's control program.[26]

### International Trade Agreements and Environmental Protection

International trade negotiations have always been the subject of political and economic debate. Although there are known economic advantages to trade, exchange between nations is nonetheless a complex undertaking. Trade negotiations are rarely if ever totally distinct from political objectives and national defense issues. The gains from trade can easily become clouded by protectionist attitudes fueled by differences in product safety regulations, labor laws, and nationalism. Recently, international trade discussions have triggered controversy of another sort—the potential conflict between the associated economic gains and a decline in environmental quality.

A common concern about foreign trade is that lenient labor laws and relatively low wage rates in less developed nations can adversely affect employment in more advanced countries. Similar apprehensions have arisen about differences in environmental regulations between trading partners. Production costs are lower in countries with lenient environmental standards, which can give producers there an unfair advantage relative to competitors in nations with more stringent controls. Another source of

---

[25] For more detail on the origin and content of the LDC, see National Advisory Committee on Oceans and Atmosphere (April 1984).

[26] For an economic analysis of this agreement, see Menz (1995).

**APPLICATION 20.3**

# The London Dumping Convention (LDC):
# An International Agreement on Ocean Dumping Rules

Signed over 20 years ago, the London Dumping Convention (LDC) is an international agreement to control the practice of dumping wastes at sea. It is the only such convention to which the United States is a signatory nation. The LDC has been accepted by 75 nations, among them the major industrialized countries that generate most of the wastes being dumped into the sea. The LDC controls ocean dumping through various means. It bans the ocean disposal of "black-listed" substances like mercury and cadmium. The disposal of "grey-listed" or less damaging substances are controlled through special permits, and the dumping of any other substances is managed through a general permitting system.

One of the convention's most significant achievements was a ban on the disposal of high-level nuclear waste in ocean waters. Another was a 10-year voluntary moratorium on the disposal of low-level nuclear waste, which was agreed to by the signatories in 1983. At the LDC's 1990 annual meeting, a consensus was reached to phase out ocean dumping of all industrial wastes by December 31, 1995. The phaseout was to be achieved without transferring the damage to some other environmental media. Each member nation was to be responsible for enforcing this resolution and for prosecuting any of its ships found to be in violation. At this same session, the delegates proposed that an international agreement be drafted to control land-based ocean pollution. This action is in direct response to the fact that more than 80 percent of ocean pollution is generated on land.

More recently, 44 of the 75 LDC signatories gathered at their 1992 meeting. The most significant decision to come out of this assembly was an agreement to update the rules of the convention in 1994. There are three major issues that the member nations must consider for revision: the disposal of low-level radioactive waste; the dumping of industrial waste; and the incineration of toxic liquid waste. Several countries, namely Denmark, Norway, and Iceland, submitted their collective proposal to ban all of these activities on a permanent basis. In November 1993, 37 of the signatories did vote to permanently ban the ocean disposal of low-level radioactive wastes. Although there were no votes against, five nations abstained, Belgium and four nuclear powers—China, France, Russia, and the U.K. Of greatest concern was Russia's abstention, since this nation had just one month prior dumped over 237,000 gallons of low-level radioactive waste into the Sea of Japan. Russian authorities have stated that they need international aid to help them build proper waste storage facilities on land.

There is little question that the LDC must address some difficult decisions in the months and years ahead. In fact, as these nations restrict or eliminate waste disposal at sea, they must develop alternatives that will allow the advance of industrial activity without simply transferring the environmental damage from the earth's oceans to some place on land.

SOURCES: U.S. Congress, Office of Technology Assessment (OTA). *Wastes in Marine Environments.* Washington, DC: U.S. Government Printing Office, 1987, pp. 73, 149; Associated Press. "Industrial Nations Ban Dumping Waste at Sea." *Boston Globe*, November 3, 1990, p. 7; Associated Press. "44 Nations Agree to Update Rules on Ocean Dumping." *Boston Globe*, November 14, 1992, p. 61; Edith M. Lederer. "Ban on Atomic Dumping at Sea Voted; 4 Nuclear Powers Abstain." *Boston Globe*, November 13, 1993; Associated Press. "Russia to Continue Dumping Nuclear Waste at Sea." *Boston Globe*, October 19, 1993b, p. 2.

controversy is the quality of imports produced in nations with lax regulations on toxic chemical use, fuel efficiency, and coal consumption.

On the opposite side of the coin, trade advocates argue that the economic gains from trade will help poorer nations afford the costly cleanup of what is in many cases severe environmental pollution. In the case of transboundary pollution, the benefits from this response may accrue to bordering countries or those located downstream along a common river. These arguments are consistent with the premise of sustainable development—that economic prosperity, in this context enhanced through trade, can bring about improvements in environmental quality.

These and other issues were part of the lengthy and often contentious negotiations associated with the North American Free Trade Agreement (NAFTA) and the latest round of the General Agreement on Tariffs and Trade (GATT).

**North American Free Trade Agreement (NAFTA).**[27] Following a difficult series of negotiations, many of which centered on environmental issues, the NAFTA was reached by the United States, Mexico, and Canada in 1992 and approved by Congress in 1993. Among its provisions are the following, which are aimed at economic advance and environmental quality:

- Explicit language that asserts the signatories' commitment to sustainable development.

- Agreement among the three nations to implement NAFTA in accordance with the aim of environmental protection and not to lower health, safety, or environmental standards to attract investment.

- Consensus to aim for congruence of each country's respective environmental regulations while preserving each nation's right to select a level of environmental quality that it deems appropriate.

- Agreement that NAFTA dispute settlement panels will solicit environmental experts for advice on factual issues as needed.

Consistent with NAFTA, the United States and Mexico also implemented a 1992–1994 Integrated Environmental Plan for the border region. The 2,000-mile border has been a source of concern because of the concentration of the now infamous *maquiladora* factories positioned there for access to American markets. Effluent releases into the Rio Grande River and air emissions far exceed U.S. standards. The plan, supported by $208 million from Congress and $160 million from the Mexican government, was aimed at improving water quality, monitoring air pollution, tracking hazardous waste, developing enforcement cooperation, and promoting pollution prevention.

**General Agreement on Tariffs and Trade (GATT).**[28] Originally executed in 1947, GATT is a major international treaty on foreign trade. Its

---

[27] Drawn from Council on Environmental Quality (January 1993), pp. 52–53.

[28] Drawn from Council on Environmental Quality (January 1993), pp. 52–53; Davis (January 10, 1994); Noah (December 16, 1993); Cough (April–June 1993); and *The Economist* (February 27, 1993), pp. 25–28.

avowed purpose is to reduce tariffs and other trade barriers. The 107 signatories, mostly developing countries, meet periodically for discussions called rounds, the latest being the Uruguay Round. This round began in 1986 and was signed in December 1993. The associated negotiations, much like those preceding the signing of NAFTA, had to consider environmental protection issues. However, most environmentalists say that the long-awaited agreement did not respond adequately to their concerns.

Environmentalists' opposition to GATT was stronger than it had been to NAFTA. Reportedly, the intense debate was fueled by a 1991 GATT panel ruling that the United States could not block imports of tuna from Mexico harvested under conditions yielding an unacceptable, incidental kill rate of dolphins.[29] However, the arguments that ultimately pitted open traders against environmentalists during the GATT round run broader and deeper than this single incident.

Fundamentally, environmentalists are wary of any agreement that promotes economic growth and hence increases the potential for ecological damage. Furthermore, they are concerned about how GATT rulings that deter trade restrictions run counter to environmental aims. A few examples will illustrate. A nation cannot use countervailing duties on imports from a country whose environmental regulations are lower, and therefore less costly to producers, than its own. An import cannot be restricted based solely on the exporter's use of a pollution-generating input or production method. Relatively high environmental standards in one country can be viewed as restrictions on free trade.

Based on the results of the Uruguay Round, countries are required to use the least trade-restrictive measures to achieve environmental goals, and in most cases, international standards should be employed rather than national ones. Economically, the concern is that such a universal set of guidelines may become a ceiling instead of a floor. Nations might recognize the incentive to keep standards and enforcement relatively low as a way to keep compliance costs down and attract foreign investment. In any case, once this pattern emerges, other countries may follow suit to maintain export competitiveness.

## Domestic Partnerships

Although the perspective is global, initiatives promoting sustainable development have to begin within national borders. Just as is the case for international agreements, domestic initiatives also require cooperation, but of a different sort. In many industrialized countries, collaborative arrangements are being developed between government and industry, between environmental groups and businesses, and among private firms and industries.

---

[29] According to GATT provisions, import restrictions may be allowed to protect biological life only in the importing country, not the exporting nation.

Sustainable development and related objectives like pollution prevention call for significant change in how firms make decisions, engineer their production, and design and market their products. If businesses perceive these changes as counter to their own self-interest, the changes will be met with resistance at best. To foster a positive evolution in thinking and business planning, governments are attempting to work with industry and environmental groups to share information, to foster needed technological development, and to find solutions that satisfy both environmental and business objectives. As these efforts have taken hold, cooperative arrangements have begun to form—some within the private sector, and others the result of government-sponsored partnership programs.

## Government-Sponsored Partnerships

**Green Lights Program** A plan that fosters partnerships between businesses and the EPA aimed at improving energy efficiency.

**Energy Star Program** A product-labeling plan encouraging manufacturers to develop energy-saving products.

**33/50 Program** A program that encouraged firms emitting one or more of 17 priority pollutants to voluntarily reduce releases of those substances.

In the United States, national efforts to achieve sustainable development are being implemented in part through the launching of voluntary partnership programs between the EPA and private industry.[30] One of these is the **Green Lights Program** launched in 1991. The plan encourages private firms to commit to using energy-efficient lighting, but only if it improves or maintains lighting quality *and* if the conversion is profitable.[31] Another is a product-labeling plan called the **Energy Star Program.**[32] Introduced in 1992, this plan urges manufacturers to develop personal computers that "power-down" or "sleep" when not in use. An "Energy Star" logo is then used to communicate to prospective buyers both the potential cost savings and the reduction in polluting emissions from lower and more efficient energy use. Among the program's participants are IBM and Apple Computer. The EPA projects that the plan will yield a 50-percent reduction in energy use with no added costs.[33]

Another government-sponsored pollution prevention strategy was the **33/50 Program,** which used the Toxics Release Inventory (TRI) database.[34] Administered by the EPA's Office of Toxic Substances, the 33/50 strategy was a noncompulsory program that called upon firms emitting one or more of 17 priority pollutants to voluntarily reduce their releases of those substances. Using 1988 as a baseline, the goal was to achieve a 33-percent reduction nationwide by 1992 and a 50-percent reduction by 1995. The 1995 goal was surpassed with releases and transfers declining by 55 percent. Although the deadlines have passed, the EPA continues to monitor releases

---

[30] Visit **www.epa.gov/partners/** to learn about the many partnerships programs sponsored by the EPA collectively called Partners for the Environment.

[31] For more detail, refer to Application 13.2, "The EPA's Green Lights Program" in Chapter 13.

[32] For online information about the Energy Star Program, see **www.epa.gov/energystar/**.

[33] U.S. EPA, Office of Air and Radiation (October 1992), pp. 8–9; *EPA Journal* (April–June 1993), p. 7.

[34] Recall that the TRI database is authorized under the reporting requirements of Title III of the 1986 Superfund Amendments.

and transfers of the chemicals covered under the program. In fact, as of 1996, the cumulative reduction of the 17 chemicals reached 60 percent.[35]

### Cooperative Arrangements within Industry

As the advantages of pollution prevention have become known, cooperative arrangements have begun to form within the private business sector—some without any intervention by government. A number of trade associations, for example, have developed pollution prevention programs for their memberships. The American Petroleum Institute devised a set of 11 environmental principles for petroleum facilities, one of which specifically sets a goal for each member to reduce emissions and waste generation. The institute also publishes reports to communicate information on trends in waste generation and management throughout the industry and to update members on waste minimization practices. A similar plan has been devised for the chemical industry, a major contributor to environmental pollution. This one, called the "Responsible Care Program," was developed by the Chemical Manufacturers Association and is the subject of Application 20.4.[36]

Other collaborative efforts are the result of corporations joining forces with environmental groups. In 1990, McDonald's formed a Waste Reduction Task Force with the environmental group Environmental Defense Fund—a coalition successful enough to win it a Presidential Environment and Conservation Challenge Award for Partnership one year later. Among the results achieved by the task force were a 42-step action plan, the formulation of a corporate environmental policy, and the integration of waste reduction efforts throughout McDonald's organization. Already, the fast-food giant has replaced its chlorine-bleached paper products with brown, unbleached paper. It is recycling corrugated boxes, which account for over 33 percent of an average restaurant's trash, and it is asking suppliers to use boxes containing 35 percent recycled material. McDonald's is also testing and experimenting with a variety of reusable or recyclable packages, lids, and storage containers. In its "McRecycle USA" program, it purchases more than $125 million in recycled products each year for restaurant operations, renovation, and construction in addition to $80 million per year for recycled packaging, tray liners, napkins, and the like. It has also integrated waste reduction into its purchasing decisions along with cost, functionality, and availability.[37]

---

[35] See U.S. Environmental Protection Agency, Office of Pollution Prevention and Toxics, **www.epa.gov/opptintr/tri/national.htm**, last revision June 23, 1998.

[36] U.S. EPA, Office of Pollution Prevention (October 1991), pp. 40–41.

[37] U.S. EPA, Office of Solid Waste and Emergency Response (Spring 1992), pp. 1, 3; U.S. EPA, Office of Solid Waste and Emergency Response (October 1993), p. 13. Visit McDonald's Web site of environmental information at **www.mcdonalds.com/community/environ/info/envinfo.html**.

## An Industry's Response to Pollution Prevention: The Chemical Manufacturers Association's "Responsible Care Program"

As a major contributor to the nation's hazardous waste stream, the chemical industry recently developed a pollution prevention program that signals the industry's commitment to a cleaner environment. In 1988, the industry's trade alliance, Chemical Manufacturers Association (CMA), launched its Responsible Care Program as a comprehensive chemical management plan to be adopted by its membership. Following the lead of the Canadian Chemical Producers Association, which established its plan in 1985, the U.S. program ushered in a series of principles to guide its members in reducing both waste generation and dangerous releases into the environment. The objectives are simple but powerful—to protect the health and safety of the workforce and to protect the environment from contamination.

Implementation of the comprehensive program is guided by a Code of Management Practices, which also includes a Waste and Release Reduction Code. The 10 guiding principles of CMA's Responsible Care Program are:

1. Establish a strong and ongoing commitment by senior management to the reduction of wastes and releases to the environment.

2. Establish a quantitative inventory of each plant's waste generation and releases.

3. Evaluate the potential impacts of waste releases on workers and the general public.

4. Inform and obtain feedback from workers and the public about the facility's inventory and its potential environmental impact.

5. After accounting for both the potential environmental impacts and the community's feedback, establish priorities, goals, and plans for waste and release reduction.

6. Continue to work toward the reduction of wastes and releases through the following hierarchy: (i) source reduction; (ii) recycle/reuse; and (iii) treatment.

7. Monitor the progress of waste reduction and releases at each facility by updating the waste inventory at least once each year.

8. Maintain good communication with employees and the general public on progress, new information, and future plans.

9. Incorporate waste and release reduction objectives in the design of new or modified facilities, processes, or products.

10. Maintain a program that promotes and supports the waste and release reduction activities by others.

Britain's counterpart to the CMA, the Chemical Industries Association, also joined the ranks of trade associations working to prevent pollution. Their Responsible Care Program came on line in March 1989—the first such plan in Europe. Not surprisingly, the U.K. program is based on a set of principles not unlike the CMA's list of 10.

SOURCES: U.S. Environmental Protection Agency, Office of Pollution Prevention. *Pollution Prevention 1991: Progress on Reducing Industrial Pollutants.* Washington DC, October 1991, pp. 40–41; Chemical Manufacturers Association. *Improving Performance in the Chemical Industry.* September 1990, pp. 9–15; Peter Simmons and Brian Wynne. "Responsible Care: Trust, Credibility, and Environmental Management." In Kurt Fischer and Johan Schot, eds., *Environmental Strategies for Industry: International Perspectives on Research Needs and Policy Implications.* Washington DC: Island Press, 1993, pp. 207–26.

# Education and Technology Transfer

**technology transfer**
The advancement and application of technologies and strategies on a global scale.

**dark green technologies** Technologies dealing directly with the remediation of pollution.

**light green technologies** Technologies that benefit the environment indirectly.

**environmental literacy** Awareness of the risks of pollution and natural resource depletion.

Critical to consistent progress toward sustainable development is **technology transfer,** the advancement and application of technologies and management strategies across economic sectors throughout the world. Environmental technologies cover a broad range of products and services. Included are the so-called **dark green technologies** such as those dealing with the control, abatement, monitoring, and remediation of pollution. In addition, there are more indirect but nonetheless important advances dubbed **light green technologies.** These refer to strategies or production changes that benefit the environment even though that is not their primary intent. An example is the use of electronic mail in place of hard-copy memos, a change that reduces waste generation.[38] All of these advances and innovations are important to achieving economic growth while preserving and protecting the natural environment.

Effecting technology transfer relies on a number of interdependent factors—among them, research, physical capital investment, communication, financial resources, and perhaps most importantly education. It is critical that society be made aware of environmental risks and the importance of responding to those risks. The aim is to attain **environmental literacy** throughout all economic sectors and across all regions of the world. Without this awareness in place, society will not understand the need for change, will tend not to support it, and may be unwilling to participate in the process.

## Environmental Literacy

In 1962, Rachel Carson's *Silent Spring* warned the world about the potential hazards of chemical use. In the early 1970s, a report of Ralph Nader's assessment of U.S. water quality awakened society to the deterioration of America's rivers and streams.[39] These and other such accounts sent shock waves through communities everywhere. For many years, most people had no idea of the extent of environmental degradation nor any sense of how rapidly the problem was advancing. As a result, society unwittingly continued to contribute to the problem. Learning from our mistakes, we now understand that **environmental literacy,** achieved through communication and education, is part of an effective strategy to protect the earth's resources.

On a global scale, efforts by the United Nations Educational, Scientific, and Cultural Organization (UNESCO) led to a 1977 intergovernmental conference on environmental education held in the former Soviet Union.[40] The international conference called for:

---

[38] *EPA Journal* 20(3, 4), Fall 1994, p. 8.

[39] Zwick and Benstock (1971), as cited in Adler, Landman, and Cameron (1993), pp. 5–6.

[40] United Nations Environment Program/UNESCO (1987) as cited in Council on Environmental Quality (1992), pp. 384–85.

". . . education directed towards the solution of practical environmental problems through an interdisciplinary approach and the active and responsible involvement of each individual and of the community."

The promotion of environmental education across the globe has grown over time and was an important theme at the 1992 Earth Summit in Rio. *Agenda 21* specifically references the importance of education, public awareness, and training in helping to implement the global agenda.[41]

In the United States, the first National Environmental Education Act was passed by Congress in 1970. This legislation sponsored a small domestic grant program and authorized funding for research and curriculum development. In 1989, President Bush along with state governors launched the nation's America 2000 Strategy—a comprehensive plan to accomplish excellence-in-education goals by 2000. To facilitate the implementation of this national strategy, the newly created Office of Environmental Education in the EPA set specific goals for environmental education. Another landmark was the U.S. enactment of the second National Environmental Education Act in November 1990. Broader in scope than its predecessor, this act targets a more comprehensive student audience and calls for international cooperation as well as collaboration between government and the private sector. Programs are also under way within the EPA and other major agencies. Private sector efforts also are contributing to environmental literacy. Some of these are taking place within educational institutions, while others are being launched by private industry.[42]

## Information and Technology Transfer

As a world economic leader, the United States has an important responsibility to promote environmental **technology transfer** both domestically and internationally. Globally, the environmental technology market is estimated to be between $200 billion and $300 billion per year and expanding at an annual rate of between 5 and 10 percent. Although the federal government supports about half of the active research undertaken in the nation, most of it is actually performed by private industry.[43]

To promote private–public research endeavors, Congress enacted the Federal Technology Transfer Act of 1986. This act supports **cooperative research and development agreements (CRADAs)** between private industry and the public sector. A recent and highly innovative environmental CRADA is one formed in 1994 with Monsanto, General Electric, DuPont,

---

[41] Parson, Haas, and Levy (October 1992).

[42] Council on Environmental Quality (1992), Chapter 9; Council on Environmental Quality (January 1993), pp. 59–70.

[43] Council on Environmental Quality (January 1993), p. 205.

and the EPA. This project is developing a new soil remediation process and has been dubbed the "Lasagna CRADA" because of its use of electrical current to move contamination through *layers* of soil. Another environmental CRADA teams up the U.S. Department of Agriculture and the EPA with a consortium of 32 pesticide producers to develop a new model for assessing pesticide risks.[44]

Transferring new technologies to developing nations is being effected in part through the **U.S. Environmental Training Institute (USETI).** Founded in 1991, the institute is a nonprofit entity that trains participants from developing countries at U.S. businesses and institutions to facilitate the transfer of cleaner technologies. Over 25 comprehensive, short-term courses were developed in 1994, nine of which were located overseas. Topics include environmental risk management, pollution prevention, bioremediation, and pollution control techniques. This cooperative effort of private industry and seven federal agencies has hosted participants from such nations as Thailand, Morocco, the Philippines, Mexico, Hong Kong, Taiwan, and India. Contributing further to this effort is an **Environmental and Energy Efficient Technology Transfer Clearinghouse** supported by the Department of Energy, the EPA, and the U.S. Agency for International Development (USAID). Its aim is to communicate information on pollution control, renewable energy, and energy efficient technologies. Pilot programs have been launched in Mexico City and Vienna.[45]

To signify an ongoing commitment to technology transfer, President Clinton launched the **Environmental Technology Initiative (ETI)** in his 1993 State of the Union Address to the nation. The aim of this initiative is to promote research and development of environmental technologies both by the government and the private sector and to enhance U.S. exports of these newly developed goods and services. These efforts are to be advanced by the EPA in cooperation with such federal agencies as the Department of Commerce, Department of Labor, the Small Business Administration, and the Export–Import Bank.[46] The primary international element of the president's initiative is an EPA-sponsored, environmental technology diffusion program called **U.S. Technology for International Environmental Solutions (U.S. TIES).** Initiated in 1994, this project brings together the supply and demand sides of environmental technology in an effort to engage private sector participation in global environmental goals. It does this by designing country-specific projects that help developing countries find solutions to their environmental problems by introducing them to available U.S. technologies. In so doing, market suppliers of environmental tech-

---

[44] Preuss (Fall 1994); Japikse (Fall 1994); Council on Environmental Quality (January 1993), pp. 205–206.

[45] Council on Environmental Quality (January 1993), pp. 187–88, 210–11; *EPA Journal* 20(3, 4), Fall 1994, p. 12. For online information on USETI, visit **www.useti.org/**.

[46] *EPA Journal* 20(3, 4), Fall 1994, p. 8.

nologies learn more about the needs of the foreign sector, and prospective demanders are facilitated in their search for needed services. Among the initial U.S. TIES projects are demonstrations of drinking water treatment systems in Mexico and air pollution control technologies in Russia.[47]

# Conclusions

Although many argue that the realization was long overdue, society is beginning to recognize the importance of achieving a balance between economic growth and the preservation of natural resources. Based on current trends, world population is estimated to increase by more than 3 billion by 2025 with 90 percent of the increase expected to occur in Africa, Asia, and Latin America—regions already struggling with poverty and inadequate food supplies.[48] Attempts to increase production to provide for this growth will place inordinate stress on the ecology and the earth's stock of resources.

Acknowledging and understanding the relevant issues is an important first step, but the real challenge is in establishing appropriate goals and in taking responsible action to achieve them. Critical to meeting this challenge is a true understanding of the interdependence between economic activity and nature. Understanding this connection is a precondition for effective policy development and informed decision making, both of which are essential elements of the environmental planning process. If sustainable development is to be achieved, there must be a cooperative and educated effort from industry, private citizens, and public officials at all levels of government.

Over the past decade or so, the United States and many other nations have made measurable progress in moving closer to what have become universal environmental objectives. But there is much more to be done. Aggregate statistics disguise those regions where environmental pollution is particularly severe. There are entire nations in Asia, Africa, and South and Central America that face extremely poor air quality, contaminated drinking water, and serious degradation of their land resources.

The need for setting a global environmental agenda and implementing it is more than apparent. Identifying an appropriate course of action is not easy, and it takes time. This collective effort calls for cooperation from every market sector and from every nation, a process that is now under way. As this important transition evolves, society must move forward to restore what can be repaired, to launch initiatives to prevent further degradation, and to educate people everywhere about the importance and fragility of the

---

[47] Koehler and Lingle (Fall 1994), pp. 32–33.

[48] Stutz (March/April 1993); United Nations Population Division (1991) and International Labour Office (ILO) (1986), as cited in World Resources Institute (1992a), pp. 245–47.

natural environment. This commitment was advanced at the 1992 Earth Summit in Rio and is articulated in the preamble of *Agenda 21*:

> "Humanity stands at a defining moment in history. We are confronted with a perpetuation of disparities between and within nations, a worsening of poverty, hunger, ill health, and illiteracy, and the continuing deterioration of the ecosystems on which we depend for our well-being. However, integration of environment and development concerns and greater attention to them will lead to the fulfillment of basic needs, improved living standards for all, better protected and managed ecosystems and a safer, more prosperous future."

## Summary

- A consensus is forming that both public and private decision making should be driven by a broader goal that is global in scope and dynamic in perspective. One such goal is sustainable development—managing the earth's resources such that their long-term quality and abundance is assured for future generations.

- Implicit in the conventional use of "end-of-pipe" command-and-control instruments is a perception that the flow of materials through the economy is linear, running in *one* direction. Hence, U.S. policy has focused on abating contaminating residuals at the end of the flow. Although this can improve environmental quality in the short run, it does not adequately address the long-run consequences.

- Sustainable development is based on the premise that economic growth and environmental quality must be reconciled. Part of the answer is to recognize that product design, manufacturing processes, and energy use can be modified so that materials flow through more of a closed system.

- In the context of the materials balance model, pollution prevention strategies change how economic activity is undertaken so that less contaminating residuals are released to nature.

- To formalize pollution prevention as an integral part of U.S. policy, Congress passed the Pollution Prevention Act of 1990.

- Two major preventive objectives for industry are source reduction and toxic chemical use substitution. Among the techniques proposed to help industry achieve these objectives are source segregation, raw materials substitution, changes in manufacturing processes, and product substitution.

- The Rio Summit in 1992 dealt with the objective of sustainable development. Among the major documents produced from the Summit were *Agenda 21* and the *Rio Declaration.*

- When pollution problems are transboundary, the preservation of environmental resources can become an international concern that may require a formal treaty among affected nations. Examples include the Montreal Protocol, the U.N. Framework Convention on Climate Change, the London Dumping Convention (LDC), and the U.S.– Canada Air Quality Agreement.

- Recently, international trade discussions triggered concerns about the potential conflict between the associated economic gains and a decline in environmental quality. These issues affected negotiations for the North American Free Trade Agreement (NAFTA) and the latest round of the General Agreement on Tariffs and Trade (GATT).

- Governments are attempting to work with industry and environmental groups to share information, to foster technological development, and to find solutions that satisfy both environmental and business objectives.

- In the United States, the national strategy to achieve sustainable development is being implemented in part through voluntary partnership programs between the EPA and private industry. Examples include the Green Lights Program, the Energy Star Program, and the 33/50 Program.

- Cooperative arrangements have begun to form within the private business sector. A number of trade associations have developed pollution prevention programs for their memberships.

- Environmental literacy, achieved through communication and education, is part of an effective strategy to preserve and protect the earth's resources.

- Critical to consistent progress toward sustainable development is technology transfer, the advancement and application of technologies and management strategies across economic sectors throughout the world.

## Key Concepts

| | |
|---|---|
| environmental quality | pollution prevention |
| sustainable development | source reduction |
| materials balance model | toxic chemical use substitution |
| industrial ecosystem | source segregation |

| | |
|---|---|
| raw material substitution | 33/50 Program |
| change in manufacturing processes | technology transfer |
| product substitution | dark green technologies |
| Green Lights Program | light green technologies |
| Energy Star Program | environmental literacy |

# Review Questions

1. Critically discuss the following statement:

   "Without a well-enforced command-and-control regulatory structure, society will not take the necessary steps toward a sustainable future."

2. Environmental technology is argued to be an important element in society's effort to achieve sustainable development.
   a. Choose a specific market-based instrument that would likely encourage the advance of "dark green technologies" *and* improve U.S. exports of these goods and services. Explain using economic analytical tools.
   b. Now propose a different market-based instrument that would foster the use of more "light green technologies" domestically and internationally.

3. a. Identify the economic incentives that motivate private firms to engage in pollution prevention activities.
   b. How might the government devise policy initiatives to exploit these natural incentives?

4. a. Critically evaluate the provision in GATT that requires that the least trade-restrictive measures be used to achieve environmental goals. Include in your answer both the environmental and economic implications.
   b. Support or refute the use of international environmental standards among trading partners.

5. In your view, does NAFTA support or hinder the achievement of sustainable development? Explain.

6. Explain the economics of how U.S. TIES attempts to bring together the supply and demand sides of environmental technology. In your view, how effective is this program likely to be for the United States? For developing nations? Explain.

# Additional Readings

Beardsley, Dan, Terry Davies, and Robert Hersh. "Improving Environmental Management." *Environment* 39(7), September 1997.

Bylinsky, Gene. "Manufacturing for Reuse." *Fortune*, February 6, 1995, pp. 102–12.

Choucri, Nazli, ed., *Global Accord: Environmental Challenges and International Responses*. Cambridge, MA: MIT Press, 1993.

Commoner, Barry. "Economic Growth and Environmental Quality: How to Have Both." *Social Policy*, Summer 1985, pp. 18–26.

Daly, Herman E. "The Perils of Free Trade." *Scientific American*, November 1993, pp. 50–57.

Flynn, Julia, Zachary Schiller, John Carey, and Ruth Coxeter. "Novo Nordisk's Mean Green Machine." *Business Week*, November 14, 1994.

Goldberg, Cheryl J. "Green Machines." *Entrepreneur*, January 1994, pp. 34–37.

Gutfeld, Rose. "Keeping It Green: In a Free-Trade Pact, Is the Environment the Big Loser?" *Wall Street Journal*, September 24, 1992.

Jaffe, Adam B., Steven R. Peterson, Paul R. Portney, and Robert N. Stavins. "Environmental Regulation and the Competitiveness of U.S. Manufacturing: What Does the Evidence Tell Us?" *Journal of Economic Literature* 33, March 1995, pp. 132–63.

Kempton, Willett, and Paul P. Craig. "European Perspective on Global Climate Change." *Environment* 35(3), April 1993, pp. 16–20, 41–45.

Lesser, Jonathan A., and Richard O. Zerbe, Jr. "What Can Economic Analysis Contribute to the Sustainability Debate?" *Contemporary Economic Policy* 13(3), July 1995, pp. 88–100.

Oldenburg, Kirsten U., and Joel S. Hirschhorn. "Waste Reduction: A New Strategy to Avoid Pollution." *Environment* 29(2), March 1987, pp. 16–20, 39–45.

O'Riordan, Timothy, William C. Clark, Robert W. Kates, and Alan McGowan. "The Legacy of Earth Day: Reflections at a Turning Point." *Environment* 57(3), April 1995, pp. 6–15, 37–42.

Solow, Robert M. "Sustainability: An Economist's Perspective." In Robert Dorfman and Nancy S. Dorfman, eds., *Economics of the Environment: Selected Readings*. New York: W. W. Norton, 1993.

Taylor, Jerry. "Policy Analysis: NAFTA's Green Accords: Sound and Fury Signifying Little." Cato Institute, November 17, 1993.

U.S. Environmental Protection Agency, Office of the Administrator. *The Greening of World Trade*. Washington, DC, February 1993.

# Related Web Sites

Chemical Manufacturers Association's Responsible Care Program     **www.cmahq.com/cmawebsite.nsf/pages/responsiblecare**

EPA's Design for the Environment Program     **www.epa.gov/opptintr/dfe/**

EPA's Energy Star
Program                               **www.epa.gov/energystar/**

EPA's Partners for the
Environment                           **www.epa.gov/partners/**

EPA's Pollution
Prevention site                       **www.epa.gov/opptintr/p2home/aboutp2.htm**

Information on President
Clinton's Council on
Sustainable Development               **www.whitehouse.gov/PCSD/**

Information on 3M's
corporate environmental
programs                              **www.3m.com/profile/envt/index.html**

McDonald's environmental
information                           **www.mcdonalds.com/community/environ/info/envinfo.html**

Pollution Prevention Act             **www.law.cornell.edu/uscode/42/ch133.html**

UN's sustainable
development Web site                  **www.un.org/esa/sustdev/**

U.S. Environmental
Training Institute
(USETI)                               **www.useti.org/**

AAA World. "CFC-Free A/C." *AAA World*. March/April 1993, p. 23.

Abdalla, Charles. "Measuring Economic Losses from Ground Water Contamination: An Investigation of Household Avoidance Cost." *Water Resources Bulletin* 26(3), June 1990, pp. 451–63.

Ackerman, B., and W. Hassler. *Clean Coal/Dirty Air*. New Haven, CT: Yale Univ. Press, 1981.

Ackerman, Frank. "Taxing the Trash Away." *Environment*, June 1992, pp. 2–5, 43.

Adams, Walter, and James W. Brock. "The Automobile Industry." In Walter Adams, ed., *The Structure of American Industry*. New York: Macmillan Publishing Company, 1990.

Adler, Jerry, and Mary Hager. "How Much Is a Species Worth?" *National Wildlife*, April/May 1992, pp. 4–14.

Adler, Robert W. "Revitalizing the Clean Water Act." *Environment* 35(9), November 1993, pp. 4–5, 40.

Adler, Robert W., Jessica C. Landman, and Diane M. Cameron. *The Clean Water Act: 20 Years Later*. Washington, DC: Island Press, 1993.

Aeppel, Timothy. "Green Groups Enter a Dry Season as Movement Matures." *The Wall Street Journal*, October 21, 1994, pp. B1, B4.

Alexander, Michael. "The Challenge of Markets: The Supply of Recyclables Is Larger than the Demand." *EPA Journal*, July/August 1992, pp. 29–33.

Allen, Frederick, and Gregg Sekscienski. "Greening at the Grassroots: What Polls Say about Americans' Environmental Commitment." *EPA Journal* 18(4), September/October 1992, pp. 52–53.

Allen, Scott. "Boston Harbor's Waters Have Started to Heal: Cleanup Helping to Shed 'Dirtiest' Label." *Boston Globe*, September 6, 1992, p. 1.

———. "Polluting Power Plants to Pay Price." *Boston Globe*, November 12, 1992, p. 29.

———. "State Touts Give-and-Take on Clean Air." *Boston Globe*, January 8, 1993, p. 1.

———. "Rights to Pollute Given Up." *Boston Globe*, March 20, 1993.

———. "Mass. Firms May Now Trade Clean Air Credits." *Boston Globe*, September 29, 1993, p. 26.

Alliance for Responsible CFC Policy. *Montreal Protocol: A Briefing Book*. Rosslyn, VA: Alliance for Responsible CFC Policy, December 1986.

Anderson, Frederick R. "Natural Resource Damages, Superfund, and the Courts." *Environmental Affairs*, 1989, pp. 405–57.

Anderson, James E. *Public Policy-Making: Decisions and Their Implementation*. New York: Praeger, 1975.

Anderson, James E., David W. Brady, and Charles Bullock III. *Public Policy and Politics in America*. North Scituate, MA: Duxbury Press, 1978.

Anderson, Robert C., Andrew Q. Lohof (Resource Consulting Associates), and Alan Carlin (U.S. Environmental Protection Agency, Office of Economy and Environment, Office of Policy, Planning and Evaluation). *The United States Experience with Economic Incentives in Environmental Pollution Control Policy*. Washington, DC, August 1997.

Andrews, Richard N. L. "Economics and Environmental Decisions, Past and Present." In V. Kerry Smith, ed., *Environmental Policy under Reagan's Executive*

*Order: The Role of Benefit–Cost Analysis.* Chapel Hill, NC: Univ. of North Carolina Press, 1984, pp. 43–85.

Arnst, Catherine. "Loophole in the Ozone Pact." *Business Week*, September 29, 1997, pp. 41–42.

Arnst, Catherine, and Gary McWilliams. "The Black Market vs. the Ozone." *Business Week*, July 7, 1997.

Associated Press. "Industrial Nations Ban Dumping Waste at Sea." *Boston Globe*, November 3, 1990, p. 7.

———. "Japanese Environmentalist Says Gas Too Cheap in U.S." *Brockton Enterprise*, February 2, 1992.

———. "44 Nations Agree to Update Rules on Ocean Dumping." *Boston Globe*, November 14, 1992, p. 61.

———. "EPA: Fish Aren't Safe to Eat from 46 Waterways." *Brockton Enterprise*, November 20, 1992.

———. "Updating Previous Big Spills." *Boston Globe*, January 6, 1993, p. 6.

———. "Quietly, EPA Drops Some Tobacco Research." *Boston Globe*, January 7, 1993, p. 3.

———. "EPA Warns of Exposure to Smoke." *Boston Globe*, July 23, 1993, p. 9.

———. "German Recycling Is Too Successful." *Brockton Enterprise*, July 27, 1993.

———. "White House to Seek Reduced Use of Pesticides." *Boston Globe*, September 21, 1993, p. 7.

———. "Voluntary Effort Pressed by Clinton on Clean Air." *Boston Globe*, October 19, 1993a, p. 12.

———. "Russia to Continue Dumping Nuclear Waste at Sea." *Boston Globe*, October 19, 1993b, p. 2.

———. "Study: Dioxin Health Threat Much Worse than Suspected." *Brockton Enterprise*, September 12, 1994.

———. "Coal Dependence Has China Looking for Pollution Solution." *Brockton Enterprise*, November 3, 1996, p. 6.

Atkinson, Scott E., and Donald H. Lewis. "A Cost-Effectiveness Analysis of Alternative Air Quality Control Strategies." *Journal of Environmental Economics and Management* 1, 1974, pp. 237–50.

Bai, Matt, and Scott Allen. "Oil Spill Spreads off Rhode Island Coast." *Boston Globe*, January 21, 1996, pp. 1, 24.

Bailey, Jeff. "Curbside Recycling Programs Divert Little Trash from Dumps, Study Finds." *The Wall Street Journal*, October 4, 1994, p. A2.

Baker, Stephen. "Mexico's Motorists Meet the Smog Patrol." *Business Week*, June 25, 1990, p. 100.

Bartik, Timothy. "Evaluating the Benefits of Non-Marginal Reductions in Pollution Using Information on Defensive Expenditures." *Journal of Environmental Economics* 15, 1988, pp. 111–27.

Baumol, W. J., and W. E. Oates. *The Theory of Environmental Policy.* Englewood Cliffs, NJ: Prentice-Hall, Inc. 1975.

Beamish, Rita. "Clinton Emissions Plan Is Mainly Voluntary." *Brockton Enterprise*, October 18, 1993.

Beckerman, Wilfred. "Global Warming: A Sceptical Economic Assessment." In Dieter Helm, ed., *Economic Policy towards the Environment.* Cambridge, MA: Blackwell Publishers, 1990.

Biers, Dan. "China Creates Environmental Nightmare in Industrial Rush." *The Brockton Enterprise*, June 16, 1994, p. 11.

Blinder, Alan S. "How to Cut Pollution and the Deficit at the Same Time." *Business Week*, August 24, 1987, p. 10.

———. "Two Cheers for Bush's Plan to Clean Up the Clean Air Act." *Business Week*, July 10, 1989, p. 14.

Block, Debbie Galante. "CD Jewel Box Only, or Alternatives Too?" *Tape-Disc Business*, June 1993, p. 12.

Blomquist, Glenn C. "Value of Life Saving: Implications of Consumption Activity." *Journal of Political Economy* 87(3), June 1979, pp. 540–58.

Bowker, James, and John R. Stoll. "Use of Dichotomous Choice Nonmarket Methods to Value the Whooping Crane Resource." *American Journal of Agricultural Economics* 70(2), May 1988, pp. 372–81.

Boyle, Kevin J., and Richard C. Bishop. "Valuing Wildlife in Benefit–Cost Analyses: A Case Study Involving Endangered Species." *Water Resources Research* 23(5), 1987, pp. 615–16.

Brajer, Victor, and Jane V. Hall. "Recent Evidence on the Distribution of Air Pollution Effects." *Contemporary Policy Issues*, April 1992, pp. 63–71.

Bratton, D., and G. L. Rutledge. "Pollution Abatement and Control Expenditures, 1985–1988." *Survey of Current Business* 70, 1990, pp. 32–38.

Bringer, Robert P. "Pollution Prevention Plus." *Pollution Engineering* 20(10), October 1988, pp. 84–89.

Brookshire, D. S., and T. D. Crocker. "The Advantages of Contingent Valuation Methods for Benefit Cost Analysis." *Public Choice* 36, 1981, pp. 235–52.

Brown, Gardner M., Jr., and Ralph W. Johnson. "Pollution Control by Effluent Charges: It Works in the Federal Republic of Germany, Why Not in the U.S." *Natural Resources Journal* 24, October 1984, pp. 929–66.

Browner, Carol M. "The Administration's Proposals." *EPA Journal* 20 (1–2), Summer 1994, pp. 6–9.

Burtraw, Dallas, and Paul Portney. "Environmental Policy in the U.S." In Dieter Helm, ed., *Economic Policy towards the Environment*. Cambridge: Blackwell Publishers, 1991.

Butler, John C., III., Mark W. Schneider, George R. Hall, and Michael E. Burton. "Allocating Superfund Costs: Cleaning Up the Controversy." *Environmental Law Reporter*, March 1993, pp. 10133–44.

Cahan, Vicky. "Waste Not, Want Not? Not Necessarily." *Business Week*, July 17, 1989, pp. 116–17.

Cairncross, Frances. "How Europe's Companies Reposition to Recycle." *Harvard Business Review*, March/April 1992, pp. 34–45.

The Canadian Institute of Chartered Accountants. *Environmental Auditing and the Role of the Accounting Profession*. Toronto, Ontario: The Canadian Institute of Chartered Accountants, 1992.

Carson, Rachel. *Silent Spring*. Boston: Houghton Mifflin Company, 1962.

Carson, Richard T., and Robert Cameron Mitchell. "The Value of Clean Water: The Public's Willingness to Pay for Boatable, Fishable, and Swimmable Quality Water." Discussion Paper 88-13. La Jolla, CA: Univ. of California at San Diego, 1988.

———. "The Value of Clean Water: The Public's Willingness to Pay for Boatable, Fishable, and Swimmable Water." *Water Resources Research* 29(7), July 1993, pp. 2245–54.

Chandler, William, Alexei Makarov, and Zhou Dadi. "Energy for the Soviet Union, Eastern Europe, and China." *Scientific American*, September 1990.

Chemical Manufacturers Association (CMA). *Improving Performance in the Chemical Industry*. September 1990.

Clawson, Marion, and Jack L. Knetch. *Economics of Outdoor Recreation*. Washington, DC: Resources for the Future, 1966.

Cline, William R. "Global Warming: Estimating the Economic Benefits of Abatement." In Organisation for Economic Co-operation and Development, *Global Warming: The Benefits of Emission Abatement*. Paris: OECD, 1992.

*Clinton's Climate Change Proposal*, **www.whitehouse.gov/Initiatives/Climate / proposal.html**, October 22, 1997.

Coalition for Environmentally Responsible Economies (CERES). "The Valdez Principles." U.S.A., 1989.

Coase, Ronald H. "The Problem of Social Cost." *Journal of Law and Economics* 3, October 1960, pp. 1–44.

Cogan, Douglas G. *Stones in a Glass House: CFCs and Ozone Depletion.* Washington, DC: Investor Responsibility Research Center, Inc., 1988.

Cohen, Brian A., and Erik D. Olson. *Victorian Water Treatment Enters the 21st Century.* March 1994.

Commoner, Barry. *Making Peace with the Planet.* New York: The New Press, 1992.

Consumer Reports. "'Greener' Cooling." *Consumer Reports,* March 1993, p. 133.

Cormier, William. "Smog Eats Mexico City's Monuments." *Brockton Enterprise,* November 23, 1992.

Cough, Paul. "Trade–Environment Tensions: Options Exist for Reconciling Trade and Environment." *EPA Journal* 19(2), April/June 1993, pp. 28–30.

Council of Economic Advisers. "The Annual Report of the Council of Economic Advisers." *Economic Report of the President,* Transmitted to the Congress February 1982. Washington, DC: U.S. Government Printing Office, 1982.

Council on Environmental Quality. *Environmental Quality—1976.* Washington, DC: U.S. Government Printing Office, 1976.

———. *Environmental Quality—1980.* Washington, DC: U.S. Government Printing Office, 1980b.

———. *Environmental Quality—1982.* Washington, DC: U.S. Government Printing Office, 1982.

———. *Environmental Trends.* Washington, DC: U.S. Government Printing Office, 1989.

———. *Environmental Quality, 22nd Annual Report.* Washington, DC: U.S. Government Printing Office, March 1992.

———. *United Nations Conference on Environment and Development: United States of America National Report.* Washington, DC, 1992.

———. *Environmental Quality, 23rd Annual Report.* Washington, DC: U.S. Government Printing Office, January 1993.

———. *Environmental Quality 25th Anniversary Report.* Washington, DC: U.S. Government Printing Office, 1997.

Cox, Meg. "Music Firms Try Out 'Green' CD Boxes." *The Wall Street Journal,* July 25, 1991, p. B1.

Crandall, Robert W. "The Political Economy of Clean Air: Practical Constraints on White House Review." In V. Kerry Smith, ed., *Environmental Policy Under Reagan's Executive Order: The Role of Benefit–Cost Analysis.* Chapel Hill, NC: UNC Press, 1984.

Cropper, Maureen L., and Wallace E. Oates. "Environmental Economics: A Survey." *Journal of Economic Literature* 30, June 1992, pp. 675–740.

Cummings, Ronald G., David S. Brookshire, and William D. Schulze. *Valuing Environmental Goods: An Assessment of the Contingent Valuation Method.* Totowa, NJ: Rowman & Allanheld, 1986.

Dardis, Rachel. "The Value of a Life: New Evidence from the Marketplace." *American Economic Review* 70(5), December 1980, pp. 1077–82.

Davies, Terry. "Congress Discovers Risk Analysis." *Resources,* Winter 1995, pp. 5–8.

Davis, Bob. "U.S. Is Hoping to Blend Environmental World Trade Issues at Morocco Meeting." *The Wall Street Journal,* January 10, 1994, p. A9.

Dickerson, Kenneth R. "At the Gasoline Pump." *EPA Journal* 17(1), January/February 1991, pp. 48–50.

Dolin, Eric Jay. "Boston Harbor's Murky Political Waters." *Environment* 34(6), July/August 1992, pp. 7–11, 26–33.

Dominguez, George, ed. *Guidebook: Toxic Substances Control Act.* Cleveland: CRC Press, 1977.

Doneski, D. "Cleaning Up Boston Harbor: Fact or Fiction?" *Boston College Environmental Affairs Law Review* 12, Spring 1985, p. 567.

Duhl, Joshua. *Effluent Fees: Present Practice and Future Potential.* American Petroleum Institute Discussion Paper #075, December 1993.

Dumanoski, Dianne. "Some See Profits; We See Obstacles." *Boston Globe*, November 5, 1990, p. 45.

———. "Nations Act to Speed Phaseout of Ozone-Depleting Chemicals." *Boston Globe*, November 26, 1992, p. 26.

———. "Activists Cite Trade Rules as a Force Shaping Nature." *Boston Globe*, July 1, 1993, p. 13.

Dunlap, Riley E., and Angela G. Mertig. "The Evolution of the U.S. Environmental Movement from 1970 to 1990: An Overview." In Riley E. Dunlap and Angela G. Mertig, eds., *American Environmentalism: The U.S. Environmental Movement, 1970–1990.* Washington, DC: Taylor & Francis New York, 1992.

Dzurik, Andrew A. *Water Resources Planning.* Savage, MD: Rowman & Littlefield Publishers, Inc., 1990.

*The Economist.* "The Greening of Protectionism." February 27, 1993, pp. 25–28.

Eheart, Wayland, E. Downey Brill Jr., and Randolph M. Lyon. "Transferable Discharge Permits for Control of BOD: An Overview." In Erhard F. Joeres and Martin H. David, eds., *Buying a Better Environment: Cost-Effective Regulation through Permit Trading.* Madison, WI: Univ. of Wisconsin Press, 1983.

Elmore, T., J. Jaksch, D. Downing, M. Podar, B. Morrison, B. Zander, and S. Sessions. *Trading between Point and Nonpoint Sources: A Cost-Effective Method for Improving Greater Quality. The Case of Dillon Reservoir.* Washington, DC: U.S. EPA, 1984.

*EPA Journal.* "'Cash for Clunkers' to Cut Pollution." *EPA Journal* 18(2), May/June 1992, p. 2.

———. "State Your Claim." *EPA Journal* 18(3), July/August 1992, p. 10.

———. "Two Faces of Risk." *EPA Journal* 19(1), January/February/March 1993, p. 19.

———. "A Step toward Ecological Risk Guidelines." *EPA Journal* 19(1), January/February/March 1993, p. 33.

———. "EPA 'Energy Star' Expands to Computer Printers." *EPA Journal* 19(2), April–June 1993, p. 7.

———. "What Is Environmental Technology?" *EPA Journal* 20(3–4), Fall 1994, p. 8.

———. "U.S. Environmental Training Institute." *EPA Journal* 20(3–4), Fall 1994, p. 12.

Epstein, Samuel S., Lester O. Brown, and Carl Pope. *Hazardous Waste in America.* San Francisco: Sierra Club Books, 1982.

Farman, J. C., B. G. Gardiner, and J. D. Shanklin. "Large Losses of Total Ozone in Antarctica Reveal Seasonal $ClO_x/NO_x$ Interaction." *Nature* 315, 1985, pp. 207–10.

Fialka, John L. "Gore Faces Cool Response to Issue of Global Warming." *The Wall Street Journal*, August 27, 1997, p. A18.

———. "Global-Warming Treaty Is Approved." *The Wall Street Journal*, December 11, 1997.

Fisher, Ann, Dan Violette, and Lauraine Chestnut. "The Value of Reducing Risks of Death: A Note on New Evidence." *Journal of Policy Analysis and Management* 8(1), 1989, pp. 88–100.

Fletcher, Susan R. "Global Climate Change Treaty: Summary of the Kyoto Protocol." Washington, DC: National Institute for the Environment, December 22, 1997.

Fortuna, Richard C., and David J. Lennett. *Hazardous Waste Regulation: The New Era*. New York: McGraw Hill, 1987.

Freeman, A. Myrick, III. "Air and Water Pollution Policy." In Paul R. Portney, ed., *Current Issues in U.S. Environmental Policy*. Baltimore, MD: Johns Hopkins Univ. Press for Resources for the Future, 1978, pp. 12–67.

———. "Hedonic Prices, Property Values and Measuring Environmental Benefits: A Survey of the Issues." *Scandinavian Journal of Economics* 81, 1979, pp. 154–173.

———. *The Benefits of Air and Water Pollution Control: A Review and Synthesis of Recent Estimates*. Report prepared for the Council on Environmental Quality, December 1979.

———. *Air and Water Pollution Control: A Benefit–Cost Assessment*. New York: John Wiley & Sons, 1982.

———. "Water Pollution Policy." In Paul R. Portney, ed., *Public Policies for Environmental Protection*. Washington, DC: Resources for the Future, 1990, pp. 97–149.

Frosch, Robert A. "Industrial Ecology: Adapting Technology for a Sustainable World." *Environment* 37 (10), December 1995, pp. 16–24, 34–37.

Frosch, Robert A., and Nicholas E. Gallopoulos. "Strategies for Manufacturing." *Scientific American* 261(3), September 1989, pp. 144–52.

Fullerton, Don, and Thomas C. Kinnaman. "Garbage, Recycling and Illicit Burning or Dumping." *Journal of Environmental Economics and Management* 29(1), July 1995, pp. 78–91.

Gianessi, Leonard P., and Henry M. Peskin. " The Distribution of the Cost of Federal Water Pollution Control Policy." *Land Economics* 56(1), February 1980, pp. 85–102.

Gibbons, John. "Moving beyond the 'Tech Fix.'" *EPA Journal* 18(4), September/October 1992, pp. 29–31.

Gibbs, Lois Marie. *The Love Canal: My Story*. Albany: State Univ. of New York Press, 1982.

Goddard, Haynes C. "Integrated Solid Waste Management: Incentives for Reduced Waste Generation, Increased Recycling and Extension of Landfill Life." Paper presented at the BioCycle National Conference, Minneapolis, MN, May 14, 1990.

Goddard, Walter E. *Just-in-Time: Surviving by Breaking Tradition*. Essex Junction, VT: Oliver Wight Limited Publications, 1986.

Goldberg, Dan. "The Magic of Volume Reduction." *Waste Age*, February 1990, pp. 98–104.

Gosselin, Peter G. "Environmental Ruling Blocks Free Trade Pact." *Boston Globe*, July 1, 1993, p. 1.

Griffin, Melanie L. "The Legacy of Love Canal." *Sierra*, January/February 1988, pp. 26–28.

Gross, Neil. "The Green Giant? It May Be Japan." *Business Week*, February 24, 1992, p. 74.

Gutfeld, Rose. "Environmental Group Doesn't Always Lick 'em; It Can Join 'em and Succeed." *The Wall Street Journal*, August 20, 1992, pp. B1, B3.

Haas, Peter M., Marc A. Levy, and Edward A. Parson. "Appraising the Earth Summit: How Should We Judge UNCED's Success?" *Environment* 34(8), October 1992, pp. 6–11, 26–33.

Hahn, Robert W. "An Evaluation of Options for Reducing Hazardous Waste." *Harvard Environmental Law Review*, 1988, pp. 201–30.

———. "Economic Prescriptions for Environmental Problems: How the Patient Followed the Doctor's Orders." *Journal of Economic Perspectives* 3(2), Spring 1989, pp. 95–114.

Hahn, Robert W., and Gordon L. Hester. "Marketable Permits: Lessons for Theory and Practice." *Ecology Law Quarterly* 16, 1989, pp. 361–406.

Hahn, Robert W., and Roger Noll. "Designing a Market for Tradable Emissions Permits." In Wesley Magat, ed., *Reform of Environmental Regulation*. Cambridge, MA: Ballinger Publishing Company, 1982.

Haigh, John A., David Harrison, Jr., and Albert L. Nichols. "Benefit–Cost Analysis of Environmental Regulation: Case Studies of Hazardous Air Pollutants." *Harvard Environmental Law Review* 8(2), 1984, pp. 395–434.

Hall, John, and Ciannat Howett. "Albemarle–Pamlico: Case Study in Pollutant Trading." *EPA Journal* 20 (1–2), Summer 1994, pp. 27–29.

Halvorsen, Robert, and Michael G. Ruby. *Benefit–Cost Analysis of Air-Pollution Control*. Lexington, MA: D. C. Heath and Company, 1981.

Hamilton, Joan O'C., and Geoffrey Smith. "Making Clean Energy Sweeter to Utilities." *Business Week*, July 15, 1991, p. 136.

Hardin, Garrett. "The Tragedy of the Commons." *Science* 162, 1968, pp. 1243–48.

Harrington, Winston, Alan J. Krupnick, and Henry M. Peskin. "Policies for Nonpoint–Source Water Pollution Control." *Journal of Soil and Water Conservation*, January/February 1985, pp. 27–32.

Harrison, D., Jr., and D. Rubinfeld. "Hedonic Housing Prices and the Demand for Clean Air." *Journal of Environmental Economics and Management* 5, March 1978, pp. 81–102.

Haveman, Robert H., and Burton A. Weisbrod. "The Concepts of Benefits in Cost–Benefit Analysis: With Emphasis on Water Pollution Control Activities." In Henry M. Peskin and Eugene P. Seskin, eds., *Cost Benefit Analysis and Water Pollution Policy*. Washington, DC: The Urban Institute, 1975.

Hazilla, Michael, and Raymond J. Kopp. "Social Cost of Environmental Quality Regulations: A General Equilibrium Analysis." *Journal of Political Economy* 98(4), 1990, pp. 853–73.

Heath, Jenifer. "Moynihan Bill Sets Goals." *Water Environment and Technology*, July 1993, pp. 28–30.

Heath, Ralph C. "Ground Water." In David H. Speidel, Lon C. Ruedisili, and Allen F. Agnew, eds., *Perspectives on Water: Uses and Abuses*. New York: Oxford Univ. Press, 1988.

Helfand, Gloria E. "Pollution Prevention As Public Policy: An Assessment." *Contemporary Economic Policy* 12, October 1994, pp. 104–13.

Heritage, John, ed. *EPA Journal* 18(1), March/April 1992.

Herzog, Henry W. "Economic Efficiency and Equity in Water Quality Control: Effluent Taxes and Information Requirements." *Journal of Environmental Economics and Management* 2, 1976, pp. 170–84.

Heumann, Jenny M. "State Recycling Programs: A Waste Reduction Emphasis." *Waste Age*, August 1997.

Hof, Robert D. "The Tiniest Toxic Avengers." *Business Week*, June 4, 1990, pp. 96, 98.

Holtermann, S. E. "Externalities and Public Goods." *Economica* 39, February 1972.

Hong, Peter. "John Henry: A Power Broker for Cleaner Power." *Business Week*, July 20, 1992.

Hong, Peter, and Michele Galen. "The Toxic Mess Called Superfund." *Business Week*, May 11, 1992, pp. 32–34.

Houghton, J. T., G. J. Jenkins, and J. J. Ephraums, eds. *Climate Change: The IPCC Scientific Assessment*. Report prepared for the Intergovernmental Panel on

Climate Change by Working Group I. Cambridge, England: Cambridge Univ. Press, 1990.

Howe, Charles W. "An Evaluation of U.S. Air and Water Policies." *Environment* 33(7), September 1991, pp. 10–15, 34–36.

Humphrey, Hubert H., III, and LeRoy C. Paddock. "The Federal and State Roles in Environmental Enforcement: A Proposal for a More Effective and More Efficient Relationship." *Harvard Environmental Law Review*, 1990, pp. 7–44.

ICF Resources International. *Economic, Environmental, and Coal Market Impacts of $SO_2$ Emissions Trading under Alternative Acid Rain Control Proposals.* Report prepared for the Regulatory Innovations Staff, Office of Policy, Planning and Evaluation, U.S. EPA, 1989.

International Energy Agency. Paris, France, **www.iea.org/stat.htm**.

International Labour Office (ILO). Unpublished data. Geneva: ILO, 1986.

———. Unpublished data. Geneva: ILO, 1993.

Japikse, Catharina. "Lasagna in the Making." *EPA Journal* 20(3–4), Fall 1994, p. 27.

Jenkins, Robin. *The Economics of Solid Waste Reduction: The Impact of User Fees.* Brookfield, VT: Edward Elgar Publishing Company, 1993.

Johansson, Per-Olov. "Valuing Environmental Damage." In Dieter Helm, ed., *Economic Policy towards the Environment.* Cambridge, MA: Blackwell Publishers, 1991, pp. 111–36.

Johnson, Edwin L. "A Study in the Economics of Water Quality Management." *Water Resources Research* 3, 1967, pp. 291–305.

Jondrow, James, and Robert A. Levy. "The Displacement of Local Spending for Pollution Control by Federal Construction Grants." *American Economic Review* 74(2), 1984, pp. 174–78.

Kelly, Kevin. "It Really Can Pay to Clean Up Your Act." *Business Week*, November 7, 1994, p. 141.

Kemp, David D. *Global Environmental Issues: A Climatological Approach.* New York: Routledge, 1990.

Kerr, Richard A. "Greenhouse Forecasting Still Cloudy." *Science* 276, May 16, 1997, pp. 1040–42.

Kharbanda, O. P., and E. A. Stallworthy. *Waste Management: Towards a Sustainable Society.* New York: Auburn House, 1990.

Kimm, Victor J. "The Delaney Clause Dilemma." *EPA Journal* 19(1), January/February/March 1993, pp. 39–41.

King, David J., and Eric Schaeffer. "EPA's Flagship Programs." *EPA Journal* 19(3), July–September 1993, pp. 26–30.

Kinsman, Art. "Fueling the Future." *AAA World*, April 1992, pp. 2F–2H.

Kirchhoff, Sue. "FDA Proposes Bottled Water Measure Up to Tap Standards." *Boston Globe*, January 1, 1993.

Kirkpatrick, David. "Environmentalism: The New Crusade." *Fortune*, February 12, 1990, pp. 44–52.

Kneese, Allen V., Robert U. Ayres, and Ralph C. D'Arge. *Economics and the Environment: A Materials Balance Approach.* Washington, DC: Resources for the Future, 1970.

Knepper, Mike. "Recycling: Investment in the Future." *BMW Magazine*, January 1993, pp. 66–69.

Knopman, Debra S., and Richard A. Smith. 'Legislative Status of the U.S. Clean Water Act,' in "20 Years of the Clean Water Act," *Environment* 35(1), January/February 1993, p. 18.

Koehler, Jamison, and Stephen Lingle. "U.S. TIES: Diffusing Technologies Abroad." *EPA Journal* 20(3–4), Fall 1994, pp. 32–33.

Kohlhase, Janet E. "The Impact of Toxic Waste Sites on Housing Values." *Journal of Urban Economics* 30, 1991, pp. 1–26.

Kopp, Raymond J., and Alan J. Krupnick. "Agricultural Policy and the Benefits of Ozone Control." *American Journal of Agricultural Economics* 69(5), December 1987, pp. 956–62.

Kranish, Michael. "Energy Tax Plan Changes Sought." *Boston Globe*, February 19, 1993, pp. 57–58.

———. "Clinton Treads into Forests Dispute." *Boston Globe*, April 3, 1993, p. 3.

Krimsky, Sheldon, and Dominic Golding. "Factoring Risk into Environmental Decision Making." In Richard A. Chechile and Susan Carlisle, eds., *Environmental Decision Making: A Multidisciplinary Perspective*. New York: Van Nostrand Reinhold, 1991.

Krupnick, Alan. "Costs of Alternative Policies for the Control of Nitrogen Dioxide in Baltimore." *Journal of Environmental Economics and Management* 13, 1986, pp. 189–97.

Krutilla, John, V. "Conservation Reconsidered." *American Economic Review* 57, 1967, pp. 777–86.

Kuhn, Thomas S. *Structure of Scientific Revolutions*. Chicago: Univ. of Chicago Press, 1970.

Lancaster, Kelvin J. "A New Approach to Consumer Theory." *Journal of Political Economy* 78, 1966, pp. 311–29.

Landy, Marc K., Marc J. Roberts, and Stephen R. Thomas. *The Environmental Protection Agency: Asking the Wrong Questions*. New York: Oxford Univ. Press, 1990.

Larson, Charles D. "Historical Development of the National Primary Drinking Water Regulations." In Edward J. Calabrese, Charles E. Gilbert, and Harris Pastides, eds., *Safe Drinking Water Act: Amendments, Regulations and Standards*. Chelsea, MI: Lewis Publishers, 1989, pp. 3–15.

Lashof, D., and D. Tirpak, eds. *Policy Options for Stabilizing Global Climate, Draft Report to Congress*. Washington, DC: U.S. EPA, Office of Policy, Planning, and Evaluation, February 1989.

Lave, Lester B., ed. *Quantitative Risk Assessment in Regulation*. Washington, DC: Brookings Institution, 1982a.

———. "Methods of Risk Assessment." In Lester B. Lave, ed., *Quantitative Risk Assessment in Regulation*. Washington, DC: Brookings Institution, 1982b, pp. 23–54.

Lawrence, Jennifer. "Mobil." *Advertising Age*, January 29, 1991, p. 12.

Lederer, Edith M. "Ban on Atomic Dumping at Sea Voted; 4 Nuclear Powers Abstain." *Boston Globe*, November 13, 1993.

Lee, David. "Ozone Loss: Modern Tools for a Modern Problem." *EPA Journal* 18(2), May/June, 1992, pp. 16–18.

Lee, Martin R. "Environmental Protections: From the 103rd to the 104th Congress." *Congressional Research Service, Report for Congress*, #95-58ENR, January 3, 1995.

Letson, David. "Point/Nonpoint Source Pollution Reduction Trading: An Interpretive Survey." *Natural Resources Journal* 32(2), Spring 1992, pp. 219–32.

Light, Alfred R. "A Defense Counsel's Perspective on Superfund." *Environmental Law Reporter* 15(7), July 1985, pp. 10203–07.

Liroff, Richard A. *Reforming Air Pollution Regulation: The Toil and Trouble of EPA's Bubble*. Washington, DC: The Conservation Foundation, 1986.

*Los Angeles Times*. "Newspaper Recycling Booming." *Brockton Enterprise*, July 11, 1995, p. 18.

Lyklema, J., and T. E. A. van Hylckama. "Water Something Peculiar." In David H. Speidel, Lon C. Ruedisili, and Allen F. Agnew, eds., *Perspectives on Water: Uses and Abuses*. New York: Oxford University Press, 1988.

Main, Jeremy. "The Big Cleanup Gets It Wrong." *Fortune*, May 20, 1991, pp. 95–96, 100–01.

Malik, Arun S., David Letson, and Stephen R. Crutchfield. "Point/Nonpoint Source Trading of Pollution Abatement: Choosing the Right Trading Ratio." *American Journal of Agricultural Economics* 75, November 1993, pp. 959–67.

Maloney, Michael T., and Bruce Yandle. "Estimation of the Cost of Air Pollution Control Regulation." *Journal of Environmental Economics and Management* 11, 1984, pp. 244–63.

Mandel, Michael J. "The Right to Pollute Shouldn't Be for Sale." *Business Week*, May 22, 1989, p. 158G.

Manly, Lorne. "It Doesn't Pay to Go Green When Consumers Are Seeing Red." *Adweek*, March 23, 1992, pp. 32–33.

Marchant, Gary E., and Dawn P. Danzeisen. "'Acceptable' Risk for Hazardous Air Pollutants." *Harvard Environmental Law Review* 13(2), 1989, pp. 535–58.

Marshall, Alfred. *Principles of Economics*. 1st ed.: 1890; 8th ed., London: Macmillan, 1930.

Marshall, Jonathan. "How Ecology Is Tied to Mexico Trade Pact." *San Francisco Chronicle*, February 25, 1992, p. A8.

Mathtech, Inc. *Benefit and Net Benefit Analysis of Alternative National Ambient Air Quality Standards for Particulate Matter*, vol. 1. Prepared for U.S. Environmental Protection Agency, Economic Analysis Branch, Office of Air Quality Planning and Standards. Research Triangle Park, NC: U.S. EPA, March 1983.

Mazmanian, Daniel, and David Morell. *Beyond Superfailure: America's Toxics Policy for the 1990s*. Boulder, CO: Westview Press, 1992.

McCarthy, James E. "Packaging Waste: How the United States Compares to Other Countries." *Reusable News*, Winter/Spring 1993, p. 3.

McCarthy, James, and Mark Reisch. *Hazardous Waste Fact Book*. Environment and Natural Resources Policy Division, Congressional Research Service, 87-56 ENR, June 30, 1987.

McDermott, H. "Federal Drinking Water Standards—Past, Present, and Future." *Water Well Journal* 27(12), 1973, pp. 29–35.

McGartland, Albert M. "Marketable Permit Systems for Air Pollution Control: An Empirical Study." Ph.D. Dissertation, Univ. of Maryland, 1984.

Menz, Fredric C. "Transborder Emissions Trading between Canada and the United States." *Natural Resources Journal* 35, Fall 1995, pp. 803–19.

Metz, Robert. "N.M. Firm Is Ready to Roll into the Tire Recycling Industry." *Boston Globe*, December 28, 1993, p. 34.

Miller, Krystal. "Big 3 to Cooperate on Efforts to Meet Clean-Air Rules." *The Wall Street Journal*, June 9, 1992, p. B9.

Miller, William. "Oil Spill Threatens North Sea Wildlife." *Boston Globe*, January 6, 1993.

Mills, Edwin S. *The Economics of Environmental Quality*. New York: W. W. Norton, 1978.

Mitchell, Robert Cameron, and Richard T. Carson. *Using Surveys to Value Public Goods: The Contingent Valuation Method*. Washington, DC: Resources for the Future, 1989.

Mitchell, Robert Cameron, Angela G. Mertig, and Riley E. Dunlap. "Twenty Years of Environmental Mobilization: Trends among National Environmental Organizations." In Riley E. Dunlap and Angela G. Mertig, eds., *American Environmentalism: The U.S. Environmental Movement, 1970–1990*. Philadelphia, PA: Taylor & Francis New York, Inc., 1992.

Monaghan, Peter. "Taking on the Tail Pipe—and the EPA." *The Chronicle of Higher Education*, March 10, 1993, p. A5.

Moore, Michael J., and W. Kip Viscusi. "Doubling the Estimated Value of Life: Results Using New Occupational Fatality Data." *Journal of Policy Analysis and Management* 7(3), Spring 1988, pp. 476–90.

Moynihan, Daniel Patrick. "A Legislative Proposal: Why Not Enact a Law That Would Help Us Set Sensible Priorities." *EPA Journal* 19(1), January/February/March 1993, pp. 46–47.

Mullen, John K., and Fredric C. Menz. "The Effect of Acidification Damages on the Economic Value of the Adirondack Fishery to New York Anglers." *American Journal of Agricultural Economics* 67(1), February 1985, pp. 112–19.

National Academy of Sciences. *Risk Assessment in the Federal Government: Managing the Process.* Washington, DC: U.S. Government Printing Office, 1983.

National Academy of Sciences and National Academy of Engineering. *Air Quality and Automobile Emission Control*, Vol. 4, *The Costs and Benefits of Automobile Emission Control.* Washington, DC: U.S. Government Printing Office, 1974.

National Acid Precipitation Assessment Program. *1990 Integrated Assessment Report.* Washington, DC: NAPAP Office of the Director, November 1991.

National Advisory Committee on Oceans and Atmosphere. *Nuclear Waste Management and the Use of the Sea.* Washington, DC: U.S. Government Printing Office, April 1984.

National Commission on Air Quality. *To Breathe Clean Air.* Washington, DC: U.S. Government Printing Office, March 1981.

National Commission on Water Quality. *Report to the Congress.* Washington, DC: U.S. Government Printing Office, March 1976.

National Environmental Protection Agency. "China Country Program for the Phaseout of Ozone-Depleting Substances under the Montreal Protocol." Report submitted to the Ninth Meeting of the Executive Committee of the Multilateral Fund of the Montreal Protocol, Montreal, March 1993.

National Research Council. *Carbon Dioxide and Climate: A Scientific Assessment.* Washington, DC: National Academy Press, 1979.

———. *Current Issues in Atmospheric Change.* Washington, DC: National Academy Press, 1987.

National Research Council, Committee on Passive Smoking, Board on Environmental Studies and Toxicology. *Environmental Tobacco Smoke: Measuring Exposures and Assessing Health Effects.* Washington, DC: National Academy Press, 1986.

National Solid Waste Management Association (NSWMA). *Recycling in the States: Mid-Year Update 1990.* Washington, DC: NSWMA, October 1990.

Newcomb, Peter. "'Ban the Box'." *Forbes*, May 13, 1991, p. 70.

Nitze, William A. "Stopping the Waste: Technology Itself Is Not the Problem." *EPA Journal* 19(2), April–June 1993, pp. 31–33.

Noah, Timothy. "EPA Declares 'Passive' Smoke a Human Carcinogen." *The Wall Street Journal*, January 6, 1993, p. B1.

———. "EPA Finds Unsafe Lead Levels in Water." *The Wall Street Journal*, May 12, 1993, p. B6.

———. "Environmental Groups Say Deal Poses Threats." *The Wall Street Journal*, December 16, 1993, p. A10.

Nussbaum, Bruce, and John Templeman. "Built to Last—until It's Time to Take it Apart." *Business Week*, September 17, 1990, p. 102.

Oates, Wallace E., Paul R. Portney, and Albert M. McGartland. "The Net Benefits of Incentive-Based Regulation: A Case Study of Environmental Standard-Setting." *American Economic Review* 75, 1989, pp. 1223–42.

Ohnuma, Keiko. "Missed Manners." *Sierra*, March/April 1990, pp. 24–26.

O'Neil, William B. "Pollution Permits and Markets for Water Quality." Ph.D. Dissertation, University of Wisconsin—Madison, 1980.

O'Neil, William B., Martin H. David, Christina Moore, and Erhard F. Joeres. "Transferable Discharge Permits and Economic Efficiency: The Fox River."

*Journal of Environmental Economics and Management* 10(4), December 1983, pp. 346–55.

Opschoor, J. B., and Has B. Vos. *Economic Instruments for Environmental Protection.* Paris: Organisation for Economic Co-operation and Development, 1989.

Organisation for Economic Co-operation and Development (OECD). *Economic Instruments for Environmental Protection.* Paris: OECD, 1989a.

———. "Recent Developments in the Use of Economic Instruments for Environmental Protection in OECD Countries." OECD Environment Monographs 41, Paris: OECD, February 1991.

———. *Global Warming: The Benefits of Emission Abatement.* Paris: OECD, 1992.

———. *Managing the Environment: The Role of Economic Instruments.* Paris: OECD, 1994.

O'Toole, Randal. *Reforming the Forest Service.* Washington, DC: Island Press, 1988.

Palmer, A. R., W. E. Mooz, T. H. Quinn, and K. A. Wolf. "Economic Implications of Regulating Chlorofluorocarbon Emissions from Nonaerosol Applications." Report #R-2524-EPA prepared by the Rand Corporation for the U.S. EPA, June 1980.

Park, Richard A., Manjit S. Trehan, Paul W. Mausel, and Robert C. Howe. "The Effects of Sea Level Rise on U.S. Coastal Wetlands." Contributing project to U.S. Environmental Protection Agency, Office of Policy, Planning, and Evaluation, Office of Research and Development, *The Potential Effects of Global Climate Change on the United States.* Washington, DC, December 1989.

Parker, Larry. "Global Climate Change: Market-Based Strategies to Reduce Greenhouse Gases." Washington, DC: Committee for the National Institute for the Environment." March 9, 1998.

Parrish, Michael. "GM Signs on to Environmental Code of Conduct." *Los Angeles Times*, February 10, 1993, p. D2.

Parson, Edward A., Peter M. Haas, and Marc A. Levy. "A Summary of the Major Documents Signed at the Earth Summit and the Global Forum." *Environment* 34(8), October 1992, pp. 12–15, 34–36.

Patton, Dorothy E. "The ABCs of Risk Assessment: Some Basic Principles Can Help People Understand Why Controversies Occur." *EPA Journal* 19(1), January/February/March 1993, pp. 10–15.

Perl, Lewis, and Frederick C. Dunbar. "Cost Effectiveness and Cost–Benefit Analysis of Air Quality Regulations." *American Economic Review* 72(2), May 1982, pp. 208–13.

Phifer, Russell W., and William R. McTigue Jr. *Handbook of Hazardous Waste Management.* Chelsea, MI: Lewis Publishers, 1988.

Pigou, A. C. *The Economics of Welfare*, 4th ed. London: Macmillan, 1952.

Porter, Richard C. "Michigan's Experience with Mandatory Deposits on Beverage Containers." *Land Economics* 59, 1983, pp. 177–94.

Portney, Paul R. "Air Pollution Policy." In Paul R. Portney, ed., *Public Policies for Environmental Protection.* Washington, DC: Resources for the Future, 1990a, pp. 27–96.

———. "Economics and the Clean Air Act." *Journal of Economic Perspectives* 4(4), Fall 1990b, pp. 173–81.

"President's Council on Sustainable Development," **www.whitehouse.gov/ PCSD/index-plain.html**.

Preuss, Peter W. "EPA's CRADA Agreements: Sharing Expertise with Industry." *EPA Journal* 20 (3–4), Fall 1994, pp. 28–29.

Preuss, Peter W., and William H. Farland. "A Flagship Risk Assessment: EPA Reassesses Dioxin in an Open Forum." *EPA Journal* 19(1), January/February/ March 1993, pp. 24–26.

Protzman, Ferdinand. "Germany's Push to Expand the Scope of Recycling." *New York Times*, July 4, 1993.

Pryde, Lucy T. *Environmental Chemistry: An Introduction.* Menlo Park, CA: Cummings Publishing, 1973.

Putnam, Hayes and Bartlett, Inc. "Economic Implications of Potential Chlorofluorocarbons Restrictions: Final Report." December 2, 1987.

Quirk, James, and Katsuki Terasawa. "Choosing a Government Discount Rate: An Alternative Approach." *Journal of Environmental Economics and Management* 20, 1991, pp. 16–28.

Radin, Charles A. "With China's 'Miracle,' Pollution Surges." *Boston Globe*, January 2, 1995, pp. 47, 50.

Raeburn, Paul, and Gail DeGeorge. "You Bet I Mind." *Business Week*, September 15, 1997.

Ramanathan, V. "The Greenhouse Theory of Climate Change: A Test by an Inadvertent Global Experiment." *Science* 240, 1988, pp. 293–99.

Ramanathan, V., R. D. Cess, E. F. Harrison, P. Minnis, B. R. Barkstrom, E. Ahmad, and D. Hartmann. "Cloud-Radioactive Forcing and Climate: Results from the Earth Radiation Budget Experiment." *Science* 243, 1989, pp. 57–63.

Raven, Peter H., Linda R. Berg, and George B. Johnson. *Environment.* New York: Saunders College Publishing, Harcourt Brace Jovanovich College Publishers, 1993.

Reese, Craig E. "State Taxation of Hazardous Materials." *Oil and Gas Tax Quarterly* 33, 1985, pp. 502–526.

Regan, Mary Beth, Joseph Weber, Chris Roush, and Kevin Kelly. "Toxic Turnabout? A Deal on Superfund May Finally Be at Hand." *Business Week*, April 25, 1994, pp. 30–31.

"The Regulatory Improvement Act of 1998: Purpose and Summary," **http://thomas.loc.gov/cgi-bin/cpquery/1?cp105:./temp/~cp105V5Sn:e3633**.

Reidy, Chris. "Economics of Recycling Paper Take a Tumble." *Boston Globe*, July 24, 1996, pp. A1, A16.

Reifenberg, Anne, and Allanna Sullivan. "Rising Gasoline Prices: Everyone Else's Fault." *The Wall Street Journal*, May 1, 1996, pp. B1, B8.

Reilly, William K. "The Road from Rio." *EPA Journal* 18(4), September/October 1992, pp. 11–13.

Reisch, Mark. "Superfund Reauthorization Issues in the 105th Congress." *CRS Issue Brief for Congress.* Washington, DC: Committee for the National Institute for the Environment, April 2, 1998.

Repetto, Robert. "Accounting for Environmental Assets." *Scientific American*, June 1992, pp. 94–100.

———. "Earth in the Balance Sheet: Incorporating Natural Resources in National Income Accounts." *Environment* 34(7), September 1992, pp. 12–20, 43–45.

Research Triangle Institute. *Benefit–Cost Assessment Handbook for Water Programs*, Vol. 1. Prepared for the EPA, Economic Analysis Division, April 1993.

Resource Integration Systems, Ltd., and Waste Matters Consulting, Portland, Oregon. *Decisionmaker's Guide to Recycling Plastics.* Prepared for the Oregon Department of Environmental Quality Solid Waste Reduction and Recycling Section and U.S. Environmental Protection Agency, Region X, Solid Waste Program, December 1990.

Reuters. "Environmentalist Predicts Marked Change in U.S. Policy." *Boston Globe*, December 7, 1992.

———. "New Emissions Plan Sought." *Boston Globe*, April 8, 1995, p. 2.

———. "Mexico's Bad Air Exacts Financial Toll, Official Says." *Boston Globe*, May 30, 1998, p. A5.

Roach, Fred, Charles Kolstad, Allen V. Kneese, Richard Tovin, and Michael Williams. "Alternative Air Quality Policy Options in the Four Corners Region." *Southwest Review* 1(2), 1981, pp. 44–45.

Rose-Ackerman, Susan. "Effluent Charges: A Critique." *Canadian Journal of Economics* 6(4), November 1973, pp. 512–28.

———. "Market Models for Water Pollution Control: Their Strengths and Weaknesses." *Public Policy* 25(3), Summer 1977, pp. 383–406.

Rosen, Harvey S. *Public Finance.* Burr Ridge, IL: Richard D. Irwin, 1995.

Ross, Karl. "Some Foul Air in Puerto Rico." *Boston Globe*, January 7, 1993.

Rowe, Robert D., Michael G. Shelby, Joshua B. Epel, and Ari Michelsen. "Using Oxygenated Fuels to Mitigate Carbon Monoxide Air Pollution: The Case of Denver." *Contemporary Policy Issues* 8, January 1990, pp. 39–53.

Ruff, Larry. "The Economic Common Sense of Pollution." *The Public Interest* 19, Spring 1970, pp. 69–85.

Russell, Clifford, S. "What Can We Get from Effluent Charges?" *Policy Analysis* 5(2), Spring 1979, pp. 155–80.

St. Clair, Jeffrey, and Bernardo Issel. "A Field Guide to the Environmental Movement." Hoosier Environmental Council, **www.envirolink.org/envlib/orgs/hecweb/archive/fieldguide.htm**, July 28, 1997.

Samuelson, Paul A. "The Pure Theory of Public Expenditure." *Review of Economics and Statistics* 36, 1954, pp. 387–89.

———. "Diagrammatic Exposition of a Theory of Public Expenditure." *Review of Economics and Statistics* 37, 1955, pp. 350–56.

———. "Aspects of Public Expenditure Theory." *Review of Economics and Statistics* 40, 1958, pp. 332–38.

Sassone, Peter G., and William A. Schaffer. *Cost–Benefit Analysis: A Handbook.* New York: Academic Press, 1978.

Scheuplein, Robert. "Uncertainty and the 'Flavors' of Risk." *EPA Journal* 19(1), January/February/March 1993, pp. 16–17.

Schlesinger, Jacob M. "In Japan, Environment Means an Opportunity for New Technologies." *The Wall Street Journal*, November 5, 1990, p. A1.

Schmalensee, Richard, Paul L. Joskow, A. Denny Ellerman, Juan Pablo Montero, and Elizabeth M. Bailey. "An Interim Evaluation of Sulfur Dioxide Emissions Trading." *The Journal of Economic Perspectives* 12(3), Summer 1998, pp. 53–68.

Schmidheiny, Stephan. *Changing Course: A Global Business Perspective on Development and the Environment.* Cambridge, MA: MIT Press, 1992.

Schmidt, William E. "Aground, Tanker Spills Oil on Shetland." *New York Times*, January 6, 1993, p. A3.

Schrage, Michael. "In Tokyo, 'Just-in-Time' Deliveries in Need of Administrative Guidance." *Boston Globe*, March 22, 1992.

Schulze, William D., and David S. Brookshire. "The Economic Benefits of Preserving Visibility in the National Parklands of the Southwest." *Natural Resources Journal* 23(1), January 1983, pp. 763–72.

Seattle Solid Waste Utility. *Seattle Solid Waste Utility Rate Sheet and Customer Reply Card.* Seattle, WA: 1988.

Seattle Solid Waste Utility, Public Information Department. *Municipal Solid Waste Management Program Description.* Seattle, WA: 1991.

Seitz, Fred, and Christine Plepys. *Monitoring Air Quality in Health People 2000,* Statistical Notes No. 9. Hyattsville, MD: National Center for Health Statistics, 1995.

Seskin, Eugene P. "Automobile Air Pollution Policy." In Paul R. Portney, ed., *Current Issues in U.S. Environmental Policy.* Baltimore: Johns Hopkins University Press, 1978, pp. 68–104.

Sessions, Kathy. "Products of the Earth Summit." *EPA Journal* 19(2), April–June 1993a, p. 12.

———. "What's in *Agenda 21*?" *EPA Journal* 19(2), April–June 1993b, p. 14.

Shalal-Esa, Andrea. "Tobacco Industry Sues EPA over Secondhand Smoke Report." *Boston Globe*, June 23, 1993, p. 41.

Shapiro, Michael. "Toxic Substances Policy." In Paul R. Portney, ed., *Public Policies for Environmental Protection*. Washington, DC: Resources for the Future, 1990, pp. 195–241.

Shea, Cynthia Pollock. "Getting Serious in Germany." *EPA Journal* 18(3), July/August 1992, pp. 50–52.

Simmons, Peter, and Brian Wynne. "Responsible Care: Trust, Credibility, and Environmental Management." In Kurt Fischer and Johan Schot, eds., *Environmental Strategies for Industry: International Perspectives on Research Needs and Policy Implications*. Washington, DC: Island Press, 1993, pp. 207–226.

Sims, William A. *Economics of Sewer Effluent Charges*. Ph.D. Thesis, Political Economy, University of Toronto, 1977.

Skumatz, Lisa. Skumatz Economic Research Associates. Unpublished memorandum to whom it may concern. March 21, 1996.

Smith, Adam. *An Inquiry into the Nature and Causes of the Wealth of Nations*. 1776. Reprint, New York: Random House, 1937.

Smith, Emily T. "Developments to Watch: Aerosol Cans That Run on Compressed-Air Power." *Business Week*, June 12, 1989, p. 63.

Smith, Emily T., Vicki Cahan, Naomi Freundlich, James E. Ellis, and Joseph Weber. "The Greening of Corporate America: 'Sometimes You Find That the Public Has Spoken and You Get On with It.'" *Business Week*, April 23, 1990, pp. 96–103.

Smith, Emily T., and David Woodruff. "The Next Trick for Business: Taking a Cue from Nature." *Business Week*, May 11, 1992, pp. 74–75.

Smith, V. Kerry, and William H. Desvousges. "The Generalized Travel Cost Model and Water Quality Benefits: A Reconsideration." *Southern Economic Journal* 52, October 1985, pp. 371–81.

———. *Measuring Water Quality Benefits*. Norwell, MA: Kluwer-Nijhoff, 1986.

Smith, V. Kerry, William H. Desvousges, and Matthew P. McGivney. "Estimating Water Quality Benefits: An Econometric Analysis." *Southern Economic Journal* 50(2), October 1983, pp. 422–37.

Smith, V. Kerry, and John V. Krutilla, eds. *Explorations in Natural Resource Economics*. Baltimore: Johns Hopkins Press, 1982.

Smith, Velma. "Disaster in Milwaukee." *EPA Journal* 20 (1–2), Summer 1994, pp. 16–18.

Snyder, Adam. "The Color of Money." *SuperBrands*, 1992, pp. 30–31.

South Coast Air Quality Management District. *Regional Clean Air Incentives Market*. Diamond Bar, CA: 1992.

Spofford, Walter O., Jr. "Efficiency Properties of Alternative Source Control Policies for Meeting Ambient Air Quality Standards: An Empirical Application to the Lower Delaware Valley." Unpublished Resources for the Future discussion paper D-118, February 1984.

Spurlock, Stan R., and Ivery D. Clifton. "Efficiency and Equity Aspects of Nonpoint Source Pollution Controls." *Southern Journal of Agricultural Economics*, December 1982, pp. 123–29.

Stavins, Robert N. "What Can We Learn from the Grand Policy Experiment? Lessons from SO$_2$ Allowance Trading." *The Journal of Economic Perspectives* 12(3), Summer 1998, pp. 68–88.

Stern, Arthur C. "History of Air Pollution Legislation in the United States." *Journal of the Air Pollution Control Association* 32(1), January 1982, pp. 44–61.

Stiglitz, Joseph E. *Economics of the Public Sector.* New York: W. W. Norton, 1988.

Stranahan, Susan Q. "It's Enough to Make You Sick." *National Wildlife,* February/March 1990, pp. 8–15.

Stutz, Bruce. "The Landscape of Hunger." *Audubon* 95(2), March/April 1993, pp. 54–63.

Sullivan, R. Lee. "Snob Water." *Forbes,* August 14, 1995, p. 192.

Tanner, James. "Carbon Tax to Limit Use of Fossil Fuels Becomes Embroiled in Global Politics." *The Wall Street Journal,* June 9, 1992, p. A2.

Taylor, Jeffrey. "Auction of Rights to Pollute Fetches about $21 Million." *The Wall Street Journal,* March 31, 1992, p. A6.

———. "CBOT Plan for Pollution-Rights Market Is Encountering Plenty of Competition." *The Wall Street Journal,* August 24, 1993, pp. C1, C6.

Taylor, Jeffrey, and Rose Gutfeld, "CBOT Selected to Run Auction for Polluters." *The Wall Street Journal,* September 25, 1992, p. C1.

Taylor, Jeffrey, and Dave Kansas. "Environmentalists Vie for Right to Pollute." *The Wall Street Journal,* March 26, 1992, p. C1.

Thaler, Richard, and Sherwin Rosen. "The Value of Life Savings." In Nester Terleckyj, ed., *Household Production and Consumption.* New York: Columbia University Press, 1976.

Tietenberg, T. H. *Emissions Trading: An Exercise in Reforming Pollution Policy.* Washington, DC: Resources for the Future, 1985.

Tietenberg, Tom. *Environmental and Natural Resource Economics.* New York: HarperCollins College Publishers, 1996.

Tregarthen, Timothy. "Garbage by the Bag: Perkasie Acts on Solid Waste." *The Margin,* September/October 1989, p. 17.

Tresch, Richard W. *Public Finance: A Normative Theory.* Plano, TX: Business Publications, 1981.

Tuxen, Linda. "EPA's IRIS Data Base: Accessing the Science." *EPA Journal* 19(1), January/February/March 1993, pp. 22–23.

United Church of Christ Commission for Racial Justice (UCC). *Toxic Wastes and Race in the United States: A National Report on the Racial and Socio-Economic Characteristics of Communities with Hazardous Waste Sites.* New York: UCC, 1987.

United Nations. *Water Development and Management Volumes 1–4, Proceedings of the United Nations Water Conference.* Mar del Plata, Argentina, March 1977. Oxford: Pergamon Press for the United Nations, 1978.

United Nations Environment Program/UNESCO, Congress on Environmental Education and Training. *International Strategy.* Moscow: 1987.

United Nations Population Division. *World Population Prospects 1990.* New York: United Nations, 1991.

———. *Interpolated National Populations (The 1992 Revision).* New York: United Nations, 1993. Diskette.

U.S. Congress. *Safe Drinking Water Act Amendments.* Public Law 104-182. 104th Congress, August 6, 1996.

U.S. Congress, Congressional Budget Office (CBO). *Efficient Investments in Wastewater Treatment Plants.* Washington, DC: U.S. Government Printing Office, 1985a.

———. *Hazardous Waste Management: Recent Changes and Policy Alternatives.* Washington, DC: U.S. Government Printing Office, 1985b.

———. *Curbing Acid Rain: Cost, Budget, and Coal-Market Effects.* Washington, DC: U.S. Government Printing Office, June 1986.

U.S. Congress, Congressional Budget Office (CBO) from Office of Technology Assessment. Statement of Joel S. Hirschhorn for the Hearing Record. Senate Committee on Environment and Public Works, 98:2 (September 10, 1984).

U.S. Congress, Congressional Research Service. *History of the Water Pollution Control Act Amendments of 1972.* Ser. 1, 93rd Cong., 1st sess. (1972), 137.

U.S. Congress, Office of Technology Assessment (OTA). *Technologies and Management Strategies for Hazardous Waste Control.* Washington, DC: U.S. Government Printing Office, 1983.

———. *Protecting the Nation's Groundwater from Contamination*, vol. 1. Washington, DC: U.S. Government Printing Office, October 1984.

———. *Superfund Strategy.* Washington, DC: U.S. Government Printing Office, 1985.

———. *Wastes in Marine Environments.* Washington, DC: U.S. Government Printing Office, 1987.

———. "Water Supply: The Hydrologic Cycle." In David H. Speidel, Lon C. Ruedisili, and Allen F. Agnew, eds., *Perspectives on Water: Uses and Abuses.* New York: Oxford Univ. Press, 1988.

———. *Facing America's Trash: What Next for Municipal Solid Waste?* Washington, DC: U.S. Government Printing Office, 1989.

———. *Green Products by Design: Choices for a Cleaner Environment.* Washington, DC: U.S. Government Printing Office, October 1992.

U.S. Department of Agriculture and the U.S. Environmental Protection Agency. *Clean Water Action Plan: Restoring and Protecting America's Waters.* EPA-840-R-98-001, Washington, DC, 1998.

U.S. Department of Commerce, Bureau of the Census. *Government Finances.* Various issues.

U.S. Department of Commerce, Bureau of Economic Analysis. "Pollution Abatement Costs and Expenditures." Washington, DC: Department of Commerce (published periodically in *Survey of Current Business*).

U.S. Department of the Interior (DOI), Fish and Wildlife Service (FWS). *Threatened and Endangered Species.* Washington, DC, June 30, 1997.

U.S. Environmental Protection Agency. *Review of the Municipal Wastewater Treatment Works Program.* Washington, DC, November 1974.

———. *Economic Report—Alternative Methods of Financing Wastewater Treatment.* Washington, DC, 1975.

———. *The Risk–Cost Analysis Model: Phase III Report.* Washington, DC, March 1, 1984.

———. *Final Report: The Cost of Clean Air and Water.* Washington, DC, 1984a.

———. *Non-Point Source Pollution in the U.S., Report to Congress.* Washington, DC, 1984b.

———. *Site Discovery Methods.* EPA Contract 68-01-6888, Washington, DC, March 1987.

———. *The New Superfund: What It Is, How It Works.* Washington, DC, August 1987.

———. *Environmental Progress and Challenges: EPA's Update.* Washington, DC, August 1988.

———. *Comparing Risks and Setting Environmental Priorities.* Washington, DC, August 1989.

———. *Environmental Protection Agency Pollution Prevention Directive* (draft). Washington, DC, May 13, 1990.

———. *Charging Households for Waste Collection and Disposal: The Effects of Weight or Volume-Based Pricing on Solid Waste Management.* Final Report #EPA/53-SW-90-047, Washington, DC, September 1990.

———. *Meeting the Environmental Challenge: EPA's Review of Progress and New Directions in Environmental Protection.* Washington, DC, December 1990a.

———. *Toxic Substances 4-Year Strategy 1993–1996.* Washington, DC, December 1990b.

———. *Superfund NPL Characterization Project: National Results.* Washington, DC, 1991.

———. *Bottled Water Fact Sheet.* Washington, DC, March, 1991.

———. "1994 EPA SO$_2$ Allowance Auction." Washington, DC, 1994a.

———. "1994 EPA Allowance Auction Results." Washington, DC, 1994b.

———. "Green Lights Program," **www.epa.gov/greenlights.html**.

U.S. Environmental Protection Agency, Acid Rain Program. *Emissions Trading and Market Trends,* **www.epa.gov/acidrain/ats/trends.html**, updated January 1998.

U.S. Environmental Protection Agency, Environmental Criteria and Assessment Office. *IRIS Data Base.* Research Triangle Park, NC, 1993.

U.S. Environmental Protection Agency, Information Access Branch, Information Management and Services Division. *Access EPA.* Washington, DC, 1991.

U.S. Environmental Protection Agency, Office of Air and Radiation. *The Clean Air Act Amendments of 1990: Summary Materials.* Washington, DC, November 15, 1990.

———. *Clean Air Act Amendments of 1990: Detailed Summary of Titles.* Washington, DC, November 30, 1990.

———. *Green Lights Program: The First Year.* Washington, DC, February 1992.

———. *The Climate Is Right for Action: Voluntary Programs to Reduce Greenhouse Gas Emissions.* Washington, DC, October 1992.

———. *The Benefits and Costs of the Clean Air Act, 1970 to 1990.* Washington, DC, October 1997.

U.S. Environmental Protection Agency, Office of Air and Radiation, Office of Mobile Sources. *Environmental Fact Sheet: Accelerated Vehicle Retirement Programs.* Washington, DC, December 1997.

U.S. Environmental Protection Agency, Office of Air Quality Planning and Standards. *National Air Quality and Emissions Trends Report, 1991.* Research Triangle Park, NC, October 1992.

———. *National Air Quality and Emissions Trends Report, 1992.* Research Triangle Park, NC, October 1993.

———. *National Air Quality and Emissions Trends Report, 1994.* Research Triangle Park, NC, October 1995.

———. *National Air Pollutant Emissions Trends, 1900–1995.* Research Triangle Park, NC, October 1996.

———. "USA Air Quality Nonattainment Areas," **www.epa.gov/airs/nonattn. html**, effective January 27, 1998.

———. *The Plain English Guide to the Clean Air Act.* "Repairing the Ozone Layer," **www.epa.gov/oar/oaqps/peg_caa/pegcaa06.html**.

U.S. Environmental Protection Agency, Office of the Chief Financial Officer. *EPA Strategic Plan.* Washington, DC, September 1997.

———. *Summary of EPA's FY1999 President's Budget.* Washington, DC, 1998, **www.epa.gov/ocfo/99budget/1999bib_htm**.

U.S. Environmental Protection Agency, Office of Communications and Public Affairs. *Glossary of Environmental Terms and Acronym List.* Washington, DC, December 1989.

———. "EPA Tightens Standards for Lead in Drinking Water." *Environmental News*, Washington, DC, May 7, 1991.

U.S. Environmental Protection Agency, Office of Communications, Education and Public Affairs. *Securing Our Legacy, An EPA Progress Report 1989–1991.* Washington, DC, April 1992.

———. *Terms of Environment, Glossary, Abbreviations and Acronyms.* Washington, DC, September 1992.

———. "Federal Actions Address Environmental Justice." *EPA Activities Update*, Washington, DC, February 22, 1994a.

———. "Major Changes Recommended in the Clean Water Act." *EPA Activities Update*, Washington, DC, February 22, 1994b.

———. "Clinton Administration Proposes New Superfund Law." *EPA Activities Update*, Washington, DC, February 22, 1994c.

———. "EPA, Chicago Board of Trade Announce Results of Second Acid Rain Auction." *Environmental News*, Washington, DC, March 29, 1994.

———. "Administrator's Statement on Superfund Reform: October 5." *EPA Activities Update*, Washington, DC, October 17, 1994.

U.S. Environmental Protection Agency, Office of Drinking Water. *Bottled Water: Helpful Facts and Information.* Washington, DC, n.d.

U.S. Environmental Protection Agency, Office of Emergency and Remedial Response. *Superfund Progress—Aficionado's Version.* Washington, DC, June 1992.

———. *Progress toward Implementing Superfund Fiscal Year 1994; Report to Congress.* Washington, DC, n.d.

U.S. Environmental Protection Agency, Office of Enforcement and Compliance Assurance. *FY 1996 Enforcement and Compliance Assurance Accomplishments Report.* Washington, DC, **es.epa.gov/oeca/96accomp/index.html**, last updated February 18, 1998.

U.S. Environmental Protection Agency, Office of Ground Water and Drinking Water. *Fact Sheet: National Primary Drinking Water Regulations for Lead and Copper.* Washington, DC, May 1991.

———. *Water on Tap: A Consumer's Guide to the Nation's Drinking Water.* "Appendix A: National Primary Drinking Water Standards." Washington, DC, July 1997.

———. "Current Drinking Water Standards," **www.epa.gov/OGWDW/wot/appa.html**, last updated September 21, 1998.

U.S. Environmental Protection Agency, Office of Human Resources and Organizational Services. "EPA's Workforce: EPA's Workforce History." Washington, DC, **www.epa.gov/epahrist/growth.htm**, last updated June 26, 1997.

U.S. Environmental Protection Agency, Office of Mobile Sources. "Clean Fuels: An Overview." Fact Sheet OMS-6, Ann Arbor, MI, January 1993a.

———. "Vehicle Fuels and the 1990 Clean Air Act." Fact Sheet OMS-13, Ann Arbor, MI, January 1993b.

U.S. Environmental Protection Agency, Office of Pesticide Programs. "Pesticide Environmental Stewardship Program," **www.epa.gov/oppbppd1/PESP/**.

U.S. Environmental Protection Agency, Office of Pesticides and Toxic Substances. *Highlights of the 1988 Pesticide Law: The Federal Insecticide, Fungicide, and Rodenticide Act Amendments of 1988.* Washington, DC, December 1988.

———. *Pesticides in Drinking-Water Wells.* Washington, DC, September 1990.

———. *EPA's Pesticide Programs.* Washington, DC, May 1991.

———. *For Your Information: Pesticide Reregistration.* Washington, DC, June 1991.

———. *Pesticides and Ground-Water Strategy.* Washington, DC, October 1991.

U.S. Environmental Protection Agency, Office of Policy Analysis. *Costs and Benefits of Reducing Lead in Gasoline, Final Regulatory Impact Analysis.* Report No. EPA-230-05-85-006, Washington, DC, February 1985.

U.S. Environmental Protection Agency, Office of Policy Analysis, Office of Policy, Planning, and Evaluation. *Unfinished Business: A Comparative Assessment of Environmental Problems.* Washington, DC, February 1987.

———. *EPA's Use of Benefit–Cost Analysis, 1981–1986.* EPA Report #230-05-87-028, Washington, DC, August 1987.

U.S. Environmental Protection Agency, Office of Policy, Planning, and Evaluation. *Environmental Investments: The Cost of a Clean Environment, A Summary.* Washington, DC, December 1990.

———. *Economic Incentives: Options for Environmental Protection.* Washington, DC, March 1991.

———. *Environmental Equity: Reducing Risk for All Communities.* Washington, DC, June 1992.

———. *State Implementation of Nonpoint Source Programs*, draft report. Washington, DC, June 29, 1992.

———. *The United States Experience with Economic Incentives to Control Environmental Pollution.* Washington, DC, July 1992.

U.S. Environmental Protection Agency, Office of Policy, Planning, and Evaluation, Office of Research and Development. *The Potential Effects of Global Climate Change on the United States.* Washington, DC, December 1989.

U.S. Environmental Protection Agency, Office of Pollution Prevention. *Pollution Prevention 1991: Progress on Reducing Industrial Pollutants.* Washington, DC, October 1991.

U.S. Environmental Protection Agency, Office of Pollution Prevention and Toxics. *Design for the Environment: Environmental Accounting and Capital Budgeting Project Update #1.* Washington, DC, October 1993.

———. *1995 Toxics Release Inventory.* Washington, DC, April 1997.

———. *Toxics Release Inventory Related National and International Programs.* Washington, DC, **www.epa.gov/opptintr/tri/national.htm**, last updated June 23, 1998.

U.S. Environmental Protection Agency, Office of Prevention, Pesticides, and Toxic Substances. "New Chemicals Program." Washington, DC, **www.epa.gov/opptintr/newchms/**, last updated June 19, 1998.

U.S. Environmental Protection Agency, Office of Research and Development, National Center for Environmental Assessment. *Dioxin and Related Compounds.* **www.epa.gov/nceawww1/dioxin.htm**, last updated February 10, 1998.

U.S. Environmental Protection Agency, Office of Solid Waste. *National Screening Survey of Hazardous Waste Treatment, Storage, Disposal, and Recycling Facilities.* Washington, DC.

———. *Solving the Hazardous Waste Problem: EPA's RCRA Program.* Washington, DC, November 1986.

———. *Recycling Works! State and Local Solutions to Solid Waste Management Problems.* Washington, DC, January 1989.

U.S. Environmental Protection Agency, Office of Solid Waste and Emergency Response. *The New RCRA Fact Book.* Washington, DC, October 1985.

———. *Decision-Makers Guide to Solid Waste Management.* Washington, DC, November 1989.

———. *EPA's Report to Congress on Methods to Manage and Control Plastic Wastes.* Washington, DC, February 1990.

———. *Unit Pricing: Providing an Incentive to Reduce Municipal Solid Waste.* Washington, DC, February 1991.

———. *Summary of Markets for Scrap Tires*, Washington, DC, October 1991.

———. *Leaking Underground Storage Tanks and Health: Understanding Health Risks from Petroleum Contamination.* Washington, DC, January 1992.

———. "The Wisdom of Waste Reduction at McDonald's." *Reusable News*, Spring 1992, pp. 1, 3.

———. *Superfund Progress, Spring 1992.* Washington, DC, May 1992.

———. *Characterization of Municipal Solid Waste in the United States: 1992 Update.* Washington, DC, July 1992a.

———. "FTC Announces Environmental Marketing Guidelines for Industry." *Reusable News*, Fall 1992.

———. *WasteWise: EPA's Voluntary Program for Reducing Business Solid Waste.* Washington, DC, October 1993.

———. *Environmental Fact Sheet*, "Recycling Municipal Solid Waste: 1995 Facts and Figures." Washington, DC, #EPA/530-F-97-015, April 1997.

————. *Characterization of Municipal Solid Waste in the United States: 1996 Update*. Washington, DC, May 1997.

U.S. Environmental Protection Agency, Office of Toxic Substances. *The Layman's Guide to the Toxic Substances Control Act*. Washington, DC, June 1987.

U.S. Environmental Protection Agency, Office of Water. *Lead Contamination Control Act*. Washington, DC, July 1988.

————. *Marine and Estuarine Protection: Programs and Activities*. Washington, DC, February 1989.

————. *Fact Sheet: National Primary Drinking Water Standards*. Washington, DC, August 1991.

————. "Is Your Drinking Water Safe?" Washington, DC, December 1991.

————. *Managing Nonpoint Source Pollution*. Washington, DC, January 1992.

————. *National Water Quality Inventory: 1990 Report to Congress*, Washington, DC, April 1992a.

————. *Drinking Water Regulations and Health Advisories*. Washington, DC, April 1992b.

————. "Phase V Rule: Fact Sheet." Washington, DC, May 1992.

————. *National Water Quality Inventory: 1992 Report to Congress*. Washington, DC, March 1994.

————. *Clean Water Act Initiative: Analysis of Costs and Benefits*. Washington, DC, 1994.

————. *The Clean Water State Revolving Fund: Financing America's Environmental Infrastructure—A Report of Progress*. Washington, DC, January 1995.

————. *National Water Quality Inventory: 1994 Report to Congress*. Washington, DC, December 1995.

————. *Effluent Trading in Watersheds Policy Statement*, **www.epa.gov/OWOW/ watershed/tradetbl.html**, last updated January 5, 1998.

U.S. Environmental Protection Agency, Office of Water, Office of Ground Water and Drinking Water. *Community Water Systems Survey*, vol. 1. Washington, DC, January 1997.

————. Drinking Water State Revolving Fund, **www.epa.gov/OGWDW/dwsrf. html**, last updated June 23, 1998.

U.S. Environmental Protection Agency, Office of Water, Office of Pesticides and Toxic Substances. *National Pesticide Survey: Update and Summary of Phase II Results*. Washington, DC, Winter 1992.

U.S. Environmental Protection Agency, Office of Water Regulations and Standards. *Introduction to Water Quality Standards*. Washington, DC, September 1988.

U.S. Environmental Protection Agency, Region 5. *A Risk Analysis of Twenty-Six Environmental Problems*. Washington, DC, May 1991.

U.S. Environmental Protection Agency, Risk Assessment Forum. *Framework for Ecological Risk Assessment*. Washington, DC, February 1992.

————. Proposed Guidelines for Ecological Risk Assessment. #EPA/630/R-95/002B, Washington, DC, August 1996.

U.S. Environmental Protection Agency, Science Advisory Board. *Reducing Risk: Setting Priorities and Strategies for Environmental Protection*. Washington, DC, September 1990.

U.S. Environmental Protection Agency, Stratospheric Protection Program, Office of Air and Radiation. *Regulatory Impact Analysis*, vols. 1–3. Washington, DC, December 1987.

U.S. Environmental Protection Agency, U.S. Department of Health and Human Services, and U.S. Public Health Service. *A Citizen's Guide to Radon: The Guide to Protecting Yourself and Your Family from Radon*. Washington, DC, May 1992.

U.S. General Accounting Office (GAO). *Siting of Hazardous Waste Landfills and Their Correlation with Racial and Economic Status of Surrounding Communities.* Washington, DC, 1983.

———. *Illegal Disposal of Hazardous Waste: Difficult to Detect or Deter.* Washington, DC, February 22, 1985.

———. *SUPERFUND: Extent of Nation's Potential Hazardous Waste Problem Still Unknown.* Washington, DC, December 1987.

———. *Water Pollution: More EPA Action Needed to Improve the Quality of Heavily Polluted Waters.* Washington, DC, January 1989.

———. *Drinking Water: Compliance Problems Undermine EPA Program as New Challenges Emerge.* Washington, DC, June 1990.

———. *Water Pollution: Greater EPA Leadership Needed to Reduce Nonpoint Source Pollution.* Washington, DC, October 1990.

———. *Pesticides: EPA's Use of Benefit Assessment in Regulating Pesticides.* Washington, DC, March 1991.

———. *Water Pollution: Stronger Efforts Needed by EPA to Control Toxic Water Pollution.* Washington, DC, July 1991.

U.S. International Trade Commission. *Synthetic Organic Chemicals, United States Production and Sales.* Washington DC: U.S. Government Printing Office, annual.

U.S. Office of Management and Budget. "Guidelines and Discount Rates for Benefit–Cost Analysis of Federal Programs." Circular No. A-94 Revised, Washington, DC, October 29, 1992.

U.S. Senate, Staff of the Subcommittee on Air and Water Pollution of the Committee on Public Works. *The Impact of Auto Emission Standards.* Washington, DC: U.S. Government Printing Office, October 1973.

*U.S. Water News.* "Utilities Getting the SDWA Bill." January 1991, p. 10.

Van Putten, Mark C., and Bradley D. Jackson. "The Dilution of the Clean Water Act." *Journal of Law Reform* 19(4), Summer 1986, pp. 863–901.

Vaughan, William J., and Clifford S. Russell. "Valuing a Fishing Day: An Application of a Systematic Varying Parameter Model." *Land Economics* 58(4), November 1982, pp. 450–63.

Vaupel, James W. "Truth or Consequences: Some Roles for Scientists and Analysts in Environmental Decisionmaking." In Wesley A. Magat, ed., *Reform of Environmental Regulation.* Cambridge, MA: Ballinger Publishing Company, 1978, pp. 71–92.

Vogan, Christine R. "Pollution Abatement and Control Expenditures, 1972–94." *Survey of Current Business.* Washington, DC: Department of Commerce, Bureau of Economic Analysis, September 1996.

Vogel, David. *National Styles of Regulation, Environmental Policy in Great Britain and the United States.* Ithaca, NY: Cornell University Press, 1986.

Wartzman, Rick. "Administration Alters Proposal for Energy Tax." *The Wall Street Journal,* April 2, 1993, p. A2.

Wernette, D. R., and L. A. Nieves. "Breathing Polluted Air." *EPA Journal* 18(1), March/April 1992, pp. 16–17.

West, Patrick C. "Invitation to Poison? Detroit Minorities and Toxic Fish Consumption from the Detroit River." In Bunyan Bryant and Paul Mohai, eds., *The Proceedings of the Michigan Conference on Race and the Incidence of Environmental Hazards.* Boulder, CO: Westview Press, 1992.

———. "Health Concerns for Fish-Eating Tribes? Government Assumptions Are Much Too Low." *EPA Journal* 18(1), March/April 1992, pp. 15–16.

White, Gilbert W. "Water Resource Adequacy: Illusion and Reality." In David H. Speidel, Lon C. Ruedisili, and Allen F. Agnew, eds., *Perspectives on Water: Uses and Abuses.* New York: Oxford University Press, 1988.

White, Lawrence J. *The Regulation of Air Pollutant Emissions from Motor Vehicles.* Washington, DC: American Enterprise Institute for Public Policy Research, 1982.

Whiteman, Lily. "Trades to Remember: The Lead Phasedown." *EPA Journal* 18(2), May/June 1992, pp. 38–39.

Williams, Marcia E. "Pesticides: The Potential for Change." *EPA Journal* 18(2), May/June 1992, pp. 15–16.

Wirth, Timothy E., and John Heinz. *Project 88—Round II Incentives for Action: Designing Market-Based Environmental Strategies.* Washington, DC, May 1991.

Wittwer, S. "The Rising Level of Atmospheric Carbon Dioxide: An Agricultural Perspective." In J. H. McBeath, ed., *The Potential Effects of Carbon Dioxide–Induced Climatic Change in Alaska: Conference Proceedings.* Fairbanks, AK: School of Agriculture and Land Resources Management, Univ. of Alaska, 1984.

Wolf, Sidney M. *Pollution Law Handbook: A Guide to Federal Environmental Laws.* New York: Quorom Books, 1988.

World Resources Institute. *World Resources 1992–93, A Guide to the Global Environment.* New York: Oxford Univ. Press, 1992a.

———. *The 1992 Information Please Environmental Almanac.* Boston: Houghton Mifflin Company, 1992b.

———. *The 1993 Information Please Environmental Almanac.* Boston: Houghton Mifflin Company, 1993.

———. *World Resources 1994–1995, A Guide to the Global Environment.* New York: Oxford Univ. Press, 1994b.

———. *1997 Information Please Almanac,* **www.infoplease.com**.

Yang, Dori Jones, William C. Symonds, and Lisa Driscoll. "Recycling Is Rewriting the Rules of Papermaking." *Business Week,* April 22, 1991, pp. 100H–101H.

York, Michael. "President Wins One on NAFTA; Court Reverses Order to Study Environment." *The Washington Post,* September 25, 1993, p. A1.

Younger, Joseph D. "Cleaner, 'Greener' Gasoline?" *AAA World,* November/December 1992, pp. 14–15.

Zwick, David, and March Benstock. *Water Wasteland.* New York: Bantam Books, 1971.

# A

**abatement equipment subsidy** A payment aimed at lowering the cost of abatement technology.

**"acceptable" risk** The amount of risk determined to be tolerable for society.

**acidic deposition** Arises when sulfuric and nitric acids mix with other airborne particles and fall to the earth as dry or wet deposits.

**action level** Manner in which MCLs are expressed, generally measured in milligrams per liter.

**air quality control regions (AQCRs)** Geographical areas designated by the federal government within which common air pollution problems are shared by several communities.

**allocative efficiency** The economic criterion that society's valuation of an additional unit of the good be equivalent to the value of the resources used to produce it.

**allocatively efficient standards** Standards set such that the associated marginal social cost (*MSC*) of abatement equals the marginal social benefit (*MSB*) of abatement.

**allowance market for ozone-depleting chemicals** A system that allows firms to produce or import ozone depleters only if they hold an appropriate number of tradeable allowances.

**ambient standard** Designates the quality of the environment to be achieved.

**anthropogenic pollutants** Contaminants associated with human activity, including polluting residuals from consumption and production.

**averting expenditure method (AEM)** Estimates benefits as the change in spending on goods that are *substitutes* for a cleaner environment.

# B

**back-end** or **waste-end charge** Fee implemented at the time of disposal based on the quantity of waste generated.

**"bag-and-tag" approach** Unit pricing scheme implemented by selling tags to be applied to waste receptacles of various sizes.

**behavioral linkage approach** Estimates benefits using observations of behavior in actual markets or survey responses about hypothetical markets.

**benefit-based decision rule** A guideline to improve society's well-being with no allowance for a balancing of the associated costs.

**benefit-based standard** A standard set to improve society's well-being with no consideration for the associated costs.

**benefit–cost analysis** A strategy that compares the *MSB* of a risk reduction policy to the associated *MSC*.

**benefit–cost ratio** The ratio of *PVB* to *PVC* used to determine the feasibility of a policy option if its magnitude exceeds unity.

**best available demonstrated control technology (BADCT)** Technological basis for effluent limits applicable to new, direct industrial dischargers.

**best available technology (BAT)** Treatment technology that makes attainment of the MCL feasible, taking cost considerations into account.

**best available technology economically achievable (BAT)** Technological basis for effluent limits applicable to existing, direct industrial dischargers of nonconventional and toxic pollutants.

**best conventional control technology (BCT)** Technological basis for effluent limits applicable to existing, direct industrial dischargers of conventional pollutants.

**best management practices (BMP)** Strategies other than effluent limitations to reduce pollution from nonpoint sources.

**biocriteria** Expressed in broad statements about the condition of an aquatic system, typically based on the findings of biomonitoring procedures.

**biodiversity** The variety of distinct species, their genetic variability, and the variety of ecosystems they inhabit.

**Btu tax** A per unit charge based on the energy content of fuel measured in British thermal units (Btu).

**bubble policy** Allows a plant to measure its emissions as an average of all emission points emanating from that plant.

# C

**capital costs** Fixed expenditures for plant, equipment, construction in progress, and production process changes associated with abatement.

**carbon sinks** Natural absorbers of $CO_2$ such as forests and oceans.

**carbon tax** A per unit charge based on the carbon content of fuel.

**changes in manufacturing processes** The use of alternative production methods to generate less hazardous by-products.

**characteristic wastes** Hazardous wastes identified as those exhibiting certain characteristics that imply a substantial risk.

**chlorofluoro carbons (CFCs)** A family of chemicals that scientists believe contributes to ozone depletion.

**circular flow model** Illustrates the real and monetary flows of economic activity through the factor market and the output market.

**clean alternative fuels** Fuels like methanol, ethanol, or other alcohols, or power sources such as electricity, used in a clean fuel vehicle.

**clean fuel vehicle** A vehicle certified to meet stringent emission standards.

**Coase Theorem** Assignment of property rights, even in the presence of externalities, will allow bargaining such that an efficient solution can be obtained.

**command-and-control approach** A policy that directly regulates polluters through the use of rules or standards.

**common property resources** Those resources for which property rights are shared.

**comparative risk analysis** Decision rule that evaluates relative risk, also referred to as risk–risk analysis.

**competitive equilibrium** The point where marginal private benefit ($MPB$) equals marginal private cost ($MPC$) or where marginal profit ($M\pi$) = 0.

**Comprehensive Environmental Response, Compensation, and Liability Information System (CERCLIS)** A national inventory of hazardous waste site data.

**consumer surplus** The net benefit to buyers estimated by the excess of the marginal benefit ($MB$) of consumption over market price ($P$), aggregated over all units purchased.

**contingent valuation method (CVM)** Uses surveys to elicit responses about WTP for environmental quality based on hypothetical market conditions.

**conventional pollutant** An identified pollutant that is well understood by scientists.

**corrective tax** A tax aimed at rectifying a market failure and improving resource allocation.

**cost-effective abatement criterion** Allocating abatement across polluting sources such that the $MAC$s for each source are equal.

**cost-effective policy** A policy that meets an objective using the least amount of economic resources.

**"cradle-to-grave" management system** A command-and-control approach to regulating hazardous solid wastes through every stage of the waste stream.

**criteria documents** Reports that present an evaluation of scientific evidence on the properties and effects of known or suspected pollutants.

**criteria pollutants** Substances known to be hazardous to health and welfare, characterized as harmful by criteria documents.

# D

**damage function method** Models the relationship between a contaminant and its observed effects as a way to estimate damage reductions arising from policy.

**dark green technologies** Technologies dealing directly with the remediation of pollution.

**deadweight loss to society** The net loss of consumer and producer surplus due to an allocatively inefficient market event.

**declining block pricing structure** Pricing scheme that allows the per unit price of different "blocks" or quantities of water to decline as usage increases.

**deflating** Converts a nominal value into its real value.

**demand** The quantities of a good the consumer is willing and able to purchase at a set of prices during some discrete time period, *c.p.*

*de minimis* **risk** A negligible level of risk such that reducing it further would not justify the costs of doing so.

**deposit/refund system** Imposes an up-front charge to pay for potential damages and returns it for returning a product for proper disposal or recycling.

**direct user value** Benefit derived from directly consuming services provided by an environmental good.

**discount factor** The term, $1/(1 + r)^t$, where $r$ is the discount rate, and $t$ is the number of periods.

**dose–response relationship** A quantitative relationship between doses of a contaminant and the corresponding reactions.

**Drinking Water State Revolving Fund (DWSRF)** Authorizes $1 billion per year from 1994 to 2003 to finance infrastructure improvements.

# E

**Economic Analysis (EA)** A requirement under Executive Order 12866 that called for information on the benefits and costs of a "significant regulatory action."

**efficient equilibrium** The point where marginal social benefit (*MSB*) equals marginal social cost (*MSC*), or where marginal profit ($M\pi$) = marginal external cost (*MEC*).

**effluent allowances** Tradeable permits issued up front to a polluting source that give it the right to release effluents in the future.

**effluent reduction credits** Tradeable permits issued to a polluting source if it discharges a lower level of effluents than what is allowed by law.

**effluent reduction trading policy** A market approach whereby an abatement objective is established for a watershed and sources are allowed to negotiate trades for "rights to pollute."

**emission or effluent charge** A fee imposed directly on the actual discharge of pollution.

**emissions banking** Allows a source to accumulate emission reduction credits if it reduces emissions more than required by law and "deposit" these through a banking program.

**Energy Star Program** A product-labeling plan encouraging manufacturers to develop energy-saving products.

**engineering approach** Estimates abatement expenditures based on least-cost available technology.

**environmental decision making and risk analysis** Assessing the magnitude of the problem and developing an appropriate policy response.

**environmental economics** A field of study concerned with the flow of residuals from economic activity back to nature.

**environmental equity** Concerned with the fairness of the environmental risk burden across segments of society or geographical regions.

**environmental federalism** The coordination and delegation of tasks among levels of government to develop and implement environmental policy.

**environmental literacy** Awareness of the risks of pollution and natural resource depletion.

**environmental policy appraisal** Evaluating policy using criteria such as allocative efficiency, cost-effectiveness, and equity.

**environmental quality** A reduction in anthropogenic contamination to a level that is "acceptable" to society.

**environmental risk** The probability that damage will occur due to exposure to an environmental hazard.

**equilibrium price and quantity** The "market-clearing" price ($P_e$) associated with the equilibrium quantity ($Q_e$), where $Q_d = Q_s$.

**excise tax on ozone depleters** An escalating tax on the production of ozone-depleting substances.

**existence value** Benefit received from the continuance of an environmental good.

**existing stationary source** A source already present when regulations have been published.

**explicit costs** Administrative, monitoring, and enforcement expenses paid by the public sector plus compliance costs incurred by all sectors.

**exposure** The pathways between the source of the damage and the affected population or resource.

**exposure analysis** Characterizes the sources of an environmental hazard, concentration levels at that point, pathways, and any sensitivities.

**externality** A spillover effect associated with production or consumption that extends to a third party outside the market.

**F**

**federal grant program** Provided major funding from the federal government for a share of the construction costs of POTWs.

**feedstock taxes** Taxes levied on raw materials used as productive inputs.

**first law of thermodynamics** Matter and energy can neither be created nor destroyed.

**fishable–swimmable goal** An interim U.S. objective requiring that surface waters be capable of supporting recreational activities and the propagation of fish and wildlife.

**fixed fee** or **flat fee pricing system** Pricing MSW services independent of the quantity of waste generated.

**flat fee pricing scheme** Pricing water supplies such that the fee is independent of water use.

**flat rate pricing** Unit pricing scheme that charges the same price for each additional unit of waste.

**free-ridership** Recognition by a rational consumer that the benefits of consumption are accessible without paying for them.

**front-end** or **retail disposal charge** Fee levied on a product at the point of sale designed to encourage source reduction.

**G**

**gasoline tax** A per unit tax levied on each gallon of gasoline consumed.

**global pollution** Environmental effects that are widespread with global implications, such as global warming and ozone depletion.

**global warming** Caused by sunlight hitting the earth's surface and radiating back into the atmosphere where its absorption by GHGs heats the atmosphere and warms the earth's surface.

**greenhouse gases (GHGs)** Gases collectively responsible for the absorption process that naturally warms the earth.

**Green Lights Program** A plan that fosters partnerships between businesses and the EPA aimed at improving energy efficiency.

**groundwater** Fresh water beneath the earth's surface, generally in aquifers.

**H**

**hazard** The source of the environmental damage.

**hazard identification** Scientific analysis to determine if a causal relationship exists between a pollutant and any adverse effects.

**hazardous air pollutants** Noncriteria pollutants that may cause or contribute to irreversible illness or increased mortality.

**hazardous solid wastes** Any unwanted materials or refuse capable of posing a substantial threat to health or the ecology.

**hedonic price method (HPM)** Uses the estimated hedonic price of an environmental attribute to value a policy-driven improvement.

**hydrological cycle** Explains the natural movement of water from the atmosphere to the surface, beneath the ground, and back into the atmosphere.

**I**

**identification of the environmental problem** Awareness of an environmental hazard and the process of convincing government to respond.

**implicit costs** The value of any nonmonetary effects that negatively influence society's well-being.

**increasing block pricing structure** Pricing scheme whereby the per unit price of different "blocks" of water increases as water use increases.

**incremental benefits** The reduction in health, ecological, and property damages associated with an environmental policy initiative.

**incremental costs** The change in costs arising from an environmental policy initiative.

**indirect user value**   Benefit derived from indirect consumption of an environmental good.

**industrial ecosystem**   Closed system of manufacturing whereby the wastes of one process are reused as inputs.

**inflation correction**   Adjusts for movements in the general price level over time.

**Integrated Pest Management (IPM)**   A combination of control methods aimed at encouraging more selective use of pesticides and greater reliance on natural deterrents.

**integrated waste management system**   An EPA initiative to guide state MSW plans that promotes the combined use of source reduction, recycling, combustion, and land disposal ranked in order of preference.

**involuntary risk**   A risk beyond one's control and not the result of a willful decision.

# J

**joint and several liability**   Legal standard that identifies a single party as responsible for all damages even if that party's contribution to the damages is minimal.

# L

**Law of Demand**   There is an inverse relationship between price and quantity demanded of a good, *c.p.*

**Law of Supply**   There is a direct relationship between price and quantity supplied of a good, *c.p.*

**light green technologies**   Technologies that benefit the environment indirectly.

**listed wastes**   Hazardous wastes that have been pre-identified by government as having met specific criteria.

**local pollution**   Environmental damage that does not extend far from the polluting source, such as urban smog.

# M

**management strategies**   Methods that address existing environmental problems and attempt to reduce the damage from the residual flow.

**manifest**   A document used to identify hazardous waste materials and all parties responsible for its movement from generation to disposal.

**marginal abatement cost (*MAC*)**   Measures the change in costs associated with reducing pollution using the least-cost method.

**marginal cost of enforcement (*MCE*)**   Added costs incurred by government associated with monitoring and enforcing abatement activities.

**marginal social benefit (*MSB*)**   The sum of marginal private benefit (*MPB*) and marginal external benefit (*MEB*).

**marginal social benefit (*MSB*) of abatement**   A measure of the additional gains accruing to society as pollution is reduced.

**marginal social cost (*MSC*)**   The sum of the marginal private cost (*MPC*) and the marginal external cost (*MEC*).

**marginal social cost (*MSC*) of abatement**   The sum of all polluters' marginal abatement costs plus government's marginal cost of monitoring and enforcing these activities.

**market**   The interaction between consumers and producers to exchange a well-defined commodity.

**market approach**   An incentive-based policy that encourages conservation practices or pollution reduction strategies.

**market demand for a private good**   The decisions of all consumers willing and able to purchase a good; derived by summing the individual demands *horizontally*.

**market demand for a public good**   The aggregate demand of all consumers in the market derived by summing their individual demands *vertically*.

**market failure**   The result of an inefficient market condition.

**market-level marginal abatement cost function (*MAC_{mkt}*)**   The horizontal sum of all polluters' *MAC* functions.

**market supply of a private good**   The combined decisions of all producers in a given industry; derived by summing the individual supplies *horizontally*.

**materials balance model**   Positions the circular flow within a larger schematic to show the connections between economic decision making and the natural environment.

**materials groups**   Categories of materials in the MSW stream identified as paper and paperboard, yard waste, food, glass, metals, plastics, textiles, rubber, and wood.

**maximize the present value of net benefits (*PVNB*)** A decision rule to achieve allocative efficiency by selecting the policy option that yields greatest excess benefits after adjusting for time effects.

**maximum achievable control technology (MACT)** The control technology that achieves the degree of reduction to be accomplished by the NESHAP.

**maximum contaminant level (MCL)** Component of an NPDWR that states the highest permissible level of a contaminant in water delivered to any user of a public system.

**maximum contaminant level goal (MCLG)** Component of an NPDWR that defines the level of a pollutant at which no known or expected adverse health effects occur, allowing for a margin of safety.

**minimize the present value of costs (*PVC*)** A decision rule to achieve cost-effectiveness by selecting the least-cost policy option that achieves a preestablished objective.

**mobile source** Any nonstationary polluting source, including all transport vehicles.

**multimedia, multichemical approaches** Proposed regulatory procedures that would replace existing single chemical regulatory actions.

**municipal solid waste (MSW)** Nonhazardous wastes disposed of by local communities.

# N

**narrative criteria** Water quality criteria expressed in concise, qualitative statements.

**National Action Plan (NAP)** A nation's policy to control GHGs and a statement of its target emissions level for the future.

**National Ambient Air Quality Standards (NAAQS)** Maximum allowable concentrations of criteria air pollutants.

**National Contingency Plan (NCP)** Set of regulations that outlines official response actions to a release or the threat of a release of a hazardous substance.

**National Emission Standards for Hazardous Air Pollutants (NESHAP)** Standards set to protect public health and the environment that are applicable to every major source of any identified hazardous air pollutant.

**National Pollutant Discharge Elimination System (NPDES)** A federally mandated permit system used to control effluent releases from direct industrial dischargers and POTWs.

**National Primary Drinking Water Regulations (NPDWR)** Health standards for public drinking water supplies implemented uniformly.

**National Priorities List (NPL)** A classification of hazardous waste sites posing the greatest threat to health and the ecology.

**natural pollutants** Those contaminants that come about through nonartificial processes in nature.

**natural resource economics** A field of study concerned with the flow of resources from nature to economic activity.

**negative externality** An external effect that generates costs to a third party.

**netting** Developed for PSD areas to allow emissions trading among points within a source for the same type of pollutant, such that any emissions increase due to a modification is matched by a reduction from another point within that same source.

**new chemical** Any substance not listed in the TSCA inventory of existing chemicals.

**new or modified stationary source** A source for which construction or modification follows the publication of regulations.

**New Source Performance Standards (NSPS)** Technology-based emissions limits established for new stationary sources.

**nominal value** A magnitude stated in terms of the current period.

**nonattainment areas** AQCRs not in compliance with the NAAQS.

**nonconventional pollutant** A default category for pollutants not identified as toxic or conventional.

**nonexcludability** The characteristic that makes it impossible to prevent others from sharing in the benefits of consumption.

**nonpoint source** A source that cannot be identified accurately and degrades the environment in a diffuse, indirect way over a relatively broad area.

**Nonpoint Source Management Program** A three-stage, state-implemented plan aimed at nonpoint source pollution.

**nonrevelation of preferences** Arises when a rational consumer does not volunteer a WTP due to the lack of a market incentive to do so.

**nonrivalness** The characteristic of indivisible benefits of consumption such that one person's consumption does not preclude that of another.

**no toxics in toxic amounts goal** A U.S. goal prohibiting the release of toxic substances in toxic amounts into all water resources.

**numeric criteria** Water quality criteria stated as concentrations of chemicals or pollutants allowed in water expressed in micrograms per liter ($\mu$g/L).

# O

**offset plan** Developed for nonattainment areas to allow emissions trading between new or modified sources and existing facilities such that releases from the new or modified source are more than countered by reductions achieved by existing sources.

**operating costs** Variable expenditures incurred in the operation and maintenance of abatement processes.

**oxygenated fuel** Formulations with enhanced oxygen content to allow for more complete combustion and hence a reduction in CO emissions.

**ozone depletion** Thinning of the ozone layer originally observed as an "ozone hole" over Antarctica.

**ozone depletion potential (ODP)** A numerical score that signifies a substance's potential for destroying stratospheric ozone relative to CFC-11.

**ozone layer** Ozone present in the stratosphere that protects the earth from ultraviolet radiation.

# P

**performance-based standard** Specifies a pollution limit to be achieved but does not stipulate the technology.

**permitting system** A control approach that authorizes the activities of TSDFs according to predefined standards.

**per unit subsidy on pollution reduction** A payment for every unit of pollution removed below some predetermined level.

**pesticide registration** Formal listing of a pesticide with the EPA that must be approved based on a risk–benefit analysis before it can be sold or distributed.

**pesticide reregistration** Formal reevaluation of a previously licensed pesticide already on the market.

**pesticide tolerances** Legal limits on the amount of pesticide remaining as a residue on raw agricultural products or in processed foods.

**photochemical smog** Caused by pollutants that chemically react in sunlight to form new substances; its principal component is ozone ($O_3$).

**physical linkage approach** Estimates benefits based on a technical relationship between an environmental resource and the user of that resource.

**Pigouvian subsidy** A per unit payment on a good, the consumption of which generates a positive externality such that the payment equals the *MEB* at $Q_e$.

**Pigouvian tax** A unit charge on a good whose production generates a negative externality, such that the charge equals the *MEC* at $Q_e$.

**point source** Any single identifiable source of pollution such as a fixed location or facility from which contaminants are discharged.

**pollutant-based effluent fee** Based on the degree of harm associated with the contaminant being released.

**Pollutant Standards Index (PSI)** Signifies the worst daily air quality in an urban area over some time period.

**pollution** The presence of matter or energy whose nature, location, or quantity has undesired effects on the environment.

**pollution allowances** Tradeable permits that indicate the maximum level of pollution that may be released.

**pollution charge** A fee that varies with the amount of pollutants released.

**pollution credits** Tradeable permits issued for emitting below an established standard.

**pollution permit trading system** Establishes a market for "rights to pollute" by issuing tradeable pollution credits or allowances.

**pollution prevention** A long-term strategy aimed at reducing the amount or toxicity of residuals released to nature.

**positive externality** An external effect that generates benefits to a third party.

**potentially responsible parties (PRPs)** Any current or former owner or operator of a hazardous waste facility and all those involved in the disposal, treatment, or transport of hazardous substances to the contaminated site.

**premanufacture notice (PMN)** Official notification made to the EPA by a chemical producer about its intent to produce or import a new chemical.

**present value determination** A procedure that discounts a future value (*FV*) into its present value (*PV*) by accounting for the opportunity cost of money.

**present value of benefits (*PVB*)** The time-adjusted magnitude of incremental benefits associated with an environmental policy change.

**present value of costs (*PVC*)** The time-adjusted magnitude of incremental costs associated with an environmental policy change.

**present value of net benefits (*PVNB*)** The differential of (*PVB* – *PVC*) used to determine the feasibility of a policy option if its magnitude exceeds zero.

**prevention of significant deterioration (PSD) areas** AQCRs meeting or exceeding the NAAQS.

**primary environmental benefit** A damage-reducing effect that is a direct consequence of implementing environmental policy.

**primary NAAQS** Set to protect public health from air pollution, with some margin of safety.

**priority contaminants** Pollutants for which drinking water standards are to be established based on specific criteria.

**private good** A commodity that has two characteristics: rivalry in consumption and excludability.

**producer surplus** The net gain to sellers of a good estimated by the excess of market price (*P*) over marginal cost (*MC*), aggregated over all units sold.

**product charge** Fee added to the price of a pollution-generating product based on its quantity or some attribute responsible for pollution.

**product groups** Categories of products in the MSW stream identified as durable goods, nondurable goods, packaging and containers, food, and yard trimmings.

**Product Stewardship Rulemaking** Proposal that would require chemical producers to share risk information with their customers and to conduct hazard evaluations on substances in use.

**product substitution** Selection of environmentally safe commodities in place of potentially polluting products.

**profit maximization** Achieved at the output level where $MR = MC$ or where $M\pi = 0$.

**property rights** The set of valid claims to a good or resource that permits use of that good or resource and the transfer of its ownership through sale.

**public good** A commodity that is nonrival in consumption and yields benefits that are non-excludable.

# R

**raw materials substitution** Using productive inputs that generate little or no hazardous waste.

**real value** A magnitude adjusted for the effects of inflation.

**receiving water quality standards** State-established standards defined by use designation and water quality criteria.

**reformulated gasoline** Newly developed fuels that emit less hydrocarbons, carbon monoxide, and toxics than conventional gasoline.

**regional pollution** Degradation that extends well beyond the polluting source, such as acidic deposition.

**Regulatory Impact Analysis (RIA)** A requirement under Executive Order 12291 that called for specific information about the potential benefits and costs associated with a "major" federal regulation.

**remedial actions** Official responses to a hazardous substance release aimed at achieving a more permanent solution.

**removal actions** Official responses to a hazardous substance release aimed at restoring immediate control.

**residual** The amount of a pollutant remaining in the environment after a natural or technological process has occurred.

**risk** The chance of something bad happening.

**risk assessment** The qualitative and quantitative evaluation of the risk posed to health or the ecology by an environmental hazard.

**risk–benefit analysis** Decision rule that assesses the risks of an environmental hazard along with the benefits of not regulating that hazard.

**risk characterization** Description of risk based on an assessment of a hazard and exposure to that hazard.

**risk management** The decision-making process of evaluating and choosing from alternative responses to environmental risk.

# S

**secondary environmental benefit** An indirect gain to society that may arise from a stimulative effect of primary benefits or from a demand-induced effect to implement policy.

**secondary maximum contaminant levels (SMCLs)** National standards for drinking water that serve as guidelines to protect public welfare.

**secondary NAAQS** Set to protect public welfare from any adverse, non-health effects of air pollution.

**second law of thermodynamics** Nature's capacity to convert matter and energy is not without bound.

**shortage** Excess demand of a commodity equal to $(Q_d - Q_s)$ that arises if price is *below* its equilibrium level.

**social costs** Expenditures needed to compensate society for resources used so that its utility level is maintained.

**social discount rate** Discount rate used for public policy initiatives based on the social opportunity cost of funds.

**society's welfare** The sum of consumer surplus and producer surplus.

**sole-source aquifers** Underground geological formations containing groundwater that are the only supply of drinking water for a given area.

**source reduction** Preventive strategies to reduce the quantity and toxicity of hazardous wastes at the point of generation.

**source segregation** A procedure that keeps hazardous waste from coming in contact with nonhazardous waste.

**State Implementation Plan (SIP)** A procedure outlining how a state intends to implement, monitor, and enforce the NAAQS and the NESHAP.

**State Revolving Fund (SRF) program** Establishes state lending programs to support POTW construction and other projects.

**stationary source** A fixed-site producer of pollution, such as a building or manufacturing plant.

**stewardship** The sense of obligation to preserve the environment for future generations.

**strict liability** Legal standard that identifies individuals as responsible for damages even if negligence is not proven.

**supply** The quantities of a good the producer is willing and able to bring to market at a given set of prices during some discrete time period, *c.p.*

**surface water** Bodies of water open to the earth's atmosphere as well as springs, wells, or other collectors directly influenced by surface water.

**surplus** Excess supply of a commodity equal to $(Q_s - Q_d)$ that arises if price is *above* its equilibrium level.

**survey approach** Polls a sample of firms and public facilities to obtain estimated abatement expenditures.

**sustainable development** The management of the earth's resources such that their long-term quality and abundance are ensured.

# T

**technical efficiency** Production decisions that generate maximum output given some stock of resources.

**technology-based effluent limitations** Standards to control discharges from point sources based primarily on technological capability.

**technology-based standard** Designates the equipment or method to be used to achieve some abatement level.

**technology transfer** The advancement and application of technologies and strategies on a global scale.

**33/50 Program** A program that encouraged firms emitting one or more of 17 priority pollutants to voluntarily reduce releases of those substances.

**threshold** The level of exposure to a hazard up to which no response exists.

**tipping fees** Prices charged for disposing of wastes in a facility such as a landfill.

**total profit** Total profit $(\pi)$ = Total revenue $(TR)$ − Total costs $(TC)$.

**toxic chemical use substitution** Using less harmful chemicals in place of more hazardous substances.

**toxic pollutant** A contaminant which upon exposure will cause death, disease, abnormalities, or physiological malfunctions.

**Toxics Release Inventory (TRI)** National database that gives information about hazardous substances released into the environment.

**tradeable effluent permit market** The exchange of "rights to pollute" among polluting sources.

**tradeable permit system for GHG emissions** Based on the issuance of marketable permits, where each allows the release of some amount of GHGs.

**tradeable SO$_2$ emission allowances** Permits issued to stationary sources, each allowing the release of one ton of SO$_2$, which can be either held or sold through a transfer program.

**travel cost method (TCM)** Values benefits by using the *complementary* relationship between the quality of a natural resource and its recreational use value.

**TSCA inventory** Database of all chemicals commercially produced or processed in the United States.

## U

**uniform rate pricing structure** Pricing water supplies to charge more for higher water usage at a constant rate.

**unit pricing scheme** Common designation for the use of a waste-end charge.

**use designation** Component of receiving water quality standards that identifies the intended purposes of a water body.

**user value** Benefit derived from physical use or access to an environmental good.

**use-support status** A classification of a water body based on a state's assessment of its present condition relative to what is needed to maintain its designated uses.

## V

**variable rate pricing** Unit pricing scheme that charges a different price for each additional unit of waste.

**vicarious consumption** The utility associated with knowing that others derive benefits from an environmental good.

**volume-based effluent fee** Based on the quantity of pollution discharged.

**voluntary risk** A risk that is deliberately assumed at an individual level.

## W

**waste-end charge** Fee implemented at the time of disposal based on the quantity of waste generated.

**waste management** Control strategies to reduce the quantity and toxicity of hazardous wastes at every stage of the waste stream.

**waste stream** Series of events starting with waste generation and including transportation, storage, treatment, and disposal of solid wastes.

**water quality criteria** Component of receiving water quality standards that gives the biological and chemical attributes necessary to sustain or achieve designated uses.

**water quality–related limitations** Modified effluent limits to be met if the desired water quality level is not being achieved, even if polluting sources are already satisfying the technology-based limits.

## Z

**zero discharge goal** A U.S. objective calling for the elimination of all polluting effluents into navigable waters.